PRAISE FOR *THE COLONY*

'This is a spellbinding saga of the beginnings o   y
is a subtle and intimate portrait of early Sydney as well as an exhilarating
exploration of imperial vision and cultural encounter. This book will change
the way you feel about Australian history.'
Professor Tom Griffiths, Australian National University

'Reading this vivid text can feel like a virtual tour of the city and its environs,
with Karskens as guide.'
Peter Cochrane, *Australian Literary Review*

'Every page is startling for the mass of human and geographical detail, and for
the extraordinary freshness of the argument. It propels Karskens straight to the
first rank of historians.'
Alan Atkinson, *The Monthly*

'Grace Karskens' picture of colonial Sydney and its environs is grounded in
reality, free of stereotypes and balanced in its judgment. It neither romanticises
nor condemns and provides a foundation story that we can all recognise.'
Babette Smith, *Sydney Morning Herald*

'[A] meticulously researched volume, with a scope that is both breathtakingly
inclusive and microscopic detail.'
Australian Art Review

'A subtle and thoughtful account of early interaction that is marked as much by
generosity and mutual concern as by violence and expropriation.'
Cassandra Pybus, *The Australian*

'Karskens tells a . . . nuanced, multi-layered tale, capturing the many contradictions
of daily life in Australia's first city.'
Fiona Capp, *The Age*

'A vivid and illuminating study of early Sydney.'
Robert Wilson, *The Canberra Times*

The generous support and assistance of the City of Sydney's History Program is gratefully acknowledged.

This project has been assisted by the Australian Government through the Australia Council for the Arts, its arts funding and advisory body.

This project has been supported by the Australian Academy of Humanities

The generous assistance of the State Library of New South Wales in the production of this book is gratefully acknowledged.

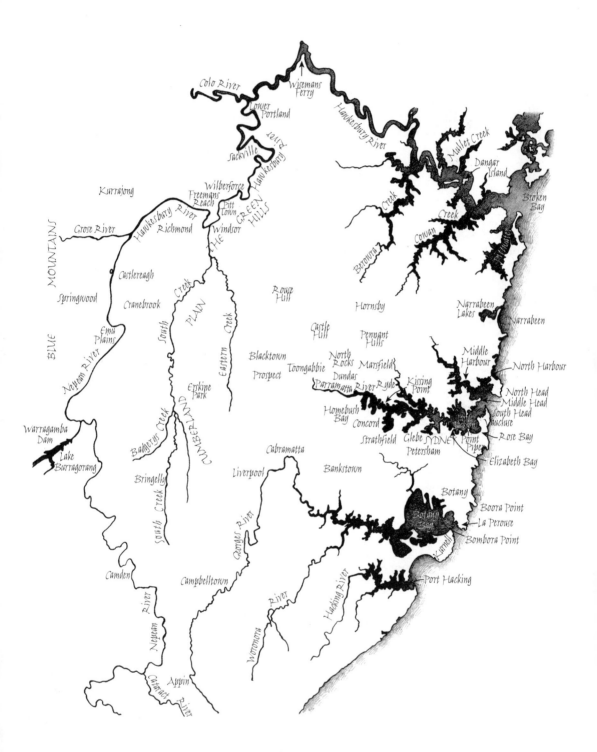

SYDNEY REGION

The COLONY

A HISTORY *of* EARLY SYDNEY

———◆———

GRACE KARSKENS

ALLEN&UNWIN
SYDNEY•MELBOURNE•AUCKLAND•LONDON

This edition published in 2010
First published in 2009

Allen & Unwin
83 Alexander Street
Crows Nest NSW 2065
Australia
Phone: (61 2) 8425 0100
Email: info@allenandunwin.com
Web: www.allenandunwin.com

A catalogue record for this book is available from the National Library of Australia

ISBN 978 1 74237 364 5

Index by Russell Brooks
Internal design by Lisa White
Map by Kate Nolan
Set in 11.5/17 pt Minion by Midland Typesetters, Australia
Printed by C&C Offset Printing Co. Ltd, China

10 9 8 7

For my parents
Francine and Bill Karskens
who made new lives in Sydney too
with love and thanks

CONTENTS

ACKNOWLEDGEMENTS

This book has been a long time coming. In the years between its conception and birth I moved home, changed my workplace and started a new career. My children became adults, my parents reached their eighties and I acquired a brood of beautiful nieces and nephews. Sydney hosted the Olympic Games with great success, global warming became a fact rather than a theory, 9/11 changed the way we think about cities, the Asian tsunami wreaked unspeakable horror. Australia went to war in Iraq, Prime Minister John Howard's reign came to an end, and there was an official apology to the Stolen Generations. The book was a sort of constant amidst all this. It endured. Thanks to all the polite and kind people—friends, neighbours, colleagues—who always asked after it and never once rolled their eyes.

The research, writing and publication was made possible by the generous financial support of a number of institutions. The early years of research were funded by an Australian Research Council Queen Elizabeth II Fellowship, while in later years I was unstintingly supported by my own institution, the School of History and Philosophy at the University of New South Wales. The publication of this book in its handsome format was made possible by generous grants from the Australia Council, Sydney City Council, the Australian Academy of Humanities and the State Library of New South Wales.

The book was made a reality by the energetic and professional people at Allen & Unwin. I am most grateful to Elizabeth Weiss, who had faith in it from the start and has been a tireless advocate and a wonderful advisor: she is an editor in the proper sense of the word. Both she and Alexandra Nahlous deserve medals for their patience and generosity. It has been such a pleasure to work with them, and also with Clara Finlay, and Karen Ward, who copy-edited the manuscript with such an extraordinary eye for detail and consistency. Thank you all.

ACKNOWLEDGEMENTS

The book is based upon the marvellous resources of our treasured libraries and archives. My heartfelt thanks, once more, to the expert staff of the Mitchell Library, State Records of New South Wales and the University of New South Wales Library. The sources for this book include the many beautiful pictures created by colonial and contemporary artists you see reproduced in these pages. I am grateful to the National Library of Australia, the Australian Museum, Queen Victoria Museum and Art Gallery, the Powerhouse Museum, Australian National Botanic Gardens, the Natural History Museum (especially Angela Thresher and Sally Jennings) and the British Library, for their prompt assistance and permission to reproduce these works. Elizabeth Ellis and Kevin Leamon made the inclusion of so many images from the great collections of the Mitchell and Dixson Libraries possible. Thanks also to artist Kate Nolan, whose exquisite pencil drawings grace these pages, and to Charles Dortch and Peter Stanbury for allowing us to use their respective works in the new drawings.

Some of this material was gathered for me by research assistants, and I want to acknowledge and thank Benedict Taylor, Rachel Davies and Alicia Gray for their intelligent and efficient assistance, their interest in the project, and their friendship.

I suspect experts in diverse fields across the nation will be heaving a sigh of relief at the emergence of this book. It means I will no longer pester them for opinions and advice on everything from plants and ecosystems to early colonial tools, from army worms to historic houses, from arcane legal terminology to blue and white china. I am grateful for the expert guidance of Val Attenbrow, Doug Benson, James Broadbent, Penny Crook, Tim Flannery, Ralph Hawkins, Don Herbison-Evans, Bruce Kercher, Mike MacPhail, Bob Salt, Barry Smith, Iain Stuart and Alan Ward.

The book was also nourished over the years by talk with colleagues and friends in history and archaeology, and flourished in a nimbus of enthusiasm and support. Many of these scholars sent me copies of their own published and unpublished works. Thank you to Robert Allen, Michael Bennet, Peter Borsay, Sarah Colley, Chris Cunningham, Graeme Davison, Shirley Fitzgerald, Lisa Ford, Geoff Ford, Rae Frances, Stephen Gapps, Wayne Johnson, Susan Lawrence, Carol Liston, Kirsten McKenzie, Hamish Maxwell Stewart, Jacqui Newling,

Naomi Parry, John Petersen, Michael Pickering, Olwyn Pryke, Noeline Pullen, Marcus Rediker, David Roberts, Bruce Scates, Lorraine Stacker and Pam Trimmer; and to my colleagues at the University of New South Wales, especially Anne O'Brien, Ruth Balint, John Gascoigne, Mina Roces and Martyn Lyons. I am especially grateful to those who also read the chapters in draft and offered such helpful advice and blessed encouragement: Tom Griffiths, Barrie Dyster, Ralph Hawkins, Heather Goodall, Vicky Haskins, Bob Salt and Keith Vincent Smith, I am indebted to you.

This leads me to the broader debt I owe other scholars. This book has its roots deep in a great mountain of existing research, thinking and histories. Historians work collectively, within a wider community of scholars. So history writing is less an individualist pursuit than a collective quest, and an ongoing process. This is one reason references are so important: they rightly acknowledge the work of past scholars, as well as guiding future readers and scholars into the literature. In the notes and bibliography of this book you will find, besides original manuscripts and archival records, maps and pictures, an extraordinary and diverse body of scholarship about early Sydney, works mainly by historians, but also archaeologists, economists, anthropologists, art and architectural historians, ecologists, geologists, museologists, geographers, biographers and local and community historians.

There is something exhilarating about exploring this 'city of words'. There are books on everything from convict work practices and popular culture to colonial paintings; from early farming practices to biographies of deeply admirable but slightly unhinged botanists; from the palynology and ecologies of creeks and valleys to the philosophies underpinning the making of new colonies. I must acknowledge my particular debt to the many historians and archaeologists, most notably Keith Vincent Smith, James L. Kohen and Val Attenbrow, who have spent many years painstakingly reconstructing Aboriginal lives and ways of living, patterns of movement and social relations, families, communities and events. I have also been privileged with the insights and guidance of Frances Bodkin, Ross Evans, Glenda Chalker, Sue Green and Aunty Edna Watson, and also Sister Kerry MacDermott of the Winga Myamly Reconciliation Group. This truly is history 'rescued out of time'.

ACKNOWLEDGEMENTS

So I hope this book will also be a gateway to the wider world of Sydney writing: it is in part a tribute, a celebration of the restless, exciting spirit of inquiry, the tireless work that Sydney scholars of all stripe and inclination do, and the joys of discovery and of telling new stories as well as old ones.

I am lucky to share these joys, and so many others, with Richard Waterhouse, who has given me constant support and encouragement over the years of research, thinking and writing, threaded like a ribbon through all else we share in our lives together. This book is dedicated to my parents, Bill and Francine Karskens, a small, loving token of thanks for everything they have given me.

CONVERSION CHART

1 inch	2.5 centimetres
1 foot	0.3 metres
1 yard	0.9 metres
1 mile	1.6 kilometres
1 acre	0.4 hectares
1 gallon	4.5 litres
1 ounce	28 grams
1 pound	450 grams
£1 (one pound)	$2.00
1s (one shilling)	10 cents
6d (sixpence)	5 cents
1d (one penny)	0.8 cents

INTRODUCTION

———◆———

In 1786, the British government decided to found an experimental colony in the lands of unsuspecting groups of Aboriginal people on the other side of the globe. It was to be a simple agrarian colony, peopled by convicted felons and run by a governor and a handful of officers. Urban development and the ills it brought were to be strictly avoided. Yet this strange venture inadvertently created Australia's oldest, largest and best-known city, Sydney, and eventually one of the world's most urbanised nations. This book tells the marvellously contrary, endlessly energetic story of the making of Sydney in those early years. It is a story about transformations, of peoples and landscapes. Not just one transformation—from a beautiful cove and valley to a thriving city—but the way that the early camp became a town, and how the town continued to be transformed by succeeding and conflicting visions of governors and people. But this is also a story about continuities: persistent habits, and threads and echoes, ways of thinking and doing transplanted, and passed on, cycles of seasons and generations and shipping, the rivers and creeks flowing on, the bushland growing back. I am fascinated by this interplay of transformation and continuity—what slips away, and what holds fast? What is forgotten and what is remembered?

To begin, let us briefly scan Sydney from either end of its two centuries. Early twenty-first-century Sydney rejoices in the status of a 'global' city, linked more closely to the network of great cities around the world by business, tourism, spin and the internet than to other cities in Australia.[1] The city works hard on its image of glamour and modernity, luxury and fun, spectacle and the good life. Its modern built environment is characterised by the glossy high-rise centre, vast low-density suburbs, the ever-expanding ribbons of highways and tunnels and the shiny new landscapes of leisure, tourism and consumption. Yet, if you visit the still-twisted streets of the Rocks, the city's earliest neighbourhood, you will see that Sydney had its origins as a preindustrial town. Early Sydney was crooked, intimate, compact. It was a walking town, reckoned by eye and worked by wind, water and muscles. Its houses, most innocent of 'architecture', faced the waters and served easily as shops and pubs, warehouses and counting houses, and the rooms had not evolved particular functions. The town's pleasures were lively, rough, exciting, cruel; they had no 'higher' purpose than enjoyment. Its people—governors and governed, masters and servants, black and white—encountered and confronted one another face to face, in the same geographic space. This first Sydney was shaped largely by people whose cultures and world views had not yet been reforged by the 'fidget wheels' of clocks and time-discipline, by steam and machines, by polite architecture, by ideas about self-discipline and self-improvement, or by notions of respectability which dictated where one lived and did not live.[2]

This book encompasses the two transformations which occurred between 1788 and around the mid-1820s. The first was from the Aboriginal landscape to an organic preindustrial town, which included Aboriginal people; the second, partial and contested, saw the preindustrial town remodelled as a more aesthetic, rectilinear, polite and self-conscious city, a project most energetically promoted by Governor Lachlan Macquarie and his wife Elizabeth. Since the growth of the town was also tied to the farming, grazing, timbergetting and town-building of the rural hinterland, this book breaks with the tradition of focusing solely on that small urban core clustered in the Tank Stream valley, and ranges out over the Cumberland Plain to the rivers and the Blue Mountains. This geographical scope allows us to explore the origins of Australian rural life and culture, as well as the way convicts made their own use of the bush as foragers, absconders, travellers, hunters and bushrangers. It also allows a proper account of the long war of Law and resistance on the Cumberland Plain fought by Aboriginal people.

INTRODUCTION

Writing the history of a city as a whole is underpinned by a great conundrum: while we can talk of 'the city' as one place—which indeed it is—it is also a different place to different people. There can be no such thing as one narrative of the city. For cities do not emerge by building alone, or by the unchallenged decrees of authority, by plans and regulations. They do not consist solely of transport systems or street grids or a series of architectural styles marching steadily over the decades. They emerge from kaleidoscopic complexity, from all these things, but more importantly from the dialogues and struggles which drove them. Different groups vied for control of urban culture, spaces and places, and for economic and social dominance, all within overarching environmental imperatives. Different people had divergent visions for this place, and themselves in it. They imagined different futures.

The structure of this book reflects this: each cluster of chapters explores the experiences and interactions of distinct groups of people. To begin with, we must know something of the human and physical landscape upon which the town was grafted. So the first cluster of chapters deals with Sydney's deep time history, the evolution of its landscapes and ecologies, and the arrivals and first encounters of Aboriginal and European settlers. The Sydney region was the country of about thirty distinct groups of Aboriginal people whose ancestors had very likely arrived in the region at least 40 000 years earlier. The year 1788 was a momentous one, but it did not neatly sever the past from the future. After all, the British were nourished by the same fish and fruits as the Eora, the coastal Aboriginal people, they used the same paths, and their most prized landscapes, the open woodlands, had been created by Aboriginal fire regimes. The rivers both demarcated and linked Aboriginal peoples: now they also shaped the white settlers' movements, boundaries and settlements.

The second cluster of chapters tracks the emergence of the town and the rural hinterland mainly through the dialogue and negotiations between authority (the governors and officers) and people (mostly convicts and soldiers). I argue that this place was not made by governors and elite settlers alone, but by ordinary men and women, white and black. It was shaped by the sinuous 'desire lines' made by walking feet as much as the straight lines plotted on maps; by the independent movements and appropriations of people, as much as official directives and grants. This story concludes at the end of the 'age of Macquarie', because the 1820s and 1830s ushered in yet another transformation: Sydney was again refashioned by the rise of a modern bureaucracy, by harsher convict regimes and by rising concerns with respectability, at times reaching the point of obsession. Increasing working-class immigration, much of it from the north of England, brought radical Chartist ideas and campaigns. After the late 1820s, then, Sydney society and culture became more divided, and this was reflected in urban patterns too, with the rise of the first suburbs.

To return to early Sydney, to reconstruct it, we must recover the factors and conditions the settlers had to contend with. In this book, the environment—topography, geologies, soils, climate, ecologies—is not simply a backdrop of 'scenery' or 'ambience'. As in James Boyce's *Van Diemen's Land*, the particular environments the settlers encountered are crucial in understanding their experience, and the sort of settlement that emerged; they are not peripheral or incidental, but core historical factors. The third cluster of chapters explores the contrasting ways in which educated colonists, convicts and women responded to the local Sydney environments: what they made of them, how they experienced them. These stories are fundamentally shaped by social standing, education and gender, yet there were shared experiences and legends too. And while the Sydney environment is traditionally described as 'hostile' and 'barren', a place that failed to nurture the colony, this is not the way the settlers saw it; or not for very long. Their environmental responses were far more complex, encompassing delight and wonder as well as bewilderment and disappointment, opportunity, free-dom and nefarious activities, covetousness and a growing sense of at-homeness. There were many ways to see nature in early Sydney.

In the last cluster of chapters we return to the story of Aboriginal encounters with the Berewalgal, as they called the pale strangers who suddenly appeared in their country, the role of Aboriginal people in making early Sydney, and the war they fought in defence of country between 1788 and 1816. I offer a brief account of the aftermath of the invasion which sketches out the impacts of hardening ideas about race, rising respectability and expanding suburbs and industries upon Aboriginal people who had already survived invasion, dispossession and smallpox. On the plain and near the coast, Aboriginal people came to live 'between' the lines of the Europeans' cadastral grids and boundaries, in areas not yet taken, or not wanted, making other histories in places which were hidden from view.[3]

––•–••–•––

Bernard Smith, in his 1974 tribute to the great collector Rex Nan Kivell, urged Australians to seek 'a more balanced, a more archaeological, a more humanist view of our history'. By 'archaeological' he wasn't talking about digging things up. He was appealing for an understanding of past and present which goes deep, which plumbs the depths and breadths of human experience. He wanted us to respond not just to words, but to material things—art and artefacts—and not simply intellectually, but sensuously and emotionally too.[4]

This book will I hope open the sorts of vistas and begin the sorts of conversations Bernard Smith was talking about. We need to know what early Sydney was like in this *holistic* sense. So, besides ecology and geology, the literature and research I have used here range beyond the standard historical sources to include archaeology and prehistory, geography, art, architecture, material culture and natural history. To avoid 'washing out the wholeness', I have sought to read these works together and to anchor actions, events and objects as precisely as I can in place and time.[5] This approach has thrown new light on many of the old stories about Sydney, and it reveals the early town as a human place, a place of movement and possibility, rather than an aggregation of structures and spaces, or the untrammelled imposition of orders and plans.

Another purpose of this deep contextualisation or 'ground truthing', as sociologists like to call it, is to escape the tyranny of the 'pendulum' view of history. The patterns of much of the historiography of early Sydney go like this: if the 'gaol town' wasn't miserable and brutal, it must have been benign and happy. If female convicts were not 'damned whores' they must have been 'good family women'. If Macquarie was not the wise, visionary 'father of Australia', he must have been a spendthrift tyrant. But by exploring the town and country in a more holistic way, with a sense of 'thereness', we may see the people of early Sydney as human beings rather than as a cavalcade of heroes and villains—though of course there were both. We may grasp the extraordinary predicaments in which people—from governors to bushrangers—found themselves. We may observe the way the mechanics of authority frayed at the edge of empire, the strategies governors had to devise to maintain some order, to make the colony work, and the realities of the complex interplay of authority, geography, imperial directives and colonial conditions. We can better assess the true political and social meanings of architecture and 'public' works. This book thus offers a reassessment of the roles and contributions of the first five governors, Arthur Phillip, John Hunter, Philip Gidley King, William Bligh and Lachlan Macquarie. Which of them followed their official instructions to the letter? Which of them, seeing what needed to be done, postponed, ignored or even subverted their instructions for the sake of economic development, good order and fairness, or burgeoning civic pride?

As well as a real city, there also exists what I like to think of as a city of stories, of words, ideas and imagination. Sydney was founded on them, they were as important as brick and stone, timber and earth. The people who sailed into Port Jackson in 1788 carried confident expectations about the new land with them. One of these stories promised a land of boundless, fertile meadows. Another was about the Indigenous people, who were few, weak, passive, did not 'really' possess the land and therefore would present no resistance to the settlers. The new arrivals were supremely confident because their stories came from impeccable sources: the illustrious James Cook and the great Joseph Banks! Significantly, these expectations also underpinned the official plans for the colony: to establish a subsistence agricultural colony, with the convicts providing the labour. As for the Aboriginal people, since they had no 'right' to the land, they were not a 'conquered' people. Phillip and the officers believed they had only to point out the moral and peaceful nature of their project, and then use the comforts of civilisation to persuade Aboriginal people to give up their savage ways and become part of British society.

Invariably, the stories were wrong, or irrelevant. The 'meadows' at first proved chimerical and settlers felt utterly betrayed. The Aboriginal people were strong and numerous, and they were also fierce warriors who not only refused to come near the English camp, but attacked and killed those unprotected by guns. The failure of those foundational stories often caused anger, bewilderment, frustration, and powerful new narratives of disappointment and betrayal. It is always hard to experience the world as we expect it to be dissolving into patternless chaos, and to find ourselves thrust into that uncomfortable realm of doubt and discovery, of having to learn anew.

But that is what happened. Soon, new stories emerged. While they raised flags, cleared, built and sowed their first crops, the literate among them were also writing first histories for eager audiences back Home. Their output was extraordinary: the birth of Sydney must be one of the best-documented settlement projects ever. They also used their writing to make sense of the place and the people, and the self-consciously historic enterprise upon which they had embarked. It wasn't straightforward—they struggled mightily with how to tell it, as we all do.

They had to think about their audience too, as good writers do, and strove to make the story fit into a plot and narrative people at home would understand. In writing this book I was struck over and over again by the significance of this: the self-consciousness of their writing, from Phillip's reports to the letters written by convicts. The narratives are moulded around the kinds of things readers were keen to hear about: is Botany Bay a very wicked place? What is the environment like? Is it topsy-turvy? Could you make money out of it? Tell us about the native people, are they very strange, exotic and savage? Are they cannibals? We must have this lens of audience always in mind as we too pore over their narratives, which became our historical sources.

Other stories blossomed: convicts told tales about going to China in order to escape, or rather to escape punishment when they were caught. They passed on rumours about wild cattle and great rivers and mysterious inland settlements they heard from Aboriginal people, and governors did not know whether to believe or ridicule them. As the decades passed, the colonists learned about the new land, let the climate sink into their bones a bit, and began to tell true stories of their own, stories about the new country, its capriciousness, its wonderful healthfulness, its sheer beauty, tales of rich river flats to the west where the soil would grow anything. Some of these became legends with wide currency: the loss of the first cattle and the way they were found once more, a fat, sleek, wild herd; the miraculous fecundity of women, proof that the environment was nourishing and beneficial. But local knowledge did not necessarily unseat some of those old tales rebounding from the 'old' country, especially the ones about passive 'natives' and degraded convicts. They were powerful, and useful, and they held fast. Neither did the home-grown stories necessarily remain in public knowledge. In later decades they were often eclipsed by new anxieties about origins, and worth, thrown back over early Sydney: tales of a population drowning in rum, of women who were whores one and all, of governors as all-powerful tyrants, and horrific tales of convict life which portrayed transportation as nothing more than brutal and agonising slavery.

This book takes these marvellous, labyrinthine, interleaved stories seriously, from those foundational expectations, to recovered legends of country, to some of the common tales about the early town we hold dear today. They are artefacts too, with histories and provenances, holograms of their time. They tell us something about how people were thinking, what they were expecting and hoping for, what they were planning. They quite literally shaped voyages and actions, street-plans, buildings and gardens. But this book is a history, not a study of texts, or a fictionalised account. It seeks to contextualise the stories, to look carefully at their sources, ask why they were told, and to triangulate them with human experience and real places and outcomes. What happened when the plan to make subsistence farmers out of convicts was actually implemented? What became of the original insistence that the colony be isolated, free of commerce, consumer goods, and alcohol? The ideas, the plans, the theories only tell half the story—the drama lies in the doing, the encounters, the collisions, the gap between expectation and experience.

I think it's important to tell the smaller-scale life-stories too: the stories of notable, extraordinary and legendary people, as well as a few ratbags. Thus these pages are also peopled by Bennelong, Barangaroo, Arthur Phillip, James Ruse and Elizabeth Parry, William and Mary Bryant, Margaret Catchpole and Mary Reibey, John Grant, George Caley, George Bruce and Moowattin, Francis Greenway, Elizabeth Macarthur, William Bligh, Lachlan and Elizabeth Macquarie, Bungaree, Mahroot, and many more. Individuals did make history in early Sydney, but what they did was bound up with the way they saw the world, their stories, the cultural 'webs of their own making', as well as by elements far beyond their control.[6] Many of these people already have stories and legends told about them; these too are re-explored.

———•◦•———

Early Sydney was not just any town, but an unusual one, established by banished convicts, their guards and their governors. So the dynamics and strategies of banishment, forced labour and punishment are germane to this history. But they are not the only narratives, for there were other, rather more glorious, visions for the colony back in England, and, still more significantly, a magnificent mismatch between the plans of the British government and those of the people they sent to Botany Bay. Military officers, along with many convicts and soldiers, considered this colony like any other: a place to make their fortunes, or at least a better life, rather than a place of banishment, isolation and subsistence. Other convicts, and a few soldiers as well, spent all their time in the colony trying to work out how to escape it. Once landed, too, Arthur Phillip and his successors found they could not keep convicts, or anyone else, fixed and controlled in one spot. The 'absence of walls and warders' meant that movement, exploration and encounters occurred out of official sight and control. The consequences were both liberating and tragic.[7]

For many decades, though, the history of this extraordinary town and its rural hinterland was eclipsed by the long, looming shadow of the 'gaol town', perhaps reaching its literary apotheosis in Robert Hughes' *The Fatal Shore*. Early Sydney was so often portrayed as a place of exile, misery and starvation, stamped by the iron fist of authority and ruled by the lash and the noose. It was exceptional, peculiar and perverse, and had little to do with patterns of 'normal' urban development, so why study it as such? Indeed, the whole convict period was often treated as separate from 'legitimate' Australian history, a kind of dark, crude 'before' period: before Macquarie, before gold, before democracy, before freedom of the press, before 'real' economic development, before free immigrants 'normalised' the colony and set it on its 'proper' historical path.[8]

Interestingly, the question that drove a lot of the earlier Sydney histories as a result was this: how could such a hideous place have been transformed into a beautiful and flourishing city, the birthplace of a nation? The search was on for the colony's 'saviour', for the historical turning point between 'convict' and 'free'. While Lachlan Macquarie, as the 'father of Australia', still reigns as the most popular contender, interestingly the latest version of the 'rescue' model is a gendered one.[9] The 2006 film *The Floating Brothel* is subtitled 'The Extraordinary Tale of the *Lady Juliana* and the Unlikely Founding Mothers of Modern Australia'. The film's historical plot portrays Sydney on the brink of extinction, disappearing into a pit of perversion, when, just in the nick of time, the *Lady Juliana* women sail into Sydney Harbour and save it. It's a sort of happily-ever-after story which, like the legend of Governor Macquarie, morphs into a tale of national destiny: in 'saving' Sydney, these women in fact founded the nation.

In this book, nobody 'saved' the colony. The seeds of its survival and shape were already there. They grew vigorously and were nurtured, manipulated, harangued, coaxed and exploited by governors as well as the people—men and women, black and white, free and unfree. They were all makers of Sydney.

In 1827 it was said that most Europeans, 'if asked to describe Australia', would 'think only of ropes, gibbets, arson, burglary, kangaroos, George Barrington and Governor Macquarie'.[10] These responses have been rather long-lived. In 1990 a large proportion of visitors to Old Sydney Town (a painstakingly reconstructed model of early Sydney built near Gosford in the 1970s, now sadly closed), said they associated the early colonial period with 'convicts and floggings'. Re-enacted floggings were among the most popular of Old Sydney Town's live performances.[11] Yet Old Sydney Town had itself emerged out of the same surge of interest in national identity, history and heritage that ended thirteen decades of embarrassed silence and shame over Australia's convict legacy. In an astonishing reversal, the convicts were resurrected and embraced. Having one or more in your family is now a badge of honour, and most revered of all are those who arrived on the First Fleet.[12] It is strange, then, that even though convicts are acknowledged as pioneers of the nation and the founders of families, the stereotypes of convicts—comical figures dragging ball-and-chain shackles, demonised criminals, degraded victims of gruesome punishment—still dominate and fascinate.

These stereotypes have so little to do with life in early Sydney. To begin with, convict men and women did not live in prisons, but in huts and houses which they built themselves or rented from others. They wore their own clothes, not pyjamas with broad arrows on them. They were consumers, interested in domestic comfort, familiar foods and fashionable clothing, and were determined to have them. Some of the energetic emancipists became wealthy traders, landholders and ship-owners. Convicts in the early period were not summarily chained and lashed unless they committed more crimes and had been tried in a court of law. (That said, governors found it so difficult to keep order in the penal colony without walls that the punishments were extremely severe for those unlucky enough to get caught.) Since the colony depended upon their labour, the convicts largely called the tune, insisting on task-work which left them time to themselves, to do as they chose. Women ensured the colony's survival by making families and fostering community and social networks, as well as through their economic contribution as workers, landladies, shopkeepers and entrepreneurs. Both men and women enjoyed the pleasures of preindustrial popular culture— gambling, drinking and fighting—and used them to resist authority. Convicts made their own distinct neighbourhoods in places like the Rocks—a recognisable community had emerged there by the earliest years of the nineteenth century.[13]

If towns emerge from the entangled strands of building, sustainable economic development, emerging families and communities, shared expectations, cultural outlooks and practices and a common knowledge of place, then the first Sydney was in large part created by convict and ex-convict men and women. *The Colony* tells this foundational story. It tracks the ongoing struggle between people and authority for control of the town, but also the confluences and accommodations in this 'dialogue of townscape', this dance of deference and obligation.[14] I also want to convey something of what it was like to live and work in early Sydney: which were the favoured places, the places scarred by evil, the places which were dangerous and wild; and how it was that property, even secured with nothing more than simple occupation, or 'naked possession', became so sacred it fuelled a rebellion.[15]

Readers may be surprised to find that nearly half this book deals with the Aboriginal people of the Sydney region, and their relations with the Europeans. This might at first seem out of proportion. I assure you it is not: it reflects historical reality. Aboriginal people far outnumbered Europeans in these years. Their early attempts to conciliate and negotiate with the invaders, and their eventual decision to leave them to their own devices at Sydney Cove/Warrane, meant that the beachhead there survived. The founding of the city, and the settlements and towns on the Cumberland Plain, was also predicated on Aboriginal dispossession.

In this book the narratives of town-building, rural settlement and environmental responses are encircled by histories of the Aboriginal people of Sydney. Of all the rich and gripping stories of what happened in the Sydney region after 1788, these are the most astonishing and the most poignant. It is time to shake off the idea that Sydney was a 'white' city, that Aboriginal people simply faded out of the picture and off the 'stage of history': it is simply untrue. The time has come, too, to recognise that Aboriginal people became urban people very quickly. But they did so in remarkable ways in these early years—by devising new ways to live which were nevertheless compatible with traditional lifeways and their own Law. Again we find those great themes, transformation and continuity, entangled. This story also challenges the common but false and corrosive assumption that Aboriginal people have no valid place in cities, that cities are by default 'white' space.[16] They have been in Sydney-town almost as long as white settlers.

The breaking of the 'great Australian silence' about Aboriginal history and dispossession led eventually to a sea change of interest and research in urban Aboriginal history and cross-cultural relations.[17] Perhaps the most extraordinary and successful of these works are Inga Clendinnen's history *Dancing with Strangers* and Kate Grenville's novel *The Secret River.* I want to briefly discuss these works because both have at their heart the quest to understand the nature of race relations in the early colony in an intimate, human way. Both allow us to talk about different ways of 'doing' history, especially history so long drowned out by the 'white noise of history making', history that seemed lost, irrecoverable.[18]

In *Dancing with Strangers* Clendinnen turns an anthropological eye upon the relationships between the Australians (as she decided to call the Aboriginal people) and the British officers, and focuses largely on what happened in and around the town of Sydney in the early years. Clendinnen does not flinch from the tragic and brutal outcomes of the invasion, but the overarching message of *Dancing with Strangers* is this: Australia's race relations did not begin with racism and violence, but a remarkable 'springtime of trust':

> There were no pitched battles between residents and incomers, but instead rather touching performances of mutual goodwill and gift-giving . . .

> . . . each initially viewed the other as objects not of threat, but of curiosity and amusement; through those early encounters each came to recognise the other as fellow-humans, fully participant in a shared humanity.[19]

If violence and racism stained Australia's history later, she says, it was not through the actions or intentions of Governor Phillip and the officers. Yet all their efforts came to nothing: the experiment ended in failure. The 'springtime' was tragically brief.

Kate Grenville says she wanted to know what happened between settlers and Aboriginal people, and specifically what her own great-great-great-grandfather Solomon Wiseman 'might have done when he crossed paths with Aboriginal people'. But while Clendinnen had her shelf of officers' journals, Grenville says she had only folders full of bits and bobs, piles of unconnected notes, dull dusty documents written in pompous, arcane language. She decided to write a novel instead of a history, and was thus free, as she charmingly and cheerfully puts it, to 'pillage' history.[20] Her story, set on the isolated reaches of the Hawkesbury River, was spun out of conflicts and atrocities which happened in other places, at other times. So Grenville argues that *The Secret River*, while fiction, nevertheless has historical validity, because these things 'really happened'. In fact, fiction is a way to 'make history real'.[21] The story tracks her imaginary settlers' relations with Aboriginal people as they spiral from grudging tolerance and cautious friendships into atrocities, poisonings and gruesome massacres. For a fiction-writer, historical details and accurate chronology matter far less than the larger underlying narrative and message. Untethered from minutiae, the novel can be seen as an archetypal story about all settlers, and settler psyche, on frontiers throughout the colonial period.

In *The Colony* I want to continue Clendinnen's and Grenville's project of re-examining and rethinking early colonial race relations, but I have taken a broader and longer view. I move beyond relations between officers and Eora in Sydney in those first years to explore those between different social groups and Aboriginal people in the period up to about 1840. In the rural hinterland, the stories are not about fictional settlers in one particular place, but real settlers in the many different places where the war on the Cumberland Plain was really fought. This approach has led to rather different conclusions. Those seemingly benign early official encounters, the 'dancing', curiosity and amusement, were underwritten by the threat of violence and guns after all. We cannot quarantine the early years from the rest of Australian history, nor quite so easily exonerate the British officers in the way they wanted us to. The experiment did not fail. Despite the disasters that befell them, Aboriginal people successfully made a place for themselves in Sydney for at least four decades.

I believe that it is possible to write of settlers without having to fictionalise them, and of Aboriginal people without caricaturing them.[22] Frontier violence, along with frontier accommodation and intimacy, really happened on the Cumberland Plain—and was recorded in newspapers, letters and archives. It seems a strange strategy, then, to borrow and stitch from other places and times. But these real events must be contextualised, considered and told in one another's light, for they have their own integrity. While there are overarching patterns as the settlers pushed further into Aboriginal land, the violence was also often contingent, dependent on place and season and the webs of relationships settlers and Aboriginal people had made with one another. So one story will not do for all after all. Time, place and chronology are essential to a genuine understanding of what happened. That said, some events and patterns remain obscure, hidden by silences and omissions. When the details get sketchy, when I am spinning thin threads of interpretation between scanty sources, I will tell you.[23]

It is important to note that *The Colony* is not an Aboriginal history of Sydney. That book still needs to be written. Much of the story of what happened in the Sydney region after the early colonial period has been retrieved, patiently pieced together by historians and archaeologists, Indigenous and non-Indigenous. But much more of this 'middle ground' history still needs to be recovered and acknowledged; the story remains, and remains to be told.[24]

———•◦•———

The noted American urban historian and architect, Dolores Hayden, writes of place as having an 'overload of possible meanings'. Nevertheless, 'it is place's very same assault on all the ways of knowing (sight, sound, smell, touch, and taste) that makes it powerful as a source of memory, as a weave where one strand ties in another'. We are back with Bernard Smith's words about a 'deeper history', and his plea for a more fully rounded, more sensual and therefore more human understanding of our past. Hayden insists that place 'needs to be at the heart of urban landscape history, not at the margins'.[25]

Novelists often say they are inspired by a 'sense of place' in Sydney—or perhaps that should be *places*. 'Place is the chalice in which the story and people grow', novelist Gabrielle Lord told *The (Sydney) Magazine* in 2007. But by place they also mean what happened in them, the history of the places. Lord gave some examples:

In the Rocks, when I see the stone in the Argyle Street cutting, I think of the tremendous violence of those convicts' lives. Or in Rushcutters Bay [the setting for her novel *The Whipping Boy*], I think of the first murders of Aborigines in the colony. Sydney is stunningly beautiful but humans have shadows as well as brightness.[26]

But as Inga Clendinnen argued in her vehement critique of Grenville's novel, you cannot divine history simply through present-day 'empathy' with place, by the way it makes you *feel*. Places and the stories that cling to them can be delicious, or poignant, or inspire a sense of unease, but they can also be seductively misleading. The men who hacked out the now dark, damp and sinister Argyle Cut in the 1840s were relics of the final days of the convict system. Perhaps they experienced 'tremendous violence' in that harsher period; but most of the convicts of the Rocks did not. They lived there in family groups, or as lodgers, in houses and they made a community there. Rushcutters Bay was not the site of the first murders of Aboriginal people. This story, though widely believed, seems to have been confused with killings of convict rushcutters by Aboriginal warriors in 1788, which happened not at Rushcutters Bay but 'up the harbour', probably around Balmain.[27] So, while there are kernels of truth in these foggy tales, places, like stories, need to be taken seriously, they need to be researched as well as visited and experienced; they need history.

At the same time, like novelists, I am keenly and constantly aware that the people of whom I write experienced Sydney emotionally and sensually, as well as intellectually and practically, that they occupied and acted in real places, which you can visit, and that some physical traces of the early town and the rural hinterland still exist. While we cannot 'post ourselves back in time', it is nevertheless important to return to places.[28] Often there remain fragments and reminders, the 'real things from the real past', insights you can only grasp by seeing the lie of the land. In some places we can still climb the hills they climbed, gaze over vistas which entranced them, or the landscapes they created. We can still see pictures they painted, the very brushstrokes, read their letters, touch the walls they built, feel the smoothness of their blue-and-white china and iridescent shell fish-hooks, or the weight of a heavy iron hoe. We can still taste sweet tea and wild spinach and saltspray, and feel the texture of bladey grass and rushes and kangaroo grass between our fingers. So this narrative is often anchored in real places and set about with things, reminding readers that these lives were lived in real geographic locations. Where places have been destroyed, where mental geographies have been lost, it seeks to retrace them and recover their meanings and histories.[29]

Perhaps my interest in locating history, especially in what seem to be ordinary, everyday places, also stems from the place where I grew up. In western Sydney, where plain, brave, self-certain, relentless new suburbs inundated the paddocks and bushland in the 1950s and 1960s, we were literally surrounded by evidence of the past. There was an old, abandoned farm at the end of our unfinished street— you could wander inside the sandstone cottage; the barns and stables were still full of tools, harnesses and horseshoes. There were reminders of later histories and land-uses too: fibro farmhouses, set back from the roads in open paddocks of long, dry grasses, their families long gone, their bare and empty rooms painted pink or blue, birds nesting high up in the corners. In a bushland gully reserve spared from development, a little creek fringed with maidenhair ferns curved around a brown beach where a great sandstone overhang provided cool shade, or shelter and a soft sand bed.

But for us these were places without memory, whether environmental, Aboriginal or settler histories. Not even foggy legends clung to these clear, bright spaces. They seemed flat, one-dimensional, they were places in transition: they only had a present and future. Cleared blocks, paling fences and an army of skeletal timber house frames overlaid the older patterns, the air was full of frantic hammering and sawing, and the sealed roads, concrete kerbs and gutters surged further forward each year. Yet it had been anything but a blank canvas. I still remember the shock of realising later that the creek *was* very likely the living-place of Aboriginal people, as I had childishly imagined it to be; of discovering the name of the settler who probably built the sandstone cottage; that a terrible war raged between blacks and whites over this seemingly bland, everyday landscape; that hundreds of Irish convict rebels marched down our local roads and were slaughtered by a few well-drilled soldiers. At school we learned a suitably sanitised version of the old ballad 'The Wild Colonial Boy', utterly unaware that our suburbs had been among the haunts of the original hero of this ballad, Bold Jack Donohoe, the most famous of the early bushrangers.

These days, 'places in the heart', places with emotional, social and cultural significance, are recognised by heritage bodies like the National Trust as just as important as the brick, stone and mortar of old buildings.[30] But it is also important to consider 'place' not as a neutral, non-contested, vaguely comforting notion ('there's no place like home') but as *territorial*. Places were contested. People competed to own, to exploit and control places, make homes or refuges in them. They often fought and expelled others in order to do so, and there were competing claims to legitimate occupation.

The struggle for country is most obviously seen in the long war on the Cumberland Plain, when Aboriginal people resisted the invading foragers, farmers and graziers and tried to drive them out. In the aftermath they came to accommodations with the white people in order to survive. Peter Read has explored the legacy of this struggle in terms of place and belonging, the ways the same country can be held as heartland by both Aboriginal and non-Aboriginal people today.[31] There were also early attempts to separate free settlers from ex-convicts, creating zones and regions closely associated with different social groups, divergent cultures and reputations for respectability or roughness. Territoriality and the politics of space underpinned the zones of early Sydney town too, from Phillip's tripartite division into civil, military and convict districts, to Bligh's abortive attempt to wrest back urban spaces for the crown. Lachlan and Elizabeth Macquarie's determined attempts to both control the urban convict population and to refashion Sydney as a place fit for genteel people were strongly challenged by Sydney's convict and working people. The Macquaries never quite achieved the transformation they so desired.

Perhaps it's also the rate and scale of change through suburbanisation and commercial and industrial development, the same processes I saw as a child, which drive my interest in the relict places, the *places where things happened*, places people used or loved or avoided or neglected. These are 'storied lands', replete with meanings so dense, so rich, so poignant, so ancient, so modern; yet so often invisible. Ordinary places and landscapes are still often assumed to be *tabula rasa*, as if there is nothing there, no histories, no human meaning.[32] Developers, planners, politicians and Sydney's wider community still act as though the remnant bushland, the old farming land, the rusty, dilapidated industrial areas are blank canvases, simply waiting to be inscribed with new development. It is strange, too, that the 'local' so often runs a poor third to 'national' and 'state' in both history and heritage assessment, when it is often the local, the familiar, the visceral, the intimate that matters most to city and suburban people.[33]

This book seeks to weave a path between past and present places, to excavate the meanings they held for past as well as present generations, to foster an historical consciousness of place. I believe it is possible, indeed essential, to recover those layered meanings. How else can we really grasp the ways in which generations of people interacted with this place? How they fought it, destroyed it, learned from it, transformed it, defended it, grew into it? How else can we understand what dispossession meant, what it still means? How else can we really understand the origins and lineaments of our city?

Chapter 1

————◆————

DEEP TIME AND HUMAN HISTORY: THE SYDNEY ENVIRONMENT

Sydney grew from a speck of European settlement pegged down on the edge of the deep, drowned valley, Sydney Harbour. The Parramatta River, flowing into the harbour from the west, is fed by a web of smaller rivers and creeks draining the flat and undulating lands of tall forests and open woodlands of the Cumberland Plain. To the south, water flowed from the Paddington ridge through a vast area of wetlands and sand dunes into Sydney's other great harbour, Botany Bay. Perhaps most strikingly, the plain is boxed in on three sides by the massive sandstone escarpments of the Blue Mountains in the west, and the Hornsby and Woronora plateaux in the north and south. In John Birmingham's memorable words: 'It was as though an irascible God, unhappy with his first try, had reached down and pressed his thumb onto the coast, leaving a rim at the edge of the land just high enough to keep out the sea'.[1] But around 20 000 years ago, the sea did begin to invade, and over the next ten millennia it reshaped both country and people. Flowing at the foot of the western and northern 'rim', the Hawkesbury–Nepean River girdles the modern city, running from still-wild highland tributaries in the south-east, flowing north through river-flat country at the foot of the Blue Mountains and then winding eastwards through a forbidding sandstone labyrinth. The river empties into the third great harbour of the Sydney region, Broken Bay.

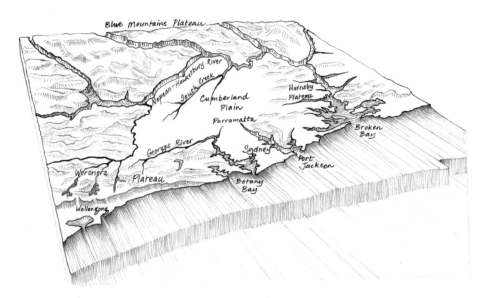

The Sydney region, showing the major geomorphic features. The Cumberland Plain is surrounded by plateaux and girdled by rivers; three great harbours indent the coast; the undersea continental shelf reaches some 50 kilometres out from the present coastline. (Kate Nolan/Doug Benson)

This natural environment shaped the early town and its hinterland profoundly. It was the exposed nature of Botany Bay and the apparent lack of fresh water there which repelled the naval men of the First Fleet. The deep, sheltered harbour to the north, with its numerous freshwater streams, lured them in. The Europeans were a maritime people, water was their element. So they searched and sounded out safe harbours for their ships, while the rivers became their routes inland, ways of exploring, travel and transport. Until the 1820s, all their towns and villages and most of their settlements were coastal, or they were inland 'islands' on rivers. They found the soils they were desperately looking for—shale soils of the Cumberland Plain and alluviums on river flats—and set up farms. Later their stock grazed over the woodlands and pastures created by Aboriginal burning.

By the 1820s, the pattern of farming and grazing lands echoed the funnel shape of the plain's arable soils precisely. But the opposite was true of the high, rough, sandstone country that encircled the plain. These areas were strictly avoided—except where settlers found remnant shale 'caps' left over from the Great Sinking. The sandstone country—the buffeted coastal areas, the Blue

Mountains, Hornsby Plateau to the north and north-west—remained largely in the state the Aboriginal people had maintained it. This avoidance would have a profound impact on ecological conservation in Sydney, for it was these once-shunned areas which became the four great, treasured national parks which encircle Sydney: Royal, Blue Mountains, Ku-ring-gai and Sydney Harbour national parks. Their ecologies became the default 'Sydney ecologies'. By contrast, very little remains of the great variety of original woodlands, tall forests and river flat brush on the arable lands which were cleared for farming or logged for timber to build huts and mansions, ships and storehouses, and then became again a 'blank canvas' for building suburbs. These forests are Sydney's lost landscapes. Suburban expansion took the line of least resistance, spreading first along the waterways, linked by small boats and ferries, and then across them as Sydney became a city of bridges. The flatter land west and south was built over with suburbs first; the steeper, rockier north shore later.

There were other significant and extensive areas which largely escaped the early settlers' axes and fires. To the south of Sydney lay the great Lachlan and Botany swamps, their vast, pure waters running through sandhills, rivers, marshes and creeks and into Botany Bay. The early Europeans found this region unpleasant and difficult, and feared swampy ground as sources of disease, though its teeming bird and animal life was later appreciated by local people and hunters, and the waters would be tapped for the thirsty city.[2] But gradually from the 1820s, and picking up momentum from the 1850s, noxious industries moved out to these 'wastelands', harnessed their waters and used the streams as waste drains. Eventually the Botany and Lachlan swamps were drained and the area became the most heavily industrialised and polluted in Australia.

———•◦•———

The topography, waters and soils which shaped the city in such fundamental ways have their own histories; these are Sydney's oldest, deepest stories. If Sydney is now coastal, its deep time origins were inland. More than 200 million years ago, the east coast of the continent lay hundreds of kilometres from the ocean in the supercontinent, Gondwana. Ancient Sydney was the vast swampy delta of a great river, flowing north from mountains; to the east were the mountains of what would become New Zealand and New Caledonia. It was hot and wet, densely covered with Australia's 'original forest'—rainforests of primitive plant, the conifers, cycads and tree ferns. Over the next 70 million years, the Gondwanan river carried vast quantities of sand, silts and clay down from those mountains, burying the earlier swamps and forests. The grains of these deposits were themselves older again—they are from rocks formed 500–700 million years ago in what is now Antarctica. Layer after layer solidified into strata of shales, claystones, mudstones and golden sandstones, a rock foundation 6 kilometres thick. Under its weight, the organic material below darkened and hardened into the beds and veins of coal. The great river slowed around 150 million years ago, but then westward-flowing streams cut deep channels through the earth and rock of the basin. Jurassic jets of molten volcanic rock thrust up through the sedimentary slab, then hardened into over a hundred breccia pipes which now dot the region, their stone eroded and weathered down to patches of fertile ground. A mass of dark dolerite bulged up from the deep at Prospect, forming Prospect Hill.[3]

These molten jets were the earliest signs of the most momentous event in Sydney's deep time history: 90 million years ago, the land that became the Australian continent began to break away from Gondwana. By 45 million years ago, the Great South Land had begun its slow voyage northwards. New Zealand and New Caledonia had drifted away, leaving behind the jagged dark cliffs lining the east coast. Sydney became oceanic, a tiny dent on the coast of a giant island. The west-flowing rivers now ran east, and tectonic forces split the thick stone strata into what would become harbours, ridges, watercourses. The highlands to the west reared up, the Cumberland Plain sagged and sank. But all of this occurred so slowly that, over millennia, the rivers 'kept pace with tectonic changes'.[4] Their waters eroded the stupendous sandstone canyons and valleys of the Blue Mountains, Port Hacking, Pittwater and Broken Bay. The Parramatta River, beginning so modestly in the little creeks of the gently undulating hills west of Parramatta, carved out the valley that became Sydney Harbour, cutting ever deeper as it flowed further east, its vast mouth guarded by the immense cliffs of North and South Heads.

The untethered land mass drifting north became increasingly arid and the

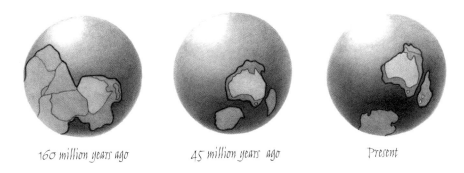

160 million years ago   45 million years ago   Present

Drifting northwards: the breakup of the ancient supercontinent Gondwana. (Kate Nolan)

soils were leached over the aeons. In these conditions, a new plant regime emerged: the fire-loving eucalypts and the dry, sclerophyll forests that Europeans would call 'the bush'. The supremacy of the gum tree in Australia is extraordinary. As Tom Griffiths writes, 'no other comparable area of land in the world is so completely characterised by a single genus of tree'.[5] And this tree found its heartland in Sydney sandstone. Over millennia, the nutrient-poor sandstone soils of Sydney came to nurture a brilliant and immensely diverse array of plants. The shale soils of the plain and the slopes, and the more recent alluvials of the rivers and creeks supported a great range of different forests. Sydney was, and still is, a botanical paradise, with over 1500 species flourishing in a 150-kilometre radius. Botanists Doug Benson and Jocelyn Howell have identified at least 30 distinct vegetation communities in the Sydney region, most of which have eucalypts as their 'keystone species'. These communities can shift subtly over just a few hundred metres, so precisely do they respond to and reflect variations in soil, aspect, shelter, wind, climate and rainfall.[6]

Perhaps most widely recognised as 'Sydney' vegetation are the sclerophyll forests which cloak the rugged sandstone escarpments and ridges. This is the home of *Angophora costata* (also called smooth-barked apple, and Sydney red gum), their twisted limbs, almost human, framing the steep, rocky country, their roots often 'growing out of the heart of rocks', their red-pink-orange trunks glowing like torches among the duller greens, browns and greys. These rocky slopes are also studded with xanthorrhoea, grass trees with wrinkled

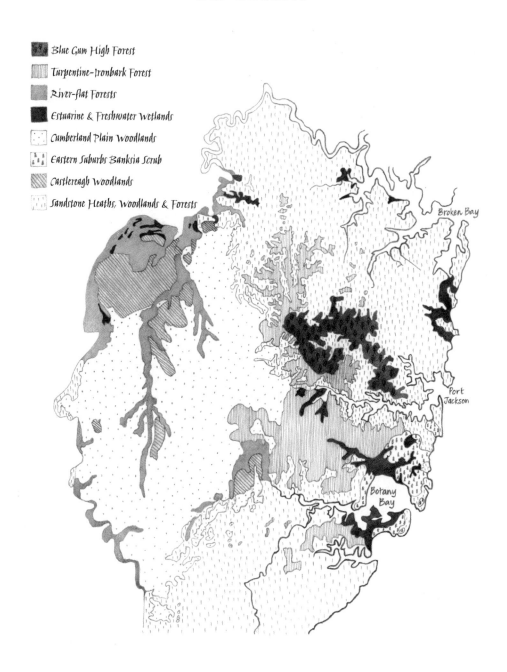

Blue Gum High Forest

Turpentine-Ironbark Forest

River-flat Forests

Estuarine & Freshwater Wetlands

Cumberland Plain Woodlands

Eastern Suburbs Banksia Scrub

Castlereagh Woodlands

Sandstone Heaths, Woodlands & Forests

Broken Bay

Port Jackson

Botany Bay

Sydney's diverse vegetation at 1788. Different soil types and variations in aspect, shelter, wind, climate and rainfall shaped over 30 different ecological communities. (Kate Nolan/ Doug Benson) black trunks, cascades of strappy leaves and long black spikes. Closer to the water's edge, safe from fire, the Port Jackson figs send roots into every rocky crevice and spread vast canopies of deep shade. But Sydney also once had tall, dark forests of massive grey-green turpentines, ironbarks and blue gums, most notably the great Blue Gum High Forest stretching right up the north shore from around present-day Ryde to Castle Hill. These forests colonised the better soils on those slopes, and also some of the eastern parts of the plain, while widely spaced grey box and forest red gums and grassy understoreys colonised the drier, undulating areas west of Parramatta. Low swampy areas supported whispering casuarinas, swamp mahogany, banksias, melaleucas with their layered, papery bark and mangroves. In the face of the triumphant army of eucalypts, vestigial pockets of ancient rainforest retreated to steep sheltered gullies to the south and west of the Sydney region.

The dynamic geological transformations over millions of years, the awesome choreography of continental drift, operate on an utterly different timescale from human history. And yet, over the past 60 millennia at least, Australia was also a peopled landscape. Geological and human history overlap. Many Aboriginal people believe that they have always been here, that their origins lie in the Dreaming with the creation of earth, rocks, stars, and other living creatures. The fossil and artefactual evidence that whitefellas insist upon has simply not been found yet, says Dharawal elder Frances Bodkin.[7] Like the scientific accounts, Aboriginal understandings of how the Sydney region came to be are about powerful forces and dramatic change, but here humans, animals, mythical creatures and country are integral (see the story of Gurangatch and Mirragan below). The stories are charged, as historian Martin Thomas puts it, with 'a fleet-footed current of dynamism and detail, a rapturous celebration of the chase'. They shudder with movement and gigantic leaps, powerful eruptions and magic, land deeply gouged and torn up, rising seas, rushing rivers, drowned valleys and flooded plains.[8]

GURANGATCH AND MIRRAGAN: THE CREATION OF THE WOLLONDILLY AND COXS RIVERS

The Gandangarra of the Blue Mountains tell of the giant Gurangatch, part fish, part reptile, who in a great contest of speed, strength and endurance created the deep rocky valleys of the Wollondilly and Coxs rivers, and each of their tributary streams and waterholes. The story was told to R.H. Matthews before 1908 by Gandangarra people living on a few acres of reserve in the Burragorang Valley in the Blue Mountains. The story, so detailed it serves as an accurate 'navigational aid', begins with Gurangatch living in a waterhole near the junction of the Wingecarribee and Wollondilly rivers. Mirragan, the tiger quoll, a great hunter and fisherman, saw his eye 'shining like a star' in the shallows, and he was determined to catch him. Realising this, Gurangatch broke out of the waterhole, 'tearing up the ground', with the water pouring behind him, creating the Wollondilly. He stuck out his tongue of lightning and in its flash saw the relentless Mirragan coming after him, so he tore down under the ranges, diving into the Wombeyan Caves. Mirragan took long sticks and poked holes down into the caves where Gurangatch was hiding, and these holes can still be seen. The creature turned left, twisting and doubling back in an attempt to outsmart and lose Mirragan, and so created Coxs River and its tributaries. Eventually both hunted and hunter called on others for help. The exhausted Gurangatch found relatives in the dark depths of Binnoomur (Jenolan Caves) and they took him to a deep waterhole, Joolundoo. There they hid him with their smaller bodies, and his head and tail became wedged in rock crevices. Mirragan, knowing where Gurangatch was hiding, called on the best divers to assist him—Billagoola the shag, Goolagwangwan the musk duck, Gundhareen the black duck and Goonarring the wood duck. Each dived down into the waterhole, surfacing with one of Gurangatch's smaller relatives, but finally Billagoola reached Gurangatch. He could not shift him, but managed to tear a great piece of flesh from his back. The hunter and the divers cooked the meat, shared 'a great feast' together and then returned to their homes.[9]

Archaeologist Josephine Flood writes that stories of the Rainbow Serpent, Gorrondolmi, are widely known in northern Australia. Like Gurangatch, Gorrondolmi is an ancestral creative being—a snake with supernatural features and powers, with a tongue of forked lightning. Gorrondolmi also 'created rivers and waterholes and left traces on the landscape along a Dreaming Track'. The Rainbow Serpent became well known, a generalised figure and story in white understandings of Aboriginal culture. Around 1958, Fred McCarthy, Sydney's pioneer archaeologist, found a 'huge-tailed creature 19-ft long drawn in solid yellow with a black outline' on the wall of a cave in the Cordeaux River catchment. He was, he wrote, 'inclined to regard it as a Rainbow-serpent'. The creature has an eel-like tail and fins but a great, thick body, more like a whale or a huge reptile. Small human figures accompany it. Perhaps it is Gurangatch: huge, powerful, but stuck fast on the rock face. Perhaps the Cordeaux and the other tributaries of the Nepean, running in their deep, rugged gullies before they were dammed for the city's water supply, were created by him or one of his relatives.[10]

Pioneer archaeologist F.D. McCarthy recorded this drawing of a huge fish-creature, over 6 metres long, found on the wall of a cave in the Cordeaux/Woronora catchment area, south-west of Sydney. (Kate Nolan/F.D. McCarthy)

Archaeologists wonder whether distant plumes and palls of smoke on the southern horizon drew the first Aboriginal people across seas and the land bridge from South-east Asia 60000 or more years ago. Moving southwards, these people colonised the entire continent. We do not know when the first Aboriginal people discovered and named Dyarubbin (the Hawkesbury–Nepean), Warrane (Sydney Cove) or Cadi (the lower reaches of Sydney Harbour). Perhaps they followed ridges or rivers down the steep-sided gullies of the Blue Mountains onto the plain, or moved down the coastline, coming upon what were then the broad beaches of the east coast. Archaeologist Val Attenbrow, who has written the most thorough study of the region's Aboriginal history and archaeology to 1788, points out the evidence for their occupation in other parts of New South Wales—60000 to 50000 years ago at Lake Mungo, and 40000 to 30000 years ago at Cuddie Springs in western New South Wales. The ancestors of Aboriginal people reached Tasmania by about 35000 years ago.

So Attenbrow reasonably argues they had settled in the Sydney region well before this time. Thousands of archaeological sites have been identified in the Sydney region, and some confirm Attenbrow's theory. For example, a heavy cobble chopper found embedded in the base of a gravel quarry face at Castlereagh on the Nepean River in Sydney's west was eventually dated to 50 000 years old. It is among the oldest artefacts yet found in Australia.[11] Attenbrow suggests that some of the earliest campsites probably existed near shorelines and waterways which were later inundated by rising sea levels. Perhaps they still lie under the waters and the earth.[12]

Through experience of place over thousands of years, Aboriginal people learned the particular climatic conditions that ruled Sydney's environment: the constant dance between drought and deluge, El Niño and La Niña, between semi-tropical luxuriance and fiery aridity. Scientists have only recently grasped that Australia's climate is not its own—it is governed by the El Niño Southern Oscillation (ENSO) effect. Ocean temperatures, currents and waves drive wind and rainfall patterns across the entire southern hemisphere, from South America to South-east Asia. Australia, as Tim Flannery points out, is the only continent held completely in the thrall of ENSO and the chaotic conditions it brings.[13] In non-drought years, the ocean's cooler temperatures mean that the great winds blow westwards, clouds form, and the monsoons arrive. But perhaps two out of seven years, the unequal embrace of the winds and waters of the Pacific reverses. The warm waters off Peru rise—El Niño, the 'little one', or the Christ child, has arrived. The winds diminish, then turn to blow the other way. Peru endures destructive floods, while on the other side of the Pacific, land and vegetation dry out, harden and wait for fire.[14] The drought breaks, often with flooding rain, when La Niña, the 'girl child', returns.

Aboriginal people developed effective ways to manage and maintain their country, subject as it was to these cycles, especially through fire. They burned parts of the country at different times and in different ways to control undergrowth. 'Cleaning up country', as it is still called in some Aboriginal communities, prevented the build-up of dry material, the fuel for uncontrollable wildfires. It also created open woodlands in some areas, while others grew dense and dark.[15] As Jim Kohen argues, their fire management must have had considerable environmental impacts, affecting the flow of water, soil composition and erosion as well as vegetation, animals, birds and insects.[16]

Traditional and ancient Aboriginal life is so often portrayed as static, as if Aboriginal people passively occupied a 'timeless land', making no impact upon it. Yet the land could scarcely be called 'timeless', for the Sydney environments the first Aboriginal people encountered were very different to those of modern Sydney. The rivers, which are tidal today, were freshwater right to the sea. Dyarubbin, the Hawkesbury–Nepean, was bigger and ran faster than today, and laid down vast beds of gravel on its banks near Penrith between 100 000 and 50 000 years ago. The Georges River, which now runs east, flowed southwards across the sandy wetland plain that became Botany Bay to join the Hacking River. The Cooks River ran due east into the ocean; now it flows south into Botany Bay.

Twenty thousand years ago, the sea level had fallen to its lowest point, 140 metres below present levels. Sydney Harbour was still a vast valley, its famous long headlands and finger-like bays were the ridges and gullies of tributary streams— the freshwater Tank Stream, Lane Cove River, Tarban Creek, for example. The coastline itself was somewhere between 15 and 20 kilometres further east from where it is today. Standing on what is now South Head, you would have looked out over a vast, gently undulating plain, stretching away from the foot of the cliffs that mark today's coastline. From Broken Bay to Botany Bay, the plain met the sea in long, broad beaches between the mouths of the rivers. Generations of Aboriginal people witnessed the formation of the vast dunes systems of the eastern suburbs, as southerly winds lifted and carried sand-drifts to cover the older sandstone of the coast, especially at Kurnell. It was a colder, drier place, too. They lived here before and during the coldest part of the last ice age (25 000 to 15 000 years ago), when temperatures were 6 to 10 degrees Celsius cooler than they are now. So the people who took shelter in the cave on Kings Tableland in the Blue Mountains 22 000 years ago lived in extremely cold conditions, since the mountains were then periglacial—on the edge of the glaciers which engulfed the Southern Alps and highlands.[17]

But the most dramatic environmental change coastal Aboriginal people experienced was rising sea levels. At the end of the ice age, the ice sheets of the polar regions began to melt in the warmer temperatures. The waters crept inexorably up the shallow slope of what is now the undersea inner continental shelf off Sydney at an estimated rate of 2 metres per year. Around 10 000 years ago, the broad coastal beach and plain were inundated and the ocean crashed at the foot of the sandstone cliffs. The coast took on its present appearance— the series of cliffs, rocky foreshores and headlands with small crescent beaches tucked between. The waters gradually drowned the ancient valleys of the Parramatta and Hawkesbury rivers, and the swampy plain that became Botany Bay. High points and outcrops became islands, ridges became headlands, and salt water mixed with fresh as the rivers became estuaries, tidal for up to 50 kilometres inland.[18]

10,000 years ago   *Present*

Drowned valley: rising sea levels transformed ridges into the finger-like headlands of Sydney Harbour's north shore, and high points became harbour islands. (Kate Nolan)

As some of the stories told by Aboriginal people today still relate, country and campsites were lost as sea invaded land—about 1100 square kilometres of land on the coast and 45 square kilometres in Sydney Harbour. One meaning of the word 'Cadi', the Aboriginal name for lower Sydney Harbour, is 'below' or 'under'.[19] Yet the loss was most likely offset by the 250-odd kilometres of extra estuarine shoreline created by the rising waters, where rich resources of fish and shellfish could be harvested. Meanwhile the inland peoples grew—or remained— marvellously adept at climbing the tall forest trees to hunt possums and other small mammals.

Aboriginal Law legends throb with transformative power; they turn on dynamism rather than stasis. This was no timeless land. Rising waters, warming climate, El Niño droughts, shifting dunes and shorelines, the changing course of rivers, temporary islands and lagoons, the bush transformed after fire or rain: all are integral to the Sydney environment and must have been central to Aboriginal people's knowledge of country, learned over generations. It was precisely this mutability—things not being as they appeared, or changing mercurially from season to season or over a few years—which confronted and confounded the second wave of colonisers, who came from the sea in 1788.

Chapter 2

————◆•◆•◆————

ENCOUNTERS IN EORA COUNTRY

When the Europeans arrived in the Sydney region, writes Aboriginal activist and elder Burnum Burnum, 'they landed in the middle of a huge art gallery'. On the shorelines today, in the national parks and reserves, and even silently underlying suburbia, are more than 10 000 artworks, carved or painted on stone. Sydney is the world's largest outdoor museum of Indigenous art. At Cowan a beached whale is swarmed by a ladder of people eager to feast; a school of fish turns as one on a rock face at West Head; lovers copulate quietly in a secluded spot there beneath the stars. In Broken Bay, fish are painted on an angled rock face not far from the heaving waterline. Is it a sign—good fishing here? Or something more, telling of fish and people and water? Kangaroos are fixed on rocky platforms beside Dyarubbin/Hawkesbury–Nepean River at Castlereagh. Sometimes *mundoes*, carved footprints, lead away to high ground: perhaps they led boys to the place where they became men or learned lessons of country and the Dreaming. These are 'emotionally charged' places, mysterious and compelling.[1]

Today the grooved and painted images, many corralled by rail fences or boardwalks or wire mesh, are the most visible marks of the first people of this place.[2] Few modern Sydneysiders realise that they also live amidst thousands of other Aboriginal sites—rock-shelters, middens, stoneworking sites, carved trees, burial sites—or that Aboriginal artefacts lie in the earth below their feet, below the masses of concrete, bricks and bitumen, under backyards and beside creeks.[3] Eora country has been damaged by the city, but not erased. Aboriginal people today say some stories and Law legends survived the maelstrom of invasion too, passed on through families. When the Europeans arrived, the country was already richly named and divided. A few of the placenames survived, by common usage or deliberate attempts to remember, in many suburban and street names. Listen to the soft, rolling sounds of the 'Sydney Language': Maroubra, Bondi, Parramatta, Turramurra, Bunnerong, Patonga.[4]

The city of Sydney is predicated upon the dispossession of Aboriginal people—their loss underpins the city's foundation and growth as it expanded over more and more of their country. Their dispossession is often seen as sad but inevitable, the price of founding a new nation and a great city. And it was instant too. The year 1788 is the fatal turning point, where black 'prehistory' is neatly sheared off so that the white 'history' of city-making can begin. It's a powerful date: some ecologists still use it as shorthand for their ideal of pristine, stable indigenous vegetation communities. Archaeologists use 'at 1788' for the way Aboriginal people lived before Europeans arrived. But the Sydney region was not suddenly transformed into white space when the first white feet sloshed onto the beaches in that year. Months passed before the Boorooberongal of Western Sydney even saw white men crashing through their country (although they had probably heard about them). It was six years before whites began building huts and planting maize on the river flats of the Hawkesbury. Meanwhile back at the Camp on Warrane/Sydney Cove, many coastal peoples were already living in the town with the Europeans, sharing their houses and food, in late 1790.

So, as well as that rich, barely acknowledged archaeological record, Sydney has an Aboriginal history, not located safely in the distant past, but unbroken, and still throbbing insistently today. The city itself would shape the destiny of thousands of Aboriginal people over two centuries, with waves of people displaced, but also arriving over the decades. It destroyed lives, communities and cultures, but then offered hope and refuge.

FIRST ENCOUNTERS

The Europeans saw Eora at the 'edge of the trees', and the Eora saw Europeans in their *murri nowie*, their strange canoes.[5] But the first *encounters* took place on the beaches of Botany Bay, Sydney Harbour and then Broken Bay. Surf, sand and the encircling bush beyond framed gestures, shouted words, gifts, raised spears, muskets at the ready. Often, the beach was empty, the fires cold. The Eora ignored and avoided the strangers, and disappeared into the bush.

When James Cook sailed the *Endeavour* into Botany Bay in April 1770 he was trying to establish whether New South Wales was already occupied, and what the nature of that occupation was. This assessment was critical to the way English settlement could 'legally' proceed in the new world. If the preliminary annexation of new territory was to be permanent, then the flags, stone cairns, blazed trees and footprints that Europeans customarily left as their marks on 'savage shores' had to be followed by settlement.[6] Annexation involved appropriate negotiations with indigenous peoples—persuasion or purchase—but only if they were deemed to *own* the land. For the English, ownership—the right to land—was not the same as mere occupation, and so arose the strange double-talk of an empty land which was clearly peopled. Leaving aside for the moment the absurdity of 'legal' invasions and land seizures, the litmus-test questions were these: did these people reside in one place? Had they earned a right to the land by exploiting nature? Did they cultivate the earth, and make it theirs by mixing their labour with it? Did they build houses and other substantial buildings? Had they developed complex social hierarchies and political organisations? Cook's and Joseph Banks' impressions of the Gweagal at Botany Bay, and also the Murri at Endeavour River in north Queensland, were scattered, ill founded and generally 'unremarkable', yet they would have such a profound impact on the future of the continent, both land and peoples, and they set a template for how the history of race relations would be understood.[7]

As the first English longboat laboured towards the Botany Bay shore, two armed Gweagal warriors, nameless but immortalised, met the strangers with a show of warning and strength. 'Their countenance bespoke displeasure; they threatened us and discovered hostile intentions, often crying to us *warra warra wai*.'[8] When a musket was fired into the air they threw stones, and when the strangers landed, spears fell between their feet. Cook ordered the musket to be fired at the warriors and one man was wounded. Abruptly the mood changed: the men were 'frantic and furious', their women and children set up a 'horrid howl'. The men ran off, leaving women and children cowering in the bark houses of their camp. The English picked up the warriors' artefacts, left little piles of nails in return, and rowed away.[9]

It seems that Cook botched this first official encounter. As historian Maria Nugent argues in her explorations of Botany Bay, the warning show of strength (as well as the way that people had earlier simply ignored the ships, as we will see) was probably a ritual prelude to meetings and exchanges of names and gifts. But actually wounding one's hosts in their own country before any meeting had even taken place clearly sent the process into a spin. Thereafter the Gweagal would have nothing to do with the strangers, and avoided them and their gifts. 'All they seemed to want', wrote Cook, 'was for us to be gone'. There may have been contacts and exchanges with others from Cook's ship, though, during visits to collect water or botanical specimens. After a week the Europeans did sail away again, which probably 'redeemed them in Eora eyes'.[10] Eighteen years/scores of seasons later the encounters would often follow similar patterns—but they were more successful: what started with a warning hail of spears would often progress to exchange of names, shared food and hilarious, if tense, games and dancing.

In 1770, Cook and Banks decided that the people of the east coast of Australia were few, that they possessed no political or social organisation beyond the family, and that they did not stay in one place, but wandered 'like Arabs from place to place'. The interior, they surmised, was probably not populated at all. Their houses showed neither art nor industry, their tools and weapons were crude and they were naked, even the women. Cook and Banks knew that they burned the country constantly—they watched the fires along the entire east coast of this 'continent of smoke'.[11] But here fire was not used to clear the ground for agriculture—its use was obvious, but the purpose and impact remained opaque. Thus, most significantly, Aboriginal people did not appear to cultivate the earth, so that New South Wales was judged to be 'in the pure state of Nature, the Industries of Man had nothing to do with any part of it'. The Europeans therefore believed themselves to be the first legitimate claimants of the land, so they had no legal obligations to compensate Aboriginal people or convince them to cede sovereignty. Besides which, Banks (whose influence as adviser to the later settlement project grew as the accuracy of his memory of Botany Bay diminished) claimed the Eora were a weak, dull and cowardly people who would not defend their country.[12]

As historian Andrew Fitzmaurice points out, the belief that a people could only 'own' land if they exploited it was part of a long tradition of natural law ideas of property, a tradition 'at the heart of the motivation for European expansion' from the sixteenth to the twentieth centuries. In Australia these ideas would underpin the spread of settlement and race relations throughout the nineteenth and twentieth centuries.[13] Yet they were founded on a few days' mistaken impressions, on not being able to see. As ethnologists and anthropologists slowly pieced together the nature of Aboriginal life and society, the terrible irony of those first reports emerged. Aboriginal people were not truly nomadic at all, but moved about limited and deeply known territory. They had developed highly complex marriage, kinship, moral and legal systems which were inseparable from land. They had successfully populated the entire continent, even the most arid and difficult places, and their 'industries' and land management had probably reshaped every part of Australia. Their ways of life nevertheless depended upon local environments and ecologies and were finely attuned to them. People developed different ways of exploiting resources and caring for country, and so mobility patterns, skills, tools, language and knowledge varied from coast to plain, mountains to deserts. Most were hunters and gatherers, though in some places they herded pelican, or harvested and cultivated in ways which ensured future crops. At Lake Condah in Victoria they constructed an extensive network of waterways, farmed, smoked and exported eels, and lived in a large settlement of stone huts. They knew country intimately, had named every place and feature, and invested all with multiple levels of mythological and spiritual meaning. Aboriginal people had mixed their labour, their spiritual beliefs, social structures and laws, their arts and industries so thoroughly with the land that they had coalesced, and were indivisible.[14] All of this was invisible to the strangers anchored at the eastern rim in 1770.

EORA AND COUNTRY

The Sydney region is just a dot on the continent, yet it offers a glimpse of this extraordinary variety. Here alone were over 30 separate groups of people, now known as clans, of which the Gweagal and Kameygal of south and north Botany Bay were two. Each was made up of around 30 to 50 people related to one another and many appear to have taken their names from their country—Cadigal from Cadi, or the south shore of Sydney Harbour from Watsons Bay to Sydney Cove; Wangal from Wanne, the lower reaches of the Parramatta River, Kameygal from Kamay, Botany Bay. Some names refer to the creatures they relied upon for food—for example the Cabrogal of the Liverpool area on the Georges River, who feasted upon the *cabro* (teredo) worms. Others may have been named for their special skills or traits—the powerful Cammeragal of the north shore and Middle Harbour were famous for the skills of their clever men (*karadji*), who were known in other places as *gomera*.[15]

These clans were woven together by women. Clan members could not marry one another—they married people from other clans. Usually the woman came to live with her husband's people, bringing her own words, toolkits and knowledge, though she also kept 'spiritual and emotional ties to her own country' and returned to it to have her babies. Women were the links, the ones who bound the peoples together. Clans that were related by marriage hunted and fished together as larger bands—these bands may also have had names, but they are lost to us.[16]

Gradually it dawned on the First Fleet officers that they had not encountered one people, but a constellation of peoples, each with their own country, distinctive weapons and tools, and ways of dressing and ornamenting their hair and bodies, all instantly recognisable. The Botany Bay people gummed their hair so that it looked to the Europeans 'like the thrums of a mop', while other groups had wavy, matted hair. On the coast people decorated their hair with the teeth of animals, while inland people glued in the 'tails of several small animals'. Overall they were strong and healthy, 'a straight well-limbed people & very active', a people who 'walk very erect'.[17] The different groups might be sworn enemies or great friends and allies at different times. What was more, languages were different, not only between Endeavour River and Botany Bay (the

Europeans brought the Murri word 'kangaroo' to New South Wales from Endeavour River via Cook and Banks, whereupon the Eora assumed that sheep, horses and cows were also called 'kangaroo'), but between some of the people of the Hawkesbury and those at Port Jackson. 'But this is not so wonderful', mused Judge Advocate David Collins, 'as that a people living at a distance of only 50 . . . miles should call the sun and moon by different names'.[18]

Collins was referring to the differences between the coastal groups and the people inland at Dyarubbin, the Hawkesbury–Nepean River.[19] The coastal Eora of Sydney were saltwater people. Fish and shellfish were a major part of their diet, and they excelled in fishing, swimming, diving and manoeuvring simple bark canoes (nowie) through the largest surf. Women were particularly skilled in all of these. They fished and paddled with fires lit in the nowie for warmth and cooking, and infants at their breasts or on their shoulders, their fishing songs carried on breezes over the waters. Joseph Banks gazing over Botany Bay at night saw scores of small lights dancing on the dark waters and realised each was a fishing nowie.[20]

Eora women had the top two joints of their little finger removed as infants in an operation called *malgun*. Removing the little finger was said to have assisted with their fishing, though many writers, then as now, have been sceptical of this explanation, because it seemed 'trivial'. As we shall see, fishing was anything but trivial. Some conclude malgun was a sign of the girl-child being promised in marriage rather than for the enhancement of fishing. It was certainly seen as a sign of status, for women who had not undergone malgun were regarded 'with some degree of contempt'. Perhaps it denoted Eora women's special status as both fishers and future wives.[21]

The word seems to echo in other languages in the Sydney region too, always associated with fingers: among the Gandangarra of the mountains and southern highlands, the great stone pillars of the Three Sisters near Katoomba are said to be a monument to malgun, their three intact fingers, and one truncated stump, reaching up from the Megalong valley. In later decades the word had more frightening associations. Among the people of the Wollombi Valley in the 1830s *Mile-gun* was an evil spirit with long fingernails for digging into human flesh.[22]

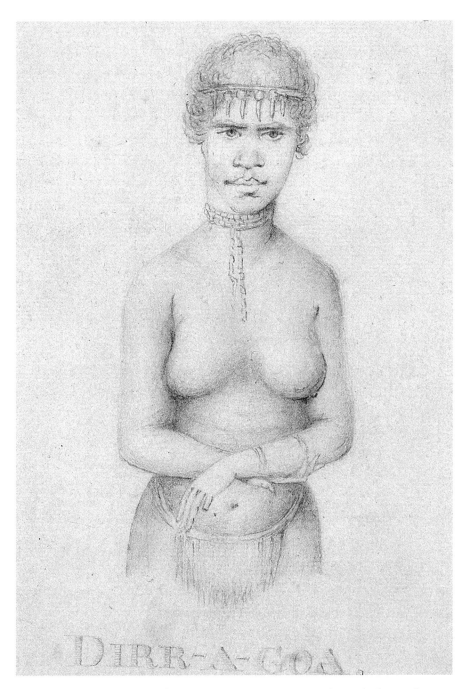

Thomas Watling's portrait of young Eora woman Dirragoa shows she has undergone malgun; she also wears jewellery and a barin, *or apron. (Natural History Museum)*

While men stood motionless in the shallows, watching for fish they speared with long multi-pronged fish-gigs, women alone used hooks and lines. The line (*carr-re-jun*) was 'nicely shredded & twisted very close and neatly' from kurrajong bark, the 'inside bark of the cabbage tree', flax plant, animal fur, or grasses 'as fine as raw silk'. They honed their fish-hooks (*burra*) from turban shells (*Turbo torquata*). In one early portrait, an Eora woman wears one of these pearly, crescent-shaped hooks around her neck.[23]

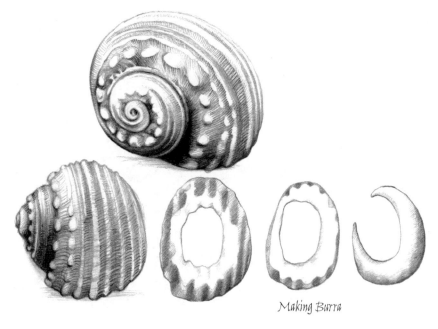

Making Burra

Making burra: Eora women honed their crescent-shaped hooks from the turban shell Turbo torquata. *(Kate Nolan)*

These hooks tell an intriguing story, a women's story. They are unique to much of the east coast of Australia and they only came into use in this region of the south-east coast between 1200 and 500 years ago. Were they invented locally? Or did they spread from the coast further north? Perhaps they arrived with Polynesian voyagers, who colonised New Zealand and the Cook Islands about 1000 years ago. Whatever their origin, women made them their own, and patterns of daily life and subsistence must have altered considerably as a result. The hooks would have changed the types of fish caught—the fish of the deeper waters was now available—and encouraged women to take their canoes further from the shoreline. As we shall see, their importance as fisherwomen is likely to have altered the balance of gender politics. Women of the distant inland clans did not undergo malgun, and these beautiful hooks have not been found on their campsites.[24]

Archaeological evidence also reveals intriguing changes in stone tool technology of the Sydney region. Around the same time as the shell fish-hooks were introduced in the region, a new kind of stone tool first appeared around the Hawkesbury: small backed blades, also called microliths, fashioned from hard stone like quartz, silcrete and chalcedony. Often triangular in section with sharp worked edges and a blunt, flat back, they included sharp points (known as 'Bondi points', as they were first found at Bondi in the 1890s), used for tipping hunting spears and as blades for shaping wood; and roughly oval or triangular tools (called by archaeologists *elouera*) which may have been fixed to a wooden handle and used for digging roots. These tools gradually became more common about 3500 years ago: in one cave alone, archaeologists found 1000 microliths and 50 000 stone flakes, the debris from their manufacture. But, just as mysteriously, these artefacts disappeared from the toolkit about 1500 years ago. Perhaps there were environment changes, such as a fall in kangaroo and wallaby populations. By the time the First Fleet arrived, the stone spear points had been replaced by the rows of lacerating stone barbs of the 'death spear', the formidable weapon warriors used in contests. Digging sticks were tipped with shell, on the coast at least.[25]

The early Europeans painted and described the coastal Eora, their fishing and implements so often that they are often presented as *the* Sydney people. That we may still look upon their likenesses, captured in paint on paper, is wondrous as well as sad. By contrast, the inland groups were relatively little recorded or painted, and the wave of smallpox which swept through the region in 1789 meant that in some cases whole groups died, along with knowledge and culture, even before the Europeans encountered them. What we know of these lost peoples will only ever be pinpricks on a darkened landscape. The surviving inland groups were known as woods people. Their men and women were famous for their ability to climb trees of 10–15 feet girth and rising 80 feet 'before there is a single branch', notching toeholds with stone hatchets to hunt small mammals like possums. They used stone instead of shell on their spears. People fished for mullet and eels using canoes, or they built traps from stone and hollow logs. The dense river-flat brush and the river banks were rich in yams (bulbs, tubers and roots) and fruits, and the waters carried floating *nardoo* fern, the spores of which were pounded into flour. The cobble-beds between Emu Plains and Richmond were the source of tools and stone for the whole region north of Botany Bay—it was a toolmaking powerhouse. The gravel beds and ancient channels of the river, creeks and river flats yielded smooth basalt pebbles, chert, mudstone, quartz and red and yellow silcrete boulders. Both inland and coastal peoples also harvested rich food sources in the vast lagoons and wetlands that backed the coast and the inland rivers.[26]

The Sydney region people had established trade relations and routes between the coast and inland and beyond. Stone for hatchets and other tools, and possum fur for belts and ligatures came to the coast and light grass-tree shafts for making spears went inland. These things travelled long distances, possibly moving through a chain of hands, and were exchanged at big meetings. News and ideas from distant places could arrive with lone messengers travelling through foreign country.[27] But from what we can glimpse, the closest links and associations between the Sydney clans and bands seemed to run north–south along the coast, rather than east–west between the coast and inland plains and mountains. Rivers and creeks, where food was more abundant, were the places of densest occupation, while high places were for ceremonial time. Rivers served as both boundaries and corridors. So coastal peoples seemed to know the central Cumberland Plain as far as the head of the harbour—the Parramatta River at Parramatta—but beyond that, country, people and languages were unfamiliar and suspicious, though not incomprehensible. In the west, Dyarubbin, the Hawkesbury–Nepean, may have played a similar role, linking different clans and bands along its long, snaking course, from the river flats and mountains around Mulgoa and Camden in the south-west to the sea at Broken Bay and its estuary Brisbane Water.[28]

The complex politics and relationships which must have existed between these Sydney region groups can now only be guessed at. We know that large numbers of people from distant places came together for feasting and celebrations, for fighting and for initiation ceremonies. The First Fleeters sometimes encountered men walking in single file, armed with spears and large stones, who 'seemed to be going to war', and they nervously observed a ferocious contest at Manly, attended by 200 people. Relationships of rivalry, suspicion and fierce animosity were common and violent, but they could be resolved into alliances and friendships through combat, payback, marriage, trade or diplomacy. As in other parts of Australia, some groups, like the Gandangarra of the Blue Mountains, were feared as powerful and ruthless warriors while others were probably more peaceable. But all these practices suggest that laws, rituals, beliefs and events were shared, they bound the peoples together. This was no peaceful, harmonious way of life; it was a 'tough warrior culture' and it was violent. But the violence had limits, and everyone observed them.[29]

Was the Sydney region in 'the pure state of nature' in 1770 and 1788? The Europeans, gazing in wonder at the hooded headlands and rocky foreshores of Port Jackson, thought so. They had no doubt they were 'taking possession of Nature . . . in her simplest and purest garb', that their axes ringing out in the 'stillness and tranquillity' were the first since Creation. They had released the original 'voice of labour' and legitimised their claim to country in the process.[30]

They could not have been expected to see the way the country was already divided into sacred and everyday and invested with myth and Law legends, which taught rules for the proper conduct of human society. Aboriginal educator Coral Edwards, writing of the area north of the Hawkesbury at Wisemans Ferry, explains the interwoven process of learning and geography as *songlines*:

> Supposing you were walking through Country with your family. There will be many things to learn along the way . . . everything will have a story and a relationship in spiritual ways—how it's connected to you . . . And there'll be stories that go back a long way . . . so in one way the songlines are a directional thing for people. They also mark out time and space. You know how far you've yet to go by how many stories there are yet to come . . . there might be songs in there too, and they're repeated. The stories go on for maybe days and then when you come to the end of those stories for that part, you know you have to make a turn to the left or right. So the songlines are like an invisible boundary, like a fence. But there's

more to it than that. That's only on the practical level. The stories also deal
with the whole history of the Country, and who the People were, and are,
within the Country and their place within it.[31]

Country was probably ordered by gender too, with sacred, secret and learning
places for both men and women. The high, rocky outcrops with their compelling
grooved images facing the sky seem to have been men's places; there must have
been corresponding women's places in the Sydney region, just as there are elsewhere.[32] This female geography is lost, but, as we shall see, it very likely focused
on the harbours and waterways. One precious hint is the word 'Birrabirragalleon'
on an anonymous word-list from 1790–91. While most clan names end in -gal,
denoting the male, the suffix -galleon meant *women*. Birra Birra is the Sow and
Pigs Reef off Camp Cove at the entrance to Sydney Harbour. Dharawal women
today still know Birra Birra, or Boora Birra, place of waters, surf and fish, as a
women's teaching place.[33]

Yet the Europeans were also surrounded by so many visible marks of human
labour and artistry; they recognised some, but not others. Close by the early
Camp, at Farm Cove, were huge mounds of shells, 'raised beaches, consisting
solely of sea-sand and shells'. Settlers in the 1840s still thought these banks were
naturally formed, that the land was new-made, emerged recently from the sea.
But they were in fact middens, vast accumulations of shells from hundreds of
thousands of meals, silent evidence of long occupation, 'deposited and struc-
tured by the unremitting efforts of woman the gatherer'.[34]

The country was crisscrossed by paths 'trod very well down'. The Europeans found them very useful, as they led along the easiest, shortest and most
accessible routes. Often they later became roads.[35] The trees were marked with
notches for climbing, chopped-out hollows, the scars of canoe- and shield-
making, and carved decorations. Bark houses (*gunyahs*), sometimes in groups,
had the customary fires and bull-ants' nests out the front; sandstone overhangs
and caves had roofs blackened by smoke, their sandy floors grey with ash and
fat, their mouths surrounded by aprons of shell middens and rich black organic
material. On the banks of inland rivers, the earth was churned up by women's
yam-digging, there were bird- and eel-traps in rivers and lagoons, and further

A large sandstone rockshelter and shell midden on the New South Wales Central Coast. (Photo: Brendan Lennard)

up on the higher ground were stone workshop sites scattered with hundreds of stone cores and flakes. Hands were stencilled onto the walls of art caves, and beautiful pictures painted or etched, which may have been the conduits, 'the veil between this world and the spirit world' and the Dreaming.[36]

Smoke was the unmistakable sign of Aboriginal presence and work, and it was everywhere. Fires kept people warm at night, and banished the darkness and terrifying evil spirits, the *mawn*. Fires in trees smoked out animals, but also left snug little shelters in the trees' bases. Cooking fires in front of them were left alight, and sometimes led to the incineration of the whole tree. The Europeans passed many of these trees, flaming like giant torches. Fire cracked stones for tools, heated wood so it could be shaped into weapons and implements, hardened shields, and melted sticky resins for fixing stone to wood.[37]

Aboriginal fires, lit ahead of the north-westerlies, raced lightly over the ground, clearing shrubs and saplings, letting in the light, creating greenpick for grazing animals.[38] The British, perplexed by the constant fires they saw, eventually began to grasp the reasons. John Hunter wrote that they

> set the country on fire for several miles extent ... for the purpose of disturbing such animals as may be within reach of the con-flagration ... [and] to clear that part of the country through which they have frequent occasion to travel, of the brush or underwood, from which they, being naked, suffered very great inconvenience.[39]

Observers rightly noted that fires were lit so that men could drive out and hunt game: later the 'hunting scene' became a favourite of painters depicting 'savage sports'. But Hunter saw something more: the fires also cleared the ground of undergrowth so that women could more easily get at the nutritious roots with their digging sticks in winter, when the fish were scarce.

It took some decades for the Europeans to realise that the great diversity of landscapes and plant communities they encountered were shaped by Aboriginal fire regimes. The dry sclerophyll of sandstone country, tall forests of ironbark and blue gum, dark, dense and tangled stands they called brush, and finally the open country of Cumberland Plain woodland, reflected soil and rainfall patterns and grades subtly according to slope, shade and wind. But this mosaic was also maintained by Aboriginal burning, a carefully calibrated system which kept some areas open while others grew dense and dark.[40]

BEREWALGAL AND EORA

What were those first encounters like for the peoples of Botany Bay and Port Jackson? We tend to view the meetings from the decks of the Europeans' ships, or in the light of what we know happened later. Some historians see the Eora as culturally vulnerable, mentally imprisoned in the long isolation of Aboriginal Australia: 'They were bound to believe that humanity consisted only of themselves and others like them', writes Alan Atkinson. 'A cosmology such as this is vulnerable to any hint that another world does in fact exist.' Doubt entered a holistic belief system, and so devastated their world.[41] The shock of first encounters reverberated and rolled into the larger shock of invasion, dispossession and death.

Did the Eora find the ships and the pale people in coloured skins completely incomprehensible? Was this shock itself toxic? Their actions on the beaches of eastern Australia suggest both forewarning and ways of dealing with new arrivals. The first tactic was to take no notice at all. Cook and Banks were perplexed and rather put out that these simple savages *ignored* them, nonchalantly went about their daily tasks in the presence of such marvellous sights, which they surely could never have seen before. But the ship looming up in Botany Bay in 1770 was probably no surprise at all. The people of Bulli further south had already seen (and ignored) it, and the news would have travelled fast up the well-worn coastal paths. When the strangers appeared, the Gweagal and Kameygal were ready for them.[42]

By at least 1790, the Eora had several names for their uninvited guests. One was *Berewalgal*, people from a distant place (*berewal*). Probably at the beginning they were also *mi-all* (*myall*)—strangers. The words remind us that strangers from distant places were conceptually and actually familiar to Eora. What they saw from the corners of their (carefully averted) eyes was also placed in the realm of the known: the ship made them think of *boorowan*, an island, or a great bird with billowed wings. The creatures climbing high in the rigging looked like possums.

(White curiosity about first contact was enduring: more than five decades later, the self-proclaimed 'last' Aboriginal man of Botany, Mahroot, told a parliamentary inquiry, 'They thought they [the English] were the devil when they saw them landed first'.)[43] As we have seen, when Cook's party came towards the shore, Gweagal men were standing ready to greet the strangers with warnings and a show of strength and had already made sure the women and children were out of sight.

Stories and talk of Cook's visit must have spread among the peoples of the eastern coastline and become part of lore. Aboriginal culture is dynamic, readily appropriating and incorporating news and ideas, so the encounter may have been commemorated in stories, songs, ceremonies, dance and art of the Sydney region. The Badjala people of Fraser Island have a song about the *Endeavour* passing their country in 1770: 'These strangers, where are they going? Where are they trying to steer?' The Badjala wondered about people who seemed to have buried themselves so far from the shore.[44] In this context the arrival of so many more ships in Botany Bay in January 1788—eleven British and two French over nine days—would have been truly alarming, but not beyond the realm of understanding. Similar rituals were enacted: shouted warnings—the Berewalgal on the decks saw Kameygal on the shore who 'by their motions, seemed to threaten; they pointed their spears, and often repeated the words, wara wara'.[45] Once more the longboat rowed towards the shore. Arthur Phillip gestured that they wanted water. The Kameygal 'pointed round the point on which they stood, and invited us to land there'.[46]

The first exchanges on that beach were not words, or names, or musket shot, but beads, mirrors, red cloth which Phillip tied about the neck of a Kameygal elder, and 'other trifling things'. Both Eora and Berewalgal were familiar with the language of things, whether as gifts or gestures of goodwill and conciliation. Such goods were not just about technology and usage: in both cultures they could cement alliances, and confer advantages and prestige. Phillip made sure every First Fleet ship carried the hatchets, beads, baize and mirrors and other simple things thought essential for opening up communication with unknown indigenous peoples, and making landing secure and safe.[47]

Before the ships had even sailed, Phillip had decided that he would cultivate good relations with the Eora. His instructions were to 'open an intercourse with them', to 'live in amity and kindness' and to punish those who harmed them or interfered with their 'several occupations'. Instead of letting fly with shot, as Cook had done, Phillip would lay down his weapons, and approach them, arms outstretched, palms open. He had lost a front tooth, and this probably accorded him some authority—the missing front tooth was the sign of an initiated Eora man.[48]

For the English, contact and conciliation should have proceeded in a lineal way. Early hostility and suspicion would be overcome with gifts, and cautious exchange would be followed by permanent trust and friendship—and assistance. But this was based on the assumption that the Eora were one group, living in one territory, and so there was much confusion over seemingly inconsistent responses and backtracking. As they crossed into different country in Botany Bay and Port Jackson, they encountered different groups, and the stages had to be repeated. After good relations were established at Botany Bay, Philip Gidley King's party, exploring along the reaches of the Georges River, was threatened with spears streaking down from a high hill, possibly opposite the mouth of the Woronora River. Gifts were of no avail and the group retreated hastily, walking backwards, downhill, to the boat. (I suspect they had blundered into men's ceremonial space on this high ground.) And at Botany Bay the 'natives seemed well-pleased with us'—until the Berewalgal started clearing a path to water, cutting through trees and undergrowth. Then they 'expressed a little Anger' and 'wanted them to be gone'. The Kameygal were clearly shocked by this vandalism in their country.[49]

DANCING WITH GER-RUBBER

Yet, when things went well, goodwill and friendliness seemed to mark the first encounters in Botany Bay, Sydney Harbour and Broken Bay. The English officers were not limited by the crude dichotomy of noble savage and brute, they were genuinely curious about the Eora, and they hoped the narratives they were living and writing would have the happy ending of a peaceful co-existence. They wanted to understand as much as they could, and they wrote endlessly about the Eora for equally eager audiences back home. Over the first weeks, and then during the exploratory journeys to Broken Bay, they described many scenes of frolicking and fun, games, laughter, jokes and 'dancing with strangers' on those beaches. It seemed that the path to friendly relations was open, though what the dancing actually signified is not clear at all. The Berewalgal liked the Eora. They made them laugh, they were 'funny, curious fellows', they could mimic wonderfully and seemed to enjoy themselves hugely.[50]

Inga Clendinnen has told this story of early Sydney powerfully and engagingly: the European officers, she says, were not racists bent on exterminating Aboriginal people. They were enlightened, tolerant and chivalrous (the convicts, however, were another matter). Those early years were a kind of blessed hiatus of cross-cultural discovery. 'Racist terror would come soon enough', she concludes firmly, 'but not in Phillip's time'. For Clendinnen, the dancing, even if the meaning is not quite clear, is the foundational emblem of early good associations: 'the British and the Australians began their relationship by dancing together'.[51]

Some of Lieutenant William Bradley's watercolours depict moments of major breakthroughs in early race relations: the first meeting with the Eora women; dancing together on Broken Bay; and later the 'coming in', when some Eora came to live in Sydney. We need to look carefully one more time at his dancing picture, set in a cove on Pittwater, on the southern shores of Broken Bay, where the series of headlands stretch down towards the crouched outline of Lion Island. The dancers holding hands are men, for the women, as always, stay out on the water, in their nowie, watching. The longboat and the schooner are close to shore, too, manned and ready for a quick getaway, the rowers resting on their oars. Underneath the surface of innocence and play, this is an edgy picture, reflecting the tensions and the watchfulness of these first encounters. And onshore, right at the centre of the happy group, are two figures who are not dancing: they are wearing red coats and have muskets resting on their shoulders. As the officers so often tell us, there could be no dancing, no rambling explorations, no meetings at all without guns and redcoats.[52]

The British officers began their relationship with the Eora by demonstrating what their guns could do. Not once, but several times. Besides firing over their heads, they would take a thick bark *elemong* or shield, point a musket and put a ball right through it. Their Eora observers learned fast. One man, just to be sure, asked whether the ball would also pass through his body? Yes, said the officers, it would. Whereupon, without flinching and with a great show of bravado, he graphically demonstrated the effect of an Eora spear on soft flesh and bone. The officers seem to have been amused by his antics and dismissed the primitive weaponry with a laugh. It would be a few more months before the horrors of a slow death by jagged spear would become clear.[53]

In any case, the musket demonstrations were highly effective: the news spread quickly. The sight of a musket, and also of a red coat, was usually enough to make the Eora melt into the bush, or paddle away. 'It is a Weapon that keeps them in great Awe', wrote George Worgan. 'Many of them will not come near You till you have laid it down which they will make signs for you to do.' By October 1788 Bradley knew Eora friendliness was not genuine, but the work of guns. He wrote wistfully: '. . . however much I wished to encourage the Idea of their being Friendly disposed, I must acknowledge . . . that they are only so, when they suppose we have them in our power or are well prepared by being armed'.[54] People without the protection of guns and Red coats—the convicts and sailors— were often attacked and killed.

So the Berewalgal had to be always on their guard to maintain the fiction of their magical, invincible guns. They could not let the Eora discover, for example, 'how little use a musquet was once discharged', nor that the guns needed powder. Worgan was frank: 'We have always been cautious in letting the natives see that it is necessary to put anything in the Gun to do Execution with it'. David Collins wrote bluntly some years later that 'it had been our constant endeavour to inspire them . . . with the terror of our fire-arms'.[55] The newcomers soon acquired another name: *ger-rubber*, which originally meant firestick, but now also meant gun.[56]

Since we rely so much on their writings to understand these early encounters in Eora country, it is also important to know that the officers were writing, and exploring, within a particular literary tradition, too—the revived tradition of 'chivalric discourse'. They saw themselves as polished and polite 'knights errant . . . wandering the world over in search of occasions on which to exercise their generous and disinterested valour'.[57] I think something of the wonder of seeing another people for the first time, the sheer joy of human contact, radiates nevertheless from their writing. But below the charming, light-filled surface, the humorous and poignant stories, was that undertow of implacable intention—

to establish a colony and take the land—backed up with 'superiority' and with guns. Chivalry, and the storytelling it allows, is 'the velvet glove which makes the iron fist of colonisation and dispossession more palatable'.[58] It makes the invasion more palatable. The officers, after all, also called themselves 'the new possessors', 'the new lords of the soil', and wrote blithely of the 'downfall of its ancient inhabitants'.[59] The perplexing thing is that they hoped the Eora would not see them as 'enemies or invaders of their country and tranquillity'.[60] They wanted to be friends.

MANLY AND EVE

The first encounters were also deeply gendered, for the initial questions had to do with the nature of men and women. Phillip, finding Botany Bay too exposed and too waterless, sailed into the harbour Cook had passed by to the north: Port Jackson.[61] All along the coast, Eora men shouted from the cliffs, 'Warra warra'. Their words and gestures, wrote Collins, could not be 'interpreted into invitations to land, or expressions of welcome'. And they were far more numerous than the officers had been led to believe by Cook and Banks.[62] The three long-boats made for Kay-ye-my, the area of North Harbour inside North Head. Near 'a point in the harbour' (perhaps Grotto Point—an important landmark for the Berewalgal), twenty unarmed black men of impressive physique waded out through the water to the longboats. They came with such confidence and curiosity, Phillip knew that Banks had been wrong about these people. They were not 'rank cowards', or apathetically uninterested. They seemed on the contrary to display the qualities most admired in English gentlemen. So Phillip named this place Manly Cove in their honour.[63]

Gender also concerned the Eora. At first they were not sure what sex the Berewalgal were, as they had no beards and their private parts were hidden. They ripped open shirt fronts and were seen to 'start back in amazement' at breastless hairy chests. They unceremoniously poked their fingers into the mouths of the Berewalgal, to see if the top incisor was missing. Since the encounters were with different groups in different places, the Berewalgal had to prove their manhood each time.[64] On the third day, on the beach around present-day Oatley where friendly exchanges were underway after the initial hostilities on the hilltop, the

Eora asked what sex they were. A sailor was ordered to drop his pants and a shout went up: they are men! Thereupon this group of Eora men pointed to the groups of women who had appeared on the shore and made it clear to the Berewalgal that 'their persons were at our service'. This was an unusual offer, and King says it was declined. He then produced a handkerchief and tied it around one woman 'where Eve did ye fig leaf'. Another amazed shout went up. It must have seemed a very strange gesture, since only Eora women who were not yet sexually active wore aprons (*barin*, made of kangaroo or possum skin) covering themselves in this way. What could the strangers be saying?[65]

On every other occasion, the men continued to keep their women well away and closely guarded by '18 or 20 stout young fellows ... besmeared with red and white clay in lines and circles'.[66] Perhaps, thought the officers approvingly, this was another sign of noble manliness: the Eora were chivalrous and protective towards their women.[67] It made them want to see the women even more. On what is now Manly Cove, the survey party, including White, Hunter and Bradley, wheedled and cajoled and used their gifts as bribes. Finally the women were allowed to come forward, 'naked as Eve before she knew Shame', standing by the boats, trembling and laughing as the Berewalgal reached over to drape them with strings of buttons and beads, and gave them presents, while their own men stood watchful and tense. They were young women, and the English officers were much taken with these 'naked beauties'. Bashful and shy, their demeanour was 'perhaps, inseparable from the female character in its rudest state'. They were the original women. The officers renamed Manly Cove: it became Eve's Cove.[68]

So often these encounters are seen first and foremost as men's business—and indeed that is what they were. In histories, and in much early anthropology, the women are usually in the background, passive and quiet, 'protected' by their men, who strut centre stage with the strangers. Yet Eora women were not invisible at all; they were a central focus of such encounters. They were after all the links between clans, the ones who knitted peoples together and the makers of children. In the coastal Sydney region they also had special prowess as fishers and canoeists. Unknown men, wherever they were from, had to be assessed before they could have access to women, if at all. These Berewalgal were obviously interested in the women, but what kind of allies, or even relatives, would they be?

William Bradley's watercolour recording the first meeting with Eora women at Eve's Cove (Manly), 1788. (Mitchell Library, State Library of New South Wales)

In the intricate and shifting web of clan and band politics, hard-headed investigations were needed: who among them were the elders, the warriors and clever men? And where were their own women?

For the English officers, the way Eora men treated their women was another way of gauging the nature and character of the 'natives'. They searched for qualities esteemed by cultured English gentlemen: chivalry, strength, protectiveness. These qualities were of course mediated by rank and social standing as well as gender. They hoped, for example, that Eora men were not like the convict men, whom they regarded as brutal, lowly and stupid; and that Eora women were indeed 'Eves', fresh from the dawn of time, and not like convict women: wanton, knowing, bossy, foul-mouthed. Then again, their urgent curiosity was sensual and sexual: they were interested only in young, comely Eora women who fitted the 'Eve' image. Old women were considered repulsive, 'dark and ugly', while a pregnant woman busy at her fishing at Eve's Cove was 'exceptionally ugly and very big with child'. The officers felt themselves at their best and most gallant fussing over young women who were in distress.[69] Over the next few years they would discover how wrong their first impressions of Eora men and women had been, and how bafflingly irrelevant their own ways of seeing.

WARRANE: COVE, VALLEY, FRESHWATER STREAM

Phillip's boat sailed around the south side of Port Jackson on 23 January, nosing into every deep bay between the long headlands, until he found what he was looking for: a sheltered deepwater mooring close to shore; gentle, sloping ground rising from the eastern shoreline, and level land beyond; and a stream of fresh water running into salt from an internal valley. This was Warrane, later Sydney Cove. And it seems to have been the one place in this complex harbour where there were no Eora waiting on the shore. Some say they must have been there, watching invisibly from the edge of the trees. But the journal entries are all the same: the ships passed black men gathered on the cliff tops and beaches, shaking spears, shouting 'Warra warra', breaking out in bouts of nervous, hysterical laughter. Tench wrote of the 'Indians' they saw among the trees at the water's edge. But at Sydney Cove itself: nobody. Here there were no angry protests when the axes thudded into the trunks of huge trees. 'The spot chosen for this purpose', wrote David Collins,

> was at the head of the cove, near the run of fresh water, which stole silently along through a very thick wood, the stillness of which had then for the first time since creation, been interrupted by the rude sound of the . . . axe.[70]

Was this simply European dreaming of silent, timeless Eden? Where were the Cadigal of this country?

It is possible that this very absence was another factor that led Phillip to select Warrane as the site for the first Camp. After all, there were numerous other freshwater streams and deep moorings in other coves and bays—you can still see them, all carefully marked on the early surveys of the harbour—and other places which offered suitable building ground.[71] But coming ashore and taking possession would present fewer difficulties, practically and perhaps morally, if there were no muscular armed Eora men wading out to meet the longboats, no-one on land, watching, shouting and remonstrating.

Tim Flannery, wondering about this strange absence, thinks that Warrane may have been a sacred site to the Cadigal, a place they did not visit much, and would never have camped on. He believes the great girth of the trees and the silence of the 'very thick wood' described by Collins and others suggests a sheltered gully, protected from summer fire by 'carefully burning round the margins'. He imagined fire-sensitive rainforest species like Port Jackson figs, cheese trees (*Glochidion fernandii*) and red ash among the fire-loving sclero-phyll trees more typical of Sydney Harbour foreshores. Did the Cadigal see and maintain this fold in the land, this hidden place, as sacred? If Flannery is right, then the city was unwittingly founded on the very place Cadigal had carefully left alone, despite its valuable fresh water and its beauty.[72]

How might we explore this fascinating idea? Let us look first at what we know of the ecology of Sydney Cove—did it support fire-sensitive plants? Here we encounter a great irony: the colony was so abundantly and self-consciously described in words, pictures and collected specimens, yet the colonists did not actually record the vegetation of Sydney Cove itself in the sort of detail needed to identify the species Flannery is talking about. They busily collected seeds, flowers and leaves from the areas around the early Camp, but made no botanical collec-tions of the Tank Stream valley.[73] And the valley was the locus of colonisation, eye of the storm of clearing and building, which altered and destroyed the native vegetation within a few short years.

Most of the First Fleet's naval men did not bother to describe the vegetation of Sydney Cove either—they were naturally more interested in water, in safe coves 'capable of receiving ships'.[74] David Collins' famous words about Sydney Cove are exceptional—most other journal-keepers moved straight on to clearing operations, raising the British colours, and toasting the King. But there are a few brief hints. The sailor Jacob Nagle, who was on that first expedition in the longboat, recalled that the west side of the cove was 'all bushes' above the rocky foreshore, but 'a small distance at the head of the cove was level'. Here were 'large trees but scattering and no underwood worth mentioning, and a run of fresh water running down the centre of the cove'. Phillip wrote later that 'in this spot

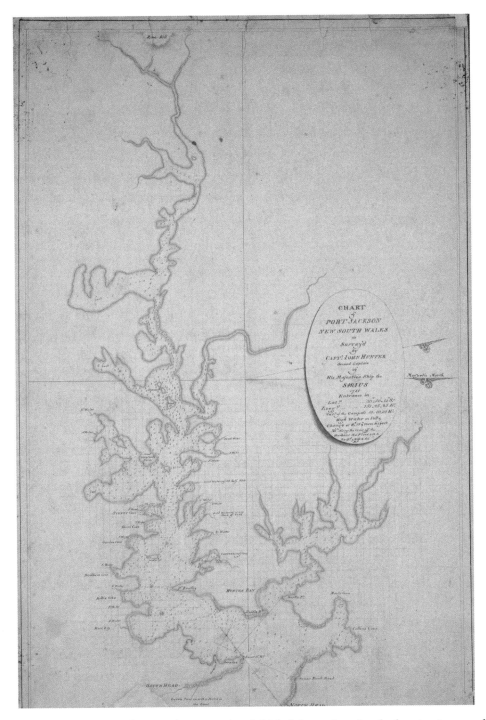

George Raper's 'Chart of Port Jackson New South Wales' shows the other freshwater streams of Sydney Harbour carefully marked in. (Mitchell Library, State Library of New South Wales)

the trees stood more apart, and were less incumbered with underwood than in many other places', though the trees were huge. The absence of undergrowth and the 'scattering of large trees' suggest an open landscape maintained by frequent cool fires, rather than a dark, moist, sheltered gully. And one last clue: Lieutenant Ralph Clark, telling his beloved wife Alicia of the dreadful lightning storms, was sure 'it is nothing else but Lightening that has burnt all the trees'. The trees of Sydney Cove were blackened by fire: but what kind of fire?[75]

Today plant ecologists like Doug Benson and Jocelyn Howell use historical and ecological descriptions of similar sites on Sydney Harbour to re-create the lost vegetation of Tank Stream valley. In the immediate settlement area, the large trees which so bedevilled the clearing gangs would have included the fire-loving sclerophylls—scribbly gums and forest red gums, with blackbutt, red bloodwoods, Sydney peppermint and the weirdly shaped, pink-trunked *Angophora costata* on the rocky slopes above. Swamp mahogany and swamp oak (*Casuarina glauca*) probably grew on the margins where the Tank Stream flowed into the harbour.[76]

But how long had this type of vegetation grown here? And was Warrane really the same as other coves? Palynologist Mike MacPhail studies the fossil pollens and spores in early soils from archaeological sites. So far, rare prehistoric soil samples from the Tank Stream area itself have proved so weathered that no plant or animal fossils survive. But further south, in what was once the valley of Blackwattle Creek (now Broadway), MacPhail was able to re-create an astonishingly detailed story, one which may mirror the Tank Stream's deep time history. Let us take the journey: during the last ice age, 15000–24000 years ago, when the sea levels were 100 metres lower, Sydney Harbour was a dry valley, and the climate was cooler and drier. The Blackwattle Creek valley was treeless, a fern- and herb-field area, dominated by coral ferns, with wire rushes in the boggy areas. When rising sea levels flooded the ancient valley between 15000 and 6000 years ago, this landscape changed dramatically. Now a warm, temperate rainforest (galley rainforest) flourished where the fern and rushlands of the wetter sites along the creek had been. Most of the species of this dense green canopy—tree ferns, hazelwood, plume bush, plum pine—are no longer found on the foreshores of Sydney Harbour. The creek was also fringed by the tall, slender cabbage tree palms, canthium and cissus, a water vine. Meanwhile, euca-lypts had invaded the drier slopes above, and among the shrubs were native hops, a species particularly common after wildfires have swept through. MacPhail found charcoal in these soils too: the forest here had burned, or been fired.[77]

Fire regimes and drier conditions appear to have spelt the end of the rain-forest. After around 3000 years ago, casuarina pollen became more common in the soils, the rainforest species disappeared and the eucalypts marched down the slopes. The valley became a dry open woodland of eucalypts with a grassy understorey—the same landscape that Jacob Nagle saw at the head of Sydney Cove in 1788.[78] It seems likely, then, that Eora would have burnt Warrane, as elsewhere.

Another way to explore the presence of Eora in Warrane is through the mate-rial evidence they left. But here again the evidence is shadowy. At first glance there appears to be a strange absence of pre-contact evidence for Eora occupation in Sydney Cove itself. For all the archaeological excavation which has occurred in Sydney, there are just two known sites. A midden high on the west side, in the Rocks area, contained the remains of meals of snapper, rock oysters and hairy mussels shared about 350 years ago. And, on the shores of the Tank Stream, deep below the high-rise, the bitumen and layers of urban deposits, archaeologists found a stoneworking site of 54 cores, flakes and fragments. The Eora here shaped waterworn pebbles, mudstone, red silcrete and quartz into tools. This also seems to be an ancient site, though no-one knows exactly how old.[79]

This archaeological silence contrasts with the wealth of archaeological evidence from the coves nearby and elsewhere in the Sydney region. Farm Cove and Woolloomooloo to the east were the sites of those huge shell middens, and another midden was found on the western side of Walsh Bay. A carved whale once swam on a rock platform at Dawes Point/Tarra at the western extremity of the cove.[80] But, as with the ecological record, this absence may simply reflect the extensive destruction caused by city building, twinned with the fact that, until very recently, it rarely occurred to anyone that Eora sites might survive in the heart of the city. Like trees, and 'nature', Aboriginal people were not thought of as having a place in urban landscapes—their sites and artefacts 'belonged' on rural and outback land. What is unlooked-for is rarely seen. Light, fragile scatters of bone, shell and stone would have been easily missed by generations of men digging ever deeper to make the foundations, cellars, sewers and tunnels of the subterranean city.

There is one final clue. As they gradually became familiar with the local groups, the Berewalgal discovered that their Camp had been founded in a boundary area—it lay in the country of the Cadigal just where it met Wanne, the south side of Parramatta River, the country of the Wangal.[81] But the status of Warrane among these groups, and their relationship with it, remains a mystery. Whether it was living space or sacred space, its destruction must have been a great shock. Perhaps the Eora gave up trying to make any sense at all of these pale arrivals: they really were strangers, savages who brought chaos to country. Eora clans and bands went on living in their own country elsewhere, and continued to use their customary spaces for gatherings and rituals. But when it became clear that the uninvited guests meant to stay, and would continue to cut trees, shrubs and rushes, to take all the food, to threaten with guns, relations soured. Spears were thrown, fish snatched from the seine nets, boats were pelted with stones, and then unarmed convicts were speared, beaten and murdered. All these attacks occurred in the areas around and away from Warrane: the beaches, the bush and the rushlands became dangerous territory. The Eora avoided the Camp itself, with its rows of tents, its gashed ground, its amputated trees. The Berewalgal fretted uneasily and wondered why.

Chapter 3

THE CAMP, THE CANVAS

REWIND COLONY

Sydney was 'born' at least three times. The First Fleet sailed into Botany Bay, made contact with the natives, located fresh water, began clearing trees for building and excavated a sawpit for cutting the timber. Stop the cameras! Rewind the film! The action runs backwards: sawpit dismantled, everything packed up, hauled back on board, and the ships retreat from Botany Bay. Begin again: the ships sail into the grander heads of Port Jackson, the natives shout at them from the shores, the scenery takes their breath away. The settlers land, raise the British flag, and begin busily clearing and erecting the tents, which look pretty nestled among the great trees. But now fast-forward three years to 1790. The Camp at Sydney Cove is unplanned and disorderly; it is the convicts' town and seems out of control, beyond salvage. Good land has been discovered at the head of the harbour, so a new, orderly centre is planned there, at Parramatta. *This* will be the centre of administration, the hub of an agricultural district. Sydney is merely a ramshackle port town. It will wither away.

It is only with the benefit of hindsight that we know where Sydney's 'real' birthplace was: in the mysterious valley at Warrane. At the time, though, this was by no means clear or inevitable. Arthur Phillip was a stickler for orders and even returned to Botany Bay to make *absolutely* sure he'd made the right choice in abandoning it as the site of the colony, thereby defying the illustrious Cook and Banks. From the start, too, those self-conscious foundation scenes of Bruegel-esque busyness in the silent forests were upended by the movement of the convicts. Large groups immediately defected and found their way back to Botany Bay, where they begged the people on the French ships to take them away. Soon more than half the convicts had left the Camp at Warrane and some were living in the bush at Botany Bay.[1] The colony, and Sydney, would emerge from movement, as well as fixing and building.

'SAFE FROM ALL THE WINDS THAT BLOW': SAILING INTO PORT JACKSON[2]

Port Jackson was another beginning, a more appropriately grand one. Once more the ships sailed along the massive cliffs and headlands of the coast, and again entered the new land through the awesome portal of Sydney Heads. The vision of Sydney Harbour was all the more powerful because of the disappointment of Botany Bay. The famous 'meadows' promised by Cook and Banks, seen fresh and green and well watered in autumn, had turned to straw in the blazing heat in the summer of January 1788.[3] There had been insufficient water for a thousand-odd invaders, the ships were exposed to the ocean gales and there seemed nowhere large enough or suitable to establish the settlement. So, as we have seen, Phillip sailed the longboats further north, the famous discovery was made, and his famous lines later written: here was a harbour where 'a thousand sail of the line may ride in the most perfect security'. At Warrane, later Sydney Cove, 'ships can anchor so close to the shore that at small expence quays may be built at which the largest ships may unload'.[4]

They stood on the decks, entranced as the ships glided past the long, finger-like headlands and secret bays. Surgeon Arthur Bowes Smyth tried to find words and images:

> ... the finest terras's ... the tallest and most stately trees I ever saw in any nobleman's grounds in England cannot excel in beauty those [which] nature now presented to our view. The singing of various birds among the trees, and the flight of the numerous parakeets, lorikeets, cockatoos

and macaws, made all around appear like an enchantment; the stupendous rocks from the summit of the hills and down to the very waters edge hang'g in a most awful manner from above and form'g the most commodious quays by the water, beggar'd all description.[5]

There were many such descriptions from the Europeans—lyrical, but also infused with a sense of being on the cusp of grand purpose, of history. They began a long tradition—for the next century at least, new arrivals would feel compelled to write of their first sight of Sydney Harbour.

VISIONS OF NEW SOUTH WALES

The reasons for the founding of the British colony in New South Wales have been hotly debated among historians for some decades now. Traditionalists insist that the primary function was as a 'dumping ground for convicts', the unwanted human refuse from England's overflowing gaols and hulks. The gaols full of prisoners dressed in rags and crawling with vermin were seen as fearful threats to public health, for they were 'so crouded . . . that the greatest danger is to be apprehended, not only from their Escape, but from infectious diseases which may hourly be expected to break out'.[6]

Economic historians accorded the colony rather more dignity, arguing that it had strategic purpose as a maritime base for ships 'following the eastern route into the Pacific Ocean' and it would establish England's presence in the Pacific, staking a claim particularly against the imperial ambitions of the French, Spanish, Portuguese and Dutch. There were also high hopes of securing the valuable natural resources of Norfolk Island: flax and pine tree spars for the masts, ropes and sails of the British navy.[7]

Phillip's Instructions and the unfolding of the settlement itself indicate that the penal motive was the main reason for the project. But as Graham Abbott points out, the term 'dumping ground' is entirely inappropriate, since the British government was looking, not for a convenient receptacle for its unwanted population, but 'for a place where a convict settlement could become self supporting within an acceptably short period'.[8] There is also some good evidence for the natural resource motives, and the two did not necessarily contradict one another. Most striking in both cases are the environmental dimensions. On one hand, the plan utilised distance and the new, 'empty' lands as a kind of safety valve, dispersing fearful urban contagion. On the other, Botany Bay also promised fair to fulfil the traditional role of colonies: it might provide natural raw material for the Mother Country to convert into manufactured goods to supply the ships of her empire. These two themes—a place where the corrupt and diseased could be sent, and the source of raw materials—were long-lived; they would pervade images and ideas about Sydney and Australia, and its relationship with Britain, well into the twentieth century.

But what *kind* of colony was this to be? We can read the original vision pretty clearly from the supplies hauled from the holds, lowered into boats, rowed ashore and rolled or dragged into tents and stores. Food and plain-but-serviceable clothing to supply the colonists for two years, cooking pots, simple tools for building and farming, seeds and plants of all kinds, and of course presents to soothe and trade with the natives. Animals and fruit trees were collected en route. The ships were arks, bearing the spores of an agricultural colony to a new land.[9]

What was not sent is significant too. The colony was not officially provided with money—though colonists soon established their customary ways of buying and selling. No treasury was established in New South Wales, and no thought given to its economic development. The convicts would breed (for both men and women were sent), establish a new society with a subsistence economy, growing food for themselves, their children and their betters, but no more.[10] They would have to lead simple lives with no need for commerce or consumer goods, or indeed large towns. Governors from Phillip to Macquarie were given urgent and detailed instructions to 'proceed without delay to the cultivation of the lands' and on the distribution of land for farms, but they had no instructions at all on town planning or leases—despite repeatedly requesting them.[11] They were also expressly forbidden to allow 'craft to be built for the use of private individuals', and ships arriving in Sydney Harbour were not even officially recorded until 1799. The colony was to be kept isolated from the rest of the world, for Phillip was instructed that 'every sort of intercourse between the intended settlement at Botany Bay . . . and the settlements of our East India Company . . . the coast of China . . . and the islands . . . should be prevented'.[12] Sydney was not to be a gaol, in the sense of incarcerating people behind walls, but neither was it officially intended to develop as a mercantile port town. Urban development and urban life were not part of the original vision for Botany Bay.

It was a rather strange, naive vision, perhaps a deliberate anachronism. Eighteenth-century England had already experienced both the rapid swelling of its cities with population increase, dispossessed rural people, and the social and economic upheavals of the commercial and consumer revolutions which pre-dated the Industrial Revolution. The convicts came from the ranks long despised as the 'hewers of wood and drawers of water'. They were the labouring classes at once essential for urban and commercial expansion, yet feared as 'loose and disorderly people', the sort who defended their common rights, and had fiercely resisted the massive environmental incursions of the eighteenth century—the land enclosures, the destruction of the forests, the draining of the fens. Since the sixteenth century, in the far-flung colonies and on the oceans, such 'motley' peoples had fought state terror with their own, resisted slavery, impressment and tyranny, and taken to swamps and mountains or to piracy to form alter-native societies. But they also 'built the infrastructure of merchant capitalism', stoked the fires of early industries, kept the ships and wharves, houses and fac-tories running. They were the targets of increasingly savage property laws which hanged thousands and swelled the gaol populations—capital punishment in the service of capital.[13]

At the same time, there was a striking counter-stream in the cultural profile of the convicts: many of them were urban working people who were participants in that new consumer culture. Employed in the quickening industries and later the factories, they bought up the new cotton prints for their clothes, ceramics for their tables, the buttons, shoe buckles and fashionable hats, cheap books. Store-bought food was replacing homemade and they drank tea, once the sole preserve of the rich, with great gusto. With spreading consumer culture came new behaviours: a sense of social worth which threatened old notions of fixed social relations based on inferiority, deference and submission. Working-class consumers could no longer be so instantly distinguished from their betters by their clothes, food and possessions. For people of rank this was as disturbing as the conspiracies and insurrections of rebels: society was being destabilised.[14]

In a way the vision for the new colony, vague as it was, expressed utopian ideas of a simpler, rural past which was felt to be fast disappearing beneath the growing commercial towns and their environmental and social problems, their rising populations of criminals and the destitute, the rising spirit of rebellion and resistance and the rising tide of consumer goods. Prosperous, handsome, modernising English cities had no place for the surfeit of dangerous, diseased, desperate working people. Conversely, the cultivation of land had powerful social and political potential, for this was to be no gentle or happy utopia. Hard agricultural toil and simple rural life, ruled with a firm hand, would surely make the convicts honest, make them pliant and deferential and separate them from the unruly pleasures of town life. From the time they boarded the ships, they were to be sober, 'debarred in all cases . . . the use of spirituous liquors', except for medicinal purposes. There would be no public houses, no ale houses, no money or goods to steal in Botany Bay. It was too far away from anywhere to rely on imported foods other than official British supplies. The logic was beautifully simple: those who refused to work would starve.[15]

Perhaps this also explains why the convicts were provided with humble, old-fashioned wooden bowls and platters, and tin plates, instead of the commonly used and reasonably priced modern ceramics. Wooden or treen ware was long out of use in England, as were the pewter and tin vessels which had initially replaced them. These vessels seem to have been regarded with contempt by convicts: they would have been old-fashioned, crude and demeaning. The cross-cut pit saws sent out were another anachronism. They were already outdated by 1788, replaced by the circular saw, patented in 1777. The pit saws ensured that timber-working in New South Wales would be a time-consuming, arduous and dirty job.[16]

The achievement of agricultural subsistence within a deadline of two years was the lynchpin of the plan—it justified the considerable initial expense of the project, and it dominated Phillip's term as governor.[17] It drove the immediate planting of crops, the frenetic exploratory journeys north, south and west in search of arable soil, and the early establishment of public farms, first at Farm Cove, then Parramatta. Unburdening the Mother Country of its financial responsibility for the colony was the *leitmotif* of Phillip's despatches home. No wonder the poverty of Sydney's sandy soils was seen as such a disaster, and so much bemoaned! Sydney had been founded in the 'wrong' place, for it soon became clear it could not be the centre of an agricultural district.

WARRANE/SYDNEY COVE: TIME'S OPENING SCENES

At the start, Warrane, with its relatively level, dry, open ground, fresh water and well-spaced trees, seemed environmentally promising. The officers saw the initial work of clearing and setting up tents as the starting point in the historical process of bringing order to the wilderness. Tench had enthused cheerfully about this historic, indeed *humanising*, mission as the ships left the Cape for the savage shores of Botany Bay:

> We weighed anchor and soon left far behind every scene of civilization and humanised manners, to explore a remote and barbarous land: and plant in it those happy arts, which alone constitute the pre-eminence and dignity of other countries.[18]

When the Fleet reached the 'longed for' Botany Bay at last, 'joy sparkled in every countenance, and congratulations issued from every mouth'. Clearing and building in Warrane was the next inevitable step, and Tench rejoiced in that scene too, as he knew his readers would:

> Business now set on every brow, the scene . . . highly picturesque and amusing. In one place, a party cutting down woods; a second setting up a blacksmith's forge; a third dragging along a load of stones or provisions; here an officer pitching his marquee, with a detachment of troops parading on one side of him, and a cook's fire blazing up on the other.[19]

The 'noise, clamour and confusion' soon wrought the happy result: 'As the woods were opened and the ground cleared, the various encampments were extended, and all wore the appearance of regularity'.[20] Improving on wild nature, however beautiful and tranquil, was integral to the colonising process; it was both action and proof, and it became the worn groove of environmental thinking. When educated Europeans first looked at the Australian environment, they saw it transformed; they saw the future.

Yet this civilising process, and the philosophical and historical ideas that propelled it, ultimately ran at cross-purposes to the scheme for New South Wales entrusted to Phillip. The isolated agrarian penal settlement may have been the British government's plan, but it was not the only vision of the new colony. In England, among people who had never seen Sydney Cove, there were rather more glorious prophecies of this colony's inevitable destiny: it would be a great city, a port of empire.[21] A year after the First Fleet landed, and the first reports had arrived back in England, the poet Erasmus Darwin wrote a poem, 'The Voyage of Hope to Sydney Cove'. It was inspired by the allegorical scenes on commemorative medallions made by Josiah Wedgwood from clay carried in the ships returning from Sydney Cove. These medallions depict 'Time's opening scene' at Sydney Cove: on a rocky eminence above the waters, the allegorical figure of 'Hope' meets 'Peace', 'Art' and 'Labour', and together they set both time and history in motion. Hope, Peace and Art are represented by female forms; significantly, Labour is male. His head is slightly bowed, his arm twisted awkwardly behind his back, as though bound.[22]

The Sydney Cove Medallion, fashioned from Sydney clay and depicting the allegorical figures of Hope, Peace, Art and Labour together setting time and history in motion at Sydney Cove. (Mitchell Library, State Library of New South Wales)

Darwin's poem, typical of the neo-classical genre of his day, expanded upon this scene and prophesied a peaceful and joyful transformation of the wild landscape through commerce, agriculture, architecture and public works. The delectable Hope calms the stormy seas and winds, and with Truth on her side and a wave of her 'snowy hand', she conjures a golden future, a 'cultured land'. The broad streets, the 'circus' and 'crescent', 'dome-capt towers' of a fabulous modern city rise, mirage-like, out of the bush. This city's energy, wealth and security is evident in the piers and quays and their 'massy structures', and the ships gliding into the harbour laden with 'northern' treasures, consumer goods to exchange for agricultural produce. The 'high-waving wood' has been replaced by the waving gold of farmlands, and by fruits from blushing orchards. Yet it is a strangely deserted place: there are no people here, no-one building, farming, working on the ships, or buying and selling goods.

The Voyage of Hope to Sydney Cove
Where Sydney Cove her lucid bosom swells
Courts her young navies, and the storm repels;
High on a rock amid the troubled air
HOPE stood sublime, and waved her golden hair;
Calm'd with her rosy smile the tossing deep,
And with sweet accents charm'd the winds to sleep;
To each wild plain she stretched her snowy hand,
High-waving wood, and sea-encircled strand.
'Hear me', she cried, 'ye rising Realms! record
'Time's opening scenes, and Truth's unerring word.–
'*There* shall broad streets their stately walls extend.
'The circus widen, and the crescent bend;
'*There* ray'd from cities o'er the cultured land,
'Shall bright canals, and solid roads expand.–
'*There* the proud arch, Colossus-like, bestride
'Yon glittering streams, and bound the chasing tide;
'Embellish'd villas crown the landscape scene,
'Farms wave with gold, and orchards blush between.–

'*There* shall tall spires, and dome-capt towers ascend,

'And piers and quays their massy structures blend;

'While with each breeze, approaching vessels glide.

'And northern treasures dance on every tide!'–

Then ceased the nymph—tumultuous echoes roar,

And JOY's loud voice was heard from shore to shore –

Her graceful steps descending press'd the plain,

And PEACE, and ART, and LABOUR, join'd her train.[23]

Erasmus Darwin and Josiah Wedgwood were the grandfathers of Charles Darwin, who would himself voyage to New South Wales in 1836. The grandson noted with some satisfaction that their prophecies had been fulfilled in the colony—or so it appeared. But his other careful observations were of *local* ecologies, and they would further inspire his revolutionary theory of evolution, a new way of understanding natural history.[24] By contrast, this poem, and the medallions, though shaped from local clay, knew and acknowledged nothing of local ecologies or landscapes, let alone peoples and politics; these were irrelevant. Sydney Cove was not a real place but an abstract space, characterised by what it lacked—culture, civilisation, agriculture, art, commerce. It was merely waiting for the Course of Empire to begin.[25] This was the philosophy of colonialism, the theory of empire, and it cast human history in four stages. The lowest and most primitive state, hunting and gathering (clearly the niche of the Aborigines) gave way to pastoralism—the grazing of stock—which was in turn succeeded by a third stage—agricultural settlement, with its golden fields and permanent 'neat, smiling villages'. The fourth and crowning stage was the development of cities, arts and commerce, signalled by buildings and grand public works. But in Sydney, as we shall see, history was strangely quickened and moved at breakneck speed; all the stages jostled together in the last of lands.[26]

In this other vision of Sydney and New South Wales, then, there could be no distinctive history. Rather than being a peculiar penal experiment in a particular place, the colony simply fitted into the grand historical narratives of European expansion, by which humankind was thought to 'progress' geographically, and through time, from the cradle of Greece and Rome to the ends of the earth.

THE CAMP

In reality, local topography and ecology shaped the rude Camp as much as compass bearings, and those first tents and paths would in turn shape the future town and city. The freshwater stream became the boundary between the two types of authority in early Sydney: civil and military. On the east side, Phillip's portable canvas house ('neither wind nor waterproof') faced northwards, while to the west were the tents and marquees of Lieutenant Governor Robert Ross, the officers, the marines, and that essential of imperial military diaspora, a ragged parade ground. Some of the convicts were housed in rows of tents behind the governor's house, men and women separated by the judge's and parson's tents, but initially most of them were placed on the west side, north of the military encampment.

By October there were still neat rows of tents running down to the west side of the Tank Stream, though huts seem to have replaced tents on the Rocks and in the east. The first hanging in Australia was from a tree between the men's and women's tents—the hanging site probably became the site of the future gaol, where a luxury hotel now stands in George Street. The dead were buried on the slopes south of the military encampment. Early plans of the Camp also show that seeding and breeding were high priorities. Garden grounds were cleared and sown immediately, even though the colonists knew it was the wrong season and were not surprised when the crops failed. Pens were built for the stock—sheep, cattle, hogs and goats—and by April the farm which gave Farm Cove its name had also been established over the eastern headland. By October the farm was simply marked 'cornfields' for the grain crops sown there.[27]

Away from the settlement to the north, on the narrow strip of land at the foot of Tallawolladah—the Rocks on the west side of the cove—the hospital tents were set up to receive the victims of scurvy and 'true camp dysentery' which broke out soon after the landing. And further north still, on the point at Tarra (Tarra means 'teeth'. Was Sydney Cove a mouth, its shorelines jaws?), Lieutenant William Dawes had a tiny observatory built by his 'own party of marines' between February and April 1788. The weather was oppressively hot, the thick brush they had to first clear tore their shoes to pieces. Dawes found it 'absolutely necessary to give them some rum and water now and then', as well as some new shoes. 'In return they wrought almost miraculously', he reported, 'as is testified with astonishment by all who have seen what they have done'. And so the authorities discovered a very useful fact: rum was not the harbinger of sloth and dissipation—it was the key to getting things done! The observatory had a conical roof made of whitewashed canvas, with a flap that opened out to the stars. Its clock was set in 'a very large solid stone', ticking in one of Sydney Cove's great rock faces. The first road in the colony was a track from the tents at the main camp, running past the hospital out to what became Dawes Point.[28]

Like many of his rank and education, Phillip was interested in town planning and familiar with the neo-classical notions of the course of empire. By July he had drafted a plan for a future town. The Camp as it stood was clearly considered a temporary arrangement, mere detritus of the rude pioneering stage. Six-month-old Sydney was still a blank canvas, awaiting inscription. Phillip's town would be named Albion, and it would be an antipodean exercise in 'baroque principles of town planning', equal to the 'extent of empire which demands grandeur of design'. A grand avenue 200 feet wide would run north–east, in a direct line with Sydney Heads, from grand public buildings and a new government house on the brow of the hill, down a gentle slope to a broad piazza at the harbour's edge.[29]

But it was a rather odd sort of town. Although there were government stores, there was no provision for merchants, shops or port workers at all. Albion's shorelines would not be 'lined with commercial buildings' but remain public space, controlled by government.[30] Like Darwin's poem, there were no people in it. This was not a plan for a real commercial port town, but a spatial fantasy about control and beauty, an abstract triangulation of authority, elegantly drawn mathematical spaces, and the sea.

It seems Phillip himself didn't take the plan too seriously. Although the grand avenue was marked out, and the lieutenant governor's house built, Government House did not migrate, but stayed in the east, where the seat of civil author-ity thus remained. In fact the east side was considered by the elite as 'the town' proper, while the west was 'clear of the town'.[31] First Government House, built

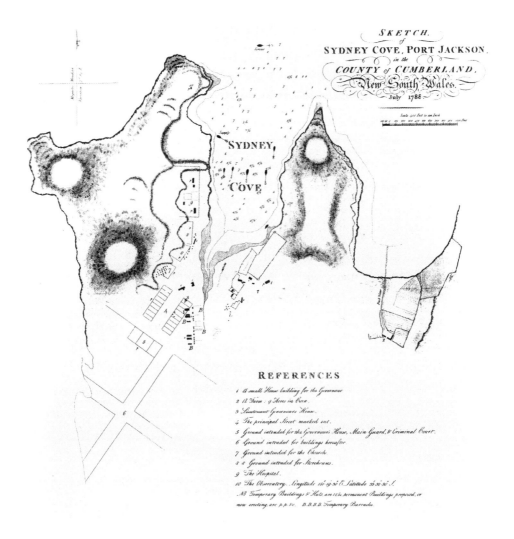

Governor Phillip's plan for 'Albion', July 1788: less a real town than an elegant abstraction of authority, mathematics and the sea. (National Library of Australia)

of imported and locally burnt bricks, rose in pared-down Palladian style, with a simple gabled bay at the centre. With various additions and extensions, it would house governors for almost six decades. Phillip built a row of handsome brick houses for civil officers, each with a flourishing garden, in what became Bridge Street: the civic side of the town was thus consolidated. New huts for convicts built further south paid no heed to the plan either; as the strange 'wheel-spoke' orientation of O'Connell Street and Bligh Street today still shows. Perhaps they were another attempt at planning: an embryonic radial pattern, with Government House at the centre.[32]

So Phillip's Albion never really left paper, while the rough, ordinary buildings and tracks shaped by hands and feet prevailed: it was these pragmatic structures and everyday movements which gave the future city its shape. Emerging roads were mainly set along the north–south axis, echoing the course of the stream, shoreline and the direction of the ridges to the west of the cove. The spaces between the military huts joined the path running north to Dawes Point that became the High Street (later George Street), the spine of the town.

On the western side, beyond the 200-foot wide corridor of trees which shrouded the Tank Stream, the military encampment also solidified. Huts replaced tents and marquees, and barracks were built by 1792. They had a good view of Sydney Cove and Long Cove (Darling Harbour) but they were 'directly in the neighbourhood of the ground for burying the dead', so a new burial ground was opened in an area of clayey ground outside the town to the south. The town's early dead presumably remained lying close to these barracks. A much more substantial brick complex was erected in the Foveaux and Macquarie periods around what is today Barrack Street and Wynyard Square. These served until 1848, when the soldiers moved out of the town to the Victoria Barracks at Paddington.[33]

Meanwhile, the convicts in the tents on the western shoreline looked up the wild, broken slopes of Tallawolladah. They called it 'the Rocks' and the name stuck. Soon they were creating their own town there, building 'little edifices', one- and two-roomed huts of split soft cabbage tree, woven wattles and clay with stubby thatched roofs and no eaves. Central doors hung on leather straps and flanking window-spaces were covered with woven wattle screens. Perhaps the building methods were introduced by rural convicts, for these houses were of ancient lineage: they much resembled the simplest traditional cottages of rural England and Ireland. Such houses were so different from the burgeoning eighteenth-century urban centres that they had become exotic, and romanticised in nostalgic scenes, complete with milkmaids and cows, on mass-produced dinner and tea sets. In Sydney the 'little huts and cots' were real, and they gave the Camp a 'villactick appearance', their whitewashed walls and orange-brown bricks and tiles 'quite romantic', especially scattered along the tree-lined road to the Brickfields.[34] As we shall see, newcomers would be amazed and delighted at the 'English' appearance of Sydney: it reminded them of a familiar, rural England.

The transmission of vernacular building styles: a traditional Irish rural cottage (left) and a cottage built at the Rocks in about 1810, itself similar in style to the earliest wattle-and-daub houses. (Author's collection; State Records of New South Wales)

SYDNEY AND PARRAMATTA: TEMPLATE OF ORDER

Looks could be deceiving in so many ways. Like Botany Bay, Warrane proved disappointing as a site for the imagined agricultural colony, and this resulted in yet another settlement—a third founding. Sydney's sandy soils did in fact support luxurious growths of vines and fruit trees, but this was not enough; it was not 'real' agriculture, because wheat and maize failed to thrive. More promising open country, free of 'underwood, Grass very long' had been observed upriver by Hunter and Bradley during the survey of the harbour in February 1788.[35] By June better soils were found in the shale country at the head of the harbour, and Phillip established a public farm there in 1789. When the crops flourished, he founded 'the first township', Rose Hill. Sending stores and provisions to the farm from Sydney would be impractical, he reported, and in any case 'The Sea-coast does not offer any situation . . . which is calculated for a town whose inhabitants are to be employed in agriculture'. Agriculture, after all, was the *raison d'être* of the colony, and the destiny of the convicts. The new settlement was later renamed Parramatta, a version of Burramattagal, the name of the Aboriginal owners from whom it had been taken.[36]

By this time, the Camp at Sydney Cove already seemed beyond official planning and control. Some huts were built under official direction, in orderly rows. These early 'official' huts were not originally intended as *homes*—spaces with emotional and intimate dimensions—but merely basic shelter for a subject workforce called to labour in gangs each day. Occupied collectively, ten to a hut, rather than by individuals, they were meant to impose order and control, not comfort, domesticity and a sense of ownership. Yards were attached—or simply appropriated—to allow convicts to grow their own food, a saving on the stores and a sign of the reforming power of gardening—for convicts and land. This echoed the urban form of preindustrial towns in their early years generally—houses set in yards which were used for work, food production and waste disposal.[37]

But on the ground, and inside those houses and yards, Sydney developed riotously, largely without order and regimentation. Convicts and soldiers chose sites in their respective zones, built houses and soon regarded them as their own. Chests containing all their possessions stood in the rooms, and they began to furnish the houses with beds, tables and chairs, and even elegant ceramic ornaments and neat china tableware.[38] By the 1810s these included blue-and-white bowls, saucers and teacups printed with those nostalgic scenes of lost rural English life, some showing cottages much like those in which their owners lived.[39] They cleared irregular patches of land, brought in better soils and planted vegetables and fruit trees. Leases were given to favoured individuals from Phillip's time on, but the vast majority had no official lease or grant at all: they held the ground by permissive occupancy, by 'naked possession'.[40]

This was not simply a matter of architectural chaos and affronted aesthetic sensibilities. It had important political dimensions. If convicts and soldiers lived in their own houses, they possessed private spaces and private lives. If they worked the ground or built structures, their labour, mixed with the earth, gave them property rights. Men and women formed relationships and raised families, and their households became essential to the convict system because they provided board and lodgings for later convict arrivals. Women retreated into their houses and simply refused to come out as ordered, protecting themselves within a mantle of private domestic space. Convicts who were tradesmen and women began to open businesses and work from these houses.

The convict settlers also created social and communal networks, and hence loyalties, with shipmates and workmates, housemates, neighbours and friends from the Old Country.

The buildings and the spaces between them, the marketplace and embryonic squares also allowed the establishment of preindustrial popular culture— the pleasures of drinking, gambling, bare-knuckle fighting and cockfighting, scenes never supposed to exist in Botany Bay. As we will see, these pleasures and pastimes also drew elite patrons, who helped organise them. The King's Birthday bonfires were another event where plebeians and the higher ranks mingled in the same urban space: Worgan wrote cheerfully that, after their own celebrations, the officers

> walked out to visit the Bonfires, The Fuel of One of Which, a number of Convicts had been two Days collecting . . . it was really a noble Sight, it was piled up for several Yards high round a large Tree; where, the Convicts assembled, singing and Huzzaing . . .

It was a rare occasion for shared loyalist sentiment and a still rarer instance of popular support for Phillip, for 'on the Governor's Approach, they all drew up on the Opposite Side, and gave three Huzza's, after this Salutation, A Party of them joined in singing God Save the King'.[41]

The next King's Birthday, 4 June 1789, brought the ranks together again. A theatre had been opened in one of the Rocks huts, where the Restoration drama *The Recruiting Officer* was performed to a highly appreciative audience by convict thespians. Phillip both permitted and attended this performance, yet he made no mention of it in his report to Lord Sydney the following day. A.J. Gray is probably right when he suggests that Phillip most likely considered it wiser not to mention the convicts' play-acting: he knew it was not quite what the British government had in mind for the convict colony.[42] The Reverend Richard Johnson wrote crossly of the urban priorities clearly in evidence in the early Camp:

> I am yet obliged to be a field Preacher. No Church is yet begun of, & I am afraid scarcely thought of. Other things seem to be of greater Notice &

Concern & most wd rather see a Tavern, a Play House, a Brothel—anything sooner than a place for publick worship.

The theatre disappeared from the official record soon after 1789, although in fact it lasted at least until 1800.[43]

So Sydney quickly developed in precisely the opposite way to the original vision for the colony: instead of a closely supervised, harsh, subsistence agricultural settlement, it was a distinctly urban place with considerable freedoms. Yet neither was it the materialisation of Erasmus Darwin's vision of the grand city with its domes and spires, and the architecture of polite society—or not yet, anyway. Much of the everyday urban landscape—buildings, paths, movements—was shaped by the tastes and habits of the convicts. And their houses had multiple meanings: they could be sites of honest work, families, independence from the stores, and 'progress'. Governors wrote with some admiration of the domestic achievements of the convict townsfolk. But they were also spaces where people made their own lives, places where stolen goods could be stashed or sold, robberies planned and liquor illegally distilled, places for riot, revelry and conspiracy out of the eye of authority. As for labour, convicts did not even work to regular hours, let alone 'what would be called a day's work in England'. They announced that they would 'sooner perish in the woods than be obliged to work' and insisted upon the task-work system. This meant that once the daily task was completed, they had free time to earn money, plant their gardens, play or wander as they chose. The authorities were faced with accepting task-work or no work at all.[44]

Of still more concern was that the military personnel living in houses thought of themselves as 'independent citizens rather than subordinate soldiers'. Soldiers who lived in huts among convicts made 'connection with infamous characters there'. These associations were forbidden by their officers to no avail, for 'living in huts by themselves, it was carried on without their knowledge'. Even when barracks were built, they were insufficient for 'accommodation and discipline', and a 'high brick wall, or an inclosure of strong paling' would have been necessary to keep them in. Unfortunately, there was not enough labour available to build either.[45]

Controlled accommodation and discipline therefore loomed large in Phillip's startover town at Parramatta. He had learned the lessons of the Camp. As Collins later explained, once convicts got into their own huts, it was too late, for 'they would be with difficulty removed when wanted; they pleaded the acquirement of comforts, of which in fact it would be painful . . . to deprive them'.[46] On this fresh canvas of kinder country Phillip decided there would be no private building or de facto ownership, no crooked rows or hidden places. No unknowable urban spaces, opaque to authorities, refuges for ne'er-do-wells. The government would retain control of land and buildings. Everything would be orderly, open and transparent. The plan laid out a broad street 200 feet wide leading up from the river's edge to a gentle rise, where Phillip planted his own house, a lathe-and-plaster version of his Sydney residence. The huts for the convicts, each placed at the same setback and distance from one another, lined the avenue below Government House in a long, straight and subordinate procession. Each hut was allotted garden ground as a 'spur to industry'. The plan also created vistas to imaginary future buildings of civic authority: the town hall, school, church, and a marketplace, which would control buying and selling. Phillip personally supervised the building of his town at Parramatta.[47]

This plan has been praised as one of 'grace, balance, charm and utility' and 'a fine Renaissance scheme in the best Classical manner'. Some say Phillip was inspired by his visit to Lisbon, and his knowledge of other European towns and cities.[48] But to view this plan only through the lens of aesthetics surely misses the point. Phillip needed a town plan which would not only be the centre of an agricultural colony, but would actually work to reinforce his authority over the convicts, and so to fulfil his instructions. And there was another model, much closer to home, which may well have inspired him.

Phillip had farmed his wife's estate at Lyndhurst in Hampshire before 1769 and then between 1784 and 1786, when he was offered the governorship of the new colony in New South Wales.[49] Nearby, in Dorset, was the new village of Milton Abbas, built in 1780 by Lord Dorchester to the design of the famous landscape architect, Capability Brown. Here, a wide street ran straight down a gentle slope, terminating with a view of the vicarage. On either side, arranged with military precision, stood rows of two-storey houses of whitewashed cob and thatch. Lord Dorchester wanted to clear the old village because it interfered with the vistas over his new parkland. The tenants apparently disliked their new houses, and Lord Dorchester, intensely.[50]

Today Milton Abbas is seen as the quintessential charming Georgian village, steeped in tradition (and hence full of tourists!). But traditional English villages do not look like this at all—they evolved over centuries and typically have an ad hoc, irregular appearance. Milton Abbas was in fact among a number of examples of modern planned housing, part of a larger landscape movement, the 'empark-ment' of the manor houses. This often involved setting the houses in sweeping, newly created open landscapes of grass and trees—and to achieve this splendid aesthetic, existing villages had to be demolished and relocated. The new villages were usually 'laid out symmetrically in systematic rows along the roadside' leading to the gates of the estate, and they formed an impressive visual prelude to the manor house itself. Earlier examples of these 'adjusted villages' included Chippenham in Cambridgeshire, New Houghton in Norfolk ('a number of well-built whitewashed cottages standing either side of the road . . . widely spaced and with particularly large gardens behind'), Harewood in Yorkshire and, most celebrated of all, Nuneham Courtenay in Oxfordshire.[51]

An anonymous soldier writing home in the early years described Parramatta as Phillip's 'country seat'.[52] He was right on the mark. Phillip was clearly creating an antipodean version of the modern and fashionable English gentleman's estate, complete with Government House set in the parklands of the Domain, the neat rows of workers' huts leading up to the gates, and the farmed fields beyond. The thatched, whitewashed wattle-and-daub huts even looked similar to those of the English model villages.

But, again, there was more to it than aesthetics. This plan was about order and control. Milton Abbas had been much publicised as the most modern, innova-tive and attractive way to deal with disorderly tenants and their messy, smelly, crooked villages. The model appears to have been adopted in other places around the globe where the control of the workers or slaves was vital. It was a template of order and modernity, at once a material expression of rank and hierarchy, a means of surveillance and control, and pleasing to eyes that sought 'balance, charm and utility'.[53] Interestingly, in both Milton Abbas and Parramatta, the occupants lived

The template: Milton Abbas, Dorset, close to where Arthur Phillip farmed at Lyndhurst.
(Photo: G. Karskens, 2002)

Phillip's startover town in Parramatta: regularity and control were to be imposed through
planning and building. (From David Collins, Account of the English Colony)

communally rather than according to individual family groups—four families to a house in Milton Abbas, ten convicts to a hut in Parramatta. The Parramatta huts, however, were not supposed to be homes: they were intended to be more like barracks, 'spread over a greater distance'.[54]

Watkin Tench was convinced that Parramatta would overtake Sydney as the centre of the colony. Sydney, he wrote dismissively in December 1791, 'has long been considered only a depot for stores'. The town of only three years was already old and worn out, for it 'exhibited nothing but a few old scattered huts, and some sterile gardens'. Cultivation of wheat at Farm Cove had been abandoned, public building was at a standstill, and 'all our strength is transferred to Rose Hill'. When more transport ships arrived, the healthy convicts were sent up to Parramatta, while the sick remained in Sydney.[55] By 1792, Phillip was making sure new arrivals did not even set foot in Sydney, so there would be no possibility 'of any attachment to this part of the colony'. For Sydney, it was said, already 'possessed . . . all the allurements of a sea port of some standing'. The newly arrived, blissfully unaware of the port's delights, went cheerfully to Parramatta.[56]

Sydney prevailed nevertheless. Phillip was still plagued with doubts in 1789, and sensitive to the charge that he had founded the colony in the wrong place. He wrote an account of the difficulties he had faced in selecting the site, and pointed out that ships falling into bad weather could take refuge in Port Jackson, so 'perhaps it will be found hereafter that the seat of government has not been improperly placed' after all. Sydney did remain 'the head-quarters of the colony' and the governors stayed there, even after Hunter built another elegant Palladian-style Government House on the site of the first house at Parramatta.[57] The town at Warrane did not wither, nor did it become a mere government depot or port of refuge alone. Instead it grew rapidly on the rising tide of trade, commerce, shipping and entrepreneurial ambition.

Parramatta, meanwhile, became the centre of Phillip's vision of rural expansion: clusters of small farms of 30 acres, hacked out of the bush.

Chapter 4

'FOOD FROM A COMMON INDUSTRY': PUBLIC FARMS AND COMMON LANDS

Before the first convict farmers were settled on their 30-acre lots, Phillip established public farms, the first stage of the colony's self-sufficiency project. His Instructions said that he was to 'proceed to the cultivation of the land' immediately,

> ... distributing the convicts for that purpose in such a manner, and under such inspectors or overseers, and under such regulations as may appear to you to be necessary ... for procuring supplies of grain and ground provisions.[1]

These big public farms were run by the government on the labour of convicts, the corn and 'other vegetable food' produced 'from a common industry'.[2] They were intended to be temporary, but they nevertheless persisted in tandem with private agriculture for 40 years. They were experiments in agriculture, and training grounds for agricultural workers, and they produced the early stores of seed grain. Despite this, public farming did not become part of the pioneer legend which focuses so strongly upon the individual men and women who battled the environment on their farms. Instead it was the makings of the other great legend: the 'fatal shore', of Botany Bay as a place of torment, slavery and starvation.

Academic historians have not been much interested in these public farms and reserves. Even the shining exception, Brian Fletcher, concludes that 'government farming and grazing . . . served only a limited purpose in New South Wales before 1810'.[3] But these public farms were an important part of Sydney's rural history, and the convict experience. Many of them, simply by being reserved lands, also left significant physical legacies which shaped the future city. Generally, their stories have been researched and pieced together by local historians, familiar with local geographies.

'THE GOVERNMENT EARTH'[4]

Phillip was taken aback by the unexpected delays in establishing agriculture. The soils were not 'all of a piece', simply waiting for seeding and breeding, but patchy—arable land needed to be located and tested. The land was 'infested' with trees and clearing was slow. The convicts themselves were obviously not going to make instant farmers and the natives were not meek, pliant or peaceful. So the public farm at Rose Hill, guarded by soldiers in a redoubt, was an important experiment—it paved the way for the first convict farmer, James Ruse, who in turn opened the way for other emancipist settlers. Hundreds of convicts were sent up the river to work the ground and plant the crops, the purpose being to establish both a food source and a seed-bank. Their success led Phillip to found Parramatta as the new centre of the colony. The site of the first wheat crop was later known as the 'Old Field'—wheat still stood there as Phillip's broad avenue approached from the east, for the new huts and the street between were built right over that first cultivated ground.[5] Similar experiments would be repeated as government farms were set up in the new districts over the mountains, the inland areas of Bathurst and Wellington for example, testing the land with hoe and seed, making a path for settlers.

Public farming on the Cumberland Plain didn't wither away as planned. As Parramatta was being laid out in 1791, new public farms were opened on creeks which fed the river, just to the north-west. The best known was the New Ground, officially named Toongabbie. On the rich, sheltered soils of Toongabbie Creek, 500 men felled the enormous turpentines, coachwood, lillypilly and scented satinwood of the rainforest brush. Some of these trees were reported to be

Port Jackson Painter, 'A View of Government Farm at Rose Hill NS Wales 1791', showing the first public farm, which paved the way for the first convict settlers. (Natural History Museum)

100 feet tall and 9 yards in diameter. The convicts piled branches around the logs not wanted for building and set them alight, sending billowing pillars of smoke into the skies. They hoed the ground and planted turnips to prepare the soil for future crops of maize.[6]

Working hours were set at first, but, as at Parramatta and Sydney, the system soon reverted to the convicts' preferred task-work, which meant that they had part of the day to themselves. By now the task for each convict was to hoe seven rods per day. It had been sixteen rods (88 yards) at the earlier Parramatta farm, and was reduced from eight at Toongabbie after the convicts sent a deputation to the governor: eight rods, they said, 'was beyond their strength to execute'. They lived communally, 500 people lodged at first in thirteen large tent huts—around 40 people in each. Tench made special mention of the fact that their labour here was 'unassisted by any liquor but water'—an unusual circumstance.[7]

By 1792, Phillip was planning another rural town at Toongabbie, a clone of Parramatta, the echo of Milton Abbas and the other model village experiments. The same regular broad street again ran parallel with the watercourse, the same allotments, the same precise rows of huts, only larger this time, barrack-shelters for groups of twenty rather than ten. The superintendent's and overseers' huts, arranged in a U-shape, stood across a bridge on the other side of the creek. Henry Brewer sketched a picture of the settlement, showing the neat rows of huts in a tamed landscape, the wheat in stack and smoke curling from a communal kitchen. The picture, included in David Collins' published journal, assured the viewer that the colony was proceeding precisely as planned. One wonders whether Phillip was planning to set more of these 'villages' across the face of the country.[8]

But in the same year, 1792, the New Ground at Toongabbie also became the colony's de facto place of secondary punishment, the first of a series that would eventually leapfrog up the coast to Coal River (Newcastle), then Port Macquarie and finally Moreton Bay (Brisbane).[9] Convicts who raided the maize harvest and hid the cobs in their huts or buried them in the bush were sent to the New Ground. They detested the place, feared it more than 'any corporal correction' because of the separation from town life at Parramatta and Sydney,

'A western view of Toongabbe', clone of Parramatta, echo of Milton Abbas. Parallel rows of huts and planted fields were carved out of the tall forests on Toongabbie Creek. (From David Collins, Account of the English Colony, *vol. 1*)

and from the fellowship of companions; and probably because of the absence of liquor.[10] After 1803 they would detest Newcastle for the same reasons.

Newly arrived convicts, particularly the Irish, were also sent straight from the ships up to Toongabbie. The farm's population reached over a thousand, as many as had arrived on the First Fleet, including 260 women, a large number of boys, and 'old and feeble men' who were assigned as hutkeepers for the rest. Eventually most of the government's gradually increasing stock of cattle, horses and sheep were kept here too. There were few legitimate reasons to leave the establishment, for the farm was largely self-contained, with a barber, shoemaker, tailor and a thatcher to mend the hut roofs, a miller to grind the wheat and maize, eight constables and a battery of overseers to run the gangs. It was easy to escape, though, and dozens were reported to have 'run off into the woods'; or they went to Sydney.[11]

But Toongabbie, site of so much activity and population, dwindled as quickly as it had grown. By 1795, as on the private farms, the soils were already giving out under continuous cultivation and the yield was failing. Despite spelling and the manure the stock provided, the soils did not recover. Toongabbie became a stock farm and a stopping place for those convicts left over from assignment—probably the least fit and able. So the New Ground became old ground in only ten years. The whole process—massive clearing, burning, planting, building—was started all over again on the hills between Parramatta and Toongabbie, and then further north, in the blue gum forest at Castle Hill.[12]

Most of the cultivated lands and livestock were still in government hands when Phillip sailed away in 1792. His successors, Grose and Paterson, wound back public farming and grazing, giving away some of the stock and taking 600 acres out of production.[13] But by the time Governor Hunter arrived, the British government was keen to revive public farming as a way of keeping costs down; private farming was only just beginning to support the colonists at this time. Hunter was also ordered to withdraw convicts from the private settlers and put them back on the 'government stroke'. He could see the folly of these measures— settlers just establishing themselves did not want to have to compete with public farms to sell their produce, and convict labour was essential to the viability of their farms. James Ruse and his fellow ex-convict farmer, Charles Williams, had both relied on the labour of convicts working on their own time. Collins had earlier come to the conclusion that subsistence farming was never going to work, and moreover that public farming robbed private farmers of their markets, for the farmer would 'find himself cut off from the means of purchasing any of those comforts which his family must inevitably require'. This would defeat the whole purpose of colonisation, for the farmer 'would certainly quit a country that merely held out to him a daily subsistence; he would look, if he was ordinarily wise, for something beyond that'.[14]

Eventually, though, Hunter gave up resisting and obeyed his orders—the convicts were taken from the farms and estates and put back into public service. This, he reported as politely as he could, resulted in 'ferment'. The farmers were 'displeased', while the workers were 'turbulent and refractory and frequently desert from their work'. Clearly, convict workers preferred private assignment over work on government projects and farms, 'the grubbing hoe or timber carriage'.[15]

By 1803 the policy pendulum had swung back, and public farming was again considered superseded by private farming. Governor King was instructed that, from now on, it was a means of employing convicts rather than primarily for food production. This remained the main purpose of the public farms: employment for those convicts left over from assignment and public works and who were not self-employed.[16] But King was concerned for the future of crown lands. He disapproved of the fact that private settlers had appropriated much of the land at Toongabbie, cleared by convict labour at great expense to the crown. By then most of the Hawkesbury's alluvial lands had been snaffled too. To help small settlers increase their stock, and to preserve lands from the officers of the New South Wales Corps, King declared a series of six commons, which settlers could use for grazing and getting firewood. Nelson, Phillip and Richmond Hill commons were located on the Hawkesbury, the Prospect and Toongabbie Temporary Common lay west of Parramatta, while the Field of Mars and Eastern Farms Common took in much of the great Blue Gum High Forest of Sydney's north shore. This common stretched over 5050 acres, from the farmers at the Ponds in Ryde right up the Lane Cove River towards the 'new ground' at Castle Hill.[17]

Castle Hill Farm was a focus of enormous activity. It was located at the junction of creeks in hilly lands in the south-west corner of the forest, a vast shaft of some 34 500 acres, taking in much of present-day Dural, Glenorie and Glenhaven. By the time visiting Frenchman François Péron visited in 1804, the earlier method of leaving stumps in the ground to rot had been abandoned on the public farms—now they cleared corridors around the new ground and set fire to it. Smoke and fire filled the skies above the great forest for days, while below ground burning stumps baked the clay hard. Péron wrote dramatically of the landscape all on fire in the Castle Hill area:

> Six hundred convicts were continually employed in felling trees to open roads through the forest, and in twenty quarters might be seen rising immense volumes of flame and smoke produced by the burning of new concessions.[18]

Like Toongabbie, the first buildings here were of bark and timber, storerooms, stock huts and, for the convicts, separate huts, each in its own fenced kitchen garden. But in 1803 King ordered a large two-storey stone barracks be built at Castle Hill: a substantial structure, 100 feet long and 24 feet wide and built upon fieldstones set in mud mortar.[19] It was the first convict barracks in the colony, for it predated Macquarie's Hyde Park Barracks by sixteen years, and was a complete departure from Phillip's plan of housing convicts in separate huts. These barracks were probably King's response to the escape of Irish men from Castle Hill early in 1803, as well as the Irish plots hatched in the huts at Toongabbie since 1800. King had also seen the way the convicts made the huts their own private spaces in Sydney and Parramatta. The Castle Hill barracks abandoned the village model, and moved towards solidity, security and surveillance. They also involved a loss of liberty for the convicts: hut-mates no longer grew and cooked food for themselves. At Castle Hill, archaeologists also found a large square building with a huge fireplace: probably a kitchen or mess hut where meals were prepared. The convicts could now be locked up, watched and counted.

King sent the Irish convicts up to Castle Hill, using isolation to quarantine them and their seditious ideas. As we shall see, the concentration of so many apart from the main settlements fostered insurrection instead. In March 1804, hundreds of convicts broke out of the farm, intent on overturning the government, taking a ship and sailing home. Instead they were betrayed, pursued, and slaughtered by soldiers on the road to the Hawkesbury at Vinegar Hill (present-day Rouse Hill). Perhaps the barracks themselves, the sense of being singled out, treated differently, had exacerbated the situation. After the rebellion, and the hangings that followed, Castle Hill Farm continued to produce wheat. But yields fell in subsequent years, and then there was a general labour shortage. Macquarie closed it in 1810.[20]

So Castle Hill was wound down, closed and converted, but when numbers of convicts rose and once more outstripped private demand for them, other farms were resurrected or opened elsewhere. Longbottom at Concord, named from the long areas of low-lying marshy 'bottoms' along the Parramatta River, took in 700 acres of turpentine/ironbark forest lands and swamps from Cabarita Point to the Parramatta Road, halfway between Sydney and Parramatta. Longbottom began as a timberyard in 1793, and was used as a stopover point for convicts being marched to and from Parramatta, to accommodate road gangs and for growing a bit of maize. From 1819 it became a more formal public 'farm', though it was used for timbergetting, grazing the government's working oxen, burning charcoal and also lime from oyster shells from the river. The convicts grew their own vegetables in an 'extensive kitchen garden'. Almost twenty years later, Longbottom was about to close when French Canadian Patriotes, exiled to Australia after the rebellions in Quebec of 1837–38, sailed into Sydney Harbour. They were sent up to its rough, verminous huts, where they felled trees, built roads, and made wooden blocks for experimental street pavements in Sydney. Some of them wrote sad journals of a miserable and desolate life there, and railed against the injustice and harshness of their treatment.[21]

Closer to Sydney, on the Parramatta Road at present-day Camperdown, was yet another government establishment, an early stock-grazing run set aside for the support of clergy and schoolteachers and as crown land, growing fodder for the government cattle. Part of this land was leased out to Major Francis Grose in 1792, and other officers appear to have helped themselves informally. The reserve, known as Grose Farm, was developed as a 'model farm' before it was handed over to the Female Orphan School in 1821. Still intact in 1855, it was ceded as the site for Australia's first university. Soon the neo-gothic sandstone walls rose under new heavens, overlooking the old huts, railed fences, the plough-furrowed paddocks and the Blackwattle swamps.[22]

In 1819, Macquarie also reluctantly opened a new farm on Emu Plains, on the fertile Nepean River flats spread below the mass of the Blue Mountains. Again, this had been an earlier depot for roadmaker William Cox and the gangs building the first track over the Blue Mountains in 1814. If Castle Hill was closed down in a period of labour shortage, this new farm was opened because of a labour glut: so many convicts arrived after 1815 that there was not enough employment for them. Emu Plains Farm surprised everyone by flourishing and even making a profit, producing tobacco, vegetables, maize and wheat, as well as flax and hemp. This landscape inspired rejoicings, for it was 'the grandest sight that has ever exhibited itself in the colony', an enormous field of wheat where, 'turn the eye which way you will, you have the most delightful and almost boundless prospect'. At last, the original vision of Botany Bay manifest.[23]

Emu Plains Farm was noted for its 'comfort, regularity and discipline'. Like the timbergetting establishment at Pennant Hills, it had some success in training young convict men in rural skills so they could then be assigned to settlers and later able to support themselves. It was a refuge too for invalids and those with weak or damaged minds. The convicts there opened their own theatre and put on fashionable plays—they made their audiences 'laugh until [they] cried'. The theatre was the talk of Sydney, where Governor Darling discouraged playhouses and censored or banned plays.[24] But this farm too closed in 1832, partly as a result of pressure from local landowners who objected to a government farm which was so successful. It was resurveyed as a township, which failed to thrive, although orchards, market gardens and dairy farms did, and the area became a great marketplace for cattle and sheep driven over the mountains from the western districts. The Great Western Road over which they came was built by gangs of convict men in the 1820s and 1830s, who toiled on the massive stone retaining walls and bridges rising from the ravines. Some of these gangs were housed in the old farm's mouldering huts and barracks.[25]

SPATIAL LEGACIES

The government farms had a chequered history—they were not meant to be permanent, yet in a maze of policy shifts and pragmatic measures, they prevailed. Thousands of men and women passed through them and the proportion of land they occupied at different times is striking—especially if considered with the other reserves: the great commons set aside by King in 1803 and by Macquarie in 1811, the vast grazing reserves, and the thousands of acres granted to the churches and schools.[26] Much of it was 'inferior' land, but nonetheless it was locked up from subdivision and other development, sometimes for decades. Thus the farms and commons often created different spatial histories and patterns, and unintended legacies.

Castle Hill Farm, for example, became the colony's first lunatic asylum. Those with mental illnesses were sent away from the towns in much the same way as the Irish had been. Conditions for the inmates at this isolated place were by all accounts appalling and after numerous damning reports, they were moved to another outlying town, Liverpool, in 1828. Ten years earlier, the larger farm itself had been thrown open to private settlers, while a 40-acre reserve went to the Church of England as glebe lands. The old barracks/asylum served as a rather clumsy church, until it was replaced, and then demolished, in the 1860s. The stone was used to build the new gothic parsonage, still standing today, while the foundations disappeared beneath grazing lands and flourishing citrus orchards.

Other farms and stock reserves eventually shrank over the nineteenth century, but often sections of them were retained as public open space. At Concord, large parts of Longbottom became playing fields, while the wetlands were filled in for golf courses beside bays which remember the unhappy Canadian exiles: Canada Bay, Exile Bay, France Bay.[27] King's great commons no longer exist, it is true, but often they were places where the bush could regenerate, in new forms, and in some cases these were protected as precious remnant reserves. To the north-west, the Field of Mars Wildlife Reserve at Marsfield remembers the old common; in the west, Scheyville National Park is a remnant of the Pitt Town Common, which was not revoked until 1890. It is the largest extant area of now-rare Cumberland woodland, and a haven for endangered species. These reserves are now small islands in unending seas of suburbs and industrial development.[28] In the east, Macquarie's Sydney Common, a block of 1305 acres of wetlands and sandhills south of Sydney, was reserved in order to get wandering stock off the streets of Sydney. It became Moore Park and Centennial Park, the vital green lungs of the densely built-up eastern suburbs.[29]

LANDSCAPES OF TYRANNY: THE PUBLIC FARMS REMEMBERED

The public farms were not established as prisons or places of deliberate punishment and torment, certainly not in the ways that later places of secondary punishment, like Norfolk Island, were. At Parramatta and Toongabbie in particular, Phillip clearly had in mind a great estate, with the convict workers housed in orderly huts of the 'village'. Although governors sometimes found it convenient to use them to punish and isolate convicts, their main purpose was to establish the initial food supply, and in the process hopefully promote reform through hard work. The farms also prepared convicts, a large proportion of whom were from urban areas, for a life on the land. Similarly, those later sent to the Pennant Hills Establishment used their timbergetting skills to get work after they served their time.[30]

But the public farms were presented and remembered as places of torment and brutality, and the tales became more lurid as each decade passed. Toongabbie in particular became associated with tyranny, torture and oppression. It was originally the Aboriginal name for this country, the word given to Phillip by the Tugagal or the Burramattagal, but it later acquired international notoriety as a place synonymous with 'Slavery and Famine'. Descriptions of Toongabbie's terrors, of mass deaths and murders, were included in the tracts of anti-transportationists and anti-slavery campaigners. As Deirdre Coleman points out, the connection between transportation and slavery was firm in the minds of the English public, and horror stories from Botany Bay were eagerly harnessed to both campaigns. Thus in the early 1790s, the anti-slavery poet George Dyer 'trawled through all the recent Botany Bay publications for the most graphic and negative accounts of the colony' and published these cobbled accounts as *Slavery and Famine, Punishment for Seditions: An Account of Miseries and Starvation at*

Botany Bay. This book included a gruesome account of Toongabbie in which the convicts were starved and worked to death, or died standing at the stores waiting for their rations.[31]

By the 1840s Toongabbie was part of a wider mythology, conjured especially by anti-transportationists, about the horrors of the early colony as

> an awful over-sea gaol, offering no prospect of advancement or liberation, where the will of the prisoner turnkey was law, where death was the punishment for the most trifling crimes, and a reproachful look was punished with the lash.[32]

There were tales of convicts buried alive, convicts eating grass, convicts summarily hanged, convicts the helpless victims of both sadistic overseers and officers, who also lusted after their wives. Stories published about the Emu Plains Farm in the local Penrith newspaper, the *Nepean Times*, in the late nineteenth and early twentieth centuries were similarly gruesome, and made their way into local lore. James Broadbent, who grew up in the old farming district of Castlereagh, remembers his great-grandfather's stories of the 'horrendous screams' of the convicts floating across the water from Emu Plains.[33]

The tales of old Toongabbie were the same. In their old age, Joseph 'Smasher' Smith and Henry Hale, both Second Fleeters who had become comfortable landholders on the Macdonald River, told the famous emigration campaigner Caroline Chisholm:

> The motto was 'Kill them, or work them, their provisions will be in store'. Many a time have I been yoked like a bullock with twenty or thirty others to drag along the timber. About eight hundred died in six months at a place called Toongabbie, or Constitution Hill.[34]

The stories Chisholm collected appeared in the work of the anti-transportationist and pro-emigration Australophile, Samuel Sidney. His *Three Colonies of Australia* set the bright and bountiful future of the colony against a dark, unspeakably evil (though undeniably fascinating) convict past, now thankfully receding into history. Sidney's book was hugely popular and, with earlier tracts like Dyer's, cemented the familiar image of old Botany Bay as a place of torture and tyranny. Such stories, as well as faked accounts of the horrors of Norfolk Island, were taken up whole into Robert Hughes' popular and influential *The Fatal Shore*.[35]

Toongabbie also lived on in Irish folk memory as an original site of Irish oppression in Australia. Nearly 80 years after the convicts were moved up to Castle Hill, in an age of steam trains, photography and mass media, bushranger Ned Kelly dictated his famous Jerilderie letter unleashing a thundering tirade of 'wild language' which placed Toongabbie in the larger story of worldwide Irish suffering at the hands of the English:

> . . . all of true blood-bone and beauty that was not murdered on their own soil . . . were doomed to Port McQuarie, Toweringabbie, Norfolk island and Emu plains and in those places of tyranny and condemnation many a blooming Irishman rather than subdue to the Saxon yoke were flogged to death and bravely died in servile chains but true to the shamrock and a credit to Paddy's land.[36]

Kelly, the poorly educated son of an ex-convict, faultlessly recited the places where convicts were sent in the early years; and he conflated the farms with the later places of banishment and severe punishment.

There is little evidence that working and living conditions at Toongabbie were like this. They were hard and primitive, and people sent there would have disliked the unfamiliar, even unnatural, structures of a public farm. But the evidence points to convict agency too: they negotiated directly with the governor, and secured their preferred task-work at a reduced rate.[37] One convict account we have of life at Toongabbie in the 1790s, that of the boy convict George Bruce, mentions nothing of torture, murder, mass deaths or starvation. He briefly recounts that he was sent to 'Towngabbe' and employed as a water carrier 'to the men that was felling the trees to clar that part of the countrey for agercultur'. When he took ill with a fever, he was cared for in the hospital, and, after he recovered, 'imployed myself in rangen the wilderness collecting of all sorts of insex for the docter'. Much of the rest of Bruce's account of his life turns on betrayal, tyranny, and his own cunning in defeating his enemies. If 'Towngabbe' had been a site of his oppression, he would have narrated it in this way. Instead he says he was cared for and allowed to roam the bush. Thomas Gilberthorpe, the emancipist settler who sheltered the fugitive Bruce at the Hawkesbury, even used his own Toongabbie experience to secure a grant of land: 'Servile Labour was my Lot', he wrote in his petition, 'To wich in a very short time I became inured, and agriculture at wich I was employed became a pleasure'.[38]

Why, then, were the public farms remembered as landscapes of tyranny? Why does memory seem to so completely annihilate history? These stories in fact have a kernel of meaning shining from them, for they expressed the deepest fears of common people. In a way the image of Botany Bay as a 'fatal shore' which would disempower men and women was created in the talk of convicts before they embarked. Convict Margaret Catchpole said as much when she reassured her old friends in England, with cheerful relief, that 'we are not driven about after work for Government Like horsen—we are free from all hard work'.[39]

That image—of people harnessed to do the work of beasts—haunted convicts from the start. It appeared in the petitions of old ex-convicts, in the stories of old Toongabbie and Emu Plains, in the reminiscences of Joseph Holt, in folksongs about Van Diemen's Land.[40] Old John Pendergrass, Macquarie's town crier, began his 1825 memorial by conjuring up the harsh early days 'daily exposed to every difficulty incident to those times, when men only did the work as there was no working cattle'. William Henry Jewell, later a teacher at Wilberforce, wrote to his brother that when he arrived in Sydney, 'the farmers and tradespeople . . . now began to pick and choose us out exactly like the Butchers do at Smithfield'.[41] Even as late as 1845, Leon Ducharme, one of the Canadian exiles sent to Longbottom, recalled that upon arrival in Sydney he 'saw miserable wretches harnessed to carts, engaged in dragging blocks of stone for Public Buildings . . . we believed in a few days we too would be employed in exactly the same way'.[42] That oxen had been used to draw carts, ploughs and timber since at least 1796 was immaterial: the vision of men harnessed like beasts was emblematic of utter degradation, dehumanisation and the loss of all rights and liberties under the law. As historian Hamish Maxwell-Stewart argues, this image also reflects the convicts' acute understanding of their economic predicament: transportation meant that 'the convict's body was expropriated by the state'. Although the state did not own the body of the convict, as in slavery, it did own his or her *labour*, in theory at least. Phillip's Instructions had spelt it out: the convicts' labour, and the products of that labour, belonged to the crown.[43]

So some of those sent straight from the ships out to the public farms must have thought their worst fears of Botany Bay realised. The farms resembled large plantations, worked by 'slaves'. Rough, male-dominated, they were far from the towns and the ships and the society of those who lodged where they wished, and those who were 'free on the ground'. Alcohol must have been difficult or impossible to come by. Many of the recently arrived convicts were still weak from the voyage, and from the deprivations of years in gaols and hulks before that. The labour of clearing and planting was monotonous and exhausting, especially in the burning hot summers. Worst of all, in the early years before there were sufficient oxen, the brick carts and timber logs *were* drawn by men. They can be seen in William Bradley's pictures of Sydney Cove—little stick figures dragging carts down to the water—and in a more comical picture drawn by the Spanish visitor Fernando Brambila. Here six convict men pull a cart with two ladies in it towards the neat huts of Phillip's Parramatta.[44]

The farms at Parramatta and Toongabbie inspired numerous escape attempts among disoriented recent arrivals. In 1792, for example, the authorities were alarmed to hear that 'a great body of convicts at the new ground' were planning to rob settlers of their arms, make their way to the coast 'destroying every person who should oppose them', build a vessel and sail away.[45] So it was the public farms, rather than the towns or the households, which were remembered as sites of tyranny and oppression, and which in turn shaped the long-lived images of early Sydney. Since many of the Irish convicts were sent to Toongabbie, it *was* the site of one of the earliest planned Irish rebellions. When the plot was discovered, or betrayed, suspected rebels were brutally flogged there to extract confessions. Local historians say the great stump of the flogging tree may still be seen in Old Toongabbie.[46] We will return to these landscapes of rebellion in Chapter 9, to explore their meanings as wrought by Irish convicts, and the Englishmen who joined them in quests for 'liberty or death'.

Chapter 5

———◆———

SEEDING AND BREEDING

Late in 1789, two years before Phillip's grand avenue at Parramatta was begun, two men could be seen labouring at opposite ends of the colony. One,
a man of the sea, sails a cutter in the harbour and hauls up the seine nets, full
of flipping silver fish in the warmer months, almost empty in winter. He is the
colony's first white fisherman, harvesting the waters for snapper, bream, jewfish,
flathead, leather-jacket and many more species that were the staple food of the
Eora; and also stingrays and sharks, which were not.[1] The other, a man of
the land, hoes the newly exposed shale soil on an acre and a quarter just south
of the Rose Hill wharf.

They are both Cornishmen, both in their twenties, both convicts still under
sentence. They were tried and convicted in adjoining towns in their native
Cornwall within two years of one another, and they both arrived on the First
Fleet. William Bryant, bred to the sea on the Cornish coastline, arrived on the
Charlotte and worked the government's fishing boat. But in March 1791 he and
his wife made one of the most astonishing escapes in colonial history—one that
achieved legendary status.[2] James Ruse, who said he was bred to farming, voyaged
to New South Wales in the *Scarborough* in 1787 and became what Tom Keneally
calls 'an Australian Adam': he became famous as the colony's first farmer.
Although his later efforts in farming seem to have been less than successful, this

original achievement created a mystique about Ruse, especially towards the end of his long life in the colony, and still more so after his death.[3]

Perhaps Cornwall's turbulent history produced men and women of peculiar character and independence of mind. Bryant and Ruse tell us about the divergent responses of skilled and determined convicts to the situations in which they found themselves in New South Wales: how they dealt with the inducements, the regulations and threats of the authorities, and how they responded to the new environments. Here we begin with Ruse and the other convict farmers who were persuaded to take up their 30 acres; later we will return to Bryant, and to all those who took their chances on land and sea as escapees, rebels and outlaws.

While Bryant was quickly learning every shoal, submerged rock and secret bay in the harbour, the currents and tides and sudden squalls, Ruse laboured on the land newly cleared by other convicts out of the forest of huge grey box and red gum. He methodically broke up clods and worked the ashes of the felled giants into the soil. At different times in the cooler months he broadcast bearded wheat and buried ears of maize in the churned earth, to see which grew best. Later this ground was named by Phillip 'Experiment Farm'. The experiment was to see how long it would take a European man to feed himself by farming.[4]

But this experiment was also focused on the man himself, James Ruse. Could convicts become farmers? Could men be redeemed by hard, simple, honest toil? Bryant in his boat was merely prosaic, practical: he met the colony's immediate need for food. He was caught selling fish for his own profit, and severely punished. But the figure of Ruse, stooped over his hoe, stood at the centre of the whole Botany Bay project. He had been supplied with seed, tools, some livestock and a hut to live in. Phillip and the officers watched the experiment intently. They visited him and were gladdened by his progress. Tench thought the fellow certainly talked as if he knew farming, though Phillip seems to have had his doubts.[5]

In September 1790 Ruse married Elizabeth Parry, who had arrived on the *Lady Juliana*, and by August the following year the first of their six children was born. (Like Bryant and many other convicts, Ruse had a spouse and two children back in Cornwall, but this was no impediment to colonial weddings: lives had to be made anew.) Eventually, around mid-1791, Ruse announced that he had produced enough maize and wheat to take himself off the stores, and his wife also in a few months more. The experiment had taken two years, and Ruse and Parry performed exactly as the British government had hoped. Parry was one of the first women to be granted a pardon for becoming an 'industrious' wife and mother, the idealised role for convict women. Ruse was granted the land he had worked so diligently: 30 acres stretching back into the woodland from a brackish creek.[6]

Soon other convicts who had served their time and were willing to try farming were placed on 30-acre plots nearby—Ruse's shipmate from the *Scarborough*, Charles Williams, settled next to him with his wife, Eleanor McCabe. This couple worked as hard as the Ruses—at first.[7] Others were sent out to a crescent of dark volcanic soil around the base of Prospect Hill about 6 kilometres to the west, and to the patches of alluvium and basaltic soils on the north side of the Parramatta River. By 1791 there were four islands of roughly cleared, primitive farms in the vast bushland, linked to Parramatta by the river or rough tracks. Collins called the little settlements 'divisions' and the governor and officers walked constantly from farm to farm, eagerly assessing the progress of both earth and people, looking for stands of flourishing crops, cottages kept snug and neat, healthy bodies, signs of industry and diligence.[8]

SYDNEY'S RURAL HISTORY

If urban development was anathema to the British government's original vision for Botany Bay, then perhaps the story of settling the Cumberland Plain is the story of Australia's *intended* origins. That is the way Phillip saw it, and Bligh after him. To these governors in particular, Sydney town was an unintended by-product, a sort of rampant root-stock sport meriting only neglect or removal because it sucked the life blood from the legitimate colony. What happened when this extraordinary experiment (bold or idiotic? humane or cruel?) was actually implemented?

The plan had antecedents. In the seventeenth and eighteenth centuries, indentured servants in the American colonies were sometimes given small portions of land after they had served their time, so that they could support themselves and hopefully create a stable yeomanry. As Fletcher observes, the governors' instructions on how the land was to be apportioned were 'in some respects identical with those applying to other colonies'.[9] With the benefit of hindsight, we might also observe that the plan of settling thieves on small acreages set a template: the perennial dreams of small-farming in Australia, dreams that recurred despite the environmental disaster and human tragedy which so often resulted from these experiments. The foundational relationship between government and settlers, where governments supplied the would-be farmers with everything to set them up—labour and land, tools, stock and seed—would be an enduring one too. Over the centuries that followed, governments would see it as their duty to partner settlers in the colonising project, opening the way, devising settlement programs and policies to encourage rural development, and providing essential infrastructure and finance, supervision and assessment.[10]

The early Cumberland Plain settlers—convicts, and later military officers, civil officers, soldiers, sailors, missionaries and a few free men and women— are often considered the founders of the agricultural and pastoral industries; that is, of Australia's rural history, and rightly so. But they were also integral to modern Sydney's story, for the vast majority of the sprawling, low-density city has rural origins. The early farmers and stockmen supplied the population with meat and grain, fruit and vegetables, and they employed most of the convicts and labouring people. For the first three decades after 1788, agriculture and grazing were the colony's main industries and employed a third of the working population.[11] Their families swelled the white population and their children once grown often pushed further into Aboriginal lands 'upcountry'. The settlers also developed a particular rural culture and way of life on the Cumberland Plain, especially in the Hawkesbury–Nepean region, with its isolated reaches and waterbound settlements. It was a way of life which increasingly diverged from urban culture over the nineteenth century. By the last decades of that century and into the 1900s, dwellers of the self-consciously modernising city were by turns horrified, amused or celebratory whenever they discovered that those older ways of being, of seeing the world, still existed in the rural hinterland. They were invariably nostalgic when they saw them passing away.

Then there is the physical legacy, and the inheritance of names. Their farms and estates underlie much of modern Sydney's landscape, from the early officers' parklike estates at Ultimo and Annandale, to the rich 30-acre riverside farms at Castlereagh on the Nepean River, cultivated continuously since 1803 but now being systematically gouged out for gravel and sand. The settlers' tracks, some overlaying Aboriginal paths, became the spines of modern road networks, their grant boundaries often shaped local street alignments. Their villages and towns became suburban centres, and their commonplace, matter-of-fact names often stuck (Blue Mountains, Blacktown, Duck Creek, Emu Plains). Sometimes their own names entered common parlance as place and road names (Withers Road, Fiddens Wharf Road, Wisemans Ferry), and their everyday destinations and workplaces too, for mills, punts, wharves, saleyards, slaughterhouses and limekilns found their way into street names which remember landmarks lost long ago.

Sydney's history is one of continual expansion, but since the early twentieth century, the citizens' deeply felt preference was for low-density, and thus land-hungry, suburbs. Suburban life became 'the Australian way of life', the ideal way to live. This has made Sydney one of the lowest-density cities in the world and it means that the city now reaches right out to the rivers and the mountains, those once distant and definitely rural places. Inevitably city growth threatens the earlier landscapes and buildings—and ways of life. Many houses of the wealthier self-styled landed gentry still stand, though closer to the city they tend to be marooned in seas of suburban houses. Further out, especially to the south-west, beyond the frantic destruction and remaking at the modern city/rural interface, gracious mansions still sit on their knolls. Their verandahs still overlook beautiful rural vistas, their tall araucarias (Norfolk Island and bunya pines) like exclamation marks in the landscape—for the time being.[12] Much less survives of the poor and middling settlers, though you can still see their vernacular farm-houses and rough slab barns, set on stilts on the low-lying floodplains, their plain little chapels and early cemeteries in places like Castlereagh, Agnes Banks, Pitt Town and Ebenezer, along the weaving reaches of the lower Hawkesbury and in the 'forgotten valley' of the Macdonald River away to the north.[13]

Some survivals are astonishing. In the gritty industrial landscape at Camellia, near Parramatta, a headstone memorial still stands in the grounds of the James Hardie factory. It remembers poor Eleanor McCabe, who drowned with her child in the Parramatta River one night in 1793. She and her babe were buried near her hut when this ground was still patches of maize and wheat in the bush.[14] At Rouse Hill in the north-west, there are two more early graves. One has a roughly carved Georgian-style headstone, but it bears no name, only a hand-picked cross. Opposite is a mound of stones and an even rougher headstone: a slab of stone set edgeways. A large rough-barked angophora sprouts from the mound. Who is buried here? When I first saw these graves in 1989, they stood in a cleared paddock on slopes above Caddies Creek, in what was then still rural hinterland. Rouse Hill has since become part of the vast North-West Sector housing release, and that older landscape of market gardens and poultry farms has disappeared under an avalanche of houses, driveways, lawns, standard roses, four-wheel drives, freeways, fast-food outlets and ersatz heritage pubs. Yet the rough graves are still there, beside the pathway in William Harvey Reserve, a local park named for its original white grantee. A row of new mansions parades on the slopes above, deserted on the weekdays, some patrolled by lonely dogs. Downhill, Caddies Creek still flows below a cave where Aboriginal people once took shelter, cooked, ate, talked, slept. The bush has been replanted, and the open paddock is now a young forest.[15]

But if suburbs relentlessly destroy the vestiges and vistas of the past, the story of the first white pioneers of early Sydney, of carving new farms and lives out of the bush, has continued to haunt and fascinate Sydney's imagination. Who were these people?

WATER AND EARTH

The settlement of the Cumberland Plain was shaped most elementally by water and by earth. As with the Eora's settlement, trade and communication patterns, the rivers shaped the earliest explorations and occupation patterns of the Europeans. The Parramatta River from Port Jackson first carried them inland to Rose Hill, just as the Hawkesbury River from Broken Bay to the north would lead them the long way round to the alluvial flats at the Green Hills (later Windsor). The upper reaches of Georges River from Botany Bay to the south were explored by George Bass and Matthew Flinders in the tiny dinghy *Tom Thumb*. They discovered the arable land around Bankstown (where both were

The mysterious graves in William Harvey Reserve, Rouse Hill. They once stood on a farm called Vinegar Hill. (Photos G. Karskens, 2007)

later granted land, side by side, though they never settled there). These rivers became the vital transport and communication links between Sydney and the settlements established in all these inland places. Most of the inland settlements were thus settled from the water; they were virtual islands, connected by the rivers. This pattern would continue as the colony sent out more spore-like colonies (often short-lived) up and down the east coast and to Van Diemen's Land in the 1800s.[16]

Fresh water also governed the placement of settlers. Rose Hill was founded at the confluence of salt and fresh waters, just as the Tank Stream had clinched Sydney Cove as the second settlement site. Farmers clustered near the myriad small creeks that ran like veins down the gullies and emptied into larger creeks and rivers. Many took land near the chains of ponds so typical of Australian water systems; they often named localities for them (The Ponds, Killarney Chain of Ponds, Second Ponds Creek). These ponds were marvellous ecosystems—they were like a series of 'holding tanks': the spongy soils, held fast with sedges and reeds, slowed down runoff. In Sydney's sudden downpours they became full streams, taking in huge amounts of water, filling quickly, releasing slowly. In drier periods they became a necklace of waterholes and in drought periods they simply dried up, until the rains came again, and swelled them once more.[17] But some farms, like that of Charles Williams and Eleanor McCabe, and ten of the thirteen farms at Prospect Hill, were placed too far from water, so the settlers 'were obliged to fetch this necessary article from the distance of a mile and a half'. When the pretty creeks gave out and the ponds desiccated in the dry seasons, settlers dug wells in the hope of water which would be sweet, not bitter or salt.[18] Ironically, too much water also forced settlement away from rivers. By 1809 it was clear that the perennial floods on the Hawkesbury–Nepean and Georges rivers were so devastating, the colony's food supply was in jeopardy. So for the next decade or so, new settlers moved into the drier forest lands, away from the luxuriant but treacherous river banks.

If you compare a map of Cumberland Plain soils with the pattern of land grants allocated up to about 1820, the fit is almost exact—the same lopsided funnel opens out towards the mountains from the same narrow neck. The most obvious reason is topography: the settlers fanned out onto the more accessible level and undulating land, and avoided the craggy plateaux, with their deep ravines. But within this big picture, soils ruled the shape and location of the farms. The smaller farms, which characterise the earliest grants of the 1790s to ex-convicts and soldiers, cluster on the richer ground, the dark fertile patches eroded out of ancient volcanic diatremes (pipe-like vertical vents filled with volcanic rock) which are scattered across the region, and on the alluvial patches and flats of the rivers and creeks. Sometimes the early farms were arranged in an irregular crescent, following the good soils obediently. Meanwhile the later, larger grants sprawl over the less fertile forest ground, especially to the west and south-west of Parramatta, and around Bringelly, Mulgoa, Airds and Appin.[19] The early Europeans are often portrayed as hopeless in their attempts to understand the land. Eric Rolls does not blame them. 'It was beyond human achievement to assess this land correctly', he writes. 'It was more a new planet than a new continent.'[20] Yet the evidence here is that they quickly located and recognised the best soils, as well as the middling ground and the severe limitations of the unyielding sandstone country encircling the plain.

Phillip's official Instructions to establish agriculture and make the colony self-sufficient as soon as possible were compelling: the invaders were obsessed by soils. In the early years the search for 'good land, well watered', the 'good' soil of 'virgin mould' they had been promised, took precedence. Everywhere Phillip and the officers voyaged, they had eyes only for soils. They had an entire lexicon to describe soils. They carried little bags to take samples for testing and blending experiments—these last proving 'fruitless', Tench reported glumly, 'though possibly only from want of skill on our side'.[21]

Unfortunately the first expeditions to the north and Broken Bay and up into Brisbane Water all led them through the rugged sandstone country of twisted angophora and bunched xanthorrhoea with their long black spikes: beautiful, but useless. So the first reports were disappointing, tinged with slight panic. Rocky ground was a particularly bad sign—not only sandy, 'barren' (in terms of European plants), dry and difficult to cross, but disorderly and impossible to regulate. But the first story was not the main story. The discovery of the better shale soils only two months later excited optimism and relief, while rich dark loams filled them with delight and hope. The explorers carried seed in their pockets—potatoes, Indian corn, melon—and planted handfuls in the promising places they discovered as parting gifts, markers, experiments, acts of faith.[22]

Most historical accounts also stress the pathetic failure of European farming in the harsh, unyielding landscape. But this too was 'first story' and it did not prevail. Botany Bay had seemed inhospitable: too open for the ships' safety, and too dry. One of Sydney's foundational ironies, though, is that Botany Bay did have good soils: the fine silts around the mouth of the Cooks River, 'one of the few areas close to the CBD of sufficient fertility to support market gardens'. This area later provided vast quantities of Victorian Sydney's vegetables, and one market garden still survives there today. But Phillip could not find sufficient fresh water in Botany Bay.[23] The first farms were established instead on the much-bewailed soils of Port Jackson, in Farm Cove just east of the Camp, along with the garden that was set out in front of Government House. Officers also planted 2-acre plots at the head of the imaginatively named Long Cove (later Cockle Bay, now Darling Harbour) in March 1788—thus they predate James Ruse as 'first farmers' by more than a year, though these allotments were not 'given to them as their Right and Property'. This attempt was not very successful either.[24]

By the end of 1788, though, things were already improving. The sandy soils in Sydney did support fruits and some vegetables and the gardens there continued to flourish with the introduction of manures and soils barrowed in. Some of this material was taken from the 'luxuriancy of soil . . . rich with shells and other manure' they found outside Aboriginal rock-shelters.[25] By September, Phillip could report that 'those who have gardens have Vegetables in plenty & exceedingly good in kind'. Tench wrote that while grain crops were variable, 'vines of every sort seem to flourish: melons, cucumbers, and pumpkins, run with unbounded luxuriancy'. In the yards of the Rocks, convict householders grew peas and beans, celery and cauliflowers for their cooking pots.[26]

The persistence of the soil-hunters inland from Sydney paid off too. Land was cleared at Rose Hill in the country of the Burramattagal and experimental crops of wheat, maize and barley were planted on the south bank of the river,[27] Ruse was installed in his hut down on the creek and Phillip built himself a house on the hill. Besides the food grains, vine-growing was a particular desideratum. Phillip planted 8000 vines on the crescent-shaped slopes below Government

House. And among the first private settlers of March 1791 was an elderly German who, it was hoped, might also establish vineyards and colonial winemaking. Philip Schaeffer had been sent out to supervise the convict farmers, but his English was so limited he could not take on the position. He seemed to know something of viticulture, though, and was granted 140 acres on the banks of the Parramatta River (at present-day Rydalmere). He named it The Vineyard, and for a few years grew grapes, wheat, maize and tobacco and made wine there.[28]

Seven years after the first clearing and planting, the view from Samuel Marsden's farm at Parramatta was one of happy promise and plenty.

> With respect to the colony it prospers much. Cultivation goes on very rapidly. At present we have the prospect of a very large crop of wheat which will be ready for reaping in November. I think it is one of the finest countries in the known world and no people I believe will be more happy than the people of this island in a short time. Our live stock increases very fast.[29]

These were the sanguine years, before the first of the great floods washed crops, barns, animals and people away, and a spell before the El Niño drought that baked the country hard and dry. Fire and air shaped the experience of the settlers too, but these were elements of much larger natural cycles of which they were not aware, and could not have been. If the colony was a 'new planet' these were the elements that made it so.

CONVICT FARMERS

But let us return to the original subjects of the Botany Bay experiment—the convicts sent to the 'ends of the earth' to be farmers and reborn men; and to the figure of Ruse toiling on his patch just north of where the F1 now roars over the suburb of Harris Park. What became of these men and women? What did they create?

Anyone who has bought a school project kit on convicts for their child, or read a popular history or novel about the early colony, will know that the image of the convict forced to labour in chains has dominated our ideas, not only of the public farms, but of early Sydney generally. This image has eclipsed the British government's original intentions: to place the convicts on small grants, thus creating a new society. There were no provisions for land grants to officers or free settlers in the original scheme at all, though grants for ex-marines who decided to stay in New South Wales had been promised as early as 1786.[30]

There is no denying the seriousness of intent here. Every governor from Phillip to Macquarie was given detailed instructions on farming and grazing. The granting of land in small parcels to emancipists continued for the first 37 years of the colony's history; it was not abolished until 1825. The first five governors were committed to this plan and devoted considerable resources to assisting, supporting and managing the convict farmers.[31] Since the *raison d'être* of the whole project was to rid England of felons permanently, they were to be encouraged by all means possible to stay on their land, to put roots down into the soil, to form families and communities. They were set up with tools, rations, grain and some stock for the first twelve months (these were promptly perceived as a right rather than an indulgence). Quit-rents, by which they would eventually become small landowners, were deferred for ten years, and they were threatened with having their grants revoked if they failed to clear and cultivate. The land, apportioned in plots small enough to manage and improve by labour, was to succour them, and thus be the basis of this new society. It was not to become a mere speculative commodity, bought and sold and meanwhile left 'unimproved' and 'unproductive'. In theory, too, these men and women would have little choice but to take the offer. There would be no money, no trade in consumer goods, no alcohol, no other way of keeping body and soul together, and no hope of returning home.[32]

The Plan as it unfolded looked uncannily like traditional English rural village life. As in the open field system, the early grants were to be strip-shaped, with the good and bad land distributed fairly, while river frontages were not to be monopolised (hence the long, narrow rectangles set out along the rivers: everyone was to have equal access to water). The convicts were to live by subsistence farming only—any surplus would go into the government stores to support the colony and newly arrived convicts.[33] Their farming was not to be concerned with profits, markets and efficiency. At a time when English commons were still being enclosed and men convicted and transported for poaching on them, Governor King set aside those vast commons for the Cumberland Plain settlers, land to be held, shared, used *in common*. The governors were also instructed to found villages, where the settlers would live, and from which they would go out each day to work their land.[34]

Sending working people across the seas to labour in distant lands always carried the risk of mutiny and secession. Such people had a long and dangerous history of insurgence, of making alternative communities beyond the pale of authority, outside its reach. Pirates and castaways formed themselves into wild banditti.[35] How would authorities keep hold in distant Botany Bay? How would disorderly, riotous criminals be made obedient, deferential and useful? How to prevent them taking to the woods and there becoming a 'nest of pyrates'? The 'work or starve' rule was one method—again, in theory at least. Unwavering supervision and the certainty of harsh punishment was another. A third and fundamental key was the emphasis on *individual* land holdings. After the more communal public farming phase, each man would, like Robinson Crusoe, make his own way in the antipodean wilderness, to stake an individual claim, to fail or succeed by his own labour, his fate tied not to his comrades but to his relationship with the government, benign or stern as needs be. Each woman would be a helpmeet, subordinate to her husband, bearer of the new society's children, essential but somehow invisible. So while the planning of the farms and villages appeared to hark back to traditional forms, at its heart was a modern individualist ethos which would guarantee productive family units and a commitment to modest private property. Dangerous combinations and alternative societies would be avoided. As Alan Atkinson points out, a number of ex-convicts and soldiers did own land communally and work it together, but this was discouraged, and King finally banned the practice.[36]

No wonder the experiment was watched with such keen interest back in England. Would villains be made into villagers? It was a subject 'affording the political philosopher new material for calculation, on a subject so interesting, so important to the civilised world'.[37] No wonder the early journal-keepers noted every small occurrence, every little triumph and disappointment, for their publishers at Home. But the colony was also highly controversial, staunchly opposed by the 'enemies' of transportation, and, of course, the source of long-lived mirth and stock jokes about the 'commonwealth of thieves'.[38]

It must have come as a shock, then, when the first group of expirees flatly refused to become farmers. No fine weather, no offer of land and tools, nothing about the colony had changed their minds. Most of them said stubbornly that they wanted to return to England. They had counted the days, done their time, were now free men and women and wished to go home. One can imagine the response of the officers. This had not been part of the Plan. Phillip, knowing the whole point of the project was to keep convicts in the colony, said they could go, but then added that they still needed his permission to leave. This was unlikely to be granted, since, as Collins added, repatriated convicts would 'be let loose again upon the public' and naturally fall back into the vices and bad company which had had them transported in the first place.[39] If ex-convicts would not become settlers, they could go on working for their rations, virtual convicts still. This is what William Bryant could not tolerate: he left anyway. He stole the government cutter, an open boat 30 feet long, and with his wife Mary Broad, their two infants and seven shipmates, rowed out of the Heads, and then 5237 kilometres up the east coast of the continent and north-west to Timor. Here they posed successfully as shipwreck survivors until betrayed by a slip of the tongue.[40]

Meanwhile, Phillip had somehow persuaded or cajoled some ex-convicts to take the offer of 30 acres in the bush, with more land for those with a wife and children.[41] One of them, Matthew Everingham, clearly considered this a contract rather than an indulgence: 'I turned settler at the Ponds', he wrote to his patron, 'on condition of his supporting me 18 months in provisions and clothing and for the first year implements for agriculture'. Others evidently had no other aim in mind but to 'raise a sufficient supply to pay their passages to England'. Phillip also emancipated convicts so that they 'might become settlers': again, a bargain—liberty in exchange for becoming a farmer.[42] Most of these little clusters were located in groups on the north side of the Parramatta River, where the more promising patches of soil had been discovered. One group was located around and opposite Ruse at Parramatta, and another at the 'Northern Boundary'—north, that is, of Parramatta—where they were laid out along a crescent of good soils around present-day North Rocks. Phillip personally inspected this ground in

April 1791.[43] Parramatta thus lay at the centre of the settlers' compass, for those at 'Eastern Farms', around today's Ryde, were the furthest east of Parramatta. Even in the 1860s people there still did all their business in Parramatta, not Sydney.[44] More settlers went to the moist riverside air and the alluvials near old Philip Schaeffer's Vineyard; to Kissing Point (where the boats 'kissed' the shoreline); and further up the slopes to The Ponds where the chain of ponds watered the volcanic soils of the Dundas valley. Most promising, but most isolated and vulnerable, were the settlers on the dark basaltic soils around the base of Prospect Hill, 6 kilometres west of Parramatta.[45]

A patch of grants was also given to eight ex-marines around present-day Marsfield and North Ryde in February 1792. Their district was called the 'Field of Mars', in honour of their former calling.[46] Perhaps it was a little joke too, bestowing the same name upon a set of bush farms for humble soldiers as graced the historic *Champs de Mars*, site of early military defences and exercise grounds in Paris. It set an amusing naming pattern in train: the non-commissioned officers and free settlers who settled directly across the river were located in the Field of Concord (now Concord and Rhodes), while, as we shall see, free settlers arriving in 1793 rejoiced in 'Liberty Plains' for their district at what became Homebush, Flemington and Strathfield.[47] Convict status, though, was not memorialised in placenames, or not officially.

The brave little squares or neat strips drawn on the maps can give little idea of the reality of these early farms. The lines were abstract, paper boundaries in the bush; they were not visible on the ground. Like Ruse, some of the settlers had huts built for them 'by the government'—rough, simple structures of wattles and clay and thatch, built square around posts, with one or two rooms and dirt floors. By 1801 they were built of timber slabs, but were just as basic.[48] These were clearly meant to be a temporary, pioneering shelter before the villages appeared. Instead they set a pattern, for the crude huts and 'tent-huts' persisted, and those settlers who stayed on their grants remained firmly in them.

The new farmers used the grubbing hoes sent out from England to break the soils and turn up the native grasses. They broadcast maize and wheat by hand between tree stumps left standing 4 feet high, for they had quickly learned that removing stumps and roots was too laborious and time-consuming. Twelve

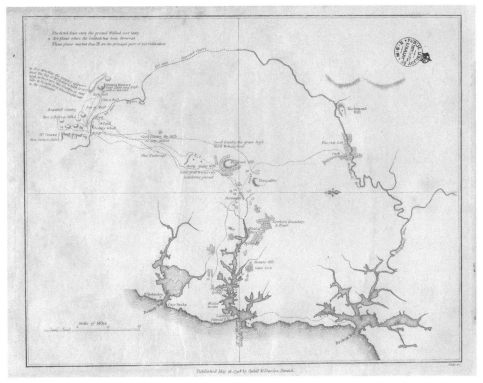

John Hunter, 'New South Wales Sketch of Settlements 20 August 1796', showing the location of Phillip's early farms and the country which had been explored by that time. Note the Eora path leading north to Broken Bay. (Mitchell Library, State Library of New South Wales)

ploughs had been sent with the First Fleet, but they were not included in the list of 'tools and utensils' intended for the convicts.[49] In any case, there were no beasts to pull them—the cattle brought from the Cape of Good Hope had escaped into the bush soon after landing. On the convict supply list, though, were enough hoes ('grubbing', 'West Indian' and 'garden') to give three to each convict. Perhaps this was deliberate: since hard work would redeem them, the convicts' farming was to be as laborious and slow as possible. To the rebel leader Joseph Holt, and to gentleman convict John Grant, the hoe represented tyranny and brutality. 'I understand tilling the ground with horses and oxen', Holt informed Major Johnston haughtily, 'but with men I do not'. The high-minded Grant had a plough specially made to work his friend's farm at Prospect because 'my Principle will not permit my hiring men to use the Hoe'.[50]

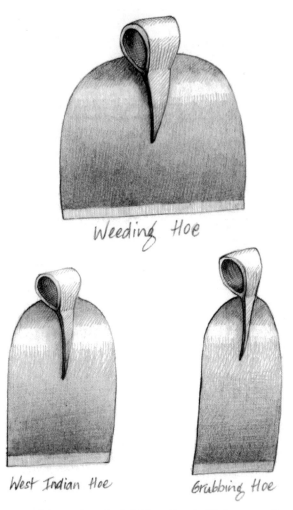

Weeding Hoe

West Indian Hoe   Grubbing Hoe

Three types of hoe used in early colonial New South Wales—weeding, West Indian and grubbing hoes. (Kate Nolan/Smith, Key to the Manufactories of Sheffield, *1816)*

But cultivation by hoe emerged as a pragmatic and successful method in New South Wales. While ploughing required considerable skills, besides expensive animals, even inexperienced farmers could use a hoe, and many had already learned to use them on the public farms. Ploughs were useless anyway with all those stumps, roots and rocks; hoes worked around them. Hoe-cultivation became a tradition; over the next 30 years or more, the 'long-tailed monkey', as it was called, was the tool of choice on the Cumberland Plain. Small-farming people in the old settlements passed the practice on to their children and ignored the beseeching of 'improving farmers' to adopt the plough. 'The plough has been tried by some, but does not seem to be preferred before the hoe', wrote botanist George Caley. 'The stumps that yet remain in the ground are against it.' He also thought there were insufficient people who knew how to use a plough.[51]

Most accounts of these early farmers portray them as hopeless, inept, lazy, sinfully wasteful, as well as hamstrung by environmental factors. They were undercapitalised, and for the main part the grants were too small to make them rich, or even comfortable. Many neither weeded nor rotated their crops, and there were not sufficient animals to fertilise the soils or pull ploughs or carry them or their produce anywhere—those on the rivers built their own small craft, and later relied on the riverboat carriers.[52] But it is also true that this image of primitiveness and hopelessness is based on what visiting observers had to say about the farmers. For the main part these observers were keen to demonstrate their knowledge of English 'improved farming', the great hobby of so many writing gentlemen; they were also deeply enamoured of the English rural idyll of the poets. The convict farmers offended on both counts: their methods seemed primitive and wasteful, and, worse, their farms were *messy*. Their crops were unfenced and their hogs rambled and rooted about at will. The settlers' clothes were poor, their persons unkempt. They were betrayed by a hostile environment: failing soils, treacherous floods, monstrous plagues. There were no manicured, neatly fenced fields, few cosy cots, and in the small-farming areas at least, no bucolic scenes of green pastures, peaceful cows or simple swains reclining in shady spots.[53]

But 'improved farming'—scientific breeding, careful rotation, enclosed fields, the intense cultivation of every inch of land—would never have worked in the conditions of the early colony (in fact it was not very widespread in England itself). Once we remove this impossible yardstick, it is clear that the settlers on the Cumberland Plain—this 'new planet'—quickly worked out a sort of rough environmental and economic logic by trial and error. The use of the hoe, as we have seen, was admirably suited to the environmental conditions and the available labour skills. The small farmers soon discovered that maize was much easier to cultivate with the hoe, thrived in roughly cleared ground and yielded better than wheat. This was another innovation, as Indian maize-growing was unknown in England. Soon the golden rippling field of wheat came to mark the better-off settlers and larger landowners with their convict workers, while the bright green crops of Indian maize was a sure sign of the poorer, hard-scrabbling farmers. Maize became the staple food of the river farmers, but remained a low-status food in Sydney, the food of the poor, rejected even by convicts in the 1840s.

There was also a great deal of experimentation with different strains of imported wheat and maize. Collins reported that the 'Caffre corn' from Africa, introduced by Lieutenant Paterson, was useful for making a 'paste like oatmeal' and as a fodder crop. The bearded 'Cape wheat' was a disappointment, though, as it was susceptible to blight, and 'not worth the reaping'.[54] The imported grains and animals also brought unwanted stowaways, including capeweed (*Arctotheca calendula*) which tainted the cows' milk, and which you can still see springing up from the newly cleared grasslands at the old Castle Hill Farm today. The farmers also complained of a species of *Lolium*, or ryegrass (they called it drake), which 'infested' the harvested wheat. Some of them tried to remove it, others seem to have let it be.[55]

The farmers on the shale soils soon learned how to deal with the limited fertility of their ground, compounded in the early years by the lack of animal manure. They adopted the 'bush fallow' method, similar to that used in the North American colonies. Despite the earnest entreaties contained in the *New South Wales Pocket Almanack*, published in 1806, they worked the land hard, two crops a year, until it was exhausted, then simply let it lie fallow to recover. Meanwhile they moved on to clear another patch. The fallow land was left for six to ten years, 'to be overgrown with mimosas . . . a nursery for rank and noxious weeds', a haven for regenerating native plants and wandering introduced ones. It was then cleared and planted again before large trees could establish themselves. This 'relieved the farmer of worrying about manuring or planting nitrogen-fixing plants'.[56] As with the public farms, and the graziers who would follow, the shift from 'old' to 'new' ground was a continuous cycle. All of these were pragmatic measures, adapted to a colony where, unlike England, land was abundant and cheap, labour was scarce and dear, and the limits to soils' fertility were discovered very early.

Emily Anne Manning, 'Maize' 1837. 'Maise, or Indian corn', wrote English settler Louisa Meredith, '... is a most ornamental crop, each plant being placed by itself, its long, broad green leaves and crowning spire of blossoms having a very graceful appearance... it is always understood by the word corn, all other corn, such as wheat, barley &c being called grain', from Notes and Sketches of New South Wales. *(Mitchell Library, State Library of New South Wales)*

BEYOND THE PALE: THE GREEN HILLS

By early 1793 there were only about 67 settlers, still mostly clustered around Phillip's 'islands' on or near the Parramatta River. Altogether the farms and gardens under cultivation totalled less than 1700 acres, and there was as yet no prospect of so few feeding so many.[57] In October of that year, Collins was disappointed to record that James Ruse, the great hope of the colonial project, had sold his farm and stock at Parramatta to the Surgeon John Harris for 40 pounds. He had held Experiment Farm for less than two years. Ruse's neighbour and shipmate from the *Scarborough*, Charles Williams, sold up at the same time to another officer, Lieutenant Cummings. This seemed a little more explicable, for Williams was considered a 'miscreant' who had 'wearied of being in a state of independence'. But Ruse! He was clearly a backslider. The two men said they wanted to return to England, but neither actually left. And early in 1794 they, together with twenty others, suddenly requested grants on the banks of the Hawkesbury River, at a place they called, with typical simplicity, the Green Hills. Acting Governor Grose agreed. He had little choice: it seems they were already there.[58]

Historians of the Hawkesbury are rightly puzzled, even exasperated, by their region's abrupt and rather strange pioneer history.[59] It does not make sense in terms of a colony ordered strictly from above. Phillip, the only governor to actually stick to his Instructions, had proceeded cautiously, experimenting, selecting men and land, carefully measuring and laying out, making sure no farm was too far from supervision and surveillance.[60] After four years, most of the cultivated lands and stock were still in government hands; of the 3470 acres granted to settlers, only 417 were actually cultivated, less than half that of the public farms. And Phillip had already ruled out the Hawkesbury for farms. It was too far away from Sydney—at least two days' journey over-land or a three-day voyage by boat all the way up the twisted rocky reaches of the Hawkesbury River, Broken Bay and along the coast to Port Jackson. The Hawkesbury lay beyond the pale of administration and the law: and a lawless, independent community of banditti had to be prevented at all costs. It was clearly subject to powerful floods, for the earliest white explorers had seen trees on the banks laid down by the force of water, and, ominously, those still standing had dry clumps of grass and reeds lodged 15 metres up in their branches.[61]

Yet, suddenly, settlement on the Hawkesbury was a *fait accompli*. In January 1794 Collins offhandedly reported that Ruse and his companions were building huts, breaking the ground for planting 'with much spirit, forming to themselves very sanguine hopes of success'.[62] How could this have happened? Was it simply Grose's negligence and slackness? A fit of culpable absent-mindedness?

We might make sense of Ruse's story and the Hawkesbury settlement in another way: it was a deliberate, and successful, attempt to do as William Bryant had done—escape the colony. The experimental acres at Parramatta, Ruse's studied performance in simple rural virtues, the abrupt sale of the land so soon after it was granted; the story about leaving the colony. Perhaps Ruse was living up to his name?

Stories and rumours were powerful in early New South Wales. News of sensational voyages, like Bligh's incredible feat of survival after the *Bounty* mutiny, raced around the colony like wildfire, and set off numerous convict escape attempts. Tales of inland settlements where people could live in happiness and peace without labour also had currency: they were colonial versions of ancient legends of Cockaigne, the mythical land where food appeared of its own accord, and people had no need to work, the recurring dream of the poor and hungry peoples of Europe.[63] But rumours—true stories—about the rich alluvial earth on the Hawkesbury would have circulated among the convicts and the settlers too: in particular, the tale of the rich river flats to the north-west, in the river's elbow at the junction of South Creek. Here the dense, viney, river-flat brush opened out into lush, grassy, lightly timbered lands—releasing settlers from backbreaking clearing work. There were large lagoons, too, teeming with ducks, swans, geese and brolgas.[64]

The settlers called it the Green Hills, probably for the gently rounded hills that overlook the flats. They are still green, the road still bobs up and down above the place where Ruse and his band settled. Today this area is called Pitt Town Bottoms, and it is the only place in Australia where you can still see the early colonial farming landscape that evolved from those first farms, though the main crop is turf for suburban gardens. Now it's a new battleground, as local people try to defend their town and country from suburban development.[65]

In any case, the Hawkesbury region was not unknown country in 1793/94. Plenty of white people had visited it in the early 1790s: officers, civil and military, and some coastal Aboriginal people as well. Convicts went there too—as part of the official exploratory parties, and on their own, unrecorded, explorations.

Its distance from Parramatta and Sydney made it still more alluring: far from the surveillance of officers and their questions, far from the courts and the floggings, and the ennui and slave-like conditions of the public farms. The soil was rich and dark and promised much more than the failing shale soils around Parramatta. The shining river beckoned.

As well, as Alan Atkinson has observed, there seems to have been a degree of deliberate communal organisation to the settlement at the Green Hills; perhaps it was simply a shared desire to get away to another place and live without interference. But there were some pre-existing bonds. Among the 22 men, who must have either walked overland with their tools, seeds, food and other goods, or sailed the winding reaches in small boats, fourteen were First Fleeters. Seven were shipmates of Ruse's from the *Scarborough*, four were from the *Alexander* and another three were from the *Friendship*. Giles Mower, whose farm lay the furthest up South Creek, was a soldier: but he was a *Scarborough* man, too, and he and ex-convict Thomas Akers were evidently friends, as they later applied to farm together. Shared voyages created bonds between men which so often played out on land—shipmates remained mates, and became neighbours. Only nine women came as wives, an early sign of the gender imbalance which would plague the Hawkesbury settlements and have serious consequences for its social well-being. Seven children, all under six years old, came with their parents, and two more were born on the river during 1794.[66]

Whatever drew them to the river—freedom, dreams, abundant food, the prospect of owning rich farmlands—the settlement of the Hawkesbury was more the result of ex-convict initiative and journeys, than deliberate government policy. The Green Hills were taken and made by the convicts themselves, and initially without any of the assistance, supervision or security measures given to the official settlers. Brian Fletcher remarks that 'Grose at first appears to have shown almost complete indifference to the whole affair'. A few months later, though, he wrote official reports in which he named himself as the instigator, even suggesting that he had sent settlers there against their will![67]

The actions and efforts of Ruse's band of settlers had important, and marvellous, outcomes. Whatever they planted grew 'in the greatest luxuriance'. One man planted and harvested a crop of potatoes in only three months. All of them raved about the 'rich black mould of several feet deep'. New arrivals were already writing home of land that bore two crops a year: the Hawkesbury soils magnified their wonder.[68] Its bounty was soon the talk of the colony too, and after some months of rain, the first land-rush in Australia swept out to the river. By the end of that same year, 1794, there were 100 settlers there, more than in Phillip's entire four-year term; six months later around 400 people 'straggled along 50 kilometres of waterways'. Farmers, bond and free, who had started at The Ponds or Liberty Plains sold or abandoned their shale soil farms for the lure of the river.[69]

Grose became more enthusiastic too. He had a rough track cut to the river from Parramatta, which reduced the overland journey on foot to around eight hours, and he began to offer convicts land there, promising them remissions of their sentences if they would take up farming. His successor, Captain Paterson, promptly made out generous grants to his brother officers, who probably never occupied them. They came out to the Hawkesbury in a party in 1795 'with a view to selecting eligible spots for farms'.[70] To the officers, these lands were, of course, 'the military equivalent of naval prize money', assets to add to their colonial portfolios.

When Governor Hunter arrived he found that Grose and Paterson had allowed large numbers of convicts still under sentence to settle without survey or title, indeed with nothing more than a note stating 'A.B. has my permission to settle'. They had kept few if any records. Trying to sort out the mess, Hunter found some struggling to farm, while others had already sold their land to avoid having it taken from them.[71] He also revived Phillip's practice of personally investigating and selecting land for new farms—the small-farming settlements at Bankstown near the Georges River in the south, and the short-lived Portland Place south of Parramatta were both established in 1797.[72]

But settlers also appear to have pushed into new country up the isolated reaches of the rivers years before any surveyor or official ever saw it. They too staked claims to the land by naked possession: felling, planting a patch of ground with maize and leaving it; or putting up a tent-hut and moving in, and suffering and repelling Aboriginal resistance and attack. These are the settler stories which have fascinated local historians and novelists, and become local lore. Eleanor

Dark's classic *The Timeless Land* (1941) and Kate Grenville's celebrated *The Secret River* (2006) both explore such convict settler experiences: Dark's protagonist Andrew Prentice recovers his humanity on the river; Grenville's William Thornhill discovers the depths of his inhumanity.

In any case, the farms, most of them small and farmed by ex-convicts, quickly reached the junction with the Colo (the Second Branch), multiplied along South Creek and south along the Hawkesbury to Richmond. The region became the settlement's breadbasket, and the Hawkesbury was dubbed 'the Nile of the colony'.[73] Expansion continued in this way, for by the 1820s the farms had spread down to Castlereagh and Mulgoa in the south. In the north small grants clung to the fertile patches all along the winding saltwater reaches, past the junction with the Macdonald where gaunt yellow sandstone cliffs shadowed the farms.[74]

From the beginning, the Hawkesbury settlers were river people. Their early names for its bends and points, superimposed on Aboriginal names, were in turn supplanted by Macquarie's gentrified ones—'Sackville', 'Windsor', 'Argyle' and so on. But in the places further downriver, beyond the reach of Macquarie's renaming project, those old, rougher, plain-speaking names survive: Halfmoon Reach, Trollope Reach, One Tree Reach, Foul Weather Reach, Sentry Box Reach.

Boat-building and owning was illegal for convicts and ex-convicts, but an exception was made for the Hawkesbury settlers, for whom the river was their road. Early on many of them built craft for themselves or their neighbours for personal use, to cross the river, or to row to neighbours' huts. These were small, clinker-built, open boats, or canoes hollowed out of whole logs. From around 1796 James Webb, ex-seaman, was building larger boats to ferry the wheat and maize from the farms to town. Soon a 'mosquito fleet' of small cutters and sloops sailed constantly down the river and coast to Sydney and back.[75] In a matter of years, boat-building on the Hawkesbury had become an important and dynamic industry and produced most of the colony's large vessels. These were the ships bound for the 'furring islands', hunting seals, or that sailed to the Pacific Islands for cargoes of pork and fragrant sandalwood. The Hawkesbury boat-builders combined their work with farming, and even in the 1860s would scour the forests for days, searching for just the right piece of timber—straight, or curved 'compass' wood—for the particular part of the boat they were building.[76]

The farmhouses and huts faced the river, the same way Sydney houses watched the harbour. When God-fearing people began to build chapels and meeting-houses, these too were raised beside the river, for people came by boat to hear the preachers. Funeral corteges arrived at the small stone Presbyterian chapel at Ebenezer by water too, a line of vessels, headed by 'a boat with muffled oars'.[77]

The great undertow of all this expansion, clearing, planting and building, this intoxicating *taking*, was that the land was already occupied when the settlers moved onto it, with or without official permission.[78] Wherever they took the river and creek frontages, the fertile floodplains, the chains of ponds and lagoons, they were also taking the areas most densely occupied by Aboriginal people, their richest food sources, their water and transport links, their sacred and teaching places. Settlers successively occupied the lands of the Aboriginal people of Parramatta, then the Hawkesbury and, as they pushed north and south, the people of the Macdonald and Nepean rivers, too. In each area, Aboriginal people waged war in defence of their country, their sustenance and their women and children. As we shall see, the Hawkesbury was in an intermittent state of war for over a decade, between 1794 and 1816. The word is not an anachronism: the settlers themselves called it a war, and travelled in groups with armed guards. In these places, it was the small settlers who bore the brunt of Aboriginal attacks and anger; and they in turn came together to respond in kind.

The abundant Hawkesbury harvests were a great relief to the authorities, nevertheless: at last self-sufficiency seemed in sight. Soldiers were sent out to 'deal with' the natives. But there was an ironic environmental twist to the Hawkesbury story, for small-farming there had opposite effects to those intended by the original plan for New South Wales. Collins reported disapprovingly that, whereas other settlers were industriously 'putting their wheat into the ground', the Hawkesbury settlers

> ... had scarcely made any preparations, consuming their time and substance in drinking and rioting; and trusting to the extreme fertility

'Baker's farm on the high bank', showing an early Hawkesbury farm, patches of crops, houses built close to the denuded river bank, together with a tent—settlers often lived in tents and they are often mentioned in court cases. Note the tree trunks rolled into the river, the dead trees on the horizon and the absence of fences. (From David Collins, Account of the English Colony, *vol. 1*)

'Saunderson's Farm' shows a more substantial house set higher up and further from the water, and a long paling boundary fence almost to the river's edge. (From David Collins, Account of the English Colony, *vol. 1*)

of the soil, which they declared would produce an ample crop at any time without much labour.[79]

Instead of ensuring a simple life of hard, honest toil, the colonial earth made possible a lifestyle far more to people's liking: luxuriant returns for minimal labour, freedom from tyranny, time for drinking and socialising and the pleasures of popular culture. It was just the sort of community the British government had sought to avoid.

Perhaps Collins was exaggerating. Were the Hawkesbury settlers debauched, delinquent and hopelessly drink-sodden? How could such a community then have been so successful in producing staple grains to feed themselves and the colony? Most historians have associated drinking with the 'low calibre' of the convicts, 'the desire for oblivion', or as an 'escape' from the 'hell' in which they found themselves.[80] A look at some of the early court cases suggests that drinking was certainly integral to that early community: it was part of the everyday. Together with other 'stimulants' like tea and coffee, alcohol was a normal part of the diet, 'the use of which they had been accustomed in England from childhood'.[81] Prolonged and binge drinking may have been a response to original prohibition. The convicts were forbidden alcohol both on the voyage out and, in theory, in the colony as well, and they must have felt sorely deprived. (Phillip tried to ban the cultivation of tobacco, their other great pleasure, too.) Collins seemed to grasp the link between prohibition and their great craving, the 'madness' that 'broke out' whenever liquor was brought ashore, often by sailors who shared it with convicts.[82]

At the Hawkesbury, settlers bought alcohol from officers or their agents on credit or in exchange for crops. They ferried it up on boats, or distilled it on every farm from maize or peaches and river water.[83] People gathered in the mean huts and tents to pass around glasses or mugs, to talk and sing and relish conviviality, especially on feast days, like Christmas and St Patrick's Day. Drinking went on for days: one poor woman, asked why she delayed telling her husband for almost a week that she had been raped, replied 'she did not do it before, as he was in a state of intoxication the most of the time, in which state she was afraid to inform him'.[84]

Court transcripts, of course, are not ideal or balanced sources. We would not like to see our own history based solely upon the sorry testimonies of alcohol-related crimes in today's courtrooms. But they do give us compelling glimpses of everyday habits, of what was 'normal', and also of the way things could flare up. Old hatreds were brought to the surface, simmering resentments inflamed, a wrong word or gesture occasionally spiralled into gruesome axe attacks and murders, or vengeful house fires. Isolation made these situations more dangerous; there were no constables, no-one but neighbours to intervene, if you were lucky. It appears that crimes often centred upon women: women attacked and raped by convict servants, or by neighbours; women the victims of brutal gang rapes, which they sometimes 'concealed'; arguments between men over women which escalated with drink. More research needs to be done, but it is difficult to avoid the implication that the scarcity of women on the Hawkesbury, and in other settlements, made them extremely vulnerable; and that drinking heightened the dangers.[85]

But we must see the other uses of drinking too: not only blessed sociability but the warm fire in the belly that gave men and women superhuman strength for hard physical labour—building and rowing boats, felling timber, splitting slabs, tilling, planting, reaping and threshing and carrying the crops to barns and boats. Recall William Dawes' marines, clearing ground at wonderful speed—and Tench's specific remark that the work at Toongabbie was proceeding *without* spirits: a novel circumstance. Even Governor Hunter recognised this: he wanted a supply of 'comforts' for the convict workers because it 'performed miracles of exertion'. Drinking, life and labour were inseparable; life was lame, incomplete, without drink. Men and women felt themselves transformed by it. Not for nothing was liquor known as 'spirits'.[86]

What Collins was also talking about when he wrote darkly of the 'drinking and rioting' at the Hawkesbury was popular culture—the lively, vital, sometimes brutal leisure pursuits of working people. At first these included, of course, communal pastimes of drinking, gambling, and the pleasures of talk, smoking and singing together. By 1795 there was already a racecourse at the Green Hills (the Killarney racecourse, around 3 miles (5 kilometres) east of the river at the Killarney Chain of Ponds). James Ruse himself seems to have been in the thick of the gaming activities, for great concourses of 'disorderly persons' (which usually meant working people) were said to have gathered at his house and outbuildings 'to gamble and Illegally Squander away their property'.[87]

Collins' words proved prophetic. The Hawkesbury became famous as a great centre, later a bastion, of preindustrial popular culture; Windsor was fondly known as a 'little sporting town'. The bloody sport of cockfighting was popular, with mills, or meetings, held in the 'Holland Paddock', the birds fitted with deadly spurs 'to tear their opponent to pieces more easily'. Cockfighting persisted, after it was outlawed, in the 'secluded spots' in the district until the 1890s. By the 1830s and 1840s the Hawkesbury was also one of the meeting places on the bare-knuckle prize-fighting circuit. The Wilberforce fights, where town fighters and bettors mixed with 'ablebodied shakebags from the Kurrajong were perhaps most memorable, and by the 1840s Windsor was nostalgically celebrated by the 'fistive' fraternity as the birthplace and heartland of colonial-born fighting champions, the true manly stock of the old colony. Now these champions were old, and benefit nights were held in city pubs to help support them and their families.[88]

In his old age, J.T. ('Toby') Ryan, grandson of convict farmers, born and bred on the river, remembered these men and the fights well too, but it was the great Killarney Races which shone most gloriously in his memory. These were rollicking festivals of boozing, betting, fun and enjoyment—the booths at Killarney were crowded with people, black and white, drinkers, dancers and tambourine players, while

> [e]very kind of amusement imaginable was going on, nine pins, poppet shows, the devil among the tailors, with lollypop and cake stalls at the front; at the back, skittles and gambling of every description, with the occasional fight through the day.

There were 'two big races' whose noble equine winners were long remembered as heroes in local lore, a 'District purse, hack races', prize-fights for 'two hundred pounds aside and the championship'. In the evening a great bonfire licked the starry night sky beside the river, Windsor was alive with music and a ball was held in the town square, while drunken soldiers picked fights with the Aboriginal men of the 'Mulgoa tribe'. On the journey homewards a motley collection of Aboriginal people and whites, including 'fiddlers, actors, old hangers-on from Penrith and Yarra Monday's Lagoon' travelled together, sharing at their camp a rich haul of 'broken tucker' from the festivities, draining every bottle and keg. 'The blacks gave a corroboree and the fiddlers played and sang "Killarney"', recalled Ryan, 'after which they yoked up again and started on the straight road'.[89]

The popular culture of the early Hawkesbury settlers, though much like that of the townsfolk, was seen as notoriously 'riotous' and 'disorderly' because it was beyond the pale of administration, and it lay at the core of this 'other' place the settlers were making there. But it was more than this: like the negotiations over task-work, popular culture in itself was a culture of *resistance*, a way of defying exhortations to sobriety, regularity, time-discipline and relentless work. In the beginning the Green Hills people lived without authority figures. Although soldiers were sent out in 1795, they were mainly concerned with hunting local Aboriginal people. There were no constables until Andrew Thompson arrived in 1796, for it seems no Green Hills settler would become one. Collins wrote in 1794 that the colony was now so dispersed that 'orders did not find their way to the settlers' in the first place.[90] There were no parsons either: the Reverend Richard Johnson did not trek out to the Hawkesbury and the fiery Methodist preachers had not yet arrived. The Reverend Samuel Marsden made an effort in 1795, though reluctantly. It was a thankless task—a rough journey of 20 miles and even when he got there he knew perfectly well that 'the people will absent themselves as soon as they know I am coming'.[91]

Occasionally the defiant stance of the Hawkesbury people broke through the stately surface of official records—to be hurriedly snuffed out, of course. Hunter reported with outrage the settlers' retort to his orders: 'that they did not care for the Governor or the Orders of the colony, they were free men and wou'd do as they pleased'. This ageing sea-captain had not forgotten how to pull a mutinous crew into line, though. Hunter met them face to face, eighteenth-century style, and soon they 'became very humble, and promised the strictest obedience in future'. They also relied on the governor to settle their differences.[92]

The British government's directive to establish villages seems to have been aimed at creating stable and orderly communities. But by the time of Bligh's overthrow in 1808 there were still really only two towns besides Sydney— Parramatta, and the unruly Green Hills. Macquarie decided to found more as a matter of urgency. Soon after landing he travelled his new domain from end to end, and with a wave of the vice-regal hand, chose sites for new towns and renamed old ones. Macquarie inscribed these declarations in his journal and despatches: this is how the Green Hills, the people's town, became Windsor, a 'Macquarie town', one of the famous five.[93]

But laying out the neatly grid-patterned towns was one thing: peopling them was another. Macquarie ordered, and then beseeched the flood-ravaged farmers to move to his towns on higher ground. Only a few moved. He accused them of 'Infatuated Obstinacy', of being obsessed with their land. Still they refused. Some of his towns were still-born. At a practical level, this was most likely because the townships (like Pitt Town and Castlereagh) were often too far from the fields to walk to work every day. In the years of frontier conflict, too, settlers literally had to defend their huts and crops as best they could by being on their land. There were probably other reasons too, which had to do with liberty and resistance. On their own lands they were out of sight, free from the surveillance of clergy and constables in the villages. When the Methodists arrived, they had to go out to the people, into their houses, and to rough bark riverside chapels, in order to spread their message of personal salvation. But there was one more reason: Macquarie believed the land itself had bewitched them. 'The Lands . . . are so very productive and Cultivated with such very little trouble', he explained in an 1817 despatch, 'it is not at all Surprising that the Old Settlers who have long lived on those Farms should be so partial to, and so unwilling to leave them'.[94]

More small-farming communities sprang up in the successively granted areas on the plain—Irishtown near Bankstown, for example, where the Irish Deputy Surveyor James Meehan 'encouraged his countrymen to settle', mostly Irish labourers who worked on the construction of the Liverpool Road.[95] There were small settlers around Campbelltown and Camden in the 1810s. But the Hawkesbury–Nepean remained the emblematic alternative place for the colony's convicts and ex-convicts. The early Irish rebels were thought to have hidden their pikes at Killarney, and, as we shall see, the Green Hills was the destination of the rebels who stormed out of Castle Hill Farm in 1804—they hoped to gather great numbers to their cause among the small settlers and convicts there.[96]

The high cost of labour, and perhaps common loyalty and personal connections, meant that the poor Hawkesbury farmers were notorious for hiding runaway convicts and giving them work; the latter in turn made the 'Oxberry' (Hawkesbury) their destination. Ironically, the small settlers also became the accomplices, as well as the main targets, of large numbers of bushrangers, who hid in the more rugged, forested country and raided the farms and roads for food, clothing and ammunition. As we shall see, bushranging became endemic on the Cumberland Plain and did not entirely subside until the 1840s.[97]

For perhaps eight or ten years, the farmed patches on the plain bloomed and colonists rejoiced in their progress; they wrote of 'beautiful and luxuriant fields', wheat in the ground 'realising golden dreams', of 'wonderfully prolific' stock and of their colony as 'the finest country in the world'. The Hawkesbury was most admired of all.[98] Then came the years when the plagues of Egypt seemed to rain down upon them.

The first decades of the nineteenth century brought previously unheard-of pests and diseases—a blight in the wheat crop in 1803–04, and in the following year the harvest suffered again when a flymoth appeared and laid its eggs in the wheat, destroying it in the stack. But the most devastating, because they were so visually dramatic, were the 'caterpillar' plagues. From 1799, and possibly as early as 1791, the fields and pastures, gardens and orchards were regularly attacked by 'a new enemy to agriculture', army worms.[99] These are the inch-long, yellowish-green and black-striped larvae of a drab brown moth, *Pseudaletia convecta*. They hatched after rains and, if no food was immediately available, would literally form a front and move, as one wriggling mass, towards a standing crop, or anything green. 'The ground was covered with them for miles', remembered free settler George Suttor, 'all travelling in the same direction . . . we were frequently obliged to sweep them out of the house in heaps'. Farmers and graziers watched helplessly as crops and pasture were devoured, leaving bare earth, and prayed for rain which might sweep the army away. Sometimes the rains only brought further hatching, and millions more erupted from the drought-parched ground.

We don't yet know the full ecological story of the caterpillar plagues, as they were called. The creatures seem to have emerged in such monstrous numbers after drought, when their natural predators were fewer. Perhaps the presence of the settlers' cereal crops also encouraged their population explosion.

Drought took hold once more in 1798. The creeks and ponds dried out, the wheat and maize shrivelled, pastures turned to straw and the 'whole country has been a blaze of fire'.[100] This drought was dramatically broken in May 1799 by floodwaters roaring into the basin of the Hawkesbury–Nepean valley from the rivers' vast catchment. Horrified settlers discovered the true import of the valley's topography: the waters tore down 'as from mountains of solid rock, filled all the low grounds and the various branches of the river, which being in a shape suddenly serpentine, cou'd not give vent so fast as the waters came down'.[101]

The river rose 15 metres, 'the torrent so powerful it carried all before it', and then the water backed up, as if the valley was a giant bathtub. The huts, crops and animals were swept away, drowned. Hundreds of people were left homeless and starving.

The shock of this first 'true' flood was profound. Yet there had been warnings—the river had risen more than 7 metres in September 1795, a settler was drowned and some people lost their nerve and 'offered their grants again to the crown'.[102] Despite this, and the warnings of Aboriginal people, flood-fear subsided as the crops flourished. After 1799, though, the massive flows returned every few years—again in 1800, and in the catastrophic year of 1806, when the torrents drowned the valley three times. Governor Macquarie arrived to a chorus of lamenting: the two floods of 1809 had again washed away the colony's food supply.[103]

The famous emancipist Margaret Catchpole, long revered among Hawkesbury folk, wrote of the swirling terror of these floods, of clinging with children to the chimney on the roof with the black waters racing just below. It made the long sea voyage to New South Wales look tame. 'I was more frightened', she wrote to her uncle, 'than all the way going over'. The Hawkesbury was a scene of devastation:

… housen and barns and wheatstacks and the indeay [Indian] corn that was not gathered it washed all away before the stream some poor creatures riding on their housen, some on their Barns Crying out for God sake to be saved, others firing their Guns in the Greatest distress for a Boat there was many thousands of head of all kind of Cattle was lost and so many bushels of all sorts was lost of grain so now these places is in Great distress for wheat.[104]

Emancipist South Creek tenant farmer, James Ward, married with three sons and hopelessly in debt, wrote plainly of the recurring nightmare in an 1801 petition: 'Now back came the floods again greater than before, leaving us helpless spectators only of our stacks, Barns, Houses and stock swimming down the current'. But officials had little sympathy for Hawkesbury settlers of Ward's type. Surveyor Charles Grimes thought he and six of his neighbours were 'worthless characters' and did not believe their debts 'have been contracted by cultivating their farms'.[105] Ward died of snakebite in one of his fields in the spring of 1812. His wife and sons left the Hawkesbury for good. But there were always more settlers—tenants and purchasers—to take the place of those who were ruined.[106]

The smallest Hawkesbury farmers, though their 'farms promised plenty', had never managed to prosper. In 1798 their 'houses and persons wore the appearance of poverty and beggary'.[107] The floods kept them poor, living on maize in squalid conditions. Perhaps many never aspired to more. Yet the waters replenished the earth too, with a thick blanket of silt:

… a vast quantity of rich mud which covers the country to the depth of several inches, so that every piece of land that the water reaches is as productive as the richest muck-heap, the corn . . . being often twenty feet high, and one stalk had been known to afford seven large cobs of corn.[108]

And so the farmers who remained stuck stubbornly to the river banks, moved back into the sodden huts, if they still stood, hoed and planted again, learned the river's rhythms and signs, and hoped they would be spared next time.

For governors, though, the lessons of the rivers finally sank in: the rich alluvials, the great hope and salvation of the colony, could not be relied upon to feed the people. In the end the waters forced new official settlement into the higher, drier forest ground away from the rivers.[109]

FATE AND OPPORTUNITY: CONVICT ENTREPRENEURS

The plots of 30 acres were originally intended to anchor men and women in this new world—this is why they were given so much practical encouragement and assistance. Land was not intended to be merely a speculative commodity, bought and sold like a cow or a bushel of wheat, with no improvement or labour investment. But by 1793 it was already clear that land *was* a commodity in New South Wales. The settlers had brought with them notions of private property, and thus the right to buy and sell. Farms were freely sold because there were people (officers in particular) interested in purchasing them. Governors could not prevent these sales, nor would they have wished to. The fact that these were *grants* rather than freehold titles, government indulgences theoretically to be paid for in quit-rents, made little difference; nor did the rule forbidding settlers to sell within a certain time, although Hunter and King occasionally revoked grants. Land grants were also increasingly used as rewards and compensations, in contrast to the original intention, especially by Governor Macquarie. Aboriginal land was regarded as a convenient, cheap and inexhaustible source of largesse.[110]

Ex-convicts certainly considered their rural grants as 'merchantable' property, to retain or sell as they wished, just as convicts in Sydney bought and sold as they pleased, even when there was no official lease at all. Some emancipists gave up on small-farming because they were deeply in debt, because they wanted to move on, or because they never had any intention of farming in the first place. James Ruse was forced, through bad luck or a 'gambling streak', or both, to sell his original Green Hills farm, and then another he had been granted nearer Pitt Town. Like many others, Ruse then simply kept requesting and receiving fresh grants in newly opened districts: 100 acres near Bankstown in 1809, another 100 acres near Riverstone in 1819. But he and Elizabeth never occupied these lands; their lives were fastened to the Hawkesbury. They held them, most likely little changed, for a few years before selling them on to the Reverend Samuel Marsden.[111]

Then there were those with a quick eye for advantage and profit. In Kate Grenville's novel *The Secret River*, the convict William Thornhill 'fell in love with a piece of ground', the knob of land at the junction of the Hawkesbury and Macdonald rivers, 'where the river turns eastward and makes a break for the sea'.[112] Interestingly, the historical appropriator of that land, Solomon Wiseman, was an entrepreneur, an opportunist. He was one of a large number of emancipists with an eye for advantage, a willingness to take risks—and, as his petitions and memorials show, he was practised in the language of demands cloaked in deferential language. A lighterman convicted of stealing rosewood, Wiseman was one of those convicts who seemed scarcely to pause for breath before launching a new career in his old trade in Sydney. He established a successful shipping business, carrying wheat, wool, coal and cedar between the settlements, including the Green Hills. After both his boats were lost in storms in 1817, he and his family moved to the 200-acre grant at Lower Portland Head. This land was granted as a kind of compensation for his loss, but it was also strategic.[113] Not only was it admirably located for the busy river trade, but as it turned out, Wiseman's headland straddled an essential node of a new road linking Sydney with the new estates of the Hunter Valley to the north, the first of the colony's ambitious 'Great Roads'. Wiseman added to his packet-boat fortune by establishing a punt there to ferry travellers across the river, and he built a substantial stone hotel where they could eat, drink and rest. He also won lucrative government contracts to repair tools (using government labour!) and to provide food for the hundreds of convict men who laboured on the road for over ten years.[114] When you drive north into the 'forgotten valley' of the Macdonald today, you must still edge down to Wisemans Ferry along the steep zigzag bends built of stone by the convicts, still pass the stone mansion Wiseman built with his profits, and you must still queue at his ferry wharf to cross the Hawkesbury River.

The conditions of life on the Hawkesbury soon sorted the ambitious and entrepreneurial from those who trusted to fate, whose meagre possessions, hogs and crops were swept away every few years by the floods. At the Hawkesbury, emancipist Andrew Thompson, the first constable, was a busy and energetic man. He acquired more farms, built boats and a pontoon bridge over South Creek, opened a store and inn, set up saltpans and tanneries. Macquarie appointed him

Wealthy emancipist Solomon Wiseman very likely commissioned this picture of his house and estate at Wiseman's Ferry, also called Lower Portland Head. The unknown artist seems to have abandoned perspective in order to show every facade of every building in as much detail as possible. Wiseman himself is depicted issuing orders to an overseer, a young man twirls an umbrella in the garden, a little girl holds up a bird and an oversized emu wanders about. A strange trio of statues adorn the garden wall: emu, kangaroo, and what looks suspiciously like a kangaroo dog. (Photographic copy: author's collection)

a magistrate, much to the horror of the free settlers of Richmond.[115] But the best known among these ambitious go-getters were Mary and Thomas Reibey— Mary arrived a convict and Thomas was a junior ship's officer. A pragmatic, restless and energetic couple, they married in 1794 and were granted land on the Hawkesbury. They tried farming life, but aspired to much more. Thomas, like several of his neighbours, soon saw the potential of trade and carrying and built a sloop (*Raven*), establishing a thriving cargo business between Sydney and the Hawkesbury. Soon the couple acquired more land in both settlements, including a key site in Sydney with a frontage onto the mouth of the Tank Stream. The Reibeys left farming and rural life behind and moved back to Sydney, though they held on to their Hawkesbury lands. More ships were built and they entered the seal fur and skin trade, carried coals from Newcastle, red cedar from the Hunter Valley, and then entered the Pacific trade. They built a handsome townhouse in Sydney and moved their growing family in. Like their more successful neighbours back on the Hawkesbury, they bought up the farms of those driven off by debts and leased them out in small allotments to tenant farmers. Mary Reibey was widowed in 1811; she nevertheless continued in business and trade and became one of the richest people in the colony.[116]

The Reibeys were typical of a particular class of adventurers, both convict and free, who saw this colony, like any other in the New World, as a place for making fortunes. People like them tied the growing town and the rural plain together, for their interests straddled both port and hinterland, maritime trade and agriculture. Butchers with slaughteryards and shops in town acquired grants or leases on the plain for their stock. Merchants and hoteliers with capital added farms to their many investments.

Sometimes the town's social/spatial configurations were echoed on the plain: tradesmen and dealers who were neighbours in Sydney seem to have acquired grants alongside one another out west too—so William Davis and Andrew Fraser, both well-known men of the Rocks, acquired grants in the Dural/ Glenhaven area, while butcher George Cribb, stonemason Richard Byrne, and William Cassidy who were neighbours on the Rocks, held land adjoining one another at Minto.[117]

The first five governors kept the original vision for the colony alive by continuing to grant small acreages to people of humble standing, and they were at pains to encourage and protect the small farmers, in spite of, even in defiance of, the interests of the wealthy. But in reality, the notion of a population entirely comprised of small-scale, subsistence farmers vanished in a few short years. What emerged so rapidly instead was a hierarchy of small, middling and large landowners. The smallest were generally wretchedly poor, the middling doing tolerably well, often diversifying with different crops and mixed farming, while the largest landowners were the least vulnerable because they had sufficient capital for improvements, to amass other investments, and to tide them over difficult periods.[118] Often they were absentee landlords and owners too, their lands occupied by their emancipist managers, sometimes with families, and their workers. When wealthy landowners did live on their estates, or retire there, they became the 'big men', the 'leading families' in their areas, dominating local affairs as magistrates who sat in judgement over local people, as directors of trusts, collectors of censuses. But how had these estates and vast accumulations of other property and capital come about in a colony meant for felons?

OFFICERS AND FREE SETTLERS

James Ruse, the 'first farmer', and Philip Schaeffer, the hoped-for vigneron, both sold their grants to officers. Ruse's went to Surgeon John Harris and Schaeffer's Parramatta River farm was purchased by Lieutenant Henry Waterhouse. Waterhouse was so pleased with his farm, he meant never to part with it, though he later sold it to Hannibal Macarthur. Macarthur retained the romantic name 'The Vineyard', in memory of Schaeffer's pioneering grapevines, while over the river, Harris kept Governor Phillip's name 'Experiment Farm'. He ran a herd of spotted deer among his cattle and sheep there—these deer later graced the grounds of Ultimo, his other estate near Sydney. Later some of them escaped and took to 'breeding and running wild in the woods'. Forty years later Harris built a pretty bungalow cottage with elegant verandahs and French windows on Ruse's old farm. It still stands today in Harris Park.[119]

The officers sent out to New South Wales were originally forbidden land grants. But they had ambitions which were fundamentally at odds with the official/agricultural project, and more in line with the business-as-usual colonies of the empire. Most of them were adventurers seeking their fortunes rather than disinterested career men. They were themselves mainly of relatively modest background, 'marginal men' on the make, for whom serving the empire in distant colonies was the path to wealth and prestige at Home. Amassing land and property was one way to achieve these ambitions, and Joseph Banks had sketched New South Wales as a land of boundless meadows, rich in easy pickings. This is the context for the officers' initial outburst of angry disappointment at the Sydney environment. As we shall see, their words were so vehement, so condemnatory that they became foundational myths of Sydney as an 'alien land' and a 'harsh environment'. But during exploratory trips and supervisory duties they saw the fertile, picturesque riverside lands, the open 'Kangaroo Grounds' around Petersham, and the open woodlands of Parramatta and beyond. To their wonder, the country looked exactly like the carefully designed parklands of gentlemen back Home. By early March 1788, they had changed their tune, and clamoured to be part of the great land-grab. The possibilities of this country were abundantly clear: here they might establish country seats, raise elegant houses in those ready-made parklands, and style themselves landed gentry in a new world, even if only for a short time.

Phillip explained that he had no authority to give them land grants, only garden and stock-feeding grounds, but he obligingly petitioned on their behalf. Eventually permission arrived—130 acres could be granted to non-commissioned officers plus more for those with wives and children. Phillip's successors were not empowered to do so, but they did anyway. Grose and Paterson made a number of grants to their brother officers at Bulamaning, the old name for the Petersham area, the 'Kangaroo Grounds' west of the town, stretching from present-day Camperdown and Ashfield down to the upper reaches of the Cooks River. This was open woodland on shale soil land, lying along the track to Parramatta, some parts watered by the creeks feeding the Parramatta and Cooks rivers, but dry elsewhere. Since the grants were far larger than the 30-acre patches, the officers were also granted ten convicts each, fully rationed, to provide the labour—and so the assignment system was born. Thus, set up with land and labour absolutely free of charge, they set about clearing and planting with great energy.[120]

Among the most acquisitive was Lieutenant John Macarthur. As inaugural Inspector of Works, charged with making sure agriculture was progressing satisfactorily, he had both 'the run of the convicts' and the opportunity to grab the best lands. He selected for himself and his wife Elizabeth 100 acres of beautiful undulating land on the river at Parramatta next to Experiment Farm. By now the better-off settlers were starting to build boxy, English-style farmhouses with jerkinhead roofs. But the Macarthurs' new cottage was long and low, encircled with fashionable drooping verandahs in the latest style. Elizabeth Farm was merely the home estate, for Macarthur quickly added more lands at Castle Hill (Bella Vista, used as a stock farm where another cottage was built, and still standing as part of a later house), Field of Mars, Dundas, Toongabbie, Prospect and Cabramatta. In 1805 he swapped 3620 acres of these grants and

Hadley Park at Castlereagh, built in about 1812, is an English-style farmhouse with a jerkinhead roof. This house has not been modernised and is a rare survivor on the Cumberland Plain. It now stands at the edge of a huge open-cut gravel quarry. (Photo: Benedict Taylor, 2006)

purchases for the greatest prize of all: 5000 acres of rich, well-watered slopes and alluvial flats on the Nepean discovered and colonised by the escaped cattle: the Cowpastures.[121]

Civil officers profited as well. The Reverend Richard Johnson's moaning about the privations and moral bankruptcy of the colony belies his extraordinary success as a farmer. Tench said he was 'the best farmer in the country', for by 1790 he had raised the colony's first orange trees from pips, garden peas, grapes, strawberries and 'at least a thousand cucumbers', as well as grain crops from the Sydney Cove soils so much bewailed by the others. In 1793 he took land near Cooks River, veined with creeks and a chain of ponds (like the emancipists, he was already farming there before the official grant was made). He named it Canterbury Vale and planted groves of citrus, almonds, apricots, guavas, vines and figs as well as growing wheat and running sheep and goats. But Richard Johnson was a sojourner after all, and returned to England in 1800.[122]

The Reverend Samuel Marsden, originally sent to assist Johnson, was still more ambitious and acquisitive. He was hyperactively busy, besides possessing 'the strength of an ox'. Finding 'all the higher ranks . . . lost to G. and Religion', and the convicts even worse, he felt redundant: 'I do not know one person who wants the Great Physician of Souls', he wrote to a friend. He threw himself instead into farming, stockraising and the 'study of the nature and soil of the colony'. His letters burst with enthusiasm for the colony's agricultural future. Indeed, Marsden found farming far more interesting than preaching: 'I may be too fond perhaps', he confessed in 1795, 'of the garden, the field and the fleece'. By 1811 he was commissioning portraits of his best bull, finest horse and stud ram and sending them to friends back home. He and his wife Elizabeth and their children lived at first on Captain Thomas Rowley's 'Kingston' at Petersham, and later mainly at Parramatta, in the big, bossy-looking rectory designed by Francis Greenway. But they amassed almost 4000 acres in grants in the opening districts—first in Dundas and the Field of Mars, where he built two more fine houses, then at the Hawkesbury. On the plains at Evan (St Marys) on South Creek, he built his English-style farmhouse, Mamre (named modestly for the biblical place where Abraham dwelt), where it still stands. Finally the Marsdens were given 1000 acres over the mountains, at Bathurst.[123]

Marsden, like the officers, also relentlessly enlarged his landholdings through purchasing the grants of humbler people like James Ruse. This was the origin of the Blaxlands' Brush Farm at Eastwood too—Lieutenant William Cox bought up the lands of the poor, debt-ridden grantees at The Ponds and sold them on to John Blaxland in 1807. So The Ponds, named for the earlier farmers' water source, became The Brush, named for the stands of rainforest that grew on the dark soils of Eastwood's sheltered slopes. While Governor Macquarie was disappointed by the mean huts of the small settlers, he thought 'The Brush . . . a very snug good Farm and very like an English one in point of comfort and convenience'.[124] Some of the small Hawkesbury farms were consolidated in the same way, as we have seen, though it remained a small-farming district overall.

Once more, names were telling, sometimes cynical. George Johnston called one of his many Georges River grants 'Foveaux's Gift'. John T. Campbell, Macquarie's private secretary, swapped his Sydney allotment for 1000 acres at Villawood and called it 'Quid Pro Quo'. Even governors indulged in little jokes like this: King and Bligh came to a mutually beneficial arrangement in which they granted one another vast tracts of land. The 790 acres Bligh granted to Mrs King was called 'Thanks'.[125]

A few free settlers—those who overcame their fear of the Botany Bay taint— also made the great voyage to New South Wales, but not many. Phillip, even as he dutifully set up the public farms and tried to implement the Plan, quickly realised that the convicts were unlikely to be transformed into productive farmers in time for the self-sufficiency deadline. Perhaps more importantly, he also lacked properly qualified people to supervise them on the big public farms.[126] He was soon asking for free settlers with knowledge of farming—good, respectable, plain-speaking yeoman stock. A few came, men and women with their children, lured eventually by free passages, promises of land and the same rations, tools and seed as the emancipists received.[127] Their presence, like that of the officer-farmers, also eroded the original scheme of a colony of felons, sealed off from the world.

Yet to begin with, there appears to have been some attempt at segregation on the part of both the government and the settlers themselves. The earliest free settlers, who arrived in groups, selected land in their own districts, away from the emancipists' farms. The first group, including the notable Rose family, arrived in the *Bellona* in 1793 and chose land between Parramatta and Petersham. To underscore their distinct status in the convict colony, they named their district Liberty Plains.[128] So often we think of new settlers feeling alienated and homesick in the 'strange landscape', but the Roses at least seem to have had high hopes of their new 'Rosedale' farm. When their son John was born in 1795 they christened him there on the land, under a shelter fashioned from 'saplings and evergreens'. A 'poetical address' was composed to celebrate the birth, and the country in which he was born:

> Fair rose the morn, bright shone the day
> The forest songsters from each green spray
> Warbl'd high to heav'n the enraptured lay
> Among the groves of Rosedale
> Wise and good thoughts, fond love and joy
> Welcom'd the birth of the darling boy . . .[129]

George and Mary Hall, who went to Portland Head, named their first colonial-born boy James Hawkesbury, for the river. This became a family tradition, for grandchildren were named for other rivers as the family spread into new country: Ebenezer Hunter Hall and Reuben Namoi Hall.[130]

Another group of free settlers, including George Suttor and Andrew MacDougall, went to the Baulkham Hills area, north-west of Parramatta, which became a famous citrus-growing region. Within three years, Suttor was also growing saplings of 'Apples, Pears, Early Peaches, Figs, Apricots, a few Almonds . . . Pomegranates, Lemons, Loquats, Raspberries, large Chilli Strawberries, Quinces, Willows, etc', which he sold to other settlers keen to plant their own orchards and gardens.[131] Suttor, telling his story for descendants many decades later, recalled the long search for land: 'Many a long and weary journey I had in continuing the search on all sides of Parramatta'. What was he looking for? Good land, yes, but perhaps still more important, a 'good neighbourhood of free families':

> This was indeed a very desirable circumstance for protection in the early days of the Colony when gangs of wild Irish bushrangers were frequently the dread of the settlers . . .[132]

It was also a place separate from the convict farmers.

Yet convicts were integral to these 'free' districts too. Like the emancipists and officers, free settlers benefited greatly from convict labour: their land was cleared and cottages were built for them at the expense of the crown. Their farms and households were staffed and worked by assigned convicts, also fed and clothed by the crown. Convicts working on their own time provided additional essential labour for free settlers' new farms. George Hall, one of the *Coromandel* free settlers, kept a brisk, businesslike journal which kept track of both work and pay on his first farm at Toongabbie. This was no mean feat, as Hall had to measure and calculate what part of the 'falling', burning, breaking up the ground, 'holing for corn', chipping and reaping was done 'on government time', and what part was on his workers' own time. Then he paid them accordingly, mostly in pork, sugar, tobacco, wheat, soap. By 1803, his workers could be paid, if they so desired, in 'ribbands', check shirts, shoes or silk handkerchiefs.[133]

Free settlers went out to the Hawkesbury too, some to take 100-acre grants, others buying up the lands of the failed and desperate. Here again placenames helped to distinguish them from the convict population. A number of free arrivals went, for example, to a stretch of the river above Yarramundi lagoon which was then called 'Free Man's Reach'. The impulse to distinguish oneself from Botany Bay criminals was once more inscribed on the landscape. Richmond, on the other side of the river, was settled by another knot of free settlers, who formed a 'tight enclave'. They did their best to exclude ex-convicts and disassociate themselves from the turbulent Green Hills people.[134] By 1806, and in the Bligh years, though, the settlers of Free Man's Reach knew that there were deeper and more destructive divisions in their little society than those between convict and free, as we will see.[135]

Other groups were more liberal, or became so. The people from the *Coromandel* (which arrived in 1802), mainly artisans and devout Presbyterians, were first placed at Toongabbie. When these farms began failing, they were reallocated land together at Portland Head, on the lower reaches of the Hawkesbury. Together with ex-convict neighbours, they built their plain stone chapel-cum-schoolhouse at Ebenezer in 1809, now the oldest extant church in Australia. Strict social avoidance was both impossible and ridiculous here. Familiarity eventually bred intimacy.

The Rose family also left their shale soil land at Liberty Plains, moved out to the river and settled again at Wilberforce. Their children married emancipists, or the children of emancipists; they were the makings of the famous Rose dynasty.[136]

As with the convicts, these settlements reinforced the shipboard and earlier relationships between the free arrivals. The *Coromandel* settlers, as they were known, asked to be 'placed together', and named the road to their church at Ebenezer after their ship. So they were neighbours, and their children intermarried. Sometimes their settlements developed truly local identities, deeply rooted in the land.[137] But many other free settlers were a great disappointment. Unfortunately, the scheme also attracted no-hopers—adventurers wanting to make a quick fortune, people with no experience or capital who were fractious as well as avaricious. They deluged governors with demands to supply their every want. By the time Macquarie was in office, the record of free settlers was so poor that the free passage scheme was abolished and settlers were required to have 500 pounds in cash before they could acquire land. Even then, they arrived with the 'cash' in speculative cargoes they had purchased on the voyage, which they could not always realise through sales. George Suttor, who had reaped the rewards of great indulgences in land and labour, later denigrated and slandered the governors who had helped him.[138]

The free settlers who had arrived with large resources (or good connections) and big ideas, like the Blaxland and Riley brothers, tended to mingle with the officer class. They took land in the same districts and followed similar pursuits—Alexander Riley built elegant and comfortable houses at Burwood, on the road to Parramatta, and on Raby, a large grant near Liverpool. He went back to England in 1817 to pursue his business interests but he held on to his lands in New South Wales, and continued to supervise them. He successfully introduced Saxon merino sheep at Raby in the 1820s by directing other family members, including his brother Edward, via detailed letters from England. In his old age, knowing that return was now impossible, he recalled his first sight of Raby, and how 'deeply moved' he had been 'by the ownership of his land and by the beauty of its situation'.[139]

Family connections were also pre-eminent for brothers Gregory and John Blaxland. They bought up estates at Newington and Brush Farm, on either side of the Parramatta River. Newington was a particularly busy place, with a salt works, tweed mill and a limekiln, besides agricultural activities. By the 1840s, as historian Barry Dyster succinctly puts it, the Blaxlands 'owned five fine houses on both sides of the river, in close proximity to each other'. From the windows of mansions and villas at Newington, Rhodes, Brush Farm, Eastwood and The Hermitage at Denistone, the Blaxland families could keep the houses of their kin always in view. It must have given them a great sense of power and success, this vista of lands, houses, mills, orchards, vineyards and paddocks spread out along the broad river, all linked by family ties.[140]

These officers and free landowners were intimately familiar with one another's properties, not only because they were often adjoining, but because they constantly bought or leased or borrowed one another's houses and estates. John Piper, for example, lived in Alexander Riley's Burwood while his own 'marine villa' at Point Piper was under construction (Riley had a verandah added especially for him). Riley himself had rented John Harris' Ultimo and his brother Edward Riley bought John Palmer's Woolloomooloo farm with its classical-style house when the Palmers hit hard times. Lieutenant William Cox bought the Reverend Johnson's flourishing Canterbury farm, built a house 'in a stylish manner' upon it, but then sold it on to the merchant Robert Campbell. The traffic in land, houses and stock was lively and constant, tied to capricious colonial fortunes.[141]

These officers, civil and military, created something more than real estate, however. They also aspired to the *lifestyle* of eighteenth-century country gentle-men, and many of them achieved it. This was not the polite, self-improving, Protestant culture of the nineteenth-century genteel classes, obsessed with status and breeding, but an older, more rambunctious male culture of 'patriarchy and paternalism, risk and style, coolness and courage'.[142] As Richard Waterhouse reminds us, men like John Piper, John Jamison, Thomas Rowley, D'Arcy Wentworth and his son William Charles after him were enthusiastic patrons of rough plebeian sports and amusements. They demonstrated elite social and cultural standing by organising the cockfights, bare-knuckle prize-fights and horse races—so not all the bettors and spectators at the races and fights at the Green Hills were emancipists and convicts. Some of those who decided to live on their rural properties even established the old tradition of the Harvest Home, when all the local workers and tenants were invited to the Big House after the harvest to feast and drink, and enjoy the paternalistic largesse of those who were, undeniably, their superiors.[143]

The officers and their friends revelled in rambling and camping out, hunting and shooting, they rode their own (rather wild) horses and raised their rummers to one another in endless toasts. They demonstrated their manhood in the vast quantities they could drink, and their honour by shooting one another in duels. Most of the officers had convict mistresses, and some, like George Johnston and Thomas Arndell, eventually married them; others like Anthony Fenn Kemp at least made sure they and their 'natural' children were well provided for.[144] As we shall see, a number of these women became property owners and successful businesswomen in their own right.

Their farmhouses were far more substantial than those of the smaller settlers, yet they were often similarly simple, comfortable and unpretentious—sprawling wings with low, shady, stone-paved verandahs, often arranged in a U-shape around a courtyard, with outbuildings, storerooms and servants' quarters. The rooms were filled with eclectic collections of empire and global trade: porcelain and silver from China, furniture and fabrics from India, cases of birds, leopard skins, 'carved ivory and tortoiseshell trinkets.'[145] Listen to the reminiscences of Emmeline Macarthur, who grew up in such a house, The Vineyard, on Parramatta River, Philip Schaeffer's early farm:

> My first knowledge of my surroundings was a long low cottage forming two sides of a large grass square . . . with a pump in the centre . . . I recollect details of . . . that delightful home . . . The . . . sofas and wardrobes were of choice Australian woods, the floors were Kouri pine from New Zealand, in the dining room the floorboards were 35 ft long without a break, & mantelpieces were of marble from the [Macarthurs' Marulan] estate inland . . .[146]

She could have been describing Lawson's sprawling Veteran Hall at Prospect, or D'Arcy Wentworth's Homebush, or for that matter, the farmhouse of free settler

Anna Macarthur's sketch 'Vineyard N. S. Wales Sept 1834' conveys the fondness of the Macarthur daughters for the old homestead on the Parramatta River. (Mitchell Library, State Library of New South Wales)

James McCarthy, at Castlereagh: prototypes of what became classic Australian rural homesteads.

But let us return to seeding and breeding, those early exigencies. The granting of land to the officers is sometimes seen as the turning point in early colonial agricultural history. After four years of slow experiments and little to show but those handfuls of ragged farms, their initial energy was astonishing and the yields were promising. At last, large-scale farming by serious, properly financed contenders! Visitors rowing up the Parramatta River, or riding through the green tunnel of the trees on the Parramatta Road were struck by the look of comfort, plenty and productiveness of these estates, evidence of the colony's 'rapid strides' and astonishing progress from 'wilderness' to 'civilisation'.[147]

But in a way such appearances were deliberately staged, and they were deceptive. Though many were working farms, and certainly the most impressive and pleasing visually, these estates were not their owners' major sources of income. In fact after that first burst of enthusiasm in 1793, the officers quickly lost interest in grain production on a large scale. It was a mug's game. The cost of labour was high, the market small, and in any case grain-growing was associated with the deeply inferior, poverty-stricken emancipist settlers. Grazing cattle and sheep was a much more appropriately genteel pursuit. It 'fitted better with their duties', was less labour intensive and, in those early years at least, the quality of the soils did not matter so much. They acquired large tracts of land on creeks and rivers on the western parts of the plain, and also around Botany and the Georges River, as stock farms, run by emancipist managers and convict stockmen. Despite all the landowners' names on early maps, these were the people who actually lived on the frontier; they were the ones who encountered Aboriginal people there. Collins complained that absentee owners defeated the purpose of the assignment system and fostered disorder. Settlers were supposed to closely supervise their workers and control their movements, but as they did not live on their farms, their convict labourers were free to go into the towns and to commit robberies.[148]

Before 1820 even the officers' grazing activities on their extensive forest-land grants were not economically significant. Although sheep numbers jumped considerably between 1800 and 1810, these were raised for the local meat market rather than for wool—for example, the larger, meatier Tees Water sheep run by the Hall family, rather than the lighter, more delicate fine-woolled Spanish merinos. A few settlers were seriously interested in wool (though wool exports did not really begin to take off until the 1820s) but, for all the appearance of pastoral splendour celebrated in poetry, art and prose, the officers still only owned 18–20 per cent of the colony's livestock. As George Parsons observes tartly, channelling the profits of their trading in town into grazing in the early years at least 'must have seemed a form of conspicuous consumption'.[149]

The officers' money came not from seeding and breeding, but largely from trade—as we shall see, they had a unique advantage in that they alone had access to sterling and could purchase goods from the ships, buying cheap and selling dear.[150] They began to amass lands on the harbour now too: Macarthur at Pyrmont, George Johnston at Annandale, Surgeon Balmain at Balmain, Surgeon Harris at Ultimo. The impact of their profiteering on the small settlers

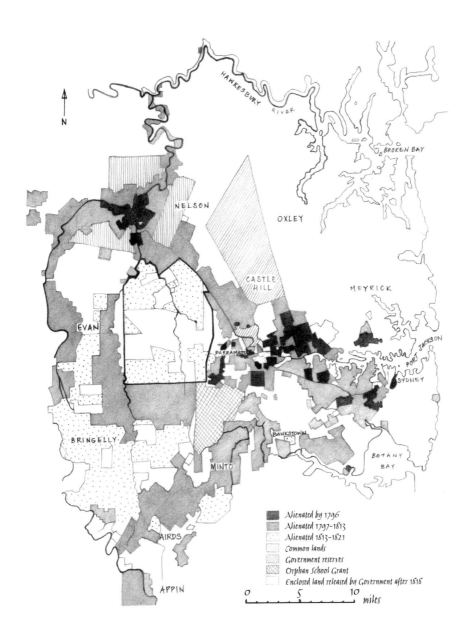

Land alienated in the country of Cumberland to 1821

*The spread of settlers over the Cumberland Plain, 1788–1821, showing the early 'islands'
before 1796, and the movement of settlers south and south-west and into the forest lands over
the succeeding decades. Note the way the alienated lands follow the arable soils precisely, and
the large areas set aside as commons and reserves. (Kate Nolan)*

was severe; the debts they racked up were crippling and persisted for years.[151] The officers' profits funded their dabbling in grazing and experimenting with grapes and wine-making, or hops, and allowed some of them (the Macarthurs, John Piper, the Blaxlands) to become obsessed with building and rebuilding ever more impressive and fashionable mansions to replace those comfortable old verandahed ones. Most never occupied their distant grants on the edge of the colony, but resided in quasi-rural splendour on the estates closer to Sydney. These were proto-suburban dream houses: they seemed idyllic and rural, but they were close to the business of the town and the port, tied by umbilical cords of river and road.[152] Meanwhile, the bulk of the grain which fed the colony was produced by the small emancipist farmers, those who were most numerous, but also most vulnerable to debt, flood and fire, and who commonly farmed less than 10 acres.[153]

THE CITY AND THE PLAIN

On the dusty track through the forest lands, a lone woman walks determinedly. It is 50 miles between Richmond and Sydney, but she has just heard that a cedar case sent to her from England months before has come to light, and so, in great excitement, she left her farm at once. After two days' walking, Margaret Catchpole arrives amidst the stone walls, houses and gardens, the bustling wharves and sea-tanged air of Sydney. She makes her way down to Woolloomooloo Farm where her friend and former mistress Mrs Palmer has the case safely stored for her. It holds treasures from her patron back at Home, Mrs Cobbold: 'some to sell, some to wear', stuff for gowns, lace and gingham, petticoats and caps and much more. 'You cannot tell the happiness it give me', she wrote later, 'and all my friends were overjoyed to hear of it, now this will give me great happiness for a long time'. Best of all is a cap which had been Mrs Cobbold's own. Back on her Richmond farm, Margaret found it 'a great comfort . . . I put it on and wear it—I Drink Tea with tears and a heavy heart'.[154]

The port and the storerooms at Sydney supplied the settlers of the inland districts with the commodities they needed, wanted, or could afford. The ships and boats carried clothing, shoes, hats, pots, tools, locks and bolts, salt meat packed in barrels, sugar, tea, kegs of spirits, hemp cloth, black cloth, calico, ticking, looking glasses and drinking glasses. As Catchpole tells us, these were not always simply to meet material needs. They had emotional meanings as well; they brought comfort, familiarity and security. Possessions also delineated all-important social standing. Before 1803 the boats from Sydney to the outlying districts brought the latest Government and General Orders from Sydney—a kind of de facto news service-cum-list of regulations. After 1803 they carried copies of the colony's first newspaper, the *Sydney Gazette*, where those who had the means and inclination could scan a cornucopia of tempting new goods offered by the Sydney dealers every time a ship came in: cheeses, hams and pickles, china dinner sets, cruets, candy, fancy hats, buttons and bobbing and hundreds of other things. Eventually the inland towns had their own stores, supplied from Sydney by boats or drays, where people shopped for themselves, or bought goods in bulk with which to pay their workers.

The *Gazette* was itself an important link between Sydney and the settlements, for it was full of lively news and stories about the events in Sydney as well as in the rural areas. Comical stories in blurry print about drunken sailors or terrible roads in Sydney jostled with reports of hailstorms or drought, or humorous tales of foolish farming bumpkins. There were items of news from Home and from other outposts of the empire. The boats and the dusty tracks eventually brought soldiers and constables, preachers and magistrates, governors surveying their domains, runaway convicts seeking sanctuary, and bushrangers. And they brought more people. By 1813 there were about a thousand more settlers outside the Sydney district than within it, and by 1820 Sydney housed only a quarter of the colony's population.[155]

Sydney in turn depended on the outlying settlements for staple foods. Many people in Sydney did grow their own vegetables in the early yards (peas, beans, cauliflower, fruit), while salt meat, tea and fancy preserved goods came from the ships. But the bulk of grains and fresh foods came on the boats from upriver—potatoes and cabbages from Kissing Point, wheat and maize from the farmers of the Hawkesbury–Nepean.[156] Once stock numbers were sufficient, cattle and sheep were driven from the plain into town, slaughtered in the butchers' yards and sold from their shops. The town consumed building materials too. With the 'edge of the trees' disappearing fast over the horizon, Sydney's buildings were raised in blue gum, blackbutt, ironbark, red mahogany and forest oak, cut out of the great Blue Gum High Forest stretching up the north shore to Pennant Hills and beyond Castle Hill. The joists and rafters of George Johnston's spreading bungalow roof at Annandale were built entirely of red cedar, which timbergetters cut out of the Hawkesbury–Nepean forests before moving up the coast in the ceaseless search for 'red gold'.[157] The town's gardens were stocked with plants supplied by nurserymen like George Suttor at Baulkham Hills, and favoured native plants were brought in too. As noted earlier, many of the ships and boats essential to Sydney's transport and trade were built on the Hawkesbury, and the men who sailed them had often learned their skills on the river. As economic historian Noel Butlin pointed out, it is difficult to make hard and fast distinctions between urban and rural populations and activities—the boundaries are blurred, for the city and the plain were inter-dependent, and so they remain.[158]

But by the time the *Sydney Gazette* first appeared, distinctions between urban and rural people in the Sydney region had already emerged. There were deep social and economic differences among the settlers, as we have seen—between officers, free settlers and emancipists; within the ranks of the emancipists; and, to varying degrees, between small landholders and the landless convicts. Now there were differences between town and country folk as well. Eating-house proprietors welcomed visitors from 'remote settlements', but the latter were immediately suspect, for householders were warned not to 'allow people from other settlements' to lodge with them without reporting them to the magistrate. Settlers arriving in town with their precious grain had reason to fear unscrupulous townsfolk, too. For if the public stores were full, they had no choice but to go to one of the pubs with a temporary granary where, of course, there were 'great temptations to dispose of the grain at a heavy loss'. Should a friendless stranger from the interior fall ill, or get badly drunk, the chances of kindness and shelter from townsfolk were exceedingly slim. Sydney was a dangerous place for rural settlers.[159] Moving the other way, out to the settlements, travellers noticed that the manners of the colonists shifted from polished politeness to rustic intimacy. In Sydney one was welcomed with 'ceremonial politeness', at Parramatta 'with friendly affability', while at the Hawkesbury visitors were embraced 'as one of the family'. Christmas well-wishes varied according to the urban/rural divide too: for the settlers at Parramatta and the Hawkesbury, there were hopes for agricultural plenty; for Sydney people, 'all concerned in trade and commerce' were wished success.[160]

At times the people from the 'remote settlements' came to town en masse, on foot, in carts and boats, and Sydney people were wide-eyed to see their streets full of upcountry strangers. The opening of Governor King's 'new and beneficial' store was one such occasion, for it 'drew a concourse of visitants together from all the settlements, scarcely if ever before witnessed'. George Howe thought this influx created an air of the great London fairs, with their licence and riot, for 'such was the consequent appearance of the town, as almost to qualify the belief that we had been unexpectedly honoured with a visit from the very eccentric Saint Bartholomew'.[161] While the pleasures of popular culture were still much the same in town and country—as we have seen, horse-racing, cockfights and prize-fights travelled wide circuits—the people from the outlying farms probably looked different from their town-dwelling counterparts. Their clothing was said to be poor, and perhaps it was also old-fashioned and simple compared to the fashionable and fine fabrics, shoe-buckles and hose that even convicts wore in Sydney. Perhaps the Hawkesbury men were already wearing 'moggasins' fashioned from kangaroo skins. Perhaps their accents, the words they used already sounded different.[162]

Over the nineteenth century, praise and celebration of the farming landscapes and rural communities of the Sydney region alternated with contempt, pity and derision. Meanwhile, country folk increasingly distrusted the big city, with its growing materialism, sophistication and disdainful attitudes, and proclaimed their own moral superiority. By the 1820s George Howe's son, Robert Howe (who inherited the *Gazette*, but none of his father's genial good humour), found Windsor's people insufferable, for the preaching circuit at the Hawkesbury was 'wretched . . . in my opinion. I would sooner go [to] the heathen a hundred times than have to preach to those miserable & filthy & hardened Cornstalks'.[163] In the 1830s, Mrs Sarah Mathew toured the isolated Macdonald River and Mangrove Creek with her surveyor husband, and in mingled horror and amusement scribbled journal descriptions of gliding past the small farms and maize patches in the sheltered coves: wretched huts, fowls cackling, shy peering women, half-naked children 'staring in amazement'. A year later, on the Colo River, a settler woman welcomed Mrs Mathew with overjoyed hospitality, proudly showed off the pigs and caged parrots. She offered her genteel visitor tea, and when that was firmly declined assumed she would like 'a drop of grog'. Mrs Mathew was mortified. Being welcomed as 'one of the family' was the height of embarrassment—though it made an amusing story.[164]

There was a world of difference, of course, between the small, isolated communities of the region and the bustling towns and villages, always keen to demonstrate their progressiveness, and increasingly well connected to the city by steamships, rail and roads. Sydney thought itself the centre, the core, upon which outlying settlements depended. But this imperial model was not necessarily the world view of people who made up the provincial towns, with their deep sense of local identity, and still less of those who made lives on distant river reaches, in the foothills of the mountains or deep in the forests. There they made their own histories, created other ways of being from the ones emerging in the town—vestiges of these ways survive to this day. The settlers of the Cumberland Plain also established rural cultures and ways of life, which, in the more isolated places especially, were little bound by urban ways but tightly interlaced with local environments. The Hawkesbury and Nepean generations, descendants of emancipists, free settlers and Aboriginal people, for example, learned to read the currents and warnings of the river, knew the limits of the soils, the properties of the timbers. Women learned how to collect and cook native foods and were still doing so in the 1940s. The Hawkesbury families intermarried, making a labyrinth of relationships spread out along the snaking reaches and tributaries; some families intermingled with local Aboriginal people too. Early Australia had been a partly literate society, just as England was, and for some, education and literacy remained in the realm of the non-essential. They knew the ways of their own world. The downriver communities especially were still hard-drinking and clannish in the 1940s and 1950s. This is also a living legacy, as there are still river communities accessible only by water, as in the 1790s, and river people who use the same local expressions and pronunciations as their great-great-grandparents.[165]

The city and plain were locked together, but their relationships and encounters continued to shift between imaginings, tensions, desires, scorn, even as the suburbs spread like a rising tide over the rural hinterlands.

————•—•—•————

Of all the thousands of settlers of the Cumberland Plain, it is James Ruse who continues to be the stuff of legend. At the beautifully restored Experiment Farm Cottage today, an exhibition for schoolchildren has recently been revamped. Ruse has been reinterpreted as the 'First Aussie Battler', a 'national symbol of survival against the odds'. This exhibition was devised in the context of the current severe drought and the resulting hardships suffered by Australian farmers. Visitors are asked to see Ruse as the progenitor of proud, self-reliant, independent farmers who waged war on a hostile environment, sometimes triumphant, often defeated.[166]

The mantle of the individualist battler farmer sits uneasily upon Ruse's shoulders. After all, at Experiment Farm he had considerable government help in clearing the land, supplying his tools, seed and stock, and he had his cottages built for him. He was not alone on the land either: as he was at pains to tell Tench, his wife Elizabeth Parry worked alongside him. Experiment Farm was not the first farm in the colony, and in any case Ruse held it for only a few months before selling up. Thereafter he lost or sold every farm and grant he possessed. Most importantly, though, Ruse's life and the lives of other emancipist settlers turned less on hardy individualism than on traditions of communalism.

In his earlier years, Ruse himself does not seem to have claimed special status as the 'first farmer'. While others demanded land in their petitions to Macquarie as a reward for all manner of 'public' service, he simply said he needed a grant because he had a large family to support. But in his old age, Ruse did begin to voice, to confirm, his own fame—and he added more material. Called to give evidence in court in a squabble between some old colonists over boundaries at Wilberforce in 1826, he reportedly informed the assembled throng that 'he was the first person to set foot on New Holland'. He claimed he had carried Major Johnston ashore on his back. Both the *Australian* and the *Gazette* published this story and so it too became part of the Ruse legend: he was not only the 'first settler', he was the 'first who trod the soil'.[167]

155

James Ruse and Elizabeth Parry stayed on the Hawkesbury for as long as they could. By 1828, their five children had produced sixteen grandchildren, and two of their daughters lived in the Campbelltown area (Soldiers Flat at Airds, and Lower Minto). Perhaps this is why the parents followed. James, at nearly 70, became an overseer on Captain Richard Brooks' farm at Denham Court. The Brooks were free emigrants who had made money in trade and were now setting themselves up as landed gentry.[168]

Elizabeth, James' life-mate, died in May 1836. Perhaps it was after her death that he began to carve his own headstone. We can still hear his Cornish accent in the engraved words:

SACRED

TO THE MEMOREY

OF JAMES RUSE WHO

DEPARTED THIS LIFE

IN THE YEAR OF HOURE LORD 1837 NATEF

OF CORNWELL AND ARIVED

IN THIS COLENEY BY THE

FORST FLEET AGED 77

MY MOTHER REREAD ME TENDERLEY

WITH ME SHE TOOK MUCH PAINES

AND WHEN I ARIVED IN THIS COLENEY

I SOWD THE FORST GRAIN AND NOW

WITH MY HEVNLY FATHER I HOPE

FOR EVER TO REMAIN[169]

It is a beautiful and moving artefact, bespeaking calm resignation and faith, but also a determination to be remembered, to leave a mark. In a period when well-heeled free settlers were beginning to flood in, build their grand houses, drive their flocks ever further upcountry, make their woolly fortunes, Ruse knew that he and people like him had been 'first'. He knew what they had wrought: the independent farming community on the rich Green Hills soils, the real site of the 'forst grain'; the planting of lively popular culture, the heartbeat of the people; and for the lucky ones, the making of new generations.

'I sowd the forst grain': James Ruse's headstone, St John's Campbelltown, photographed about 1910. Part of Elizabeth Parry/Ruse's headstone appears on the left. (Dixson Library, State Library of New South Wales)

Chapter 6

———•◆•———

VIEWS FROM FLAGSTAFF HILL

In some places in Sydney it is still possible to see key signs of the city's development. Flagstaff Hill, now called Observatory Hill, is one of these special places. Crowning the Rocks on the western side of the cove, it was the highest point in the town, a place where you could see both outwards and inwards, out to the Heads and the ocean, and up the rivers and roads into the interior. It was always a place for watching the waters, for receiving and sending signals, first from the flagstaff, later by telegraph wire. It was a lookout place to guard against insurrection from the inland and invasion from the sea. A windmill built there in 1797 harnessed the winds to grind the colony's wheat. Then in 1804 an octagonal stone fort was built around the mill to defend the town against both external attack and Irish rebels storming down the road from Parramatta. In the 1850s a handsome stone Observatory, complete with Government Astronomer, rose above the old fort to scan the skies. The telegraph wire looped up to the Observatory brought standard time to Sydney, linking the young city still more closely to the world.

But for many years the surrounding area on Flagstaff Hill remained unfenced, unalienated public space, and local working people used it as common ground, a kind of big backyard. This could not last, of course. Trustees were appointed in the 1870s to gentrify and control. They banned goats, washing, roaming children, indolent and immoral people and cricket matches. They erected iron-

Flagstaff Observatory, set atop what remained of Flagstaff Hill in the 1880s. (From Picturesque Atlas of Australia, *1886)*

haft fences round the rim of what remained of the hill, planted lawns and fig trees and banished the darkness, and what it could hide, with gas lamps.[1]

Today Observatory Hill, still known as 'the Flaggie' by local people, is a kind of island in the midst of high-rise and freeways at the north end of the city. The figs are spreading giants now, and the lawns roll down to abrupt drops where the hill was carved right away to perpendicular cliffs by nineteenth-century quarrying and twentieth-century road construction. There is that sense of quietness, the lofty airiness that high ground has. The city's huge towers of glass, concrete and steel are close by, but somehow distant too. The Observatory is now a museum, opened on special nights for stargazing. In nearby Millers Point, a tall concrete tower rises up from the remaining terrace housing, still watching

159

the shipping in the harbour and the river spread out below. And this is where the 'proud arch' of the Sydney Harbour Bridge springs over to the north shore, the traffic a distant roar.

Two hundred years ago, Flagstaff Hill, this lookout place, was already bald, stripped of its angophora, spotted gum, all gone for hearth fires and bread ovens and building. People had already started hacking into the great outcrops of wrinkled, grey-weathered sandstone to build better houses and storerooms. And the views to each compass point would have told of the kind of town Sydney was then: a maritime town, only a few kilometres long, the horizons to the south still clothed in bush. It was already a thriving commercial port town, a place that followed preindustrial patterns, divided into civil and military zones, but also roughly concentric circles of the different ranks of townsfolk. It was a dynamic town, emerging from the creative, constant tension between authority and people, control and independence, between commonality and possessive individualism.

OCEAN, HARBOUR, COASTS, RIVERS: MARITIME TOWN

Perhaps the most important vista from Flagstaff Hill was to the north-east, over the harbour to the Heads. On a clear day you might even glimpse what many early artists included in their paintings—the flagstaff and tower at South Head, marked as tiny but significant vertical lines on the horizon. When ships were seen out to sea, the flag was run up, spotted from Flagstaff Hill, and answered by more flags fluttering here above our heads. From the early years well into the 1840s the glimpse of these flags caused hysterical joy amongst the towns-folk. Sometimes a ship appeared and then vanished again for some days, and there was talk of nothing else. Ships brought news, new people, longed-for goods, the prospect of profits. Ships meant the colonists had not been forgotten. Ships were like friends, like living things, like lovers, greeted with 'rapture and exultation'. When the ships of the Third Fleet were sighted off the Heads, the officers could not contain themselves, but sprang into a boat and rowed out into the open ocean to meet them. Lieutenant Tench wrote of the ship *Supply*, 'we had learned to regard [her] as part of ourselves'.[2]

No wonder the houses on both sides of the cove mostly faced the water, rather than streets or one another. No wonder those who built on the higher parts of the Rocks boasted in real estate advertisements that their houses had good views to the Heads. This was a town whose eyes strained constantly to sea. The ocean was not simply a vast, imprisoning barrier, it was the link with Home and the world. In the earliest years, the colonists were so fearful of missing a ship, of a vessel sailing past Port Jackson oblivious to them, patrols of marines marched back to Botany Bay every week for eighteen months to keep watch. Officers had signs painted on 'some conspicuous rocks near the entrance', telling new arrivals 'that the settlement was made at Port Jackson'. In July they made more signs, 'boards of direction', and fixed them on Bare Island in case a ship should come into the north part of Botany Bay. Hunter and the surgeons went to South Head early in 1790 to raise a flagstaff and build a lookout house. Next to the flagstaff Phillip built a whited column to signal ships: we are here.[3]

Once the ship entered Port Jackson, the mad race was on to get to it. Flotillas of small boats streamed out from the cove and soon surrounded the hull.

The view over the town from the Rocks around 1808. The rear yards just below are occupied by Aboriginal people. (Mitchell Library, State Library of New South Wales)

There were shouted greetings and people clambered aboard, exchanging vital information well before the official parties arrived. Aboriginal people, who had once stolen the coloured flags from South Head, perhaps in the hope that with no signal there would be no more arrivals, soon established a tradition of greeting the ships too. Their swift nowie circled the vessels with the others, and the new arrivals stared in wonder at their nakedness. This tradition continued into the 1820s, when Bungaree, the elder and leader of the 'Sydney Tribe', climbed aboard the vessels to welcome newcomers to his country.[4]

Sydney was also a maritime town because it was founded and run by naval officers. Look at the early maps they made: the first priority was to survey the harbours, beginning with Captain John Hunter's careful plotting of the shorelines, shoals and bottoms of Port Jackson in January and February 1788. This survey was used by ships entering the harbour for many years.[5] By contrast when William Bradley drew the first map of the settlement in March, the high ridges, steep slopes and the Tank Stream valley might as well have been a pancake. No topographical features are shown at all. Yet the harbour is scattered with depth soundings, and every vessel is carefully drawn in position, right down to the anchors and ropes. The safety of ships was paramount, and despite the survey, Bradley was still worried about submerged rocks; the shape of the land was immaterial.[6] Convict Francis Fowkes' more naive yet stylised plan, drawn in April, has more detail about land-based activities and building locations, but these are inaccurate and the cove's topography is still absent. The ten ships, shown as pictures, are beautifully drawn, complete with furled sails, webs of rigging and fluttering flags.[7] Tench also wrote that the officers transferred methods of ship's reckoning to keep track of where they were on land, 'where one hill, and one tree is so like another'. Like the ocean, the seeming sameness made counting paces and drawing up traverse tables imperative to avoid 'fatal wanderings' and to know always 'how far you are from home'.[8]

The officers also brought ship-like ideas of authority, chains of command and rule by terror onshore with them. The British navy was founded on harsh conditions and brutal punishments for seamen. As well, a ship's safe passage through oceanic dangers was only possible when the crew worked tightly as one. Instant obedience to orders was paramount, since any slacking off or defiance put the

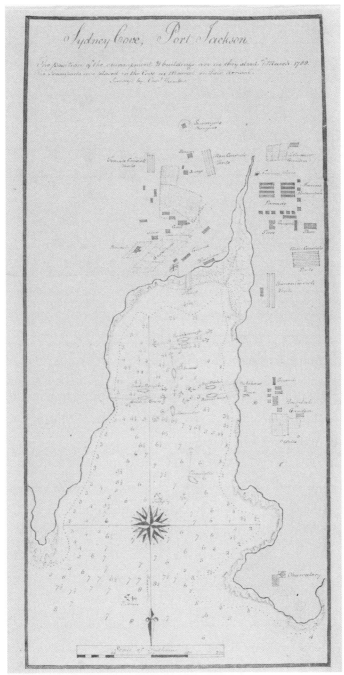

William Bradley, 'Sydney Cove Port Jackson 1 Mar 1788'. The buildings in the civil, convict and military zones are colour coded, but no topography is shown. By contrast the Cove is marked with depth soundings and the ships are accurately plotted, anchored and named. (Mitchell Library, State Library of New South Wales)

163

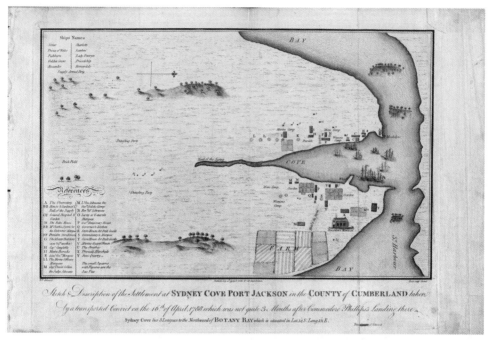

*Francis Fowkes, 'Sketch and description of the settlement at Sydney Cove Port Jackson . . .
16 April 1788'. (National Library of Australia)*

whole company in peril. Severe and humiliating punishments, including floggings, were instantly meted out to recalcitrant seamen. Mutinies were common;
if discovered, mutineers were hanged.[9]

Strong strands of this world view—that of the 'wooden world'—were
transferred onto land in Sydney Cove. The convicts were expected to work—
cheerfully!—like a ship's crew at clearing, building and cultivation. When
they did their 'duty', negotiated as task-work, they were for the main part left
to their own devices. Skilled men who were cooperative and showed promise
were placed in positions of authority. (Others were made overseers because the
marines sent out refused to supervise.) The days were marked out by the beating of the taptoo drums, and later the clanging of bells. Like sailors at sea,
convicts were given weekly rations (salt meat, flour, peas) similar to ships' rations,
precisely measured out, and in the earliest years cooking was done communally
at designated cooking places.

But the convicts seemed to have little experience of rules and regulations
of any kind, let alone the barked orders and instant punishments meted out

by naval officers. And Sydney Cove was not enclosed by wooden walls, or gaol walls; even the walls of the stores were flimsy. When convicts wandered into the bush, shirked work, bartered away their tools or stole food from one another or the stores, the officers were confounded and outraged at their unseamanlike insubordination.[10] They described them as incorrigible, lazy, stupid and improvident. Although the number of corporal punishments was 'surprisingly few', those who *were* caught and convicted of serious crimes— mostly thefts—suffered severe public floggings or were stranded on the small islands of Sydney Harbour. The officers brought judicial terror on shore from the ships and wasted no time demonstrating that thieves would hang in New South Wales. By May 1788 these demonstrations were still more gruesome. Thieves 'were flogged at the Tree' while another executed convict was 'hanging over their heads'. The purpose was plain: 'to strike these abandon'd wretches with Terror'. I suspect the authorities' impotence in the face of the convicts' de facto freedoms and movements, and the impossibility of imposing strict naval discipline, had much to do with this savagery.[11]

At the same time, as historian Alan Atkinson points out, a good number of the convicts *were* seamen, or otherwise bred to the sea. They too had knowledge of winds and currents, ports and ships' routes, and so they were valuable in the early colony. They became the fishermen, the crews of sea-going exploratory expeditions, the harbour police and the navigators of coastal and river vessels. But their seafaring skills and the brotherhood of sailors also meant they were the ones who had the best chance of escape, either by stowing away on labour-hungry ships, or by stealing boats and sailing down the harbour and out to sea. For them in particular, the colony was not at the ends of the earth, nor was it a place of no return. The ocean beckoned constantly.[12]

From Flagstaff Hill the view circling from north-east to west spanned the harbour dancing around Dawes Point into Cockle Bay (later Darling Harbour), and the river winding westwards. This is the Parramatta River, the head of the harbour, its islands and finger-like headlands still clothed in eucalypt forest, fringed with casuarinas at the edge of sandy beaches, and the little creeks lined with grey-green mangroves. Small bumboats and dinghies, rowed by tiny figures, made their way up- or downriver. From the early 1800s, enterprising emancipist

Ann Mash ran a passage boat service up to Parramatta, her vessel joining the small sailing boats laden with fruit and vegetables from the upriver farms, bound for the wharfside markets. Ferries would carry on the river trade and allow the expansion of waterside suburbs throughout the nineteenth century.[13]

Our eyes are so often fixed on the Australian outback as the source of history, identity and mythology, we forget that the earliest European colonists were maritime people. Water was their element and early Sydney was waterborne and waterbound. Water travel, even long roundabout voyages, was quicker and smoother than going by land. Boat- and ship-building flourished despite the original instructions and subsequent rules forbidding their construction. Many people, great and humble, owned boats and ships, and both Hunter and King allowed and even encouraged ship-building. Like the Eora, the Europeans rowed and sailed to visit friends, to do business, to fish and collect oysters, to fetch wood. By these small, everyday voyages and eventually through contact with the Eora, people came to know the configuration of the harbours and the rivers. Many worked and lived by the tides and currents and daylight hours more than by clocks and bells. Water linked the town to natural rhythms.

The sea and rivers offered work, food, mobility and the evasion of authority, but also constant danger and risks. Unlike the Eora, most European people, even sailors, could not swim. When their boats capsized in squalls, or they missed their footing and slipped, they often drowned. Those in liquor were especially vulnerable. The bodies were recovered, where possible, and laid on the wharves, or on their own beds. The drowned were lamented, the small boats on tossing waters watched uneasily.[14]

Sydney's oceanic location shaped the coming city economically, socially and physically, but it shaped mindsets and sensibilities too. Early Sydney, intended to be simple, harsh and unbending, was marked by a pervasive sense of fluidity and movement, of things not being fixed, the restless possibility of return, of escape in one form or another. As a penal colony, the ocean settlement had ironic outcomes. Twenty years later Commissioner Bigge, sent to review the colony, observed the constant passage of ships and thriving trade they attracted, all of which in turn increased the opportunities for convicts to escape. The fundamental problem, he concluded, was geographic. The seaboard position of Sydney raised 'discontent' in the minds of otherwise well-behaved convicts; the constant movements of the port kept longings and restlessness alive. These, he believed, were feelings and possibilities that only *true* remoteness 'might gradually suppress'. Sydney, by virtue of its maritime position, was not remote.[15]

LANDWARDS: PREINDUSTRIAL TOWN

From Flagstaff Hill, the arc running south to east took in the growing town. It lay in rough concentric bands, from the bustling centre along the mouth of the Tank Stream, through the rows and clusters of small houses of lesser folk, until it reached the fringelands, the ragged 'skirts of the town', before the receding blanket of forest grounds.

Imagining ourselves in this place in 1800, one fundamental point is immediately clear from the vanes of the windmills creaking over our heads: this is no modern industrialised settlement. The colony is powered by wind (the 'precarious element') and the muscles of humans and beasts, not by coal, steam and machines. There will be no steam power to turn millstones here for another decade and a half. Dickon's Steam Mill will be erected at the head of Cockle Bay to the south in 1815, but for now that land still terminates in the low, swampy ground where creeks from the Brickfields flow into this arm of the harbour.[16] The town's windmills became distinctive early landmarks, crowning the ridges east and west of the town until the late 1820s and early 1830s.[17]

Away to the south, too, banished to those fringes, was the burial ground, a collection of wooden crosses, earthen mounds, round-shouldered gravestones and one or two handsome tombs, set in the bush. It was opened in 1793 when the new barracks for the soldiers were built over or near the first burial ground. The hanging grounds were also set at the periphery, somewhere on the east side of the road to Parramatta opposite the burial ground. Hangings and burials were public events, accompanied by processions of townspeople. Jeering crowds followed the condemned in their rough cart, coffin at their feet; pallbearers and mourners walked southwards in solemn columns to inter the dead in the hard clay of the burial ground.[18]

Neither of these unpleasant sites would stay isolated for long because the town again crept up relentlessly to surround them: the long history of leapfrogging to the edges had begun. This second burial ground soon filled up, was closed, and a new ground, the Devonshire Street Cemetery, was opened in the bush at the site of present-day Central Railway Station. The hanging ground had been moved further west, too, also closer to the Brickfields. By the 1820s public executions were abandoned and hangings were hidden behind the walls of the gaol in George Street below the Rocks. But topography defeated the purpose: people gathered on the steep hill behind the gaol to view the jerking death-throes and jeer as before. If there was a last-minute reprieve, they went away disgruntled. The spot where they gathered in Cambridge Street became known as Gallows Hill.[19]

Closer by Flagstaff Hill to the south was the military zone, with its mean barracks and two rows of soldiers' houses lined up behind them, the makings of present-day Clarence and Kent streets. Although the majority of soldiers lived in huts among the convicts and mixed with them in the pubs and streets, these were nonetheless often edgy, tense encounters. Meanwhile, the military parts of the town were largely off-limits to convicts and ex-convicts and later citizens. It was soldiers' territory and those who dared set foot over the invisible boundary risked a bayonet in the guts. Their broad, dusty parade ground had migrated southwards from that first one in front of Lieutenant General Ross's house— the new one became today's Wynyard Square. Handsome new red-brick barracks rose on the southern edge from 1808–09.[20]

The old parade ground had been a public space, where petty offenders were set in the stocks. Sydney's climate meant it was also used as an outdoor reception area for officers from visiting ships: women in fashionable dresses and men in full dress uniform thronged and chatted. After the military camp moved south, it became a kind of irregular square, leading up a broad path to Church Hill (now the still-steep Grosvenor Street). On the north side, the old stores, in stepped formation, marked the boundary. Further up on the southern side stood a strange clock tower, the first stage of a new church, begun in 1800. The rubble-stone, hipped-roof body of the church was attached to this tower in 1802–04, whereupon the tower collapsed and was replaced by an equally odd round one. St Philip's, the first substantial church in the colony, thus had the 'rare distinction of having been built downwards'. It was rather squat and stubby, though light pouring through those large, arched, multi-paned windows must have bestowed a sense of grace inside. Visitors unkindly dubbed it 'the ugliest church in Christendom'. Nevertheless, for many decades, men and women came here to marry, and in the early years Protestants and Catholics alike climbed Church Hill to have their infants baptised.[21]

Across the High Street (now George Street) from Church Hill, the path which became Bridge Street led to the bridge over the Tank Stream. The bridge had symbolic as well as practical importance, for it linked the two sides of the cove, military zone with civil district. The first simple timber structure was improved with struts and handrails in 1792, and replaced with a stone arch bridge from 1803. This bridge took four years to build and then fell down. The builder tried to flee the colony. Bridge Street climbed the opposite slope, passing the solid brick houses of the senior civil servants to terminate at Government House, where another road turned sharply left and ran down to the government wharf.[22] Beyond was the rocky foreshore bushland of the Governor's Domain.

The governor's house had been extended and a verandah, a concession to the blasting sunshine, now shaded its rather gaunt facade. Mrs Anna Josepha King, the first governor's wife to live here after a series of vice-regal bachelors, added a long drawing room to the east, and then the shady verandah crept over its facade too. Mrs King brought polite gardening to Government House as well: the geometrically laid-out vegetable gardens, so much a feature of early paintings, had long been ploughed in for formally arranged ornamental shrubberies, fruit trees and rolling lawns.[23]

Beyond the governor's house, the Domain stretched around to Farm Cove, the haunt of those seeking cover for nefarious purposes, but also a kind of common, used for grazing and quarrying stone—the eastern equivalent of Flagstaff Hill and Cockle Bay. A few houses had risen untidily on leases here too. Out on the point, a square brick hut, built by Phillip for his friend and ally Bennelong in late 1790, had stood for some years, but by 1800 it was long gone.[24]

THE HEAD OF THE COVE: MERCANTILE TOWN

But look down to the cove, to the water's edge and the mouth of the stream: this is the town's heart. Already by 1800, the decrepit hospital and the gaol, which had been deliberately set outside the town, were surrounded by the brick and stone townhouses and warehouses of traders and merchants, though their wharves were still fairly primitive. The early merchant class vied for the irregularly shaped leases fronting the stream and, on a continent of such vastness, began to create more land by filling in its scoured and silted-up channel.[25]

Officers had already grown rich on the profits of imported foodstuffs, and rum, bought by the barrel, sold by the bottle. They had picked out the premium spots, bought them from existing occupants or leased from agreeable governors. While most concentrated on building genteel homes on their rural holdings, a few had built town villas in the most fashionable styles. Lieutenant William Kent built a fine Palladian mansion with symmetrical flanking wings and rectangular garden beds running down to the water. North towards Dawes Point, Ensign Nicholas Bayly's house had a French-style mansard roof lined with dormer windows to light the attic rooms. Further north again stood the capacious wharf and stone warehouses of a newcomer, the officers' rival in trade: the merchant Robert Campbell. He and his wife Sophia lived with their growing family and servants in the Indian-style verandahed bungalow which stood on the go-downs to Campbells Cove. White peacocks roamed their walled waterside gardens.[26]

But still more stylish and impressive were the houses built by the emancipist traders—men and women who had arrived as convicts. The elegant, flat-roofed Regency mansion of emancipist trader James Underwood faced the High Street, but its rear yard sidled down to the cove, and a turret gave access to the 'Captain's walk' on the roof, from which Underwood could watch the waters. Largest and most impressive of all, but more conservative in style, was the sandstone, brick and cedar-lined pile erected by emancipist traders and entrepreneurs Simeon and Mary Lord. Set on a key site beside the bridge in Bridge Street, their mansion rose to four storeys and became 'as much a Sydney institution as a residence'.[27] As in most of these early colonial houses, business and domestic life were thoroughly fused, for a counting house, auction room and offices occupied the ground floor, bedrooms and dressing rooms the middle floors, while fourteen small rooms on the top floor welcomed visiting sea-captains staying on shore with their goods. This house was draped with a two-storey verandah, and the Lords' front door was crowned with an enormous semi-circular fanlight. These audacious houses put the plain bulk of Government House in the shade, and they underscored how slow, short-lived and often inept was progress in public building.

This vista of Sydney Cove—the busy foreshore building—was celebrated in many paintings of early Sydney. Sometimes artists would add dramatic sunrises in the clear blue Sydney skies to express the rising glory of another British colony; meanwhile the foregrounds often showed Aboriginal people who represented the fast-receding past. Like Erasmus Darwin's poem and the Wedgwood medallion, these paintings seem simple and transparent, for they reveal a town on a predetermined historical trajectory. The evidence is, after all, right before our eyes, in the 'massy structures' and the 'embellish'd villas' as well as the boats being built and the ships in the harbour. There was joy and optimism in these pictures too, for they defied the image of Botany Bay as a place of tyranny, misery and isolation.

What the paintings cannot tell us is *how* these impressive houses, this jostle of private wharves, warehouses, outhouses, slipways and gardens, had been built. How had this thriving mercantile town sprung up in a settlement where shipping and trade had been expressly forbidden, and for which hard subsistence agriculture had been the plan? At least four founding factors, implicit in those original conditions of settlement, made the emergence of the port town inevitable: access to land and sea; access to money and monetary transactions; geographic position and existing trade routes; and the consumer culture of the convicts.

At first Phillip stuck to his Instructions and discouraged contact and commercial development. Even those early ships which did call for refreshment were deflected to other coves—Careening Cove, Neutral Bay—to keep them away from the Camp. Some days before he sailed away from Sydney forever, Phillip declared that all the land around Sydney, falling north of a line from the swampy head of Cockle Bay to the head of Woolloomooloo Cove, would remain crown land, with no leases or freehold grants ever to be permitted. Then he promptly broke his own rule by granting leases within this line to some officers, including Captain William Paterson, Lieutenant John Macarthur and Quartermaster Thomas Laycock. His successors followed suit, granting fixed-term leases to men and women who either wished to occupy and 'improve' land, or to those who had already done so, and were in residence. By 1807 there were 99 official leases, but, given that there were around 250 houses in Sydney, it is clear that the majority were occupied—as well as avidly advertised, bought and sold—without a lease.[28]

While no money had been sent with the First Fleet, people nevertheless wanted to acquire goods and services in Sydney, and so a lively and relatively sophisticated monetary system soon emerged, combining barter, a riotous variety of specie brought privately in pockets and purses, credit, and promissory notes. Phillip recognised this unruly, hidden internal trade only gradually, and eventually tried to regulate it (as well as the lively trade in stolen goods, of course) by establishing public markets where 'anyone, including convicts was permitted to trade in articles and produce legitimately owned'.[29] Public markets were first opened at Parramatta, and then in Sydney near the Hospital Wharf at the foot of the Rocks. This was probably an informal market space earlier; now it became a great gathering place. On market days the riverboats unloaded produce in the early hours, butchers and bakers sold their wares, townspeople mingled with settlers from the inland, miscreants were punished in the stocks. Today George Street near Circular Quay West still widens in memory of that first marketplace.[30]

Another key factor was that military officers alone had access to sterling for foreign exchange, through their pay. Seeing the hungry market and the opportunities for profit, they used their salaries to buy up cargoes of imported goods.[31] In 1792 the officers commissioned the corpulent Captain Raven of the *Britannia* to import a speculative consignment. When he returned with their goods, they celebrated by hoisting his vast bulk into a chair and parading him joyfully around the town, with the military band playing 'He Comes, He Comes, the Hero Comes'.[32]

Since codes of honour forbade officers from retailing, they wholesaled to smaller dealers, often soldiers, convict servants or convict mistresses. These smaller players became the myriad dealers who in turn sold the goods to the populace from the front rooms of their houses. The officers' monopoly on sterling made them rich in these early years, though their grip would be loosened by the arrival of private merchants like Robert Campbell from India, and by the rising emancipist traders who petitioned successfully to be allowed to buy from the ships themselves. Soon the officers' wealth and their houses were matched by the equally entrepreneurial emancipists: the Lords, Kables and Underwoods were joined by Thomas and Mary Reibey, Sarah and Edward Wills, and Australia's 'first millionaires', Samuel and Rosetta Terry. Of the 127 ship-owners in Sydney between 1800 and 1821, over 100 were either emancipists, descended from convicts, or otherwise related to convicts.[33]

The ambitiousness of the mansions rising from the shorelines in the early 1800s surprised and amazed visitors expecting to see a gaol town, and they still surprise and amaze us. The fancy roofs, fashionable filigree balconies and elegant fanlights, the pretentiousness of flanking wings: it all seems delightfully out of kilter. These were unambiguous statements of aspiration and taste, but they were also about frenetic activity, 'an absolute inability to relax', which had its origins in the humble social backgrounds and urgent ambitions of people stalked by social and economic insecurity.[34] As we have seen, the officers of the New South Wales Corps were mainly from modest backgrounds, and for them the colony was primarily a place to advance their fortunes. Impressive houses helped create the sense of having made it; they were also good investments. The emancipist traders were perhaps still more driven, and built still more elaborate houses. They had come from similarly lowly origins, and had endured the stigma of conviction and transportation. Many in early Sydney would struggle hard for social acceptance to match their wealth. They built up their businesses, bought fine clothes and carriages, educated their children, donated to good causes, only to have their status promptly repudiated by prejudice, hardening social boundaries and the demonisation of convictism, which darkened over the decades.[35]

Sydney's third founding factor was its geographic position. Rather than remaining a remote, shunned speck, or merely a refreshment port for ships, Sydney Cove was soon drawn into the existing global network of shipping routes, despite the fact that trade and shipping were both forbidden, and in any case illegal because of the East India Company's monopoly. The market was tested with the arrival of the Second Fleet in 1790. Sydney's people watched in horror as the human cargo of sick and dying prisoners crawled ashore, but then they flocked to inspect the goods the ships' masters had brought: 'articles of grocery, glass, millinery, perfumery and stationery'. By 1802 visiting Frenchman François Péron described 'this assemblage of grand operations, this constant movement of shipping' with wonder and admiration.[36]

The British government's decision to supply the colony from India in 1790 also opened up ocean links with places besides England. Soon private ships from Bombay and Calcutta sailed for Sydney Cove with speculative cargoes of live-stock, sugar, meat and rum (and convicts fleeing Sydney were setting themselves up in enclaves in Calcutta). In 1794 two ships from the United States arrived with food and spirits. By the first decade of the nineteenth century, ships from the Cape of Good Hope, India, the United States, China, as well as the expanding and lucrative southern whale fisheries arrived in Sydney at the rate of between 23 and 33 a year, some making two or three visits per year. Each brought an ever-increasing array of consumer goods to 'gratify the inhabitants', including 'many elegant articles of dress from Bond-street', from ribbons and bobbing to telescopes and musical instruments, from Tahitian pork to toys, jewellery and candy, and tens of thousands of gallons of rum. Soon observers were remark-ing the intense materialism of this society—that spirit of ruthless, never-ceasing entrepreneurialism, the abiding interest in making money.[37]

So those audacious houses were built on a hunger for food and spirits, and desire for decencies and luxuries. And they were built on sealing. The Sydney traders were soon in desperate need of a staple: a local product, a raw material for exchange and to send away on their ships. When the hopes for the Norfolk Island resources quickly evaporated (the flax was unworkable and pine spars too shaky and rotten for masts), the Cumberland Plain became a great experimental ground for various crops, from grapevines to tobacco and the first stirrings of the wool industry.[38]

But the first real solution came, once more, from the sea. On his voyage to Sydney with the officers' cargo in 1792, Captain Raven left a party of men in Dusky Bay in New Zealand to slaughter and skin seals. They killed 4500 of the creatures, easy prey, and a valuable haul in skins, fur and oil. The wreck of Robert Campbell's first ship, the *Sydney Cove*, in Bass Strait revealed that the islands there were also home to colonies of elephant seals and fur seals. From 1800, parties of men recruited in Sydney signed up with traders for sealing voyages. They were left on these bleak islands for months to endlessly club and skin seals—sometimes the men were completely abandoned. Land and sea were awash with blood and the shorelines bristled with thousands of bleaching skeletons.[39]

In the years 1801–07, up to a third of the ships visiting Sydney were involved in sealing, or the more capital-intensive whaling, and by 1806 almost 200 000 seals had been slaughtered by the Sydney sealers. The fur went to make English-men's beaver hats and clothing in China, the skin was used for shoes, and the clear, scentless oil rendered from their bodies lubricated machines, burned in street lamps, and went into commercially produced foodstuffs. The exploitation was so thorough and so ruthless, that the once-myriad, teeming seal colonies were eventually hunted out, some never to recover.[40]

But the fourth, and perhaps most fundamental factor in the emergence of the port town was the invisible baggage brought by the convicts: consumer culture. Contrary to the visions of British administrators, the convicts were not simply bodies and minds which could be remoulded into a deferential agricultural popu-lation, any more than the colonial earth was a blank canvas. Neither were they pathetic, beast-like creatures, the poorest of England's abject poor. The majority were working people of the lower orders, a large proportion from the burgeoning urban centres of England: they were urban people. Despite Phillip's attempt to shift the focus to Parramatta and the farming settlements, the initiative of the Hawkesbury farmers, and the fact that most work available was rural work, many convicts preferred Sydney. It was safer, more secure and more convivial than the lonely, isolated farms. In Sydney there was a softer life, or the chance of one. There was work, there were neighbourhoods, taverns and the motley population of working people from different parts of England and Ireland, black Africans, Jews, Aborigines, visiting sailors from the Pacific Islands, India and America. Men or women could be close to the excitement and opportunities of the port, the company of friends, the chance of finding a partner and the pleasures of popular culture.

One of the best-known letters from early Sydney was written by an anony-mous convict woman from the Camp in November 1788. The wording and style suggests either a woman of some education, or a heavily improving editorial hand, for she writes of wanting to 'acquaint' her audience 'with our disconsolate situation in this solitary waste of creation':

> ... the inconvenience suffered for want of shelter, bedding, &c are not to be imagined by any stranger. However we now have two streets, if four rows of the most miserable huts you can possibly conceive of deserve that name. Windows have they none ... no glass could be spared; so that lattices of twigs are made by our people to supply their place ... as for the distresses of the women, they are past description, as they are deprived of tea and other things they were indulged in in the voyage by the seamen, and as they are all totally unprovided with clothes, those who have young children are quite wretched.[41]

This letter is often cited as evidence of the horrors of the early 'gaol town'. Yet what is this writer saying? Her complaints concern the *lack of material things* and the uncomfortable nature of pioneering. She bemoans the crudeness of latticed shutters, the absence of window glass, sugar and clothing—print gowns, proper hats and shoes—and the constant women's lament, the absence of tea. Women especially suffer deprivation, she says, for they are accustomed to such comforts.

If the colony had been founded a hundred years earlier, these would not have been her complaints: the notion of comfortable, weatherproof houses and the practice of tea-drinking were at that stage unknown to working people. But by the latter half of the eighteenth century, they were familiar with ideas of comfort and fashion and with the fruits of the commercial revolution and eighteenth-century global trade. A revolution of things had spread mass-produced commodities like glass, tea, sugar, printed cotton, gilt buttons, ceramic dinner sets, glass tumblers and a thousand other objects into the lives, and thus the expectations and self-definition, of the lower orders. Tea is the classic example: transformed from a luxury enjoyed only by the wealthy, to a necessity consumed by all but the poorest, its absence was sorely felt by women in New South Wales. 'I never have known anything of punishment since I have been here', convict Margaret Catchpole assured her aunt, 'only that I cannot get no tea'.[42]

And even in that first year, when Phillip was doggedly setting up the earliest farms, our anonymous female letter-writer was already sanguine about sea-borne commerce, commodities and urban opportunities. 'We are comforted with the hopes of a supply of tea from China', she wrote, 'and flattered with getting riches when the settlement is complete'. By 1799 William Noah assured his relatives back in Shropshire that 'the Town Dayly Increases in Wealth & in a few Year more it will be inhabited by a Vast number of individual'. So, even among some of the convicts themselves in those earliest days, Sydney was seen in Erasmus Darwin's terms, rather than as a subsistence agricultural colony, let alone a gaol. And they were an instant and eager market for much-missed consumer goods. The archaeology of early convict houses reveals that those who managed to establish households much preferred the smooth, coloured ceramic dishes, bowls, cups and saucers brought in the ships from England and China, over the clumsy, primitive wooden ware sent out for their use.[43]

'A PLACE SO VERY LIKE MY OWN NATIVE HOME': THE CONVICTS' TOWN

What kind of town did the convicts make? The spectre of their squalid, beast-like existence in early Sydney is deeply engraved in the historical imagination. Convicts remain forever suffering and starving in the crude huts, sleeping on dirt, hemmed in by the hostile bush and tyrannised by the lash and the ball and chain as well as hostile, spear-carrying Aboriginal warriors.[44]

But the voices of at least some of the convicts themselves beg to differ. New arrivals sailing into Sydney Harbour were astonished to find Sydney such a flourishing, English-looking place.[45] They said they felt at home, and were mightily relieved after the rigours of the voyage and the horror stories they had heard about 'Botany Bay'. Margaret Catchpole found Sydney a familiar sight in 1801, just as it had been a 'long and wished-for country' to William Noah in 1799. We might imagine Catchpole, looking intently from the ship's deck, eyes tracing around the blocky shapes of the warehouses and stores, and the smaller houses behind clustered on the Rocks right up to Flagstaff Hill. This vista 'put me in very good spirits', she wrote, for it was 'a place so very like my own native home', and 'a great deal more like England than I ever expected to have seen'.[46] In just twelve years, a familiar-looking place had been created on the other side of the globe.

Not surprisingly, some convicts never accepted banishment from their native place and regarded New South Wales only as a prison and a place of misery. There were desperate mutinies on the transports en route, while escape attempts from the colony were very common, particularly among the newly arrived and those with life sentences. Convicts also resisted their fate in New South Wales by refusing to work hard, or at all, and occasionally by burning down public buildings: the early gaols at Sydney and Parramatta went up in flames and the first church ended in ashes too. The arrival of Irish convicts brought a series of insurrectionary plots and a daring rebellion. Many came from the ranks of the dispossessed, the poor, the propertyless; a good number were sailors, some were black Africans, ex-slaves, Irish rebels. Given the centuries-long history and traditions of insurrection, mutiny, revolt and piracy against slavery, tyranny and capitalism among just such peoples, the question to be wondered at is not why they resisted in these ways, but why the colony was not burned to the ground, or taken in violent uprising?[47]

The view down the rocky slopes from Flagstaff Hill reveals one reason: Sydney Cove was a canvas for the convicts themselves. They took this 'outskirts' land and inscribed their town as deeply in earth, stone and wood as did the elite with their plans and mansions. Out of direct surveillance, under the cover of 'industrious-ness', they created a place welcoming to newcomers because it had been built and occupied in ways which were familiar to working people. Ironically, some convicts then became property-owners: shopkeepers, publicans and household-ers who called for constables, feared their servants would rob them, sided with the elite officers against Bligh, and joined the volunteer militia to put down Irish uprisings. Yet the Rocks nevertheless also remained an enclave, to some extent outside the surveillance of authorities, a refuge for runaways, a gathering place for thieves.

So while merchants and traders clustered on the premium sites at the water's edge, the surrounding zones in the west and to the south of the cove belonged to the restless ranks below them. Convict and emancipist shop-keepers, tradesmen and women, and publicans vied for the land closest to the commercial heart, or the houses on the heights where they could watch the harbour out to the Heads. Humbler folk—labourers, washerwomen, seamstresses, hairdressers, watermen—lived or lodged in the streets between and beyond. On the east side where the land was more level, regular rows of houses ran north–south beyond the civil precinct, each separate with yards front and back. During the first decade of the nineteenth century, some small manufacturing concerns were established here: breweries in Castlereagh Street and Upper Pitt Street and a boot and shoe factory, using kangaroo leather, in Pitt Street. Some tanneries and soap-and-candle establishments, always found together, opened too—these are likely to have been associated with slaughter-yards and butchers' shops. In Pitt Street and at the Brickfields, potteries were turning out clay pipes and the plain, chunky, pale orange earthenware jars and dishes we commonly find on early colonial archaeological sites today. These were very much preindustrial-style concerns, for they were small scale, mixed into the urban fabric and often integrated a number of different operations on the same site. Sydney's manufacturing history would remain tied to natural and rural products—grains, livestock, clay and timber—for many decades.[48]

Over on the Rocks, some of the rows and jumbles of early wattle-and-daub huts still stood in the 1800s (at least one was still in use in the 1820s!), some threatening to buckle under the weight of salmon-coloured clay roof tiles burnt at the Brickfields. These houses were not very stout, but neither were they as flimsy and ephemeral as so often described. Rather than symbols of pitifully crude origins, they were simply practical buildings constructed along traditional lines. Later, they became a bit of a local joke: the *Sydney Gazette* referred to them as 'ancient colonial architecture'.[49]

By the end of the eighteenth century the early huts were being overlaid by more substantial houses of rendered rubble stone and sawn weatherboards. They remained vernacular in style, without a skerrick of architectural pretension, the foundations laid down by eye, the walls raised in stone quarried nearby, the mortar mixed with shells from Aboriginal middens, or the bones of birds and small animals. Their face-like facades—central doorway and flanking windows—still commonly looked out over the water, and they had that same blunt, stubby look as the earlier huts, with their hipped roofs of cascading casuarina shingles and cropped eaves. The better houses now boasted the luxury of glazed multi-paned windows and proper hearths and chimneys of stone or brick, doors which swung on iron hinges, and locks and keys to make people and property secure. As families, businesses and custom grew, extra rooms and skillions, bread ovens and forges were added at the back and sides, wherever there was space. With rising land values, houses were increasingly semi-detached and some were double-storeyed.

From above, the yards on the Rocks looked like crazy paving: irregular shapes fitted together at odd angles on the rocky slopes. These yards were really extensions of the households, practical rather than ornamental spaces, where food was grown, water collected, trades carried on, soap made, fowls killed and plucked and household waste (including human waste) disposed of. Some yards were green with vegetables (peas, beans, cabbages) and fruit trees, particularly peach trees, privet for hedges, exotic weeds like medic and probably also regenerating native plants. Deep wells cut through the sandstone often stood on one side of a central path in the frontyard—a bounty for households, but a constant danger to small children.[50]

There was no sharp spatial division between work and home either. The yards housed stonemasons' tools, blacksmiths' forges, water cisterns needed by the bakers. They were used as slaughteryards, with pens and sheds, and piles of guts, heads and bones. The (mainly non-legal) boundaries of these yards were increasingly marked by ubiquitous pointed paling fences: signs of occupation and claims to ownership, but also practical in keeping out the packs of dogs and semi-feral pigs which roamed the town. Smells of baking and slaughtering and sometimes distilling wafted over and through fences. Seeds floated, alighted, sprouted. At night laughter and singing erupted from the pubs and houses where people sat drinking together, and fiddles scraped out music for dancing.

Those who opened hotels and businesses in their houses hung out shingles with pictures on them—a punchbowl with ladles announced the long, low Punchbowl Hotel, for example. Though literacy rates were relatively high compared to England, the population here was nevertheless only partly literate. So information and news was visual, oral and aural, carried by flags and pictures, word of mouth and sound. The town crier shouted the latest decrees from Government House, the constable bellowed the hours of the night from dark streets. People were called to their labour by the beating of the taptoo drums, to church services by the bells at St Philip's, to the shoreline and arriving ships by the boatswain blowing his 'long wishful call' across the water. Sights and sounds, seen and heard in common, made the town too. In 1803 the colony's first newspaper, the *Sydney Gazette*, appeared (and immediately became a collector's item). Editor George Howe's humorous asides, pseudo-pompous word-play and puns were perfect for reading aloud in the hotels. As we have seen, the paper connected Sydney and the plain, gave the town a sense of itself, and its place in the world.[51]

Private development flourished, but public amenities remained fairly limited and crude. Tanks cut by government order into sandstone to create reservoirs on the Tank Stream served the eastern side, but were too far away to be of much use to those on the west. Householders there organised their own water supply, drainage and waste disposal, a tradition carried on for decades. The paths of the walking town could scarcely be called streets—they billowed dust in the hot summer months and became bogs in the wet, despite government attempts to mobilise the population into carting broken bricks to make them, or to assign householders sections to keep in order. On the west side, the paths were inaccessible to vehicles, jumping up and falling steeply with topography and rugged sandstone outcrops. Kent Street was still so rocky and uneven in the early 1840s that carriages could not pass at the northern end.[52]

Sydney began with little sense of public civic responsibility: energy was focused upon those private yards and houses. The public spaces, where people gathered, were full of movement, exchange and performance rather than neatness and order. Joseph Foveaux raged about the 'total disregard of everything tending to public utility and ornament' among the townsfolk. In many cases governors who attempted environmental conservation and urban decorum fought a losing battle: the Tank Stream grew thick and brown with pollutants despite the orders; the paling fence around the burial ground, which should have protected the graves from wandering stock, was repeatedly stolen for firewood.[53]

How should we see this town, which was to some a place of banishment, squalor and tyranny, to others home-like and reassuring, and to still others rich in potential for trade, land and profit? Our vistas from Flagstaff Hill reveal that the lineaments of the modern city—street patterns, domestic spaces, the reshaping of the foreshores, and an intricate mercantile capitalist network—were laid down in these early years. But the town growing below the windmills and the Fort looked pretty much like late seventeenth-century New York. Sydney was founded much later than the American city, when commercial capitalism and consumer culture had already begun to transform some English cities forever, yet physically it followed those older, preindustrial patterns of urban evolution: the wealthy and powerful clustered at the centre, surrounded by the next bands, the houses of tradespeople and shopkeepers, and the dwellings of poorer householders, with the wilder, disorderly badlands beyond.[54] Commons were set aside and much land was unenclosed, open to all. The single houses set in large, self-sufficient yards are sometimes mistaken for a prototype of the modern Australian suburb, but this form too is typical of the early stages of towns and cities. True suburbs did not appear in Sydney until the 1820s.[55]

Nourished on modern modes of trade and consumption, rife with entrepreneurialism and exploitation of the natural environment, Sydney was a New World colony. Yet, because it was built largely by ordinary people, its physical patterns had more in common with crooked, organic medieval towns than with polite Georgian planning, let alone emerging industrialised urban patterns. In the modern industrial cities of England, the wealthy and powerful would abandon the centres to the dense-packed homes of the working class, and fashion for themselves new suburban worlds in sylvan settings at the fringes. Sydney retained the jostling, mixed neighbourhoods of a mercantile town until the 1870s. With its 'ancient architecture', its 'mossy roofs' and its easygoing pace, Sydney would be seen by newcomers as an 'old-fashioned town' with the 'appearance of an old establishment' for decades, a little bit of older England sprouting on New World shores.[56]

'PROPERTY IS TOO SACRED TO BE TAKEN AWAY . . . MERELY AT THE WILL OF A GOVERNOR'[57]

Already, the origins of Sydney are looking complex and wonderfully contrary: a place meant to be a simple agrarian penal colony, grew instead as a port, and looked constantly to sea. It was a town of modern mercantile capitalism which followed old urban patterns; a town where governors had extraordinary powers but could not control urban development, and where a constant dialogue of negotiation between people and authority was played out. Into this mix, add the discontinuities of governors and civil officers leaving and arriving, and, conversely, the persistent idea of the colony as *tabula rasa*, of Sydney as a blank canvas, despite the buildings, gardens and streets spreading over the slopes and down the cove, and the human meanings already invested in the place.

The erosion of official control had stemmed partly from the contradiction (and impracticality) in Phillip's mandate: the unresolved difference between a place of banishment and a colony, when in the original plan they had been one and the same. But prisoners who became settlers, who made families, and built houses which were clearly homes, were not all reborn as farmers in New South Wales, and nor could they be treated as prisoners. In Sydney they were house-holders, townsmen and women. Although governors were supposed to maintain strict control, they were also bound by the English reverence for private property rights and the duty to reward initiative and respect investment, particularly in a place like Sydney. If mixing one's labour with land—building, fencing, cultivat-ing—gave rights to that land, then private property, even in the shape of 'naked possession', *was* sacred. Both leaseholders and those in permissive occupancy knew this. They defended their houses and yards with all the vigour of freehold property-owners. The discourse linking land, labour, liberty and rights which justified the dispossession of the Eora had deeply ironic outcomes.

The assemblage of huts, houses and mansions, the yards, wells, gardens and outbuildings which greeted new arrivals represented a conundrum for gover-nors. On one hand private development was identical to the public interest in a new colony, not separate from it. The settlement was rising through the efforts of people of different ranks. Robert Campbell knew this when, requesting permis-sion to land vast quantities of spirits, he pointed out the boon his trading ventures had bestowed in both economic and aesthetic terms. He had ended the officers' monopolies (and had a grateful memorial from Sydney consumers to prove it) and pioneered the sealing industry. His warehouses provided employment for many 'labourers and mechanicks' and his shady bungalow was 'ornamental to the harbour'. Economic development and urban enhancement went hand in hand. Lieutenant Colonel Foveaux drove home the point to his superiors some years later. It was obvious: colonists 'who had speculated with such confidence and spirit upon the precarious tenure of a lease' deserved both encouragement and reward, for it was they who set an example to others and were responsible for the 'extension and ornament of the town'.[58]

But private property and investment meant that the authority of government to regulate the town's growth, to make effective laws for the public good and the urban environment, was severely curtailed. Streets that had grown from rough footpaths could not easily be realigned now that houses and business concerns had solidified them. Sydney's long history of piecemeal attempts at planning and improvement in a town of bustling private enterprise was already well established at the close of the eighteenth century.

Whatever their initial plans, the governors who followed Phillip quickly realised the economic and social realities of the emerging town and tried to impose order and authority upon it. They invariably reported on finding the town in disarray (Hunter, for example, wrote of a town 'in decay' and its people 'very disorderly' with 'frequent disgraceful breaches of the peace'), a suitable prelude, of course, to catalogues of their own improvements.[59] Their tools for urban order included counting, lists and numbers, patrols and passes, and endless rules regulating movement and activities. Some of these regulations were about controlling bodies and movement, others tried to protect water, land, wildlife and vegetation from destruction and pollution. They were only ever partly effective; all were eroded by time and geography, and all had to be repeated over and over again. Hunter reinforced constables' patrols in the different town quarters and authorised the arrest of loiterers and people travelling without passes to the outlying settlements.[60]

Upon landing, Governor King (1800–05) found he did not even know how many people there were in the colony, there being 'no general list whatever of the inhabitants', and ordered that musters be held.[61] He established Registers of Assignments (now known as the Old Registers, the joy of colonial historians) to notarise land and other agreements in an attempt to mitigate the chaos of conflicting claims based on verbal contracts. He had the houses of Sydney renumbered, imposing some external order on an arrangement that had grown along the pragmatic, organic lines of need, taste and topography and the search for profit. Numbering was also a way of control, a means for authorities to find their way around and to locate people. It worked where houses stood in rows; but failed comically where the houses were scattered hugger-mugger over broken ground and where new houses were constantly being built.[62]

Governor King's own background was commercial and urban, and he was committed to encouraging the commercial development of the port town. Like Hunter, he clashed with the officers (most notably John Macarthur, who tried to organise a military boycott of Government House: no-one to entertain in Anna Josepha's new drawing room), but he allowed traders and merchants to build bigger ships in their yards and encouraged the exploratory voyages in search of seals, even though such activities were still strictly illegal. When merchant Campbell's audacious shipment of oils and skins was impounded in London in 1805 because it flagrantly defied the East India Company's monopoly on trade, King asked Sir Joseph Banks himself to intercede. Banks—and indeed the British government—seemed only vaguely aware of the way Sydney had developed, but the ensuing debate did result, eventually, in the legitimising of New South Wales as a trading port within the Navigation Act.[63] King's policies and measures to build up agriculture and assist the struggling small farmers on the plain were also impressive: he resurrected public farming, and introduced the plough on the public farms, imported and purchased stock and distributed animals among the settlers, and set aside the commons for public use. In 1803 he was lauded in a New Year's address from the Hawkesbury settlers 'for his anti-monopoly stance, the maintained wheat price, the premiums in livestock awarded to encourage agriculture'.[64] Given his energetic and hands-on policies, and the way he, unlike Phillip, grasped the here-and-now of the colony's economic development and social conditions, King deserves to be better recognised for his advocacy and contribution to the growing town and the rural settlements. However, his governorship would be eclipsed by Lachlan Macquarie's powerful self-conscious narratives of 'building' and 'regulating' the town, and of himself as the 'father' of the colony.

William Bligh, who succeeded King, seemed by contrast determinedly oblivious to the politics and economics of the existing town. He stepped ashore in

August 1806, long preceded of course by the famous story of the mutiny on the *Bounty*. News of Bligh's astonishing survival and longboat voyage from Tofua (Tonga) to Timor had caused a sensation in Sydney (and inspired similar escapes!), but his reputation for unbending 'tyranny', and for 'bad language' was also common knowledge. Leaseholders and permissive occupants watched the arrival of every new governor nervously, but Bligh must have made them doubly so.[65]

Bligh's short, volatile period in office marked one last attempt to reinstate the original agrarian vision in New South Wales, and ended in rebellion—the so-called 'Rum Rebellion'. Only rum was not as vital a factor as land, and who controlled it. Bligh wanted to sweep away what had grown in Sydney and to reclaim the town for the crown. He was a rules man. His vision turned on a simple, moral/environmental duality of rural and urban, too, for he believed unswervingly in the virtues of the small settlers, the 'plain sensible men' farming in the outlying settlements. Conversely, he saw the Sydney traders, particularly the emancipists, as vicious, the 'sharks preying on merchants and ships captains'. He made strenuous efforts to help and protect the settlers of the Hawkesbury and Parramatta, especially after devastating floods washed the riverside farms and livestock away in 1806. Although many continued nevertheless to live in poverty, and although he had little time for emancipists who he said 'wallowed in vice', Bligh championed the small farmers as 'the industrious settler-farmers who feed us'. They in turn wrote, signed and presented long addresses which praised his 'arduous, just, determined and salutary government over us'.[66]

But the ideal of a paternalistic governor presiding over a race of humble, loyal farmers could never work if Sydney continued to grow as a commercial town. Bligh decided that, in strictly legal terms, the town belonged to no-one but the crown, and he took it upon himself to restore official control over the urban environment. He resurrected Phillip's abstract, commerce-free plans and orders, apparently unaware that Phillip himself had abandoned and also breached them.[67] Despite the material imprint, the busy trading interests, the lives made and remade in this place, in Bligh's eyes it was still an empty land.

So, besides antagonising the officers and men of the New South Wales Corps, as well as the wealthy emancipist traders, Bligh set about undoing Sydney. He issued orders for householders who were living on the Governor's Domain to quit so their houses could be pulled down, though for them compensation was offered and the deadline extended. He was much less conciliatory with the more prominent, powerful and wealthy leaseholders. He threatened John Macarthur, George Johnston, Garnham Blaxcell and several others, arguing that their leases interfered with the public amenity of the town: the church, the gaol, the lumber yard, the parade, the space for the government boat crews. Government functions were to take priority over private. He lashed out at men like emancipist trader Simeon Lord, forbidding him to build on land he had purchased, threatening to pull down any unauthorised structures. He also had Lord, Underwood and Kable heavily fined and gaoled for a month, merely for daring to request that they be permitted to tranship goods without landing them. Bligh charged at them all, using violent, intemperate and humiliating language. Those who were natural rivals or enemies soon became allies against him. They easily turned his bad language back on him at the later court hearings, for it perfectly fitted the rhetoric of tyranny and monstrous interference with liberty and private property.[68]

On 26 January 1808, twenty years to the day since the founding of the colony, 300 officers and soldiers marched up Bridge Street to Government House in the evening sunlight, flags flying and the regimental band playing 'The British Grenadiers'. They searched the house and eventually found and arrested Bligh, deposed him and declared themselves the new rulers, with Major George Johnston as acting governor. That night the town blazed with 'illumination, bonfires, burning effigies, roasting sheep', fires to celebrate the deliverance of Sydney's property-holders. At the Green Hills, Bligh was burnt in effigy at the gallows. Propertyless soldiers claimed later that the celebrations were theatre, orchestrated by the officers, whom they saw parading arm in arm, silhouetted by the bonfires' flames. The officers supplied the soldiers with wine and brandy, 'which cause general intoxication'. The rebels and their supporters used grog and threats of withdrawing convict labour to extract Hawkesbury settlers' signatures on an address which 'recanted praise of Bligh and hailed Johnston as deliverer'.[69] For the next twelve months, Bligh remained under house arrest at Government

House, pacing, fuming and plotting his revenge, refusing to budge. As in the *Bounty* mutiny, he never reflected upon his own role in the events, only the treachery of others.[70]

Historian Tim Bonyhady has argued that this rebellion was Sydney's first major loss of environmental planning control, the action of a cartel of a few privileged officers bent on their own profits, at the expense of good government and wise urban management. Or was it, as the rebels argued, generally supported by the townspeople, who 'trembled for the safety of their property, their liberty, their lives'?[71] It is difficult to cast Bligh in the role of urban environmental crusader because his vision was so profoundly anti-urban. His actions were not for the benefit of the town's people, but for the reassertion of authority: it was a 'unilateral attempt to return . . . Sydney, bustling and anarchically developing, to a pristine state'.[72] This was to be, once more, a government town, ruled from above, merely servicing the port for the benefit of the agrarian hinterland. In fact, the leaseholders whom Bligh actually threatened *were* a minority of occupants in Sydney—they only made up a seventh of the total number of householders, and very likely less.[73] But the threats and demolitions reverberated among the hundreds who were permissive occupants, from those in 'naked possession' of flourishing businesses and solid homes right down to the residents of the meanest huts. Anxiety over tenure must have been still greater among them. So Macarthur's melodramatic rhetoric about trembling townsfolk had little to do with urban well-being either. But he was touching upon what those who had scrabbled for a foothold in Sydney perceived as vital to their interests: the right to the land they had taken and the homes they had built, the right to make a decent material life, and, for some, the freedom to pursue wealth.

Chapter 7

—◆◆◆◆◆—

LANDSCAPE ARTISTS: THE MACQUARIES IN SYDNEY

Fireworks and bonfires blazed against Sydney's night sky once more to welcome Lachlan Macquarie, Bligh's replacement. The new governor sailed into Port Jackson with his wife Elizabeth aboard the *Dromedary* in late December 1809. Macquarie was accompanied by his own regiment, the 73rd, sent out to replace the Rum Corps, as the NSW Corp was known. On the day he first came ashore, New Year's Day 1810, Macquarie had his soldiers line the streets up to Government House, their volleys of gunfire answered by the guns on Dawes Point. Later, in the gathering darkness, the windows of Sydney's grander houses shone with candlelight and brilliantly coloured pictures, 'transparencies' painted on light fabric and lit from behind.[1] On the highest street of the Rocks, near Flagstaff Hill, wealthy trader Garnham Blaxcell's house proclaimed his fervent loyalty: his windows framed a glowing portrait of the King, a painting of a ship encircled with ears of wheat, representing 'Commerce and Agriculture' harmoniously united, as well as other symbols of 'Love and Unanimity'. But appearances were deceiving: these gleaming visual declarations were a ruse. Blaxcell had supported the rebels in Bligh's overthrow. Now the rebel administrators were bound for England, to be tried for treason, and Sydney people felt their rights to the properties they occupied were again in jeopardy.[2]

Macquarie served as governor for twelve years, from 1810 to 1822, far longer than any of his predecessors. Along with Arthur Phillip, he is the best known of the colonial governors. In the search for national history, origins and father-figures over the twentieth century, Macquarie morphed from 'The Last of the Tyrants' to the 'Father of Australia'. Autocratic behaviour became wisdom; obsession with building became a vision of nationhood. 'What William the Conqueror was in English history', wrote architectural historian Max Freeland grandly in 1968, 'Lachlan Macquarie was in Australian'.[3] Although the 'Age of Macquarie' is associated with enlightened social attitudes, improved morals and economic expansion, it is *building*—bricks and mortar—which lies at the heart of this nationalist recasting of Macquarie as the heroic figure who transformed the colony 'from a penal camp to a young nation of the future'. He is said to have taken a mean, ramshackle, disorderly camp and transformed it into an orderly town, a town endowed with fine, worthy buildings which lent permanence, confidence and purpose.[4]

Macquarie's aura is reinforced by the fact that some of the buildings he commissioned have survived the ravages of subsequent city-making: a precious legacy. From Flagstaff Hill today, you can still glimpse the imprint of the Age of Macquarie if you know where to look. Just south of the freeway that coils deep through Gondwanan sandstone towards the Sydney Harbour Bridge, the National Trust headquarters sits like a pretty iced cake above the roar of bridge traffic. Its exterior shell is a Romanesque 1840s school building with large arched windows, but inside Macquarie's military hospital is intact. The keystone over the arched fanlight still bears the inscription 1815, and the inner rooms retain the great multi-paned sash windows which once opened onto airy columned verandahs.

The handsome military hospital, set above the barracks on the west side of town, is still mirrored by the grand colonnades of Macquarie's great public hospital in Macquarie Street, to the east. Two wings of this hospital also survive: one served for decades as the Mint, and has recently been reverently restored as the Historic Houses Trust headquarters. The other became Parliament House, its two additional wings (1843 and 1856) neatly illustrating the stages of establishment of democratic government, the great story of how and when men got the vote in New South Wales.

This mirror-image pattern—as though the town were an inkblot, folded in half along the seam of the Tank Stream—was echoed in other Macquarie projects as well. By 1822, when the Macquaries set sail again for England, the extensive red-brick barracks for the soldiers rose on the east side, while the barracks for convicts—also brick, and still extant—stood on the west. St Philip's to the west was left as it was, but the elegant, steepled St James appeared on the east, as refined and elegant as St Philip's was homely and crouching. Even Macquarie's fortifications were doubles: small crenellated battlements adorned the batteries on both Dawes Point and Bennelong Point.[5] It seems the Macquaries saw the town as an *artefact*, an object in itself: something which could be refashioned according to their visions of art, architecture and landscape.

If you stand between Hyde Park Barracks and St James, their pedimented facades facing one another so precisely across Queens Square and Macquarie Street, the meaning of Macquarie's urban geometry is still clear. Here is the combined authority of church and state—and polite architecture is clearly on their side. By contrast, almost nothing remains of that earlier Sydney, the one he and Elizabeth found in late 1809, above ground at least. The Commissariat, an ambitious structure built of solid stone to deter thieves, was commenced in late 1809 by Lieutenant Governor Foveaux. It was completed under Macquarie's direction, rising to four massive storeys, arranged in three wings around a stone wharf studded with great iron rings. The Commissariat guarded the west side of Circular Quay for 130 years but was torn down in 1939 for the construction of the Maritime Services Board building (now the Museum of Contemporary Art).[6] St Philip's church was demolished much earlier, in 1854, for a less interesting gothic church (itself now marooned between gritty freeways). Today a plaque in shady Lang Park alone remembers the old church. First Government House, the living space and headquarters of the first nine governors, was pulled down, unlamented, in the 1840s—though you can see some of the foundations under glass in the windswept modern forecourt of the Museum of Sydney. A new Government House—an exact copy of a baronial castle, designed by an Englishman who never set foot in Australia—was built in the Domain to the east. One by one the early merchants' mansions, with their offices, stores and wharves, were demolished, mostly for wharf expansion, road widening, public buildings and commercial development. Simeon Lord's costly four-storey pile survived until 1908. The only major standing relic of those first twenty years are the venerable stone walls of Fort Phillip, on Flagstaff Hill, commenced in 1804 but never completed.[7] So the heritage of early Sydney is skewed to the Macquarie years: in the absence of the structures of the first twenty years, his buildings serve as tangible symbols of the nation's birthplace. In many academic and popular histories, Macquarie's Sydney is where the nation's history 'really' began.

The legend of the Macquarie era was also ably nourished by Macquarie himself. He and Elizabeth were certainly conscious of their roles as the bringers of taste, order and civility to the wilds of Botany Bay, though their visions were of course colonial and imperial rather than national. Macquarie's journals and despatches were perfect for the narrative. They brimmed with great symbolic gestures, they were tailored for immortality.[8] Perhaps his best-known and most quoted piece of writing is this passage:

> I found the colony barely emerging from infantile imbecility, and suffering from various privations and disabilities; the country impenetrable beyond 40 miles from Sydney; Agriculture in a yet languishing state; commerce in its early dawn; Revenue unknown; threatened by famine; distracted by faction; the public buildings in a state of dilapidation and mouldering to decay; the few Roads and Bridges, formerly constructed, rendered almost impassable; the population in general depressed by poverty; no public credit nor private confidence; the morals of the great mass of the population in the lowest state of debasement, and religious worship almost totally neglected.[9]

Powerful, uncompromising words, which have become received wisdom. Few question the notion that Sydney before Macquarie was, indeed, ephemeral, imbecile and crude, a 'difficult infant'. But this passage was in fact written in 1822, as part of Macquarie's long, vigorous defence of his record as governor, and of his astonishing building program, when he was under attack for misman-agement and wasting public funds. When he arrived in Sydney Harbour in

1809, Macquarie's response was quite the opposite. He reported the colony as being in a 'state of perfect Tranquillity', albeit anxious about his arrival. He praised Lieutenant Governor Foveaux, who had 'promoted the interests of the colony', and reported 'Public Works and every other Department of Government under his control in a state of Great Improvement, and conducted with a degree of regularity, economy and industry that reflect great credit to him'. True, there were not enough barracks to keep the soldiers housed and under control, the older public buildings needed replacement and there was a food shortage as a result of the 1809 floods. But Macquarie proposed to build upon what had already been well established.[10] His early despatches do not depict a squalid colony languishing in hopeless poverty and brutality, because this was not the case. That image was invented twelve years later by a man fighting desperately to save his reputation.

The Macquaries were great *improvers*. Energetic and ambitious, their rollcall of improvements included establishing new towns and extending old ones, building turnpike roads to the interior and the coast, issuing endless orders and regulations for moral and civic improvement, security and control. But best of all, they loved building. The scale and ambition of their ideas became evident soon after they arrived, with a fashionable new villa for Judge Ellis Bent, and the commencement of a vast new hospital in 1811. With the arrival of trained architects—most notably the convict Francis Greenway—and rising numbers of convicts after 1815, the Macquaries' ideas and plans grew more elaborate, their determination to reshape both urban and natural environments on a grand scale increasingly obsessive. Sydney was their focus, their crowning achievement. The city became an artefact of the way the Macquaries saw the world, and themselves in it.

But how *did* they see the world? What had shaped their visions and aspirations? Lachlan Macquarie, like many men who went to New South Wales, was born into humble circumstances. He was the son of a poor tenant farmer on the Isle of Ulva in the Inner Hebrides, Scotland. His mother was probably illiterate. He volunteered for the army at fifteen, became an ensign at sixteen and rose through the ranks to lieutenant colonel, seeing service all over the world, in the United States, Canada, the West Indies and India, and in war

with France in Egypt in 1801. At 42 he was wealthy through his first marriage (his first wife died in 1796) and through the prizes of war, and lived 'grandly—
and expensively—in London'. Elizabeth Campbell, whom he married in 1807,
was the daughter of his second cousin. She too had been born into modest
circumstances, spent most of her life in Appin, in Scotland, but she was well
connected, well educated, capable and self-sufficient. Both of them were
familiar with the language of fashionable architecture and landscape design
as a true marker of social standing, taste and gentility. Elizabeth had already
impressed Lachlan with her redesign of the grounds at Airds House in Argyll,
with its winding paths and glimpses of the loch. Theirs was a modern marriage,
of mutual admiration and affection, the felicitous union of equal but different
qualities in the genteel husband and wife.[11]

One wonders when the realisation that New South Wales could be their canvas
occurred to the Macquaries. When they embarked it was in their minds a place of
disorder, immorality and rebellion: Lachlan Macquarie was specifically charged
with remedying these defects.[12] But when they encountered Surgeon John Harris

*'Much higher style than expected': Elizabeth Macquarie was impressed by a picture of John
Harris' mansion, Ultimo. Note the arcadian setting and the spotted deer. (Mitchell Library,
State Library of New South Wales)*

at Cape Town, en route to New South Wales, Harris proudly displayed a portrait of his house, the two-storey Ultimo, rising in the arcadian riverside landscape, complete with that essential of landed opulence, a herd of spotted deer. Elizabeth was most surprised. Ultimo, she wrote, was 'altogether in a much higher style than anything we would have expected to find in the new world'.[13] Did it set her wondering? Perhaps their first sight of Port Jackson excited their imaginations. The wild, ruined cliffs and rocky foreshores, the tumbling woodlands, the glimpses of azure bays: here, surely were perfect picturesque settings, only waiting for romantic architectural embellishments. Elizabeth, gazing from the deck, may have seen her turrets and crenellated ramparts rising in the hazy harbour air.[14]

And in Sydney Cove, the massy warehouses, the wharves, those waterfront mansions in their lush gardens and the solid foundations of the new Commissariat may well have surprised them too. Perhaps they were even taken aback. It was obvious that this was no pathetic camp full of thieves and rebel soldiers, but a port town, winking with potential for profit and improvement. If the natural environments of Sydney Harbour inspired gothick visions, the architecture of emotion and imagination, the urban environment of the town proper demanded the opposite style: the polite, rational, classically inspired architecture of England's modern cities. Here pediments and loggias, pilasters and round-headed windows could be successfully transplanted: the architecture of professional men based on fixed rules and proportions, which signified at once authority, superior taste and gentility.

These, of course, were two different ways of seeing, and refashioning, the environment; and they were also two different views of history. The romantic gothick buildings were set into receptive natural landscapes: on the rocky shorelines, or glimpsed amidst embowering trees. Buildings and nature complemented one another perfectly. Nature could be appreciated for its beauty, while history was a reservoir of ruined castles and abbeys, a medley of nostalgic and patriotic styles with which to imagine and play, to indulge intuition, and inspire the spirit. The picturesque eye sliced through the environment, it 'saw nature as a series of potential landscape paintings', different vistas unfolding from vantage points along a journey. This is the way Lachlan and Elizabeth would view the natural and rural landscapes of New South Wales.[15]

Urbane classical architecture was just the opposite: it sought to triumph over a hostile environment, transforming its waywardness into 'civilisation' through mathematical order and 'rational' control. After all, towns, with their grand buildings, infrastructure, commerce and arts, marked the highest stage of civilisation, the furthest point from wilderness and barbarism. So to raise such buildings was to *make* history, to demonstrate great 'historical forces' at work, to fulfil the course of empire, and the prophecies of Erasmus Darwin for Sydney Cove.[16] One viewed such structures head-on, their facades were impressive and immovable. They filled the picture, while nature was insignificant, a remnant of the past, a mere backdrop.

In both these visions of future Sydney—gothick and classical—aesthetic sensibilities were not merely decorative superficialities: they were drivers. To the Macquaries, Sydney had the potential to become a fit subject for landscape art.

But to begin with, the town had to be brought to order, or at least some semblance of it. Macquarie was instructed to revoke the leases and grants made by the rebel government, and to make grants 'if you see not any objection'.[17] Accordingly, he cancelled them all, including the great flood of last-minute town leases made by Foveaux, and demanded that each leaseholder and grantee submit a petition stating why they were entitled to their land. An avalanche of petitions arrived at Government House. From the clamour of obsequious assurances emerged the unanimous view: never in the history of the British Empire had there been such a paragon colony as this. Could there possibly have been a more law-abiding, sober, hardworking, family-loving population anywhere? Satisfied that government control was seen to be restored, and with an official paper trail to prove it, Macquarie ratified all the town leases.[18] It was, of course, official gloss on what had long been material fact. Some of these townspeople had been in residence as permissive occupants for twenty years, their children grown to youths and adults in the houses and yards. In the following decades, after a long, tortuous process of sorting out ownership and tenure, these leaseholders eventually became freeholders. Macquarie's acquiescence to de facto occupation rights finally fixed Sydney as a town of private property holders, with commonly understood rights to do as they pleased upon their own land.[19] The environmental impacts for the future city would be profound.

Macquarie also had specific orders to secure the food supply, encourage marriage, education and morality, suppress the trade in spirits, and prevent convict women from living 'indiscriminately, first in one family, then in another'. He was to end public farming, but to foster *rural* development by establishing new towns, with streets, allotments, spaces for town halls, churches and glebe lands. And so he did, as we have seen.[20] In November 1810 he established Liverpool to service the newly opened forest lands of the south-west. But, ironically, like all his predecessors, Macquarie had no official instructions on urban development in Sydney at all. Nothing on commerce, trade or finance, no word on planning or building. In fact his official orders still carried the original injunction forbidding contact with other ports and ship-building. Though the importation of goods was acknowledged (and problematic), the bustling town of Sydney seems to have remained in an official blind spot, for the British authorities were still fixed upon transportation, agriculture and cost-saving.[21]

Nevertheless, beginning in January 1810, Sydney's people were bombarded with orders and rules concerning their everyday life, printed in the *Gazette* and bawled out by a town crier 'so none may pretend ignorance of them'. The streets were a particular focus. Their irregular, organic patterns had grown up from footpaths and 'desire lines', dog-legging around houses, yards and creeks. The new governor found them insufferable. Wayward crookedness was akin to social and moral disorder. Macquarie was a grid man. He tried to straighten, widen and level the streets, make them turn at right angles. Some older houses were demolished to allow for straightening and regulating streets and their owners compensated (though no records were kept of who these people were).[22] He banned wandering pigs, goats and dogs. He appointed more constables to patrol the streets at night. He bestowed regal and vice-regal names upon the crooked paths and dusty rows—George, Charlotte, Cumberland, Gloucester, Cambridge—erected finger-boards and ordered everyone to use the new names. In the east, a procession of governors' names graced the 'streets': Hunter and King were parallel cross-streets and Phillip Street ran next to the broad, newly laid-out Macquarie Street, for Macquarie had already begun to memorialise both himself and Phillip, and to associate himself with the first governor. Bligh Street was the shortest.[23]

The creation of Macquarie Place, a new, fashionably elegant square in Bridge Street opposite Government House, demonstrates the way Macquarie reversed Bligh's tactics. Bligh had threatened everyone by attacking the most influential. Macquarie did the opposite: he demolished the dwellings of humbler people and flattered the wealthy traders (Simeon Lord, Mary Reibey and Andrew Thompson) by incorporating their town houses as the new square's northern boundary.[24]

Macquarie Place itself was emblematic of what the Macquaries were trying to do in Sydney. With its dwarf walls and railings, it mimicked the genteel urban squares of England's fashionable provincial resorts—cities like Bristol, Cheltenham, and most famous of all, Bath. But such elegant squares demanded stylish stuccoed villas. The existing judge advocate's house was solid brick and only five years old, but it was oafishly unfashionable and simply would not do. The new judge, Ellis Bent, was permitted funds, materials and a contract to sell spirits in order to build an expensive new house. The design, with its Regency verandah and flanking rounded wings, came straight from a pattern book which Elizabeth Macquarie had brought with her, Edward Gyfford's *Design for Elegant Cottages and Small Villas*. Despite a huge cost blowout on this extravagant house, another

Macquarie Place in 1829, showing the elegant, expensive pattern-book houses of the judge advocate and the colonial secretary. (Mitchell Library, State Library of New South Wales)

was begun next door in 1813 for the colonial secretary, the design again taken from Gyfford's book.[25]

But the other side of the town, the Rocks, was largely untameable and remained ungentrified. Commissioner Bigge, sent to investigate the colony and Macquarie's administration in 1819, concluded it was 'chiefly inhabited by the most profligate and depraved part of the population', the one exception to the general 'tranquillity of the streets' in Sydney. Surveyor Meehan told Bigge in 1819 that regularity could not be imposed without 'removing several Houses and a Great Part of the Enclosures'.[26] To start with, there was that great difference between official orders and the 'lived town'. Some people used the new street names, others ignored them and continued to use the common local parlance, saying they lived 'on the Rocks' or 'behind the Windmill'.

Archaeological evidence and early maps suggest that, where they could, surveyors simply drew lines between existing buildings on the Rocks rather than laying out new, straight streets. Subsequent buildings, increasingly conjoined, mostly obeyed these lines and were built along a uniform frontage. But those older houses jutted at odd angles into the streets and lanes, which grew up around them, as a tree will eventually grow around something embedded in its trunk. They were the anchor points, they still marked a town innocent of geometry. The houses, shops, stables and stores built by Rocks people in the 1810s and even the 1820s looked much like those of earlier years too: solid, unpretentious with hipped roofs and simple symmetrical facades set out like faces, with window-eyes and door-mouths. Vernacular building continued here while desperately fashionable architecture sprouted in the east.[27]

So it can be said that, rather than completely remaking the town, the Macquaries actually presided over two Sydneys: the older, preindustrial areas of the Rocks and Cockle Bay, which remained resolutely unrespectable, and the more regular, genteel and fashionable zones to the east and south, as well as the military zone to the west. These were the new foci of the town, a modern ring around the old core. To the south, where the land was more level, the long rows of houses and yards were regulated into the grid now so familiar to Sydneysiders. This grid could be replicated and extended almost indefinitely over the horizon; and it was, right out over the old hanging grounds and the scattered village of the Brickfields area, and then beyond, towards Redfern. Macquarie also moved the wharfside markets from the west side of Sydney Cove to a less congested site to the south, connected by Market Street to a new wharf on Cockle Bay. The new markets stood next to the once-distant and noisome cemetery.

But the real showcase areas were the ridges east and west, that extraordinary mirror-image development, which reinforced the original civil/military divide. The town's horizons, crowned with the great hospitals and barracks, were a painter's delight. These earliest of the Macquaries' public buildings were in the 'international style' of the British military, of colonies and empire. The long, colonnaded facades of the Rum Hospital (so named by the colonists because Macquarie paid for it by giving the builders a monopoly on the importation of spirits for three years) might as well have been in Madras or Port Royal in the West Indies: these were the familiar styles of Lachlan Macquarie's tour of duty.[28] They were so different in scale and style from the blunt, bare facades of the older public buildings.

The Macquaries were clearly conscious of this contrast, and deliberately played upon it. Elizabeth's 1810 sketch of the earlier St John's Church in Parramatta, for example, shows the 'odd barn', as she called it, as crude, dilapidated and, worst of all, old-fashioned (it was very similar to St Philip's in Sydney). It had in fact been an object of some pride to the earlier colonists—Collins described it as 'handsome' and listed it among Hunter's many achievements. But in Elizabeth's picture the tower had collapsed, the belfry was crooked, the picket fence decrepit. Her new St John's featured pointed windows and ambitious twin towers, a direct replica of the celebrated ruined Saxon church of Reculvers in Kent, of which she had magazine prints and a watercolour. Elizabeth's 'after' sketch of St John's in 1819 celebrates the transformation she had wrought: the steeples reach heavenwards, and the churchyard is enclosed with a neat stone fence. The new St John's also ornamented the view from Government House at Parramatta. Art became landscape, landscape became art. Visions materialised, and these newly minted buildings and landscapes were then the subjects of picturesque paintings. John Watts, the architect of the church, and John Lewin, Macquarie's emancipist artist, painted views of the new church and Government House at Parramatta.[29]

The Macquaries' building plans were given a fillip by the arrival of Francis Greenway, architect, painter and convicted forger, in 1814. Greenway was born into modest circumstances, the son of a long-established family of West Country stonemasons and builders. His early life and training is obscure, but there is good evidence he worked under the illustrious John Nash. He and his brothers set up in business in Bristol and Greenway designed the handsome Assembly Rooms there. But for some reason he was not credited with this work, and another ill-judged housing project ended in bankruptcy. In 1813 Greenway forged a contract, was arrested, tried, sentenced to hang, reprieved and given a seven-year sentence of transportation to New South Wales.[30]

There is something suspiciously *organised* about both the crime and the manner in which Greenway embarked on his voyage of exile. The forgery attempt was so stupid that his exposure and trial were inevitable; and even if it had succeeded, the proceeds would have gone to his creditors, from whose debts he had already been released. 'The singularity of this forgery', reported a baffled Bristol journalist, 'is that it is impossible to trace the motive which could have actuated the prisoner to commit it'.[31] In Bristol prison, Greenway did not lament and rot, but painted pictures, in oils, showing the prisoners at leisure and holding a mock trial. He depicted himself dressed in superior clothing, a cut above the rest—much as the 'gentlemen' convicts sent to New South Wales all thought of themselves. When he boarded the transport *General Hewitt*, he carried with him a copy of Chambers' *Treatise on Civil Architecture*, a portfolio of his work and a letter of recommendation from none other than Arthur Phillip himself.[32]

During the voyage Greenway most likely met fellow passengers John Harris and Captain Piper, both interested in building elegant colonial mansions; he appears to have secured a contract to extend Harris' old Ultimo mansion even before he reached Sydney. Greenway's wife Mary and their children sailed out to join him the following year. Historians have judged his crime as the result of stress, or an irrational act committed on the spur of the moment, spawned by bitterness at the way he had been treated. But perhaps Francis Greenway committed forgery deliberately, in order to start again in New South Wales.[33]

Like other skilled and educated convicts, Greenway lost no time establishing his practice in the colony. Upon landing, he immediately sent the governor his portfolio of designs. Lachlan and Elizabeth must have been excited by these, and by the prospect of employing a trained architect at a bargain price. With a real architect at their service they could move beyond pattern-book copying and military designs. Greenway was asked to copy a design for a courthouse. Was he humbly flattered? No. He responded by criticising the design severely and giving the governor a lecture on taste. Talented, well trained and ambitious, but also impossibly opinionated, peevish and tactless, Greenway was playing the deadly politics-of-taste card. It could easily have backfired, but it worked. After some evident admonition from the governor, and a few months of private work which demonstrated his abilities, he was appointed in 1816 as Civil Architect on a salary of 3 shillings a day. His first job was to survey the newly completed General Hospital, Macquarie's pride and joy. He proclaimed it not only structurally defective but of inferior and ill-educated design: the columns were all wrong.[34]

But in Greenway the Macquaries found a conduit for their tastes and their expanding ambitions. His skills were versatile. For the towns he designed the urbane, restrained, squared-off buildings for which he is best known: domed markets in Sydney, stores for Parramatta, and classical square-towered churches and severe pedimented rectories for the country towns. In Sydney, a building which started as a courthouse became St James' church, while a new school became the Supreme Court. Greenway also designed the brick barracks finally built to house Sydney's male convicts. But Elizabeth's gothick fantasies materialised too, spun over the forts at Dawes and Bennelong points at the harbour's edge—though whether their guns could actually inflict any damage on an enemy was highly doubtful. The tollkeeper on the new turnpike road to Parramatta rejoiced in a medieval lodge, complete with pointed windows, crockets and turrets. A baronial castle rose too, bowered in the sylvan setting of the Domain. But this building was a 'palace for horses'—government stables meant as a prelude to an even more splendid palace for the governor, drawn up by Greenway but stymied by Lord Bathurst in 1817.[35]

Greenway's output was impressive and his architecture raised the standards of both design and building techniques in Sydney. The town's new face reflected his training, and a whole spectrum of fashionable English styles. But the work for which he is most famous—the neo-classical public buildings

John Rae, 'Supreme Court and St James, from Elizabeth Street', 1842, showing Hyde Park on the right. (Dixson Galleries, State Library of New South Wales)

of brick and sandstone—echoed the sensible, straightforward architecture of the major provincial cities of England, specifically Greenway's own city, the booming port of Bristol. These cities had emerged or grown rapidly in the eighteenth century in the wake of commercialisation and early industrialisation, and they had themselves only recently been transformed. The new, increasingly wealthy middle classes of Bristol, Bath, Edinburgh and Cheltenham had copied the polite culture of metropolitan London in everything from language to elegant parks to theatres, and in architecture too, for they 'built new towns imitating neo-classicism and abandoning vernacular architecture and materials'.[36]

What we are looking at in Greenway's buildings is this same process of urban mimicry, working itself out on the other side of the globe over the 1810s and

TOLL GATE, AND THE NEW POOR HOUSE ON THE PARRAMATTA ROAD.

Gothick tollgates at the edge of the town near Brickfield Hill, a later sketch showing the 'new Poor House' (Benevolent Asylum) and the forests and farmlands of Chippendale, beyond the town limits. (Mitchell Library, State Library of New South Wales)

1820s. His architecture is admired for its abstract and transcendent values: balance, harmony and restraint. Yet this is chimera. These buildings were not above messy, profane reality at all, nor innocent of social and political purpose. In the English cities this was the architecture of social distinction and exclusion, a means by which the new middle classes might firmly set themselves apart, culturally and spatially, from the lower orders. In Sydney, as we shall see, it served not only to make a town suitable for genteel folk, but the purposes of urban social and political control and exclusion too.[37]

As the decade progressed, Macquarie increasingly employed the language of colonial improvement and the 'need' for public works to give himself a *carte blanche* for ever more fanciful or ambitious buildings, including some delightfully crazy ornamentalism. These were the 'fugacious toys' (as Macquarie's enemies called them), the romantic and picturesque 'eye-catchers' set fashionably in various urban and natural landscapes, just as an estate-owner might indulge her whims and demonstrate taste by building follies. In Macquarie Place a miniature Greek obelisk served as a milestone, the purported starting point for the roads radiating south and west. A water pump in the soldiers' parade ground was dressed up as a classical Greek temple. Ships carrying banished felons to the coalmines at Newcastle were guided by a light shining from a Chinese pagoda, set high on the rocky headland. A darling domed pigeon house, probably designed by Greenway, peeped out from the treetops of the Domain.[38]

For South Head, where the flagstaff and Phillip's white tower had signalled ships, Greenway designed a beautiful classical lighthouse. It rose on the highest ground some way back from the point, the great oil lamps set in parabolic reflectors and turned by clockwork throwing an arm of light 35 kilometres out to sea. Macquarie named it 'Macquarie Tower'. Inside, Greenway intended to install a tribute to the winds, a frieze 'on which will be carved the four winds in *alto relievo*, distributing their different good and evil qualities from their drapery, as they appear to fly around the tower'.[39] One wonders how the southerly buster would have been portrayed—or the burning north-westerlies.

But the South Head lighthouse had another important function besides guiding ships: it was a 'prospect tower'. After enjoying the drive along South Head Road, ladies and gentlemen could climb the tower and gasp at the views along the awesome cliffs, out to sea and back along the sandy road to town. The building included a domed room 'for the governor's pleasure', a geometric staircase and decorative enclosing fence, but it failed to provide enough room for troops stationed at South Head. From here, Macquarie's emancipist artist Joseph Lycett completed the circle by painting the view back to the town, carefully including Macquarie's barracks, hospitals, forts and castle-stables, all set on the shores of the beautiful winding harbour. In subsequent decades artists were often drawn to South Head to paint the elegant lighthouse in its wild romantic setting.[40]

So South Head, that early, lonely, vital contact point, was now a landscape of pleasure and leisure. The Macquaries were first to create such landscapes and they used public funds to do it. They formalised and marked out places for recreation as separate space from building, industry and work and protected them from exploitation and development. Hyde Park was the rather lofty name bestowed upon the area the townsfolk had referred to as the Common—an unprepossessing edge-place where people played cricket, raced horses, turned their stock loose to graze, and collected firewood. Brick and pottery carts trundled across it from the Brickfields to the town. In 1810, Macquarie declared it the colony's first official racecourse and defined the boundaries, and his regiment promptly organised the colony's first government-sanctioned race meeting. This three-day carnival was a resounding success, attended by all ranks of colonists, including 'the fashion and beauty of the colony', and featuring races for all kinds of horses, from thoroughbreds to hacks. But rather than fostering decorous public behaviour, it was also an opportunity for a three-day carnival of drinking, gambling and general carousing.[41]

The carts and stock were banned from Hyde Park, and the brickmakers forbidden to dig out clay from the southern end. But this was no park in the modern sense—early Sydney people would not recognise today's garden beds, lawns, statuary and fountains, nor the grand rows of figs, their lacy leaves touching in the vast green tunnel over the main avenue. There was 'not a tree upon it', no plantings at all, and the space remained bare and open well into the 1840s, when one less-than-enchanted English observer described it as 'merely a large piece of brown land fenced in'. Locals regarded it with great affection. Hyde Park, unencumbered by shrubs and trees and utterly unlovely, remained public open space for walking, races, exercise and games, the most popular by far being cricket. It was also a place where people of different ranks continued to mingle.[42]

Perhaps still more celebrated is the Macquaries' remaking of the old Domain, spreading over the two headlands embracing Farm Cove (the present-day Botanic Gardens and Domain—the city's green lungs), but also all the area around Government House in Bridge Street, down to the foreshore and back to Bent Street. Unlike Hyde Park, this was meant as a space for passive recreation, for rational and genteel pleasures of the respectable classes, not the boisterous games of the people. So this landscape demanded certain activities and behaviour. Macquarie banished signs of industry by ordering the removal of a windmill and other buildings which had sprouted there.[43]

Elizabeth, having built a copy of her ancestral home in Scotland as the Female Orphan School at Parramatta, and remodelled the gardens at Government House, now turned her considerable skills to the Domain. The landscape, thickened with vegetation perhaps in the absence of Aboriginal burning, was partly reshaped with artistic groves of trees and shrubs. Sinuous pathways led out to the point at Yurong, where a seat carved in sandstone became

'Merely a large piece of brown land, fenced in': the unlovely but much loved Hyde Park. Artist John Rae painted a series of views of the park in 1842, delighting in the many games and pastimes people enjoyed there. This lively scene of the southern end (near Liverpool Street) shows games of cricket and football underway, one man spruiking to a group on the right, and a crowd gathered around what appears to be a cockfight. The lightly sketched seated group are possibly Aboriginal women. Otherwise, this is clearly men's space, for white women remain outside the fence—the two walking inside are chaperoned by a man and stay well away from the games. (Dixson Galleries, State Library of New South Wales)

'Mrs Macquarie's Chair'. Here, away from urban noise and vice, nature in all her grandeur could be contemplated.

The Domain's deliberate separateness from the town marked a new consciousness of nature separate from the urban in Sydney. This was underscored by a 10-foot stone wall running from Sydney Cove at Government House, along the back yards of the Rum Hospital and the barracks, all the way down to the stream running into Woolloomooloo Bay. Lined by an avenue of English oaks, this wall was intended to keep out ne'er-do-wells, thieves and lovers. Fashionable promenading, fresh sea breezes and harbour views unfolding among the wild rocks

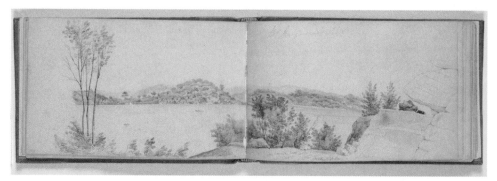

Emily Anne Manning, 'Mrs Macquarie's Seat', 1837. (Mitchell Library, State Library of New South Wales)

on the foreshore and slopes were now, seemingly, open to all, though the area directly in front of Government House was marked 'Pleasure Ground'—and some sources suggest that the Macquaries considered the Domain as a whole to be their own private pleasure ground.[44]

Urbane churches, pompous hospitals, huge military barracks, ornamental objects and landscapes of leisure: all of these fell under Macquarie's official heading of 'public works', his greatest claim to fame and immortality. Most were paid for with public funds of one kind or another, all were justified as being of 'great Benefit' to 'the Public at large' and many were very expensive.[45] But what was the connection between these structures, spaces and places and the 'common good'? If Hyde Park was for 'the people', for whom were the polite and romantic landscapes intended? How did the hospitals and barracks benefit Sydney's people? How were they received?

'A FINE, LIVELY TOWN': THE BROOKS FAMILY IN SYDNEY

Young Jane Maria Brooks and her family were well pleased with Macquarie's Sydney. Jane wrote of her father, Captain Richard Brooks, as a 'fine navigator and sailor' despite having gone to sea at the age of ten and possessing 'not much book learning'. Brooks was also utterly ruthless and possessed of a keen eye for getting on. He had been visiting Sydney with speculative cargoes and transports since 1802 and it was his negligence and his overcrowding of the convicts on the *Atlas* to make room for his own personal cargo which resulted in the high convict death rate on that voyage. By 1813 Brooks had decided to settle, as he baldly stated, 'to make a good fortune by supplying the ships with stores'. In short, he was an adventurer. But he arrived to discover that Macquarie had resumed the land he had purchased on Farm Cove and added it to the Domain. Unlike Bligh, though, Macquarie's manner was patriarchal, genial and conciliatory. He offered Brooks land of equal extent in Cockle Bay as compensation, and Brooks accepted it. The family and their servants moved into a stone cottage set in a garden on the corner of Hunter and Pitt Streets, acquired a pew in St Philip's and no doubt benefited from the rising numbers of convicts available for assignment after 1815.[46]

Jane's mother, Christiana Brooks, found society 'small but agreeable', and Mrs Macquarie a 'fine sensible woman'. Sydney was, on the whole, a 'fine, lively town'. The children after their daily studies went out on walks with their governess, and a favourite walk was Macquarie's 'raised terrace walk under the Government Domain Wall'. They strolled out to the seat cut in the rock and up a steep flight of steps to the heights above Woolloomooloo. Fixed in Jane's memory was the sight of Aboriginal people still living there, in the Domain, 'in their little gunyahs made of bushes'. The governess kept the Brooks children well away. And on early morning strolls along the waterfront, Jane remembered seeing 'the very tiny canoes with a gin fishing in them, quite alone, sometimes with a streak of smoke from it, and we supposed she was cooking'. Twenty-five years after the invasion, Eora women were still fishing in Warrane.

Newcomers of acceptable social background, with the right manners, clothes, tastes and aspirations, were eagerly welcomed into the fine homes which had spread out along the harbour, the headlands and hinterland. The Brooks were invited to John Palmer's Woolloomooloo residence, on the other side of the Domain, now occupied by Acting Commissary Allen. Guests passed through the iron gates and along the stone palisade and groves of Norfolk Island pines and kurrajong trees to the classically inspired house. At Dr Harris' Ultimo (extended by Francis Greenway for Mrs Harris, much to Elizabeth Macquarie's envy and Dr Harris' apparent dismay) the children picnicked happily under spreading lillypilly trees and ate their mildly sour pink fruit. They walked through the bush out to the old Macarthur windmill creaking on Pyrmont Point.[47]

Best of all was the elegant, double-domed Henrietta Villa, perched on the harbour at Point Piper, a house said to have cost 10 000 pounds. Here Captain John Piper, the Naval Officer who earned twice as much as the governor, entertained ladies and gentlemen lavishly and with great flair and imagination. Piper had returned to Sydney and his family on the *General Hewitt* with Greenway. He was inspired by the 'grandiose suburban visions' of Regency London, and passionate about creating an enchanting and elegant social life, with himself its gregarious host. His friend Major Johnston once lamented in a letter to him that 'Sydney is duller (if possible) than when you left us', but those early days of dusty, grinding boredom were over.[48] Now it was time to dance. Piper ferried his guests to the point in a barge, where they were welcomed by liveried servants playing gaily on musical instruments. Jane remembered feasting on 'an excellent well-cooked dinner, French Wine', as well as the fruits of the cross-shaped garden carved out of the bush on the slopes behind the house. They sipped 'wine coolers and finger glasses with scented geranium leaves', danced beneath the ballroom dome and gazed at the harbour views from the French doors opening onto cool, flagged verandahs. But the Brooks sisters bristled when they overheard a judge's wife sniffing that the house was 'too good for NS Wales'. Henrietta Villa, and the social life it allowed, was after all a great model, 'showing others that had to seek a Home what might be made of this Faraway country'.[49] Like Macquarie's public buildings, Piper's house was a beacon of promise: it proved that the environment of New South Wales could be made elegant, polite and opulent.

Such houses and events were not only about pleasure, of course. They were also about the politics of social inclusion—and exclusion. The salons and drawing rooms were created as exclusive spaces, their doors already firmly shut against those who were never on the guest lists: emancipists, pretenders to 'society', despite their wealth and their own great houses. That the Macquaries themselves welcomed and entertained successful emancipists at Government House was considered by some a betrayal and an abomination, and gave their enemies much useful ammunition. Yet it did not do to be too hard-line in 1820s Sydney. After all, John Piper himself had married Mary Anne Shears, the daughter of a convict, after she had borne their first four children.[50]

Augustus Earle's portrait of a suave Captain John Piper, with Henrietta Villa on its romantic headland in the background. Piper has the look of a man who has made it. (Mitchell Library, State Library of New South Wales)

Meanwhile, the Brooks' business in Sydney was booming. By 1822 the family had made their money, paid their debts and were ready to move on to the next stage of colonial success: the lives of landed gentry. They moved out to a cottage at Denham Court in the Airds district to the south-west, and by 1828 had eighteen convict servants working for them, including labourers, house servants and skilled tradespeople. If Richard Brooks had disliked Macquarie's convict barracks in Sydney because it 'condense[d] these men', he and masters like him were glad of it once they moved upcountry. The barracks lessened the attractions of Sydney for convict servants sent to the hinterland.[51]

In 1832 the Brooks family commissioned fashionable architect John Verge to build them their own house. Denham Court still stands today in the suburb that took its name, its splendid porticoed façade flanked by two rounded wings. The Brooks sons and daughters married the offspring of other aspiring landed gentry, expanded the holdings and spread a net of families, homesteads and properties over the Cumberland Plain and beyond.

CONVICT SYDNEY IN THE MACQUARIE ERA

The landscape of public works, domestic environments and public open space had quite different meanings for convicts arriving in Sydney in the Age of Macquarie. Ankles freed of shipboard irons, they were mustered in the gaol yard and assigned to government work gangs or to settlers. Those assigned to well-off settlers and townsfolk went to live with them, and so became familiar with the grand houses, their dining rooms and drawing rooms, kitchens and gardens, the whims of their masters and mistresses. Others knew the bare huts and scrabbling lives of the small-farming emancipist settlers on the plain and the rivers. Still others found themselves in the more familiar domestic environments of the publicans and tradespeople of the town: the plain, solid stone houses of two or three rooms, the jumble of furniture, household goods and tools in every room, and masters and mistresses of much the same rank and cultural outlook as themselves. They worked for their masters and mistresses, but those who were artisans often also paid their masters to be allowed to work on their own account.[52]

As Naval Officer, John Piper probably managed to get the pick of the new arrivals as servants for his own establishments: strong men for the boat crews, men and women with high levels of domestic skills, people who would look well in livery—and could play musical instruments! And of course skilled tradesmen to build his dream villa. Their work, and that of the hundreds who fetched and carried, chopped, cooked, served, washed and went slowly mad tending sheep, made the elegant houses and leisured landscapes of the gentry possible, as well as the wealth amassed in town and on estates by the Brooks and people like them.[53] At Newington on the Parramatta River, John Blaxland's servants not only farmed, tended stock and ran the household, but worked at the salt pans, limekilns and in the small woollen mill he had established on the estate. The mill turned out the fabric from which their clothes were made. The busy free and emancipist entrepreneurs needed labour for their new ventures too: John Dickson's steam mill down in the Haymarket valley at the head of Darling Harbour, and lonelier workplaces like Simeon Lord's new Fulling Mill down on the Lachlan Swamps, which cleansed and thickened cloth, and the Waterloo Flour Mill nearby on Sheas Creek.[54]

The Macquaries themselves acquired skilled servants for their retinue at Government House: a gardener named Thomas Curry in 1816 to tend their grounds and the Domain; a confectioner named David Douglass, snapped up to prepare sweets and cakes for their balls and parties.[55] Increasingly, Macquarie also kept skilled tradesmen in Sydney to work on his public works program, which expanded in tandem with the rising numbers of convicts who arrived after the end of the Napoleonic Wars in 1815.[56]

For the first 30 years of the colony's existence, men assigned to the work gangs on buildings, in quarries, at the brickworks or the great hive of manufacturing activity that was the lumberyard, were not housed in gaols or barracks, but told to go and find their own lodgings in the town and turn up for work when the morning bells were rung. They went to the older neighbourhoods, like the Rocks, rented rooms together or dossed down in the kitchens and skillions of established householders. The urban conditions in which they lived were not much affected by Macquarie's improvements: the streets here were still uneven, pubs were everywhere. Some houses were much improved and had proper wells and privies; others were hastily put up as mean 'rents' with few amenities, if any.[57]

Night-time might be hazardous for the careless, though, as convicts were subject to a curfew and could be arrested and thrown into the watchhouses after 9 pm. Macquarie had revived the division of the town into districts, each patrolled at night by constables with rattles and sabres, who called out the hour. But Sydney also had a free population, so there were bound to be frictions. As convicts did not wear distinctive clothing, it was difficult for constables to tell the difference between them and free labourers or artisans, and the curfew was a constant source of irritation and indignation to non-convict townsfolk. Although the increased policing of convicts was still only partly effective, it nonetheless jarred with the free, and Sydney people resisted by refusing to be arrested. They tore down Macquarie's first notices about new rules and regulations. Macquarie expressed his 'astonishment' at this and declared with characteristic drama that the culprits caught would be tried as 'traitors'.[58] The knowledge of people's whereabouts and movements was also fundamental to urban control, so the townsfolk were ordered to inform their local constabulary when they or their servants moved. They refused. We can compare this with the vastly expanded, eagle-eyed bureaucracies of the later governors, especially Ralph Darling. Under these regimes convicts' movements *were* strictly controlled, and accurate records of their behaviour were kept. But during the Macquarie years, despite the bluster, this level of surveillance and control was not yet in place, nor even possible.[59]

It would not have taken new arrivals long to become familiar with the lineaments and particular places of Sydney town. Strangeness gradually settled into patterns and landmarks: the stores where rations were distributed, the quarries and brickworks, and the scaffolds of new buildings. To them, of course, Macquarie's buildings meant work rather than aesthetic improvement, though the contrast between the fine airy rooms of the new residences and hospital and the stinking, filthy, crowded gaol where prisoners were housed could not have escaped them. There were places to be seen, like the marketplace, alive on Saturdays; and places to avoid being seen, like the ambivalent, often dangerous military zone, and all the guard houses and sentry boxes manned by soldiers and constables who were authority's eyes in the town. They stood to attention, or lounged or dozed, at the wharves, the forts, at Government House and the Domain gate, at the Main Guard in George Street and the barracks.

For the first two years or more after their arrival, convicts were perhaps most conscious of the shorelines, the wharves, the Heads and horizon. Throughout the period of transportation to the colony, they were the most likely group to attempt escape. The sea was their link with Home: the harbour and ships offered the hope of return. They must have listened eagerly for news of when ships sailed, which labour-starved captains might be prepared to take stowaways, which seamen might be bribed to hide them.[60]

For others there were bright possibilities in Macquarie's Sydney, and for many there were the consolations and enjoyment of popular culture, much of it carried on out of doors, in public spaces. The streets and old squares remained places for mobs to gather and fights to break out. By the end of the 1810s there were pubs and drinking houses on almost every corner, with drinking, dancing and music, while illegal carts trundled around the town selling spirits. Everyone who owned a horse, even the most broken-down old carthorse, wanted to race it and wager on the result. The streets were used for reckless horse-racing, even after Hyde Park was set aside as a racecourse. Cockfighting, dog-fighting, bare-knuckle prize-fighting and footracing with the runners carrying weights also attracted great crowds. The locations for illicit meetings, usually isolated, fringe places, were passed by word of mouth among the patrons. Unruly mobs of both white and black people commonly gathered at the Kings Wharf—at the bottom of the Rocks—or in the old square outside the new Main Guard, much to the consternation of the constables and soldiers on sentry duty.[61]

So by the 1810s Sydney's people had inscribed the urban landscape with cultural meanings, meanings made by common actions, repeated over time, which had become common knowledge. Other public spaces were more unsettling, marked by death or the expiation of crime. The crowded, malodorous old burial ground next to the new market was closed in 1820, but people continued to use it for illegal or covert purposes. Thieves buried stolen goods there, fathers quietly buried stillborn babies. The hideous hanging ground on the far fringe received the bodies of executed criminals. Angry townsfolk also dragged the body of a young woman who had committed infanticide out here too, to lie among the hanged. Fire was sometimes used to cleanse places after gruesome murders. Near Brickfield Hill to the south, the house where poor Reverend Samuel Clode was murdered by soldiers in 1799 had been burned to the ground. The bodies of his killers were strung up on gibbets nearby: public reminders, public spectacles, places suffused with evil and stench. Sometimes private land was ill-omened by a death. Catherine Cotton complained in 1810 that she had gone to considerable expense to clear her land on the north shore, but now could not improve it further because 'a man happen(ed) to be killed on it'. No-one would work there for her. And at the points where the cart-tracks crossed in Hyde Park lay the bodies of suicides. They were excluded from consecrated ground and buried there with stakes driven through their hearts.[62]

For Sydney's convicts and labouring people, the Macquarie era was also marked by walls. Walls of rubble or ashlar sandstone (squared blocks) rose relentlessly to heights of 9, 10, 12, 14 feet, encircling new buildings and old, cutting off access to yards and the waterfront and common ground. At the Dockyard, the 'battered railing and gates' were replaced by a 'high stone wall, nine feet tall'. A stone wall rose around the churchyard of St Philip's. The old hospital at the foot of the Rocks had no walls at all; in the new hospital, inmates were confined by another 9-foot wall.[63] This was a new phenomenon in a town where, apart from the gaol wall and paling fences, the demarcation of space had been largely mental, and fluid. The walls had to do with the control of bodies and movement, with enclosure and exclusion. How did people deal with them? In places of confinement, they sometimes scaled or jumped over them, literally risking life and limb. But more often they simply made holes in the walls, and walked through.

The Domain wall, snaking right across the neck between Sydney Cove and Woolloomooloo Bay, became a flashpoint for the struggle between governor and people over the uses of urban space. The Aboriginal people seen by the Brooks children on their daily walks were not the only ones still using the Domain in the older ways. People came in to cut firewood, to bathe naked in the waters, to meet or simply to walk. Couples seeking some privacy went there for sex. Thieves dumped or hid stolen goods, convicts hid there after the curfew hour, young women were clandestinely spirited away on ships from its dark shores at night. While the Macquaries considered the Domain transformed into a pleasure ground, a place of 'rational amusement', in the minds of the people it was still 'the skirts' of the town, still a place for practical and nefarious activities.[64]

It was bound to be problematic, this double reading of space. People were in fact able to enter the Domain legally—either through the official gate, with its lodge and constable, or over a stile on Bent Street. But they defied Macquarie's rules and surveillance by repeatedly making convenient holes in the wall from Hyde Park, or behind the hospital, and by continuing to use the 'pleasure ground' for what were now defined as 'improper' purposes. Elizabeth's carefully designed 'new shrubbery and young forest trees' were trampled and broken. Perhaps it was deliberate; or perhaps the 'intruders' had not really noticed them. Either way Macquarie was incensed. He decided to demonstrate his authority and teach the reprobates a lesson. Constables were ordered to hide near the wall and arrest anyone who came through. They obediently pounced on two young women, one a servant to Sophia and Robert Campbell, with a child in her arms. And they arrested two convicts and three skilled free men—a stonemason and caretaker named Reed; a respectable blacksmith, William Blake, who went to relieve himself; a coiner named Henshall who was working for Macquarie converting Spanish dollars into holey dollars and dumps. Henshall was after some white sand for his metallurgy.[65]

When Sophia Campbell opened her door at Wharf House she found her servant with the infant, trembling and 'much alarmed'. She hurried her inside, slammed and locked the door and told the constables outside that she would not give her up. The chief constable had to threaten Mrs Campbell with a warrant before the girl was surrendered, and both young women went to gaol for 48 hours without trial. In the gaol yard outside the women's cell, the men were summarily flogged: 30 lashes for bond and 25 for free. The flogging of convicts meant little to the free townsfolk, but the flogging of free men without trial 'created a great degree of alarm among all classes of inhabitant', especially those who had received pardons from Macquarie. What were the rights of free men if a governor could pardon or flog as he pleased? A petition to the British House of Commons was already in circulation: the case of the Domain victims was added to it, along with the names of many emancipists.[66]

Commissioner Bigge, while not unsympathetic to Macquarie, saw the Domain incident as a turning point, for 'it made a deep and lasting impression upon the minds of all, and has become a sort of standing reproach against the system by which the government of the colony has been administered'.[67] In insisting on these new uses and the control of public space in this way, Macquarie provided ammunition for both his own enemies and the enemies of the colony. The

Domain became synonymous, not with the public good and equal access for all, but with tyranny and the infringement of individual liberty.

The summary punishments were not even effective as deterrents. Three months later, people were still breaking down the wall and 'trespassing' on the Domain. The wall was strengthened and raised still higher, and eventually they gave up.

The Domain featured in a collection of beautiful watercolours painted in this period. For the past two decades, art historians and curators have attributed this collection to Sophia Campbell. But when these pictures were purchased by the Mitchell Library in 2009, it was discovered that they were in fact painted by Lieutenant Edward Close, who was related to the Campbells by marriage. The son of a Bengal-based merchant, Close arrived in Sydney with a detachment of his regiment aboard the *Matilda* in 1817. Given their common background, it is possible that he and the Campbells knew one another—in any case, he married Sophia's niece, Sophia Susannah Palmer, in 1821. While most paintings of Sydney in this period are stiff, bland or clichéd depictions of empire and authority, many of Close's Sydney watercolours shine with acute human observation and mischievous humour. For example, his picture of the back of the Main Guard and St Phillip's church features a red-coated soldier who is supposed to be on guard duty, dozing off in a chair in the Sydney sunshine. His watercolour of the massive, pompous red-brick military barracks, complete with the Macquaries' Grecian-temple well, includes a woman washing clothes and a soldier chasing ducks.[68]

Close was evidently interested in colonial politics. He painted a most unusual interior view of the Sydney courtroom—then installed in the 'Rum' Hospital—showing many of Sydney's well-known figures at the infamous 'Philo Free' trail, the first libel case in New South Wales. One of his paintings of the Domain may have some connection to the arrests there the previous year. It shows the rear view of the new hospital and the convict barracks, arraigned proudly on the horizon and framed by picturesque shrubberies: the Macquaries' natural and urban visions. Right at the centre of the picture stand a wall and gateway.

Another of Close's pictures shows the vista towards the Domain from the battery at Dawes Point. A forest of masts cluster in front of the Campbells' sub-stantial home and warehouses in the foreground, while the Macquaries' Sydney parades along east side of the cove. There stand the elegant villas on Macquarie Place, and the much enlarged Government House, and the splendid arrangement of trees and open ground of the Domain, adorned with a domed pigeon house and the curious hexagonal house built for Macquarie's favourite, the Jamaican ex-convict Billy Blue. The three verandah'd pavilions of the hospital rear up on the horizon in this picture too (though having the windmills poking out of the Domain still higher and larger would have irritated the Macquaries no end). But the title, 'Sydney in all its Glory', written with flourishes along the top, adds a humorous, ironic edge. Was it a comment on the grandiose ambitions of the governor and his wife for what was, after all, a penal colony?

If gothick stables and classical pigeon houses were properly set among trees, the opposite was true of the sterner buildings meant to house and control convicts and labouring people—the hospital and barracks. Seriously authoritarian, they stood in the centre of bare, walled yards, with not a tree or shrub in sight. Such spaces had nowhere to hide. They were fashioned for surveillance, for mustering people, for lining them up and for flogging miscreants before their assembled fellows. Ironically, but unsurprisingly, most paintings of these buildings do not show the people they were built for, though they often feature the odd frock-coated figure pointing at them.[69]

But if we could zoom in on those handsome hospital verandahs in 1816 or 1817, they would not have been stately, quiet and deserted at all. The women patients used these spaces to wash and dry their clothes: gowns and undergarments flapped between the columns. And the verandahs really came alive on the days the inmates received their meat rations. Crowds of townsfolk thronged in to barter, buy and haggle for the beef with the bandaged, the aged, the venereal, the dysenteric and the scorbutic. Those patients too sick to walk crawled on the floors amidst the hubbub. With the proceeds, patients could then buy other supplies—tea, milk, sugar, spirits.[70]

The alleged confluence of grand public works, the common good and the improved environment of public health were celebrated in poetry as well as painting. The Macquaries' 'Poet Laureate', Michael Massey Robinson, included a panegyric to the new hospital, this time including its happy inmates, in his 'Ode for the King's Birthday' in 1817:

To rear you fabric, that with stately Boast
Shews its white Columns to the distant Coast;
Within whose Walls, pale Sickness rears its Head
Fresh, with calm Slumbers, from the cleanly Bed
Nursed with Humanity's consoling Care,
And cheer'd with currents of salubrious Air
Til rosy Health expands its vivid Glow
And new-born Hope pervades the smiling Brow![71]

Surely this poem would have been read aloud from the *Gazette*, perhaps in rolling, pseudo-pompous voice, in the crowded, stifling wards? The patients, bred on the humour of inversion, would have loved it. They had only moved from the old hospital little more than a year earlier, in April 1816, and the new one was overcrowded, unhygienic and disorderly. Much of the building had been appropriated for other purposes—two wards for courtrooms, another for a retiring room. Artist John Lewin occupied yet another floor. Macquarie himself came to inspect the building when it was under construction, but he rarely visited once it was occupied and seems to have taken no interest in its management.[72]

There were only two hospital wards for men and one for women, with around 40 patients in each, their cots lined in four rows. When it was discovered that male and female patients were having sex, bolts were placed on the ward doors and another storeroom was converted to a syphilitic ward. The other spaces were chaotic too—one kitchen was used to house the overseer and the other as a dead-house (morgue), so all the cooking was done in the wards themselves. The storerooms were so untidy and crammed that much-needed medicines were lost under piles of other stores. Convict clerks stole medicines from the dispensary and sold them to quack-doctors and chemists in the town. There was never enough jalap, tincture, calomel and laudanum for the patients.[73]

In the wards themselves, fires were kept burning day and night in those impressive fireplaces, while the multi-paned sash windows were always locked shut to prevent inmates escaping (so much for the 'currents of salubrious air'). Visiting surgeons were shocked, felt their stomachs heave in protest at the stench, the heat, the slabs of meat thrown down in the dust, the slovenly, untrained convict nurses, the soiled bandages kicked under the beds—and the pans full of excrement. Somehow the architects and builders had neglected to include privies in the building. Wooden commode chairs were installed at the top of the handsome stairs. The bedpans were emptied out the windows.[74]

Who in their right mind would enter such a hellish place? Nobody, if they could help it. Certainly not the elite, nor the middling and artisanal townsfolk; nor even labourers in regular work. The hospital was a last resort for those who had exhausted all other options: the weakest and poorest, the friendless, those with no sustaining social networks to shelter and nurse them. While people did come up to the hospital for medicine and advice, the proper place for the sick and injured was in their own homes, or the homes of friends. To enter the hospital, or indeed any institution, was feared and stigmatised. They called it the 'Sidney Slaughterhouse'. One man wracked with a terrible cough in 1822 said 'he would rather die than go to the hospital'.[75]

Besides the fact that it was a deadly environment, the hospital represented the surrender of personal independence—an independence predicated on spatial mobility. Despite its vast size, the new hospital had fewer patients than the old one. This was probably a result of the fact that wards had been commandeered for other purposes, but it also had to do with confinement—the forbidding 9-foot wall around the bare, dirty yard, the gate locked at six every night. The old hospital at the foot of the Rocks, set in its expansive garden ground, had no walls at all and was a sort of drop-in centre for the old and indigent, 'a mere skulking place for Pensioners, who used to come in at night and take shelter after committing robberies'.[76] Now the poor preferred to take their chances on the streets rather than succumb to the horrors and restrictions of the new hospital.

The freedom of the streets, the freedom to live independently and find one's own lodgings, was a double-edged sword of course: it made people vulnerable too. Irregular food and sleeping rough wore down their bodies, made them susceptible to disease. While the doctors rejoiced in the general absence of serious infectious diseases in Sydney, they agreed that dysentery was endemic, and a killer. Men (and some women) who were 'in the habit of lying in the street' at night were particularly susceptible to 'bad bowels'. They weakened quickly, dying in the most abject conditions. The doctors generally opined that their indulgence in drink was the cause.[77]

Accommodation for convicts generally became a pressing issue when their numbers rose dramatically after 1815. Shipload after shipload arrived in the unprepared town, sometimes unannounced, a total of 78 ships carrying 13 221 convicts. The colony's population more than doubled in the six years between 1815 and 1821, from 12 911 to 29 783, a greater increase than in its whole history until that time.[78] A severe labour shortage suddenly became a glut, and free settlers could not take all the men as servants. Macquarie's greatly expanded building program in Sydney was one solution—it provided employment, but it also kept the convict workers tied to the town. Existing housing stock was stretched to the limit, the streets were full of strangers. The older inhabitants must have wondered what was happening to their town.

The rising population of homeless and probably disoriented convicts, and the urban disorder they caused, soon made convict accommodation a priority. Macquarie also wanted to make convicts work a full day rather than the customary task-work arrangements which had prevailed since the foundation of the colony, and which left the convicts free to do as they pleased after three o'clock in the afternoon.[79] The new barracks in Macquarie Street were built to address both problems. The foundation stone was laid on the land next to the hospital in December 1817, and the three-storey walls of soft orange bricks, set in mortar bonded with bits of shell, rose steadily to Greenway's design. A handsome clock was set in the centre of the pediment, symbolic of the time-discipline the building would impose on its wayward inmates. To those with pretensions to architectural taste, the barracks were an object of 'towering grandeur . . . the most elegant proportions of the Greek school'. The public benefits were self-evident: 'much good must be expected to result to the Prisoners and to the Public at large from this humane, this highly salutary, and excellent institution'. But to the convicts, it must have looked much like a workhouse, those dreaded places of detention and regulation.[80]

Macquarie now had a problem: while 130 men had moved into the unfinished building in May (probably the most desperately homeless and hungry), how could the majority of convicts be lured into his handsome new barracks? How could they be persuaded to exchange their private lodgings, the freedom of the streets, for longer hours of work, routines, surveillance and confinement? A suite of inducements was offered: barracks men would have their rations increased by half, and they would still have free time to work or enjoy the pleasures of the town on the weekends. Macquarie added a final, and character-istic, incentive: a spectacular welcome feast on the King's Birthday. So on 4 June 1819, 598 convict men sat down in the mess hall to mountains of beef and plum pudding and half a pint of rum punch each, eaten and drunk from tin platters and pots. (One thinks of the logistics: cooking, carrying and serving beef and plum pudding for nearly 600 hungry men; and the incredible roar in the room, the eating, drinking, talking, shouting, singing, the fug of bodies, the aromas of food and the smoke from 600-odd clay pipes). Lachlan and Elizabeth and their young son Lachlan, together with all the important officers and judges of the colony, called in on the feast. Like the landowners at Harvest Home feasts back in England, Macquarie toasted their health and happiness. He noted in his diary later that the men 'all appeared very happy and Contented, and gave us three cheers on us going away'.[81]

But after the feast was over, the doors were shut and the convicts became barracks men. Their trunks and possessions were taken away and put into storage, they were assigned hammocks slung over rails on the upper floors, much like the hammocks for sailors on ships. They were to rise, muster and march to their places of work, labour a full day, mess together and retire to their hammocks. The constables were to put out the oil lamps at 8.30 at night.[82]

An impressive facade and a bevy of rules: but appearance belies the reality of life in the barracks, the measure of looseness which still allowed convicts some action and movement. Their time there was certainly more regulated, and the working day for all convicts was now longer. Their space was patrolled and men who committed offences were brutally flogged in the yard. Yet these were barracks, not a prison. The overseers and constables were not gaolers, but there to keep order. They themselves were 'well-behaved' convicts and ex-convicts, little more accustomed to precise regimentation than their charges, and they often ignored the rules. On Sunday the barracks men were marched across the bridge and up to St Philip's for Divine Service. After that, those who hadn't skived off already could amuse themselves in the town as they pleased. 'They run immediately to the Rocks', as one disgusted officer later reported, 'where every species of Debauchery and villainy is practised'. As the punishment books show, convicts continued to commit crimes despite the fact that so many were confined and controlled, though the numbers of robberies in the town fell, during the weekdays at least. The downside, according to a cranky Francis Greenway, was that the overfed and regulated barracks men made poor workers, for 'nor will you or I or all the World according to the present System get them on fast with their work'. The barracks also meant that free workers charged more for their labour—'they do not work for less than 5s to 7s 6d' (5 shillings to 7 shillings 6 pence). When the government wanted a job done quickly, they reverted to the old task-work system.[83]

At night the overcrowded barracks were not silent and orderly, but rang with conversation and arguments, singing and oaths, the men probably playing cards and drinking. In later years they made cabbage-tree hats to sell, walking about the town with them stacked four or five high on their heads. It was probably not until the 1830s that the 'squints' you can still see at the barracks today were cut through the walls, high up in the corners. These were face-sized gaps most likely installed to allow observation of sexual activity between the men (which was apparently common, and by that period was a subject of some obsession to authorities) as well as gambling, drinking and fighting.[84]

But in the Macquarie years and early 1820s, the barracks men were not under this sort of surveillance. One Sunday night in 1820 after the day's carousing, the hubbub of talk was so loud that the groaning and crying of a desperately ill man leaning on the hammock rail was not even noticed; such raving usually simply meant a man was drunk. Eventually a fellow prisoner sent for the clerk, and Matthew Hyard, a quiet man who worked at the lumberyard, was carried down to the courtroom and placed in a chair by the fire. He was in such pain he begged them not to touch him, he frothed at the mouth. Asked what was wrong, he gasped about a lump in his stomach, and that he had been sent away from the dispensary as an 'impostor' and was 'afraid to go in to the hospital lest he should not be properly treated'.[85] He died in agony a few hours later.

Matthew Hyard probably had no choice but to go into the barracks. While men 'who could get a living by their work were discontented' there, it was a refuge for 'those who could not pay for their lodging'. The more acquiescent were glad of the food and shelter. The restless and 'dissolute' wanted to be among the favoured ranks of around 300 to 400 'best behaved men and men married legally' who were still allowed to 'sleep out in the town'. Some of these men ran shops and worked at trades as well. Skills, capital, intelligence, a wife, and willingness to work for the authorities were still factors which decided where and how convict men would live in Sydney after 1819, not their convict status. Confident demeanour, physical height and initiative helped too.[86]

<hr />

The Age of Macquarie is often seen as a period of harmony, order and tranquillity after the early wretched, starving days. Yet the economic and social realities of Macquarie's decade were tumultuous. The retail market collapsed in 1811–12, followed by a major economic depression which ruined many of the early Sydney traders. Drought and caterpillar plagues jeopardised food supplies, destroyed grazing land and threatened the tenuous hold the rural settlers had established on the farms. A severe labour shortage was followed by a tremendous glut as the colony was swamped by those thousands of newly arrived convicts. Macquarie's own enlightened policy of accepting emancipists—or the wealthy ones at least—back into society and to his own table, and even elevating them to positions of high office, was utterly rejected by the military and civil officers, and free arrivals. They undermined and betrayed him by sending outraged complaints to influential people in England. His impulsive and authoritarian actions over the Domain also caused unease among the lower orders of free and freed. The Age of Macquarie was also a period of war and massacre: the war waged by Aboriginal people on the Cumberland Plain settlers was reignited, and in 1816, when Macquarie ordered a retributive raid which resulted in the massacre of at least fourteen men, women and children at Appin.[87]

The appearance of order and 'progress' often hid unruly reality: over half a million acres of Aboriginal land was generously granted to settlers, but two-thirds of it remained unsurveyed and no titles had been issued at all, leading to endless litigation. Quit-rents were never collected; the agreements about settling and building were unsupervised and many grantees soon sold their land on to speculators. Currency was still chaotic, with a mixture of different specie, notes of hand, and the barter of goods, though Macquarie did proclaim sterling the official colonial standard in 1816 and presided over the establishment of the first bank, the Bank of New South Wales.[88] In the town of Sydney, beauty, taste and appearance largely took precedence over pragmatic needs and humane concerns: the conditions in the gaol and hospital were appalling and filthy and the gaol was insecure, while the public wharves were in a state of ruin. Macquarie's penchant for naming places and buildings after himself or members of his family was much ridiculed, and his elaborate public works which diverted funds and attention from more basic necessities provided powerful ammunition for enemies, who portrayed him as an extravagant, self-indulgent martinet and watched his every move.[89]

Nevertheless, Macquarie remained in power for twelve years and evidently won the affection and loyalty of many Sydney people. When he returned from a brief visit to Hobart Town in July 1821, the entire town was lit up in 'one continued blaze of light' to welcome him back. Candles, tapers and lamps shone from the windows of mansions and cottages alike, and the evidently well-to-do emancipist butcher Thomas Harper commissioned a transparency from the artist Richard Read junior depicting a likeness of 'our respected, our paternal GOVERNOR'.[90] Despite all the rules and regulations, the temperamental outbursts and his insistence on subordinate behaviour, Macquarie seems to have exerted a personal influence upon the people: there was a relationship between them. He was a negotiator, often imaginative and flamboyant. He made verbal promises face to face with people of humble standing. He understood the nature of public ritual and performance. He insisted on being present when people gathered to be counted at the musters 'to see and be seen by the people'. Like earlier governors, he personally selected land where settlers could establish farms. They saw him travel the colony from one end to the other over the years, inspecting, naming, instructing, proclaiming. There were agendas of deference and obligation on both sides of course: this was no unanimously grateful and cowed population. But nobody could have missed his profound interest in the colony and the town, whatever they thought of his improvements and buildings. To emancipists, who made up the largest section of the population, his unwavering support of the wealthy men among them had great moral and symbolic power. And despite the continuance of floggings, convicts must have known that Macquarie was the first governor to reduce the savage floggings ordered by the naval governors, limiting the number of lashes to 50 (although magistrates still ordered 100) and instigating the alternative punishment of spells in the gaol gangs.[91]

If Sydney itself was an artefact of the Macquaries' artistic and authoritarian visions, it had nevertheless also remained a space for negotiation over urban life and forms, as well as a vehicle for the expression of popular feeling: celebration, enjoyment, rage, mourning. After he left the colony, Macquarie grew rosier in memory, especially with the arrival of far less engaging, more impersonal and bureaucratic governors. Petitioners often wrote nostalgically of his benevolence, and his personal promises of indulgences. 'Declining life few consolations bring', wrote his ageing, crippled town crier John Pendergrass in 1825, 'for when I lost Macquarie I lost a friend'.[92]

John Thomas Bigge, lawyer and former chief justice of Trinidad, was sent out in 1819 by the British government to investigate Macquarie's administration and the state of the colony. He spent two years collecting information, travelling the colony and interviewing people, and produced three reports summarising his findings. These reports presented a kind of history of the colony and a blueprint for its future. Bigge tends to be portrayed as the villain to Macquarie's hero, but in fact he was at times quite sympathetic to the governor, his program of improvements and the stressful nature of his office. He praised some of the buildings and thought the outburst over the Domain simply an instance of irrational behaviour which had unfortunate impacts.[93]

But it was clear to Bigge that the British government's original purpose and plan in founding the colony had been well and truly perverted. Instead of a place of dread which would deter crime, the colony bore a certain degree of laxity and liberty, most obviously seen in the pleasures and freedoms of the town. Some convicts were writing back and encouraging relatives to join them— Sydney had become familiar rather than strange, a place of opportunity rather than terror. A great many other convicts, unmoved by good weather or colonial possibilities, escaped on the rising numbers of visiting ships, despite the great, cumbersome edifice of port regulations. Instead of a subsistence agricultural colony, free of money and trade, and quarantined from the rest of the world, the colony was decidedly urban, unambiguously commercial and already tied into global trade and capital—and vulnerable to its vicissitudes. The Macquaries' improvements had ironic outcomes too—intending to transform and gentrify the urban fabric, they kept convicts in the town, which the convicts themselves preferred. Sydney pulsed with their movements, familiar networks and popular culture, its pleasures a constant beacon for those assigned to the inland settlements. Perhaps worst of all was Macquarie's fiscal irresponsibility. The costs of maintaining the colony had spiralled rather than diminished and many of the Macquarie buildings were inappropriate, improvident and an extravagant waste of government funds.[94]

LEAVING SYDNEY

Lachlan and Elizabeth and their young son, together with their servants, their favourite horse and cow and a menagerie of native birds and animals, sailed from Sydney in February 1822. The streets that day were crowded with 'an immense concourse of people' to farewell them: schoolboys wearing medals, soldiers lining the road down to the wharf. On the harbour a motley flotilla, boats of every size and description, bobbed and sailed around and after the *Surry* as it made its way down the harbour, the cheers fading on the wind. After days of delay, the ship finally cleared the Heads. The Macquaries watched their beautiful lighthouse on South Head receding, until it disappeared from sight.[95]

The publication and wide circulation of Bigge's massive tomes on New South Wales was devastating for Lachlan Macquarie. He spent a great deal of time and energy, indeed the remainder of his life, trying to rescue his reputation. As the Macquaries were in much reduced circumstances, he also wanted to secure a pension. It was granted in 1824, but he died five weeks later. Elizabeth buried him on his family estate on the Isle of Mull, and erected a handsome monument over his grave. The stone was inscribed 'The Father of Australia'.[96]

When news of Macquarie's death reached Sydney, the town went into mourning. The shutters were drawn, and a funereal procession of his former officials and friends, complete with mutes, marched slowly along George Street (his enemies stayed away). Later there was talk, mainly among the emancipists, of raising a monument to him, the first ever proposed in Sydney. Such a memorial would have continued a tradition Macquarie himself had established and encouraged: the anniversary celebrations, the memorials to Phillip.[97] These had been in effect the first stirrings of self-conscious historical sensibility in the city, formalising the sense of historical moment the earliest white arrivals had felt.

But the idea petered out. No memorial was built to Macquarie, or any other governor, until grateful colonists erected a statue of Richard Bourke in 1842. Moreover, Macquarie's most self-conscious legacy, the buildings, however ambitious, fine and costly, were never necessarily permanent: they might at any time be merely obstructions in the path of new development. Soon Greenway's refined, fashionable structures were regarded as ugly and old-fashioned; an unsavoury air of the old convict days increasingly hung about them. Macquarie's and Greenway's buildings set new standards for the town but their perceived role as the 'foundation stones' or 'building blocks' of the nation is quite recent. Much altered and chopped about, the big bluff military-style buildings and the early hospitals, orphanages and barracks survived largely because they were useful for pragmatic and often rather grim reasons: for immigrant barracks, for poorhouses, for insane asylums, for rabbit-warrens of government and legal offices. (The gothick stables which had caused so much grief were considered rather a nuisance when the grand new gothic Government House was eventually built.) The tide of taste only began to turn when architect William Hardy Wilson published his *Old Colonial Architecture* in 1924, with its exquisite, dappled drawings and the extravagant prose of architectural rediscovery.[98] But it was a slow turning: Macquarie buildings did not really achieve their present highly revered status until the 1970s.

Those elegant and expensive private houses of the first decades fared little better. At Point Piper, the music and dancing ceased and the lovely domed Henrietta Villa was shut up in 1826. John Piper's creative borrowing against his future commissions as Naval Officer had eventually caught up with him and he went bankrupt. The beautiful house was sold to emancipist merchants and demolished before it was 40 years old. Piper himself was helped by friends and retired to a property near Bathurst, where he died in 1851.[99] At Woolloomooloo, the hospitable Palmers also got into financial difficulties, lost their household goods and furnishings, sold their mansion in 1822 and took land grants at Bathurst and Parramatta. The house was later leased to the Anglican archdeacon, but by the late 1840s, it stood empty. A dense tea-tree scrub reclaimed the estate, followed shortly by a suburban tide of bricks and mortar, and by 1854 the house was gone. Dr Harris' Ultimo survived longer and remained in the family. Remarkably, descendants built another crop of fine houses on this land in the 1880s, close by the factories and modest workers' terraces that now spread over the peninsula. Eventually, though, Ultimo was resumed by the state government for Sydney Technical College and was lost from sight behind modern buildings. In 1933 it too was demolished.[100]

The fates of the ex-convicts and emancipists who had built and run the town were often more severe than those of the elite, who had well-to-do friends or relatives to help them. Francis Greenway, who betrayed the Macquaries in his interviews with Bigge, was dismissed from his official position in 1822. He went on living in a ramshackle old house at the foot of the Rocks with his family, surviving on commissions from older colonists. They seem to have put up with his irascible temper and unwavering self-importance out of a sense of loyalty. But the work dwindled, his wife Mary died in 1832 and he was evicted from the house two years later. The family retreated to a hand-to-mouth scrabbling life in a bark hut on a grant of poor swampy land near Raymond Terrace. Francis Greenway died there of typhoid fever in 1837. He was buried in an unmarked grave at the Glebe burial ground in East Maitland.[101]

———•◦•———

Let us climb Flagstaff Hill once more, to gaze upon Macquarie's Sydney. In about 1819, Major James Taylor of the 48th Regiment did likewise. From a point between the fort and Macquarie's new military hospital, he made sketches of the views over Sydney from the four compass points, deftly distorting topography to include as much of the harbour as possible, and to showcase impressive buildings.[102] Joined end to end, his paintings presented a 360-degree prospect of Sydney—they were intended for exhibition in London in Robert Burford's Panorama. So in 1823 and 1824, when Lachlan Macquarie was fighting for his reputation, curious Londoners might have visited the Panorama building in Leicester Square, ascended a darkened spiral staircase and emerged at the top into a brightly lit virtual town. Much classicised and refined in the lithograph versions, the illuminated images presented a well-ordered, prosperous and handsome town, set on the picturesque harbour.[103]

Major Taylor's panorama was a loyal defence and vindication of Macquarie's governorship and his urban aspirations, and a challenge to notions of Botany Bay as a vile and disorderly penal colony. It directed the gaze through time as well as space, for as the viewers turned from west to north, they could see those still wild, ragged Sydney outskirts yielding to the remarkable and sanguine influences of civilisation upon nature and people. Blasted vegetation and tree stumps on the rocky foreshores at Millers Point give way to fences, neat cottages of warm red bricks, flower gardens and vegetable plots. These in turn frame the next phase, a glorious view to the east over the town proper. There are the public buildings—hospitals, churches and barracks rising proudly, there are the handsome private residences and commercial buildings of Sydney, all spread genially under the antipodean sun. Here there are no ale houses or gin taverns, no cockfights, no poverty, no riot.

There was plenty of picturesque human activity in Major Taylor's panorama to intrigue and amuse viewers too—but these conveyed another overarching message about the influence of civilisation and urbanisation. Beyond the fence-lines and on the peripheries of Cockle Bay, Aboriginal people still go stark naked and squat on the ground around their bark gunyahs or by the shoreline, while idle convicts gather in little knots, lounging, sleeping and chatting—or plotting. Closer to town, convicts have become workers, cutting and carting stone in the quarries to build the town—but some still sit around or nap in the sunshine. Within the fences, though, the transformation is complete. The convicts are obedient workers, the men toiling diligently in gardens or carrying lumber; a modestly dressed female servant minds a child. And within the grounds of the military hospital, Aboriginal people now stand upright, some in classical poses, and cover their nakedness with improbable white loincloths. Urban development has civilised and controlled convicts and Aboriginal people, made them useful.

This image of Sydney extolled Macquarie, but it also assured genteel visitors that Botany Bay was a civilised place, that their tender sensibilities would not be offended by naked savagery, and that convicts could provide the docile labour they required in New South Wales. Commissioner Bigge, who had seen Sydney, knew it was fantasy. Like the Macquarie buildings, Major Taylor's painting privileged appearance over substance. Bigge had also been commissioned to find out whether it was possible for New South Wales to be made into an 'object of real terror' which would deter criminals, whether a system of 'general discipline, constant work and vigilant superintendence' could be established. He thought both were possible—but only if Sydney was excised from convict experience, and they from it. Like Phillip in that early attempt to remove them from the embryonic town to the rural setting at Parramatta, Bigge recommended that convicts be separated from the urban environment and the port as much as possible:

> [the] accumulation of convicts in a Town is the worst possible mode of providing for them . . . rural labours and occupations are at once the most fitted for accomplishing change on their moral habits.[104]

Bigge's solution sketched an elegant fusion of capitalism, colonial expansion, punishment and reform, all turning on environmental vistas: empty land, waiting for capital, flocks and agriculture. The urban environment, the real bustling streets and wharves of Sydney, the anonymity and social networks it offered, were incompatible with discipline and punishment. The city did not subdue and civilise convicts, it nurtured their society and freedoms; thus they could have no place in it. Rather than growing food for themselves as originally envisioned, they would be sent out to the estates of large landowners, providing the closely supervised, unpaid labour for agriculture and pastoralism. The skilled artisans would be taken off the government projects and sent to private masters too. Their masters, in turn, would come from the ranks of free immigrants with capital, lured by promises of free land—and by images like Major Taylor's panorama. Convicts who re-offended, who were recalcitrant and hardened, were to be banished to the road gangs, to hard labour in irons, building a network of Great Roads, radiating from Sydney to the inland.[105] Boundless lands, considered to be unoccupied, twinned with the existence of Sydney, would underpin colonial expansion, the rising severity of the convict system, and the continued dispossession of Aboriginal people over the next two decades.

Chapter 8

THE FACE OF THE COUNTRY

The face of the country is fair.
WATKIN TENCH

The face of the country is deceitful.
THOMAS WATLING

We are rightly fascinated by the story of how the Europeans of the First Fleet encountered the Sydney environment, a place they had never seen before, but which was already so intimately known by the Eora. The imaginings, discoveries, hopes, disappointments, encounters and gradual acclimatisation of voyagers and settlers are great themes in human migration and settlement. But the environmental stories told in most histories, exhibitions, novels and popular books about early Sydney are depressing ones. Despite the temperate climate, lush vegetation and beautiful waterways, the Sydney environment is depicted as hostile and barren, a hated place. The early Europeans found the 'landscape . . . harsh and forbidding; the vegetation and soils were unproductive'. Their experience was blighted by terrible deprivation and starvation. It was a portent: life in Australia would be 'difficult and often tragic'. The convicts 'stumbled ashore in a land of inversions where it was high summer in January, where trees kept their leaves but shed bark, where squat brown birds roared with laughter'.[1]

Some studies connect inner lives with environmental experience and impacts. The Europeans, suffering the pangs of banishment, must have been ill at ease and homesick in an 'alien landscape', where nature was 'upside down' and flora and fauna were so unnervingly weird. They 'hated trees'. Artists and

writers 'struggled . . . to come to grips with this new, totally alien environment', for the brooding, menacing bush 'crushed the eye with its monotony'.
They found plants and animals 'odd and perverse'.[2] A sociologist has recently
argued that Australian national identity, 'what it is to be properly Australian',
is neither resolved nor well defined because the first settlers failed to bond with
the native fauna. Worse, some say they failed to put down roots, develop any
sympathy or affection for the land. Art historian Bernard Smith thought that
no colonist before the 1880s really felt at home or spoke the language of the
land, and when they did it was a language of defeat and resignation. In their
hatred and disappointment, the settlers committed acts of environmental
vandalism by clearing, planting, building and polluting. The First Fleeters
became the original environmental sinners, first perpetrators of Australia's
appalling despoliation. In short, they were ignorant, clumsy-footed and they
did not belong; at least in the way the Aboriginal people belonged. This idea
still haunts some non-Indigenous Australians.[3]

Yet, even the most fleeting look at what the first Europeans actually wrote
and painted of the Sydney environment reveals just the opposite: their admiration, enjoyment, fascination and sometimes awe of the place. The land *was* new
and strange, and the wildlife like nothing they had seen. Sometimes they did
struggle, in words and watercolours, to describe it, and they wondered where
these creatures fitted into their own understandings of the animal kingdom.
People endured primitive conditions, suffered homesickness and boredom in
the Camp and they complained long and loud. They were disappointed by the
soils of the sandstone country, after what they had been promised. But the
expectations of exotica, of strange and marvellous plants and animals, were
more than fulfilled. As we shall see, so often the responses to the local landscapes, flora and fauna were eager curiosity and wonder rather than existential
unease. The idea of 'inversion' was expressed by a few writers, but it was quite
rare in the early years, and nobody attributed their troubles to the world being
'upside down'. They can hardly have been surprised to find the seasons reversed,
since they had ample knowledge of other southern hemisphere colonies. Antipodean inversion seems to be a trope more common to the 1830s and later, and
tended to be expressed by visitors.[4]

LANDSCAPES OF WORDS

Let us begin with a few of those early responses. Perhaps most striking were the rapturous descriptions of Port Jackson which so many felt moved to write down, despite the fact that its beauty, as First Fleet Surgeon George Worgan wrote, 'beggared all description'. These early accounts have sometimes been dismissed as mere mouthings of European notions of landscape—the picturesque arrangements, the romantic islands, the deep safe coves 'all thrown together into a sweet Confusion by the careless hand of Nature'.[5] Yet all people make sense of what they see through the cultural ideas and the words in their possession; and after two centuries, the succession of headlands, the scattering of islands, deep blue bays and glittering waters of the harbour still have the power to move.

Once landed, the colonists found not a desolate wilderness, but a wildflower garden, 'surpassing in beauty, fragrance and number all I ever saw in an uncultivated state', as Watkin Tench described it.[6] Even those with little botanical knowledge exclaimed over the brilliant colours, the way the perfume of flowers wafted in the air. Here is Judge Richard Atkins, rambling along the forested road to Brickfield Hill (now George Street around Haymarket) one autumn morning in April 1792:

A very good road is made the whole way to it, through the wood where trees of an immense size border it on both sides their lofty and wide spreading branches look beautiful . . . The underwood is mostly flowering shrubs, some of whom are new in blossom of the most vivid and beautiful colours imaginable and many of the most delicately formed. An arm of the sea appears thro' the wood & beyond it another wood rising gradually to a moderate height terminates the prospect. [7]

The natural landscapes of the interior were inspiring too. Tench, though thirsty and shivering after a cold night camping beside salty Prospect Creek to the southwest, could nevertheless describe a misty dawn on a clear winter's day with deep admiration:

The sun arose in unclouded splendour, and presented to our sight a novel and picturesque view: the contiguous country was white as if covered with snow, contrasted with the foliage of trees, flourishing in the verdure of tropical luxuriancy . . . the exhalation which steamed from the lake beneath it contributed to heighten the beauty of the scene.[8]

The new landscapes wrought by settlement were also celebrated, especially the farms and gardens of Parramatta and its district. Six years after that first, slow journey up the harbour, and after the Europeans had endured their first El Niño drought (1791–93), a New South Wales Corps soldier praised the bounty of Parramatta and the botanical treasure-trove of the colony generally:

The garden that surrounds [Government House] is beautiful, abounding in the season, with grapes, melons, pumpkins, and every other fruit and vegetable. The florist may also amuse himself. In short, the country may well be called Botany Bay; for the botanist . . . may here find the most beautiful shrubs and evergreens that produce very fragrant flowers.

Indeed, he thought that nature here had trumped the work of landscape artists, for 'the Governor's garden at Parramatta is so situated by nature that in my opinion it is impossible for art to form so rural a scene'.[9]

Why, then, have most historical accounts portrayed the Sydney environment as hell on earth? Historian Eric Rolls thinks we must have projected the gloomy bush literature of Henry Lawson and Adam Lindsay Gordon backwards onto early Sydney.[10] The disasters and tragedies of selection and small-farming over the nineteenth century overspread the preceding period. Seeing the nineteenth century like this, ahistorically, as a single block, is a mistake. We cannot project the responses of one generation backwards or forwards upon the whole; we cannot assume what happened later must have characterised earlier experience. Present preoccupations with alienated white settlers in the 'weird' Australian bush, and with the landscape's 'absence of ghosts', also shape assumptions of how it must have been. Another explanation is that the *idea* of the brutal 'gaol colony' looms so large. In such a place, the environment could only have been cruel and harsh.[11]

There were of course many negative responses. These are mainly found in the accounts and letters of the officers, and also in those of some newly arrived convicts. Historians found that Surgeon John White's words fit perfectly with the 'barren gaol' image, for he raged against '. . . the ingratitude and poverty of the soil and country at large . . . a country and place so forbidding and so hateful as only to merit execration and curses'. White was echoed by Lieutenant Governor Robert Ross, the Reverend Richard Johnson, Surgeon John Harris and Master David Blackburn. Most of them complained about the rocky, barren soils: they had of course been expecting rich 'meadows', the lands promised by Cook and Banks. The 'meadows' soon became their literary shorthand for betrayal and abandonment. Later it became an (unwarranted) historiographical metaphor for the hare-brained nature of the entire settlement project.[12]

Their initial disappointment was compounded by the undeniably primitive and uncomfortable conditions of the first few months—though one wonders what else they could have expected. The town was a muddy quagmire when it rained, and blazing hot at the height of the burning summer. Rations were short. The bored, disgruntled and homesick officers were soon heartily sick of the whole experiment, and unleashed tirades condemning the colony and everything in it. Those who had been ordered to come, and had obeyed unwillingly, like Master of the brig *Supply*, David Blackburn, never went back on their pessimistic opinions.[13]

But for most of them, as we have seen, these were initial responses to a *particular* environment: the sandstone sclerophyll country of the immediate area of Sydney. It was, as we know, only one of many Sydney ecologies. Soon exploratory expeditions found the longed-for 'fine Meadow Ground' and within weeks the officers were agitating for land grants.[14] Many of them eventually acquired vast tracts, where they built their charming, rambling houses. White himself had 'considerably modified his poor impression of the colony' by the time he approached a publisher with his journal. Those blasting pages had been written, he explained, 'when Hunger was very pressing . . . from the distress of the moment'. Now he wanted them suppressed in the publication. But those first stories of New South Wales as an environmental hell were vehement, and they were powerful: they captured the narrative ground. As a result, later arrivals expected to find themselves in a barren desert. When Major Francis Grose sailed into Sydney Cove in 1792 to succeed Phillip, he was surprised and delighted. 'Instead of the rocks I expected to see', he wrote, 'I find myself surrounded with gardens that produce fruit of every description'.[15]

Both Phillip and Collins were taken aback, puzzled and a little hurt at the stories rebounding from England about the colony as utterly sterile and a hopeless failure. By mid-1794, after all their pioneering work, the establishment of gardens and public farms, and the settling of the ex-convicts and soldiers on their 30-acre plots, Collins proclaimed that 'it might be safely pronounced that the colony never wore so favourable an appearance'. The storehouses were full of 'wholesome provisions', and there was

> wheat in the ground to promise the realizing of many a golden dream; a rapidly increasing stock; a country gradually opening, and improving everywhere . . . with a spirit universally prevalent of cultivating it.[16]

It came as a shock, then, to learn that the people of the newly arrived *Halcyon* were 'fraught with the dismal and ill-founded accounts . . . of the wretched and unprofitable soil of New South Wales'. Phillip was also disturbed by these 'extraordinary accounts' and responded in a characteristically earnest way. Worried that he would be seen as misleading his superiors on the nature of the soils, he appointed an 'independent expert', the gardener David Burton, to complete a survey of all the farms. He sent Burton's mainly positive report back to England as objective evidence justifying his own decisions in selecting the farm sites. Collins meanwhile thought the true stories reaching England would soon do the trick, and then 'every attempt to mislead the public would cease'.[17] But the positive counter-stories never did entirely succeed in setting the record straight. The 'dismal and ill-founded accounts' of the officers, easily accessible in their letters and journals, made a deep and lasting impact. They would shape the historical view of both the environment and responses to it.

It is also important to remember that the descriptions colonists wrote were often deliberately fashioned for their audiences, and for their authors' own purposes. The colony was famous before it was born, a hotly debated experiment, a site for the exotic and strange, for imagination. The well-known letters of the Scottish convict artist and coach painter Thomas Watling are a good example. Art historians, and historians seeking to reconstruct settler reactions to the environment, have found a rich source in his *Letters from an Exile*, published in 1794. Some offer him as the artist unable to appreciate the beauties of the Australian bush and struggling with the new forms. Or he was the first of the 'unwilling occupants of . . . gloomy terrain . . . the first of the wounded ones, crying out in self-pity and anguish at a land that did not seem to want them'.[18] Watling was assigned to Surgeon White, who commissioned him to paint landscapes, birds, animals and plants. In his long letters to his aunt, he proclaimed both the artistic merits and deficiencies of the local Sydney environment, and opined on most other things as well. The landscape, he said, failed the test of 'picturesque' status, for there were allegedly no 'bold rising hills' or 'azure distances' (strange, given the vistas the Sydney region offered!). He wrote that an artist would have to 'select and combine' to avoid the monotony of the 'extensive woods'. The country also failed in a utilitarian sense, for Watling declared, 'the face of the country is deceitful': it had 'every appearance of fertility; and yet [is] productive of no one article in itself fit for the support of mankind'. He thus ignored the native foods that had kept people in health. But it was true in another way: as the exploratory parties also noted, the large, dense, green mantle of the sandstone sclerophyll forests that clothed the headlands in fact grew in the poorest soils and 'out of the heart of rock'.[19]

But wait a minute: Watling's letters also *praised* the Sydney landscape lavishly, often in passages directly following the negative ones! The 'sameness' of the 'extensive woods' was paired with a wondrous meditation on the artistic beauty of the trees, with their 'old fantastical roots on high', their different tints and foliage, the way they stood in 'glimmering groves in the glooms of twilight'. His description of the Parramatta River was a hymn of praise, replete with suitable classical allusions:

nothing can surpass the circumambient windings, and romantic banks of a narrow arm of the sea . . . the Poet may there descry numberless beauties; nor can there be fitter haunts for his imagination. The Elysian scenery of Telemachus; the secret recesses for a Thompson's musidora; arcadian shades or classic bowers, present themselves at every winding to the ravished eye. Overhead the most grotesque foliage yields a shade, where cooling zephyrs breathe every perfume. Mangrove avenues and picturesque rocks, entwined with non-descript flowers.[20]

Why were Watling's descriptions of the colonial environment so utterly contradictory? And why did he paint these extravagant, sensual word-pictures? The answer is not that he was in a 'love–hate relationship' with Australian nature, nor that he was confused and disoriented.[21] It is connected to the fact that his letters were published by his aunt or agent in 1794, as he without a doubt intended. An address at the end of this publication advertised his proposed 'highly-finished set of Drawings, done faithfully upon the Spott, from Nature, in Mezzo, Aqua-tinta or Water Colours', and requested that prospective patrons 'send their names to Mrs M. K—', his aunt.[22] The letters are not an innocent and direct account of the colony's environment: they are a long and enticing advertisement for Watling's paintings. By pairing the country's 'deficiencies' with vivid passages proclaiming its beauty, he was not only piquing interest and curiosity, he was letting patrons know that his painterly genius could deliver them wonderful and picturesque paintings, even from the most unpromising material. Like so many others in New South Wales, Thomas Watling was on the make.

As historians have noted, there were similar contradictions and motivations in other letters and journals; words were also belied by actions.[23] Watkin Tench and John White responded in both positive and negative ways. The Reverend Richard Johnson, another bemoaner, in fact became one of the most successful farmers in the colony, and wrote to his friend Henry Fricker: 'My little garden also begins to flourish and supplies us daily with one kind of vegetable or another'. Then again '. . . the greatest part of the country is poor, barren and rocky . . .' The otherwise miserable Ralph Clark wrote that he was 'quite charmed with the place' and, of the glossy black cockatoos (the Eora's name for them was *carate*), 'they are a most beautiful bird'. He desperately wanted to capture some alive to take home to his dear wife Alicia. The black swans (*mulgo*) discovered in the lagoons elicited not anxiety but wonder and amazement (and, inevitably, gunfire).[24]

Port Jackson Painter, 'The Black Swan, native name Mulgo'. It looks as surprised as its European discoverers. (Natural History Museum)

How could the Sydney environment be both 'very romantic, beautifully formed by nature' and 'the worst country in the world'? The contradictions should not be ignored, nor mined selectively, nor written off as 'ambivalence', for they are a key to grasping the colonists' responses to the new land.[25] In the first place, the 'Sydney environment' was not a single entity, it was not 'all the same'. The Europeans encountered a diverse range of environments: harbours, rivers, beaches, wetlands, forests (tall, open, brush, scrubby), plains, slopes and, eventually, mountains. It is important to track the encounters with these different landscapes—not only with the sandstone country of Sydney Cove. The climate of Sydney varied radically too: the First Fleet arrived in the wild storms and downpours of a La Niña event, but three years later experienced the drought and heat of the succeeding El Niño.[26]

Second, the European reaction was not one 'response', but a complex layering of different, sometimes contradictory, responses. What they saw and experienced was not only fundamentally shaped by pre-existing ideas, expectations and hopes, but by social standing and education. Their responses also changed over time with more exploration, acclimatisation and the rapidly growing store of environmental knowledge.

SEVEN WAYS OF SEEING NATURE IN EARLY SYDNEY[27]

How can we make sense of these tangled, but vitally important, responses to country? Environmental historian George Seddon suggested that they are 'easily sorted': the unfavourable ones are 'utilitarian', while the positive are 'picturesque', the aesthetic response.[28] But people see, experience and learn about their environments in more ways than economically and aesthetically. A third lens was regulatory: the early governors issued orders, mostly from utilitarian concerns to protect natural resources from the pollution and wastage caused by the people.[29] A fourth, political and philosophical lens turned this last around: some saw the evils of all-powerful governors and the transportation system as the true corrupters of an Edenic, fertile, beautiful country. A fifth lens was natural history, accompanied by the mania for collecting that had everyone out eagerly scouring the country for specimens, and a great outpouring of art. Sydney was a 'scene of novelty and variety', a paradise for botanists and painters alike.[30] But colonists did not only pickle, press, preserve and paint, they began to reshape the face of the country, planting local and imported seeds and plants, and interacting with animals and birds. The sixth lens, then, is this making of 'new natures', and their unfolding environmental impacts. A seventh lens, deep-seated and elemental, yet rarely mentioned in histories, is the visceral and emotional response. The Europeans experienced the new environment through their bodies, senses and emotions: their words, pictures and actions convey this too.

Each way of seeing and learning could, of course, cross over, as we have seen in Thomas Watling's case, but each also had its own language: the language of Locke and Adams, concerning rights to land through use, and the historical trajectory of the course of empire; the language of tyranny and liberty; the language of improvement and progress; the languages of science and art, intertwined but slowly separating; the language of emotion and the sensual. Inevitably, the colonists slip and slide between these ways of speaking, writing and thinking.

UTILITY, BEAUTY AND PROMISED LANDS

George Seddon thought that these divergent views of utility and beauty set an unfortunate template for the perception of the Australian environment, because they have become 'sharply defined, alternative categories' as a result.[31] He argued that early colonists saw either beauty *or* usefulness, whereas the two should be fused.

In the urgency of the early years, the utilitarian eye does seem to dominate. Where were the soils suitable for agriculture, the clays for bricks and tiles, the stone, lime, gravels and sands for building? The environment was often anatomised, with earth, stone, trees and so on assessed with seamanlike thoroughness for their practical usefulness. But as many historians have noted, the Europeans *did* respond that second way, aesthetically, too, and were often moved by the great beauty they found around them. Some wild places were indeed beautiful but 'useless'. Elizabeth Macarthur was aware of this. She resolved it by deciding that Sydney Cove's beauty was undeniable but only skin-deep, a superficial beauty.[32] Other elements could have multiple meanings—for example, sandstone outcrops and overhangs could be awe-inspiring and bring to mind romantic ruins; they could also be cursed as 'barren' and 'useless' ground *and* be very useful for building, all at once. Some landscapes were seen in both ways simultaneously: the beauty and utility of Port Jackson inspired euphoria, as did the rolling expanses of open woodland on the Cumberland Plain.

The utilitarian responses of the First Fleeters were shaped by the interplay of experience and a whole raft of expectations of the 'new' land and its possibilities. These had been built up by the reports of Cook and Banks of 1770 and subsequently by the extrapolations of Sir George Young, one of the proposers of the colony, from countries of similar latitudes. The colonists were fully expecting a country which would be easy to clear and cultivate, because it was 'formed of a Virgin Mould undisturbed since the Creation'.[33] They sailed towards a promised land of boundless 'meadows', pastures for stock, a climate similar to the south of France, waters teeming with fish and shellfish. The expectations of officers and seamen were also cued by other colonial experience in the Americas and the West Indies, the Cape of Good Hope, India and the East Indies and the islands of the Pacific. Banks had reported that there were no large, dangerous animals, but they watched for 'quadrupeds' all the same. And were there mines of marble, slate, ore or salt? Where were the mighty rivers, flowing from the interior, great arteries suitable for trade and transport?

Perhaps the most fundamental, and ironic, assumption was that Botany Bay was a wilderness, in Cook's words, a 'Country in a pure state of Nature, the Industry of Man has had nothing to do with it'. As we have seen, the country was already managed, harvested and known by Aboriginal people, but to the Europeans it was supposed to be a new Eden, waiting for improving human hands, waiting for history to begin. Improving hands set to work immediately, only to discover the 'deceitfulness' of the country—created, of course, by these expectations. The sandy soils at Sydney Cove, so rich in natural biota, were unsuitable for grain crops. As we have seen, in the first months, the search for the promised 'good' soil of 'Virgin Mould' overshadowed all else. Meanwhile, crops planted in what the settlers knew was the wrong season sprouted but then failed to thrive. Worgan, disappointed with his garden, still thought it unfair to judge the climate 'before a round of seasons'. The rivers they followed seemed to end mysteriously in 'shallows and swamps', though when the colonists looked west they knew 'they must rise in the mountains'. It was a landscape of speculation and curiosity, as well.[34]

They had also expected 'a considerable Space of Land together'—large, open tracts where vast fields could be planted, where farms could be allotted. This was another reason the early verdicts were often that the country was 'deceitful', that good country and soils were interrupted, as Worgan put it, by 'a rocky, or a sandy or a swampy surface crowded with large Trees, and almost impenetrable from Brush-wood'. This meant that 'it will necessarily require much Time and Labour to cultivate any considerable Space of Land together'—that vision splendid of boundless fields of wheat was dashed. Still, here again, Worgan contrasted these 'interruptions' with the 'fine black Soil, luxuriantly covered with

Grass, & the Trees at 30 or 40 Yards distant from each other, so as to resemble meadow lands'. So it was the expectation of *unbroken* expanses of 'meadow' lands that was the problem.[35] They disliked the swampy areas intensely—these were believed to be sources of disease, as well as difficult and treacherous to cross. Tench wrote with some vehemence of the great Lachlan and Botany swamps stretching between Sydney and Botany Bay as 'a rotten spongy bog, into which we were plunged knee deep at every step' (and added the by now obligatory 'so much for the meadows').[36]

Clearing land is often presented as evidence that the 'invaders hated trees'. They allegedly hated them because the eucalypts were alien and un-English, and because they found the bush 'oppressive' and dismal. 'The settlers' desperate need, together with the fact that they had not developed a sympathy for the land, meant that there were no barriers to destruction.'[37] But many of the First Fleeters admired the trees of Sydney for their immense size, their stately spreading branches. The cabbage palm, wrote Worgan, 'is a beautiful tree'. Even the greatest lamenter Surgeon White thought that 'when standing, they look fair and good to the eye'.[38] Again, as eighteenth-century people, their world view rarely separated the natural world from human use and benefit, so this admiration did not prevent them from cutting down and burning trees and shrubs to create space for building and cultivation, much to the shock and anger of the Eora.

In Sydney Cove, too, there were far more trees than they expected, and they were perversely monstrous. They had great snaking networks of roots which repelled tools and they bled sap like blood: 'I have seen this Gum gush out like Blood from an Artery', wrote Surgeon Worgan.[39] Each one took days to remove, and there were hundreds of them. Once the great labour involved in felling trees and removing stumps became evident, the trees were also described by some as 'pests' which 'overran' the land, and the stumps were left in situ. As we shall see, those early landscapes of amputated trees came to convey certain meanings about order and authority. Tim Bonyhady, telling the story of Louisa Meredith, points out that settlers later also cleared relentlessly around properties, not because they hated trees, but for fear of fire and attack from Aboriginal people and bushrangers.[40]

Another often-told environmental story in the 'deceitful country' mode is that, once felled, the native timbers of New South Wales were useless to the settlers. They were hollow, 'rotten', full of gum whorls, too hard to work with the English tools and 'fit only for the fire'.[41] Again, this is a 'first story': the initial response to the unfamiliar timber, and also a reflection of the unfortunate fact that the Camp was established in one of the few areas where useful timber *was* scarce! The way this 'first failure' has so often eclipsed the vast and significant history of timbergetting in the Sydney region is almost comical. In fact, the settlers learned fast. Lieutenant William Bradley included lists of useful timbers and their properties in his journal in March 1791, including blue gum and the 'brown bark'd gum' of the Kangaroo Grounds (Petersham) and around Parramatta (probably box); and mangrove, which provided perfect compass-wood for boat- and ship-building. High ground mahogany was best for furniture, while casuarina (called 'pine' or 'she-oak') was already recognised as good for framing, laths, shingles and flooring.[42] The shingles made excellent roofs—almost the entire town, and then the city, was shingled right up to the 1860s. By 1794 the official boat-builder, Daniel Paine, was cutting and using local timbers for his craft. Historian Ralph Hawkins thinks Paine probably talked to Aboriginal people to find out where the best stands were. By 1803 timbers like 'she-oak, swamp oak, red gum, blue gum, blackbutt, stringy bark, ironbark, box, mahogany, cedar, lightwood and turpentine' were considered 'commercially useful species' for buildings, ships and furniture.[43]

Sydney's sandstone was also much maligned as a hindrance to farming and town planning—'Sydney Cove . . . may justly be termed one of the most Barren Rocky Situations for a colony under Heaven' was a common refrain. Yet it was also of 'excellent quality' for building, for the men who knew stone, the 'Mason & Stone-Cutters' pronounced it 'as being well-adapted for Buildings'.[44] Sandstone foundations were laid for the first European building, the governor's house, and by the early 1800s, convicts and ex-convicts were literally building the town from the sandstone. They quarried the outcrops in their own yards to build everything from capacious rubble-stone houses and shops to ovens, cisterns, drains, burial vaults and gravestones. Later, of course, sandstone became the celebrated and emblematic substance of the city, the golden stuff of pompous public buildings and civic statuary.[45]

Meanwhile, the colonists had discovered, and rejoiced in, another Sydney landscape entirely: the open woodlands beyond the head of the harbour at Parramatta, which reminded everybody of a gentleman's park in England. Like Port Jackson, these woodlands (now called Cumberland Plain Woodlands) were especially praised because they offered both aesthetic beauty and economic potential: the two were, once more, inseparable. These landscapes made covetous hearts leap with desire. In contrast to the rocky, dense bushland of the sandstone country, the tall forests and the impenetrable thickets of river-flat 'brush', they offered open vistas of level or undulating land, 'the trees being a considerable distance apart and the intermediate space filled not with underwood but a thick rich grass, growing in the utmost luxuriancy'. Here, at last, was the promised 'vast Extent of fine Meadow Ground', ready-made for farming and grazing, needing no laborious clearing, and easily traversed on horseback or even by carriage without the trouble of making roads.[46] The sightlines made them feel more secure—one could see all around for miles. Perhaps best of all, these landscapes 'resembled a beautiful park', 'a wilderness or shrubbery, commonly attached to the habitations of people of fortune'.[47]

Artist Jacob Janssen celebrates Sydney sandstone near The Gap, *South Head, in 1846. (National Library of Australia)*

The actual 'gentlemen's parks in England' they referred to were not 'natural' areas at all, but the fashionable landscape designs of Capability Brown and his successor Hugh Repton. The idea was to replace the earlier formal gardens on the estates of noblemen with 'natural'-looking landscapes of grassy expanses, clumps of carefully arranged trees and shrubs, and winding streams or artificial lakes. As Tim Bonyhady observes, the English were 'soon identifying parks across the globe', locating landscapes which were not only familiar, but coveted, for they were associated with nobility, wealth and fashionable good taste. So the wonder of this for the Europeans—or at least the elite, literate and ambitious—was that here in New South Wales, God and nature appeared to have provided what in England was a deliberately constructed landscape, available only to the very wealthy. Perhaps New South Wales was a promised land after all.[48]

Soon people who could never have aspired to such a prospect in England, like the Macarthurs and the Marsdens, were settled on grants around Parramatta, where they themselves became 'people of fortune', elevated by their estates and the economic returns of farming, grazing and trade. If we now think the harbour's edge much more beautiful than the plains of western Sydney, in the early period the reverse was true: people of means much preferred the parklike scenery around Parramatta to the rocky slopes, dry forests and swamps of Sydney Cove. Over the next century, people with wealth, aspiring to the lifestyle of landed gentry, would follow these early estate-holders onto the Cumberland Plain, building increasingly grand mansions set in the undulating open forest lands.[49]

EARLY ENVIRONMENTAL LEGISLATION

In *The Colonial Earth*, Tim Bonyhady argues that if early Sydney set a pattern of environmental damage, it was also the site of some of the world's earliest environmental legislation. The busy clearing and building going on there were considered unmistakable signs of improvement and progress, but the environmental damage arising from them did not go unnoticed. Phillip, realising that the Tank Stream was 'only a drain from the swamp at the head of it', had ditches dug on each side and a paling fence erected 'to keep out stock and protect the shrubs'.[50] The tanks by which Sydney's stream became known were cut in the stone to capture water from the springs, altering its flow. Phillip had also forbidden the felling of trees within 50 feet of the Tank Stream in March 1788—not for its own sake, but to conserve the water supply for the town's use. This order appears to have been actually enforced, for in 1792 a corridor of timber still stood along its banks. Not long after Phillip sailed away, though, the precious Tank Stream forest vanished forever—you can see this abrupt destruction in the pictures of Sydney Cove.[51]

Now you see it . . . the disappearance of Phillip's protected Tank Stream forest. The tree-corridor is clearly visible in the middle of the 1792 picture (top), the year Phillip sailed away. But by 1795, when Thomas Watling painted Sydney town, the trees had vanished and the slopes were bare. (Natural History Museum and Mitchell Library, State Library of New South Wales)

Governor Hunter continued Phillip's attempt to protect the stream—one of his first proclamations in 1795 forbade the pollution of the stream by roaming pigs and ordered householders to fence them in. But by 1796 householders above the tanks had broken down the fence, and 'with dirty vessels take the water they want . . . and thereby disturb and thicken the whole stream below'. More proclamations were issued. The Tank Stream was already choked with sand and rubbish in 1803, although the townsfolk tried to keep the dirty flow separate from the clean.[52] Macquarie also issued a barrage of protective orders and regulations. With continued urban growth, it was a losing battle. By the 1840s the waters were 'thick and turbid', the western bank bare, slumped ground. The foundational urban stream, which had drawn and succoured the first settlement, was a virtual sewer. It was covered over and buried in the 1860s.[53] Today it runs silently through arched stone culverts under the city streets.

Regulations were also issued to conserve timber and prevent soil erosion on the Hawkesbury. Hunter remonstrated with the settlers over their river bank clearing via a government order in 1795, reminding them that trees fit for naval purposes remained the property of the crown, grant or no grant. The settlers had cleared the land right to the river's edge, often rolling the trunks into the stream. This not only created hazards for shipping—one settler complained that South Creek was completely choked with timber and rubbish in 1803—but when the floods struck the unprotected banks, rich lands were washed away. Governor King set aside the six great commons, preserving them from private alienation. He too denounced the settlers' hacking as 'improvident', forbade the further removal of trees and shrubs from the river bank, and urged the settlers to replant their banks with 'such binding plants and trees as they can procure'.[54]

But settlers, racing to take land north and south, were mostly well beyond the reach of inspectors and courts. The axe and fire prevailed and the river banks continued to be stripped bare. Over the decades parts of the river became wider and shallower as the banks slumped and caved in, and silts and sands were washed into its channel. Eventually in the 1860s the Windsor reach—the place where Ruse and his group had first settled—silted up. Ships could no longer reach the town, and the population in the valley fell as people left to try farming elsewhere under the new Selection Acts.[55]

Bonyhady is right in arguing that Australia 'began with a form of colonialism alive to the importance of environmental protection'. But it is important to note that the early governors were alive to long-term *conservation*, rather than *preservation*—making sure natural resources were conserved for human use, rather than preserved for their own sake. The settlers and townsfolk themselves apparently possessed no such long view—their use of land, timber, birds and animals and their fouling of water was immediate, lavish, thoughtless, wanton. They evidently paid no heed to the future—even the short-term future of turbid, dirty streams and strangled, unnavigable rivers. Again, this does not denote a hatred of or disdain for the environment—if anything they revelled in its bounty, its seeming boundlessness.[56] They acted as though they believed the country's resources were limitless, that it could withstand any incursion or disruption. So while early Sydney had some of the earliest environmental legislation in the world, based upon recognition of environmental limitations, mostly it failed. Governors lacked the means of enforcing regulations in the so-called gaol colony—the townsfolk and farmers flouted them, the orders had to be repeated several times. In the end these early regulations did not save the streams, the river banks and the forests. It was the commons, defended over the nineteenth century by local people, which kept alive the practice and ideal of public lands, shared in common, and which preserved islands of bushland.[57]

'O COUNTRY BEAUTEOUS': EDEN, TYRANNY AND SLAVERY

There were people in the colony who saw it the other way round: the governors, not the people, were the polluters and defilers of a pristine and promising environment. Men such as the educated, if eccentric, 'gentlemen' convicts like John Grant and Sir Henry Browne Hayes, and the few political exiles, including Maurice Margarot and the Reverend Thomas Fyshe Palmer, railed against the tyranny and despotism of governors given too much power in New South Wales. Colonists were already writing of the need for reform in 1791, for 'nothing can be so truly acceptable as freedom and a trial by jury in all cases'.[58] Palmer made the link between environment and polity explicit in a letter to the Reverend Jeremiah Joyce in 1794:

The reports you have had of this country are mostly false. The soil is capital, the climate delicious . . . I will take it upon me to say that it will soon be the region of plenty, and wants only *virtue* and *liberty* to be another America . . .[59]

Palmer could see the potential for a new, free society in this place: it lacked not environmental bounty, but moral and political virtues.

John Grant, who arrived in 1804 and was deeply impressed with the 'Beauties of this colony', went further. From the start he equated the position of convicts with slavery: 'the moment I require Provisions I become harnessed at their disposal as a Slave', he wrote. So he made sure he never 'required provisions', mostly by imposing on his friends, who looked after him. Grant himself lived a life of idleness and pleasure and became a favourite with some of the ladies. He went shooting, wrote poetry and played his violin in the beautiful tree-fern groves on his friend Charles Bishop's farm at Prospect. Grant was much taken with this place. 'If I had a little independence', he told his mother, 'I never would quit this spot'. The soil seemed poor, but the farm had 'such a sweet house' which 'commanded a fine prospect of land and water'.[60] Despite his undeniably soft landing, Grant's letters and journals were written in the language of the oppressed: he saw himself as the victim of tyranny and injustice. (He was in fact transported for shooting a solicitor with a pistol-full of swanshot. The solicitor had implied to a young woman Grant kept harassing that he was a homosexual.)[61]

When Grant's hopes of making a quick fortune did not materialise (King refused to allow him to land and sell a consignment of rum), his stance became increasingly radical. He decided that the governors in fact had no right of authority over convicts or free people. There were legal opinions which supported this stance.[62] But Grant wasn't prudent enough to use this knowledge wisely, sending numerous rude and inflammatory letters to King ('by what right do you make Slaves of Britons?') and to several others, including the people who had sheltered, fed and otherwise helped him. 'Why do you espouse in this way the cause of the prisoners?' wrote a baffled and hurt Judge Richard Atkins, one of these patrons-turned-targets. 'We have never treated you as a prisoner!!!' But Grant had assumed the mantle of the noble political martyr. While he had earlier utterly disdained the ordinary convicts (referring to them as 'abominable villains' and 'rogues'), he now styled himself their champion.[63] Eventually, in June 1805, his outbursts, insults and dangerous claims saw him packed off to Norfolk Island, where a number of dissidents, treasonous plotters and annoying people were sent. (His close and similarly aggrieved friend, Sir Henry Browne Hayes, soon joined him there, along with Maurice Margarot.) On the deck of the ship during the voyage, in a fever of sickness and righteous conviction he wrote *Ode on His Majesty's Birthday 1805*. This is the fourth verse:

O Country beauteous, Climate healthful, Mild!
O George (unlike some Kings beloved) abus'd!
O People into slavery beguiled
O rulers guilty of a power misused!
When shall All cry Britannia rules the Waves
And Free-born Britons are no longer Slaves . . .

As he had earlier written to his mother, 'the fertility of the soil, the fineness [of] the climate etc are far superior to yours in England; but the Truth is, this Slave system blasts all exertion and until this is done away with, this Country can never flourish'.[64] The environment of New South Wales was not the problem. Grant saw it as a perfect Eden poisoned by transportation and the tyranny of an all-powerful governor, who trampled the rights of British men (he didn't mention women). When Sir Henry Browne Hayes and Maurice Margarot were removed from Norfolk Island to Van Diemen's Land, the grieving Grant drew up a 'Bond of Union' denouncing the colonial authorities and calling for the restoration of rights, freedom of the press and trial by jury.[65]

Poor Grant did suffer for his new-found convictions, his habit of writing inflammatory petitions and publicly censuring the authorities on behalf of himself, his friends and other convicts. On Norfolk Island he was flogged and sent to four months' solitary confinement on Phillip Island, a rocky knoll off its coast. When he returned to Sydney in 1808 his health was impaired. Sir Henry returned to Sydney from Van Diemen's Land, and Grant went to live with him in a fine stone house at the mouth of Port Jackson. If governors could use distance to separate troublemakers from the main settlement, Sir Henry could respond in kind. He used his considerable wealth to purchase land inside South Head in order to create a refuge far from the 'prying eyes' and eavesdropping spies of Sydney. He named it Vaucluse, after the refuge of the self-exiled fourteenth-century Italian poet Petrarch. Here the two men lived quietly, immersing themselves in domestic and farm chores, letting the hair on their top lips grow long in a kind of protest, which gave them a 'formidable and grotesque appearance'. Grant became increasingly religious, kept his journal and continued to agitate for signatures to his Bond of Union. He was pardoned by Macquarie in 1811, and sailed back to England.[66]

Romantic, secluded and a haven from 'prying eyes': a view of Vaucluse House in about 1817. (Mitchell Library, State Library of New South Wales)

A LAND OF WONDER AND DELIGHT: NATURAL HISTORY, COLLECTING AND ART

The establishment of the colony of New South Wales coincided significantly with another birth: the foundation of the prestigious Linnaean Society in London. In Britain, interest in natural history was raging among the genteel and wealthy classes, with the flowering of numerous societies, a publishing explosion and a proliferation of private museums and collections. The Linnaean Society championed the revolutionary system of classifying the natural world developed by the famous Swedish botanist Carolus Linnaeus. The great power of this system was its universality, for it seemed to be 'an explanatory framework for the natural world'. Every living thing, once carefully observed, could be pinned down in its 'proper' family and place according to genus, species and sometimes variety. Linnaeus also proposed a whole new scientific language, the Latinised double names for plants and animals which scientists and aficionados still use today.[67]

Although it seemed admirably 'objective' and universal, this new framework for understanding nature was inevitably a centralising system, and it placed Europe at that powerful 'centre'. Since animals and plants had to be closely observed in order to be classified, natural history had already become 'the great enterprise of collecting the world'. It was also, as Denis Byrne observes, a practice utterly consistent with imperial expansion, for they were parallel world systems, together forming a 'giant catchment . . . for objects, information and wealth', which moved 'resolutely to where power lay'. Specimens—from rocks and butterflies to the bones of indigenous people—moved from the colonies back to the museums and collections of Europe.[68] Classifying them one by one as part of the great system of genera and species also meant that they were divorced from their own particular ecological and social contexts. And while the new language on one hand seemed to make consistent information accessible to all, it was also a way of excluding those who would not or could not master it, and of invalidating other ways of talking about nature.

Before the colonial project was even conceived, the Australian continent was already a site of great popular scientific interest in Europe. Curiosity was aroused when the scientists and artists of the *Endeavour* returned with an impressive haul of exotic never-before-seen specimens, drawings and written descriptions. Cook had renamed Stingray Bay on the east coast Botany Bay in honour of the botanical treasure trove Joseph Banks found there. Given this widespread popular interest, and Sir Joseph's support of the colony, ecological historians are still puzzled that no official botanist or artist was sent on the First Fleet. These absences, like others, seem to indicate the British government's single-minded focus on setting up the convict colony.[69]

The 'rage for curiosity' spilled nevertheless from the ships as soon as the Europeans disembarked. Everyone was soon collecting plant specimens, catching birds, chipping bits of rock, and stealing the tools and implements of the Eora to send home or to sell to sailors on the ships. Everyone who could write, or dictate a letter, took the trouble to describe the plants, animals and native inhabitants of the new land for their friends and relatives back home, or in the manuscripts they were preparing for their publishers. The European foundations of Australia were marked by a great outpouring of art and writing by the 'eager curiosity' of these self-conscious discoverers. Collected specimens, remarks Richard Neville, became 'Australia's first export industry'. Banks, as the leading naturalist and the colony's patron, naturally received the greatest bounty: stuffed and preserved kangaroos, kegs containing more kangaroos, kangaroo rats and echidna, live possums and parrots, stuffed birds, the skin of an emu, dried flowers, seeds and scores of tubs of plants. Lesser patrons and friends also received parcels and crates of much-desired specimens: tokens of deference, homage or friendship.[70]

The talented amateur naturalists among the officers also sketched, painted and described specimens they collected from the bushland around Sydney and on their exploratory trips. The botanical riches were dazzling. Surgeon John White 'collected in the distance of about half a mile 25 flowers of plants and shrubs of different genera and species', evidently choosing the most colourful and eye-catching flowers. Collectors were not taken aback by weirdness or strangeness, but by the sheer variety. Worgan thought that collecting and categorising them all was simply impossible. 'As to the Shrubs and Plants and Herbs of this Country', he wrote, 'Tis beyond the Power of Botanists to number up their Tribes'.[71] White's first journal was published with 65 plates, and its success encouraged him to continue with the project. When artist Thomas Watling arrived in October 1792, he was assigned to White, and evidently given some of the work of the anonymous artist we know as the 'Port Jackson Painter' to copy. He then set to work on watercolours of birds, animals and plants for White's next volume. Watling himself had rather ambitious plans for his own art, as we have seen, but White appears to have stymied these. He considered Watling arrogant for signing his paintings, and told his publisher to leave his name off them.[72]

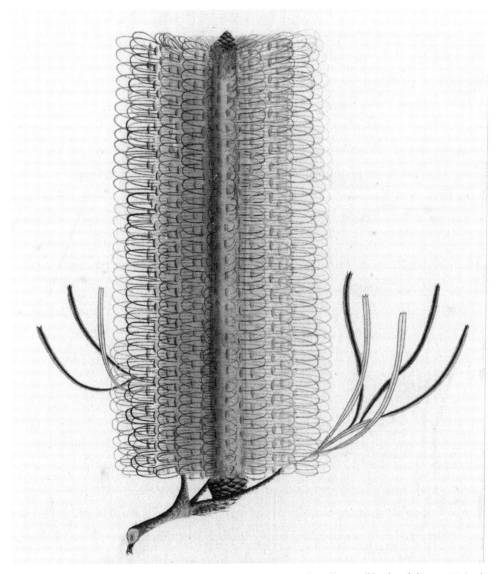

Port Jackson Painter, 'Banksia Spinalosa native name "Wallangre"', the delicate Hairpin Banksia. (Natural History Museum)

This great movement of animals and plants was not restricted to the elite and educated: convicts not only did a lot of the collecting, but sent boxes of curiosities and specimens home too. Margaret Catchpole had evidently been asked to collect specimens for her patron, Mrs Cobbold. Such collections were not only about scientific knowledge, then: being both exotic and fashionable, they were a great asset to the social standing of gentlefolk. Catchpole set about dutifully putting together a collection, only to have it stolen from her house by 'wicked Creatures', as she wrote crossly, just when it was 'in readiness to a sent to for you my good Lady'. In the meantime, two 'mountain cocks and a hen pheasant' had been despatched across the ocean in a cedar case at Mrs Cobbold's request. And in return? Catchpole's next paragraph contained her humble request that the Cobbold family petition Governor Bligh 'that something would be done for me'.[73]

So Sydney's natural environment had this social dimension: it was a cornucopia of desired objects which could be used to lubricate social relationships and patronage networks, all the way down the ranks and orders. Some collectors were entranced by what they found; others were completely instrumental; still others found the time-consuming business of collecting rather irksome. Samuel Marsden wrote apologetically to his friend and patron Mrs Stoker that he had been too busy to collect many seeds for her, and besides, 'I don't profess any great Botanical knowledge myself'. Still, he packed some up and sent them to her, with 'a branch belonging to each kind according to their number . . . they are all new and fresh and gathered with my own hand'.[74]

The alternative was to buy curiosities and specimens from the collectors themselves—often Aboriginal people, convicts and ex-convicts. But by 1791, the market for specimens was fierce, as the collectors clearly well knew. Elizabeth Macarthur was annoyed to discover that 'every person here sets up for Sir Joseph', and that ersatz 'botanists' gave 'high prices for every curiosity brought them'. The newly arrived would continue to complain of such high prices into the 1810s. By the 1820s several Sydney dealers were making very good livings putting together collections and selling them to departing visitors.[75]

But as far as serious botany was concerned, to be a colonist, sending pictures and specimens back Home, was to be by default in a deferential position. One offered specimens humbly and deferred to the far greater knowledge and status of the great institutions and personages. The latter did not always respond with appreciation or generosity—they had no need to. Despite all the gifts, Banks himself was 'reluctant to involve himself with the amateurs' at Botany Bay. He supported instead ventures like Matthew Flinders' *Investigator* voyage in 1801–03, which included the professional artists William Westall and Ferdinand Bauer.

Earlier Banks had also sent out his man on the ground in New South Wales, George Caley.[76]

George Caley, son of a Manchester farrier, was one of those extraordinary self-educated men who rose from humble beginnings through his intelligence, utter dedication and relentless work. He gave himself utterly to his passion for botany and its proper collection, recording and preservation. Yet Banks did not choose him for his knowledge or dedication, but because of his physical strength and stamina—qualities thought to be peculiar to the lower orders, suitable for the strenuous life in the colonies. Caley was not considered an equal: he was firmly outside scientific circles. His hopes of publishing a natural history of New South Wales were not encouraged and came to nothing. He later lamented that the 'language of Linnaeus' was 'above my reach'.[77] Caley was also eccentric, took offence easily and combined hyperactivity and ineptitude in often disastrous ways. He lost things, stormed about, inadvertently started bushfires and was 'a menace to equipment'. Banks, thanking Governor King for putting up with him, added: 'had he been born a gentleman, he would have been shot long ago in a duel'. Even William Bligh found him 'a most strange creature', and was taken aback by his 'wildness'.[78]

Banks instructed Caley to investigate the resources of the new colony in order to discover their commercial potential. But Caley's efforts on that score were minimal. From his house in Parramatta, with its established botanical garden, he threw himself into collecting, preserving, pickling, pressing, describing and classifying the colony's plants, animals and birds. 'Every inch of ground I consider as sacred', he wrote to Banks, 'and not to be trampled over without being noticed'.[79] (If only Caley had been in the valley of the Tank Stream early in 1788.)

Naturally, everything was far more difficult and complex than it had seemed. Paper was in perpetually short supply, which, he wrote, 'threw a gloom on me that I cannot describe in words'. He drove everyone mad trying to get it. A flood carried off his garden, though by the time Péron visited it in 1803, it was again in a flourishing state. Flies got into his bird skins and ruined them. The animals he caught usually managed to escape. His attempts to catch the platypus Banks hankered for were unsuccessful and he could not afford to buy one from the dealers in Sydney. The trees of the inland areas were so large, they were impossible for him to climb, so he had to rely on the parrots which, he observed, 'throw down numerous bits of branches'. But then Caley worried that the seed capsules and flowers might not belong to the tree he was recording. He was often frustrated that he had little to show for all his frenetic activity, and believed that he had 'never had a fair trial'.[80]

But Caley was utterly convinced of the noble nature of his calling, and the importance of making permanent records. He knew his own limitations, and sought not individual fame, but to contribute to a larger endeavour. 'We should not only be eager to collect, but to preserve what we collect', he lectured Banks, but for himself, 'I shall content myself by thinking that I have erected a line of beacons as a guide for future botanists, and rendered the road more easy to travel'.[81]

If Caley was Banks' collector, he in turn had collectors working for him. Some were assigned convicts, one of whom had very good relations with Aboriginal people. Another was likely to have been the boy-convict-turned-sailor-turned-fugitive-cattle-thief, George Bruce. Bruce appears to have been an experienced collector, for he said he had 'employed my self in rangen the wilderness collecting of all sorts of insex for the doctor of the hospital'. In later life he boasted of knowing the country from end to end as a result of his 'collicking'. We will learn more of Bruce's adventures in Chapter 9. But Caley relied most of all on his Aboriginal assistant and friend, Daniel Moowattin, whose intelligence and usefulness he praised. Aboriginal guides were of huge help to naturalists, he declared, for they stopped collectors 'getting lost or bewildered', they pointed out the tracks of animals, they were 'excellent marksmen and quicker-sighted than our people'. The 'bush natives', as he called the people of the inland, could climb trees too. When Caley sailed back to England in 1810, Moowattin went with him.[82]

Caley became intimately acquainted with the ecologies and landscapes of the Sydney region. He made a number of fatiguing exploratory journeys, and met more Aboriginal people, occasionally in rather edgy circumstances. But he always said he was drawn to mountains. Once in the colony, it was his greatest ambition to explore the rugged plateaux which encircled the Cumberland Plain.

He jealously watched the attempts of others to cross the range, and finally set out on his own expedition in November 1804. Like the others before him, Caley soon found himself climbing for days up and down an endless maze of rugged, steep, rocky gullies, accompanied by a party of increasingly unhappy convict men. The weather was freezing and foggy, the country like a 'devils' wilderness'. One valley, he wrote, 'put me in mind of looking down a coal pit . . . [I]ts great depths, darkness damp and the hideous noise . . . some frogs or toads made, cause me to call it Dismal Dell.' The view seemed to be unanimous. The convicts in the party declared 'they would sooner prefer the worst cell they had ever seen in prison' to this awful place. The party reached Mount Banks, overlooking the Grose Valley, where Caley decided to turn back, much to everyone's relief. Later he wrote to Banks of the extreme roughness of the country, which he found 'beyond description' and 'like going over the roofs of houses in a town'. Yet he thought restlessly of the undiscovered plants still waiting for him in the Blue Mountains.[83]

Caley wrote long and rather baleful reports of the colony's level of progress and potential. Farming was primitive and the farmers lived in poverty, and he did not think the natural productions would ever amount to much. Perhaps he, then, was the archetypal homesick settler, unable to adjust to the local environment? Banks terminated his appointment in 1808, and Caley decided to return to England. There he struggled to get his collection properly documented and preserved. It took years. But instead of feeling he was home, Caley felt out of kilter, a stranger in England. The country was 'now so much increased in population and the customs there so opposite to mine, that I scarcely now call myself a native of it'. What had caused this deep shift in Caley's being? He knew: 'the Forest undoubtedly had been the cause of this and whose wilds I now prefer before the most civilised place in the world'.[84]

And of all those forested lands of New South Wales, it was the Blue Mountains which haunted him most powerfully, and called him back. 'If it were not for the thoughts of seeing my collection put in a state of preservation, all my thoughts would be engrossed with New South Wales', he wrote to Banks, 'for in the mountains of that country, my desiderata—and I believe I shall never rest till I have visited some places there I have years ago marked out'. Earlier he had written: 'The mountains of the country I believe have bewitched me'.[85]

'Like going over the roofs of houses': a view over the Blue Mountains from the top of Grose Head, the country George Caley and his party crossed. (National Library of Australia)

But George Caley, torn between the enchantment of lost country and his dedication to botany and posterity, never returned to New South Wales. At the age of 46 he married, then from 1816 to 1822 served as superintendent at the Botanical Gardens at St Vincent in the West Indies, where his wife died. Caley returned to England, where he died in 1829. His collection was broken up and dispersed after his death.[86]

The earlier newcomers to New South Wales found themselves enchanted as well. They were inspired to capture the beauty of what they saw, bursting to tell their family and friends about it, and mustered whatever writing and artistic skills they possessed to do so. Most used not the language of science but the language of wonder, beauty and emotion. In their descriptions and paintings, then, the local became central. Much of the colony's early outpouring of art depicted birds, animals and plants, particularly flowers. The pictures and the notes on them do not convey fear, loathing or alienation—if anything the artists sometimes admit to feeling inadequate to the task of showing the true beauties of what they were painting. Newton Fowell apologised that his sketch of 'a Lorequet' did not match the 'brilliancy' of their plumage, so he sent his father a stuffed specimen as well. Thomas Watling confessed of his leaf-tailed gecko: 'the Beauty of its colours are but very humbly imitated'. The artists did struggle with the unfamiliar shapes of the larger animals—there were some extremely unlikely pictures of kangaroos and emus, for example. Another problem was that they often worked from dead specimens—inevitably they look lifeless in the pictures too, sometimes propped up in odd positions. But it is exciting to observe the way these artists learned through experience and observation, and the way painting and ecology coalesced. Watling and White in particular combined written observations with the images, inscribing paintings with descriptions of the creatures, their encounters with humans, as well as information they had gleaned from Eora informants, including the 'native name'.[87]

Meanwhile, midshipman George Raper, who at first was so lacking in confidence he did not sign his pictures, grew wonderfully proficient under John Hunter's tutelage. Some of his paintings, recently rediscovered and acquired by the National Library of Australia, reveal his serious attempts at botanical art—they include the requisite flower-structures or root-systems. But the paintings which really shine are those which eschew specific names and taxonomic classifications—they were instead immediate and sensitive responses to 'the exotic and its strange beauty'. His pictures of birds—the glossy black cockatoo with his head turned back, a honeyeater with the blue flash around his yellow eye—had only the most general titles: 'Bird of New Holland', for example. Raper was entranced by their gorgeous shapes and colours, by the sinuous lines and the pictorial arrangements he could create with them on his page. He alone among the First Fleet artists used 'glittering bronze paint' to capture the sheeny feathers of a bronzewing pigeon.[88]

The anonymous Port Jackson Painter (Bernard Smith describes him, or them, as a 'cluster of stylistic traits') also created pictures of extraordinary beauty—a coiled diamond python, a striking black swan—which convey 'an authentic feeling of surprise and sense of wonder'.[89] Some of John Hunter's paintings were striking for another reason: while most natural history paintings set their subjects in abstract space or in 'natural' settings, he sometimes acknowledged that the act of painting them involved encounters between creatures and humans. A great tuna lies gutted on a table. Fish still hang by hooks and lines. Three feathers of a black cockatoo's tail are tied up with a string. A king parrot swings down from a loop of rope to accept fruit from a human hand.[90]

So the colony's birds, mammals, fish and plants were first collected and painted by amateurs and convict artists. By the turn of the century professional artists were starting to make the voyage to New South Wales as well. The first of them was John Lewin, who arrived with his wife Anna Maria in 1800. Lewin planned to study and paint local plants and animals and publish books. His patron was Dru Drury, the London entomologist who had collectors 'scattered in many lands'. Drury had also been responsible for nominating Lewin as a Fellow of the Linnaean Society, though Lewin was not a scientist.[91] In Sydney, Lewin soon met John Grant, who was entranced with his talent, and promptly wrote an ode in his new friend's honour, including the verse:

Whether thine Hand delineating draw
Insect, or Bird, or crimson Warrataw
In each, in All, thine Art we can forgive
when things inanimate appear to live.

Grant also promised to write scientific descriptions for Lewin's paintings, because the artist, he said, was 'unable to clothe his Ideas with adequate correct language'.[92] Lewin, supported by Anna Maria, busied himself with an extraordinary range of painting, including beautifully observed insects and birds (published as *Prodomus Entomology* in 1805 and *Birds of New South Wales* in 1808), other animals and plants, but also charming 'theatrical paintings' of kangaroos, koalas, insouciant brush turkeys and dramatic still-life arrangements of local fish. These were commissioned and enjoyed by his colonial patrons, and hung proudly in the main rooms of Government House. Lewin also painted the illuminations that shone from windows during public celebrations, and landscape paintings commemorating Macquarie's inland excursions.[93]

Lewin wanted to paint directly from nature, 'on the spot', not from desiccated specimens or 'notes still more abstruse'. He wanted his paintings to 'appear to live', just as Grant said. But before he could observe his subjects' habits, let alone paint them, he had to find them, and he soon discovered that 'every thing in Naturall History is contrary to our known knowledge on England and in fact I was greatly puzzled to find any'. Did this contrariness elicit feelings of dread or distaste? Just the opposite: by careful observation, Lewin eventually discovered that the larvae he was after

> feed by night and secret themselves knawing a hole . . . in the body of a tree . . . and there lie hide all day . . . They cover hole with a web in a verry artfull manner so that it requires a careful person to find their hiding places.

Lewin's delight at the creatures' cunning was matched by his delight in having solved the mystery. He let his patron know that he had 'got such an insight into their manners' that he would now be able to 'procure you some of the most beautiful and rare moths'. His letter was suffused with the sheer joy of discovery.[94]

John Grant's poem did not exaggerate, and art historian Richard Neville is right: one look at Lewin's glowing sheaf of feathery gold wattle tumbling diagonally across the page 'gives lie to the idea that early settlers could not "see" distinctive Australian flora and fauna'.[95] Here was an artist who immersed himself in colonial nature, and in turn delighted, informed and inspired others with his paintings. But, as in Caley's story, his work did not rate as 'science' of the sort promoted by his Linnaean fellows, because he did not possess the language of science. The same had been said of Watling's paintings, brought to England by Surgeon White in 1795 and delivered to a publisher two years later. The descriptions were too simple, the pictures not detailed enough. It is ironic, then, that many of Watling's paintings, and those of his contemporary anonymous colonial artists, eventually did became the 'type material' for the first scientific descriptions of the Australian fauna and flora they depicted. Meanwhile most of Banks' Australian material collected on the *Endeavour* voyage was never published.[96]

CHANGING THE FACE OF THE COUNTRY

The settlers themselves were changing the face of the country with their farms, gardens and orchards, their plants and animals, their quarrying and timber-getting and fires. Observers read the cleared and cultivated patches and groves, the country opened by clearing as 'improvements', welcome, happy signs that the country's potential was being fulfilled. Gardens and gardening in particular were an integral part of the colonising project—even convicts were allowed time off to tend them. Their huts were surrounded by practical vegetable patches and fruit trees.[97] Many of the officers and free settlers were passionate about gardening, about growing things. The gardeners saw the colony less as a place to slavishly replicate English gardens than as a great testing ground for a cornucopia of plants from all over the world. Péron admired the wonderful gardens he saw in Sydney. Behind the lieutenant governor's house to the west was 'a vast garden which is worth the attention both of the philosopher and the naturalist, on account of the great number of useful vegetables . . . which have been procured from around the world'. At Government House he explored

> a fine garden which descends to the sea-shore: already in this garden may
> be seen, the Norfolk Island pine, the superb Columbia, growing by the side
> of the bamboo of Asia: farther on is the Portugal orange, and Canary fig,
> ripening beneath the shade of the French apple-tree: the cherry, peach,
> pear, and apricot, are interspersed amongst the Banksia, Metrosideros,
> Correa, Melaleuca, Casuarina, eucalyptus, and a great number of other
> indigenous trees.[98]

The gardening colonists did not despise, supplant or exclude native trees and shrubs. On the contrary, they left them in situ or planted them deliberately among the exotic species, creating new hybrid communities.

Plants sent to the colony in the ships travelled in better conditions than the convicts, for special hothouses and beds were built for them, and every care taken to ensure their safe arrival. The settlers not only sent seeds and cuttings back Home, their letters were full of requests for seeds, cuttings and more plants, and news on how these vegetable pets were faring in the colonial soils. They boasted of their successes and lamented the plants that died in transit, or shrivelled in the dry years. There were emotional dimensions too: Eliza Marsden always associated her ripening melons with a fondly remembered relative: 'We often talk of him when we are eating the melons', she wrote, 'the seeds of which he was so kind to give me'. John Grant's beloved mother gave him seeds to take on the *Coromandel*—'I shall always be thinking and talking of you', he told her, 'particularly when any produce [of] your present of Seeds appears on my table in New South Wales'.[99]

The gardening colonists developed a mania for the majestic Norfolk Island pines, which had proved such a disappointment as mast material, but made fabulous landmarks for their estates (another example of the confluence of aesthetics and utility). Towering over the eucalypt canopy when mature, the pines were visible for miles, and eventually they marked out many of the Cumberland Plain mansions. (The next fashion in huge trees was the still weirder-looking bunya pine from Queensland.) Captain John Piper seems to have been single-handedly responsible for this invasion of green giants, for he must have spent a great deal of time while on duty on Norfolk Island packing up young trees and shipping them to his friends in Sydney. Eliza Marsden received some, and probably so did D'Arcy Wentworth, for the pines stood sentinel at Homebush for many years. A disappointed George Johnston wrote to thank Piper from Annandale in 1804: 'I am extremely obliged to you for the Pines but Mr Pendleton, or Serj't Guise took so little care of them that I received three empty boxes & one with only two live plants in it'. Piper immediately sent more and Johnston planted them along the avenue to his house. For the next hundred years, travellers along the Parramatta Road saw this lofty green avenue on the ridge leading to the old house.[100]

Some of the exotic plants the colonists introduced found the environment extremely congenial. They escaped from farms, and began to make their own way in the colony. Travellers reported abandoned acres and fallow fields infested with introduced weeds like the 'cotton plant', a downy-seeded grass which produced a silky 'cotton', originally planted in the hope of a useful cash crop for making fabric. (Gentleman convict John Grant was convinced these plants represented a fortune just waiting to be made, and urged his Mam to send out

Augustus Earle, 'The Norfolk Pine, N. S. Wales'. (National Library of Australia)

a carding machine.) By the 1830s it was growing everywhere, along roadsides and in paddocks.[101]

Other plants were garden escapees. By 1804 the geraniums brought by Surgeon Bowes Smyth on the First Fleet were growing as hedges 7 feet high in Sydney, and had already spread through the bushland, splashing their homely petals as far as Parramatta. By the 1840s geraniums 'of the old-fashioned kinds are almost like weeds'.[102] Peach trees were another great coloniser. They were so prolific they grew in every garden, town and country, 'wherever stones drop', bearing fruit within months, their leaves filling the air with 'exquisitely fine' fragrance. Sometimes the trees fell under the weight of their swelling fruit, and there were far too many peaches for people to eat. Pigs grew fat on them and settlers crushed them for cider (often very bad), or distilled them illegally to make spirits. They may have been one inspiration for early accounts of New South Wales as a land of fruit-fulness and plenty. Possums, bats and birds must have loved them. The peach stones slipped through the fences, hitched rides on the currents and formed their own communities, growing in wild thickets along the rivers. 'Peachtree corner' became a common riverside placename, and Peachtree Creeks abound. They may also have been deliberately planted in groves near camps by Aboriginal people, who did this elsewhere with large-stoned native fruits.[103]

The stories of the blackberry, the privet and the willow were similar: at first celebrated for their food or aesthetic value, and for the simple fact of successful acclimatisation, their berries, stones and seeds were spread by birds, or in the winds or waters, took root and became part of everyday landscapes. Eventually their bad behaviour—they strangled bushland and waterways—became clear, and they were reviled as pests.[104]

The early colonists encountered native animals and birds, not only as speci-mens to paint, preserve and describe, but as living creatures which became part of urban and rural life. They admired dingoes and tried to tame pups, but found them too wild, for they 'snapped the heads off poultry'. By the 1820s dingoes were thought to have become taller through breeding with domestic dogs, and by the 1830s they were 'a nuisance in Sydney streets'. They flourished on the graziers' stock and were hunted relentlessly at least to the 1850s.[105] Governor Phillip kept kangaroos at Government House and in quieter moments enjoyed hand-feeding a bat, which would 'hang by one leg the whole day'. The settlers tried to raise young emus, but most eagerly sought after were the colourful birds, many of which perished aboard the ships when settlers tried to send them home. By at least the 1820s the doorways and awnings and verandahs of Sydney and Parramatta were festooned with cages full of whistling, screeching, scrambling parrots and lorikeets. Tall cranes, called 'Native Companions', stalked, dignified and unconcerned, among the residents of Parramatta in the 1830s.[106]

Animal, bird and insect populations themselves were altered by the presence of new foods, crops, exotic animals and buildings—some declined with the destruction of their habitats, but others thrived on new food sources and shelter. Rats flourished on the stored grain food to the point where they were described as 'our enemies, the rats'. The writers don't say whether these were native species or those they had brought with them on the ships, though Tim Flannery believes they were *gnar-ruck* (*Conilurus albipes*), the white-footed rabbit rat. By the end of 1791 they had almost disappeared, though the colonists did not know why. Their reports and pictures were the last record of gnar-ruck in the Sydney region.[107] For a time the settlers' fowls probably boosted the population of quolls, the 'spotted tiger cats' and 'eastern native cats' as the settlers called them (*Dasyurus maculatus* and *Dasyurus viverrinus*). They were 'very destructive to our eggs and poultry'. The Port Jackson Painter's picture shows them, decidedly weaselish with blood-stained muzzles, in the act of dragging away a dramatically slumped chicken.[108]

The creation of more grazing land and farmland meant the loss of habitat for open forest and woodland animals and birds, as clearing still does, but some birds probably increased in number. King parrots, bowerbirds, rosellas, crows and currawongs swooped and feasted on the early grain crops, and ripening peaches attracted flocks of 'all our varieties of parrots'. Cockatoos got into the maize. Small birds the colonists called white-tailed warblers (possibly Jacky Winter, *Microeca leucophaea*) 'follow the Gardeners and Workmen picking up Worms &c and [are] very familiar', the same way egrets today will stand unperturbed beside enormous, roaring excavators in quarries, waiting for the great blade to turn up a bounty in grubs.[109]

Birds and mammals as well as reptiles, amphibians, insects and all sorts of plants must have come and gone as bushland regenerated and was re-cleared on fallow and 'waste' ground. Even in the town of Sydney itself, the bush grew back only a few years after that first extensive clearing—not the original forest, but a new one. Dawes Point, so laboriously cleared in 1788 for the Observatory, was covered in 'shrubs and brushwoods' in 1796, when they caught fire. (The fire also came within metres of the powder magazine, so the gunpowder was hurriedly moved onto the *Supply*.)[110] In the 1820s, petitioners wanting town grants alleged that there were unused allotments in Sydney covered in bushland.

So, rather than sliding inexorably towards ecological devastation from January 1788, the face of the country around Sydney was in constant flux. But in the later decades of the nineteenth and into the twentieth century and beyond, the 'new natures' set in motion by the settlers took a terrible toll. Habitat destruction, degradation and fragmentation and feral animals have resulted in the increase of some species, but disappearance of others across New South Wales. To date the unrolling cost of the colony's establishment includes the loss or severe reduction of many vegetation communities, and the extinction of 125 species or subspecies of plants and animals, especially small ground-dwelling marsupials. The ferocious, fowl-hunting eastern quolls have dis-appeared from Sydney—the last one was found dead on the road in Vaucluse in 1963.[111] And while Sydney's suburbs, parklands and bushland are still alive with birds, many of those painted so beautifully by the early artists are no longer found in the Sydney region: the tall, red-headed, rail-legged brolgas which once stalked in the lagoons; the magpie geese that flew in great V-shapes overhead. The striking, noisy blue-faced honeyeater, the plump scarlet robin, the glossy cockatoo with its crested yellow head, the hovering brahminy kite were all common in the 1790s, but are now vanished from the Sydney region. Populations of Sydney's gorgeous turquoise parrot 'crashed' in the early twenti-eth century—though there have been scattered sightings recently. 'Where have all those lovely singing feathered tribes gone?' lamented Hawkesbury identity Toby Ryan, the grandson of convict settlers, in his old age. 'Alas! They have disappeared from their old haunts.' Yet he himself had relished hunting them in his boyhood and youth.[112]

Surprisingly, the plants of the Sydney region appear to have survived more successfully. Benson and Howell's exhaustive 2002 study found that, despite extensive clearing, only two Cumberland Plain woodland species had completely disappeared—perhaps the toll is higher for other plant communities.[113] What did change dramatically over the early colonial period were the forest *ecologies*. On the Cumberland Plain, most of the tall forests, rainforests and open wood-lands were dramatically altered through clearfelling, grazing, new plants and animals, and through timbergetting. The great swathe of the Blue Gum High Forest, set aside by King as the Field of Mars Common in 1803, was transformed in the lifetimes of the first white settlers. Blackbutt, ironbark, some blue gum, mahogany and forest oak was cut out and dragged to the mills by timbergetters, while local settlers and leaseholders cut firewood, shingles and fencing posts. This after all had been one of the original purposes of the common. But by the 1850s this forest had been cut and recut so often that 'the roots have thrown up numberless saplings and low scrub, which has destroyed the grass that might have been on the ground when it was open forest'. By this time, too, these were common laments: not fewer trees, but more; not easier to travel through, but harder. 'The Field of Mars Common', concluded an old colonist in 1862, was now 'in a wild state . . . covered with timber, old stumps and young saplings'.[114]

It was truer than he knew. It had gone wild since the settlers arrived, but it was not only timbergetting which had caused this. The other great element now missing from the forest lands was fire. Not the fires caused by lightning strikes of the great Sydney storms, of course—they continued—but the fire regimes of the Aboriginal people. As these fires were extinguished with the spread of settlement, the open 'park-like' woodlands so prized by Europeans also thickened with vegetation. Around Sydney itself, Surgeon Joseph Arnold was already complaining in 1810 that the bushland 'was so thick as to be in many places impassable'. By the 1840s, Sir Thomas Mitchell remembered the old, open forests where 'a man might gallop and see whole miles in front of him'. Now it was covered in 'thick forests of young trees . . . the grass choked with underwood'. By then he knew that Aboriginal burning had kept the country open.[115]

These new thicker forests had another serious environmental consequence. As early as 1791 Watkin Tench could see what every Sydney gardener knows: the climate of Sydney meant that 'the progress of vegetation never is at a stand'. Then as now, both native and exotic plants grew rampantly, opportunistically. This is why the early gardeners rejoiced in the good years of rain, sunshine and clear blue skies: everything grew so wonderfully well. But when the dry years returned this vegetable exuberance desiccated: it became fuel. In the unburned, dense bushlands, straggly bark, dead limbs, twigs and crackling, explosive gum leaves accumulate rapidly, a crisp, airy pyre. Lightning strikes ignited them, fires escaped from houses and camps and set the country ablaze. The settlers had unwittingly created the conditions for the terrible wildfires which destroyed their farms, houses and crops, and which still threaten the city, the plain and the mountains every summer.[116]

'HERE WE FEEL WE ARE ALIVE': VISCERAL AND EMOTIONAL RESPONSES

The Sydney environment is often assumed to have harmed the physical and emotional well-being of the colonists. Most histories, popular and academic, portray the early years as the 'starvation years', brought on by a combination of a lack of local foods and the cruelly disorganised nature of the whole project. Europeans are said to have stupidly shunned what pitiful local produce there was and slowly starved on the reducing rations of weevilly flour and rancid salt pork; or so the story goes. But convicts and soldiers spent a great deal of time collecting native foods in the bushlands surrounding Sydney, especially coastal food plants. Midshipman Daniel Southwell laboriously listed the useful, therapeutic or tasty native species:

> we find many salutory herbs that make wholesome drink and of g[reat]t use to our sick. Balm is here in plenty and sevral vegitable have been lately found that are of the same kind tho' not so good as at home. Here is Spinach, parsley a sort of B[roa]d Beans several wholesome unknown vegetables. Many of the productions of the country are Aromatic and have medicinal Virtues and it yield a variety of things proper for Foementa and other external applications, a Sort of green Berries that are procured and m[ake an] Excellt Antiscrobutick are gathered in abundance, and a species of sorrel &c, all of a peculiar fine acid.[117]

The other officers wrote such descriptions and lists too, and often mentioned the gathering of vegetables, berries and tea; Phillip wrote of heart-shaped transparent red berries (probably native cherries), wholesome and agreeable, and eaten in 'great quantities'. Surgeon White included pictures of sweet tea (a native vine whose leaves were used as a tea substitute) and tea-tree in his journal. Tench and Worgan waxed lyrical about the delicious green turtles brought in from Lord Howe Island. Worgan listed the beautiful birds they shot, and the animals and fish—all of which 'made no despicable meal'. An anonymous convict woman wrote: 'Our kangaroo rats are like mutton, but much leaner, and there is a kind of chickweed so much in taste like our spinach that no difference can be discerned'.[118] In summer local fish were often abundant, although the supply could be uneven; in winter they were scarce. Oysters—both the large mud oyster and the smaller Sydney rock oyster—were certainly devoured with gusto; they were a major part of the diet. The officers dined on kangaroo and emu and relished both—the kangaroo equal to 'good mutton', and the beefy emu meat 'a delicious meal'. On exploratory trips ducks, crows, cockatoos and anything else they could shoot went into the cooking pots or onto roasting spits. By the early 1800s Sydney was considered wonderfully healthful, a sanatorium, where a fine climate and abundant fresh fruit and vegetables could even bring half-dead victims of scurvy back to life.[119]

It is strange that those constant early references to native foods have been largely ignored or dismissed in historical accounts. The spectre of the colony, abandoned and starving in a hostile, barren environment, seems to have over-shadowed them completely. But as Alan Frost and others point out, the colonists were on the whole in good health, and the mortality rate was low, except when ships brought weak and diseased people and pathogens. Mr Lowe, the Surgeon's Mate of the *Sirius*, reported in 1790, 'Our births have far exceeded our burials'. Frost thinks the consumption of the nutritious local foods was the key to this well-being. The vitamin-C rich berries in particular are likely to have contributed to a wondrous phenomenon: the births of healthy babies to convict women who had reputedly been 'barren'.[120] As we shall see, some of these foods were also the staple foods of the Eora. The tragic side of this story is that the invaders probably monopolised the native produce, leaving the Eora hungry and weakened.[121]

Yet hunger and starvation stalk the written accounts of the white settlers, and most of the histories. Why? As James Boyce suggests was also the case in early Hobart, it probably had to do with imported food supplies. In the early years these official foods did run very low at times, something which obsessed most journal-keepers. After all, rations of salt meat, flour, dried peas, and sugar or butter were not just about nutrition, they were of psychological importance.

They were also considered a right by convicts and therefore a flashpoint of nego-tiation—and rebellion. Nobody wanted to have to deal with hundreds of hungry, aggrieved, rebellious convicts, upon whose labour the colony depended.[122]

Climate is often presented as yet another hardship the early colonists had to bear in the 'gaol town'. Expecting a green and pleasant Eden, they sailed into a raging La Niña. Ferocious lightning storms (which killed some of their precious stock) were followed by cracking thunder—'the most Terrible I ever herd', groaned Ralph Clark. The 'heavy Gloom [that] . . . hangs over the Woods' was a prelude to tremendous Sydney downpours. The storms made them wonder what kind of wild place this was. But then the summers of 1979–93 were scorching, with temperatures in the forties and the blast of hot winds from the north-west. Birds and flying foxes fell dead from the air.[123] Judge Atkins tracked the heatwave of early December 1792, and worried about the source of the furnace-like winds:

4th [Dec] Excessive hot, a hot Westerly wind, whether the heats proceed from the country being on fire or from traversing hot sandy deserts is yet to be discovered.

5th [Dec] a burning westerly wind, obliged to keep the windows shut, unless we have rain soon the late crops of Indian Corn will be totally burnt up 10 oclock a heavy gale from the w.ward and as hot as the mouth of an oven. At 12 oclock ther in the shade 99 [degrees Fahrenheit] in the air 114 It begins to thunder—light shower

7th Dec 1792 . . . 12 oclock 107° in the shade the whole country was in a perfect blaze, but whether it proceeded from the intense heat of the atmosphere or whether it was set fire to by the Natives is a doubt . . .[124]

The searing air bore ominous messages about the new land—its interior must either be a barren sandy desert or ablaze with fire. Over the next two centuries, European expectations of four predictable seasons revolving in every year would collide with the non-annual Australian climate, parched and deluged in El Niño cycles of seven to ten years. This would also loom large in the conceptualisation of Australia as the baffling 'unparalleled continent', where nothing behaved as expected, and where experience alone could teach.[125]

Richard Atkins' diary was also a meteorological record. Thermometer and barometer readings were carefully noted, and gave shape to the days. Entries for April 1792 track both weather and wellness:

> 12 [April] The rain still continues but with less violence than before . . . It has pleased God Almighty to inflict on me these last three weeks more sickness than I have experienced these last 30 years . . .

> 13 [April] This day our usual good weather is returned & with it as it should soon returning health. I feel the principal of life strong . . .[126]

In good weather he rambled, collected and went fishing; rain made him miserable; hot drying winds were irritating and fearful. But experience of climate—air, clear sky, winds, temperature, humidity—was more than merely a matter of superficial bodily comfort. During the eighteenth century, European ideas about climate as a determinate of social organisation were in ascendance. So the Europeans in early Sydney used 'their own bodily sensations . . . their feelings of comfort and unease, to judge whether the land they coveted was properly British territory'. They used their bodies to judge whether it was possible for Britons to live here. They were linking climate directly with physical health, reading their internal states in external weather conditions.[127]

In spite of their dramatic initiation, Sydney's climate was the element most praised by the colonists. They continued to acknowledge its capricious changeability—sudden squalls which so often overturned boats, the abrupt drops in temperature 'with no warning', the massing of dark clouds and dramatic downpours. Collins thought the common inflammation of the eyes was probably due to 'variable and unsettled weather'.[128] But they also discovered the clear air and still blue days of autumn months, and how few winter days were truly cold, dark and miserable. In fine weather they were content and filled with a sense of well-being. Most of the early writers agreed that the climate was 'healthful', indeed 'no climate, hitherto known, is more generally salubrious'. By 1795, Commissary John Palmer declared simply that the climate was 'delicious, the airs so salubrious'. Many people attributed the births of so many healthy children directly to the climate. When one considers infant mortality rates in England, the significance of this becomes clear: children were safer, and thrived here. The pleasant air temperature was linked directly with the absence of 'dreadful putrid fevers by which new countries are often ravaged' such as those of the East Indies and the southern states of America.[129]

At the end of his sojourn in New South Wales, Watkin Tench provided a remarkably observant summary of Sydney's climate which sounds very much like modern descriptions: it was 'changeable beyond any other I ever heard of . . . clouds, storms, and sunshine pass in rapid succession'. There was often not enough rain, but when it fell there were wild torrents. Thunderstorms were common but 'have ceased to alarm, from rarely causing mischief'; the Europeans had adjusted to them, as they would to hot weather. The air was 'purged' by strong breezes, and with them came a 'hard, clear sky'. Overall, no other climate *'affords more days on which those pleasures, which depend on the state of the atmosphere, can be enjoyed'* (my emphasis).[130]

Tench was perhaps the first European to write down that Sydney's weather fostered outdoor 'pleasures'. For the early Europeans these included collecting botanical specimens, picnics, boat trips for pleasure and discovery, fishing, shooting, and the exploratory rambles men like George Worgan were so fond of:

Our Excursions put me in Mind of your going a Steeple Hunting, We sometimes, put a Bit of Salt Beef, or Pork, Biskit, a Bottle of O be joyful, in a Snapsack throw it over our Backs, take a hatchet, a Brace of Pistols, and a Musket, and away we go scouring the Woods, sometimes East, West, N.S. if night overtakes us, we light up a rousing Fire, Cut Boughs & make up a Wig-Wam, open our Wallets and eat as hearty of our Fare as You of your Dainties, then lie down on a Bed, which tho' not of Roses, yet we sleep as You do on down; I enjoy these little Rambles, and I think you would . . .[131]

If any piece of writing squashes the image of the alienated, fearful, indoor-dwelling, bush-hating European settler, it is George Worgan's letter. Surgeon Joseph Arnold wrote of his 1809 sojourn in Sydney: 'My greatest diversion is to run among the woods and rocks; and also go a fishing with lines and a net, at which we have the greatest sport, catching great numbers of the most curious fish'. Men such as these obviously relished the environment, and probably never forgot the sensory experiences of the bush—the scents, the breezes, the sun on one's back, the sounds of the bush at night, the sight of moonrise over water and the lagoons and rivers alive with fish and birds. In the 1830s a travelling 'Gentleman' wrote of his deep sense of well-being in the Australian climate. He declared simply, 'In England we exist, here we feel we are alive'.[132]

Over the next two centuries many more 'outdoor pleasures' would be taken up and enjoyed by Sydney people, especially swimming, fishing, sailing, hunting and walking, as well as cricket and horse-racing.[133] The demand for spaces to cater for them would shape the physical city as it grew, and the organisations and cultural meanings attached to sport and leisure would be woven into the urban social fabric. Sensual experiences and the Sydney places which allowed them would fascinate artists, photographers and novelists. These 'pleasures', enabled by climate and environment, moulded the city's cultural identity, a sort of sensual undercurrent in the harder-edged clamour of city-making.

But here I have written mainly of the responses of those of means and at least some education, and those in authority. There was another layer of environmental experience and meaning entirely: that of convict men. For them, the land and waters became places of refuge, escape and rebellion, of pleasure and freedom, and of nefarious geographies.

'Away we go, scouring the woods.' John Lewin's picture of camping out in the Australian bush. (National Library of Australia)

Chapter 9

NEFARIOUS GEOGRAPHIES

I f the 'invaders hated trees', surely the convicts of the First Fleet had most reason to do so.[1] Those assigned to the clearing gangs wrestled for days with the tough maze of roots snaking for metres just below the surface, grubbing out the stubborn stumps. Looking up from this sweaty work, they would have seen dozens more monsters nearby, hundreds in the surrounding valley, the grey-green army of thousands beyond: surely this—the bush—could only have filled them with despair and loathing?

The reactions of the convicts to the Sydney environment have been assumed rather than explored. The first assumption is that they left no records (John Birmingham writes, astonishingly, 'the views of convicts weren't sought and aren't recorded'), so we must interpret for them. Let us review this received wisdom one more time: the gaol town was a terrible place of banishment, the environment was harsh and unyielding, and could only have compounded the convicts' suffering and privation. It must have been hated and frightening. Historians are fond of saying that the hostile bush was the gaol, or that the encircling sandstone escarpments were the prison walls—thus there was nowhere to run. Bush and stone were in league with the authorities; the Australian environment was therefore repressive, menacing and confining. Convicts sent to this terrible place had no escape but alcohol or madness.[2]

There is a picture which begs to differ. It's a rare painting because it shows both convicts and the bush, and seems to speak of the relationship between them. Its official name is 'Major Johnston with Quartermaster Laycock One Serjeant and twenty-five Private of ye New South Wales Corps defeats two hundred and sixty six armed Rebels, 5th March 1804'. Its commonly used name is 'Convict uprising at Castle Hill, 1804', although the action is not taking place at Castle Hill, but along the road to the Hawkesbury at Vinegar Hill.

This picture, much reproduced and studied during the bicentennial and re-enactment of the uprising in 2004, was most likely painted soon after the event, probably to celebrate the 'military glory of the New South Wales Corps'.[3] It is a sort of 'time-travel' picture, telling the story of the brief, savage battle fought on that road during the Irish uprising in March 1804.[4] On the right, the vast and chaotic mob of Irish rebels emerges from the dense, dark bushland—there are hundreds pouring out from between the trees. On the left are ranks of red-coated soldiers, with loyal citizens behind them. Their numbers are much smaller, but they are armed with guns and they stand in regular, orderly lines. Centre stage, the rebel leaders Philip Cunningham and William Johnston have been arrested. The soldiers fire on the rebels, they return fire, then turn to run away in panic and confusion. The last part of the picture, on the far left, shows the bush thinning out, the trees further apart, more orderly, and light shining through. Among the trunks stand the gallows, the 'fatal tree', where the bodies of rebels William Johnston and Samuel Humes are hanging.[5]

In this picture, then, the bush is associated with convict rebellion, with darkness and disorder. It is the rebels' sanctuary. Conversely, cleared bushland, the creation of more open, sunlit landscapes, represent the imposition of order and control by authority, here associated with the legitimate violence of the state. The picture suggests that by 1804, the bush was in league with the convict rebels, and was the enemy of authority. How did this come about?

Let's look at what else historians tell us about convicts and the environment. The convicts sent to Botany Bay are supposed to have been geographically ignorant and ill-equipped to appreciate the local environment. Those who tried to escape were allegedly misguided fools who thought China lay within some days' walking distance of the colony. They are said to have been unable to live in the bush, and those who ran away inevitably starved, or tottered half-dead back to the Camp. While officers, protected by armed soldiers, happily went off on exploratory camping trips into unknown country, it was assumed that such journeys were fatal for convicts.[6]

In fact, convicts were not as geographically ignorant as their superiors liked to believe. Cook's voyages had inspired catchpenny publications, broadsides and pictures, just as the early accounts of Sydney would. These were crude, sensation-alised and inaccurate, but they brought the Australian continent and the Pacific to the consciousness of common people in England.[7] And while there were rumours and stories circulating about the country being joined to China, or India, this does not mean they were taken literally by everyone. Among the convicts were many sailors, who of course knew their global geography; convicts also talked with sailors on board the transports. Clare Anderson, in her study of New South Wales escapees, shows that convicts shared in the knowledge of empire: ships, routes, ports and colonies, knowledge carried on the oceans.[8]

It is assumed that convicts were unable to admire the colonial environment. 'Most of the newcomers were products of the slums who had never been in contact with the soil', writes Eric Rolls. 'They were artificial people, grown on bricks and flagstones.' Geoffrey Bolton points out that England's savage anti-poaching laws meant that the common people who became convicts 'lacked built-in protec-tive attitudes' towards animals; they had no love of wildlife.[9] Again, as convicts banished to an unknown, alien land, their response is presumed to have been hatred.

Convicts' responses to the environment are hard to gauge because relatively few left the sorts of records which tell us such things. Yet those who did write letters and keep journals did not express loathing and alienation at all. William Noah, writing to his sister in 1799, was one of the few early observers who used the idea of inversion to describe the environment, for he wrote of all being 'quiet Opposite to England & and everything in nature plainly appears so, even the Moon is Top side Turvy your summer our winter'. But there is no sense of angst or dislocation here—Noah is unperturbed: he is simply explaining the antipo-dean world. He also wrote panoramic descriptions of the harbour and detailed accounts of mammals, birds, fish and timber.[10]

Emancipist Matthew Everingham was an early Hawkesbury settler who explored the Blue Mountains from 1795. In his letters he wrote of a sublime landscape, of seeing the hand of the Creator in those awesome chasms and ridges. One night he and his companions took refuge in a cave, 'a Cavity like an Oven Capable of holding 200 men', and a great thunderstorm rolled in:

> In the night there was some little Rain with a deal of Thunder and lightning. Never in my life was my soul Struck with such awful admiration, the echoing of the Thunder about those terrible Rocks and mountains was sublimely grand . . . as if the very rocks and mountains were rending from their bottoms, each flash of forked livid fire seem'd regularly to keep time with each dreadful report; when first the flash appeared I could see all the Country before Me . . .[11]

Even when the storm calmed, the men did not sleep, but talked together of the 'awfulness and majesty of [the] Supreme being' whose power they had witnessed, and of their own 'littleness and insigifficancy', watching in wonder and awe from the cave.

When the fugitive convict George Bruce recalled his times in the bush, on the run from floggings and police, he spoke of nature as beautiful, a solace, an inspiration, proof of an ever-present God. One of his stories can stand for many: Bruce, exhausted and fearing for his life, is hiding out on the edge of one of the lagoons by the Hawkesbury. Overcome by despair and grief, in 'floods of Tears', he prays to his Redeemer to 'lead me thro thous woods'. Then, a sign:

> I Lookt up to heaven and saw one of the most Boutfulest sites that ever mortel eyes beheld. it was A body of gees . . . six or seven thousand . . . I stood Confounded with my eyes fixed on the object. they Descended so low that I perfectly beheld them in their Elequince. they whar perfectly as white as snow. the circumfirnince of theis body of water was A bout three miles . . . of which these butful creasures covered one without moving a fether or wing they went their cirket Three times round the lagoon . . . as if Jehovah had mead A String fast to ech of those butful creatures and was playing with them out of the winder of heaven.

Bruce believed his prayers had been answered: the birds were 'Gods Holy masinger . . . surely sent on purpes to shou me wat road I chould go'. The dazzling geese massed, and as 'straight as a line they followed one another'. And Bruce, filled with hope, 'set out through the woods in the same Directshion'.[12]

Clearly, the convicts' responses to Australian nature included fear, but fear was mingled with admiration, enjoyment and wonder; there were deep spiritual dimensions too. But look again at that mob of rebels, pouring out from the dense, dark bush along the side of the road to Windsor. Here the relationship with the environment was not about aesthetics, but harder, more urgent realities of power and subjection, evasion and capture. It concerns the spatial underside of colonial history; it is about nefarious geographies.

This history began as soon as the convicts were disembarked at Sydney Cove. Rather than huddling in their tents, terrified of the alien landscape, a large number of the First Fleet convicts promptly left Sydney Cove, found their way back to Botany Bay across the swamps and dunes, and begged to be taken on board La Perouse's ships.[13] And then, instead of skulking shamefaced and starving back to Sydney, some of them had 'taken up their residence near Botany Bay'. Despite having marked out 'the Lines for the Encampment' and ordered that any convict stepping outside the line be arrested, Phillip reported that in the first two weeks, up to 400 convicts had gone missing from the settlement. Since the total number of First Fleet convicts was 778, this means well over half the convicts were out in the bush, out of sight and control. Bradley reported in early February that four convict women were seen 'straggling about the Rocks' from a boat 'up the harbour', that is, up the Parramatta River. One of these women 'made her escape into the Woods', he said 'and no doubt perish'd'.[14]

What prompted these movements? The first and primary reason was the desire to escape the colony, to return home. Escape would remain a great 'spirit of emigration' among convicts throughout the period of transportation. The search for native foods was a second reason, and convicts seemed to have foraged largely when they wanted to, though some had permission from officers. In later months Aboriginal attacks forced governors to declare Saturday as the official foraging day, and convicts went out with an armed guard. With wild foods constantly drawing convicts away, no wonder the cultivation of European foods in regular, fenced gardens in the settlement became so important.[15]

And third, the convicts, like everyone else, were collecting animals, insects, plants, rocks and Eora artefacts to sell, barter or send back to their own patrons. They 'were everywhere straggling about', wrote Collins, 'collecting animals and gum to sell to the people of the transports'. Ironically, the pursuit of scientific and fashionable collecting, the 'rage for curiosity', fostered the convicts' mobilities and geographic knowledge.[16]

It *was* easy for novices to become lost in the bush; some disappeared, and were assumed to have starved or been killed by Eora. A few more staggered back like walking skeletons, and were always held up as examples of foolishness. But the majority of convicts were learning about the country, journey after journey, until topography, paths, creeks, rivers and vegetation were familiar.

Each of the many landscapes of the Sydney region was used and seen in different ways by both Europeans and Aboriginal people. None was 'neutral' or merely an inert backdrop: each was invested with intense human meaning—with fear, delight, hope, greed, desolation, awe, with a sense of danger or feelings of safety. To add to this kaleidoscope, the same landscape could be seen in opposite ways by different social groups, by the convicts and those in authority. And it was the convicts through their movements and actions who increasingly shaped the meaning of the bush.

THE LEGEND OF THE WILD CATTLE

If the bush was no prison for convicts, this was true also for cattle, and the movements of cattle and convicts became entwined. The earliest escapees from the Camp included four-footed ones: the cattle the First Fleet had taken on board at Cape Town. They were humped Afrikaners, red with white spots or perhaps black, with long, sweeping horns. Those who sailed to New South Wales were hornless, though, since they had been polled for the sea voyage.[17]

A bull, a bull-calf and four cows absconded into the bush and headed southwest, perhaps following the rivers and creeks, until they reached cow-nirvana: the rich pastures, open woodlands and lagoons on the western banks of the Nepean River near Camden. Over the next eight years, the herd went feral, and was amazingly fecund—by 1795 there were more than 60 beasts ranging over what became known as the Cowpastures, with Mount Taurus rearing up above them. By 1811 they numbered 5000.[18]

The Muringong people of the Cowpastures region must have been astonished and probably terrified by these huge, lowing, lumbering beasts crashing through country, churning up the river and lagoon banks, muddying waters, tugging at and chomping down the long grasses. Some reportedly quickly climbed trees whenever the animals approached; but there were other, constant rumours that they were herding them. When the black Madagascan convict John Caesar was brought in from Parramatta pierced with spear wounds early in 1790, he said he had seen the cattle 'under the care of 8–10 natives' who 'attended them closely'. Three years later, stories of the lost cattle were still circulating. Now Aboriginal people told the whites that the cattle had all been killed by the people down south. They even offered to show them the bones.[19]

In a cave above a creek near present-day Campbelltown, the Muringong artists sketched the mighty bulls in red clay and charcoal on the rock walls. The cave-bulls have no horns, so they must represent those original escapees. Perhaps there was cattle dreaming, explaining origins and place in the world. Or perhaps by making their image the artists sought to exert some powerful magic over them. They called them *gumbukgooluk*.[20]

The rumours of the wild cattle which travelled by word of mouth back to Sydney were regarded with both scepticism and quickening curiosity, so eventually exploratory parties were despatched to investigate. Finally Governor Hunter went to see for himself. Imagine the wonder of this first vista over the herd of huge, sleek, well-fed cattle, grazing in 'one of the finest countries in the world'.[21]

For at least a decade, the wild cattle were considered by successive governors almost reverently, as a great and valuable, indeed miraculous, asset for the colony, and protective regulations were immediately passed forbidding anyone from molesting them. The Cowpastures became one of Sydney's famous early tourist attractions. Parties of gentlemen and ladies, their servants and guides, travelled south from Prospect to view the wonders of the herds grazing in country which 'exhibited a beautiful appearance of a luxuriant and well-watered pasturage'.[22] Along with the fecundity of convict women, the story of the lost cattle became a white legend in early Sydney, told and retold, written and rewritten. These beasts had gone forth and multiplied without the husbandry of men, and were found again in what the Europeans saw as an Edenic wilderness. The Cowpastures held profound environmental promise.

They held a different sort of promise for convicts. The problem was that *they* had already been to the Cowpastures and killed cattle there. Governors saw the beasts as public property, but convicts seem to have thought of them as 'common property', perhaps in the way poachers saw pheasants and rabbits on the gentlemen's estates in England. Convicts and bushrangers continued to kill them for food—and if the Cowpastures was open, 'safe' woodland country, it adjoined the rugged sandstone country of the Nattai Ranges, which was a 'favoured retreat of absconding convicts'. The fabled cattle appear to have become part of the fallback plan for Irish rebels—the means by which they could survive in the bush while they planned the next rebellion. As well, the small farmers along the east Nepean—mostly emancipists—increasingly crossed the river and raided the herds for calves to add to their own herds.[23]

Instead of being a sort of insurance policy for the colony's future, the wild cattle were a magnet for disorder and crime, even a kind of emblem of freedom. Governor Macquarie had soldiers and constables patrolling along 40 miles of the Nepean River to try to prevent crossings—but the herds roamed across an even larger range. Cattle theft became a capital offence in 1817, with 'no benefit of clergy, pardon or mitigation'. Crossing the Nepean without permission was made illegal to all but the landholders there—John Macarthur and Walter Davidson. The Cowpastures and lands beyond became forbidden territory. In the end Macquarie decided that convicts and wild cattle were an untenable combination, so the cattle were rounded up into extensive enclosures by stockmen working on horseback, and kept there until they were tame enough to add to the government stock. The remainder were ordered to be killed in 1824, though a few evaded the massacre. They escaped further west, thundering into the 'deep ravines of the Nattai', the same sandstone country where convicts and bushrangers hid out, as well as the Burragorang and Guououng valleys. Their shaggy progeny, 'all horns and balls', could still be seen in the 1930s.[24]

The COLONY

EARLY BUSHMEN

Despite the real dangers and privations, convicts continued to explore the Sydney region and to develop bushmen's skills. They made these journeys legally as hunters or as part of official exploratory parties. We forget that all those men who rowed boats, put up tents, fetched and carried for their superiors did have eyes and ears, and mouths to tell others back in Sydney about what they had seen. Convicts also increasingly lived illegally as 'bushrangers'. This word first appeared in the 1790s and it simply meant men who lived in the bush. By the mid-1790s Collins reckoned that two convicts absconded every week. Some seem to have travelled far inland, for in later decades explorers often met Aboriginal people who were already familiar with Europeans, and so they knew others had preceded them.[25]

The extraordinary convict explorer John Wilson lived with Aboriginal people for some years, and spoke their language. Wilson took the name Bunboee and even underwent ritual scarifying. He became a superb bushman and explored the country perhaps 240 kilometres inland—far further than anyone else in the 1790s. When he and four others were ordered to come into the settlement in 1797, John Wilson actually complied. Dressed only in kangaroo skins, he marched into Parramatta, his chest glowering with scars.[26]

As geographer Chris Cunningham writes, Wilson/Bunboee was the quintessential convict explorer, the original white bushman. Remarkably strong and robust, he knew the country for a 100-mile radius around the settlement. In 1798 Hunter sent him on an official expedition which was intended to scotch rumours rife among the convicts that there was fine country and an inland settlement on the other side of the Blue Mountains. Hunter wanted Wilson to demonstrate, once and for all, that the mountains were an impassable barrier. Instead, Wilson showed that the interior was easily accessible, and led the party to fine country. With two hapless companions staggering after him, he marched over the gentle ramp from the low-lying plains at Camden to the highlands of Mittagong. From the end point of the journey, the three explorers could see the Great Dividing Range and the expanse of the Taralga tableland away to the south; on the return journey they discovered the fine grassed country around Bowral.

Besides being an extraordinary explorer and bushman, Wilson was very voluble. Cunningham thinks he probably started the rumours about the 'better country' inland in the first place![27] Detailed written accounts of these discoveries were handed to Hunter, but they were then lost and forgotten. Nevertheless talk of his discoveries must have raced around the colony like wildfire. When the convict William Noah arrived in 1799, he soon picked up information about the country and people from old hands and 'those here that have travel'd and Lives in the Bush with the Blacks', clearly a reference to Wilson and the 1798 expedition. Fourteen years before Blaxland, Lawson and Wentworth made their officially recognised journey over the Blue Mountains, the townsfolk of Sydney already knew of the 'fine open Country with Grass Land but at a great Distants from here'.[28]

Convict bushmen, with their knowledge of country, were invaluable both to botanists, like George Caley, and to graziers, like the Macarthurs, who used them to scout for new lands.[29] George Bruce, alias Joseph Druce, who had arrived in 1792 at the age of about fourteen, later claimed he had 'bine from one end to the other of all the settlements' collecting for 'Dr Caley'. In his reminiscences, the country and its creatures were described with deep reverence and appreciation, as we have seen. But geographic knowledge was valuable for nefarious purposes too. Besides escaping from gaol and working illegally for small settlers, Bruce got involved with a gang of cattle thieves, stealing from the government stockyards and presumably hiding the beasts in isolated gullies and reaches.[30]

But Bruce's gang was betrayed and raided one night—three were arrested, two later hanged. Bruce and two others, Farr and Meredith, fled into the bush. It was his knowledge of both 'my trails through the woods', as he called them, and of the location of the isolated settlers' farms at Prospect that saved them from starvation and capture. As we have seen, Bruce was also possessed of a fiery religious faith, much given to preaching and inspired by the visions, signs and omens he witnessed in the wild and settler landscapes of New South Wales. He believed that 'Great and mircyful God . . . brought us three out of the gully of hell', but here he was not referring to 'hostile' bush, but the deadly raid at the campfire two nights before. 'God brought us out of the hands of our enemies', he declaimed, so He would surely protect them from betrayers. (It may have worn a little thin—one of his fellows retorted impatiently, 'it is no time for priching now'.)[31]

This was no easy journey—the men had been naked when they were raided, and they remained naked, as well as hungry and cold, and could not light a fire for fear of discovery. They must have moved through fairly dense brush, as their legs and feet were 'tour in A most dredful maner by the brambiles and buries'. Worse, Joseph Luker, the settler they trusted, betrayed them by going for the police. Fed, warmed, clothed and warned by another settler family, Joshua Peck and his wife Mary, whom Bruce called 'my Loving Sister Peck', the fugitives managed to evade the search party crashing through the bush. Eventually they made for the 'rever Ocsbery', the Hawkesbury settlements, walking in silence all night along the dark track through the forest to the river.[32]

If some of the colony's elite felt betrayed by the new environment, it seems for convicts betrayal was the province of humans, not nature. Bruce's account is visionary and visceral—his story of escape, pursuit and salvation weaves together nefarious geography, trust and betrayal. The bush was known, navigable, the refuge of the hunted, although for naked white fugitives it was neither kind nor bountiful; it tore their legs and feet to pieces, the cold froze their bones. Nor did it offer them nourishment, warmth or shelter. These were only to be had at the settlers' huts on the patches of cleared ground at Prospect and on the Hawkesbury. Within the context of increasingly familiar geographies, the greater question for convicts and ex-convicts, and for the cattle duffers and the bushrangers who followed, was: in whom should they place their trust?

CONVICT ESCAPES

The same question lay at the heart of the many convict escape attempts. Most historians have taken the convict stories about 'going to China' or 'paradise' literally—that is, that the convicts believed them literally. Most portray convict escapes as foolishness, doomed to failure, and evidence of mental 'otherness'. They were minor, if picturesque and rather comical, diversions in the larger, serious story of colonisation and progress.[33]

But escape attempts were serious. They were quite common in early New South Wales, and resulted in a barrage of complicated rules and regulations aimed to stop them. Escapes were not necessarily futile exercises either—in an estimated one in four cases, the escapees succeeded in getting clear of the colony. One might reasonably gamble on a one-in-four chance. And most convicts, when they did escape, did not run over the mountains, whatever they told their captors later: they went to the water. Escapees (including some women) headed towards coastlines, rivers and headlands and tried to stow away on ships—they could hide in the bush for weeks, waiting for a ship to set sail.[34] Alan Atkinson points out that many of the convicts had been sailors or otherwise bred to the sea, so had skills in sailing and navigation. These were the men who stole fishing boats, longboats, rowboats and sailboats and took their chances on the open sea. By 1789 convicts were seizing larger colonial vessels plying the Hawkesbury and Broken Bay between Sydney and Windsor. While some were never seen or heard from again, other escapees from Botany Bay surfaced all over the world: they formed an enclave in Calcutta before 1800, and turned up in Mauritius, New Zealand, South America, the ports of the Pacific rim and Indonesia, Fiji, Ceylon, and the islands of Bass Strait.[35]

As for tales of China to the north or over the mountains, convicts were probably quite familiar with China as a real place, if an exoticised one. Their houses and huts in the colony were after all full of Chinese earthenware—mainly bowls of different types—brought by the ships. Talk between convicts and seamen was common, so knowledge of ships' routes was most likely also well known. And it was quite possible for convicts to get to China—some probably did. It was the next destination for the *Scarborough*, *Lady Penrhyn* and *Charlotte* after they sailed from Port Jackson. Phillip himself lamented in 1790 that 'every ship that stops here on her way to China will carry off some of the best convicts'.[36] So why did they tell the authorities fantastic stories about *walking* to China? And why were they believed? Pathetic tales of geographical ignorance, paired with terrible privations evident on famished bodies, tended to mitigate punishment—a flogging might be reduced, for example. Sometimes would-be escapees got off scot-free and were allowed to recover from their ordeals. (Often they then tried to escape again.) The stories neatly confirmed what their educated betters already suspected of convicts: their minds were different, they were stupid, ignorant, delusional, probably—

hopefully—harmless. The vast superiority in geographic knowledge of those in authority was thus affirmed.

But escape attempts had little to do with hare-brained delusions or crazy dashes into the trackless wilderness. They required the same elements as rebellions, bushranging and cattle-stealing—geographic familiarity, careful planning and a network of people who could literally be trusted with one's life. As in George Bruce's story, geography was folded into social networks; both had to be intimately known. Escapes were meticulously planned. Stores, tools and equipment were stockpiled at secret locations, often an isolated river cove; the time of day or night arranged for rendezvous, shipmates carefully chosen, and an overland route to water worked out. And although there were some (very impressive) individual bolters, escape was overwhelmingly a *collective* action. Most escapees made the break in groups of between three and 60 people, and there usually had to be a larger network of sympathetic others to assist them by looking the other way, keeping mouths shut, creating diversions or even passing on stories about walking to China. Escape was characterised by this co-operation between people of the same rank, and involved a level of trust between escapees themselves and those they relied upon.

So, in order to prevent disorder, nefarious activities, rebellions and escapes, authorities had to deal with these two great factors in early Sydney—the social contracts of loyalty and trust between people, and the bush—forest, gully, river, cove—which had become their refuge. Promises of rewards and personal gain, even emancipation, were used to encourage convicts to betray one another. They must have been partly effective, since so many escape attempts were discovered. Commissioner Bigge wrote in 1821 that officials 'have always depended upon the treachery of accomplices for information'. These were the original Australian dobbers, loathed then and ever since.[37]

THE CASTLE HILL UPRISING, 1804

Dobbers and the bush played pivotal roles in the Castle Hill uprising of 1804. Although it is called a 'rebellion', the aim of the insurgents—Irish and some English—was not to rule, but to escape. They wanted to overcome their gaolers, take a ship and sail away. Historians like John Hirst dismiss the Castle Hill uprising as exceptional, proving that New South Wales was never truly in danger of insurrection. Yet this was the last of at least six such uprisings planned, or rumoured to have been planned, by the Irish exiles and convicts. Geography and social networks were the arenas of this short, restless, violent history. Word of plans was carried by convicts from farm to farm, house to house, from Parramatta to the outlying government station at Toongabbie, from Castle Hill to the Hawkesbury. Escapees who lived in the bush around Parramatta—especially around present-day Harris Park—were useful go-betweens and sources of information. Passwords and hand-signals were devised, instructions memorised.[38] When Governor King allowed the Catholics to attend mass, the Irish had legal means of coming together.

The plans were not necessarily wild and ridiculous. They usually involved a coordinated breakout, collecting weapons, marching on Parramatta, overpowering soldiers through strength of numbers, and putting those in authority and 'private families' to death. There was a wider vision here too: one which transcended ethnicity, calling and rank. All disaffected men would join them—convicts, free, soldiers, sailors, constables, prisoners, Irish and English—all would throw off the shared yoke of oppression, and together they would march on to Sydney, take a ship and sail for freedom.[39] Should the rebellion fail, there were fallback plans: the rebels could scatter, vanish into the bush 'and subsist on wild cattle'.[40]

But the settlements' authorities—especially the Reverend Samuel Marsden at Parramatta—had equally effective networks of informers. Every one of these plots was betrayed and discovered, and all but one was abandoned before they began. Brutal floggings were ordered, information extracted, caches of weapons hidden on farms or underwater in streams were hunted out, pike-makers accused, arrested and locked up, leaders identified and shipped off to Norfolk Island. From 1801 Governor King also tried to use geographic distance to remove the Irish troublemakers within the main colony. Ordered to revive public farming, he opened the new farm at Castle Hill, north-west of Parramatta, and sent the Irish convicts there to clear the massive blue gums and blackbutts. New arrivals joined old hands at Castle Hill—by 1803 there were over 300 men living there. King was already confident their 'wild schemes' would not get beyond talk, because the 'lower classes' were 'kept as separate as possible' from those who might lead them.[41]

But the concentration of so many men, the majority Irish, living and working together at Castle Hill was a very unusual circumstance. The official strategy backfired; it is one reason the Castle Hill uprising actually happened when others were so quickly snuffed out. The Irish insurgents had learned from their mistakes, and being together in one place made sharing plans easy and seems to have strengthened their resolve. On the evening of 4 March 1804, a bell rang out loud and urgent, and a hut was set alight. At these signs, the convicts turned on the few constables at Castle Hill, most of whom then joined them. They broke into raiding parties to steal weapons and ammunition from settlers over a great arc of Sydney's Hills district, from the settlers in the loom of Prospect Hill to the west, round through Rouse Hill and eastwards to the Field of Mars.[42]

At Parramatta another group was to take up arms to join them, and a third group was to rise in the Hawkesbury. Once Parramatta had been taken, a symbolic tree, a tree of liberty, was to be planted in the grounds of Government House. It would take root in the colonial earth, on authority's ground, and grow strong as a reminder of the struggle, while the rebels themselves would long ago have taken to the sea and sailed away.[43]

Informers doomed this rebellion too. Communications went awry—those at Parramatta and the Hawkesbury never got the messages, though the authorities did. Geographical knowledge also failed the rebels. Two of the parties became hopelessly lost in the darkness and were scattered in the bush.[44] Those still gathered on Constitution Hill near Parramatta waited in vain for the signal— another hut in flames—but none came. They marched instead to the old Toongabbie station, intending to make for the Hawkesbury and raise support. But by now they were pursued by the contingent of 28 red-coated soldiers armed with muskets, and 67 armed civilian volunteers. They had marched from Sydney through the night and were gaining fast.

So we return to that painted scene on the road to Windsor, its strange, frozen sequence of violent encounter, and its smug depiction of savage inevitabilities. The rise on the right later became known as Vinegar Hill for another hopeless, bloody battle in Ireland in 1798. Major George Johnston persuades the Irish leaders to come forward and parley—with nearly 300 armed rebels, it seems that Philip Cunningham and William Johnston were still hoping to negotiate for a ship.[45] It was a trap. Pistols were placed at their heads and they were marched towards the line of soldiers, who were then ordered to open fire on the rebels. The rebels returned fire but then turned to flee, with eager soldiers and volunteers after them, shooting, and slashing at those already on the ground. Later Major Johnston, bursting with pride at their 'spirit', wrote that 'the only fault I had to find with them was their being too fond of Blood'. The soldiers would have butchered more rebels, he said, 'if I had not presented my Pistols at their heads and swore I would shoot them if they attempted to kill them in cold blood'.[46]

The anonymous battle-scene painter wanted us to know something suppressed in the official accounts: the painting shows Quartermaster Laycock slashing the rebel leader Philip Cunningham with his sword, this terrible blow slicing away part of the man's head and face. Cunningham, said to be still alive, was dragged to the Hawkesbury and summarily hanged from the staircase at the new Windsor stores.[47]

In the following week most of the other rebels scattered in the bush surrendered or were captured. Rather than calling the common people to revolt and liberty, that week showed how despised these Irish were among some settlers, how keen the desire to hunt them down. Settlers eagerly offered to take up arms as 'true Englishmen' for the cause. The bodies of the fifteen killed at Vinegar Hill are said to have been left to rot on the ground where they fell. If this was so, it reinforces the contempt of settlers and travellers. Quiet burials would have been easy. To lie unburied, left to the elements, birds and animals, was deeply feared by Europeans as a most ignominious fate.[48]

Twenty-two years after the massacre, an Irishman named Hugh Kelly bought land in the area and named it Vinegar Hill Farm. Kelly was a settler in the area at the time of the rebellion and it seems he named this farm in memory of the battle, and to mark the site. 'Toby' Ryan in his reminiscences recalled that 'in Governor Macquarie's time, a large quantity of human bones were collected on Vinegar Hill and were duly interred by the Governor's direction'.[49] The name 'Vinegar Hill' was erased when local landowner Richard Rouse insisted the area be known as 'Rouse Hill'. Local historians wonder whether one of those strange, rough, anonymous graves still standing today on what was once Kelly's Vinegar Hill Farm might be their final resting place.

If trees could be the rebels' haven, their escape route, and even planted as a parting gesture of defiance and liberty, they could equally be used by the authorities to symbolise the might and terror of the law. Though they had killed no-one, and only stolen arms, nine rebels were hanged. The executions were spread around the gallows of Parramatta, Castle Hill and Sydney, so that all could watch in awe, or laughter. Two, Johnston and Humes, were sentenced to be hung in chains, one strung up in a tree in a hollow on the road to Prospect near Parramatta, and the other probably near Johnstons Bridge at Toongabbie on the road to the Hawkesbury. Gentleman convict John Grant wrote in his protest to King of the 'skeletons of my fellow Creatures creaking in the winds upon the tops of trees . . . methought I smelt the bones and heard the groans of Dying Patriots'.[50]

The roads, and the farms and huts they connected, were thus taken back from the rebels. Local historian Dorothy Sargeant wrote in 1964 that the 'witch hunt' after the uprising 'produced deep psychological repercussions which echoed down through the minds of generations of Australians to the present time'. Legends about the 'hanging trees' at Toongabbie were long remembered by local people too.[51] But in the official annals of the colony, the Castle Hill uprising, the bloodshed and atrocities, soon receded into the past. The event was diminished, treated as a joke, an aberration, and forgotten.

Authority and control could be symbolised and created through landscape in broader, subtler and seemingly more benign ways. Another picture, probably painted about 1803, shows the Castle Hill establishment with the undulating land around the timber buildings completely cleared.[52] Most striking are the stumps of the Blue Gum High Forest dotted in their hundreds over this ground. Ranks of trees on the horizon are minuscule; the stumps in the foreground are huge. Much of the land is greened with shoots of post-fire grass or young wheat; the darkened foreground suggests the ground has recently been burned.

To us this is a picture of environmental devastation: the forest has been destroyed and the stumps resemble gravestones in some vast, gaunt cemetery.[53] At the time it was painted, though, it carried a different environmental message: one of reassurance, security, the triumph of authority over the mighty forest— and the possibility of human defiance. The picture implies that the work will go on, beyond the borders right and left, and over the distant hills. The dark refuges of the bush will be cut away; there will be nowhere to hide. The colonial earth will be freed of trees for agriculture—after all, 1804, the year of the uprising, was also the year of highest grain yield from the Castle Hill farm. Visitors were impressed with the 'vast tracts of cultivated land'.[54] The beauty was that this massive work was achieved by the forced labour of convicts themselves. Yet here they are invisible, both workers and rebels, for this is a landscape emptied of struggle, bland in its assurances of historical inevitability, a landscape bathed in light.

DISTILLERS AND CATTLE THIEVES

Sydney and the outlying settlements remained surrounded by bushland for decades, and so convicts, ex-convicts, bushmen and settlers continued to explore, occupy and use the bush for their masters, but also for their own purposes. Their activities and presence also overlaid continuing Aboriginal occupation: the same places were used as shelters, refuges, hideouts and to stash stolen goods.

Of course, there were still opportunities for legal exploration and travel as well. Convicts accompanied official touring or exploratory parties, carrying and fetching, lighting fires, cooking, and erecting and dismantling tents. They travelled the colony from end to end with the surveyors sent out on the arduous business of measuring and mapping the country. It seems that these convict workers at least enjoyed rambling bush life and camping, and especially the joys of companionship and talk. Surveyor Felton Mathew, in the words of his wife Sarah, listening to their 'stories and songs' from around the campfire, glimpsed an entirely different world view from his own:

> I am sometimes rather amused, as I sit in my tent in the evening, to hear the songs and stories circulating among my men. They are very merry and very happy, plenty of food, regular work—and no care. To them it is not a tythe so like transportation, as it is to me. But for every state of life there is a source of consolation and support, adapted to its peculiar trials. The sense of duty, the consciousness of usefulness, ambition, and the prospect of the future support me—carelessness, love of ease, and the hope of liberty consoles them.[55]

High in the rugged, isolated Wollombi valley north of Sydney, it is the dutiful, educated middle-class man who feels banished into the wilderness, not the convicts, who live for the moment, look forward to their liberty and seem to revel in bush life.

Closer to Sydney, the bush provided space for illicit economic activities from the early years, most notably distilling and cattle theft. Distilling was extremely lucrative and very common—10 gallons of peach cider from the trees now bearing abundantly on settlers' farms would make 1 gallon of brandy, and 20 gallons of brandy fetched 50 pounds in 1805. Out of sight at isolated Manly (also called 'Little Cabbage Tree'), Gibber Jack's soap- and candle-making seems to have been a front for a distilling operation—but his assistant dobbed him in and led police to the still. He was convicted in 1812.[56] Earlier, exile Joseph Holt (who, like many others, saw nothing wrong with distilling—in fact, it demonstrated one's industriousness) went prospecting for a suitably secluded spot for a still near his property, Mount Hester (now the exclusive Kings School at North Parramatta). He found it in a clear stream at the Rocks of Jerusalem. This was an old name for North Rocks, a gigantic outcrop of sandstone on Hunts Creek, the picturesque destination of genteel picnic parties. Later this place became the retreat of Aboriginal resistance fighters and a bushrangers' haunt. Holt recalled it fondly as 'a very fine place' where 'the water came off the rock in my flake stand and there was a small brook to take away my feints'. He was later arrested, betrayed, he said, by others in the same game but jealous of his success. The Rocks of Jerusalem are no more: the outcrop was sold off, blown up and quarried in 1841 to build Parramatta Gaol.[57]

Cattle theft continued; it became the most common form of crime. In the early years—those of George Bruce and his gang—thieves worked on foot to steal and hide the animals. Stolen beasts were either quickly sold to settlers, or slaughtered immediately and the meat consumed or sold. This last was problematic, though, because of the perishable nature of meat and the unmistakable signs (and smells) of slaughter—hidden caches of rotting meat and holes full of secreted hooves, hides and heads formed the evidence used to convict cattle thieves. Historian Paula J. Byrne observes that 'intense policing created its own intricate activities of hiding, planting, and "fences"'.[58]

Although these practices continued, from the 1810s and 1820s cattle theft also became decidedly more sophisticated. It was regarded as a scourge on the colony—one observer remarked darkly that it was a 'sort of science'. The key lesson learned from the wild cattle of the Cowpastures was that cattle could fend for themselves in the bush, and so stockholders turned them loose, only mustering them once a year—a practice not so different from Aboriginal game management. Cattle, wild, semi-wild and tame, became 'the shock troops of empire'. Like the First Fleet escapees, they were first into Aboriginal country and pioneered the way for flocks by eating down the longer grasses, leaving new shoots for the shorter bite of sheep. Often stockholders did not know how many cattle they had, let alone what they looked like. The mustering and droving required stockmen skilled on horseback and wielding stockwhips—skills 'that were unknown in the land of their parents' birth'.[59]

Cattle thieves, now usually ex-convicts and emancipists who as stockmen had learned to ride horses, followed the mobs. They exploited both landscape and the fluidity of boundaries between 'wild' and 'tame', and the fact that cattle ran not on 'settled' ground but in the bush. Some 'planted' stolen cattle, and horses too, then came forward to claim a 'reward' from owners for their safe return. The stock route along the narrow Macdonald River, a northern tributary of the Hawkesbury, became notorious for this game, as well as for driving stolen cattle north. The valley's historian claims such activities continued right up till the end of the nineteenth century. Other horsemen engaged in 'gully-raking'—they stole the unbranded stock which had evaded muster. The semi-wild and difficult beasts were rounded up from their refuges, and driven into rough, broken, more inaccessible country, or isolated river reaches, well away from clear, open expanses.[60]

But the doyens of the stock thieves were the cattle duffers, who 'stole intelligently', carefully selecting the tamer branded stock and skilfully altering the brands on their hides. The beasts were hidden until the wounds healed, then sold, or driven as the duffer's own herd along stock routes at a rate of 20 miles a day. Cattle theft was rife from Liverpool south to Minto and Appin in the late 1820s and early 1830s. The area around Kurrajong in the Blue Mountains, with its dark turpentine forests, was well known for cattle duffing. From here stock could be driven to the 'ready market' on the Hawkesbury, or northwards 'over the Bulga' along an isolated inland track to the Hunter Valley.[61]

Cattle thieves no longer stole simply to sell live beasts or their meat as in George Bruce's day. By the time he was telling his story to his fellow patients in Greenwich Hospital in the late 1810s, cattle duffers were amassing their own herds—their 'primitive capital'. They were snaring a share in the emerging pastoral economy for themselves. Since their herds were illegal, the duffers and gully-rakers constantly pushed them further out, beyond the limits of settlement. They drove the cattle deep into Aboriginal lands in the interior, and became the original squatters.[62]

BUSHRANGERS

Increasing numbers of convicts ran from the road gangs or from their masters in the wake of the harsher and more bureaucratic convict system of the 1820s. Yet starvation, overwork and floggings do not seem to be the causes for absconding. Ironically it seems the threat of banishment to distant parts itself was enough to make some take to the bush. Others were assigned servants or road gang men who were already involved in crimes—they absconded when their crimes were discovered. Some of these men became bushrangers as a means of support and for profit. They forged gangs out of older connections—shipmates who had voyaged out together, men escaping from the barracks together, men from the road and ironed gangs. From a word which originally meant a man who could live in the bush—today's 'bushman'—'bushranger' came to mean those who robbed settlers and travellers, acting alone or in gangs. Bushranging in Australia continued throughout the nineteenth century, but, by sheer rate of conviction per head of population, the period of most intense activity was in the late 1820s and early 1830s.[63]

Bushrangers had maritime equivalents in the pirates who plagued some of the rivers and coastal areas—both found safe 'harbours'. Mullet Island in Broken Bay (now Dangar Island) was the early haunt of pirates who preyed on the boats from the Hawkesbury, and later for escapees from the penal station at Newcastle.[64] The Manly, Middle Harbour and Pittwater areas, although well known and often frequented in the earliest years, became great resorts for hordes of bushrangers, smugglers and pirates in the 1820s—*Gazette* editor Robert Howe suggested that a 'gun-brig' be stationed at Middle Harbour against the 'piratical visits of those desperadoes'. Sometimes pirates became bushrangers, as when the men who stole the brig *Wellington* escaped custody in Sydney and took to the bush and robbery.[65]

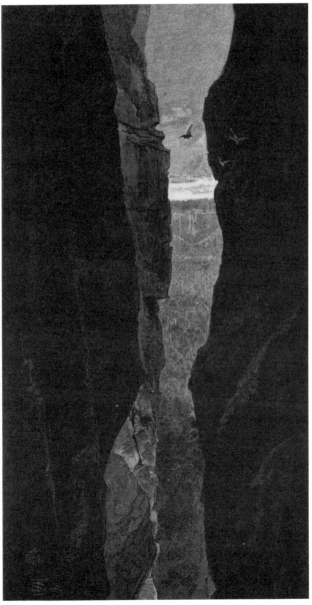

Frederick Schell, 'Bushrangers Cave, Mt Victoria', 1886. (Author's collection)

Meanwhile, gangs of men hung around the inland settlements of the Sydney region and watched the isolated roads for lone drivers with laden carts. Few appear to have been bushmen in the true sense—there appear to have been no John Wilsons among them. They worked on foot, relying on robbery for food and clothing, and were unable to survive independently in the bush. Paula Byrne suggests some may not have possessed much geographic knowledge either, citing cases where bushrangers relied on sympathetic settlers to hide them in back rooms, and one case where a bushranger became lost in the bush around Pennant Hills at night and was forced to return to a settler's house. The military, mounted police and bushrangers alike were 'dependent on Aboriginal people to get from place to place'.[66] Yet local geographies of the gullies, ridges and tracks must have become as well known as the social geography of roads, farms and houses. Areas of dense 'brush', like the valley of the Duck River Bridge on Parramatta Road and the Bargo Brush, were favoured places to launch attacks. Caves were important as shelter and places to hide stolen goods, though most bushrangers appear to have camped in the open.[67]

Bushranging in the Sydney region was amazingly long-lived, spanning the years between the depredations of the escaped convict 'Black' John Caesar in the 1790s to the late 1830s, when writer and naturalist Louisa Meredith reported that the Parramatta Road near Homebush was 'infested with bushrangers', though she added (slightly disappointedly?), 'we were never molested'.[68] The places where bushrangers were gaoled and convicted also indicate that the Sydney region was a hive of bushranging activity, for between 1816 and 1831, over half of all bushrangers arrested were tried in the towns on the Cumberland Plain—Sydney, Parramatta, Penrith, Windsor and Liverpool. The largest proportion by far was tried in the courthouse at Parramatta.[69]

For the bushrangers themselves, once more, geographic knowledge was inseparable from social networks: they walked the knife-edge of trust and betrayal. William Geary was 'most successful and notorious', remaining at large for two years in the 1820s, striking settlers and travellers along the arc of country from the upper north shore to Rouse Hill and the Hawkesbury. He and his gang hid out in a cave in present-day Gordon and stashed stolen goods with local settler-accomplices. They robbed houses and held up the carts of Hawkesbury farmers returning from Sydney with money and goods from the sale of their harvests. The whole gang of six men were hanged together in Sydney on 24 August 1821. Near Parramatta, the still-wild and rugged areas around North Rocks sheltered the notorious McNamara gang until they were 'wiped out' in 1830. Hawkesbury people suffered depredations throughout the 1830s. John Armstrong was 'chief of a lawless murdering gang and had his headquarters in the Kurrajong, a hilly district abounding with fastness'. He was shot dead by police in 1837. In isolated valleys like the Macdonald, bushranging continued well into the 1840s, and in the 'wild mountainous part' of the Wollombi, still further north, the part-Aboriginal bushranger William White had the sympathy of 'nearly every settler' in the 1860s.[70]

A few among these hundreds became famous—Jack Donohoe, originally a young Irish convict, was the inspiration for a ballad, 'Bold Jack Donohoe', a song so popular and so subversive it was banned. (It survived nonetheless as 'The Wild Colonial Boy', still taught to schoolchildren in the 1960s.)[71] Donohoe's bushranging career began with a highway robbery on the Richmond Road in 1827. The Nepean south to Bringelly and Cobbity and north to Richmond was his range, though his harbourers were scattered all the way from around Pennant Hills in the north-west to Appin in the south, and clustered most thickly along South Creek and the Windsor Road around Castle Hill. Toby Ryan, born at Castlereagh in 1818, recalled that at one stage Donohoe and Geary teamed up, and 'robbery after robbery was committed'. This gang had a number of hiding places, including 'one at Chain of Ponds, near Windsor, the Grose, Castlereagh and the Nepean'. They and others who joined them 'kept the whole of the district in terror for two years'. Donohoe was shot dead by police at Greendale near Bringelly in 1830.[72]

William Westwood was a later bandit who captured the public imagination. He robbed in the area around Goulburn and Bungendore to the south in the late 1830s, but was seemingly unable to resist crossing back into the territory of authority and civility, and came to Sydney. In 1841, Westwood rode into town, dressed in elegant clothes, and stole a horse from the old Grose Farm. He chatted and drank with the tollkeeper on the Parramatta Road, and then galloped off southwards again. Westwood was later captured and sent to Cockatoo Island,

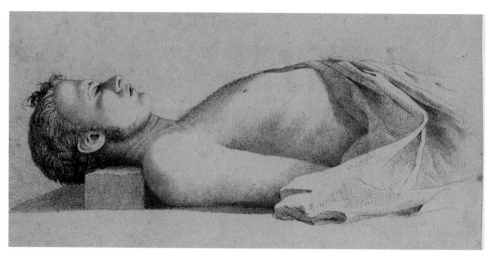

Thomas L. Mitchell, pencil sketch of the bushranger Jack Donohoe after his death. (National Library of Australia)

where he attempted, with 25 other prisoners, to escape by swimming to Balmain. They were fished gasping out of the river and sent to Port Arthur. Westwood ended up on Norfolk Island, where he was hanged with eleven others in 1846 for his part in an uprising there.[73]

The careers of both Donohoe and Westwood were punctuated by several spectacular escapes, which fuelled popular fascination and tales of supra-human powers. These were self-conscious outlaws; they possessed, or were perhaps possessed by, a sense of theatre, tradition and symbolism. They knew the stories would be reported in the press, that their exploits would be the talk of the towns, the pubs and the campfires. For those bushrangers who aspired to the immortality of legend, traditions of Robin Hood and the romance and derring-do of the highwayman evidently loomed large. Donohoe, in particular, is said to have mainly robbed from the rich and left the poor alone. Violence was to be avoided unless necessary and gallantry towards women was a hallmark. But John Hirst, Jennifer McKinnon and others argue that these flamboyant outlaws were atypical—they were the exceptions who proved the rule. The majority were merely desperate and decidedly unromantic robbers who did not hesitate to intimidate, to use violence if resisted, and who sometimes assaulted, raped and murdered their victims.[74] As for taking from the rich and sparing the poor, in the end it was the small settlers, not large estate holders, who bore the brunt of bushrang-ing, even though they were also the accomplices on whom outlaws relied.[75]

Yet Paula Byrne's meticulous reading of the early court records reveals that even among the ordinary bushrangers, symbolic gestures and performances were common. They often dressed in fine and extravagant clothing—cloaks, sashes, feathered hats—which they probably enjoyed for its own sake, but which also mocked the trappings of wealth and status. Bowd says that on the Hawkesbury, bushrangers were often better dressed than their victims.[76] They sometimes blackened their faces, wore masks made of bags with holes cut through for the eyes, and spoke in disguised voices. Others took none of these precautions and were completely unconcerned about being recognised. They might order their victims to kneel and say their prayers, or force them to swear their silence on the Bible, or make them drink until they were drunk. Here, in this brief space and time, the world could be turned upside down: they could 'sentence' a magistrate or constable to be flogged; they would leave a rich man stripped of his clothes. Defiant gestures and words were reported in the press and translated into stories and songs. And there were some to whom, in Hirst's words, 'the inevitability of death gave . . . a magnanimity and grace'.[77]

Tracking Sydney's convict geographies—the bush, rivers and harbours they made their own through exploration and journeys—is like seeing the region through another set of lenses entirely from those of authority and order. As geographer Chris Cunningham observes, early exploration and environmental knowledge was more a process of diffusion of people and animals than official explorations and despatches. Rumours, stories, hope and imagination, as well as successful escapes, played important roles in sparking official exploration.[78] And the discoveries, experiences and talk of the first sixteen years or so were the foundations for convicts' nefarious activities and geographies over the following twenty years.

Ironies abound. The unknown forest lands, the rugged sandstone country, the sea, distance and hunger were supposed to act as prison bars and walls. Instead they fostered mobility. For convicts and ex-convicts, the Sydney environment was neither naturalist's paradise nor terrifying wilderness, but offered all sorts of possibilities. Geographic knowledge and bushcraft might save one's life, lack of it could lead to starvation, or abort a rebellion; so much depended on learning and familiarity. There were opportunities to explore new country, forage and hunt, to make deadly enemies and intimate relationships with Aboriginal people, and to make money. A range of environmental knowledge developed—bush experience produced some superbly skilled bushmen and 'guides'. Other runaways simply used the bush as a refuge, and remained tied to the emerging network of farms and roads for sustenance. From their ranks came the hordes of bushrangers who plagued the Sydney region in every direction well into the 1840s and even later. For the humbler outlaws among them, dressed in ragged clothes or stolen finery, the bush was fundamental to the chance, usually short-lived, for what they imagined to be an easier life, a life of liberty; and for a few to aspire to immortality, despite the musket ball and the gallows.

So it is clear that long before the surveyor, the road, the official report, the Sydney region was mentally mapped and known by whites as well as Aboriginal people. Very occasionally, an echo of convict geographies lives on in placenames—Cattle Duffers Flat, on the isolated reaches on the banks of the Georges River, for example.[79] Or Bushrangers Cave, near Bents Basin on the Nepean River to the south-west, and Donohoes Cave, above Nortons Basin at Wallacia. Bushrangers Hill, on the rocky heights at Newport to the north, still overlooks the ocean to the east and Pittwater to the west. Local people still knew Gearys Cave at Gordon in the 1920s.[80] But these are faint echoes, local talk. For the main part, it is the names bestowed by authorities and surveyors, or of settlers or their estates, which were written onto the maps, and over this earlier geography, later to become suburb names, and destinations, and part of the everyday parlance of the city.

Because of convicts' activities, the bush—especially the denser forests, and the rugged sandstone areas shunned by settlers—eventually became deeply implicated in lawlessness and disorder. 'By taking to the bush', landowner John Jamison declared flatly in 1835, 'the prisoner cannot be expected to have any honest means of support in the wilderness'.[81] From the perspective of authority, the bush came to be synonymous with threats to the social and moral order; it was a dangerous wilderness in which men regressed to criminals and savages. It was inimical to civilisation and the making of a respectable society—the sort that any city worthy of the British Empire must develop.

If new, negative attitudes to the bush emerged, it was not simply the result of angst or homesickness or prejudice or artistic taste, but because convicts, as well as Aboriginal people, made it dangerous space. No wonder the sight of open, parklike country, cleared land and smoke curling from chimneys evoked joy and reassurance in the minds of literate, genteel travellers. These were signs of busy industry, a promising future of agrarianism, a race of hardy, independent, law-abiding farmers. Mile after mile of what was now so often seen as monotonous and menacing bush conjured an alternate, frightening vista of a land which might easily revert to savagery, crime and violence. As we have seen, settlers relentlessly cleared every tree from around their houses. Fire was one threat, bushrangers and Aboriginal attack the others.[82]

The convicts' nefarious geographies also shaped the emerging towns. They were inseparable from social and economic networks, and powerful vectors in shaping legal landscapes and in the physical shape of Sydney itself. The Irish rebellion of 1804 resulted in a landscape of surveillance and savagery. After the Castle Hill uprising, King realised that Fort Phillip, then rising on Sydney's highest point, Flagstaff Hill, could also defend the town against internal insurrection.[83] The fort commanded a view down the road to Parramatta, where the rebel convicts had planned to march shoulder to shoulder with the soldiers and constables. In the west, the rotting bodies of the rebels themselves inscribed the land, not with victorious symbols of freedom and peace, but blunt messages about the futility of rebellion, and the brutality of the law.

Escapees, bushrangers and cattle thieves always prompted official responses: laws, proclamations and regulations, new structures for surveillance or incarceration or death, new police forces and search parties. Tollgates were the 'eyes' of the towns, nerve centres of information about people, stock and goods on the move. Cockatoo Island became a prison where escapees were incarcerated and marooned. It was notorious for brutal conditions. New gaols, police stations, lockups and watchhouses appeared in the towns.[84]

The practice of hanging criminals near the place where they committed crimes was revived in the 1820s. Scaffolds were erected at Burwood, and at the Western Road Gate at Parramatta near Parramatta Park in 1826 for the execution of five men, all 'in the prime of life'. At Burwood the convicts from nearby Longbottom and the local road gangs were marched out to watch, while at Parramatta a 'great concourse of inhabitants' turned out for the 'novel sight'. The bodies of the bushrangers, dressed in white with black-ribboned caps, 'remained suspended until sunset'.[85] By the 1830s, the condemned were again mostly brought to the towns, usually Sydney, and hanged behind the gaol walls, first at the old gaol in George Street and from 1841, at the new Darlinghurst gaol on the urban fringes. The old George Street gallows loom black and exaggerated in Thomas Woore's detailed panorama of Sydney in the early 1830s. But, perversely, the gaols and hangings could also be sites of disorder, defiance and the expression of popular loyalties. When bushranger Edward 'Jew-boy' Davis was hanged with five of his associates in Sydney in 1841, soldiers had to hold back a vast, emotional crowd of his supporters.[86]

Part of Thomas Woore's panorama of Sydney, about 1831: a neat and pretty town, a busy harbour, yet the black gallows rise up from the gaol (middle far left). They are exaggerated in size, and there are bodies suspended on them. A flag flies from Fort Phillip on Flagstaff Hill above. (Mitchell Library, State Library of New South Wales)

The convicts' activities and journeys continued nonetheless. Escapes on ships were so frequent they resulted in a massive edifice of port regulations. By 1820 Sydney had provisions unknown anywhere else in the British Empire, making it perhaps the empire's most inconvenient and expensive port.[87] By the 1820s bushrangers were pursued by specially appointed 'police runners', like the legendary 'thief-taker' Israel Chapman, who said he saw the bushrangers' lairs in his dreams, and always got his man. Search parties of constables, Aboriginal trackers and eventually mounted police were sent out, constantly scouring the wild parts of the Sydney region to deal with what was seen as a bushranging crisis. The success of these measures contributed to the gradual decline of bushranging in the 1840s. But the Bushranging Act introduced in 1830 also corroded basic civil liberties. Any house could be ransacked, any man arrested merely for being unknown to the constables or dressed in rough, working clothes. As John Hirst argues, the burden fell heaviest on itinerant free workers, who, unlike convicts, had no ticket or pass to prove their freedom.[88]

From the beginning, nefarious geographies also shaped the talk of the towns, the information circulating, mouth to ear, about the bush, the rivers, Aboriginal people, the tales of what lay beyond the mountains. Later, news of bushrangers' exploits—feats of daring, cunning escapes, strength, courage and gallantry— were also spread through the print media and fired the popular imagination. They became the material for stories and songs, melodramas and musicals, and for early film. They were the stuff of a shared urban popular culture, shaped both by traditional outlaw legends and modern media, eternally fascinated with defiance, evasion and upending of authority, and with the ideas of liberty, inseparable from the bush.

Chapter 10

---◆•◆---

'A VERY BOUNTIFUL PLACE INDEED': WOMEN AND COUNTRY

HOUSE, HOME, HEARTH

Fugitive George Bruce and his companions, naked, shivering and hungry, longed for a 'good warm at the fire'. The house of his 'Loving Sister Peck' at Prospect drew them out of the concealing bush like a magnet. The domesticated, tamed fire of the hearth gave comfort to cold bodies, provided familiar food, warm and filling to shrunken, shrieking stomachs. The hearth itself, built of stone or brick, with its large blackened terracotta or iron pot hanging over the fire, was the focal point of colonial rooms. In some rural houses, rooms had only three sides, the hearth standing in the open air at one end. Outside, smoke curling from chimneys of plastered timber, or rubble stone, were airy, vertical landmarks, signalling welcome islands of 'civilisation' and human contact to travellers for whom the bush was a featureless, endless ocean of drab green and grey. Domestic spheres and spaces—clearing, fence, yard, house, room, hearth—were the counterpoint to the bush, and they were strongly associated with women, the bringers of 'abundance and cheerfulness'.[1] Home-fires and houses symbolised a sense of European 'at-homeness' which grew with the creation of families and communities, the physical and emotional ties which in the end helped stem the flow of escape attempts.

Clearing, hut and smoking chimney. A woman hangs out washing by the Cowpastures Road. (Mitchell Library, State Library of New South Wales)

The houses and hearths of Sydney town were important in these ways too. Newcomers sailing into Sydney Cove remarked in relief that the town looked so much like home. It was not the public buildings that made it so, but the houses. These were by far the most common structures in the town; they were its everyday fabric. Apart from detailed descriptions of how they were built, the domestic vistas of Sydney have not been the subject of much attention. One reason is that in the plethora of pictures of the town, and in histories, the structures and artefacts of men, authority and empire loom so much larger. Flagpoles and huge flags, ships, hospital, storehouse, clock tower, church, the governor's house with its rectangular garden beds dominate. The construction, enlargement and replacement of these structures have been equated with the 'growth' of the town, while the houses of convicts, huddled in the background, or marching in anonymous rows along the slopes, tend to stay in the background, unimportant, crude and ephemeral. In most accounts, they are pitiful hovels of cabbage tree, clay and thatch, 'temporarily sufficient single-cell shadeless shelters', doomed to wash away in Sydney downpours. These houses were clearly not the stuff of foundational city-making.[2]

But this is exactly what they were. The huts, and houses which succeeded them, and the couples, families and lodgers they sheltered, remind us that New South Wales had always been imagined as a colony, albeit a curious, experimental one, with a population that would settle and grow. In the clumsy social planning of Botany Bay, convict women were sent to normalise sexual relations and to conceive children; they were the human clay of this rather strange branch of imperial expansion. Women, domestic environments and families were thus fundamental to the whole project.[3]

Houses were also the basic unit of the early convict system. For the first 30 years, and even after, convicts sent to New South Wales lived in houses, either as householders, with or without families, or as lodgers or assigned servants who slept in kitchens or skillions. The normal experience of convicts in early Sydney was not the gaol or barracks, but the house, and within a few short years of arrival, these households were often run by women. Women provided shelter and food for the town's convicts and ex-convicts, and cared for the colony's rapidly growing families. Both men and women used their houses to make a living too, as seamstresses and washerwomen, stonemasons, bakers, blacksmiths, prostitutes, teachers, publicans and shopkeepers. Work, home and family ran together; fires blazed in forges and bakers' ovens as well as hearths.[4]

What were their houses like? By the early 1800s those of convicts and emancipists generally were solid and unpretentious, built of sawn weatherboards or rubble stone, sometimes incorporating the earlier hut. They usually had two or three rooms, and sometimes only one. These rooms were large compared to the tiny spaces of the later terraced houses, but in the earliest years they were not used for particular functions in the way we think of rooms today (for example, bedroom, dining room, kitchen). All the activities of the household—trades, cooking, domestic work, child-rearing, socialising—were carried out in the same room. So a room in early Sydney might contain table and chairs, or forms, for eating and drinking, china dinner sets, a cot by the fireside, ticking mattresses for lodgers, tools of trade, square panes of glass, large earthenware storage jars, chests full of clothing, silver teaspoons and money, buckets and washboards and many other things. Where there were more rooms, people tended to think of them as 'outer' and 'inner'. The outer room was the public one—for socialising, cooking and work; the inner room was the more private space, with the bed, chests and any valuables hidden away in it.[5]

Because they were considered private property, houses and yards in town and country were also places which could overlap with nefarious geographies. After all, bushrangers and runaways found shelter in them, and they were used

312

as brothels, to hide stolen goods, carry out illegal distilling, hold seditious meetings and sell sly grog.

'DAMNED WHORES' AND THE LEGEND OF THE FOUNDATIONAL ORGY

In his famous popular account of convict Australia, *The Fatal Shore*, Robert Hughes began by stoutly refuting the old 'damned whore' view of the colony's women. Yet he could not resist telling the legend of the 'foundational orgy', said to have occurred during a furious Sydney storm, after the convict women first disembarked on 6 February. The women, he writes, 'floundered to and fro, draggled as muddy chickens under a pump, pursued by male convicts intent on raping them'. It was perfect comic and libidinous material:

> Out came the pannikins, down went the rum, and before long the drunken tars went off to join the convicts in pursuit of the women . . . It was the first bush party in Australia . . . And as the couples rutted between the rocks, guts burning from the harsh Brazilian *aguardiente*, their clothes slimy with red clay, the sexual history of colonial Australia may fairly be said to have begun.[6]

These are powerful, seductive images—the burning rum, the awesome storm, the bodies 'rutting' like beasts in the wilderness of rocks, rolling wildly in clay as red as blood. But this last is, of course, a bit of environmental fiction; and it sends up a warning flag. Sydney Cove has no red clay; its soils were light, loose and sandy.

The legend of Sydney's foundational orgy is now very popular, and so well known it is widely accepted as part of the lore and history of early Sydney. But all legends have provenances, and the origin of this one is quite recent. It first appeared in Manning Clark's *A Short History of Australia* (1963); after Clark re-read the source, he quickly recanted. But it was too late, the story was out. 'The orgy', writes feminist historian Marian Aveling, 'had entered the historical consciousness of all students in Australian history, including mine'. But in Hughes' retelling of Clark's story, the sex was no longer consensual: it was rape.

313

Zoologist Tim Flannery opened *The Birth of Sydney* with a suitably dramatic account of the orgy, and in 2005 it got another run by sports journalist and writer Peter FitzSimons in the *Sydney Magazine*'s 'place in time' series.[7] Histories of Sydney and early colonial Australia routinely include the orgy. Even the imaginary red clay seems to have taken on a life of its own. After her closely researched and deeply human account of the voyage of the convict women on the *Lady Juliana* in 1790, travel writer Sian Rees imagined the newly arrived women as they 'squelched up paths between the rocks to the convict huts, red mud oozing between their toes and clinging to the hems of their skirts'. The orgy has even been re-enacted for television: a lascivious, silhouetted scene in the docu-drama *The Floating Brothel*.[8]

The problem, as Manning Clark soon realised, is that there is no real evidence that the orgy actually took place. The star (and only) witness, Surgeon Arthur Bowes Smyth, wrote that 'the men convicts got to them very soon after they landed' but that it was 'beyond my abilities to give a just description of the scene of debauchery and riot that ensued during the night'. The reason he said it was 'beyond his abilities' was because he wasn't there. He was on his ship, the *Lady Penrhyn*, moored in the harbour. The drunken revellers he described were very likely to have been the sailors on board this ship, carousing and fighting *after* the women had left. The convicts themselves were not issued with grog at all.[9]

There are a few vague and general references to convict men and women having sex—the educated ranks generally assumed that the lower orders were sexually depraved and beastly. Ralph Clark predictably described the women's tents as a 'Seen of Whordom' and a 'whore camp', but he called all convict women whores as a matter of course, and these jottings were made days after 6 February. Their contexts are ironic too: he was writing about the first convict marriages, and then noted the punishment of two sailors and a boy found in the women's camp. Clark also reported that a convict was sentenced to 200 lashes 'for striking one of the convict women because She would not go up in the woods with him and do X–'. On 20 February, three soldiers were punished 'about going to these d . . . . . B . . . . . . of convict women'. Naturally these floggings were the fault of the women, for 'they will bring our men into many Such Troubles'. For

6 and 7 February, though, Clark mentions nothing much except the crashing thunderstorm.[10]

We have myriad detailed accounts of almost everything that occurred in those first days and months, particularly accounts of convicts' moral failings, but there is no other evidence of this fabled 'orgy'. (Tench even remarked that, contrary to expectation, 'nothing of a very atrocious nature appeared' in February!)[11] It is simply impossible that the busy chroniclers, as well as scores of letter-writers of all ranks, failed to mention such a sensational event (which would have provided such salacious copy back home!).

Does it matter that it probably didn't happen? Isn't the story a harmless bit of colourful entertainment? A rollicking tale to liven up an otherwise rather dull story about landing and taking possession and running up a flag? I think it does matter, for two reasons. First, the modern orgy story as told by Hughes is about rape, and it is told as rough comedy about loose whores and randy drunken men in a way that validates certain types of male behaviour as 'normal', funny even. But there is more than this. As Aveling also pointed out, Hughes was saying that these were the *foundations* of sexual and gender relationships in early Australia. Brutal, drunken rapes, sex lacking in any kind of commitment or feeling; this is how it would be. But Hughes was wrong. Besides the extensive studies on women, men and family relations by historians such as Portia Robinson, Monica Perrot, Deborah Oxley, Alan Atkinson, Kay Daniels and my own work on the early Rocks neighbourhood, Tina Picton Phillips has recently shown that the convict men, sailors and soldiers were not psychopathic rapists. Most acknowledged their partners and children and supported them if they could. The lucky ones formed families and households which became the basis of the town. Given the unbalanced gender ratio, many men never got that chance.[12]

The second reason is that the orgy story eclipses a real legend: the story of an environmental miracle which amazed everyone. As we shall see, equivalence *was* made in early Sydney between the colonial environment and women; however, it did not revolve around rape, exploitation and abandonment, but just the opposite: fruitfulness, and wondrous life uncurling in earth, in animals and in women's bodies.

'Black-eyed Sue and Sweet Pol of Plymouth taking leave of their lovers who are going to Botany Bay', c1790, a cartoon lampooning convict farewells which depicts enduring stereotypes of working-class women—and convict women: buxom wenches, bottles, bad teeth and black eyes. (National Library of Australia)

Despite the essential role women played in the early colony—envisaged and real—for many years most historians took the condemnatory words of elite male chroniclers quite literally. They quietly ignored the fact that many of the writers upon whose testimony they relied—David Collins, Ralph Clark, Arthur Bowes Smyth, John White, Philip Gidley King, and most of the other civil and military officers—themselves had longstanding relationships with convict women, and fathered children by them. In any case, as Marian Aveling points out, the women selected as sexual partners by officers and sailors were not the ones they considered 'damned whores'. The term had to do with defiant behaviour, with rebellious working-class women possessed of short tempers and big mouths, women who effectively used language to retaliate against and humiliate men. Many of these same women became wives and mothers in New South

Juan Ravenet's 'Convicts of New Holland' is a more realistic picture of a convict woman—especially the penchant for shoe buckles and fashionable tall black hats. (Dixson Galleries, State Library of New South Wales)

Wales, too, though they were not meek paragons of respectability and wifely subjection.[13]

'Gentleman' convict John Grant perfectly demonstrates the way women were viewed through the lenses of double sexual standards and rank. To Grant, women only came in two types: 'London whores' and virtuous beauties. The women of the colony, he told his mama, were not wife material, though he did 'amuse myself as I please' with them. He took them to his bed, had them do his laundry, but called them bitches in his letters. His heart was reserved, he said, for those rare colonial commodities, beautiful and virtuous women. (Beautiful and virtuous women, however, wisely rejected Grant's proposals.)[14]

Other literate convict men echoed these views, even those who married convict women or their daughters. Irish rebel Michael Hayes (who married Elizabeth Baker, the daughter of convict Susannah Huffnell) warned his sister not to join him, for her 'life would be a solitary one without you were to associate with prostitutes. In this country there is Eleven Hundred women I cannot count Twenty . . . to be virtuous.' Worse still, they were shamelessly open about their 'high way of life' and talked freely of their 'lude acts'. William Noah (who married convict Catherine Lines) explained to his sister that the women avoided working by 'living with Useful men', but that they were 'sadly given to drinking and whoring'.[15] Why were these men so taken aback by the women? What was it about their behaviour that made them write like this?

The Irish rebels and would-be escapees add a more sinister note. In mutinies and at least one escape plot, at Norfolk Island in 1800, the men planned to kill all the women, including the convict women. (Ironically they planned to take a ship and sail for Tahiti, that eighteenth-century paradise of erotic fantasies.) The rebels of Norfolk Island were betrayed by other men who 'loved their brothers too little, and the women too much'. Perhaps in the rebels' world view women were seen as vile and treacherous, while men were uncomplicated and loyal. Perhaps womanly ways, their mysterious allure, trapped men into being husbands and fathers, softened them with affection, domesticity and town life. How could such men be brothers and rebels, men who said they would have nothing but 'death or liberty'? Irish exile Joseph Holt certainly made the choice between these two paths clear in his memoirs. When convict plotters 'hinted' to him of a rebellion, he wanted nothing to do with it. 'Having my wife and childer', he wrote, 'made me easy in my mind'. Stonemason Richard Byrne's life story was similar: he was involved in several rebellions until he met Mary Kelly, made a family, settled on the Rocks and followed the 'quiet path'.[16]

Men in authority were wary of convict women too, because of their power to seduce soldiers away from their duty and sailors from their ships. Sian Rees tells the story of the *Lady Juliana* sailors begging to be allowed to stay in the colony with their shipboard 'wives', and the dramatic scene of their final parting, when marines were called in to drag them apart.[17] Both Collins and Tench were curious about the private lives of the lower orders, not quite believing that such people might possess emotions and intimate attachments, and laboriously found ways to dismiss evidence to the contrary. They wrote scornfully of soldiers who decided to stay in the colony and take up land because 'the majority of them had formed connections with women' and had developed 'infatuated affection to female convicts'. Convict escapees who left their women behind could surely not have had any real affection for them; yet when William Bryant did take Mary and their infants in the longboat to Timor, Collins decided that it must have been because he thought she would betray him. When six marines, 'the flower of our battalion', were hanged in March 1789 for robbing the stores, Hunter blamed their women. 'It appeared from the trial of these infatuated men', he wrote later, 'that they had carried on this iniquitous . . . practice . . . several months; and all originally occasioned by some unfortunate connections they had made with women convicts'.[18]

As we have seen, the soldiers of the New South Wales Corps also married or lived with convict women in their years in the colony. Many had children by the time their regiment was recalled in 1810. Macquarie considered this less than ideal, recommending that regiments only serve for a short time to prevent them 'forming matrimonial, or less proper connexions with the women of the country, whereby they lose sight of their military duty and become in a great degree identified with the lowest class of inhabitants'.[19] Infatuated soldiers were hard to keep disciplined. But some of their officers, including George Johnston, William Lawson and John Piper, also decided to return to the colony and marry their convict mistresses after the Rum Rebellion trial. As Carol Liston observes, they probably 'recognised that their future lay with their colonial women, children and estates'. Perhaps Philip Gidley King was expressing something of this when he baptised his sons by convict Anne Innet 'Norfolk' and 'Sydney' for their birthplaces.[20] Here we have the seeds and vectors of the real colony—not an imagined site of order, toil, reform and silent subservience, but a place where 'infatuated' men of all ranks would stay for their women.

In the colony, the constant derogatory remarks about 'whoredom' and 'prostitutes' centred on both 'transgressive behaviour' and on the commonplace fact that women often lived with men without being officially married. Again,

Augustus Earle, 'Ann Piper and her children', c1826. Earle painted the Piper family inside Henrietta Villa, surrounded by the trappings of taste, opulence and fashion. (Mitchell Library, State Library of New South Wales)

this written legacy meant that, until the 1980s, historians tended to write off convict women as lewd prostitutes who were a burden to the colony, inimical to its 'progress'.[21] This in turn made invisible all those women who were householders, workers, business- and tradeswomen, mothers and makers of community in early Sydney. Infatuation, passion, and the relationships and commitments of men and women were also eclipsed. Instead, the 'imaginary prostitute' thoroughly tainted the colonial environment. The myth that the colony was nothing more than a giant brothel was in a sense more powerful than the real history of women in Sydney, for such images were key factors in the decision to end transportation to Australia in 1838.[22]

These ideas, and the stereotyped binaries about 'damned whores' and 'virtuous women', are important windows onto eighteenth-century gender relations and constructions. They tell us about some of the contradictory ways eighteenth-century men saw women, and explain the ways they acted towards them and spoke and wrote about them. They also sketch out the particular colonial situation in which women found themselves as a result: a place where they were met with both contempt and desperate desire; a place where the severe sex imbalance meant they were sought after as partners, yet also vulnerable to sexual assaults; a place where their work was praised on one hand but ignored or belittled on the other; a place where they were essential for the creation of a new community yet considered subversive of authority in the garrison town and treated as an unwanted nuisance.

But men's views and actions cannot explain the women of Botany Bay themselves, or how they responded to the colonial environment, or what they did there.

CONVICT WOMEN AND COUNTRY

If the domestic sphere of home and hearth transformed the natural environment, made a place for Europeans in it, how did European women respond to that environment in the first place? It is not a question often asked. Many writers, perhaps seeking to empathise with women banished to a strange land, assume that convict and elite women alike hated the 'harsh' environment and suffered severely. 'It was all so strange, so weird, so different in the bush', wrote Mary

Reibey's biographer. 'In the small clearings, under the burning sun and set about by the brooding bush, the pioneer women undertook the pathetic . . . task of keeping house, and maintaining their self respect': this is how a landscape architect imagined Elizabeth Ruse's experience. They write 'as if the whole continent was hostile to women', an environment where their efforts were feeble and doomed, where they themselves would wither and wrinkle into lonely 'dust women', lose their 'femininity', and, in the words of Henry Lawson, end up 'Past Carin''.[23]

It is also often assumed that convict women, like men, left no records of their experiences. But as 'fallen womanhood in chains', female convicts were a subject of fascination in England, so, like men, some of them wrote letters about their experiences to 'patrons' as well as to their relatives back Home. Those whose letters have survived wrote according to their immediate experiences—letters from the El Niño years complain of heat, the furnace-like north-westerlies and drought. But this is not the whole story, for on the whole these first settler women did not write of a harsh or alienating environment, but a 'very bountiful place'. And as Maggie MacKellar writes of the women who came later, they too 'walked, rode, touched, smelt and felt the new reality around them'.[24]

What women seemed to miss most was comforts and commodities. We have already heard one woman complaining bitterly in the first year of the roughness of the housing, lack of clothing and, worst of all, the dearth of tea. But the colonial environment itself held promise and nourishment. Besides listing the palatable wild food available, this woman had hopes for 'the hemp which the place produces'. Other women echoed these impressions and priorities. An anonymous voice from the *Lady Juliana*, arriving in 1790, also lamented the want of material things, especially clothes, and she had heard that 'the ground won't grow anything, only in spots here and there'.[25]

These initial impressions changed very quickly, as they did in the accounts of the elite. By 1797, Sarah Bird wrote to her father that 'the climate is very healthful and likewise very fertile, as there are two crops a year of almost everything'.[26] Four years later, Margaret Catchpole was delighted to find the town's gardens were 'very beautiful', planted with 'stuff of all kinds', vegetables and fruits, and geraniums growing 8 feet tall. Sydney still felt like an island, surrounded on all sides by seemingly endless bush, for 'if I go out any a distance here is going through woods for miles'. But the 'woods' were not monotonous, nor threatening. Like the gardens, 'they are very beautiful, and very pretty birds'. The fluttering, jewel-like lorikeets, parrots and rosellas entranced her as much as they did the painters.[27]

For those who had arrived, the horror of 'Botany Bay' was not environmental at all, but social. It had to do first and foremost with tyranny—the unjust use of power. In 1790 the colonists' worst fears were realised: they watched aghast as the wasted, filthy, half-dead victims of the Second Fleet staggered or crawled ashore, some only to die on the shingly beach. The deprivation and mistreatment they suffered at the hands of the ruthless, inhumane shipping contractors, and their utter helplessness, sparked outrage which was shared across the ranks. 'The governor was very angry', one woman wrote, 'and scolded the captains a great deal . . . for I heard him say it was murdering them'.[28]

Women dreaded tyranny and the loss of their rights in the same way that men did—in the gaols and hulks their forebodings about Botany Bay centred on fears of slavery and cruelty too. Once arrived, though, many women found themselves virtually free—recall Catchpole reassuring her relatives and friends that they were not, after all, 'driven about after work like horsen'. Mary Talbot wrote to her patron in 1791: 'We are much better off than we expected, and have as much liberty as our unhappy situation possibly allows'. New arrivals heard and retold the tales of harder times, though: legends of the years when men were half starved and had no heart for the work, had 'their poor head shaved' and were sent to Norfolk Island with 'steel collar on their poor necks'.[29]

Women who had been fortunate enough to voyage on healthy ships rejoiced in that fact. 'Sir we had not one died', wrote Catchpole to Dr Stebbens, 'no not all the passage out in so many a women'. The number of babies born and the 'great care taken of them' were also matters of pride and joy to women. And on land, women's fecundity was the talk of the town:

> The crops of wheat is very good in the Country for it produces forty bushels per acre—it is a very Bountiful place indeed for I understand them that never had a child in all their lives have some after they come here.[30]

It was these women, the ones who 'never had a child', who were the objects of wonder. They had probably earlier stopped menstruating because of poor and inadequate diet. In the Sydney environment, and on Norfolk Island, even in the so-called 'starvation years', they were restored and became pregnant. 'It is a wonderful Country for to have Children in', wrote Catchpole in another letter, 'very old women have them that never had none Before'.[31] The births of their 'charming children' would be celebrated in reports and letters. Collins reported with some pride in December 1797 of 'not less than 300 young people at this town of Sydney, none of whom, with the exception of a few, had been born in England'. By eighteenth-century standards, Sydney was a great place for children.[32] And so often the stories of women and the bounty of the soil are told in the same breath. 'That country will soon be able to multiply of the natural breed of itself', Joseph Holt predicted, 'and a fruitful country it is. I seen women of sixty have a young child.' Like the legend of the wild cattle thriving in the arcadian wilderness, the double crops of wheat and maize, the 'delicious fruits of the Old taking root . . . in our New World', women's fecundity, mysterious and marvellous, converged with rising optimism about the Sydney environment. After all, seeding and breeding, multiplying over the new land, lay at the heart of the colonising project.[33]

Those curious to see what had come of the Botany Bay experiment took a special interest in convict women, as well as the rising native-born 'Currency' generation, and the impact of the colony and the new environment upon them. French visitor François Péron reported in astonishment and delight the miraculous changes the colony had wrought in these 'degraded' women, for 'after residing a year or two at Port Jackson, most of the English prostitutes become remarkably fruitful'. Apparently oblivious to the food, medical treatment and healthful climate which were helping members of his own crew back to health, Péron speculated that this remarkable phenomenon was probably due to the fact that the women were having less sex, since 'an excess of sexual intercourse destroys the sensibility of the female organs'. Péron also delighted in women's mothering skills and parental affection, for he and his companion often called in at settlers' cottages, where

[w]e were everywhere received in the most obliging manner; and when we observed the tender care of the mothers towards their children, and reflected that only a few years before these very women, destitute of every tender affection and delicate sentiment, were disgusting prostitutes, the sudden revolution in their moral conduct, gave rise to reflections of the most gentle and philanthropic nature.[34]

Among officers and governors, acknowledgement of convict mothers was more grudging, and usually negated by the old spectre of the 'damned whores'. Collins remarked in 1798 that their 'fine children should have meant that they deserved value', but, alas, their vices were 'too conspicuous'.[35]

GENDERED SYDNEY

Sydney has always been a city of women, shaped by them and partly for them, too. On one hand, the spatial configuration of the early town reflects the ways women were seen by the men in power: in need of protection, but also in need of control. Hence the earliest tents were segregated by sex, and, in contrast to the orgy legend, men who harassed and assaulted women, or were caught in the women's tents, were humiliated and flogged. Later, ships were careened on the north side of the harbour (Careening Cove) because those in authority were pretty sure their men could not resist the temptations of women and liquor in the Camp.[36] The waters separated men from women and kept them at work. As we have seen, Parramatta was intended to play a similar role for newly arrived convicts. Phillip hoped—in vain, as it turned out—that it would 'do away with any attachment to the port' and its allurements.

But part of the original scheme for the colony was that convict men and women would couple and produce families—and they did. Men in authority seem to have seen convict women rather like commodities which were in short supply. When the *Hunter* arrived in 1798 with 94 convict women and a herd of cattle on board, Collins drew parallels, remarking that the cattle sold at auction 'were not greater objects of contest than were these females'.[37] Ironically, the fact that most of the officers had 'taken their pick' first meant that convict men were lucky to get wives. Those who were unskilled and lacked capital or prospects had little chance. For their part, many women also kept their options open—they did not marry officially, but 'lived tally', that is, in de facto relationships. This was quite common among the urban working class in the Old Country (though it shocked those observers who came from rural regions and Ireland). It meant that women kept their own property and could leave an abusive or otherwise unsatisfactory relationship.[38]

Where did women live? Upon arrival, some were assigned to settlers or emancipists, others were kept on the stores and given government work to do. Those with their own resources and sought-after skills were free to live and find work where they pleased, though the dearth of work was a problem and women could find themselves in a vulnerable position as a result. Although women of the lower orders were accustomed to work, particularly as domestic servants, they were in fact given very little work to do compared with the men (a fact the elite grizzled about endlessly). On the ships and on land, they were freer than men. This was especially true if they had children and/or if they had brought some capital with them, like Sarah Bird, or if they married well. Margaret Catchpole had much-wanted skills and went back to a familiar environment—she worked as cook, dairy maid and nurse for free families of means. She was proud to be both 'off the stores' within two days of arrival and mixing with her betters in their comfortable homes—the Palmers down at Woolloomooloo. She told her relatives that 'They make as much of me as if I was a Lady'.[39]

Variability is important. The majority of women came from rural areas, though they generally had already moved at least once, to towns and cities, in the search for work. A large proportion were domestic workers. But beyond these broad commonalities, convict women came from different backgrounds, and regions, had different skills, inclinations and dispositions. In the early period, these factors, rather than their convict status, shaped their colonial experiences. Catchpole's friend Sarah Barker, for example, was still on the stores, and had to 'spin for government'. Others were 'set to make shirts, frocks, trousers &c. for the men, at a certain number per day'. The system was task-work, as for the men, and if Sarah worked hard at it she could finish by twelve or one o'clock.[40]

As was the case for male convicts, there was no place set aside to house women before the first Female Factory was established by Governor King in 1805.

Before that, women, like men, were told to find their own lodgings in the towns. Opened in the top floor of the new gaol at Parramatta, this first factory was a rather crude attempt to address the reported problem of homeless, workless women. Or perhaps these were the most 'disorderly' women, the ones who insisted on their pleasures of drinking and fighting and singing in the streets—dressed in the most fashionable clothes, of course—as if they owned them. It is also true that women were the only convicts treated like this: men were not incarcerated in their workplaces. The women at Parramatta were set to work producing 'linen, duck, blanketing, flannel, sacking and sailcloth' and they slept in the same space as the looms were set up. This first Factory soon became overcrowded and unsanitary.[41]

Most women did find shelter in the houses of Sydney and Parramatta—those growing rows of cottages stretching along rudimentary streets steadily became their domains. Some historians say that these houses must have been oppressive to convict women because they were forced to 'exchange the authority of the government for that of a husband', forced by homelessness into sexual relationships with men. Indeed, by 1804 around two-thirds of women still under sentence were living in houses as wives.[42] But can we see all these women as victims? In the first place, men did not own or control all the real estate. Women were among the earliest de facto property-owners, energetically buying, selling, building and leasing. By the early 1820s women made up a third of the population of the Rocks, Sydney's most populous neighbourhood, and 85 per cent of them were independent householders. Some emancipist women, like the entrepreneurial Mary Reibey, built houses and cottages all over the city and in the early suburbs. Others who arrived with capital rented their own houses and many took in convict lodgers. Some of them became the 'big women of early Sydney', the formidable ex-convict landladies who 'had special relationships to the Sydney constables' and 'ran rackets to get women out of the Factory'.[43]

If men saw women as sexualised beings, then women, finding themselves in great demand, took opportunities to better their conditions and make a life for themselves and their children through their relationships with men. Some of the wealthiest and most successful emancipist women in Sydney secured land grants, licences and houses through their relationships with officers as well as their own

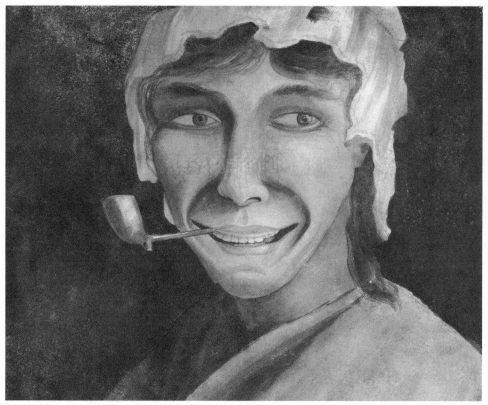

W.B. Gould, 'A Landlords Wife' enjoying her pipe. (Queen Victoria Museum, Launceston)

skills. Many of the houses that changed hands in early Sydney were gifts from men to their women, given as tokens of 'love and affection'. As Paula Byrne points out, it is impossible to separate the early colonial economy from sexuality—and love, and intimacy—both 'because sex could be used in buying and selling' and because women thought of houses 'in terms of cash and value'.[44]

Women clearly preferred living in houses to institutions like barracks or factories. They were also keen on the opportunities for trades and business that houses provided. With furniture, bedding, curtains, chests, crockery, fires and cooking, and with the pointed paling fences around their gardens, they upended the official intention that the houses be no more than barracks, and made these domestic spaces their own. They often referred to their homes proprietarily as 'my house', 'my yard', 'my paling'. They also used them to defy government orders, refusing to come out for work or Divine Service. They exasperated officials because they 'took advantages of indulgences' and did not 'feel' their lowly condition, as women or convicts.[45]

What about the idea that women were forced to submit to the 'authority' of convict husbands? The lack of employment for women and the arrival of children undoubtedly made women economically dependent on men they chose (and they demanded to be supported as a right). But, despite the occasional male voice bellowing from the page that he was 'lord and master', relationships between plebeian men and women did not work like this. Couples lived more as partners, albeit in different spheres. It was normal for both men and women to work, to keep 'separate chests' and have different circles of friends. Some women were outspoken on the issue of their husband's authority. When Eleanor Lawler's husband tried to keep her out of his dealings with cattle thieves at Prospect, she retorted that 'she would not be governed by him'. While couples often fought, women rarely spoke or acted as though they considered themselves subject to their husband's authority. In fact they frequently took husbands to court for violence, stealing their property or failing to maintain children, and they often won. As Alan Atkinson observes, the court's power could 'override that of the men they [women] saw around them, the courts took the place of men'. The courts also upheld women's rights to their own property, independent of their husbands, and women defended their property vigorously. Thus women in Sydney enjoyed legal rights unknown to their married sisters in England, who were, in the eyes of the law, one person with their husband.[46]

Then there was the fact that women (and their children) could also 'go on the stores' or be given government rations, though this meant they were expected to do some work in exchange. Many regarded being 'on the stores' as a loss of status, and preferred to live independently if they could. But the rations (commonly exchanged for other goods), like the courts, did provide an important safety net. They were a genuine alternative to dependence on a man, so 'living tally' may therefore have been a matter of choice, preference and strategy—and passion— rather than necessity.[47] Men of all ranks seem to have been resentful of this reversal of the 'natural' gender order of female dependence and subservience. Perhaps this resentment partly explains the way they, to a man, wrote condemnatory descriptions of convict women and their colonial situation.

Nevertheless, negotiating the labyrinth of government orders, high rents in a strange town, and male competition for women, as well as competition from other women, took considerable skill, a certain hard-headedness and audacity. It wasn't a place for the faint-hearted. Paula Byrne puts it succinctly: 'Tough girls ... are the ones I think did well in colonial New South Wales'.[48] Women took chances in all their dealings with men, and some of these men were short-tempered, bullying and violent. Soldiers in particular acted as though they were immune to prosecution for attacking women. When Lydia and Timothy Ragin's landlord, Corporal Anderson, swaggered into their house in York Street with Private Collins in 1817, they demanded the rent and spirits and sat down to drink. The Ragins simply tried to be quiet and amenable. They had little option: she was a free woman, the leaseholder, but he was a convict, assigned to her. The soldiers were armed. As they got drunk Collins became more aggressive, until, in Timothy Ragin's words, he repeatedly 'said he should like to fuck my wife'. When Timothy remonstrated with him, saying it was no 'bawdy house', they called him a 'bloody convict', and beat him, knocking him senseless. They raped Lydia and then stabbed her in the stomach with a bayonet. She died a few days later. Anderson and Collins were convicted of killing by misadventure.[49]

So women must also have understood the town environments spatially and corporeally, with zones of relative safety and danger. Houses, shops and pubs were the most secure, but they could nevertheless be volatile places. On the 'skirts' of the towns, the unbuilt, ragged fringes where the bush began, as well as on the roads and isolated farms, women were vulnerable to attack, robbery and rape. It was not the bush itself which threatened—women seemed to know their way, and enjoyed walking through it. But some men clearly saw these areas as their chance to attack; they made the bush and hinterland dangerous.[50]

Sydney town was shaped, created by women themselves, by their very presence, their determined, ceaseless activities, the way they re-established old ways and forged new ones. From the beginning, European women preferred to live in towns rather than going out to the frontier. This is not to deny that some women made lives in the bush, and did most of the things that men did, but simply to point out that in towns and, later, cities, the number of women came much closer to the number of men, despite the notorious and perennial sex imbalance. Towns and cities were their favoured places; they were women's places. Like the houses of the early town, they represented relative safety, security and comfort compared with the rigours, loneliness and dangers of going 'up the country'. This would later have great bearing on the masculinist idea which located national character and mystique in the bush, rather than the cities where most Australians lived.[51]

MARY REIBEY AND MARGARET CATCHPOLE

If the mobility of male convicts fostered geographic knowledge and nefarious activities, as well as white myths and legends, women's concerns with material life, domesticity, economic opportunity, children and communal relations were germane to the growth of towns and settlements. Mary Reibey and Margaret Catchpole are both famous and celebrated convict women of early Sydney, and their lives trace out the way women responded to the colonial environment and their roles in the evolution of town and country in the Sydney region.

Both Reibey and Catchpole were transported for horse-stealing and both appear to have dressed as men to evade capture. Many years later their identities were confused by purveyors of stories about convict women. But their remarkable colonial careers diverged significantly. Reibey arrived at age fifteen in 1792 and Catchpole arrived in 1801 aged 39. Mary married after she arrived, built up a fortune in business and property, lived in splendid houses at the centre of Sydney, built houses and raised a large family. Catchpole, though courted by a botanist, always said she was 'not for marrying'. Highly skilled in domestic work, dairying and nursing and a fine horsewoman, she lived with various wealthy families and was much esteemed by them, before farming land at the Hawkesbury in her own right. As midwife, healer and nurse, she was the kind of pioneer woman who brought the blessings and rituals of comfort, decency and dignity so often missing in crude frontier life, especially when it mattered: during birth, illness and death.

Mary Reibey arrived as Mary Haydock, or Haddock (alias James Burrows). She hailed from Lancashire, was convicted at thirteen for horse-stealing and sailed to New South Wales on the *Royal Admiral* in 1792. Upon her arrival she wrote simply that 'it looks a pleasant enough place' and cut her letter short because 'we are in a hurry to go on shore'. Mary Haydock was always in a hurry. In 1794 she married junior ship's officer Thomas Reibey and the couple embarked upon their remarkable entrepreneurial ventures in shipping and trade, as well as amassing land and buildings in Sydney and farms on the Hawkesbury. Mary managed their properties, the business and a pub, as well as raising seven children; Thomas sailed to Feejee (Fiji), returning with cargoes of salt pork and sandalwood. His voyages to India brought back the goods white women desired so much: fine tea, sugar, calico and china.[52]

Thomas Reibey died suddenly in April 1811 and Mary buried him in the George Street burial ground, erected a handsome altar tomb over his grave, and grieved for him. But she soon returned to her business and family and went on successfully running and expanding her interests on her own. Three months after his death she advertised a cornucopia of plain and luxury goods for sale from her new house in the commercial centre of town—George Street near Kings Wharf. In later years she went into property development, building houses in Castlereagh Street and cottages at Hunters Hill.[53]

By the late 1810s Mary Reibey had also expanded her land holdings into Van Diemen's Land, where she settled her sister and brother-in-law, the Fosters. Her attitude to land, wherever she held it, appears to have been one of sheer utilitarianism, of land as commodity and source of capital. In a letter to her cousin Alice Hope in 1818 she wrote simply: 'Mr Foster expects to get his land and indulgences and proceed with the cultivation of it so that he can either let it or sell it'. Here we see the same complacent expectations of promised lands and 'indulgences' as the free settlers displayed. Much of the remainder of her long, dense letter concerns the things she had built upon the 'colonial earth': her family, her business matters and their prospects.[54]

In 1820, Mary Reibey made a triumphant tour of England, visited all the right places and fulfilled all the rituals of respectability; then she sailed back to live in Sydney content in the knowledge that she had made it in terms of Home. In 1828 she told the census collector, quite correctly, that she 'came free' to the colony in 1821. She was wealthy, well known and widely respected, a founder of the Bank of New South Wales, a governor of the Free Grammar School, and her children married well (though not always happily). She did her utmost to obscure her original convict status by displaying the hallmarks of gentility. Her

Mary Reibey, c1835. (Mitchell Library, State Library of New South Wales)

miniature shows a respectable round-faced, bespectacled lady in lace cap, collar and brooch. Nevertheless, Mary Reibey was 'capable of conducting her business affairs with the utmost vigour', to the extent that she assaulted a man who owed her money at Windsor.[55]

But by the mid-1820s and 1830s Sydney had developed a more acutely status-conscious elite. Origins became crucial where once they had not mattered so much. As Linda Young writes, 'Ex-convicts like . . . Mary Reibey were never received into Sydney society, partly because of their legal status, but also because they never acquired the cultural capital to pass muster in a genteel drawing room'.[56] Perhaps Mary was hinting at this when she described the smallness and gossip-ridden nature of colonial society: 'no one will do well that is not thrifty correct and sober', she wrote. 'This place is not like England You are under the Eye of every one and your Character Scrutinized by both Rich and Poor.' But now, wealth, stately homes and possessions were not enough—besides an unblemished reputation and complete freedom from 'the convict taint', one had to know the intricacies of etiquette in every word and gesture, and make it all look effortless. Though a pillar of the community and a founder of important institutions, Reibey probably did not possess all of this, the finely nuanced manners, the way of speaking. And she would always be an emancipist. In spanning the preindustrial convict period and the succeeding age of obsessive respectability, Mary Reibey outlived her own era and occupied uneasy social ground.[57]

In 1842, at the age of 65, Mary Reibey moved to the new suburb of Newtown. This quintessential townswoman, who had rejoiced in her house full of daughters, their families and servants, sold her townhouse and moved to a two-storey mansion on what were then the rural south-western outskirts. In 1850 she built or bought a still more elegant house nearby for her favourite daughter, Betsy, and her family. This house was within sight of her window; like the Blaxlands on the Parramatta River, the residences set in the bush literally represented her family links etched in the landscape. She lived quietly in this retreat until her death in 1855. In that year, the first train ran from Redfern to Parramatta, the gleaming steel rails curving close by the Reibey homes. Mary Reibey was buried beside her long-dead husband, a daughter and grandchild at the Devonshire Street burial ground. Thomas' altar monument, moved earlier from the Old Sydney Burial Ground, marked their resting place until 1901, when the cemetery was moved.[58]

Mary Reibey seemed largely oblivious to the colonial environment, though of course she could not have been: it was the unremarked clay with which she worked. Land, crops, cedar, ships, oceans had to be exploited, managed and made to grow, flourish and profit. All of it was inseparable from family. She represents the unreflective tradition of utilitarian pragmatism that was such a powerful strand in the making of Sydney and its hinterland—the culture of 'spoils and spoilers', but also the engine of urban development—wharves, warehouses, counting-houses, shipping and the vast circulation of goods.

By the 1820s the Reibey family enjoyed spending time together by the water, reading, and gathering and eating oysters. (J.S. Prout, 'The cove in which the coves enjoyed themselves'. National Library of Australia)

Pencil and wash drawing of Margaret Catchpole. (Dixson Library, State Library of New South Wales)

There is a fleeting counter-image of her, though. Her daughter Jane wrote to a disappointed suitor in 1825 that the Reibey family scoffed at the pretentious assemblies of 'society'. They preferred instead 'spending a few hours in a boat of an afternoon', or sitting on a rock by the waterside, reading 'while others employ themselves with eating Oysters which we gather from the rocks ourselves, my Mother, Elizabeth and cousin Eliza frequently accompany us'.[59] So we have this one glimpse of Mary Reibey, excluded from fashionable circles, relaxing with her family at Sydney's waterfront and relishing oysters chipped straight from the rocks.

During the eighteen years she lived in the colony, Margaret Catchpole often described and reflected upon the physical environment in which she was immersed—partly because she knew her English audience was eager to hear about 'the country'. (She even dangled promises of information as a way of cajoling people into writing to her! 'If I can get a letter from your dear hands', she wheedled, 'I will send you a list of the whole country'.) Hers is a rare voice in that it is sustained—there are letters from 1802 to 1811—and because she wrote of women's worlds. Her narratives revolve around women of different ranks—her patron, mistresses, her patients, her friends. It was a world in which men seem to be rather distant and incidental figures.[60]

She wrote of the beauty of the bush and the birds, the fertility of the soils, and in later years of her own little flock of goats and sheep, as well as fowls and pigs. Cattle and horses were the sole preserve of governor and 'gentlemen'. Carriages were the preserve of the elite too. Men and women like Catchpole walked the country—even the long roads between the Hawkesbury and Sydney. Their feet burned on the hot ground in summer and crunched through winter frosts. They prided themselves on being great walkers, boasting of the distances they strode. They were founders of the proud tradition of long-distance walking carried on by colonial generations that followed.[61]

Longer experience taught harsher lessons, though it must be said Catchpole had a good eye for a story. 'This is a very Daingres Country to live in', she wrote dramatically, pairing the attacks of 'Black men and women' with 'Black snakes' which 'fly at you like a Dog, and if they bite us we die at sundown'. Snakes were not thought to be venomous until convicts labouring in the field and moving through the bush became the victims of snakebite. Working people, who were in the front lines of colonisation, developed a dread of all reptiles. Joseph Arnold wrote with some amusement that 'the people' would not come near his ship until a snake twirling around the figurehead had been knocked off into the water. English travel writer and settler Louisa Meredith scoffed at the conviction of 'vulgar people' that the blue tongues of harmless lizards meant they surely must be venomous, and was greatly amused at her servants' foolish terror of black-and-white goannas.[62]

The much-celebrated colonial sunshine could be savage. On one of her long walks, Catchpole was burned so badly, 'I Come out with Blisters on my back . . . and swelled so Bad that I thought I should a been dead very soon'. She thought it cold in winter, too, and believed it had become colder since so much land had been cleared in this 'woody country'.[63] Then, as if suddenly remembering, she wrote that it was 'nothing like your snow that was very shocking indeed'.

In Catchpole's mind the sexual maturity of the Currency girls ran together with the 'forward' state of cultivation—'the young Girls that are born in this Country marry very young at 14 or 15 years old everything is very forward in this Country', but, then again, 'very uncertain—we may have a Good Crop of Grain on the Ground to Day and all Cut off by the next in places by a haill storm or a Blight or a flood'. The country's promise and beauty could be unreliable and capricious. Catchpole survived floods, saw hailstones 'as big as pigeons eggs' cut off the wheat 'just as it was in bloom', and witnessed wild winds flatten acres of standing timber 'and trees that were of very great size'.[64]

Yet wildness and destruction, and the despair and want they caused among ordinary people, were gradually offset by more stable food supplies, the spreading areas of cleared land, steadily growing fruit trees, a few oak trees. 'Dear uncle I wish you could see this place', she wrote in 1806, 'for at this time the peaches are all on the trees, the wheat all the ear'. By 1811, when she wrote her last surviving letter, the colony was 'getting very plentiful'. But Catchpole often contrasted progress, bodily health and natural bounty directly with the 'wickedness' of colonial society. She certainly considered herself superior to other convicts and kept herself aloof by making sure 'that my company is good all ways better than my self'. She also prided herself on never marrying 'as other women do' (observing tartly that 'some women do very well indeed by it').[65] Hers was a very 'honest' life in the farming community on the rich river soils at Richmond, rather than in the port town of Sydney.

Catchpole's letters also reveal that intimate ties of personal relationships were paramount. Through her letters she strove, as many women did, to maintain those links with her 'owen native home', with family and friends in England, to keep herself with them somehow, so as not to be forgotten. 'For Gods sake and my sake, let all that is livin see this letter', she implored. When her aunt sent her a lock of hair she was deeply moved: 'O how I did kiss your Dear hair and cry over it for I thought that I had you that minute in my hand, I have been very happy ever since'.[66] As we have seen, the goods her patron Mrs Cobbold sent her in 1811 had deep emotional dimensions too.

In all her letters, Margaret Catchpole wrote of her 'heavy heart': her longing to return, the dreams of seeing her own people and land again. Yet, unlike Mary Reibey, she never did, even though she was pardoned in 1814, and had the means to do so. The story of her staying is gently interwoven with the narrative of loss and homesickness, for Margaret made good friends among the families she worked for, her fellow servants, the women she nursed to health and through their births, and her neighbours at the Hawkesbury. Some of her friends' children came to stay at her house and called her 'grandmother'. She was very fond of children, and seeing them grow up must have been a consolation for the 'dear cousins' she had left behind. As midwives usually also laid out the dead, she was probably with her friends and neighbours at these times of need as well. 'I have a good many of my friends that I go and see when I think proper such as I have nursed when they lay in that Cannot do without me', she wrote. 'I am looked upon very well.' The new country, which she at first resolutely decided she did not like, 'no, nor never shall', became more comfortable and familiar, and in it Margaret Catchpole re-created what she had lost: webs of intimate personal and community relations, for herself and for others, rooted in the Hawkesbury soils. In 1819, at 58, she nursed an old shepherd through a bout of influenza, caught the disease from him and died. She is buried in an unmarked grave in Richmond, in a plot belonging to her friends, the Dight family.[67]

'Out of the heart of rock': the typical vegetation of Sydney region sandstone country—pink-trunked *Angophora costata* (Sydney red gums) cling to the rugged foreshore in Broken Bay.
(Photo: G. Karskens, 2002)

Fish Rock, Broken Bay. (Photo: G. Karskens, 2002)

Port Jackson Painter, 'Method of Climbing Trees'. The people of the inland areas of the Sydney region were renowned for their skills in climbing trees to hunt small animals. The artist shows the men carrying *mogo* (stone axes) to cut toeholds. (Natural History Museum)

The Port Jackson Painter's portrait of an Eora woman and child shows her wearing a burra, or fish hook, around her neck. (Natural History Museum)

Eora and Berewalgal men dancing together on the shore at Pittwater, 1788. Note the red-coated soldiers in the centre of the painting and the women sitting in their nowie. (Mitchell Library, State Library of New South Wales)

William Bradley, 'Sydney Cove, Port Jackson, 1788'. Paling fences protect the precious first crops; tents and the first buildings are scattered among the large trees on the west side; an oversized flag flies below the governor's tent-house on the east. The all-important ships loom large in the cove. (Mitchell Library, State Library of New South Wales)

George Raper's watercolour of the east side of the cove c1789, showing Government House, the houses built for the civil officers along what became Bridge Street, the land cleared and planted, and the bushland beyond. (National Library of Australia)

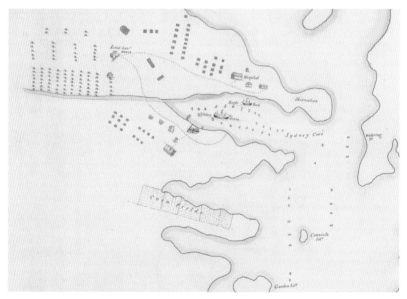

The Camp in October 1788, showing rows of tents, the earliest huts, and the hospital at the foot of the Rocks, while the governor's house stands on the east side of Sydney Cove. The 'cornfields' have been planted in Farm Cove, and Mattewanye/Pinchgut is called 'Convicts Island'. Note how the earliest tracks echo the shape of the cove. (Natural History Museum)

Francis Wheatley's portrait shows Arthur Phillip holding a 'plan of New South Wales' in 1786, just before his departure with the First Fleet. The artist captures Phillip's earnestness, and something of the momentous nature of what he is about to undertake. (Mitchell Library, State Library of New South Wales)

Left: John Hunter, the colony's second governor (1795–1800), knew how to pull mutinous convicts and settlers into line. (National Library of Australia)

Centre: Philip Gidley King, third governor of New South Wales (1800–06), encouraged and championed commerce, shipping, trade and small-scale agriculture in the colony. (Mitchell Library, State Library of New South Wales)

Right: William Bligh, fourth governor of New South Wales (1806–08). His attempt to restore Sydney to the control of the crown resulted in rebellion. (National Library of Australia)

John Lewin painted the fertile river flats and farms on a reach of the Hawkesbury in about 1810—
perhaps the flats around the Green Hills, or further east at Wilberforce. Note the extensive forest
clearance which has occurred, parts of the banks already slumped and bare, and the small boats, the
easiest mode of transport. (Dixson Galleries, State Library of New South Wales)

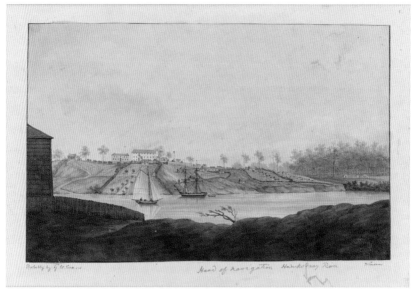

George William Evans (attrib.), 'Head of navigation Hawkesbury River', showing the town of Green
Hills around the time Macquarie proclaimed Windsor c1810, when ships could still reach this far up
the river. The more substantial buildings are set back from the water on high ground, dwarfing the
clusters of smaller huts. Some settlers have planted avenues of trees, but otherwise the slopes are bare
and the banks eroded. Beyond the banks, the river-flat forest still stands behind the farms. (Mitchell
Library, State Library of New South Wales)

Drowned country: the 1816 floods at the Hawkesbury. The artist wanted to tell us what lay beneath these waters. (Mitchell Library, State Library of New South Wales)

'I may be too fond perhaps of the garden, the field and the fleece.' Richard Read junior's portrait of the Reverend Samuel Marsden, 1833. (Mitchell Library, State Library of New South Wales)

RABY.
A Farm belonging to Alexander Riley Esqʳ

New South Wales.

Joseph Lycett's painting of Alexander Riley's farm Raby, near Liverpool. Riley later wrote that he had been deeply moved by 'the ownership of his land and the beauty of its situation'. (National Library of Australia)

We are here. The flagstaff and signal tower on South Head, c1790. (National Library of Australia)

'The ugliest church in Christendom', but pretty enough to adorn this 1850s folding tea-table. Perhaps the artist was recording quaint old St Philips's, built in 1802–04, just before it was demolished in 1854. (Dixson Galleries, State Library of New South Wales)

Sydney's original mercantile heart: George Street near the King's Wharf, much as it looked in the 1810s. Many of the buildings in Stanley Owen's 1847 picture were built in the convict period. (Mitchell Library, State Library of New South Wales)

Simeon Lord, emancipist entrepreneur. (Mitchell Library, State Library of New South Wales)

'So like my own native home': the view southwards over the Rocks on the west side of the Cove in about 1808. By now the early small huts still seen here standing in rows are being replaced by more substantial stone houses. (Mitchell Library, State Library of New South Wales)

The pubs, streets and houses of the early town. The Punchbowl Hotel in Gloucester Street on the Rocks was opened by Irish ex-convicts Andrew and Charlotte Coss. (Dixson Galleries, State Library of New South Wales)

Left: Lachlan Macquarie, a portrait by Richard Read senior in 1822. (Mitchell Library, State Library of New South Wales)

Right: Elizabeth Henrietta Macquarie, 1819. (Mitchell Library, State Library of New South Wales)

Joseph Lycett, 'Convict Barracks Sydney N. S. Wales', c1820. (Mitchell Library, State Library of New South Wales)

Ornament and utility, lighthouse and prospect tower: the beautiful classical lighthouse at South Head designed for the Macquaries by Francis Greenway. (Mitchell Library, State Library of New South Wales)

Augustus Earle's dramatic study of the Macquarie Lighthouse, South Head and the great coastal cliffs against the backdrop of an oncoming southerly squall. (National Library of Australia)

C. Cartwright, 'Map of the Governor's Desmesne' (1816), an extraordinarily detailed map showing the new pathways and trees and the line of the wall reaching from Sydney Cove to 'Woolloomoolla'. (Mitchell Library, State Library of New South Wales)

Realising colonial ambition and environmental potential: Jane Maria Brooks and her sisters may have been among the visitors ferried out to admire Captain Piper's almost complete Henrietta Villa in this 1820 view. Note the gardens established on the slopes above the beach. (Mitchell Library, State Library of New South Wales)

Elegant partying in the domed salon of Henrietta Villa. (Mitchell Library, State Library of New South Wales)

Edward Close's picture of the 'Sydney Barracks' shows the pompous brick facades and the Grecian-style well in the parade ground, but also includes a washerwoman at work and a soldier chasing some ducks. (National Library of Australia)

Edward Close's 1817 watercolour of the new public building in Macquarie Street, framed by the trees and shrubs of the Domain. Note the fence and gate at the centre of the picture. (National Library of Australia)

From savagery to civility, from disorder to control: Major James Taylor's paintings of Sydney in about 1817 were reportedly exhibited at Burford's Panorama in London in 1823–24. (Mitchell Library, State Library of New South Wales)

Portals to the new land: Augustus Earle's painting of Sydney Heads and the harbour which inspired so many enchanted descriptions. (National Library of Australia)

Vision splendid: the Cowpastures. Augustus Earle's 'View of farm of J. Hassall, Cow Pastures', c1826. (Mitchell Library, State Library of New South Wales)

George Raper, 'Bird & Flower of Port Jackson', blue-faced honeyeater, native iris, *Patersonia* sp., and a sundew, *Drosera* sp. (Natural History Museum)

John Hunter, 'Gomah (Murry)', the king parrot. (National Library of Australia)

'. . . and secret themselves by knawing a hole in the body of a tree.' John Lewin, 'Dappled grey—Cryptophasa Irrorata', a pre-publication plate from his *Prodromus Entomology*. (Mitchell Library, State Library of New South Wales)

John Lewin's sheaf of green and gold acacia, c1805. (Mitchell Library, State Library of New South Wales)

A landmark avenue of mature Norfolk Island pines announces Annandale House in 1877. (Dixson Galleries, State Library of New South Wales)

Spotted quolls (*Dasyurus maculates* and *Dasyurus viverrinus*) feasted on the settlers' poultry in the earliest years of settlement. (Natural History Museum)

'Convict uprising at Castle Hill, 1804': a time travel picture which tells us about the relationship between convict rebels and the bush. (National Library of Australia)

A view of the Castle Hill farm in about 1803: a graveyard of stumps, relicts of the Blue Gum High Forest which once covered this area. (Mitchell Library, State Library of New South Wales)

Convicts and wild cattle: Joseph Lycett's 'View upon the Nepean River at the Cow Pastures' (1825) is unusual in his work in that it shows bushrangers camped by the Nepean, feasting on illicit beef. (National Library of Australia)

Augustus Earle was one of the few artists interested in painting nefarious geographies—the 'other side' of the history of progress and improvement. 'Skirmish between bushrangers and constables, Illawarra' (1827) shows early bushrangers, who moved about on foot, exchanging musket fire with constables, who have found their creekside hideout in a dark forest in the Illawarra region south of Sydney. (National Library of Australia)

'They were just leaving when they saw four canoes coming towards them': the Port Jackson Painter's picture of the historic reconciliation between Bennelong and Phillip in 1790. The figure in the second nowie is probably Barangaroo. (Natural History Museum)

Attributed to G.W. Evans, but possibly by John Lewin, 'Sydney from the West side of the Cove' shows the vista from the back of the old hospital at the foot of the Rocks, the most populous part of the town, in 1802. Aboriginal people—men, women and children—are shown talking, gathered around a fire, or throwing spears, alongside the European townsfolk. (Mitchell Library, State Library of New South Wales)

The Port Jackson Painter's picture of Bennelong 'when angry' after the wounding of Botany Bay Coleby. (Natural History Museum)

A hidden history?: the Port Jackson Painter's 'Mr White, Harris & Laing with a party of soldiers visiting Botany Bay Colebee at that place when wounded near Botany Bay'. (Natural History Museum)

Natives returned from Fishing

Port Jackson Painter's version of the fish picnic, 1790: women bring and cook fish, man lies around. (Natural History Museum)

Eora women in their nowies at the base of South Head/Taralbe (also called Burrawarra) where the European men 'hollowed' to them from the cliff tops in May 1788. (Mitchell Library, State Library of New South Wales)

Augustus Earle, 'Portrait of Bungaree, a native of New South Wales'. Bungaree, dignified in jacket, breastplate and bare feet, raises his hat to artist and viewer, as to newcomers. The ships he welcomed to Sydney lie in the cove below. (National Library of Australia)

Alphonse Pellion, 'Tara et Peroa': Aboriginal men of the Nepean River in 1819 wearing jackets. (Mitchell Library, State Library of New South Wales)

Joseph Lycett's painting of a contest around Newcastle or Lake Macquarie, c1817. Women and children are shown watching from the edge, though written accounts claim they took part in some of the fighting. Men fight with clubs and the man standing trial by spear appears to be handing a womera (spear-thrower) back to his opponents. (National Library of Australia)

Augustus Earle, 'A View in Parramatta N. S. Wales looking East', showing the massive commissariat by the river. The soldier seems to be gesturing towards the Aboriginal family seated on the ground: they are still here, still naked. (Mitchell Library, State Library of New South Wales)

Augustus Earle, 'Natives of N. S. Wales as seen in the streets of Sydney', presents the stereotypical images of Aboriginal men drinking in the streets, though Earle also includes a visual comment on the hypocrisy of the outraged white drinkers outside the hotel. Black glass bottles and broken pottery lie in the foreground. Interestingly the women are not drinking, and one of them carries a large fish. A man, dressed in a jacket and shirt, carries a traditional club. (National Library of Australia)

A punchbowl, made in China for an unknown person about 1818, showing a panorama of Sydney on the exterior, and a group of Aboriginal people inside. (Mitchell Library, State Library of New South Wales)

Augustus Earle, 'The Annual meeting of the native tribes at Parramatta, New South Wales, the Governor meeting them', c1826. (National Library of Australia)

Augustus Earle, 'A native family of New South Wales sitting down on English settlers farm', c1826. (National Library of Australia)

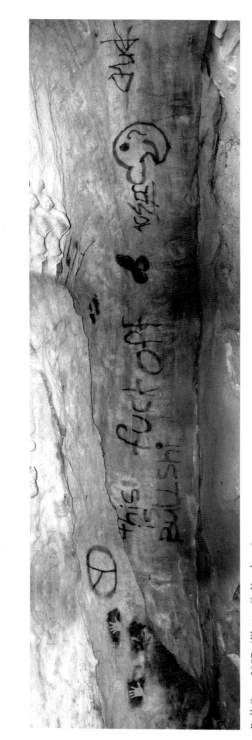

Bull Cave, 2007. (Photo: G. Karskens)

GENTEEL WOMEN AND CONVICT WOMEN

While convict women were creating culture, businesses and community in town and country, the wives of military and civil officers, clergymen and the earliest merchants were similarly busy with their homes, families, gardens and farms, as well as public projects. They too were writing home about the new country, about fears of being forgotten and about their own colonising projects.

Curiously, one could conclude from reading their letters that they were the only women in the colony. Elizabeth Macarthur, who was only 21 when she arrived, lamented in 1791 of 'having no female friend to unbend my mind to'. When suitable ladies did arrive, she was exultant: 'our little group has grown quite brilliant'.[68] The first was of course not literally true: genteel women had female convict servants, like Margaret Catchpole, and probably ordered goods from businesswomen like Mary Reibey. After November 1790, they were visited by Aboriginal women, who sometimes stayed in their houses. While the exotic 'natives' were sometimes described in letters, the lower and middling orders were utterly invisible. Just as convict collectors were essential to George Caley, yet anonymous 'servants' in his letters, genteel women rarely if ever mentioned

A female servant minds a child; her mistress returns home, shaded by a parasol. (Detail from Major James Taylor's panorama, 1817, Mitchell Library, State Library of New South Wales)

the women who washed, ironed and cleaned for them, cared for their children, ran their kitchens and dairies, laid the food on their tables, nursed them when they were sick and assisted when they gave birth. The lives of women of different ranks were so intimately entwined in the houses, gardens and estates, but genteel women wrote as if their social world was hermetically sealed off from these other women. A world of conversation, friendship and intimacy could only be created among women of their own rank.

From the beginning and throughout the nineteenth century, women's letters track the transition from sea to land. Some wrote of not wanting to leave the womb-like wooden world of the ship: cramped, but familiar and secure. The first pages of Elizabeth Macarthur's first known letter home were given over entirely to the sea; her days were haunted by the failure of the *Gorgon* to appear and the constant anxiety over the fate of those on board: 'each succeeding sunset produced among us wild and vague conjectures of what could be the cause of the *Gorgon*'s delay'. When there was no ship anchored in the harbour Elizabeth Paterson felt uneasy, 'cut off from all communication with any part of the World'.[69]

The ships brought the greatest desideratum: letters, full of hungered-for news, but which more importantly testified that one had not been forgotten. After the exhilaration of a ship's arrival, the disappointment of receiving nothing was unbearable. Poor Margaret Catchpole reproached her relatives for not writing to her. 'It's enough to make me go out of my mind', she wailed, 'to see so many Letters come from London and poor I cannot get no not one'. For some their sense of self, even of existence, seems to have been aligned with remembrance and being remembered. Eliza Marsden wrote to her friend Mrs Stoker of a surreal sense of detachment:

We seem in our present situation to be almost totally cut off from all connexion with the world especially the virtuous part of it. Old England is no more than like a pleasing dream. When I think of it it appears to have no existence but in my own imagination.[70]

Writing and ships were the means of keeping Old England real in the new environment, of keeping relationships alive. Letters were frantically written when ships were about to set sail, and ships were carriers of these flimsy paper emissaries, the stream of information and intimacy between new and old worlds.

While convicts feared tyranny and oppression, genteel women feared convicts. For Elizabeth Paterson, writing in 1800, the Irish convicts and their plots meant gentlefolk were 'uncomfortable and harassed'. But her real terror was the violation of her home, of 'private assassins breaking into our houses in the dead of night—in which they were all too successful in their own country'.[71] These women were also anxious about the moral and social environment into which they sailed. If Botany Bay was truly a sink of immorality and depravity, how could they create all-important genteel environments, maintain their respectability and virtue, and bring up their children properly? For the first few years Eliza Marsden, like her husband, praised the natural environment, but bemoaned the 'loss of religious society'. This was what made New South Wales a 'dark benighted part of the world'. Evil-minded men seemed to take delight in frightening genteel women: Mrs Mary Pitt, a widow with a grown family, in 1801 boarded the *Canada* where a 'gentleman from New South Wales' told her a 'shocking account . . . the whole land is full of corrupted, wicked people'. She was seized by panic and despair, declaring dramatically that she 'would rather fall into the hands of a merciful creator [that is, presumably, die] . . . than fall into the hands of wicked people'. Mary Pitt received a 100-acre grant at Windsor, where she was cared for by Margaret Catchpole and grew fond of her. The Pitt children married well and prospered, and Mary Pitt lived to a good age of 72, dying in 1815.[72]

Women who arrived as wives of governors and officers did not remain cloistered in their drawing rooms. They turned critical eyes and improving hands to the environments outside their own homes and estates: to both colonial society and the colonial landscape. In what was often an overwhelmingly male environment—one Alan Atkinson has described so well as 'brotherhoods' of sea and soldiering and rebels—these women began to make spaces for female society and conversation. They added drawing rooms to houses; they held their own dinners and hosted sparkling balls; they reshaped gardens to reflect fashionable English taste. Their works were the antecedents of the embellishments and architectural triumphs of Elizabeth Macquarie.[73]

Landscapes created by women, for women. Elizabeth Macquarie's Palladian-style Female Orphan School on the river near Parramatta was based on her ancestral home in Scotland. A lady and some gentlemen enjoy a boating excursion in the foreground. This building still stands by the river in present-day Rydalmere. (National Library of Australia)

Elizabeth Paterson (wife of Lieutenant Governor William Paterson) and Anna Josepha King (wife of Governor King) poured their energies into the first Female Orphan School, believing that 'if we ever hope for worth or honesty in this settlement, we must look to them [colonial-born children] for it, not the present degenerate mortals'. True reformers, these women saw *beyond* the existing social environment—the town the convicts were creating—to a future where an orderly urban environment would support an orderly and deferential society. The convicts' roaming children would be transformed into skilled, obedient and useful servants, and then good wives and dutiful workers and husbands. (They were of course working from their own assumptions about convict parents, utterly oblivious to the parenting and affection convicts did give their children.)[74] Convicts' children were not the only ones seen in this way, of course—as we shall see, Aboriginal children were also separated from their parents and placed in schools, largely for the same purposes.

The responses of elite women to the natural environment were for the main part full of praise and wonder, particularly those who arrived after the El Niño years of the early 1790s. The way they observed and experienced it was often very different from convict women. Like Margaret Catchpole, Elizabeth Macarthur wrote of walking in new country. But her walks were not purposeful 50-mile tramps between settlements on business or errands, but short 'excursions', taken for pleasure, for air and views, and as a way of familiarising herself with the country. She was accompanied, too, by soldiers to guard against attack, and servants who carried 'our tea equipage' so that the party might 'drink tea on the turf', under shady awnings 'upon some pleasant point of land'. Excursions and picnics by boat would become important and pleasurable parts of genteel socialising: 'We are constantly making little parties in boats up and down various inlets of the harbour, taking refreshments with us'. Over the nineteenth century, such outdoor pleasures would be enjoyed by all classes, and coves and beaches transformed to cater for them. But when it was hot in those early years, Elizabeth Macarthur did not walk at all, not for a whole summer, but stayed indoors and kept the twelve-paned windows shut tight against the burning winds.[75]

Both Macarthur and Catchpole wrote of the colony as a wondrous botanist's paradise, but Catchpole collected and packed up specimens as a way of maintaining her social links with patrons in England, while Macarthur thought of botany as an 'easy science' to busy her mind and fill the empty hours of her day. She delighted in matching the plants she collected with the 'theory I had gain'd before by reading', bringing this environment to order, and so to familiarity and 'calmness'. So one fundamental difference was the idea of leisure: respectable genteel women, by definition, did not work, and part of their task was to find suitably refined and improving pastimes.[76]

Places could have very different meanings for women of different rank. Botany Bay, already richly invested with myth and association, is an example. Catchpole played mischievously with the difference between the imagined place—the place of slavery and starvation feared by prisoners in the English gaols and hulks—and the real geographic one she discovered once she arrived: Botany Bay was not the site of the colony at all! She made a marvellous joke of this, sending her 'best respects to all my old fellow prisoners and tell them never to say "Dead Hearted" at the thought . . . of coming to Botany Bay', for after all, 'it is likely you may never see it for it is not inhabited, only by the Blacks'. But to Elizabeth Macarthur, Botany Bay was already a historic site. On one of her rambles she climbed a hill between Sydney and Botany Bay 'where I could command a prospect of that famous spot'—her eyes sweeping across the sheet of water to the place where Cook had landed, setting colonial history in motion.[77]

Within this historical frame, genteel women also wrote with eyes fixed firmly on a future of comfort and prosperity for themselves, their families, and other families of their rank, with whom they intermarried. This, after all, was the purpose of the colony as they saw it. 'We have every reasonable expectation of reaping the most material advantages', Elizabeth Macarthur confidently told her mother even before she had embarked.[78] Their own role was to create gentility in this new environment; they wrote now of land rather than sea. The environment was lovely and salubrious—the harbour was so beautiful 'the most fanciful imagination must tire . . . and yield the palm to reality and simple nature'. Yet natural beauty could not be left as it was. It is as if they constantly saw *through* it, beyond its raw but promising state, to a future of 'improvement' and embellishment. The course of empire, inevitable and virtuous, was most clearly manifested in the 'opening up' and 'improving' of the country through clearing. For women who lived on the farms and grazing estates handed out to officers after Phillip's departure, the removal of trees was the initial step in creating the wealth, security and pleasures they expected. 'I [do not] think there is any probability of my seeing much of the inland country', wrote Elizabeth Macarthur, 'until it is cleared'. After all, there was nothing there but 'native paths', criss-crossed like veins, 'very narrow and very incommodious' to a genteel walking lady.[79]

The estates of the Cumberland Plain represented the achievement of 'improved' nature. Genteel women described their homes, the sprawling single-storey affairs 'of the cottage type' with six-panelled doors and French windows symmetrically arranged. Increasingly they were shaded with the new fashion in verandahs which looked like broad-brimmed hats, pulled down over cool stone-flagged floors. These houses themselves became features of the picturesque landscape, symbols of beauty and progress, set in the idyllic 'gentleman's park'. Their estates had flourishing vineyards, dairies for milk, cheese and cream, poultry for meat and eggs, kitchen gardens and orchards full of vines and fruit trees, and of course the free labour of convict servants to run and maintain it all. As we have seen, practically every letter home begged for the seeds of practical and ornamental plants—a quickening green invasion to match the human and animal ones. Packs of mean, muscular greyhounds were used to hunt wild ducks and kangaroo at the Macarthurs' Elizabeth Farm. The dogs killed an average of 300 pounds of meat a week, a massive drain on the foods of Aboriginal people.[80]

Elizabeth Macarthur, like the early officers, wrote soon after her arrival of the drought and wretched soils of Sydney Cove. By 1795, only four years later, she could write in total contentment of the colony's plenty and beauty:

> The necessaries of life are abundant and a fruitful soil affords us many
> luxuries . . . It is now spring, and the eye is delighted with a most beautiful,
> variegated landscape; almonds, apricot, pear and apple trees are in full
> bloom; the native shrubs are also in flower, and the whole country gives
> a grateful perfume.

Elizabeth wrote the poetry of place and sought to convey scents and vistas, what it felt like to be on this land, in this air. When she included some of her husband's descriptions in her letter there is an abrupt change in tempo and expression. He boasts of the extent of his possessions, of acreage under crop, head of stock, number of rooms. As Alan Atkinson observes, Elizabeth 'thought of her children as native inhabitants long before John did'. She wanted their horizons broadened so that they would truly appreciate 'this retirement' and their place in it. By 1805 John Macarthur told Governor King that he too considered his family 'attached to the soil' of New South Wales.[81]

One historian said of Eliza Marsden's letters that 'she speaks with the voice of all those who were aware of the deeply alien quality of the Australian environment'. This is what Eliza Marsden actually wrote:

Eliza Marsden, 1821. (Mitchell Library, State Library of New South Wales)

The Climate is fine & healthy and agrees very well with my constitution. I have not suffered one single day of sickness since we came here. The country is very romantic beautifully formed by nature and will be most delightful when it becomes a little more opened. It abounds with Beautifull Shrubs, and Firns of various kinds . . . . There is a fine river which runs up from Sydney to Parramatta and boats continually passing to and fro so that we can easily visit each other.

Clearly, genteel settler women found this country agreeable, healthy, beautiful and convenient. Most of them rejoiced in their good fortune and bright prospects, and they wrote with such pleasure of the natural environment. Yet this is not the whole story either, for their environmental experiences and responses *were* profoundly mediated by rank and economic standing, as well as by the vicissitudes of country and climate. In later years there would be few empty, idle hours for the extraordinary Elizabeth Macarthur. In the absence of her men, she would play a crucial role in managing the family's estates and grazing interests, sometimes staying over in bark huts and working closely with her overseers. Others suffered privations they had never known at home; many relished new freedoms too.[82] But on the whole, genteel women were sheltered from the harsher aspects of the land and the rigours of outdoor work. They were not likely to have been badly sunburned while walking the colony's roads in the blaze of summer, they probably did not feel the frozen ground through the soles of their shoes, they were unlikely to die from snakebite working in an isolated field. As Susan West observes, working people throughout the nineteenth century had the rawest relationship with the land.[83] When genteel women wrote of the colony's fruitfulness and beauty, their words hide the pyramid of social and economic structures which made such lives, and such vistas, possible. And they were for the main part sublimely unaware of the environmental impacts of clearing, building, planting, grazing and hunting, and of the impacts of Aboriginal dispossession.

Pure landscape, untrammelled by convict workers, Aborigines, or even stock. A lady and gentleman walk side by side, enjoying the parkland vistas of Elizabeth Farm around 1825. (National Library of Australia)

EUROPEAN WOMEN AND ABORIGINAL WOMEN

Of course, their husbands' influence, connections and positions ensured genteel women's exclusive access to thousands of acres of Aboriginal land. Many of the pictures of these early estates match Elizabeth's description of splendid contentment in a parklike and secure landscape. Whereas early pictures of the colony featured Aboriginal figures in the foreground, now they increasingly showed respectable people. In Lycett's painting of Elizabeth Farm, probably commissioned by John Macarthur, a little bonneted woman and a top-hatted man promenade in the foreground, an arm raised in admiration of the parkland vista, picturesque and empty of both workers and Aboriginal people. The promise of the antipodean environment has been fulfilled, the landscape has been cleared, pruned back, brought to light and perfection. The way they walk, side by side, she upon his arm, he her protector, expresses the ideal relationship between respectable couples, and the proper way to be in this landscape, itself in turn the proper environment for them.[84]

A miniature dating from 1785–90, thought to be Elizabeth Macarthur. (Dixson Library, State Library of New South Wales)

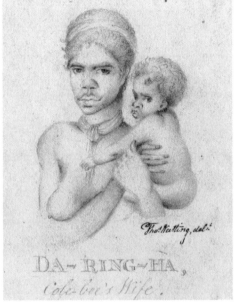

Thomas Watling's beautiful portrait of Daringa and her baby, c1791. (Natural History Museum)

Elizabeth Macarthur said as much in reverse when she described the way that Aboriginal men and women walked together. 'The natives are certainly not a very gallant set of people, who take pleasure in escorting their ladies', she wrote. Instead the women humbly followed their men 'Indian file like'. She thought this lack of gallantry symptomatic of Eora women's oppressed situation, for they seemed to her to be 'slaves to their husbands', and carried out the 'most laborious part of their work'. Macarthur was of course writing from the perspective of a leisured middle-class woman. Nevertheless, she was quick to observe the gendered nature of Aboriginal society and economy, and the way women did the bulk of the work—fishing, collecting food, cooking, making tools and implements, as well as bearing and caring for children.[85]

When Daringa, the wife of the well-known Cadigal warrior Coleby, came to her door with her newborn baby, Elizabeth thought she 'appeared feeble and faint'. She gave her food and 'had her taken proper care of for some little while'. This was the female equivalent of male gallantry: kindness and bounty to the poor—but it was also a way of expressing female empathy. Daringa and the baby visited regularly, and Elizabeth discovered and delighted in her 'softness and gentleness of manners'.[86]

European women's responses to Aboriginal people were expressed in a double view—in towns and houses the Eora were familiar, friendly, known by name. But they also described and feared them as dangerous savages, because of the attacks on convicts and settlers. Hence 'we take care not to venture walking to any distance unarmed, a soldier or two always attending when we make any excursion'. Echoing the dangers of the town's bush fringes, picnic parties and exploratory journeys too far from known country were cut short for fear of unseen attackers. When Eora women began to move between the households of the whites and their own people, some equated their increasing presence in the town as a sign that they were 'gettin' very civil', compared with attacks of earlier years.[87] As we shall see, this perception had more to do with space than time. While the whites in Sydney were beginning to complain of Aboriginal over-familiarity, a savage war was still raging between settlers and Aboriginal people out on the Cumberland Plain.

Relationships between black and white women were of course shaped by rank and racial assumptions—and white women considered themselves and their ways of life superior. There is little consciousness of Aboriginal people as occupiers and owners of their country. When Margaret Catchpole wrote that Botany Bay was 'not inhabited', she meant not inhabited by whites, or not 'really' inhabited, for she added that 'only' black people lived there. Yet relationships like the one between Daringa and Elizabeth Macarthur did grow, especially after the Eora 'came in' to the towns after November 1790. Visits were made, babies admired, food was given or shared, things, like soft bark baby wraps, were touched and exchanged; eyes must have met, words and conversations haltingly shared. In later decades settler and Aboriginal women of the Sydney region would learn about food, medicine and healing, and probably about birthing from one another.[88] Here is an aspect of cross-cultural relations not much explored—especially compared with the negotiations, fighting and sexual activities of men—yet it was fundamental to everyday life in the colony.

Chapter 11

———•◦•———

SOFT COLONY

If places are inscribed with human meaning by people's actions and intentions, then early Sydney was an Eora town. Peer into that first, rather ramshackle hospital at the foot of the Rocks on the west side—the surgeons are briskly assessing the possibility of removing jagged spears from the bodies of black warriors, who stoically endure their probing. Further up the slopes, young Eora people often sleep in the skillions and kitchens of the private houses, and some children have been 'adopted' by officers and merchants. In the early years, the east side of the cove was still more Eora country. Bennelong's square brick house, built at his own request, stood on the point that would take his name. Crowds of Eora people dropped in to the yard of Government House for a feed. And look through the multi-paned windows into the elegant dining room: Eora men and women, friends of the governor, are sitting at the table with him, talking, sharing food and wine, and taking dishes of coffee.

Certain urban public spaces became still more thoroughly associated with Eora and other Aboriginal people. From at least 1791 to the 1820s their great contest ground was 'a clear spot between the town and the brickfield', a flat, open area on the southern fringe.[1] Here crowds of people, black and white, gathered to watch the ritual contests and the bloody, cathartic battles. Often reports on these contests, detailing winners, losers, deaths and injuries, were published in

Sydney in 1800: a nowie *paddles near Mattewanye (Pinchgut), once a favoured picnic place of the Eora. Now the remains of murderer Francis Morgan swing from a gibbet on the island, his irons creaking and clothes flapping in the wind. (Surgeon's Log of the Minerva 1799–1800, ref. no. 13880, British Library)*

the *Sydney Gazette.* Out on the harbour, the Eora women fished from their bark nowie until at least the mid-1820s, plumes of smoke rising from onboard fires. The little green harbour islands had been favourite picnic grounds for Eora— Bennelong and his wife Barangaroo were very fond of Memil (Goat Island).[2] But the Berewalgal tended to despoil these places—the Eora dreaded and avoided the pyramid-shaped Mattewanye (Pinchgut, now Fort Denison) after the body of a murderer was strung up there to rot in 1796, 'his clothes shaking in the wind', his irons creaking.[3] Other islands were used to imprison re-offending convicts, and denuded of their vegetation. In the 1830s, Memil/Goat Island became a prison for ironed convicts labouring in the quarries and building a powder magazine and barracks there. They were joined by Aboriginal men, arrested and brought to Sydney from their Brisbane Water country to the north. They were taught to speak English and given some training in stonecutting. Their voices, reciting English words and singing hymns, floated over the waters.[4]

From December 1790 right up to the 1830s and beyond, the sight of Aboriginal people in the streets of Sydney, naked except perhaps for an old jacket or a blanket, was commonplace and unremarkable. White visitors were often shocked and offended by them, and wondered why they were tolerated, but townsfolk and officials took their presence, and their activities, largely for granted. Sydney people wrote of 'our natives' and knew them by name, knew locals from visiting strangers. After the arrival of Bennelong and his family and friends in November 1790, they were part of the town, for better or worse. They fashioned particular, often ingenious, ways of living in it, and certain places, now forgotten, were very much their own. In later years, Aboriginal people from all over the region, the colony and then the state would follow them to Sydney.

This inclusion of 'the natives' in the town had been official policy as well as the genuine hope of Phillip and several of the officers from the start; Tench called it 'this much wished-for event'. Tench, Collins and Bradley in particular tracked the progress of race relations painstakingly in their journals, and their narratives were driven partly by the great aim of 'reconciling' the Eora to them, and of living in 'amity and kindness with them'.[5] David Collins thought the Eora's early 'sociable and friendly' conduct seemed to indicate that they did not think of the strangers as 'enemies or invaders'. He added a wistful note: 'How grateful to every feeling of humanity would it be if we could conclude this narrative without being compelled to say, that these unoffending people had found reason to change both their opinions and their conduct!'[6] The irony of their eventual success, of course, is that Aboriginal people did come to live in Sydney, and made a place for themselves in it, not as Europeanised people, but very much on their own terms. As the decades of the nineteenth century passed, governors, city councillors and respectable citizens became less tolerant and increasingly discomforted by the presence of Aboriginal people in the city, tried to control their behaviour and eventually to banish them altogether.[7]

How were 'the natives', these 'Adamites and Evites', to be won over? The officers were sure it would be quite simple. Besides demonstrating the power of their guns (highly effective), there was the softer persuasive power of civilised comforts. Tench was blunt: 'Our first object was to win their affections, and our next was to convince them of the superiority we possessed: for without the latter, the former we know would be of little importance'. The initial rituals on the beaches had to be carried out successfully first—the laying down of arms, the stately open-handed approach, the giving of presents, the offering of wine, and then the nervous, edgy playtime of words, mimicry and jokes, jumping and capering. Shyness and fear would be overcome by kindness and restraint—not overt violence and brutality.[8] Phillip issued orders, as instructed: shooting or otherwise molesting them was strictly forbidden. After this, the Eora, a people from before time, would need only to see and experience the comforts of highly advanced civilisation to understand what a blessing had befallen them. Warm clothes, abundant food and drink, snug houses, tools and trinkets would do the work of colonisation and dispossession: New South Wales would be a soft colony, though underwritten by the hard power of guns.[9] Civilised manners, language and Christianity would swiftly follow: and then the crowning gift of British justice. The Eora would leap the aeons of human development, straight to the apex! Phillip hoped a native family would live in the new settlement, and he planned to shower them with 'everything that can tend to civilise them, and give them a high opinion of their new guests'.[10] These fortunate people were to be agents of civilisation, for they would then go out to their countrymen and women with the news of wonders.

So, at the first meetings, Eora men were not only given lessons in British firepower, but also jackets, hatchets and knives, beads and mirrors, strips of white linen and red baize. They were offered food and wine. It was a template: gifts of food, drink and clothing would mark the relationship for years. Later the Berewalgal encouraged the curious Eora to inspect their boats, and then urged the black men to sit in them and try rowing. They tried to persuade them to board their ships, their 'wonderful canoes', too, and to come to Sydney with them.[11]

The early responses were less than encouraging. A man who tried on a shirt 'appeared to be deprived of the use of his limbs while within it'. They spat out the bread, perhaps in distaste at the doughy stuff, or fearing poison, or perhaps because they also spat out the remains of fibrous starchy fern roots after they chewed them. The wine was also rejected or spat out. The Berewalgal were disgruntled to note the lack of interest in the 'trinkets', beads and mirrors—they were accepted politely, but left on the sand. 'They look at our objects with a kind of vague indifference', wrote George Worgan. They were like children, the way they so quickly tired of these childish things. River people pointed out that they could see their own faces reflected in their waters just as well as in a proffered mirror (and hence the name Looking Glass Bay on Parramatta River for one place where this happened!).[12]

But knives and especially metal hatchets were of immediate and keen interest—one man given a hatchet promptly turned up the sole of his foot and used the blade to shape a piece of wood on it. Soon spears were being tipped with metal blades and edged with broken glass, and hatchets became the much desired and prized possessions of warriors, 'the most valuable article that could be given them'. Jackets were another item which appealed; later they became coveted possessions. The Eora were curious about the small craft too, and 'run all over our boats'. They liked the Berewalgal's dogs—the yappy spaniels and terriers made better night-watchdogs than their own non-barking dingoes.[13]

The Eora clearly were not much interested in frivolous and useless things, though; or in clothing in general, which must have felt very uncomfortable and restricted their strong and active bodies; or in unfamiliar tastes and textures. The Berewalgal were confounded. They even watched the Eora to see if they *felt the cold*, and they did, they shivered miserably like other human beings, yet they rejected clothes![14] These seemed ominous signs of intractable barbarity—perhaps these people were incapable of appreciating the wonders of civilisation?

In the responses to these small things, then, it is possible to glimpse the cultural differences between the two groups. And it is possible to see that, in formulating the 'colonisation by kindness' plan, it did not occur to Phillip and the officers that the Eora might have a different way of seeing the world, and hence all the things they were offered. It was assumed that any existing culture would simply collapse in the face of European superiority. This is the great, contrary theme running through their journals: that genuine anthropological impulse, the quest to *know* these people, but at the same time an inability to see Aboriginal culture as instrumental in shaping action and reaction. Watkin Tench, a man who could observe their customs even in the most dire of circumstances, did glimpse something of this by the time he left the colony in 1791. 'They resist knowledge and the adoption of manners and customs differing from their own', he wrote, though this was because 'all savages hate toil, and place happiness in inaction'. Yet he defended his Eora friends against those who accused them of 'stupidity and want of reflection', pointing out that they understandably ignored unfamiliar and pointless 'artifices and contrivances', but were interested in and admired things which made sense to them. Thus they were impressed by collections of weapons, animal skins and stuffed birds they saw in a gentleman's house: these denoted the owners as a 'renowned warrior or expert hunter'. The surgeons, with their ability to heal bodies and to save lives, earned their admiration and respect too, and elicited shouts of true wonder. 'If these instances bespeak not nature and good sense', wrote Tench defiantly, 'I have yet to learn the meaning of the terms'.[15]

But I am getting ahead of the story. For the first twelve months, there was no way to demonstrate the marvels of ships and houses, farming and surgery. After a brief, early visit from two elders in February 1788, the Eora avoided the settlement at Warrane almost completely.[16] In the surrounding country, the British seemed to only ever encounter them 'by Accident', and in small groups, even though they knew the Eora were numerous. There was something odd and unnerving about it. The Eora were always on their guard, kept their distance. They would never board the ships (the strange floating country of the Berewalgal) either, though they constantly paddled their tiny nowie close by the steep wooden hulls.[17] The meetings, the good fellowship and dancing on the sand, even the breakthrough in meeting the women at Eve's Cove, had not led anywhere. The official relationship stalled before it had really even begun.

CONVICTS AND EORA

Meanwhile, a completely different set of negotiations and relationships was emerging. The officers were not the only ones interested in making contact, much as they would have liked to have been. We have seen the way that convicts immediately began their own explorations and journeys overland. They collected food, found paths back to Botany Bay, and learned about country, until topography, paths, and the 'two coastlines'—the outer of cliffs, headlands and harbour, 'ghosted by an inner coast of lagoons, meandering tidal estuaries and self-draining lakes'—were familiar.[18] And they were learning about the Eora, and how they lived.

Given this geographic mobility, especially that of the hunters and fishers, there must have been a whole history of relations between convicts and Eora. I write 'must have been' because, while we have detailed accounts of relations between the officers and the Eora, this other, larger, history of convict–Eora relations is far more shadowy. We must read between the lines, and the small glimpses we have seem all the brighter and more intriguing for it.

It is likely that the convicts, as well as the sailors and ordinary soldiers, had more in common with the Eora than did the officers. This is not to suggest any sort of true cultural commonality, only that there were probably more recognitions and resonances. Although around three-quarters of the convicts sent to New South Wales could read and/or write, theirs was still largely an oral and visual culture. They used writing for petitions and memorials, and well knew its power, but for many it was the medium of their betters and oppressors.[19] For them, as for the Eora, news and ideas came by word of mouth, by songs, stories and performance. Probably both watched for signs, interpreted dreams and avoided ill-omened people. Both admired cunning and the ability to outwit enemies.

Convicts in early Sydney held a world view revolving around fate and opportunity, rather than their betters' cause-and-effect model of lineal progress. They were opportunists, boldly taking risks when the odds seemed good, resigned to misfortune and failure when luck was against them. Eora culture also bore powerful elements of resignation and fatalism: when people submitted to the Law through payback and ritual punishment, for example. But there are glimpses of dynamic opportunism too: the Eora watched and learned quickly, paying particular attention to names, repeating words, accents and actions perfectly. Soon they worked out strategies to seize fish and animals from the Berewalgal, and they manufactured artefacts specifically for the insatiable white collectors. The Eora were described as being quick to anger, violent in their responses and sensitive to insult, but their great good humour, generosity and sense of fun was equally quick to return. Such mercurial behaviour could also be observed in any of the early pubs or sly grog shops, especially where Irish and English, or soldiers and convicts, drank together. Good-humoured socialising could turn in an instant: a word, a song, a sneer could end with a bayonet in the guts.[20]

At the same time, both groups took great enjoyment in what Clendinnen calls 'expressive good humour'—in coming together for socialising, eating, relaxing, singing and dancing, storytelling and jokes: for fun. Conviviality was close to the essence and meaning of human existence. The officers and their entourages were not the only ones to 'dance with strangers', to play with the Eora, or to give them presents. In those very early days when the First Fleet was still anchored in Botany Bay, sailors blithely went ashore 'without Arms of anything to protect themselves, sailor like' and introduced themselves to Eora families. The Eora were 'very friendly, met them without fear & eagerly accepted of a jacket which one of the Sailors gave them'. Someone took a fife on shore, and 'played several tunes to the Natives who were highly delighted with it espetially at seeing some of the Seamen dance'. In later months, an Eora family living in a cove adjoining Sydney—either Farm Cove or Long Cove (Darling Harbour)—'were visited by large parties of convicts of both sexes' where they 'danced and sung with apparent good humour, and received such presents as the convicts could afford to make them'.[21] There is a crucial difference: these convicts were socialising with the Eora despite the fact that they had no muskets, and there were no red-coated soldiers standing watchfully by.

Physical violence was part of interpersonal conflict, popular culture, and the course of justice in both cultures. There were some striking parallels, too, in the excitement, blood and violence of the great Eora contests and the European prize-fights. Both were tests of manly strength, skill and courage, and stoicism in bearing pain. As we shall see, European spectators gathered to watch the Eora men parrying and dodging spears, just as they followed the prize-fight circuit from one end of the colony to the other. Phillip thought there was an equivalence: 'The natives throw their spears and take a life in their quarrels', he wrote, 'as readily as the lower class of people in England strip to box, and think as little of the consequences'. The Eora's incredible power and accuracy in throwing spears (Bennelong could hurl a spear almost 100 yards into a gale) must have impressed as well as terrified the convicts. Being hit by a spear felt like being struck a massive blow.[22]

The Eora contests were, however, the execution of Aboriginal Law. The accused had to face the spears or clubs of the family and friends of the person they had wronged. Aboriginal Law demanded payback for crimes and this could be inflicted on the relatives of the offender—therefore guilt could be collective as well as individual. Once the crime had been expiated, and the world thus righted, the combatants were often the best of friends.[23] Ideas of revenge, collective guilt and the need to right wrongs were familiar to the white lower orders of Sydney.

Certain crimes—infanticide, suicide, murder, for example—were abominable acts which disrupted the natural order and made the populace uneasy and anxious. They too demanded expiation to right wrongs: through public shaming, violent attack upon the body of the transgressor, and execution. And if their courts would or could not deliver such resolution, they would take matters into their own hands.[24]

Most strikingly, both cultures held beliefs in the sentient corpse. Aboriginal people, believing that all deaths were unnatural, interrogated the dead, asking them how they had come by their death and who was responsible. When murders occurred among the whites, suspects were brought close to the body of the victim, to see if it bled. Higher and lower orders alike believed that a corpse could identify its killer by bleeding in their presence. In deathways generally, there were probably also parallels in beliefs about the spirits of the dead, and what Ruth Richardson calls 'an uncertain balance between solicitude of the corpse and fear of it'—uncertainty about the power of the dead—which made proper post-mortem rituals so important. The white townsfolk avoided places polluted by murder and suicide. The Eora avoided graves, and burned the places where people died. Tench knew that the Eora 'believe the spirit of the dead not to be extinct with the body', and they told him of the *mawn*, the ghosts of the deceased, which might suddenly rise up and seize them by the throat. They were 'sadly afraid of the dark'; Holt recalled that 'they make fires to prevent the devil of coming to them by night. So I found that they are afeared by night, like feeble minded people in Ireland.'[25]

Most convicts, who would refer to themselves as 'freeborn Englishmen' despite their predicament, no doubt felt themselves superior to the 'intirely naked' Eora, and scorned 'savage' Eora ways of life in the way their superiors did. But not all. As we have seen, some convict men became aware early on that it was possible to live another sort of life in this country, and took to the bush, despite the threats and cajoling of their superiors about the dangers and horrors of the bush, and the ridicule they heaped on those who tried to escape. The Eora's hunting, fishing and fighting must have seemed exciting and enjoyable compared to work at the brickyards or the quarries, or the backbreaking labour of clearing and hoeing ground on the public farms.[26]

Stories and glimpses from the Sydney region suggest all sorts of ways that Eora and European practices, knowledge, things and words crossed over among certain groups of people. Some Europeans soon learned to build shelters of 'boughs' similar to the Eora's 'hunting wigwams', and by 1801 the Eora of the Manly area were building solid gunyahs using 'timber procured from the wreck of a small vessel'.[27] As we have seen, metal hatchets were much prized, and worked glass, and perhaps pottery and porcelain, were used as tools and spear points. Knowledge about what foods were good to eat and how to prepare them was probably also shared—Collins' servant told him witchetty grubs were 'sweeter than any marrow he had ever tasted'. Hunting certainly became a shared passion of men, and by 1803 there were incidental, everyday reports of Europeans and Aboriginal people hunting kangaroos together at the Hawkesbury. Convicts were reported as working without clothes in the heat—perhaps the clothes had worn out or been gambled away, but George Bruce's story suggests that white men in the bush went naked when it was hot.[28]

Words ran together too. Governor Phillip's gamekeeper, John McIntyre, learned to speak the language of the coastal people. John Wilson, who lived with Aboriginal people on the Hawkesbury River, developed a pidgin language and took an Aboriginal name, Bunboee. Names not only crossed from Europeans to Aboriginal people, then, they went the other way too, like 'Gibber Jack' at Manly, and a man known as Wanga Jemmy (meaning James the Liar). In the 1840s a white Hawkesbury prize-fighter took the Aboriginal name Bungaree.[29] Some words crossed over into English, though not many: *wombat, warrigal* (large dog) and *dingo, cooee, gunyah* (shelter/house) and *patter* (to eat, food), as well as water-words like *bogey* (from the Eora word to dive or swim—now bogey-hole) and the lovely word *bombora* (the waves which crash over submerged offshore rocks or reefs). The governor himself used *pattagorong* (kangaroo) and *baggaray* (wallaby) without inverted commas in his reports. Meanwhile the Eora soon adapted English words for some of the things for which they had no names: 'badal' (bottle), 'gandle' (candle), 'winda' (window), 'badaduh' (potato). Or they made their own quite sensible constructions: *murri nowie*, 'big canoe', for the ships, and *naa-moro* (or *muru*) for compass, meaning, literally, to 'see the way'.[30] That many of the Eora words dropped out of use again bespeaks the constantly shifting nature of Sydney society: so often those who acquired words, ideas and insights sailed away again, or moved on. Sometimes they carried Eora words inland with them.[31]

The convict–Eora relations which are better known, however, are just the opposite: brutal attacks and killings. These incidents are better known because the officers wrote about them. The bush could be an extremely dangerous place for convicts, because they bore the brunt of Eora anger and resistance to the invasion of country, the shots fired at them by the soldiers, the blundering onto sacred sites, the desecration of graves by curious officers who were themselves protected by guns and red coats. From March 1788, unarmed convicts were threatened and attacked with showers of stones, clubs, spears and *womeras* (spear-throwers). Some were simply warned by spears whistling over their heads, others were chased, terrified, for miles through the bush, still others were stripped, beaten and left to crawl back to the Camp.[32]

On 22 May 1788, the killings began. Two convicts, William Ayres and Peter Byrne, were attacked while out gathering greens. Ayres staggered back to the Camp but Byrne was dragged off, his clothes left hanging on bushes. Eight days later, William Okey and Samuel Davis, sent to cut rushes in Darling Harbour, were killed. Okey's body was mutilated—limbs broken, eyes chopped out with an axe, skull smashed in, brains spilling out. Davis, a youth, was found dead among the rushes. He had been hit on the head, but seems to have died of shock. Most of the officers did not question the reasons too closely, assuming that 'there was too much reason to believe that our people had been the aggressors' and that the Eora 'must have been provoked and injured by the convicts'.[33] But William Bradley did, and discovered that it was, indeed, payback: a convict had slashed an Eora man across the belly and killed him. 'I have no doubt but this Native having been murder'd occasioned their seeking revenge', he wrote, '& which proved fatal to those who were not concern'd'.[34] Another convict, Cooper Handley, was killed on the road to Botany Bay in October when he straggled from a party of vegetable-getters. His body was repeatedly exhumed, as if to keep the image before European eyes, to haunt them.[35] The convicts and soldiers sent out to bury and re-bury him must have come back to the Camp with terrible stories.

By the end of 1788 the journal-keepers were noting that convicts were con-stantly attacked 'where they [the Eora] think they can get the better of them'. Clendinnen dismisses these attacks as 'spasmodic gestures of hostility' which were 'no threat to the British'. But they were serious threats to unarmed convicts. On the other hand the Eora 'never meddle with a redcoat'. Attacks on parties with officers, protected by soldiers and guns, were very rare, though the occasional warning spear arced over their boats.[36] As we have seen, the Eora quickly grasped both the hierarchy and weaponry of the whites, and they must have seen that Phillip, though he lay down his own arms and approached their elders open-handed, could not control his people. For the main part the convicts lost out on all counts. They quickly developed some defence strategies, though. By March 1788 they had worked out that by heading for thick brush—areas of dense semi-rainforest—they had a chance of escape. Bradley noted that these were places 'the natives don't like to go into', but whether this was because they were uncomfortable for naked people, or because these were the unburned, non-visited or sacred spaces, we don't know.[37] In July a sailor being pelted with stones picked up a stick and pointed it at them 'in manner of a Musquet'. This was effective too—his pursuers 'stopped & by that means he got away clear of them'.[38]

So the authorities were right when they constantly warned convicts about the real danger of going into the bush. But in this awful succession of reports, we can see that the attacks were not inevitable, or indiscriminate; nor were they all the same. Edward Corbett, the convict blamed for the escape of the colony's cattle, said he 'frequently fell in with the natives'. They didn't like him much, but they didn't 'treat him ill' either.[39] Some convicts were simply threatened and warned, others stripped, beaten and left trembling, white and naked on the tracks. Still others were killed and horribly mutilated. What would explain this? On one hand it seems that the Eora Law of payback was in operation, as Bradley said of the dead rushcutters, and it is likely convicts paid the price for others' offences. Eora people had been shot at as early as February 1788, when the crew of the *Sirius* fired on them on Garden Island. At Botany Bay, La Perouse built a fort and had been 'forced' to shoot at the 'malevolent savages'. When his ships sailed away, the Gweagal pulled down the board marking the grave of Père Receveur, who had died during their sojourn, and 'defaced everything around'.[40]

But the different types of attack also suggest that some victims may have been personally responsible for various crimes against the Eora. When the warrior Pemulwuy speared the governor's convict gamekeeper, John McIntyre, in December 1790, it seems to have been the result of his own wrongdoing—Bennelong loathed him in a way that suggests some terrible crime. What sort of crimes could have demanded such retribution? The most likely were violent attacks, abductions, illicit sex, theft and trespassing. Phillip's excursion to Broken Bay in March 1788 seems to have been a cue for an outbreak of absconding and violence at the white settlement. He and his party landed at Camp Cove on the return trip and were surprised to see the Eora, instead of welcoming them, running away. Eventually a man came forward and showed them 'the marks on his body where he had been beat' as well as cuts and stab wounds 'from a barbed spear'. The man said he had been attacked by white men who had arrived in two boats. At other meetings thereafter, men would come forward to show Phillip their injuries, and complain of his people's behaviour.[41]

By 1799, the convict William Noah could report that some of the Aboriginal people around Sydney were 'Very friendly, & will take you from tribe to tribe', so it appears that, despite the killings, early friendliness between Eora and convicts had also been sustained. But there was a vital coda: 'You must not touch their Gins as they are very Jealous and Desperate Cruil to their Woman'. The gross sexual imbalance among the convicts meant that Aboriginal women were desired by white men from the start of the invasion. Exploration, moving through Aboriginal territory, was powerfully charged with sexual undercurrents, as it would be for the rest of Australia's European history. In this shadowy period of early convict–Aboriginal history, the nature, meaning and import of sexual relations remain obscure and open to speculation. We know that Eora women at first kept away from officers and convicts alike. But babies with lighter skin were born, and there are sad stories of Aboriginal mothers trying to darken these infants with smoke and ashes.[42] Assaults, abductions and rapes would have been violently avenged.

The explanation often given for the violence and killings involved that other lust—'the rage for curiosity'. Daniel Southwell concluded that the eagerness to collect Aboriginal artefacts 'and the unjust methods made use of to obtain them' was the source of 'misunderstanding'. Convicts were well aware of the market for Eora tools and weapons and some of them, along with soldiers and sailors, stole the spears, shields, lines, hooks, bags and tools left lying under rocks or by their huts. There is no doubt that these were considered by the Eora as thefts of personal property—they taught their own children not to steal. The loss of essential, carefully made and personalised equipment and tools must have been infuriating, making fishing and hunting still more difficult than it was already. When Eora retaliated by picking up European artefacts and taking their goods— axes, shovels, jackets—the whites were outraged. They shot at them, slapped the faces of elders, kidnapped their children and held them to ransom.[43] Phillip banned the trade in artefacts to no avail. Yet the officers were also keen to acquire such goods—for loftier aims than mere 'curiosity' and profit, of course, and with attempts at fair exchange. Nevertheless, they lusted after 'curios' too, and, tellingly, knew where to find goods which had been stolen. They were at least partly complicit in the process.[44]

Nevertheless, during the first months, Phillip and the officers usually decided the thieving, straggling convicts had brought the attacks upon themselves. A picture painted by the Port Jackson Painter seems to capture one aspect of this

The Port Jackson Painter's version of an attack by Eora warriors on a sailor or convict gathering sweet tea. (Natural History Museum)

attitude. It is almost comical, like an illustration for a nursery rhyme: the cowardly blue-coated convict or sailor, some greenery (probably the vine known as 'sweet tea') under his arm, is running away as fast as he can from the spears of the black men. Worse, the convicts could jeopardise the project of 'soft colonisation': their unenlightened brutishness and violence would negate the officers' kindness and civility, and send out the wrong message entirely! This outcome had been feared even before landing—when parties were sent ashore for water and grass that first day in Botany Bay, 'an officer's guard was placed there to prevent the seamen . . . from having improper intercourse with the natives'.[45]

In later months and years, the crimes and misdemeanours of convicts and seamen also became a convenient retrospective explanation for the eventual 'failure' of Phillip's plan. In a brief peaceful interlude in February 1789, Collins wrote that 'very little molestation was . . . given by the natives: and had they never been ill-treated by our people, instead of hostility, it is more probable that an intercourse of friendship would have subsisted'. Dispossession and colonisation were not the reasons for interracial strife: the gross, uncivilised convicts were entirely to blame.[46]

Meanwhile this tendency to regard the convicts' ordeals and horrible deaths as deserved, and the authorities' inability or unwillingness to punish the attackers, can only have fostered other, dangerous undercurrents in the Camp. These were later exacerbated when convicts saw the governor's Eora friends given food (which they devoured in huge quantities, while the colonists were on short rations), clothing (which they often gave away or traded) and shelter—both at Government House, where a privileged few were 'guests of the governor', and later in a solid brick-and-tile house built especially for them. Fear and hatred, and longing for payback, must also have begun to writhe among the convicts of the town.[47]

SWEET TEA

The sweet, liquorice-flavoured tea the convicts brewed from the leaves of *Smilax glyciphylla* must have been delicious: a pick-me-up, an anti-scorbutic, a great comfort, perhaps addictive. The Eora name for it was *warraburra*; the convicts and soldiers called it sweet tea, or Botany Bay tea, the brew so sweet it needed no sugar. Tench said it was 'drank universally'. It twined among the bracken and other ferns on the floors of the open turpentine–ironbark forest which grew on gentle sheltered slopes in sandstone country. This forest was found just to the south and south-west of the Camp—today the areas stretching south-west from Hyde Park past the Brickfields towards Chippendale.[48]

But the settlers' delight in sweet tea meant that, only a year after the Camp was established, the plant had disappeared from the immediate environs, and convicts had to go further afield to gather it. Horticulturalists today say the seeds are difficult to germinate and the plant is very slow growing; evidently it could not regenerate quickly enough to keep up with the relentless harvesting.[49] Despite the attacks on unarmed convicts, no risk seemed to deter the tea-seekers. In February 1789, a convict from the Brickfields went out searching for tea. He was killed and his body mangled by Eora, possibly the Gomerigal or Cadigal, whose country this was. His brother brickmakers had had enough. They formed a revenge party and marched along the road to Botany Bay (now Oxford Street) armed with 'work tools and large clubs'—only to be met with a body of 50 Eora warriors ready and waiting for them. If they tried the stick-as-musket strategy this time, it didn't work. Seven of the convicts were speared, one was killed, a boy had his ear almost cut off and the rest ran for their lives back to town. 'Our heroes', Tench wrote sardonically, 'were immediately routed'.[50]

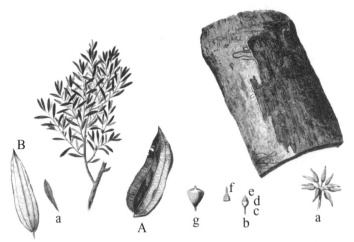

Dangerous, desired plants: Surgeon White's pictures of sweet tea (native sarsaparilla, Smilax glyciphylla, A and B) and tea-tree (left). On the right is the scribbled bark of the Sydney redgum (Angophora costata). (From John White, Journal of a Voyage to New South Wales)

This was dangerous comedy, for their brutality and stupidity would undo every good intention of their superiors. The able-bodied would-be vigilantes were flogged before the assembled town as a savage lesson on who would carry out retribution in this colony, after which they had to wear fetters. The wounded were allowed to recover in hospital. Then they were flogged too.[51]

Once more, the convicts were the problem. But a thirst for sweet tea had lured the man out. At the heart of the hostilities lay not only the trespassing on other people's country, but the immediate fact that the Berewalgal were destroying the vegetation and relentlessly consuming the foods of the Eora—fish, birds, game, seeds, legumes, berries and fruits. As the months passed they moved further and further out from their own Camp and onto other people's lands, their waters and the Kangaroo Grounds. These days urban scientists call this process a city's 'ecological footprint'—they calculate the amount of the surrounding hinterland a city uses to support itself. Sydney's 'footprint' today reaches from Batemans Bay in the south right up to Port Macquarie in the north—a monstrous tread with a radius of some 330 kilometres.[52] The process began, of course, as soon as the Berewalgal discovered the tasty and nutritious local produce, felled trees for firewood and building, cut rushes for thatching, and began gouging out the clay at the Brickfields for their bricks and tiles.

The pressure on the food resources in particular meant that some food plants and shellfish could not regenerate quickly enough and were soon exhausted in the immediate area of Warrane. Already by April 1788, the 'esucculent vege-tables' were reportedly becoming scarce around the Camp. By May, Phillip reported that many of the food plants 'had failed us'. (I suspect their rapid disappearance is one reason officers like Tench dismissed them with such contempt).[53] While it is unlikely that the Eora ate the leafy vegetables and drank the sweet tea enjoyed by the Berewalgal, we know that both groups relished oysters, both the smaller Sydney rock oysters and the large, unctuous mud oysters in their plate-like shells. But archaeological evidence indicates that the slower-reproducing mud oysters disappeared from the waterways soon after 1788. Convicts foraging for food and cutting rushes moved steadily further afield: the forested country between Sydney and Botany Bay, and the foreshores of the Parramatta River at Long Cove and Balmain. The attacks upon them soon began. By October they were told to get their vegetables, tea and herbs only on Saturdays, accompanied by an armed guard.[54]

It is possible the Eora at first thought these rather ill-mannered and odd strangers were transients—that they would camp temporarily at Warrane and then move on, leaving the locals in peace. As we have seen, Phillip had unwittingly located the Camp around the boundary between the country of the Cadigal and the Wangal, for Warrane lay between Cadi (lower Sydney Harbour) and Wanne (the upper reaches of the harbour, now called Parramatta River).[55] But months passed and instead of leaving, they not only ate and destroyed everything in their host country, but were starting to rob other people's country. In a flash of insight after the Brickfield Hill posse incident, David Collins realised that the attacks in areas away from the Camp were attempts at containment: they were trying to restrict the colonists to Warrane. To the British this was an outrageous proposition. On the same day, Phillip sent out two armed parties to march to Botany Bay and 'elsewhere', Collins wrote defiantly, 'that the natives might see their late act of violence would neither intimidate nor prevent us from moving beyond the settlement whenever occasion required'.[56] There could be no concessions: besides the fact that the town needed these resources, the whole territory had been officially claimed and was now British. Leaving the Eora their own country and respecting their boundaries, as they seem to have expected, was beyond the pale. The British would go where they wished.

So the vegetables were eaten out, the foragers moved further away, and as the weather grew colder, the once-plentiful fish seemed to vanish from the harbour as well. At the same time, the chronicling officers noticed that the Eora looked increasingly hungry and thin. They were perplexed at this, and then deeply concerned when they met people—often old men and children—who seemed to be literally starving, for they looked like 'walking skeletons'. They would kindly shoot birds for them (which were devoured, guts, bones and all), or give them bread and salt meat, and leave again.[57] But the officers tended to see the Eora's predicaments as part of their 'savage' condition: lacking the comforts and securities of civilisation, these primitive people suffered severely and could not even feed themselves. They were to be pitied.

It never occurred to any of them—or not in their official journals, anyway—

that the sudden appearance of over 1000 people, who relished many of the same foods as the Eora, had overstretched the local food supply. It is likely to have been a delicate enough balance before the invasion. Eora women spent much of their time gathering or catching the day's food, and shortages of fish in the winter months were expected. It is also likely that food plants were less plentiful in winter. When they were hungry, people tied their bellies tight with ligaments to stop the pangs (hungry soldiers later copied them). It was a matter of surviving these leaner months, of making do with fern roots and suchlike, until the fish returned in the plentiful warmer months. It is unlikely, though, given their excellent health and the 'great age' they attained, that starvation was a normal part of this cycle.[58]

Fish was their staple food and so fish became an early flashpoint. The Eora were amazed by the Berewalgal's seine nets when they first saw them drawn up, bursting and leaping with fish of all types and sizes, taken in one deadly drag. Sometimes the seine nets were so full they could not be taken ashore, but had to be staked to the sand for the tide to leave behind. The Eora were probably shocked by the sheer volume of fish taken—they speared or hooked fish one by one, enough for the group or family for the day. They also regarded the fish of their waters as their own. The first time they saw the nets hauled up, they came forward to claim them, only to be forced back and given a portion. Soon they knew when the fishing boats were going out and were waiting for them on the shore, helping to pull up the nets for a share of the catch. The British thought approvingly that this signified both good relations and industriousness. But as the fish and food generally became scarcer, cooperation turned to aggression— the share of what the Eora considered to be theirs in the first place had probably grown meaner. In July the officers were shocked to hear that a group of Eora, backed up by a row of armed warriors, attacked and beat the crew of the *Sirius'* fishing boat, and took half the catch. After that, a petty officer was ordered to accompany all fishing expeditions. In later incidents on the beaches, spears were thrown and the large fish demanded instead of the small fry that were offered.[59]

These raids were clearly carefully planned and staged. The Eora were also watching the Berewalgal and their animals on land. In August a group of men in five canoes came ashore at Dawes Point/Tarra on the west side. While some of them distracted the officers there, others dragged off and killed two goats which were grazing on the hospital grounds. They got clean away with the kill, paddling swiftly back round Long Cove and away up the river.[60] How did they know that these animals were good to eat? Probably through careful observation, and contacts with convicts. Besides, Surgeon White had had a very pleasant conversation and singsong with a group on Long Cove behind the hospital just three weeks before—a man had come ashore, although the women stayed in their nowie. The man had been very friendly, and shown him certain edible figs—and then he'd asked him about a dead sheep he saw lying nearby. The surgeon no doubt happily explained what sheep were for. Interestingly, a month after the goat raid, Phillip ordered the first breastwork to be built on Dawes Point, and had the *Sirius'* guns installed there.[61]

So the Eora were not only trying to stop incursions into their country, they were learning about the newcomers' methods of fishing and hunting, and their food supply. In March 1788, one of the governor's gamekeepers—it was probably John McIntyre—went out on his own expedition for five days. Upon his return he said 'he had been taken a considerable distance into the Country by the Natives, that he had killed a Kanguroo which they took from him, broiled it & eat it all together'. It was a mutually beneficial excursion: McIntyre was probably led to what became known as the Kangaroo Grounds, around Petersham; and his friendly Eora companions got to see more of how those muskets worked.[62]

There was one seafood in which the Berewalgal were mercifully uninterested. Whales, occasionally thrown up onto the beaches by the sea, were a great bounty, and people who feasted upon them seemed to get ecstatically drunk on the glorious fatty blubber. But we know that on one occasion at least, at Manly Beach in 1790, the feast did not include all those who wanted to eat. People who had come all the way from Parramatta for a share were attacked and possibly killed by those who claimed the whale. Was this a traditional response, or had it been created by severe food shortages?[63]

The wild food became scarcer and the Eora hungrier over 1788—probably the older people especially were weakened. There was of course a new source of food, a lifeline: the bread, salt meat, fish, vegetables and fruit at the Camp of the white men. The ruthless politics of food, dependence and dispossession, which shaped the next two centuries of race relations, were about to begin.[64]

SMALLPOX/GAL-GAL-LA

Among the crowds forced to watch the flogging of the vigilante brickmakers was an Eora man, dressed in European clothes. He wore a fetter around his ankle, as the flogged men soon would. This man had been held a prisoner at Government House since his kidnapping at the end of December the previous year. His captors had only just learned his name: Arabanoo. They wanted to demonstrate that English law, the course of justice, was on the side of the Eora in this case, but Arabanoo was disturbed and sickened by what he saw.[65]

The Brickfields was very much a locus of conflict in the earliest years. It was the first, rough outpost, occupied by unarmed convicts, and it was near the track to Botany Bay which the food-gatherers followed. On 18 December 1788 the brickmakers saw an attack party coming towards them (reported numbers ranged from 2000 to 400 to 50, perhaps according to the level of terror felt by the witness). Bloodshed was narrowly averted when the convicts picked up their shovels and spades and pointed them at the warriors, who melted into the scrub.[66]

This was a military-style attack and it seemed to mark a new, still more serious phase in deteriorating relations. Phillip had had enough of the attacks and killings, the weird silences. He still did not even know how many Eora there were in the region, let alone what their intentions were. Even the convicts, after all, were 'our people' and they themselves would be difficult to control if this situation continued. Phillip decided on a new strategy. They would kidnap Eora men, and force them to understand the kindness, peaceful intentions and generosity of the Berewalgal, as well as the advantages of civilised life. These men would become envoys who would then pass the all-important information to their countrymen. Tench was more resigned: they would either succeed, or know the worst. At least this terrible uncertainty would be at an end. Twelve days later, the longboat was rowed to Manly beach. In the midst of friendly talk a man was grabbed, a rope thrown about his neck. He was dragged to the boat, thrown in and rowed away while his people howled in anger, distress and fear on the beach.[67] Isabel McBryde and Inga Clendinnen point out that the kidnapping strategy had a 'long history in the annals of imperialism'.[68] But Arabanoo and his people were not to know this.

Arabanoo turned out to be a quiet, dignified and gentle man who eventually seemed to be resigned to his fate. Not that he had much choice. They scrubbed off his outer skin of fish oil, soot and dirt, cut his hair, put him in shirts and trousers, and kept him in a specially built hut at Government House. His leg was ironed and he had a 'keeper' looking after him, guarding him day and night. They were bursting with questions and eagerness to learn his language, but Arabanoo seemed not much interested in learning English. They took him on board the *Supply*, hoping he would be impressed. He jumped from the deck and tried to swim back to his people, but floundered when his unfamiliar clothes ballooned in the water, and so they hauled him back again. They rowed him round to visit his friends and family, hoping he would tell them how comfortable he was and what generous hosts they where. They heard him explain to them where he was, and, pointing to his ironed leg, why he could not return. The next time they rowed around for a visit, no-one was there. Eventually they noticed some happier moments: Arabanoo loved to be with children, and shared his food with them; he liked petting and playing with cats and dogs.[69]

When Captain John Hunter sailed back into Port Jackson in May 1789 after a voyage to the Cape of Good Hope for supplies, he immediately noticed an ominous absence. There was no-one on the little coves and beaches, no nowie out fishing, no little fires cooking shellfish, no children. At Government House he found Phillip taking tea with friends, among them an Eora man, 'decently cloathed' who 'managed his cup and saucer as well as though he had been long accustomed to such entertainment'. Hunter asked about the Eora: where were they all?[70]

Phillip told him about the smallpox epidemic that had broken out among them in April. The fishermen and the timbergetting parties had come in with shocking reports of whole families dying of the disease in caves, of pustule-covered bodies abandoned in the open, found lying between dead fires, with water left beside them. Sometimes family groups were found, some dead, some still alive. The living were brought into the Camp, where the surgeons placed them in a separate hut next to the hospital and tried to make them comfortable. The older men died, but a boy of about seven and a girl of about fourteen recovered.[71]

As Judy Campbell points out in her history of the disease in Australia and Asia, smallpox outbreaks provoked tremendous fear. The disease spread quickly in densely populated areas and there was no cure. It is simple to write 'smallpox epidemic'. Perhaps we should remember what the disease did to people. After an incubation period of about twelve days, the person suffered a very high fever, chills, severe headaches and backaches, vomiting and colic. Children had convulsions. After two or three days, a rash appeared all over the body and in the mouth and throat. The rash developed into lesions or pustules which broke down in the throat, releasing the virus into the saliva—this is how it was passed to others. 'There were limits to the relief that even devoted care provided', writes Campbell. 'Feverish and very sick people couldn't breathe or speak properly, or swallow anything, even water, despite agonising thirst.'[72] Among those who were very likely cared for in the hospital hut, and died there, were 'Gomil, Gora-moa-bou, Gnoo-lu-mey, Yendaw, Yarre-a-rool and Baid-do'. But this last man was probably not saying his name, but crying out in thirst: *bado* is the Eora word for water.[73]

Arabanoo was taken back down the harbour to look for his Cammeragal family and friends. He found his country deserted:

He looked anxiously around him . . . not a vestige on the sand was to be found of human foot . . . not a living person was anywhere to be met with. It seemed as if in flying from contagion they had left the dead to bury the dead. He lifted up his hands and eyes in silent agony for some time; at last he exclaimed 'All dead! All dead!' and then hung his head in mournful silence.[74]

When the pustule-covered bodies were discovered on the shorelines, Arabanoo unsurprisingly hung back at first. Unlike the Europeans, he had never seen such a disease, and must have been horrified. But as more victims were brought in to the Camp, Arabanoo carefully tended them alongside the surgeons. For those Eora who not only suffered terribly but were dying in an utterly alien environment among strangers, his voice and face and hands must have been an immeasurable comfort and blessing. The officers learned his words and used them to soothe a young woman they found sick and shivering some months later. But by then Arabanoo was dead. He had caught smallpox from those he nursed. He died on 18 May 1789 and was buried in the governor's garden, in the heart of Berewalgal country.[75]

As they explored the country around Port Jackson, Broken Bay and the Hawkesbury River over the next months, the Europeans read the spread and ravages of smallpox in the weakened bodies and pockmarked faces of survivors, and the unburied, desiccated corpses still lying in the caves where they died. The pretty coves and bright crescent beaches of the romantic harbours had become landscapes of death. King thought the disease was 'a distemper natural to the country', but most others—Phillip, Collins, White and Tench—disagreed, yet were utterly bewildered about its origin. They had not seen a pockmarked face among the Eora they met. There had been no cases aboard their ships or those of the French, and none since they had arrived.[76] Yet here was this catastrophe, following hard on the heels of their own landing. And why had the people of their own Camp not contracted it, the children especially? The only person among them who caught smallpox was a native American sailor.[77]

Of course they thought instrumentally as well: Collins considered the epidemic an opportunity to demonstrate goodwill, through the care and kindness shown the victims. The recovered children might prove useful as go-betweens, so instead of being returned to their families (some of whom we know did survive) they pretended they were orphans and fostered them out in the town. The boy Nanbarry went to Surgeon White (who promptly renamed him Andrew Snape Hammond Douglas after his patron. Mercifully everyone ignored this). The girl Boorong was taken by Reverend and Mrs Johnson. The officers also realised uneasily that the Eora most likely associated this terrible catastrophe with their own arrival. It became still more imperative to open communication, to tell them of their innocence and good intentions.[78]

The Eora probably did link the arrival of the Berewalgal with *gal-gal-la*, their name for smallpox. The belief that the British brought smallpox, and either deliberately or accidentally infected the local population, is still widespread

Thomas Watling's portrait of the boy Nanbarry. (Natural History Museum)

'Abbarroo a moobee at Balloderrees funeral', a later portrait of Boorong, painted in red clay for the funeral of her brother Ballooderry in 1791. (Natural History Museum)

among Aboriginal and non-Aboriginal people today. Given the terrible toll of diseases generally upon Aboriginal communities this is perhaps not surprising—one of the 'larger truths' that Peter Read writes about. Besides plants and animals, the invaders brought pathogens—tuberculosis, measles, influenza, venereal diseases and many others.[79]

The source of the smallpox epidemic of 1789 still remains unresolved. There were no recorded cases on the European ships, and the 'time lag' between their arrival and the outbreak of the disease is far too long for the virus to have been incubated by individuals—this took a maximum of seventeen days. One recent explanation is that it had swept down from the other side of the continent. Judy Campbell believes the virus originated with the Macassan fishermen from the island of Sulawesi after the terrible outbreaks there in the early 1780s. She argues that the disease moved south then east over the continent along the trade and communication paths. However, this explanation has been strongly challenged by Craig Mear, who points out that such a rapid spread of the disease in the sparsely populated north is contrary to the way it normally behaved. The notion that it turned eastwards is even less likely. Mear suggests an alternate infection source: the possibility that smallpox scabs—or fomites—clinging to old clothing and blankets may have carried the disease ashore. We know that even before the official contacts between Eora and Berewalgal, convicts were socialising with local Aboriginal people, and gave them 'presents', probably clothing and blankets they had brought with them. Mear also points out that deliberate infection among Indigenous peoples by giving them fomite-laden blankets and clothing was common practice in other New World colonies.[80]

We know very little about what gal-gal-la must have been like for the Eora, or how they understood it. In his conversations with Sydney Aboriginal people in 1802, French visitor Péron learned that they 'had a sort of religious terror of the Blue Mountains: they think them the residence of a kind of evil spirit, whom they represent by a variety of grotesque figures'. The evil being hurled 'thunder, inundations and burning winds' down upon them, in fact 'all the plagues which infest the country'. And smallpox? Did they understand it to have swept down from the west, from the ragged blue heights? Smallpox appears to have been seen as sorcery, engulfing, wild and furious. By the 1840s it was known among Sydney's Aboriginal people as devil-devil. The Blue Mountains, too, were long considered 'a place in possession of debbil debbil'.[81]

Historians have argued for many years over the source of the smallpox epidemic, and whether or not the British were to blame for unleashing it. Yet so little attention has been given to the immediate and wider impacts of this catastrophe. Smallpox would have threatened Eora society and culture in the most fundamental ways, for it undermined cultural and healing practices, law and cosmology. Traditional medicine was ineffective, and righting the world by avenging the dead through payback was irrelevant. The familiar bodies of family and friends suddenly erupted horribly, as though the evil had entered and claimed them. The living fled their own country, taking contagion with them. The sick, instead of being tended, were abandoned and left to die of the disease, or starvation or thirst.[82] The dead, normally carefully interred or cremated with appropriate funeral honours, were left unburied, their spirits free to walk about the earth and haunt the living. We have some archaeological evidence, silent but compelling. In the early 1960s, some home-owners in Gymea Bay in Port Hacking discovered skeletal remains in a rock-shelter on their property. Archaeological investigation revealed them to be those of a young woman, aged about 27, who appears to have been one of the victims. She had not been buried, but lay on her left side across a shell midden, 'face down, arms under her chin, legs sharply flexed'.[83] Given that death—so many bad deaths—invaded everyday places—caves where people lived, beaches where they fished and shared food—I wonder what this maelstrom did to country, and their relationship with it.

We don't know how many people died in this, the first of three epidemics which swept through the Australian Aboriginal population over the nineteenth century. Bennelong later told his British friends that half the Sydney popula-tion had died, including all but three of the Cadigal. Campbell thinks this must have been an underestimate, though, given the disease's impacts on similar populations elsewhere. Some scholars estimate that 80 per cent of people died in the 1789 epidemic. It is also likely that the disease did not strike evenly. Tench thought that the dominant and powerful Cammeragal of North Harbour were still strong because they had not suffered as much as the people elsewhere. Perhaps this was because their food supplies had not been depleted as much as those of the groups on the south side of the harbour.[84]

The Europeans often found men with children: their women were already dead. In late 1790 Phillip noted that 'the females bear no proportion to the males'. As in later epidemics, women were likely to have been more vulnerable and had less chance of survival. The implications were serious. Campbell suggests that 'the loss of women food-gatherers and child-bearers may have delayed a return to customary life'. Anthropologist R.G. Kimber explores a whole suite of interlinked impacts of smallpox in Central Australia, including groups moving and re-forming, 'concentrated where foods were most plentiful', and, in the initial aftermath, 'men fighting over women' because there were so few women. He might be describing the Sydney region in the 1790s. Phillip thought the shortage of women explained why most of the Eora wives were taken by force from enemy tribes; but he and the other officers thought this practice was customary, and not created by the ravages of smallpox.[85]

We know too that the disease came upon a people already weakened by hunger, and among them the old people had perhaps least resistance of all. This was mirrored by the patients at the hospital: the old men died, the young recovered. It is striking in the written records too: in 1788, every meeting between Berewalgal and Eora was hosted, conducted and firmly controlled by old men.[86] After 1789 we see very few old people.

By late May the canoes of the Eora were starting to appear once more on the river and the harbour. Bradley saw six nowie near the Flats (Homebush Bay) on the Parramatta River, and then on 2 June, he recorded twenty more paddling swiftly down the harbour past Sydney Cove, 'the first time any number of them had been seen together since the small pox'.[87] The population was starting to return, to resume fishing, hunting, and rebuilding communities. But it must have been a reduced and much-altered society: far fewer old people, fewer mature women, proportionally more young men and youths. The politics and relations between the local groups were severely disrupted: some groups (Cadigal and nameless others) were practically wiped out; the Cammeragal stayed strong. The people the governor and officers cultivated in Sydney, who became the first Sydney Eora—Boorong, Nanbarry, Bennelong and Coleby and their partners and friends—were already marked out. They were special, distinct from the world as it had been before: for they were young, and they were survivors of smallpox.

WALKING WITH WARRIORS

Without Arabanoo, the Camp was again without lines of communication with the surviving Eora. Nanbarry and Boorong were useful, and much liked, but they were only children. Despite Arabanoo's unhappy experience, the Berewalgal were soon on the lookout for a replacement. Phillip's original idea of having an Eora family ensconced in the town and lavished with 'everything that can tend to civilise them' was nearly realised during the excursion to Broken Bay and the Hawkesbury River in July 1789. On their outward journey the party had found a terrified young woman, so weak after surviving smallpox she had not been able to run from them. They made her comfortable, brought her food and water, lit a fire, spoke the soothing words they had learned from Arabanoo. On their return to Broken Bay they found her again, much recovered, with her husband

and child. Care and concern nearly turned to opportunism. 'This Family would have been taken by force', wrote Bradley, 'but the wind not being fair, the Officer in the Boat did not think it a proper opportunity'. Possibly they had not the stomach for it.[88]

During July and August the boats went down Sydney Harbour with the children Nanbarry and Boorong on board, trying to persuade some Eora to come back to Sydney. The children were asked to tell the people on the beaches how well they were treated, how happy they were. Poor Nanbarry's longing for his own people was such that he 'was much inclined to join the naked tribe'. Unsurprisingly, no-one agreed to get into the boats. Using the children as spokespeople was probably counterproductive, since they were not Cammeragal and had no status.[89]

By September 1789, the Eora had resumed their attacks on the Berewalgal roaming in their country, and now they were boldly theatening armed officers and fishing boats too. Even the power and mystique of muskets seemed to be diminishing. The *Sirius'* quartermaster Henry Hacking was menaced by a group of warriors despite his musket. He shot into the group, and thought he hit two of them, but if so they were quickly carried off.[90] In November, after another attack on a boat, Phillip decided to repeat the experiment: he ordered another kidnapping raid. Again the longboat rowed to Manly beach. Tench writes breezily that two men were secured 'without opposition', but Bradley, who was in charge of the operation, described it with deep distaste. 'They were dancing together', he wrote later, 'when the signal was given by me and the two poor devils were seized'. The bellowing of the men, 'the crying and screaming of the women and children together was most distressing', and the captured men 'were much terrified'. Those on the beach 'followed the boats on both sides as far as the points of the cove' as the boat rowed away. A spear was flung so hard it pierced 'four layers of sail and struck the apron of the boat's stern with such violence as to split it'. But, oddly for people in paroxysms of rage and fear, they then returned to the beach and picked up the fish which had been dangled to lure the victims.[91]

Who had they captured this time? Back at the Camp, among the crowds of curious onlookers, the Eora children were deliriously happy to see the two men and announced their names: they were Coleby (Nanbarry's uncle), and

William Bradley, 'Upper part of Port Jackson'. This is Wanne, Woollarawarre Bennelong's country. (Mitchell Library, State Library of New South Wales)

Woollarawarre Bennelong. Coleby was about 35, a survivor of the decimated Cadigal, the 'great warrior and a leading man among them' of whom Nanbarry had often spoken. Woollarawarre Bennelong was about 25, a Wangal from the south shores of the Parramatta River.[92]

The fact that the officers happened to snatch these particular men is deeply ironic, and suggests some shadowy yet powerful possibilities. For of all the men on Manly beach that day, the men who came forward were not Cammeragal, but warriors from the country directly east and west of Warrane/Sydney Cove.

Why did Phillip send the boats to Manly? Although they knew that Eora elders held authority, the British wanted to deal with younger men, warriors, from the group that had impressed Phillip most: the 'manly', powerful-looking Cammeragal they had first encountered at Kyeemay/Manly. Every time the boats went out to either persuade or abduct, they rowed down the harbour to that same beach in North Harbour. Phillip's instincts were right: the Cammeragal, besides being the most numerous and the most 'robust and muscular,' dominated the tribal politics of Sydney's coastal region. They were karadji, clever men and doctors, they ran the big male initiation ceremonies. 'Many contests or decisions of honour', wrote Collins after years of observation, 'have been delayed until the arrival of these people'. And when they arrived, their 'superiority and influence' was impossible to miss. Their survival of smallpox may well have enhanced their status.[93]

Why not send the boats upriver, to the much closer country of the Wangal, to abduct a cross-cultural hostage/envoy? Or to the country of the Cadigal on the south shores of Port Jackson? Probably because these people had suffered most of the incursions into their country, and had attacked convicts so often, and so ferociously. Coleby and Bennelong had without doubt been in the attack parties.

And what were they doing there on the beach, out of their own country and among the powerful Cammeragal? Carrying out honorary and reciprocal visits? Negotiating tribal politics in the wake of smallpox? Seeking women? Since the kidnapping of Arabanoo and the visits of the longboats, they must have known the intentions of the Berewalgal. Was Bennelong in particular 'unwittingly thrust into history by his abduction', as Keith Vincent Smith says; or was he at least partly instrumental in his own abduction, as Inga Clendinnen suspects?[94]

In Sydney the warriors were bound with leg irons fixed to ropes and locked with their keepers in the small hut at Government House. One night they chewed through the ropes and were found crawling about in the dark trying to find a way out. Seventeen days later, Coleby managed to escape—but Bennelong did not. His leg rope was replaced with a chain which was attached to his keeper.[95]

Bennelong seemed much more at ease in his new situation once the more senior Coleby was gone; indeed, the officers noted with interest, he took to it with great enthusiasm. In Coleby's presence he had remained silent: now he seemed to come alive, and they could scarcely hush his loud voice. Unlike Arabanoo he quickly learned English words, and answered all their eager questions. He told them of the powerful Cammeragal, his sworn enemies, boasted of his conquests in his two favourite pursuits—love and war. He often talked of a woman with whom he was enamoured, a Cammeragalleon called Barangaroo. He told them

of his enemies: the Botany Bay men, and the Cammeragal, and asked his hosts
to help him kill them. He ate their food with great relish and soon learned to
enjoy a glass of wine, and to raise it to 'The King', though he detested spirits.
He was good-natured enough to ignore the fun they sometimes made of him,
and was a superb mimic. When they asked him to dance, he obliged with one
that started slowly but ended in 'madness'. King was taken aback to recognise it
as the same furious dance the Eora had performed as 'a sort of defiance' on the
cliff tops and beaches when they had first sailed in, accompanied by shouts of
'woroo woroo, go away'.[96]

I wonder whether Bennelong had been among the group who greeted Phillip's
exploratory party up the river in Wangal country in February 1788, the time
before gal-gal-la and the invasion of Parramatta. Bradley noted one particular
warrior who met them on a 'neck of land' where they went ashore for breakfast,
perhaps Breakfast Point near present-day Mortlake. This man was different. He
'had more curiosity than any we had before met with, he examin'd every thing
very attentively & went into all our Boats from one to the other'. The governor
gave him a hatchet and a mirror.[97]

By early 1790, Bennelong's curiosity, brilliance and enthusiasm appeared to
the officers to be the longed-for breakthrough in relations. He seemed so open
to being civilised, so admiring of all they did; he seemed to understand them.
He came aboard the *Sirius* 'without the smallest apprehensions'. Finally, they
could show off the wonders of their ships. Bennelong was appropriately impressed. Soon he and the governor were seen walking everywhere together, or
making little trips to South Head by boat. Bennelong called Phillip *Beanna*—
father, or male elder—and Phillip called Bennelong *dooroow*—son.[98]

Phillip was moved by these father–son names and may have considered it
akin to a real familial and intimate relationship—with himself as the gentle, wise
father and Bennelong as a strong but respectful son, whom he could guide into
civilisation. For Bennelong, young, powerful, ambitious and vastly talented, it
was most likely more a political and social term: perhaps something like the 'skin
names' Aboriginal people in traditional communities today give to outsiders
'so [they] can interact and converse with them'.[99] Later 'Beanna' would take
on its more powerful kinship meanings, as 'foster-father' to Bennelong's baby

daughter Dilboong. For the moment, Bennelong had embarked on a relationship with the Berewalgal, learning of their ways, and of their fighting power, with an enthusiasm calculated to please.

By April 1790 Bennelong's loyalty and friendship were considered so reliable that the fetter was struck from his leg. Less than a month later, he stepped out of his clothes, abandoned the Camp and returned to his own people. The chroniclers were deeply disappointed and concerned. How he could return to the savage state after all the comforts they had showered on him was beyond them. Another experiment seemed to have failed. They rowed up and down the harbour calling his name, their voices mimicked by higher, thinner voices of Eora women making fun of them. Boorong and Nanbarry cheerily told them he would never return.[100]

Some thought perhaps he had gone to woo the woman Barangaroo. They were probably right, for during his sojourn at Warrane, she had taken up with Coleby. But, as later dramatic events would indicate, Bennelong was most likely also busily negotiating his own political position among the different tribal groups, along with that of his new allies, the Berewalgal. Perhaps he felt he had learned enough about them, their political structures, their firepower and their seemingly inexhaustible supply of food. The strange was now familiar. It was time to make an alliance, and a bid for a foothold in the boundary country they occupied.[101]

Occasionally there were reports of Bennelong and Coleby seen with fishing parties. The Europeans always begged them to come back to Sydney, but they declined. So when, in early September, Phillip received a present of stinking whale meat and a message to meet Bennelong at a whale feast at Manly Cove, he did not hesitate to row there immediately, with just a few old muskets for defence. After he landed, the muskets stayed in the boat, because Phillip knew a genuine interview, a true conversation, was unlikely otherwise. A man came forward from the people feasting upon the great carcass. Bennelong was thin, his hair and beard long and matted, and he bore fresh scars. Phillip did not recognise him until a bottle of wine was produced and he raised the glass to toast 'The King'. There followed much good-natured conversation, reminiscing about Bennelong's Sydney days, gossip about people, hilarious mimicry. Presents were given and hatchets promised.[102]

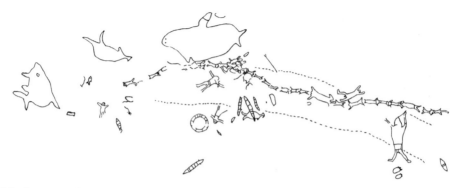

This drawing of a rock carving at Cowan shows a whale feast with a 'ladder of warriors' reaching up to the stranded whale. (Kate Nolan/W.D. Campbell)

What happened next shocked and terrified the officers and men who were there that day. The warriors formed a semi-circle which gradually closed in on Phillip. He noticed a strange man, stockier than the rest, who seemed agitated. Phillip approached this man, open-handed, to reassure him (in a fatherly way?), but in a flash he picked up an unusual spear with a barbed wooden head (*billarr*) and hurled it at Phillip. It pierced his body through the shoulder. The shaft was so long that he could not run down to the boat without the end hitting the ground. He shouted at Lieutenant Waterhouse, 'for God sake to haul the spear out!' Waterhouse, sure they would all die that day on the beach, fumbled with the tough shaft. Another spear whistling between the fingers of his right hand gave him a rush of strength to break it: Phillip was bundled into the boat and the men rowed for their lives the 5 miles back to Sydney.[103]

By this time Surgeon White had seen enough spear wounds to know that this one was not fatal: the point lacked the jagged stones of the death spears, it came out smoothly, and no vital organs had been hit. He immediately announced Phillip would recover. Within ten days, Phillip was up and walking about again.[104] The relief among the British must have been enormous.

Both the spearing of Phillip and the events which immediately followed were and still are matters of divided opinion. Collins was angry at the flightiness and treachery of the savages, and hoped Phillip had learned his lesson. Phillip at first thought the spearman—Willermering—acted from panic and out of fear of being seized, though he was hurt and puzzled by the way Bennelong seemed to collude in the attack and then ran away. Was this the way a son should treat his father?[105] Reading ethnographically, W.E.H. Stanner, Keith Vincent Smith and Inga Clendinnen make sense of the spearing from the Eora perspective. They argue that what Phillip underwent was ritual punishment for his crimes—as the Eora saw them—and perhaps also for the crimes of his people. If the Berewalgal were to be accepted as allies, something for which Bennelong was probably agitating, payback had to be carried out first.[106] Did Bennelong, pointing out the white men's cluelessness in the use of shields for parrying in self-defence, negotiate for the use of the smooth *billarr* rather than the usual jagged spear, and the aim at the shoulder? Phillip Jones thinks this interpretation is rather 'too neat', for it does not sufficiently reflect the often unpredictable nature of such encounters, 'turning on a sideways glance or a glint of metal'. And how had Bennelong orchestrated all this in the space of a single day?[107]

And yet, some deep resolution had occurred, for a miraculous breakthrough soon followed: friendly relations were established with Bennelong and his people, and the Eora finally 'came in' to Sydney. From that time on, Aboriginal people were always among the city's population. Whatever the mystifying details, Phillip perhaps came to think of his ordeal in a larger light: somehow, he, the 'father', had paid a blood sacrifice for the greater good of both peoples and the future of the colony. He also refused to retaliate, at least at first, which made sense and made peace in both Christian and Eora terms.[108]

Chapter 12

———◦•◦———

TAKING POSSESSION

Phillip's spearing also turned out to be satisfying in a narrative sense. Those who were self-consciously writing the first drafts of the colony's history told the story as climactic conflict followed by resolution, hopelessness turned to salvation. The attack, which seemed to spell utter disaster, was in fact a transforming moment, marking the end of hostilities and the opening of communications. It was the unlikely portent of 'peace and amity', which had been the underlying quest in their narratives all along. At last, Tench wrote delightedly, they could 'cultivate the acquaintance of our new friends, the natives'.[1] But they soon found that the more they learned, the more bewildered they became.

The process by which the 'peace' was made was a complicated choreography of visiting, signs, gifts, expressed good intentions, dancing and games, concessions, and a test of wills between Phillip and Bennelong. Bennelong controlled most of the action. A week after the spearing, Eora people were making polite inquiries after the governor's health, and a few days later, smoke was seen rising from a cove on the north shore, close to Sydney. (I wonder where this important first reconciliation site was—Kirribilli? Or somewhere on the shoreline of Milsons Point?) It was a sign, and the officers lost no time in forming a party, filling a boat with wine, beef, bread and barbering implements, and rowing over. The day began with greetings, wine and food, moved on to beard-shaving and clipping, and culminated in dancing, frolicking games and hilarious tests of strength. The girl Boorong introduced her white friends to her father, Maugaron, and was herself courted by Bennelong's young kinsman Yemmerrewanne. Eventually they persuaded the proud and striking Barangaroo to come forward too. Bennelong was now her husband.[2]

Phillip and Tench have different accounts of the next few days' events, but both revolve around a series of arranged and broken appointments between Bennelong and Phillip. The governor said he arrived at Bennelong's cove on 17 September, only to find Bennelong had left to go fishing down the harbour with Barangaroo. But just as Phillip's party pushed off back to Sydney, the Eora dignitaries arrived in a splendid procession of canoes, captured forever in a picture by the Port Jackson Painter. We know the first person, pointing his paddle towards Phillip's party, is Bennelong, but this picture very likely also includes the only image we have of Barangaroo—most likely the woman in the next canoe. Her posture is typically erect but, significantly, her expression is slightly worried and she holds back a little from the longboat that is approaching like a great spider.[3]

So good and friendly relations were re-established, both sides reassured of the other's peaceful intentions. Bennelong promised he would visit Sydney, a promise he broke repeatedly until he finally came ashore in Warrane in early October, accompanied by a retinue of four friends (but without Barangaroo). He was like a king returning in triumph, marching 'with boldness and unconcern' through the crowds of people flocking to see him, up Bridge Street to Government House. He greeted Beanna with 'honest joy', embraced his old friends, and raced around the vice-regal rooms, shouting, introducing people and things to his friends, and, when they stared in incomprehension, shouting at them for their stupidity.[4]

After being shunned for so long, the British suddenly found the Eora constantly among them. 'The natives were becoming very familiar and intimate with every person in the settlement', wrote Hunter upon his departure, 'many of them took their rest every night in some of the gentlemen's houses'. Tench wrote, 'with the natives we are hand in glove' though already their 'clamour for bread and meat . . . are become very troublesome'. William Bradley returned from Norfolk Island in February 1790 to find he had missed all the excitement and that 'the Natives had lately become familiar; several of them staying chiefly in the Camp

& at the Governors'. Bradley, as we have seen, often painted the great events in race relations in early Sydney. So in his 1791 picture of Government House he included little stick figures of Eora and British shaking hands—the first depiction of Eora in the town. Indeed, from this point on, the pictures painted of Sydney often included Aboriginal people—not only as exotic 'pictorial embellishments', but because they were there.[5]

Those who slept in the skillions and kitchens were the young people and children. Some were 'adopted', like young Boneda, who went to live with David Collins, while others lived with the soldiers at the barracks. As Jakelin Troy points out, at least some of the officers were inspired by evangelical ideas about 'domestic experiments'—the children would be civilised by immersing them in domestic environments. Eora children played games in the gardens and the rough streets. Older people came to visit each day and ask for food. After their early distaste, they had developed a great liking for bread, and asked for it constantly. They often called at the hospital for Surgeon White to stitch their wounds— White noted ominously that the injuries were increasingly metal hatchet wounds. At Tarra, the western point of the Cove, Lieutenant William Dawes built his small observatory and scanned the night skies. He befriended a young Eora woman, Pattyegarang, and the two taught one another their languages. Dawes wrote fleeting snatches of his conversation with her and others in a notebook, which survives. In these small fragments, some touching, others disturbing, we hear the criss-cross of the words and voices of the two groups as they tried to understand one another. Pattye, as Dawes called her, appears to have spent at least some of her time living in the secluded house on the point under the stars.[6]

The artists were finally able to ask the Eora about the animals, birds and plants they were collecting and painting. Thomas Watling described his inform-ants with a torrent of ugly words: 'Irascibility, ferocity, cunning, treachery, revenge, filth and immodesty are strikingly their dark characteristics'. Yet Watling's portraits of the Sydney Eora are beautiful and sensitive. He also wrote that they were 'extremely fond of painting, and often sit hours by me when at work'. The pictures of local animals, reptiles and birds reveal that the Eora were not merely passive observers at the artist's elbow. Watling pumped his contacts for information about animals and birds, he included the 'native names' in his pictures and sometimes transcribed notes as well. The leaf-tailed gecko (*Phyllurus platurus*), for example, 'is not very common in N.S. Wales and never seen or at least seen very rarely except in the Summer. The Natives will not touch it, because they say it emits a fluid that stings like common nettle . . . Native Name Pae-ginn.' Coleby seems to have been the main informant and it may be that he grew tired of the relentless interrogations. When Watling wanted to know about echidnas, he told him they 'principally live on the dew which they lick in with red-fleshed tongue', and that they emitted a 'constant single whistle', which he probably then proceeded to 'imitate'. Watling wrote down every word on the painting. But as ecological historian John Calaby points out, dew is not food, and echidnas do not whistle.[7]

The locus of Eora presence in Sydney was on the east side, at Government House and down on Tubowgully, the eastern point of the cove. Bennelong and Barangaroo came nearly every day, along with two children they had adopted, and often ate at Government House with Phillip. Barangaroo remained defiantly naked, though Bennelong probably donned the red jacket with silver epaulets which he 'used to wear when at the settlement', a gift which had 'pleased him more than anything else'.[8] Remembering the power—literal, symbolic, visual—of red coats among the Eora, the jacket probably reflected and reinforced his meteoric rise in status. Soon a house was being built for him and his people on the point that would take his name. This was not an initiative of Phillip's, as so many historians assume, but of Bennelong himself. He requested it be built and selected this site close to the water, with a good view of the town, and strategically aligned with Government House. It was a stake in the town, an Eora place. The house rose 12 feet square in solid brick with a hipped roof of clay tiles. Inside family, friends and guests slept on the ground all tumbled together as they did in their own gunyahs. The fire was outside the door.[9]

Bennelong's Point also became the site for the Sydney Eora's dances (corroborees). The earliest, held in November 1790, was the first one to which the British were invited, having dropped hints to Bennelong about their eagerness to witness such a performance. He cheerfully 'assembled many of his friends for the purpose of entertaining us'. Hunter earlier described the dramatic appearance of white clay bodypaint on black skin: it gave the 'most shocking appearance . . . they were exactly like so many moving skeletons'. Now he watched the young women 'employed with all their art in painting the young men', striking designs which glowed luminous in the firelight as they danced to the clapsticks and the songs with 'regularity & good order in them, so much that if any of the fires were in their way they danced through them'. Afterwards they all agreed it was a 'boojery Caribberie' (a good dance) and the British bade them farewell, taking several sleepy children back to their houses with them.[10]

Government House itself was incorporated into the itineraries of Eora people on the move—going to and from dances, on hunting trips or other business— for it was a place where they knew there would be a friendly welcome, fire, and abundant fish, meat and bread. As Clendinnen observes so beautifully and with such an eye for comic situations, Phillip was besieged by his new house guests:

> Two youths in full ceremonial fig chose to stay in the yard to prepare for a tooth-drawing ceremony, and came back afterwards to recover; children were parked there under the governor's care while their parents went off on essential travels unimpeded; and at least one redundant wife fetched up in the governor's charge when her husband dumped her for another woman.[11]

And Bennelong himself was impressively busy—so busy, Tench wrote, only half joking, that it was impossible to get an interview with him.[12] As he was their main and essential go-between, this was not the situation the British had envisaged. He went off to the Cammeragal and returned without the clothes he had just been given. He tried to enlist a party of soldiers out searching for an escaped convict in his fight against Pemulwuy and the Bidgigal. He went down to Botany Bay for a great corroboree, where, he told Phillip proudly, a new song had been sung about 'his house, the governor and the white men at Sydney'. New places, people and events were being incorporated into Eora cultural and knowledge traditions, so gaining legitimacy and acceptance. He brought a delegation of people back from Botany Bay to see his new country and British-style gunyah. The purpose behind all this activity was probably the shoring up of his new status and authority and his people's right to the country at Sydney.[13]

As we have seen, women were the links between the different groups, and made kin out of rivals. Bennelong appears to have sought to cement his alliances in this way too. He had already won Barangaroo back from Coleby, and thus had a foothold, or better, with the powerful Cammeragal. (His strategies must have been effective, for at the end of 1790 he performed the male initiation rituals which were said to be the exclusive right of the Cammeragal.)[14] During his time at Botany Bay he abducted another woman, Kurubarabulu, from the people there (the other 'enemies' he so often mentioned), and brought her back to Sydney with the others. Bennelong had fought a contest against her father, an elder called Metty, and in a show of authority back at Government House, tried to publicly punish Kurubarabulu for daring to attack him during that fight. He was stopped by a horrified Phillip, who snatched the girl away to safety. Soon after, she became Bennelong's second wife.[15]

Bennelong's people might have been physically identifiable too: the men were shaven or had clipped beards—or regrowth, as we see in some of the portraits. Some women at least seem to have agreed to have their heads shaved. They sometimes wore some articles of clothing—petticoats or caps, given to them by white friends. The Sydney Eora seemed to have clothing and food in plenty without having to hunt, fish, forage or make anything. And they had access to objects which had already become very desirable among warriors: sharp metal hatchets which were slung in waistbands instead of the old-style stone ones.[16]

Collins insisted that the Sydney Eora were 'always allowed to be their own masters', for they 'live with us as they were accustomed to do before we came among them'. But that was 1796 and by then he was probably writing after the fact: the Eora did live as they chose in Sydney. Despite the sense of breakthrough and resolution of October 1790, the sort of 'peace' and cohabitation sought by the British was chimerical. They most wanted an end to the hostilities and killings of course, but had also envisaged the Eora living harmoniously in their community, settling down in houses, wearing clothes, learning to speak English, being clean in their persons and meekly grateful for the great bounty of European food and shelter. Collins also thought that with 'kind treatment' they might be made quite a 'serviceable people', sailing boats or tending stock. Phillip hoped to bind them into the white community economically, through simple commercial ventures, like the fish-trade he encouraged young Ballooderry to take up at Parramatta.[17]

Underpinning all this was the assumption that the Eora would shed their savage culture and ways (fascinating as they were) and become like the British in thought and action, respecting British laws. Unsurprisingly, they did not. For some people in the town, the novelty was already wearing thin. Surgeon John Harris, who arrived in mid-1790, wrote wearily that 'The Whole Tribe with their visitors have plagued us ever since nor can we now get rid of them they come and go at pleasure'. By 1792, the townsfolk 'could scarcely keep them out of their houses in daytime'. Some of the powerful young men behaved like bullies, and were becoming increasingly rough and demanding, for they 'made a practice of threatening any person whom they found in a hut alone unless bread was given them'.[18] They acted as if they owned the place.

More seriously, convicts continued to disappear, and the Sydney Eora never seemed to know anything about them. Phillip and the officers still had little inkling of Eora Law—they thought the Eora were a people 'from before time' who had no real system of legal or political authority. After nine years of observation, Collins could write: 'We found the natives . . . living in that state of nature which must have been common to all men previous to their uniting in society, and acknowledging but one authority'. At this stage they seem to have attributed payback to a primitive (that is, pre-social) desire for personal revenge, and probably thought of ritual combat as male sports and contests, akin to their own prize-fights and duels.[19]

SHOWDOWN AT BOTANY BAY

With two systems of law at work in the same geographic space, with the Eora punishing the British according to theirs, a showdown was inevitable. It came in December 1790, with the spearing of the governor's gamekeeper, John McIntyre. McIntyre was one of only three convicts who were armed in order to shoot game for the officers. He probably had the best knowledge both of the country and the Eora, for he spoke their language, and copied their ways of building shelters. But McIntyre had apparently committed some atrocious offence against them. One day while out hunting, this ill-omened man paid the inevitable price:

he was speared with a *cannadiul*—the jagged, stone-studded death spear. The spear was thrown by Pemulwuy, a powerful warrior of the Bidgigal people. McIntyre knew enough of spears to know he was a dead man. But not yet—he lingered painfully for weeks, and finally died at the hospital on 20 January 1791.[20]

What happened next is one of those key events in early race relations which historians have interpreted in very different ways. I think it is worth revisiting. Phillip seems to have reached the end of his tether at this killing. McIntyre was different from all those nameless, stupid convicts who had disappeared or been found speared and mangled. He was Phillip's own servant, he had been armed, and his knowledge of the country and the Eora had evidently been invaluable. When the official parties went out, they had often taken McIntyre to guide them. To make matters worse, both Bennelong and Coleby seemed little perturbed by the event—Bennelong promised he would find the killer, but went off to the north shore on initiation business instead. Phillip decided that the 'peace' or 'agreement' he had so doggedly forged with the Eora had been broken, and that the tribe responsible had to be taught a terrifying lesson. He ordered Tench to

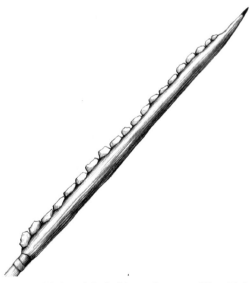

Cannadiul—the death spear, studded with lethal jagged stones. (Kate Nolan/Charles Dortch)

take a party of soldiers, march to Botany Bay and capture two men of the Botany Bay tribe and march them back to Sydney for execution. As well, Tench was to bring back the heads of ten more men. Tench managed to have the number of intended victims reduced, bargaining for six heads or six captured warriors, with two of the latter to be executed at the 'fatal tree'.[21]

The Botany Bay people were targeted as the culprits because Bennelong had said that Pemulwuy was from that area. But which Botany Bay people? In fact, Pemulwuy's people, the Bidgigal, were a 'woods tribe' of the inland Georges River area. The Georges River runs into Botany Bay, which itself had at least two other groups living on its shores—the Kameygal on the north, and the Gweagal to the south. Just to the north around Long Bay was another group, including the well-known leader Moorooboora, for whom Maroubra is named.[22] But Phillip only heard 'Botany Bay' and aimed his reprisals there.

The party, 'a terrific procession' of over 50 men laden with muskets, hatchets to behead warriors, and bags in which to carry the heads, marched out of Sydney on 14 December. They headed for Botany Bay, but lost their way in the maze of swamps and dunes. Arriving eventually on the shores of the bay, they saw five Eora, who promptly ran away. Boiling in their heavy woollen coats in the hot weather and laden with weapons and packs, they gave chase, but the 'unencumbered' Aboriginal people vanished. Another group they surprised near the huts also made off in canoes. They did find one man fishing, and Tench tried hard to ignore him, but the man hallooed them cheerily. It turned out to be their friend Coleby, who shared a meal with them, blithely informing them that Pemulwuy had fled long ago to the south—most likely tipped off by Coleby himself. The party camped the night by a 'sandfly and mosquito infested swamp' before returning to Sydney, a sorry, tired and itchy band.[23]

Undeterred, Phillip sent Tench out again with a smaller party on 23 December, this time leaving at sunset and marching by moonlight. Hoping to ambush the same huts and take prisoners and heads, they were crossing the Wolli Creek estuary as a short-cut when three of them, including Tench, began sinking in the muddy quicksand. Struggling only made them sink faster. Finally a terrified soldier shouted to those on the banks to cut and throw in tree branches so they could save themselves. With these and the ropes they had brought to tie up the captives, they managed to haul themselves out; but their weapons were unusable. When they finally crept up on the huts, they found they had been deserted for some time. Defeated by the swamps, rivers and tides, and by swift Eora communications, Tench returned, again empty-handed, to Sydney.[24]

Though they were unsuccessful, these expeditions sound eerily like the terrible reprisal parties which later marched or rode out to kill Aboriginal people, whether or not they were responsible for attacks, or to 'quieten the country', as the euphemism went. So it is unsurprising that the anthropologist W.E.H. Stanner wrote of this 'headhunt' as the commencement of a long history of racist terror in Australia. But was it? Clendinnen, in the spirit of Tench, retells the story as ludicrous farce, with the pathetic, long-suffering, lumbering British at the mercy of the much cleverer, light-footed Eora. Clendinnen concludes just the opposite to Stanner: this was not racism at all, but grand theatre. It was a show of force intended to warn and impress the Eora for their own good, as well as to reassure the convicts. Further, by making the guilt, and therefore the punishment, collective rather than individual, Phillip was using 'authentic anthropological insight': attacking the whole tribe rather than the individual responsible would make a far greater impact in their terms. But it *was* mostly theatrics, for Clendinnen says Phillip also knew that 50 men crashing through the bush would have little chance of shooting anyone, let alone capturing them. And finally, to ensure no-one would really get hurt, Phillip put the likeable and sympathetic Tench in charge. 'Phillip knew his man', she writes. 'Tench would be loath to shoot.'[25]

But Tench did shoot. Or he ordered the soldiers to shoot. Collins, all the while explaining endlessly why the party could not *possibly* have harmed anyone, mentioned that the fleeing Eora were 'fired upon', but adds too hastily, 'without doing them any injury'.[26] Keith Vincent Smith points out that someone probably was hit, however. A painting by the Port Jackson Painter, whoever he was, seems to refer to this incident: it is a striking portrait of Bennelong, entitled 'Native name Ben-nel-long, as painted when angry after Botany Bay Colebee was wounded'. Bennelong, painted with stripes of red and white clay down his arms and chest, still glowers from the paper. A second painting, 'Mr. White, Harris and Laing with a party of Soldiers visiting Botany Bay Colebee at that place, when wounded' may also be connected. Art historian Bernard Smith thought it could be a scene from the head-hunt expedition. While we know that the surgeons White and Harris accompanied Tench and the soldiers, Surgeon Laing did not arrive in the colony until February 1792, so the painting may depict a later event. However, close inspection reveals that several different hands have added words to this picture. The different spelling of Coleby's name on the two paintings may indicate the titles were written at different times, and the title may have been added later, the writer misremembering the surgeon's name.[27]

Either way, this painting is intriguing. It shows an Eora family group lying at their ease around a fire. Coleby, the victim referred to in the title, seems to be the figure sitting alone on the log to the right, the name 'Colebee' pencilled above.[28] But look closer: the three surgeons are gathered closest to someone lying on his side on the ground, being comforted by another man. Surely this is the injured man, Botany Bay Coleby? The surgeon is tapping or poking the seated man with the butt of his musket. But then who is the man on the log, evidently not part of the immediate family circle? This would be the other Coleby, Cadigal Coleby, the namesake of the injured man. He is also a friend of John White's and an admirer of the surgeons' healing skills. Perhaps he asked them to attend the wounded man, and led them to him.[29]

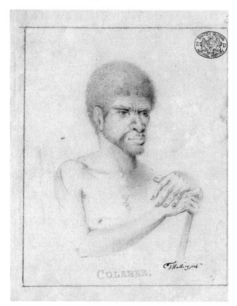

Thomas Watling, Cadigal Coleby.
(Natural History Museum)

Thomas Watling, Botany Bay Coleby, Warungin Wangubile. (Natural History Museum)

As Keith Vincent Smith points out, Botany Bay Coleby, or Warungin Wangubile, was the *damelian* (namesake) and therefore a kinsman of Cadigal Coleby, whose wife Daringa was from the Botany Bay area as well. Botany Bay Coleby was also the brother of Kurubarabulu, Bennelong's second wife, and thus Bennelong's brother-in-law.[30] This is consistent with Bennelong's red-painted anger and his subsequent defiance of Phillip. If the paintings do indeed depict this event, they suggest that the man Tench managed to shoot was a kinsman of the very people Phillip relied on as envoys and peace-keepers.

We are reminded that Tench, White, Dawes and the others, the people who actually had to carry out Phillip's orders, were faced with the prospect of having to pursue, shoot and behead people they may well have come to know intimately, if not deeply. Or they may have been strangers and enemies. Out there in the maze of bush, rivers and swamps, the gulf between the chain of command which governed their lives, and the reality of being unable to tell between the different bands, let alone guilty men and 'some unoffending family unconnected with them', must have become increasingly, incongruously clear.[31] The shooting of Botany Bay Coleby would have realised these fears. Perhaps this explains the silence and denial in the written records; and the downplaying of the whole affair in both Tench's and Collins' accounts.

A final clue in this half-told history is the response of Lieutenant William Dawes. Dawes was sympathetic to the Eora and a skilled linguist, and initially he refused to follow Phillip's orders. But in the end he did go with Tench, having been persuaded to change his mind by the Reverend Richard Johnson. Whatever he saw, he found it morally unpleasant or repulsive, for he later returned to his first conscientious objection, angering Phillip by stating publicly that he 'was sorry he had been persuaded to comply with the order'. Both Dawes and the colony paid a high price: he wanted to stay, to pursue his scientific and linguistic research, and to farm. But he would not retract his statement and Phillip refused to forgive him. He was threatened with a demotion if he remained in New South Wales. So Dawes sailed away with the marines in December 1791, and never returned.[32]

The head-hunt of December 1790 was not play-acting, nor a grandiose show, nor intentional farce. Phillip's harsh orders were given for a reason: to demonstrate and shore up his own authority in this precarious colony. And his actions were not inconsistent with the humane patience, tolerance and kindness he had shown the Eora: these were two sides of the same coin. In the same way that convicts were generously rewarded for certain types of behaviour (hard work, sobriety, enterprise, steadiness), but savagely flogged or hanged for quite trivial infractions, the Eora were similarly treated kindly and indulged when they behaved well (or when there was hope of it), but if they persisted in killing and thieving, they too had to be given a terrifying lesson in the awesome might and ruthlessness of eighteenth-century British justice. It is hard to avoid the fact that, in theory at least, Phillip intended the lives of the innocent to be taken in the stead of the guilty. This is a measure of war, not law. And race must be a factor. Would such an order have been made against his own refractory people?

As it turned out, Botany Bay Coleby recovered and his kin did not insist on retribution. Perhaps they decided the wounding was payback for McIntyre's death, or some other infringement, and the matter could rest there. In 1791 he was a 'frequent visitor to Sydney'. He also seemed to desire an alliance or favour with Phillip. In July he rescued an armed soldier lost in the bush between Parramatta and Sydney, though first insisting the soldier give him his gun. The soldier, no doubt with deep dread, but without other options, handed the weapon over. Botany Bay Coleby did as he promised, led the soldier back to town, and returned the gun. He then made sure Phillip heard about it by specifically instructing the soldier to tell 'Beanah' that 'he was Botany Bay Colebe'.[33]

In Sydney and Parramatta there was more strife, skirmishes and fatal altercations. While the headhunt was proceeding in the Botany swamps, two of Bennelong's mates, young men named Bangai and (probably) Bi-gong, decided they would help themselves to potatoes from a convict's garden on the west side of the cove. In this they were merely harvesting the food of their country, as they had apparently been doing for some time, though the convict gardener naturally saw it as a brazen theft of his hard-won produce. A fishing spear whistled towards the irate convict, and a party of soldiers was hurriedly ordered down. In the confrontation which followed, a club was thrown and a musket fired in response. Bangai was shot. The surgeons went out to attend him, but they were too late.

Thomas Watling, 'Bi-Gong'. (Natural History Museum)

They found him already lying in a beach grave, a young sapling arched over his body. He had bled to death.[34]

Bennelong was furious over this shooting. He attacked some people in a fishing boat and when Phillip tried to remonstrate with him, he bellowed repeatedly 'about the man who had been wounded'. 'Where's Bangai?' he shouted. 'Where's Bangai?' But he also offered his hand to Phillip. Phillip, unmoved, refused to take it. Bennelong then ran off in a violent temper of frustration, stealing a hatchet from a blacksmith's shop on the way. He did return, still sullen, to Government

House, and was admitted to the yard with the other people. But Phillip for now forbade him entry to the house.[35]

It was early in 1791, only three months since the 'coming in', and so much cross-cultural interaction was entirely at cross-purposes. The British were confounded by the refusal of their 'guests' to stop the violence, attacks and murders, and must have wondered whether Bennelong and Coleby had any authority at all among their own people. They in turn must have thought the same of Beanna. Phillip felt his authority constantly challenged and his trust and friendship betrayed. After the death of Bangai, they began to suspect that Bennelong's people 'did not desire any of the other tribes should participate in the enjoyment of the few trifles they procured from us'. This would, ironically, 'retard the general understanding of our friendly intentions towards them', the whole purpose of the exercise. They worried uneasily that Bennelong would 'represent them in an unfavourable light' to other groups.[36]

Collins had a rare flash of insight at this point too. He realised that at the heart of the ongoing attacks was the dispossession of country:

> We had not yet been able to reconcile the natives to the deprivation of those parts of this harbour which we occupied. While they entertained the idea of our having dispossessed them of their residences, they must always consider us as enemies; and upon this principle they made a point of attacking the white people whenever opportunity and safety concurred.[37]

'We had not yet been able to reconcile the natives': did he think there was still hope of convincing the Eora they were not invaders, but rightful, peaceful and friendly settlers? That taking land was just and proper and involved no crime? Or was this an early 'whispering in the heart', a deep disquiet over dispossession? With so much riding on the new farms up the river, and the whole agricultural project to follow, the implications of this observation would have been appalling. Did Collins allow himself to go there? We don't know.

Bennelong and his people must have been similarly confounded by the violence of the British, which seemed lawless to them. They were survivors of the terrible, disruptive gal-gal-la, and had taken possession of this reshaped country—as they had been repeatedly invited to do. They had taken the food on offer as their right (for they were no grateful, passive recipients). They had continued to carry out their Law and punishments upon wrongdoers, as they were compelled to do. Bennelong had worked hard to forge tribal alliances, but these would have been jeopardised if his supposed British allies shot at his Gweagal kin, and then his friend Bangai too. As Clendinnen so often observes, misunderstandings compounded misunderstandings.

But despite these conflicts and ongoing strife, the endless game of cat and mouse as soldiers pursued and Eora warriors taunted and evaded them, the Eora stayed in Sydney, and soon people from other regions and kinship groups joined them, especially after Bennelong sailed away with Phillip in December 1792. The emergence of Aboriginal Sydney did not revolve only around guns, spears, killings and men's struggles for authority and power. There were other stories unfolding as well.

EORA WOMEN

There was one Eora woman whom the British officers found very striking, and a little frightening too: Barangaroo. While they described other women generally as quiet, passive drudges to their 'tyrant' husbands, Barangaroo was different. After an initial humiliating incident with a petticoat, she refused to wear any clothes whatsoever, even at the governor's table. She was clearly unhappy about Bennelong's consorting with the Berewalgal. She was so angry with him on that first occasion when he went to visit Sydney that she broke his fishing spear. Every time he tried to visit Rose Hill she refused to allow it, and neither was he permitted to go on an exploratory excursion to the Nepean in April 1791 (Coleby and Ballooderry went instead). When Bennelong hit her, which he often did, she hit him back. The officers were perplexed at how a couple who were obviously so fond of one another could be so violent to each other. They put it down to savage gender relations, and Tench said she deserved her beatings because 'she was a scold and a vixen and nobody pitied her'.[38]

We owe Inga Clendinnen a great debt for recovering this woman, Barangaroo, from the 'great condescension' of male-dominated history. It is partly because of her insightful, deeply human reconstruction that the eastern shoreline of Darling

Harbour has recently been renamed Barangaroo by some enlightened people at the Sydney Harbour Foreshore Authority. Yet Clendinnen herself concludes that Barangaroo was the exception that proved the rule: she was not typical of Eora women, for she was a 'natural-born loner, a natural-born rebel' as well as violent and touchy: in short, 'always a woman with attitude'. It is one of those historical ironies, she writes, that 'the woman who emerges most vividly from the documentation we happen to have is, simply, atypical'.[39]

Clendinnen's portrait is intriguing; it invites further exploration. Was Barangaroo really different from other Eora women? And, more specifically, why was she such a 'difficult' woman, trying to stop Bennelong's politicking and movements? Could there have been reasons for her stubborn opposition other than her own cranky character?

In fact, Barangaroo was not the only rebel, for, as Clendinnen notes, the officers recorded a number of instances where the women did not behave meekly. After the initial joy and enchantment of meeting the beautiful, bashful 'Eves' at Eve's/Manly Cove, they were slightly disconcerted by the way the women burst into rather rude laughter and furious chatter when safely back at the edge of the trees together. They then energetically 'threw themselves into indecent attitudes'.[40] The Berewalgal thought this marked an 'opening' of communications, but then the women promptly shut it down again, mostly (though as we shall see, not entirely) avoiding them, paddling away in their nowie as fast as they could. Worse, after relations had deteriorated some months later, officers in boats were dismayed to realise that both women and men wanted to harm them. The women tried to lure them ashore using 'lewd tricks' so the waiting warriors could attack them. Bradley wrote of one of these incidents in North Harbour in November 1788:

> A great number of Natives then appear'd, the Women came close to the rocks & used every wanton lure to entice our people to land, when the Women came forward a party of Men were observed to walk away, no doubt to be ready for an attack if our people had been so improvident as to land, this artifice having been practised by them before, the people were well aware of it.[41]

The implications were disturbing: they were not innocent Eves at all! They were wanton temptresses, sirens calling men to their doom.

Barangaroo might well have been among these women—she was Cammeragalleon, this was her country. By the time the officers met her in late 1790, the world had changed. She had lost a husband and two children, she had survived smallpox, and she now had a new, younger husband: the ambitious Bennelong.[42] They estimated her age at about 40, and I think this is significant. She was older, and therefore more mature, and possessing wisdom, status and influence far beyond many of the other, much younger, women the officers met. If smallpox had indeed taken many older women, then Barangaroo was one of a reduced number who had the knowledge of Law, teaching and women's rituals. She certainly had presence and authority. When they sent Boorong as go-between to persuade her to come to Sydney, she instead gave the girl a firm talking-to and told her it was time to rejoin her own people. Boorong wanted to obey, and sulked when the British would not let her go.[43]

There was a number of reasons for Barangaroo to distrust the Berewalgal, to be alarmed about them, as she seems to be in the Port Jackson Painter's picture. She knew of course of the kidnappings and the shootings and had no doubt heard of the bizarre goings-on at Warrane. The Berewalgal seemed to have more influence over her new husband than she did. He seemed bedazzled by them. It is also possible that what may have really triggered Barangaroo's anger that first day of reconciliation was fish. The meeting on the north shore coincided with a massive haul of 4000 Australian salmon, hauled up in two nets, and 40 fish of 5 pounds weight each were sent as a present over to Bennelong's group.[44] Two hundred pounds of fish may well have been far more than the small group could eat, an extravagant gift, given from men to men. As an Eora fisherwoman, winning fish one by one through skill and patience, Barangaroo may have felt insulted. She may have seen ominous implications too: future alliances with these food-bearing Berewalgal meant that women would lose their essential role, and their control over the food supply.

Why would this be important? Wouldn't both men and women benefit from British largesse? We need to look, once more, at fishing. We know that women's work was different from men's, and that Eora society had these gendered

403

distinctions. The officers were fascinated by the women, they wrote as though utterly absorbed by what they saw, lost in it. George Worgan, peering through his spyglass from the deck of his ship, watched a group of eight or ten men and women arrive in five canoes. The men got out near the rocks on the shoreline—'I could see them very busy in striking the Fish with their Spears, and I saw them take two or three tolerably large ones'. Meanwhile the women stayed in the nowie and fished with hook and line, and caught somewhat smaller fish. When they had enough, they 'went on shore a little way up in the Wood, lit a Fire, and sat down round about it, in the Afternoon, they got into their Canoes, and returned . . .'[45]

Tench wrote of the men on the shoreline too, and the women pushing off into deep water . . . regardless of the elements, sometimes 'several miles into the open ocean'.[46] How did they control these 'contemptible skiffs', with their 'ticklish formation', so narrow and long and unstable? He watched their posture carefully: they dropped to their knees, backs straight, their bottoms on their heels, and pressed their knees against the sides of the nowie 'so as to form a poize'.[47] Collins said that the women sang together as they fished, and kept time with their paddles when they rowed. The officers worked out that the strange red bubbled scars on the smalls of their backs were caused by the onboard fires they kept burning on clay pads behind them, ready to cook fish. Collins remembered watching a picnic one sparkling summer's day at Tubowgully (Bennelong Point) where Bennelong, minding an infant, waited for his sisters to bring lunch. They nosed their canoes onto the shore, carried up the fish, cooked it over the fire and shared it. Then they all lay down to snooze in the sun.[48]

Hunter wrote of the women's extraordinary boating skills too:

In this necessary employment of fishing, we frequently saw a woman with two or three children in a miserable boat, the highest part of which was not six inches above the surface of the water, washing almost in the edge of the surf, which would frighten an old seaman to come near, in a good and manageable vessel.

How did she manage canoe, paddles, fishing gear, struggling fish, fire and three children in a pounding surf? Older children sat in front, a small child might sit upon her shoulders, clutching her hair; and the littlest 'lies across the mother's lap, from whence, although she is fully employed in fishing, it cannot fall'.[49]

The women were sometimes seen fishing all day, and at night too. Children grew up on the water from their youngest days, and the swell of the waves and rocking nowie must have been just as familiar to them as the solidity of the earth, or their mother's heartbeat—water was their element. The girls learned to line-fish as they grew—there are glimpses of young girls in canoes with older women, learning the fishing places and songs, how to burley with chewed cockle, how to lure and snag a fish with the pearly, crescent-shaped burra. Women dominated the waters of the harbours, and the coastlines in between—for they 'make much more use of [nowie] than the men'. Men, said Worgan, 'get into them only when they want to cross from one cove to the other'.[50]

Men fished too, but only with spears, and usually on shore. Sometimes they struck fish from a canoe, sticking their heads underwater to see them. But the decided opinion of the officers, and archaeologists and anthropologists today agree with them, was that most of the food was gathered by the

An Eora woman fishing in her nowie with her baby on board and a fire at the small of her back. (Dixson Galleries, State Library of New South Wales)

women—fish and shellfish from the waters, small animals and lizards, and the winter-food of fern roots from ground cleared by summertime burning. For men, 'the procuring of food really seems to be but a secondary business'. Real men's business was fighting and contests:

> The management of the spear and the shield, dexterity in throwing the various clubs . . . agility in either attacking or defending, a display of the constancy with which they endure pain, appearing to rank first among their concerns in life.[51]

These observers were deeply impressed with the women's fishing and canoeing skills, their stamina and stoicism. Worgan thought their hooks and lines showed 'the greatest ingenuity' of all the Eora implements. They also quickly learned that gifts of fishing tackle were much more acceptable than useless beads or buttons, and they learned to respect the value of women's fishing gear—these were not female frippery, 'trifling things in a fishing way', but serious and important, like men's spears and clubs. Officers started collecting the hooks as well as spears and fish-gigs. Convicts caught stealing fishing tackle were severely punished.[52]

But the officers concluded, as had Mrs Macarthur, that women's fishing and their role in supplying food generally was a terrible burden on them. They often described them as 'slaves' to their 'tyrant' men, who simply lay about on the shore waiting to be fed.[53] Partly this was the result of their own gendered world views, in which women should not work but be supported by men. Paid work was unthinkable for genteel women. They even gave the convict women, for whom work was a fact of life, a relatively easy time of it.

Still, what they observed had elements of truth. They could not have known— and it is only a dim awareness from our own vantage point—that women's fishing, made possible by the pearly burra, was linked to gendered politics and the balance of power over food. Until Sandra Bowdler's path-breaking essay 'Hook, line and dilly bag' appeared in 1976, archaeologists tended to leave these hooks aside in their analyses, in favour of stone tools. But Bowdler pointed out that in many traditional Aboriginal societies, women did the bulk of the food collection, while men controlled much of the food, particularly meat. This control of labour and food was probably crucial to the development of 'male secret ceremonial or political life'. When the new fish-hook appeared on the east coast of the continent between around 1200 and 500 years ago, she says, 'women doubtless seized gladly this opportunity to provide themselves with more fish than they had probably been getting'.[54]

In 1988, anthropologist Ian Walters suggested a still more startling scenario: women's hook-and-line fishing was 'a bold move' by which they were able to expand their economic and social base. He points out that the shell hook was not taken up in all areas—there is no evidence of it in the vast central arc between the Keppel Islands off Queensland in the north and Newcastle in New South Wales to the south—yet it was taken up both north and south of this stretch. Walters argues that where women did not adopt it, men monopolised the fishery, vigorous polygyny continued (the men took five or six wives each), men 'closed off' areas as their own, and the great sacred and ceremonial gatherings, like the bunya nut feasts of south-east Queensland, were exclusively male (though made possible by the labour of women). By contrast, where women did take up hook-and-line fishing, and caught fish for themselves and their children, men's social and ritual dominance was moderated. Polygyny was not so extensive (in the Sydney region men rarely had more than two wives). 'Closed off' areas were not the norm (there is only one recorded instance of an Eora man claiming this: Bennelong said that Memil, Goat Island, belonged to him and was his to pass on to whom he chose). Women and children did take part in the contests and corroborees and were present at the male initiation ceremonies. If Walters' hypothesis is correct, women's taking some control over food would also have nourished their own secret ceremonial life, their claim to their own places.[55]

The officers would argue, with good reason, that Eora men still dominated the food supply—they simply took the fish the women caught as well as their own. Took, or were given? Were they tyrants or dependants? (I think of Diane Bell's story from Warrabri in the Northern Territory. Women return to the married camp from a hunting trip: 'men say tentatively "Anything for me?" and accept what was given'.) It's still a fair point. But remember those little fires on the clay pads in the nowie, ready and waiting to cook the fish as they were hauled out:

women ate their fill and fed their children before they returned to the shores and their men.[56]

Of course we cannot know why Barangaroo tried so determinedly to discourage Bennelong's relationship with the Berewalgal, why she sabotaged his excursions to unfamiliar country with them. But I would say that the status and self-esteem of Eora women were inextricably bound up with fishing and canoeing, as well as a certain level of independence and control over their places and their work. She must have been aware that the Berewalgal's abundant and unstinting supply of food represented power, and observed the way they dealt officially with Eora men, not women. Living with them, relying on their food, plainly meant dependence on men, white and black.

Meanwhile there had been yet another level of cross-cultural contact: unofficial encounters between the British men and Eora women. It too is a history in hints, tiny glimpses, offhand remarks. The official meetings were strictly controlled by the men, while the women stayed behind the trees, guarded by warriors, or bobbed in their nowie on the water.[57] But men could not control the women's movements all the time, and the Berewalgal were nothing if not persistent. During one early encounter at Camp Cove, the Eora men placed their spears on the beach between the Berewalgal and the women in their nowie. The white men then rowed out past both the spears and the men to get to the women, who promptly paddled for shore and ran into the bush! On another occasion the longboat pursued an older woman and a girl in a nowie. The poor woman was so terrified that she threw all her fish out of the nowie in panic. Surgeon White proudly assures us that they managed to catch up, calm the woman and bestow 'trifles'. Tellingly the older woman remained 'petulant' while the young girl seemed highly amused, laughing and smiling.[58]

But White also recorded, in a rather roundabout way, that there *were* other, accidental meetings, out of the gaze of the Eora men (and mostly out of the official narratives), for he wrote that the men were 'very jealous of the women being among us *when we happen to fall in where they are*'. They had their spears ready *'when we do not come unawares upon them'* (my emphasis)—so there must have been other times when they did 'come unawares' on women, and the women did not paddle away or run into the trees.[59]

George Worgan in his letter to his brother wrote most marvellously, and with delightful self-mockery, of an encounter at South Head/Taralbe in May 1788. He was there with Hunter and Bradley, fixing the latitude of the great promontory. Looking down giddily from the 'tremendous precipice' they saw the women in the nowie far below, riding the glassy green waves rolling and crashing at the base of the cliff. The men and women 'hollowed' each other from cliff top to sea, and Worgan, ever the gallant romantic, wrapped his handkerchief around some wood, and tossed it down to them. Far below, a woman paddled over and plucked it from the water, but instead of being thrilled with his chivalrous token, she held it 'between her Thumb and Finger as if it was —— and after turning it round two or three times, gave it a Toss . . . into the dirtiest Corner of the canoe'. Worgan was mortified: 'If that is the Way You treat my Favours Madam, says I, I'll keep my Hankerchiefs . . .'[60] And then he ruminates to his brother of the women's alluring but puzzling behaviour—were they Eves or strumpets?

> There is something singular in the Conduct of these Evites, for if ever they deign to come near You, to take a Present, they appear as coy, shy, and timorous, as a Maid on her Wedding Night . . . but when they are, as they think out of your Reach, they hollow and chatter to You, Frisk, Flirt, and play a hundred wanton Pranks, equally as significant as the Solicitations of a Covent-Garden Strumpet. I cannot say all the Ladies are so shy and timorous on your approaching them, for some shew no signs of Fear, but will laugh and Frisk about You like a Spaniel, and put on the Airs of a Tantalizing Coquet.[61]

It was still only July 1788 when he wrote this. Officially there had been little or no contact between Eora and Berewalgal, apart from the killings, yet Worgan could describe and ponder such intimate meetings. (We might also ponder what Eora women made of the British men: curious, some of them attractive maybe, but so *earnest*; and inconsistent, sometimes friendly and intimate and other times frightening, with so many mystifying gestures. And the constant giving of ridiculous trinkets, what were they about?) Another tantalising glimpse of this hidden history also relates to fishing. By May 1790 the Berewalgal's stocks of fishing tackle were running low, so a convict ropemaker was employed to make Eora-style fishing lines.[62] How did this man know how to pound and spin the kurrajong bark unless shown by Eora women?

After the 'coming in' or 'taking possession' of October 1790, women and girls were among those who visited the Camp, and some of them may have already known people there. Most came with their husbands or family groups which passed through, collecting food, dropping off children at Government House. Some of them seem to have lived in the town, although they were obviously not 'settled' there in the way the British had envisaged, for they often left for fishing trips when the fish were running, for dances and no doubt for women's business. The Reverend Johnson complained that Boorong, of whom he had grown quite fond, became less pliant and 'ran off into the woods' far more often once the Eora 'came in'.[63]

One circle of related women became very well known to the officers: Boorong and Pattyegarang, of course, but also Boorong's half-sister Warraweer Wogul Mi (Warraweer One-eye), who may have also lived with the Johnsons; Coleby's wife Daringa Barangaroo (she was Barangaroo's namesake); Bennelong's sister Warraweer and another female relative called Worogan, who was Pattyegarang's friend. There was also a little girl named Gonangulye (Collins spelt it Go-nang-goo-lie), who was taken in by the soldiers and officers at the barracks. The first thing to note about them is that they were young women and girls—old women are rarely glimpsed in Sydney in these early years.[64] And they were different from the mature Barangaroo, more open and curious, less suspicious, more naive and impressionable. Certainly less prickly! Like the men they took advantage of the town as a rich source of food. 'Why don't you learn to speak like a white man?' Dawes asked Pattyegarang, and quick as a shot she replied: because you give me food, drink, everything I want, without my having to ask. When the beauteous young woman Gooroodeanna visited Tench at his house, she was hungry and asked for food.[65]

These were the women who helped the studious Dawes learn and transcribe their language, and corrected his pronunciation. They were setting a precedent, for as linguist Jakelin Troy points out, Aboriginal women were often the first go-betweens in cross-cultural contact, and thus played an essential role in the

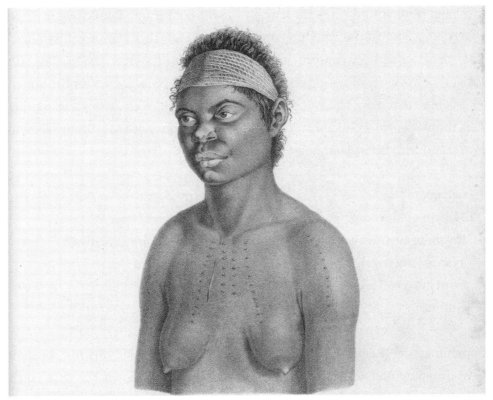

Nicolas-Martin Petit's 1802 portrait 'Oui-re-kine', or Worogan, one of the young women in William Dawes' circle. (Mitchell Library, State Library of New South Wales)

emergence of pidgin languages. In Sydney they and all the nameless female visitors and sojourners helped create a new language, a dynamic mix of 'English and the Port Jackson dialect', used between whites and Aboriginal people. David Collins lamented this new patois: it was 'nothing but a barbarous dialect'. After all those months of waiting and watching, somehow the chance of capturing 'pure' language had flashed past, and was gone forever. Meanwhile the Eora had the advantage, for they understood 'everything they hear us say'. Dawes also recorded the way they readily ran English words like petticoat, jacket, tea, breakfast and sulphur into Eora sentences. Sometimes the words were modified, as in 'breado tunga'—she cries for bread, 'gunin'—guns, 'kandulin'—candle.[66]

Dawes' extraordinary notebook records simple, intimate and pleasurable moments, but there are darker threads too. Nanbarry and Boorong are always at play. Little Gonangulye wants to wear Pattye's petticoat, which Dawes says is too long. Never mind, she says sensibly, 'I will hold it up'. Bennelong is being shaved and Barangaroo, laughing and playing, teases that Dawes will cut him. Someone, perhaps Warraweer, has brought a baby to show Dawes. 'Minyin tunga?' he asks: why does she cry? 'Yabunga' is the reply: she cries for the breast.

There were times when Pattye had to be very patient with Dawes. He asks her why the black men wounded a white man coming from Kadi to Warang (Cadi to Warrane), and she explains:

Gulara	*(Because they are) angry.*
Minyin gulara eora?	*Why are the [black men] angry?*
Inyam ngalwi [whitemen].	*Because the white men are settled here.*
Tyerun kamarigal.	*The kamarigals are afraid*
Minyin tyerun k-gal?	*Why are the [kamarigals] afraid?*
Gunin.	*(Because of the) guns.*

Sometimes she seems to want to speak to her friends without his constant eavesdropping and scribbling and questions—he writes down her curt reprimand: 'We two are talking to each other; that is, we did not say anything to you'. At other times they grew angry with one another. 'I will watch you through the window because you did not give me any bread', she says menacingly after Dawes 'gave her a blow on the head out of the window'. Along with words about play, fishing and food, Dawes recorded the frequent beatings his informants suffered, often at the hands of Eora warriors, but also of white men. 'A white man beat us three, Pundal, Poonda', Pattye tells him. Noting her words, Dawes wonders why she constructs the sentence without including herself in the three.[67]

Even as the spearings and the beatings continued, Eora women in Sydney were forming mutually beneficial friendships with convict women and men as well as officers and their wives. The notebook mentions other people they knew in town—men who gave them petticoats, servants who washed their clothes for them. When William Bryant's fishing boat was upset on the harbour in February 1791 a young Eora woman, Carrangarrang, a sister of Bennelong's, was on board with a girl and two children. Bennelong and his friends rescued the white men, while she and the girl swam to safety with the children. As Clendinnen suggests, Bryant had probably 'formed a fisherman's alliance with Baneelon's [Bennelong's] sister, who exchanged her local knowledge regarding fish movements and local habits in return for transport to the less accessible fishing spots'.[68] The fishing boats had been important sites of contact from the start, so Bryant, like McIntyre, had probably built up some knowledge and personal relationships. But his were with the fisherwomen of the harbour, rather than the land-based male hunters.

Convict Margaret Catchpole at first found the Eora's nakedness highly embarrassing: 'I for my part do not like them—I do not know how to look at them—they are such poor naked creatures'. Yet later she reported that they were 'gittin very civil', and came into her house, behaving 'well enough'. She used their word for food, *patter*, in her letters.[69] When Warraweer went into labour with her first child, she had a retinue of convict as well as Eora midwives to attend her, just as convict women helped one another in childbirth. These women, wrote Collins, were 'favourites with the girl', suggesting friendship and trust. Some Eora women even appear to have left their babies 'in perfect security' with convict wet-nurses who, as Daniel Southwell wrote disgustedly, were 'suitably rewarded by government'. When Coleby's wife (not Daringa) died in the town, probably of consumption, 'her corpse was carried to the door of every hut and house she had been accustomed to enter during the latter days of her illness' so her white friends could pay their respects, and make their farewells.[70]

Eora women also used Sydney as a temporary refuge from angry and violent husbands. Phillip and the other officers were horrified at the way Bennelong and Coleby and their friends hit their wives, even when they were heavily pregnant, and then laughed and boasted about it as though it was the most normal thing in the world. Phillip used Government House and the hospital to shield Kurubarabulu from the enraged Bennelong, and the yard became a shelter too. Barangaroo went to Tarra, to Dawes' house, when Bennelong was angry and she was ill, possibly because he had bashed her. Tench hoped Gooroodeanna's beauty had protected her from violence but found to his grief her head was criss-crossed with scars too (one wonders uneasily whether he thought it more explainable in ugly wives). Collins was so disturbed by Eora women's lot, he thought it might well be better for female infants to be 'destroyed' rather than face such a fate. The British were further mystified, and disappointed, when, after tempers had cooled and heads were stitched, the women they protected always rejoined their husbands.[71]

As Clendinnen observes, this was a 'tough warrior culture', and violence was integral to it, just as it was in so many aspects of British culture. Certainly those convicts who wrote about the Eora agreed—recall William Noah's observation: 'they are very Jealous and Desperate Cruil to their Woman'.[72] At the same time it is likely both that the officers' view was somewhat skewed by the type of Eora men they associated with, and that the level of violence had escalated in the wake of invasion and smallpox. In the first place, the British dealt almost exclusively with privileged young men, warriors, and the most ambitious and aggressive among them. By contrast there were other men who were known for their gentleness— Arabanoo, and Gnunga Gnunga Murremurgan ('Collins'), for example. But these qualities were regarded as exceptional, and they probably were.[73]

Second, the officers portrayed the Eora women as helpless victims of male violence as well as exploitation. Yet women themselves used violence (though, except for Barangaroo, not usually against their husbands). Like convict women, they were often rivals for the affections of men and did not hesitate to attack other women they considered to be encroaching on their relationships. They took part in the mass brawls which followed ritual contests and in violent payback when their Law demanded it—and not merely throwing 'feeble spears', but inflicting horrific injuries. Against their men they probably used piercing words to humiliate and shame: Tench said they 'often artfully study to irritate and inflame the passions of men'.[74]

And, perhaps more importantly, the officers were observing a society in the flux of recovery and readjustment. We don't know precisely how the invasion and the smallpox epidemic had altered Eora sexual politics and relations, or how the presence of Sydney itself, and the alternative refuge and protectors it offered, may have affected behaviour. As we have seen, the arrival of hundreds of white men who had no hope of finding a partner among their own women certainly meant that Eora women were much desired. The smallpox epidemic would have exacerbated this by carrying off a disproportionate number of women, and competition for them thus became even more intense. Women were vulnerable to abduction and rape at a younger age (the officers noted how young they were). But as Tench himself noted, violent abductions had *not* been the norm, but a last resort when elaborate courtship rituals and dances failed to secure the desired woman as a wife. Now they increased, along with constant and violent public demonstrations of male possession and dominance. As we will see, overtly male ceremonies were very prominent in early Sydney too. Yet all of these things were reported by the officers as the 'traditional' and 'natural' customs of the Eora.[75]

Collins nevertheless hints at the centrality of women, the desperate competition for them, when he commented that they were very often at 'the head of men's quarrels', the focus of their struggles.[76] Bennelong probably quit the Camp to win Barangaroo back from Coleby; or perhaps it was Kurubarabulu. When Eora men sailed away on the ships to distant places with the Berewalgal, they knew their wives would find new partners in their absence. When sailors and sojourners returned they had to fight the new husband, often a younger man, to recover their wives (and their honour). And even if the first husband triumphed, the woman might still decide she preferred her younger partner.[77]

Despite the violence, which was without a doubt widespread, some women at least seem to have kept the upper hand some of the time and made their own decisions about their relationships. Some were greatly desired. Kurubarabulu, abducted by Bennelong, became his wife. When she took refuge in the yard of Government House, he and Coleby, along with two other men, tried to abduct her, she said in order to rape her. They scaled the paling fence but were stopped by the soldiers. When Bennelong sailed to England with Phillip in 1792, Kurubarabulu took a second, younger husband, Caruey. Although Bennelong beat him severely when he returned, she stayed with him, and there was nothing Bennelong could do about it. She was abducted a second time by Botany Bay man Collinjong in 1798, and a great contest between him and Caruey followed. When Caruey was killed in a fight in December 1805, Coleby 'bore off the widow' and Bennelong, once more, tried to win Kurubarabulu back by fighting his old friend and rival.[78]

Eora women also made Sydney their own by choosing to give birth there. As the officers were just as fascinated by women's childbirth rituals as by everything else they did, we have two descriptions of Eora births in early Sydney (this is two more than we have of births to convict women). Warraweer, Bennelong's sister, gave birth 'in the town' before 1796, although we don't know where. Perhaps at the home of a friend, but I think it more likely to have been a place outdoors: somewhere secluded, with soft groundcover and water nearby, a fire ready and a small hole dug. As Warraweer laboured, Boorong poured water on her stomach, and another woman eased her pain by transferring it through a string passed from neck to lips. But in birth itself, Warraweer was 'unassisted', and the baby dropped to a soft bark blanket on the ground. She then squatted over the 'small hole' awaiting the placenta. Boorong and the others protested when the white women cut the cord and washed the infant, but Warraweer was so exhausted she let her white friends prevail.[79]

For Bennelong, and perhaps for other men who wanted a stake and a future among the British at Warrane, wives provided this precious possibility: they could give birth to babies in this place. The new generation would belong to this Sydney country because they were born in it. So there was much more fanfare before the birth of Bennelong and Barangaroo's baby some time in 1791. Bennelong told everyone he was sure it was a boy, and informed Phillip that Barangaroo had decided to do him the honour of giving birth at Government House. Given Barangaroo's temperament, and what actually happened, it seems much more likely that this was not her idea, but Bennelong's—his child's birth on this ground would bind him and his people still closer to his powerful friend and ally. But Phillip demurred, suggesting that the best place for the birth would be with the surgeons at the hospital. Barangaroo would have been even less enamoured with this place of disease and death as a birthing place than Government House. Birth was women's business and men had no right to interfere in any aspect of it. Bennelong beat her again, badly, on the morning of the birth, but she defied him one more time: she gave birth alone, in a secluded place somewhere in the bush nearby. Collins, perhaps having been tipped off by Boorong, came quietly to see her afterwards, and was astonished to see her 'walking about alone, picking up sticks to mend her fire', the tiny reddish infant lying on soft bark on the ground. It was a daughter, who was named Dilboong, for a small brown bird.[80]

Barangaroo did not live long after the birth. The officers were uncharacteristically silent on why she died. She was cremated, with her fishing gear beside her, in a small ceremony. Bennelong buried her ashes carefully in the garden of Government House. He then asked Phillip to act as foster-father to the child Dilboong, and Phillip found a wet-nurse for her among the convict women. But while white babies were thriving, Dilboong died, and was buried at Government House garden with Arabanoo and Barangaroo. In December 1791 the body of young Ballooderry would be interred there also, 'with full Australian warrior honours'.[81] I wonder where this significant, sad burial ground was, and where it is now, and how long it remained visible among the regenerating trees and shrubs before it was swallowed up by streets and buildings and indifference.

Through the other, younger women, a female social landscape was emerging in Sydney: a network of friends, lovers and patrons. But it was emerging, as far as I can see, within what we generally think of as white structure and spaces, or in unmarked, informal places in the bush nearby. The harbour was their arena and remained so for many years. By contrast, Eora men were making deliberate, unmistakable, almost hyper-masculine claims to urban space, through their rituals and public battles. Perhaps the most striking of these demonstrations was the great male initiation ceremony of tooth evulsion, the Yoolang Erah-Badiang, held in January and February 1795 at Wogganmagully (Farm Cove). These initiation ceremonies were controlled and carried out by the powerful Cammeragal men, and we know that the previous one was held in their country, on a bay 'down the harbour'. But this time the initiates included Sydney Eora boys—Nanbarry, Caruey, Boorong's brother, Yerranibe Goruey and Daringa's brother Boneda. Somehow the Cammeragal were persuaded to come over to the south side to perform it—perhaps Coleby had used his influence. They kept everyone waiting for over a week, but eventually swept into the *yoolang*, the ceremonial space which had been cleared on the cove, probably beside the government farm there. Keith Vincent Smith, looking closely at Watling's detailed pictures, says it was 'a typical bora ring of two circles joined by a path'.[82]

David Collins was present among the women and children watching and he wrote a detailed description of the long and complex rituals and dances that followed, which culminated in each boy's front tooth being knocked out with

New initiates, painted and crowned in reeds, hold their mouths after undergoing the tooth evulsion ceremony at the yoolong *on Wogganmagully/Farm Cove in 1795. (From David Collins,* An Account of the English Colony, *vol. 1)*

a wooden wedge and stone (one poor eight-year-old couldn't endure the pain and 'made his escape'). The successful initiates were crowned with reeds, painted, and finally they all 'started up', running through the town, 'driving before them men, women and children, who were glad to get out of their way ... everywhere as they passed along setting the grass on fire'. They charged up to the Brickfields ground for their first games, leaving flames in their wake. As newly made men, they were now 'privileged to wield the spear and the club'. And, Collins was told, they could now 'seize such females as they chose for wives'.[83]

What did the young Sydney Eora women think of this extravagant demonstration of masculine power, stoicism and chest-beating prowess? Extraordinarily, Warraweer and Daringa dared defy their own men and the Cammeragal to please their British friends: somehow they got hold of three of the teeth and delivered them to David Collins. Daringa said one of them was Nanbarry's and asked him to give it to Surgeon White, who had cared for the boy. Was it a secret protest, a little thumbing of the nose? These small things, now lost, hint at such large and complex gendered tensions. It must have taken some nerve—the two women were terrified. Collins said, 'they were given to me in such secrecy and great dread of being observed' and they told him never to tell anyone, as they would be severely punished. He published the story in 1798.[84]

Inga Clendinnen wonders whether coming in to Sydney was perhaps an attempt by some young Eora women to emancipate themselves from men. The release of young people—women and men—from their elders' control would be another recurring theme of frontier contact and conflict. Besides language, friendship and food, sex soon became another fact of cross-cultural relations. Sexual relations between European men and Eora women had already changed. In 1790, Phillip reported that an Aboriginal woman had 'granted favours to several of the convicts', and by 1796, Collins wrote darkly that some Aboriginal women 'were ready to exchange their chastity' for 'a loaf of bread, a blanket or a shirt' and that some, who now lived in the settlement, went on board ships to spend the night with sailors, coming ashore in the morning with 'spoils'—presumably food and clothing.[85]

There were other stories, especially after the two groups became more familiar with one another. Some white men formed relationships with unattached Aboriginal women, which from the Eora point of view would then bind them in reciprocal relationships with their Eora kin. The rules and decisions about sexual relations probably varied from group to group and according to circumstance. The four convict escapees who lived with the Gampignal at Port Stephens in 1790 were allowed wives. But John Wilson/Bunboee, who lived with the Aboriginal people at the Hawkesbury, was not, and in the end this was his undoing. It seems his Aboriginal hosts insisted he get a wife of his own race. So, in March 1795 he and another man, Knight, were arrested, probably at Parramatta, while trying to drag away two young white girls with the help of Aboriginal friends. The method was very similar to that younger Eora men sometimes used to abduct women from other groups. Wilson escaped again and rejoined his Aboriginal friends, but later he tried to keep an unwilling Aboriginal woman for 'his own exclusive accommodation'. Her friends drove a spear through his body 'when he was not in a condition to defend himself'.[86]

In other unwritten cases, relationships became permanent. Joseph Holt, the Irish exile in the colony between 1800 and 1811, recalled: 'I have seen toneys [mixed-descent children] in that country, for I assure you that some of the convicts . . . cohabits with the blacks and gets childer with them . . .' In later years there were numerous marriages between Aboriginal women and ex-convict men, and their children intermarried as well.[87]

Meanwhile, town life for young Aboriginal women became risky; the notion of early 'emancipation' and agency is overshadowed by their vulnerability. They were without mothers and aunties to guide and teach them, without their own menfolk to protect them. By at least 1817, soldiers stationed at the barracks gave young Aboriginal servant girls rum and copper pennies to have sex with them underneath rocky overhangs on the still-wild edge of town at Cockle Bay. On one occasion, a 'little girl' named Nanny Cabbage, and her friends Norry and Currumburn, went with soldiers to Cockle Bay. After the men 'were done', they drank rum together. Later Nanny Cabbage was found near the house of her mistress in Kent Street, moaning in the darkness, a wound gaping from thigh to stomach, almost separating her leg from her body. Her mistress, Elinor Brown, was 'considerably alarmed' when she was told in the morning, but by then it was too late. The men who found Nanny did not help her; they went back inside and left her on the ground to die alone. Another woman complained that Nanny's terrible moaning disturbed her sleep. An inquest was held. Although the two soldiers were ordered to be charged by the coroner, no-one was convicted of her murder.[88]

What became of those early intimacies, the deep wonder and admiration for women's skills, the early officers' gallant gestures, and Phillip's and Dawes' attempts to provide a safe haven for Aboriginal women? One by one, the officers sailed away; their actions and words failed to become a template for the future town. Although some high-profile women were well known and received a modicum of care and sympathy, the townsfolk became utterly indifferent to girls like Nanny Cabbage. White men and white laws afforded some white women privileges, but offered Aboriginal women little protection. White women found Sydney a safer and more congenial environment than the frontier, a place where they made households and homes. But from what glimpses we have, the same was not true for the Aboriginal women who also occupied urban space.

And I wonder whether this lost girl, Nanny Cabbage, knew how to keep a ticklish nowie steady, to paddle swiftly through the largest swell. Did she know the fishing songs, and how to catch snapper and bream with kurrajong line and shining crescent hook?

RETURN

Bennelong and his young kinsman, Yemmerrewanne, left Sydney for England with Phillip in December 1792. The Eora voyagers 'withstood the dismal lamentations' of their distressed wives and friends as the longboat pulled away from the wharf towards the *Atlantic*. In England they would be presented in court, spend a fortune on knee breeches, spotted silk waistcoats and the like from fashionable shops, dress like dandies, ride in carriages, and endure dismal weather in the cold rooms of mansions. Someone must have taken them 'slumming' too, because Bennelong learned the bloody art of bare-knuckle fighting. But Yemmerrewanne became ill in October 1793. He died on 18 May the following year and was buried in St John's churchyard at Eltham, where his carefully tended headstone still stands along the churchyard wall. Eventually Bennelong sailed home again, arriving in Sydney Cove on the *Reliance* with Governor John Hunter in November 1795.[89]

Eora voyagers: silhouette of 'Yuremary' (Yemmerrewanne) and portrait of Bennelong in his London finery, about 1793. (Dixson Galleries, State Library of New South Wales)

421

His first actions were classic Bennelong theatre: he swept a regal arm over 'his' people and declared that he would no longer tolerate them fighting and 'cutting each other's throats' like savages. He berated his poor sister Carrangarrang when she came all the way from Botany Bay to see him with her child on her back but forgot to put on clothes. The foppish, arrogant persona did not last long, and perhaps they knew it wouldn't. To the white observers' astonishment and dismay, within weeks of his return he threw off his fine clothes and returned 'to the woods' (though he was careful to put them on again when he came back to Government House). He fought Caruey in an attempt to win back Kurubarabulu, using his fists, English style, to knock him down. According to Collins, this was 'to the great annoyance of Caruey who would have preferred meeting his rival fairly in the field armed with the spear and club'. He attempted to abduct Coleby's wife Boorea, and Coleby beat him so badly he had to stay away from the town to recover, sending for food and his clothes.[90] In later months and years, the white observers saw him shouting and abusing people in the streets, a loud-mouthed, aggressive drunk who nevertheless had the protection of wealthy patrons and the governor himself. When he died in 1813 the *Gazette* published a damning obituary: he was an intractable savage, the classic backslider. He had been shown the light, and turned away.[91]

In settler history we seem to be searching constantly for beginnings: the first white foot touches the soil, the first white child is born, the embryonic outline of the future town is visible. But in Aboriginal history of the colonial period so often the search is for endings: the annihilation brought about by disease and violence, the 'last' of his or her tribe. Bennelong's life after his return from England is often presented as an ending. His fate seems to mark the dismal conclusion of that first phase of cross-cultural relations, the destruction of hope for 'peace and amity' between the two peoples. And his story tends to be seen as a gloomy portent of the weaknesses of Aboriginal people, their 'inability' to change and 'be civilised'. It is instructive and important to note, then, that stories of Bennelong as the 'first drunken Aborigine', shunned by women of both races, a man hopelessly and helplessly 'caught in a void between two cultures' are myths.[92] Bennelong got his life back together. As the careful research of Smith and Kohen revealed some years ago, he had remarried by 1797 and there is strong evidence that Boorong was his third wife. He had at least one child, a son named Dicky. He returned to his people and a lifestyle that was traditional in many ways, for until his death in 1813 he was an elder of the 'Kissing Point tribe'. This was the new name adopted by the people, including Boorong's family, who had moved or been forced from Parramatta and resettled on the flats at Kissing Point on the Parramatta River after their own country was invaded in 1790. Bennelong also regained his former authority. He was regarded as 'King of the natives' in the Kissing Point/Eastwood area, according to Joseph Holt, and he officiated as the last recorded Yoolang Erah-Badiang ceremony in Middle Harbour in 1797. The people of Botany Bay also 'acknowledge Bennil-long for their chief'.[93]

The Kissing Point tribe appears to have camped on the lands of white friends and absentee landholders—at The Vineyard, for example, the old Schaeffer farm, now owned by Bennelong's patron and Nanbarry's old commander, Henry Waterhouse; and at William Kent's farm at Kissing Point. People camped at Brush Farm, where Joseph Holt sometimes invited Bennelong and Boorong in 'for breakfast and a glass of grog'. The band also continued to occupy the riverside flats, land granted to an emancipist, James Squires, in 1795, who established the colony's first brewery on it in 1812. Publican, hop-grower, local constable and father of a large family, Squires became renowned for his role as 'friend and protector of the lower class of settlers', always willing to 'lend money to local farmers'. He must also have been another of the early settlers to accept coexistence with Aboriginal people, and he became a friend to them. As for Bennelong, he had returned to an area close to his own ancestral country, Wanne, which lay opposite, on the south side of the river—land there having been granted to small farmers and the 'Parramatta River gentry', as we have seen. When he died in 1813, he was buried with Boorong among the orange trees of Squires' orchard, overlooking the river. When Nanbarry died in July 1821 he was buried with Bennelong and Boorong as he had requested. The grave was still visible and locally known around 1900, but disappeared after the area was subdivided. Somewhere beneath an ordinary allotment in suburban Putney lie the bodies of these three extraordinary cross-cultural pioneers.[94]

What does Bennelong's story tell us about the larger relationship between Aboriginal people and early Sydney? His return to the river with Boorong's family does not signify the winding down and 'incompatibility' of Aboriginal people with town life, but just the opposite. During his absence in England, increasing numbers of new people had arrived from distant places, people outside his sphere of influence. Coleby appears to have taken on a key role as elder and negotiator for some years, though there is no record of him after 1806. Meanwhile, Bennelong steadily recovered his status and authority. When he died, his people were bereft, and deeply mourned him.[95]

Bennelong also found his house had disappeared. It had been gradually abandoned after he left, and the acting governor allowed visiting Spanish officers to use it as a temporary observatory in March 1793. In August 1795 a storm damaged Phillip's signal column at South Head, and the bricklayer and gang sent out to repair it salvaged bricks from Bennelong's house, which was by then 'altogether forsaken by the natives and tumbling down', carted them out to South Head and used them to repair the tower. Whitened with lime burnt from shells, it 'became a more conspicuous object at sea than it ever had been before'. Perhaps fragments of Bennelong's house still lie somewhere below the surface at the lookout on that windswept promontory.[96]

But the house's destruction does not mean Aboriginal Sydney had been wiped out, simply that the spatial focus had shifted. Details are sketchy, but it seems that they camped in family and clan groups in the open, unbuilt and still-wild areas around the town—the Domain in the east, the Rocks and Cockle Bay (Darling Harbour) in the west, around the Brickfields contest ground to the south, and across the water on the north shore around Kirribilli. They would continue to do so into the 1820s and 1830s.

Historians often talk of the 'void' between the two cultures: Bennelong is the epitome of those lost and degraded souls who, in attempting to cross, fell into it. But if this is not true of Bennelong, who returned to his people, is it a valid way to think about what happened to Aboriginal people in early Sydney as a whole? Were they merely lost, cultureless fringe-dwellers? Certainly there were people who found themselves condemned to live out lives between the two societies, accepted by neither, never able to 'go home' (think of the stories told by Deborah Bird Rose of young Aboriginal men lured by uniforms and guns into the Native Police to hunt their own people).[97] But for Bennelong and for the people who came to Sydney, not only was it possible to maintain semi-traditional ways of life, but the space 'between cultures' was not a void. It was full of possibilities. As archaeologist Denis Byrne writes, Aboriginal people in colonised landscapes were faced with an immediate, practical problem: 'How do you live in a landscape that no longer belongs to you?'[98] In Sydney, some Aboriginal people found ways to live among the invaders and in the newly configured spaces which were nonetheless compatible with their own ways and Law, and which were comfortable to them. The most adventurous, innovative and influential among them were those who went to sea.

ABORIGINAL MARINERS

A number of young Aboriginal men from the Sydney region trained as sailors and became voyagers to distant lands, and explorers, envoys and peace-makers in their own right. Some women also boarded ships, but these were often illicit movements, so their stories are even more obscure. These voyages are all the more astonishing when we think of the geographical limitations of Eora people, apart from the messengers. They knew their own and affiliated country intimately, but Coleby and Ballooderry, for example, had apparently never been much further west than the head of the Parramatta River, and they had never seen Dyarubbin, the Hawkesbury River. The nowie crossed the harbours and rivers, and hugged the coastlines but could not take them more than a few kilometres out to sea.

But from February 1791, they embarked on pelagic travel. Young Bondel (later known as Bundle), an orphan boy, was 'the first who has had the confidence & courage' to go to sea. He 'attached himself to Captain Hill' and sailed to Norfolk Island, returning unwillingly in September 1791 with a 'smattering' of English which he fused with his own language. His stories of abundant food led others to sail there: three 'natives' voyaged to the island on the *Britannia* in August 1792. And in September 1794 Warraweer, with the wife of Yemmerrewanne, went there to escape the violence in Sydney.[99] Bondel became an experienced sailor, working on colonial vessels, but also went on notable exploratory voyages. He sailed with George William Evans to Jervis Bay on the New South Wales coast in 1812, and with Phillip Parker King on a survey voyage to the north coast of Australia in

Gnunga Gnunga or Collins, warrior, mariner, husband of Warraweer. (Mitchell Library, State Library of New South Wales)

1821. He may have been the unnamed Aboriginal youth who sailed to England with David Blackburn in 1791.[100]

Nanbarry went to sea too, after Surgeon White left. He was a seaman on the *Reliance* in 1795 and went with Bondel to Norfolk Island in 1799; he later reached the Great Barrier Reef with the famous navigator Matthew Flinders in the *Investigator*. Broken Bay man Gnunga Gnunga, Warraweer's husband, sailed much further: he voyaged to Nootka Sound on the sub-arctic Canadian coast on the *Daedalus* in 1793–94, calling in at Hawaii on the return voyage. David Collins, writing of his namesake, says he was supposed to learn English and teach the ship's officers his own language in return. But while Gnunga Gnunga learned English, and understood all that was said, he did not reciprocate with Eora language lessons. A youth known as Tom Rowley, after one of the officers, voyaged to Bengal in the *Britannia* in 1795. By 1805 the *Gazette* was reporting approvingly that 'several of their youths [were] employed in the various sealing gangs in the Straits... and evince an ardent inclination of contributing every possible exertion to the common advantage'.[101]

But the most famous and intrepid Aboriginal mariner and explorer was Bungaree. As a young man he left his Broken Bay country and sailed in 1799

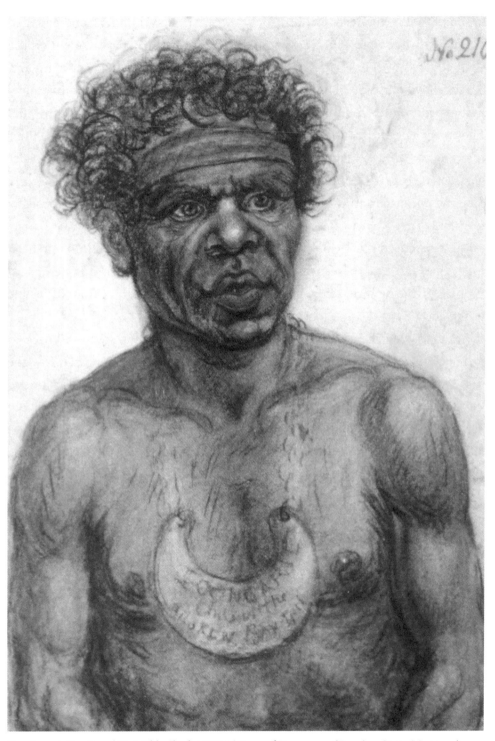

Russian visitor Pavel N. Mikhailov's 1820 picture of Bungaree. (Russian State Museum)

to Moreton Bay (now the site of Brisbane) with Matthew Flinders, and he sailed on the *Lady Nelson* in 1801 to assist in founding a new penal settlement on the Coal River (now Newcastle). Flinders described Bungaree as 'a worthy and brave fellow' and was happy to take both him and Nanbarry on the famous first expedition to circumnavigate Australia aboard HMS *Investigator* in 1802. They were not only sailors: they were scouts and cross-cultural envoys, their role was to 'bring about a friendly intercourse with the inhabitants of other parts of the coast'. Bungaree excelled in this difficult and dangerous work, meeting and negotiating with Aboriginal people who were as much strangers to him as they were to the whites. He was also an 'agent of cultural change' for he introduced the spear-thrower (womera) of his own region into northern Australia, and may have been instrumental in bringing the boomerang to Sydney, throwing it expertly, much to the 'wonder and admiration' of people in Sydney.[102]

Nanbarry left the Flinders expedition before it was complete to sail back to Sydney. Since the other expedition members were British, Bungaree was the first Australian to circumnavigate the continent. In this he was also among the first in a long line of extraordinary, but largely uncelebrated, Aboriginal explorers who went into unknown country, guided the parties, found them food and water, and saved their lives by acting as peace-makers and emissaries. During the recent bicentennial celebrations of the *Reliance*'s historic voyage, Matthew Flinders was rightly honoured. His charming cat, Trim, was a star too. But Bungaree 'scarcely rated a mention'. 'You have to be tolerant', said his descendant Warren Whitfield mildly; though he would have liked 'a little more recognition for the man Governor Macquarie called a king'.[103]

When Bungaree left his country to go to sea, he was not driven out by settlers or redcoats. Land grants in Broken Bay/Brisbane Water were not made until over two decades later, and even then the area was not intensively settled or radically altered; the rugged land was not considered very desirable for farming or grazing. What attracted these young men to sailing was probably talk with sailors, the lure of adventure, the realisation that people could go beyond the horizon. The havoc wreaked by smallpox must have loosened bonds and traditions, and heightened a sense of change, or chaos. Perhaps still more attractive was the culture and world view of seafarers: the equality and communality of sailors at sea, who depended utterly on one another for their lives, who lived in cramped spaces where privacy and individual space were dissolved, who divided the profits from sealing trips equally into lays to pay each man, and divided their food right down to the last pea. Officers sometimes observed the confluence of sailors' and Eora's superstitiousness. And it crossed both ways, for sometimes white sailors adopted Eora beliefs—Flinders wrote that one of his sailors 'learned many of the native habits, and even imbibed this ridiculous notion respecting rays and sharks'. The sailor, like the Eora, refused to eat stingrays and sharks.[104]

David Dickenson Mann, surveying the colony in 1811, wrote of notable Aboriginal sailors 'Bull Dog, Bidgy-Bidgy, Bundell, Bloody Jack', who 'made themselves extremely useful on board colonial vessels employed in the fishing and sealing trades, for which they are in the regular receipt of wages'.[105] Significantly, the dress and pleasures of sailors were adopted too:

> They strive by every means in their power, to make themselves appear like the sailors with whom they associate, by copying their customs and imitating their manners; such as swearing, using a great quantity of tobacco, drinking and similar habits.[106]

Phillip and the officers had striven to introduce their Eora friends to elite culture, and they had constantly bemoaned the 'corrupting' contact between them and the lower orders. But it was the culture of ordinary sailors which resonated with these young men, and it became a dominant strand in the lives Aboriginal people made in what was after all a maritime town. Notable sailors often became 'chiefs' or leaders of their people—Bungaree of his group on the north shore, Bidgee Bidgee at Kissing Point, Bondel/Bundle of the Cowpastures tribe, and later Mahroot (Boatswain), who described himself in 1845 as the 'last of his tribe', on Cooks River at Botany Bay. Most of the writing visitors to Sydney who encountered the Sydney Tribe commented on 'the magical allurements of spirits and tobacco' for them, pleasures 'stronger than all the delights of a fixed, plentiful, and quiet life'. Such things were written of

Bidgee Bidgee, who went to sea and later became a 'chief' of the Kissing Point tribe. 'A well known character at Sydney, speaks very good English and mimicks the manners of every Officer and person in the colony.' He was the younger half-brother of Boorong. (Mitchell Library, State Library of New South Wales)

sailors too, of course. Hyacinthe de Bougainville watched them fishing from European boats when the mackerel were running in August 1825: the men wore the wide trousers, round jackets and straw hats of sailors. 'A sailor's life would suit these blacks more than any other', wrote Roger Oldfield in 1827, 'except a gentleman's'.[107]

Their Sydney lives were adjusted to the rhythms of the port, for the nowie were always among the flotilla of small boats first out to the newly arrived ships, and they are still seen whizzing among the ships, skiffs and bumboats in paintings of the harbour in the 1820s. By then Bungaree had well and truly formalised the welcome. Dressed in the cocked, feathered hat which became his insignia, and one of the elaborate coats from his wardrobe of military castoffs, Bungaree clambered barefoot onto the decks to welcome newcomers and introduce his family. 'These are my people', he said to them. And, pointing to the north shore, 'This is my shore'.[108]

'CARRIERS OF NEWS AND FISH'

Watching the waters of the three harbours, Sydney's Aboriginal people were the eyes and ears of the town. They spotted the sails of ships labouring towards Port Jackson before anyone else. Soon after the great 'coming in' they were salvaging wrecked boat parts and saving the drowning from shipwrecks.[109] In the early 1800s, Broken Bay people raced down the paths to Sydney with the news of coastal ships that came to grief on the rocks of Broken Bay during great storms. When the unfortunate George Legg, a baker from the Rocks, drowned in Sydney Harbour after his boat upset in a squall, his Aboriginal companions came to tell his wife, Anne Armsden. Six weeks later Aboriginal people spotted his remains in the shoals—so Anne could at least recover what was left of him and arrange a decent burial. When shopkeepers were robbed, they helped search for the missing goods, demanding rewards in return. They uncovered the hiding places of fugitives in caves on Cockle Bay, and later tracked escaped convicts and bushrangers. We must begin to imagine early Sydney as polyglot rather than as 'British' space, for Aboriginal people, as well as Lascar (Indian) and Islander sailors and African convicts, were the life of the streets; they were among the mobs of people that gathered in the public spaces and for the fights. On the evening of Christmas Day in 1821, a disorderly mob collected around the Main Guard in George Street and a fight broke out. One of the injured men, Private Thomas Elliot, later told the court that freeman James McAllister 'took a waddy from one of the blackfellow's hands and made a blow at the corporal & hit me in the shoulder'.[110]

Judge Barron Field, who lived on the salubrious Bunkers Hill at the north end of the Rocks, was one of the many educated observers of the 1820s who despaired of 'civilising' the Aboriginal people. 'Perhaps it is better that their name should pass away from the earth', he wrote complacently. And yet Field was among those who watched the Sydney Tribe more carefully, saw more deeply:

> They bear themselves erect, and address you with confidence, always in good humour, and often with grace. They are not common beggars, although they accept our carnal things in return for fish and oysters, which are almost all we have left them for their support. They are . . . the carriers of news and fish; the gossips of the town; the loungers on the quay. They know everybody; and understand the nature of everybody's business, although they have none of their own—but this . . . They have bowing acquaintances with everybody, and scatter their How-d'ye-do's with an air of friendliness and equality, and with a perfect English accent, undebased by the Massa's and Missies and me-nos of West Indian Slavery.[111]

Bungaree was one of these confident, straight-walking people. Strangers could see he was a person of authority by the way he carried himself.[112] When he said to them, 'This is my shore', he was not talking about ancestral lands, but this new-made country near Sydney, where Aboriginal people had woven themselves into the urban fabric. Most had left their traditional country, either dispossessed and driven off by settlers, or drawn by the sea or the opportunities and pleasures of the town. They were peoples dealing with some of the most fundamental changes humans can undergo. Their lands had been invaded by people who were utterly alien to them, their populations decimated by smallpox, their ways of understanding the world and the way humans ought to live in it challenged to the core. They had learned to eat bread and maize, to savour tobacco and alcohol. The balance between men and women appears to have shifted, for men now manned the European-style fishing boats, and fished from them, though women still lit fires and cooked in them. And men had created places on land, within the town, for rituals and contests. Anthropologist Tony Swain believes Aboriginal people were also constructing new ontologies which resulted in the emergence of sky-heroes, new concepts of laws and morality, and the belief that salvation and power lay in the heavens.[113]

It is scarcely possible to imagine more serious challenges to ways of being, nor more dynamic and resilient responses.

And yet most observers, including Barron Field, concluded that the Aboriginal people of Sydney had not changed at all, that they were in fact unchangeable. They were 'firmly anchored to their customs, faithful to their traditions', wrote Bougainville, 'they have remained absolutely the same since the Europeans set foot here'.[114] Most used the yardstick of 'civilisation' to gauge the Aboriginal people's 'progress' (or 'lack' of it), and the key indicators were of course the same ones Phillip had hoped would seduce and civilise them: clothing, food, housing. 'Usefulness' to white society through menial labour, decorous public behaviour, speaking English and holding Christian beliefs were also markers of advancement from the savage state. The Europeans also expected them to be *grateful* for the gifts of food, clothing and kindness. They never were.[115]

Most distressing initially, particularly to the French visitors, was that Aboriginal people refused to wear clothes. Like Margaret Catchpole, the gentlemen simply did not know where to look. John Grant, gentleman convict, was discombobulated: 'I met a native today—a tall, black stark naked Man! By Job, it startled me at first, for the fellow turned a corner suddenly near to me, in the town.' Years later French visitor René Lesson spluttered, 'The stubbornness of this race in rejecting even the narrow loincloth would deeply astonish the moralist'. They could plainly see proper modes of dress and modesty all around them, and yet it had no impact on them whatsoever! It was the Europeans in town who had to adjust instead: 'one soon gets accustomed to looking at them, and does so without disgust', wrote the Russian Captain Bellingshausen mildly in 1820 of Aboriginal people who worked naked. While some of the men wore hats and jackets, 'they especially hate clothes for the lower part of the body', which was unfortunate for the Europeans, since that was the part that bothered them. French artist Alphonse Pellion's beautiful 1819 watercolour 'Tara et Peroa' shows this precisely: the two men from the Nepean wear a torn jacket, and a blue tailcoat and undershirt respectively—and nothing else. When it was cold, some of the women wore the striped blankets issued by the Commissariat—they cut a hole in the middle and wore them 'mantle style'.[116]

By the late 1820s those who came in to Sydney were apparently ordered to wear clothes, but they still made a nonsense of the whole business by putting on whatever they had acquired every which way:

> In the same group we . . . see a man with only a pair of trowsers, another with a shirt, another with a jacket . . . or a female wearing a full-bodied gown with flounces; another wearing only a skirt with a frilled cap stuck on her hair obliquely; another has perhaps a red or yellow jacket over a skirt; everyone in short wearing what the humour of individuals has bestowed, no matter how motley or fantastic.[117]

Clearly the purpose of wearing clothes had not been internalised, let alone ideas about fashion and appropriateness. 'They are the only savages in the world', sighed Judge Field, 'who cannot feel or "know they are naked" '. Even after dress rules were introduced, clothes were shucked off as soon as possible. An 1829 engraving shows a group of people camped in a paddock outside Macquarie's gothick tollgates to the south of Sydney. Apart from Bungaree, resplendent in his feathered hat, jacket and tattered pants, and one person with a blanket, they are naked.[118]

J. Carmichael, 'Sydney from the Parramatta Road', showing Aboriginal people camped on the edge of town near the Macquarie tollgates in 1829. (National Library of Australia)

European-style housing had little appeal for Aboriginal people either, for 'they cannot bear to be confined to a hut or tent', and 'only breathe at ease under the vault of the sky'. Some, as we have seen, lodged in 'the houses of gentlemen', probably in kitchens and outhouses. But for the main part, instead of settling permanently in houses, they returned each night to campsites in the bushland surrounding the town. Curious night-time voyeurs found families asleep, cuddled together around fires, or sheltered in bark-and-bough gunyahs, exactly as they had done before the invasion. Children and youths who lived with families and patrons in houses usually returned to their families and outdoor life once they reached their mid to late teens. In the eyes of Europeans this was more evidence of Aboriginal intractability, for even after years of kindness and inculcation, children were not Europeanised.[119]

The remarkable, strange and paradoxical achievement of the first generations of urban Aboriginal people is that they 'failed' in most of these signs of 'civilisation'—or succeeded remarkably in maintaining their own customs, depending on your perspective. Yet they had combined this with such vast physical and philosophical adjustments. Within dynamism and adaptation, there was this stable core, a sense of rightness in one's skin, and complete indifference to appeals for improvement, to shame and guilt. They made some concessions to respectable European ways but these were superficial, polite gestures and not internalised. The Europeans were not fooled by the clothing so easily slipped on and off as they moved between the town and the bush. They wanted more than that; they wanted nothing less than complete transformation.

As we have seen, Phillip and Collins had hoped that the Eora would be integrated into the town and the colonising project, through simple commercial ventures like selling fish, and by being 'useful' to the Europeans in performing menial labour. Early attempts to make them 'useful' were not at all encouraging: Coleby and Ballooderry not only refused to fetch wood or draw water for the exploratory party marching to the Hawkesbury in April 1791, they also declined to carry their own packs, and skipped along, laughing and joking, while some unfortunate soldiers staggered and tripped under double loads.[120]

But by 1793 a few were reconciled to such tasks: they brought in firewood to barter with the townsfolk, and carted water from the tanks on the stream.

What they demanded in return was tobacco and alcohol, though food and old clothes were also common payments.[121] Transactions and agreements were made on a personal, reciprocal basis. Visitors often wanted artefacts and botanical and geological specimens, and Aboriginal people obliged—for a price. (They had already been making 'second-rate' artefacts especially for the 'tourist trade' for some years!) Surgeon Joseph Arnold wrote smugly in 1810:

> We can only get things cheap from the savages, who bring cord, shells, etc and are glad to take old cloathes, biscuits or wine for them. We often take one or two of these fellows into the woods and make them carry our things, for they will do anything for rum.[122]

Aboriginal people sometimes worked for publicans, and by the late 1810s they were claiming the empty spirit barrels, filling them with hot water to make 'bull', which they then shared together. (*Bool* was the word for a sweet drink made of flower nectar and water.) Slightly rum-tinged water was unlikely to make anyone drunk, yet derogatory caricatures of Aboriginal people drinking 'bull', staggering drunkenly and fighting became a common trope for artists, portraying their allegedly degraded condition and incompatibility with urban life.[123]

It is likely that fishing provided far more income and goods than washing out casks, however, just as it would in coastal areas for decades. Ballooderry's early attempt to sell fish at Parramatta ended in disaster when a gang of convicts destroyed his canoe and he was outlawed by Phillip for spearing another convict as payback.[124] But in later years, Aboriginal people found a ready market for fresh fish and oysters among the townsfolk in Sydney. By the 1810s and 1820s, women still paddled bark nowie in the harbour, but men had also mastered European fishing boats. Boat-owners made deals with them whereby they took the boats out each day in return for a portion of the catch. The rest they exchanged for 'drink and tobacco', 'old clothes, bread and rum'. It seems that nobody was paid in money, except those who went sailing on the ships, and even their lays were sometimes not paid to them. Visitors watched these 'carriers of news and fish', wood and water, the obliging procurers of specimens and artefacts, the girls living with families as servants, the black men and women cleaning glasses in pubs, or helping out 'people who have helped them' by chopping wood and drawing water with the servants. But they were not sober, steady, modestly clothed, industrious workers, and they were black: therefore they were judged lazy, indolent and 'want nothing to do with any sort of heavy work'.[125]

Fish continued as their major source of food well into the 1820s, despite the acquired taste for bread and maize. It was still caught in largely traditional ways, still cooked entrails and all over a fire, scales flicked off and eaten immediately. In the early 1800s, Holt recalled that when he was stationed on Cox's property, Brush Farm, near Eastwood, in the early 1800s, the women went to get *mogra* or fish. The Russian visitors of 1820 noted that after the north shore Aboriginal people visited their camp at Kirribilli, 'the women went to fish, while the men sat making fishing implements', probably fish-gigs, 'which they smoothed down with pieces of bottle glass'. Bellingshausen wrote that mothers still taught their daughters 'to twist fishing lines and how to harpoon fish'—this last very likely a mistaken observation. He echoed the early officers' condemnation of women's fishing as 'slavery', for 'the poor women have to sit all day in little craft and

John Lewin's 1808 sketch of an 'Australian and his wife', watching the waters together from the rocks. (National Library of Australia)

fish while their menfolk wander about or sleep'. When Bellingshausen collected artefacts, though, they were men's things: 'a pronged fishing spear, a wooden spear and a small wooden shield'.[126]

This new generation of observers was not interested in women's fishing skills and implements in the way the early officers had been. Their nowies might still appear in scenes of the harbour, but there were no more portraits of them paddling and fishing, babies in their laps, or with burra and fishing lines hung about their necks. Newcomers simply assumed men were and had always been the chief food-gatherers, that women were reduced to mere fishing because the Europeans had appropriated their hunting grounds, and 'destroyed the greater part of the game that served for food for these wandering tribes'. In fact kangaroos and wallabies had not been a major part of the coastal diet, but, as James Urry convincingly argues, Aboriginal men's hunting was by this time seen, admired and depicted as 'savage sports', a rough equivalent of the venerable traditions of English hunting and shooting. Even if women's fishing was recognised, it was now considered to reflect very poorly on their men. 'The natives of the interior exhibit a much stronger power of ingenuity than the tribes of the seacoast', opined a *Sydney Gazette* correspondent in 1808, 'as the latter depend more upon the dexterity of their women in their mode of fishing than on any exertion of their own'.[127] By at least the 1820s, women's skills and role as food-suppliers had been eclipsed, even as their fishing and boating continued.

We can see this in art painted in the colony, or at a distance. It was already clear in William Westall's 1804 painting 'Port Jackson, Sydney', evidently an amalgam of earlier sketches and picturesque invention. An imaginary tableau, set in the bush high above the waters, shows an Aboriginal man, fish-gig over his shoulder and stone hatchet slung in his belt, carrying a large fish home to his family. His wife sits passively in front of the (Tasmanian-style) gunyah with the children, awaiting her husband and provider. In John Heaviside Clark's series *Field Sports . . . of the native inhabitants of New South Wales* (1813), men's hunting and fishing is glorified as exciting, manly and noble. (Clark had 'undoubtedly never seen an Aboriginal at first hand' and the kangaroos look suspiciously like foxes.) Sent to the penal settlement at Newcastle, the convict artist Joseph Lycett produced a series of pictures of the 'traditional' activities of the Awabakal of the

Joseph Lycett's watercolour of Aboriginal people fishing by torchlight on Lake Macquarie (probably Kooroora Bay) and cooking fish on campfires. (National Library of Australia)

region—hunting, fishing, contests and corroborees. In all of them men spear, fight, parry and dance, while women sit on the sidelines watching. Even in his beautiful moonlit study of fishing by torchlight at night, men spear the fish from the canoes while women cook them on the shoreline.[128]

What became of this true story of women, water, fish and fishing? When did Aboriginal woman stop launching their nowie to skim these waters? I don't know the answer—towards the late 1820s the nowies no longer appear in paintings of the harbour. But this may be put down to painterly preference, for there are echoes of their fishing in other pictures and artefacts. Augustus Earle's well-known painting of Aboriginal people in Sydney shows two men drinking from a wooden bucket, but the women are not drinking, and one of them carries a large fish. 'Queen' Cora Gooseberry, the wife of Bungaree, who lived in Sydney until her death in 1854, owned two brass breastplates. Both have fish engraved in their corners.

Another, rather more startling image of Aboriginal men and women appears inside an elegant punchbowl, made in China before 1820 for an unknown person, perhaps as a memento of Sydney.[129] Edged with gorgeous, gilded Chinese floral designs, the outside of the bowl depicts the rising town in all its glory: it is a marvellously intricate topographical view swinging from Government House in the east right round the cove to Dawes Point, taking in the bustling Rocks, the windmills and flags, the ships and nowie. Inside the bowl, though, is a picture of a group of Aboriginal people. A woman holds a child, three warriors fight with spears, hatchets and shield, and, right in the centre, a man is about to beat a cowering woman with a club.

It is bizarre to think that this violent vignette embellished fine and fashionable china, meant for elegant dinners and gatherings. Perhaps it relates to the same tradition which made ugly, degrading pictures of Aboriginal people amusing and popular—although the figures here are not caricatures. Perhaps it's a play on the function of the bowl—holding alcohol. But the punchbowl, with its double depictions, the inside and the outside, does convey a fundamental tension in race relations in Sydney in the 1810s—that between the older tolerance and sympathy for urban Aboriginal people on one hand, and new, urgent, deeply felt ambitions for an elegant, refined town on the other.

Aboriginal Sydney was perhaps best known for the great public contests and fights which continued from the 1790s throughout the 1800s to the 1820s. David Collins at first offered this as a victory for interracial tolerance and understanding, for 'when they assembled to dance or to fight before our houses we never dispersed but freely attended their meetings'. He added that this was 'agreeable and useful' to them, because the surgeons present would then tend to the wounded, who displayed 'great bravery and firmness [as] they bore the knife and the probe'. Well-known warriors also had white friends who tended them when they were wounded and sometimes even intervened to rescue them.[130]

Most often used, and most well known, was the contest ground 'near the Brickfields': a flat, open space surrounded by bushland (the Brickfields was also the site of prize-fights and cockfights). Where was this significant site? The location, 'the Brickfields', the small collection of early houses which stood around today's Haymarket, is misleading, since the colonists called everything to the south of the town 'the Brickfields'. More specific directions were given by René Lesson: 'in a field between *la route de Botany-bay et Brich-Field*'), that is, not at the Brickfields, but *between* them and the old South Head Road, which branched to Botany Bay. It was a level, open area still surrounded by bushland in the early 1820s. The Aboriginal sailor Mahroot gave another clue in the 1840s. Asked about the old contests, he replied, 'They used to turn out all . . . about the race course'. The great contest ground was located at the southern end of what became Hyde Park, near Liverpool Street, once the common and the racecourse. Today this is the site of the Sydney War Memorial.[131]

Fighting Eora men also claimed significant 'white' spaces in the centre of the town, holding contests and battles near the new bridge over the Tank Stream in 1804 and outside the military barracks in 1797, and when they were rebuilt in 1809. Further away, fights were held from at least 1795 at Pannerong (meaning blood), later called Rose Bay, and also on Farm Cove and at Botany Bay.[132]

Fights held at the Brickfields ground could continue over three evenings, and the town was 'amused by it', for 'it appeared to afford much diversion . . . they were constantly well-attended by all descriptions of people notwithstanding the risk they ran of being wounded by a random spear'. The contests had become part of the round of events, the rough and violent pleasures of the preindustrial town. And they were the means by which more Aboriginal people came into contact with Europeans, and Sydney, for contests attracted 'prodigious numbers' of people from increasingly distant places. By 1795 they came from 'the woods' and 'a great distance inland'; 25 years later people travelled from as far as the Illawarra in the south and the Hunter Valley in the north. They converged on the Brickfields site to mingle with the newly formed local 'tribes' as well as the white townsfolk.[133]

The British watched men they knew well stand trial by spear. Cammeragal man Carradah ('Midger Bool', the damelian (namesake) of Mr Ball, commander of the *Supply*) dodged and parried skilfully over two nights in December 1793. Then the fighting became general, 'men women and children mingling in it, giving and receiving many wounds, before night put an end to their warfare'. Carradah was speared in the hand, but this did not satisfy his enemies. Eventually he was murdered in his sleep 'by people inimical to his tribe'. His friends assured the whites that his killers would be discovered at his funeral, and then the whole cycle would start again.[134]

By now the white townsfolk grasped the underlying laws of payback, and blood for blood. Collins was still puzzled as to how people who 'were friends and allies' could fight 'with all the ardour of the bitterest enemies' and then afterwards, when things were settled, declare that 'one another were good and brave and their friends'. Men who had speared and bashed one another would help each other back to town, blood still flowing from broken heads.[135] As he recorded the grim catalogue of violence, injuries and midnight murders over the years, Collins' tolerance began to fade. Payback did not spare women, children or old people: Warraweer Wogul Mi was murdered in 1798 and another woman, who had grown up in the town, was beaten to death by her husband and Coleby. The girl Gonangulye, 'much beloved in the town', was beaten and stabbed to death after her relative Wattewal killed a man named Yelloway. Her killer was a woman, Yelloway's widow, Noorooing. This death seems to have settled the matter, presumably because a female child was not important enough to be avenged. Another girl-child of six or seven brought in from the Hawkesbury was taken by local Aboriginal people to the Domain, speared and had 'both her arms cut off'. The British buried her sadly at their burial ground.[136]

Eventually, as Clendinnen tells us, Collins decided that the whole cross-cultural experiment had been a mistake. The Aboriginal people were 'monsters of cruelty, devoid of reason, guided by the worst passions'. It would have been better 'to keep them at a distance and in fear' from the outset. But by the turn of the century, Collins had also begun to romanticise their lives before 1788 as innocent, simple and happy. Referring to a romantic engraving showing people dancing and sitting around a fire by moonlight at the harbour's edge, he wrote with sorrow and wistfulness:

It were to be wished, that they never had been seen in any other state than that which the subjoined view of them presents, in the happy and peaceable exercise of their freedom and amusements . . .[137]

Did Collins really wish that the great clock of history could be rewound, to return to the land 'before time'? He of all people knew that it bore little resemblance to the imagined world of the noble savage, that 'phoenix of the European imagination'. Perhaps he was haunted by memories of the earliest days, of watching people picnicking, and fishing, and gathered about fires to dance, or eat and talk or sleep; and those first days of dancing together on the sand.[138]

In fact, Aboriginal people's 'freedoms and amusements'—and the exercise of their Law—*were* respected, or at least tolerated, in the towns. As Samuel Smith wrote succinctly in 1802: 'It is not allowed to meddle with their affairs as they settle their own affairs in a Very Severe Manner by Spears'. Margaret Catchpole told Dr Stebbens in the same year: 'They very often have a grand fight with themselves 20 and 30 altogether and we pray to be spared, some of them are killed—there is nothing said to them for killing one another'. When excited spectators interrupted proceedings 'by crowding in too close' during a battle outside the military barracks in 1805, it was the 'Officers and Gentlemen' who intervened, ordering the crowds back, for 'no interruption should be offered to their customs'.[139]

At the same time, Sydney's Aboriginal people were excluded from British justice. Although they were in theory British citizens, protected by British laws, in practice they had no such protection, and their legal status remained ambiguous for decades. They could not give evidence in British courts because they were not considered capable of taking the Christian oath, nor of understanding the proceedings.[140] Among themselves, then, they upheld their own Law, even when they occupied 'white' space. The two systems operated concurrently: payback killings were not challenged in a British court of law until 1829 and were not finally judged illegal in British terms until 1836.[141] People who died or were injured had to be avenged, and for the main part victims, often relatives of the perpetrators, accepted their fate. Again, we don't know whether this confronting level of bloodshed and murder was customary or typical, or whether it had spiralled in the wake of dislocation, disease and hunger, and been exacerbated by the disproportionate number of men and the adoption of alcohol.[142]

The contests and fights continued, but the reports were increasingly framed in terms of savagery. From 1803 George Howe at the *Gazette* reported every gory detail (many of the readers were, after all, avid spectators) and described their 'unconquerable attachment to barbarous usages and utter dislike to civilised customs'.[143] The familiar names fought and fell in the pages of the *Gazette*— Coleby, Bennelong, Nanbarry, Caruey, Blewit, Wilamanan (another sailor, who took his name from the ship *William and Ann*), Old White, Old Collins (Gnunga

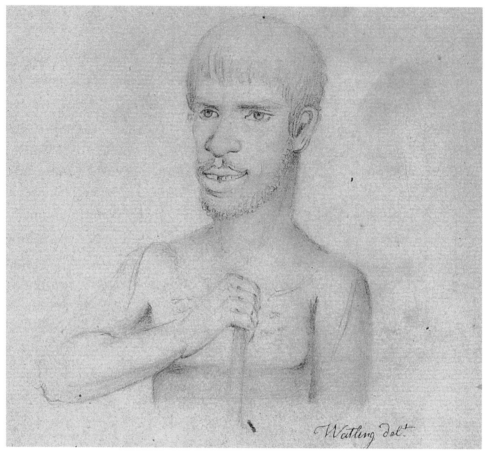

Caruey, a young warrior initiated at Wogganmagully/Farm Cove in 1795, killed in a contest and buried at the Brickfields contest ground in 1805. (Natural History Museum)

Gnunga) and his brother Old Phillip (all of whom must have been early name-sakes of long-departed First Fleet officers). Occasionally Howe tartly pointed out that the European spectators were not much more 'enlightened' than the combatants, for if nobody was slain or fell in the fights, it was 'no trifling disappointment of some of the more "civilised" observers'.[144] On one occasion, the fighting was followed by 'a contest for the wife of one of the deceased'. The men were pulling the poor woman from one another, 'her arms almost dragged from their sockets', when she was suddenly snatched and 'borne in triumph from the field' by an Irish tailor.[145] If there is an emblematic moment in the competition and violence between black and white men over Aboriginal women in early Sydney, this must be it.

Governor and Mrs Macquarie were genuinely interested in 'civilising the natives', and, like Phillip, they welcomed Aboriginal 'chiefs' into Government House. But the long-held tradition of non-intervention in 'their affairs' must have become increasingly irksome. How could Sydney emerge as the elegant, progressive and virtuous colonial city they envisaged if visitors were confronted with naked savages spearing and clubbing one another in the public streets? Worse, the foreign visitors were clearly all preparing manuscripts for publication. Macquarie's establishment of Hyde Park and the racecourse there may have been an attempt to discourage or supplant the big contests, and to dislodge them from their Brickfields grounds. If so, it didn't work. Finally, in his 1816 proclamation, Macquarie banned payback and contests altogether, and the practice of Aboriginal Law in the process:

> The practice of assembling in large Bodies armed, fighting and attacking on Plea of inflicting Punishment on Transgressors of their Customs and Manners, at or near Sydney and other principal Towns and Settlements . . . wholly abolished as a barbarous Custom, repugnant to British laws, strongly militates against the civilisation of the natives.

Men and women avenging friends and relatives would now be classed as disturbers of the peace. Aboriginal people everywhere were 'enjoined and commended to discontinue this barbarous practice' not only in the settlements but also in their 'wild and remote places of resort'.[146]

And so the *Gazette* ceased reporting on contests and fights. But this did not mean the orders were obeyed; nor that we have yet reached an 'ending'. Visitors still included accounts of contests in their itineraries. French artist Jacques Arago, enchanted by Sydney's magnificence and tasteful elegance, and apparently unaware of the ban, was outraged by the contests:

> What can be the aim of the English in permitting, and even encouraging and provoking these hideous struggles? . . . do they wish . . . to let this race annihilate itself? . . . does not humanity also have its duties, and should such scenes be allowed in the midst of a beautiful city, flourishing and well-policed?[147]

Cultured and high-minded visitors no doubt confronted the self-conscious Macquaries with such uncomfortable questions—the contradiction of the punchbowl. What place could such people have in Sydney? They were surely the negation of urbanity, restraint, beauty and elegance, everything the rising town promised, everything the vice-regal couple had worked so hard for, their grand obsession. As in other emerging cities on other continents, indigenous people were 'made scapegoats for urban disorder'.[148]

But these were sojourners; and even the Macquaries sailed away. Many long-time Sydney people knew Aboriginal people by name, were accustomed to their nakedness and motley clothing, their feuds and politics. They still provided food and fish-hooks, clothes and boats, continued to exploit them as workers and listened to the news they carried. And they upheld the Sydney tradition of non-interference in Aboriginal business, for 'within law, English administrators do not harass them'. It might also be interpreted as indifference, of course—the same indifference displayed after the murder of Nanny Cabbage. There was no outrage, no grieving for her, in the way there had been for earlier victims of payback. Complacent predictions of the disappearance of the race by their own hands were already creeping into European observations.[149]

In 1824, two years after the Macquaries had left, French visitors Dumont d'Urville and René Lesson were cordially invited by Bungaree to attend 'a great gathering' of the tribes at the old Brickfields ground. The visitors saw a great concourse of people from Parramatta, Kissing Point, Sydney, Liverpool, Windsor, Emu Plains, Broken Bay, Five Islands (Illawarra), Botany Bay and the Hunter River. Each group was painted in distinctive designs, red and white, and each was headed by a 'Chief'. The guilty stood trial by spear and club and suffered according to their crimes, the wounded were tended by their friends, there was 'general fighting . . . with admirable order and precision', women ran through the ranks 'to stir up the men'. A young man, identified as a killer in the dream of a chief, stood bravely against a hail of spears. The tribes had been re-formed. The Law was upheld.[150]

Armed with spear, shield and club the warrior Norougalderri is ready for the contest. (Nicolas Martin Petit, 'Norougalderri s'avancant pour combattre', 1802, Mitchell Library, State Library of New South Wales)

Chapter 13

WAR ON THE CUMBERLAND PLAIN

INTIMATE ENEMIES

In the winter of 1805 Elizabeth Chambers, settler of the lower Hawkesbury, saw smoke rising from her house. She raced inside, into the blaze, to snatch her baby son from the flames. Two convict servants came running to help, but the family's dwelling, shed, clothing and crops went up in smoke. The *Gazette* reported that the 'natives' were responsible. They were said to have waited until Elizabeth's husband, ex–New South Wales Corps soldier Henry Lamb, left, then climbed the ridge of rock above the farm and showered it with 'firebrands' using lighted 'montang' (*mutting*) or fishing spears.

The newly destitute Lamb family—parents, three infants and a teenage girl—took refuge with their neighbours, the Youlers, on their 30 acres further up Sackville Reach. But the warriors struck again, setting this house on fire too. The hapless family then moved again, to Thomas Chaseling's farm next door. The Chaseling farm would have been burnt to the ground as well, except that the perpetrator was caught in the act: it was an Aboriginal girl of about thirteen, about to torch the dwelling with a firebrand. She said she had set the Lamb family's house alight, too. But this girl was no stranger from the bush: she had been adopted by the Lamb family when an infant, had grown up in their household with their own children. The *Gazette* claimed she had no knowledge of 'the dialect [or] the manners of her kindred', though she had been seen talking to a young Aboriginal man shortly before. The Lambs had unwittingly carried their would-be assassin with them from farm to farm.[1]

The settlers of the early colonial period called the sustained attacks and raids by Aboriginal people a war. Military historian John Connor argues convincingly that hostilities on the frontiers, from the Hawkesbury–Nepean in the 1790s onwards, were indeed wars: mobilisations to defend territory, the 'use of force to make others do your will'.[2] Violence and bloodshed underpinned the spread of settlers over stolen ground; modern suburbs are built over battlefields. Yet what kind of war is it when the antagonists often know their attackers and their victims by name and face, when they share language and food, houses and beds with them, or even, as in the Lambs' case, when they bring them up from infancy? And what were this girl's motivations? Are the reasons for attack always the same, or do they vary, do they have multiple reasons? What, in other words, is the *history* of this war? We are entering a zone of shifting alliances and complex negotiations, for this was not a 'lineal frontier' with united opponents facing one another 'on either side of neutral ground'.[3] Aboriginal people and settlers in early New South Wales occupied the *same* ground in the hinterlands as well as in the towns: their lives had already become entangled. This social space was a version of what United States historian Richard White calls a 'middle ground', a zone of cultural exchange, negotiation and hybridisation.[4]

The Lambs had been among the second wave of settlers—some ex-soldiers, some ex-convicts, some free—who tried to retake the downriver land around Portland Head. The first batch had settled on the narrow banks on the other side of Sackville Reach in 1796 and been driven back by intense Aboriginal attack. Their isolation and the topography of the narrow river flats, hard up against the steep rocky ridges, made them easy targets. But the Lambs' land on the east bank was less vulnerable. The river flats were broader, and the tree-covered higher ground you can still see there today must have been much further from their riverside house—too far, in fact, for flaming fish-gigs to reach.

While the Chaselings remained and became a well-known Hawkesbury dynasty, the Lambs gave up farming after they lost everything in the fire. But, unlike some of their neighbours, they don't seem to have harboured a hatred of Aboriginal people. In fact they continued to associate with them and these connections spanned important developments in the Aboriginal history of the Sydney region. The *Gazette* reported that they still offered the firebrand-wielding girl 'refuge', though whether she stayed with them is unknown. Henry Lamb later became overseer at a new Aboriginal farming settlement out on the Richmond Road near Blacktown, helping the Aboriginal people granted small allotments by Governor Macquarie. The Lambs lived with the Aboriginal people there until at least 1823. Their son-in-law John Ezzy probably carted lime for building the new Native Institution, a school originally established in Parramatta by Macquarie to 'civilise' and educate Aboriginal children, moved to the 'Blacks' Town', as it was called, in 1822. The Lambs would have known Robert Lock, a convict carpenter assigned to work on the building. Lock later married Maria, one of the institution's first and brightest scholars. She was the daughter of Yellomundy (originally spelt Yallahmiendi), the renowned Hawkesbury warrior and karadji who welcomed Phillip and Tench to his country on their exploration in April 1791. Maria Lock became the matriarch of a vast family, and her descendants now number in their thousands.[5]

'WE CALLED THEM IN THEIR OWN MANNER'

The earliest encounters between Europeans and the inland groups differed dramatically from those with the Eora. Instead of standing on headlands and cliff tops dancing furiously and shouting 'Warra warra!', the inland people avoided them altogether. The first time the officers saw footprints, they were shocked to realise that the interior was occupied, that they were not alone. Then they began to see signs of people everywhere: flaming trees with animal traps at the bottom and notches cut way up the trunk, old canoes, shelters made of bark sheets folded in half, half-chewed bones left by still-warm fires. They wondered over carvings on the rock platforms between Middle Harbour and Pennant Hills, 'representations of themselves in different attitudes, of their canoes, of several sorts of fish and animals'. They ran their fingers through the silky fur of platypus- and possum-skin rugs and noted the curious patterns cut into the underside.[6]

In early July 1789, the boatloads of 40 well-armed Europeans rowing up the twisted reaches of the Hawkesbury and Macdonald rivers came upon a single woman, who fled into the bush, leaving 'two small helpless children' in a gunyah. The children were terrified at the sudden appearance of giants in their hut, looking at everything, touching everything, talking in their strange 'hissing' language. The next day the family was gone. The hatchet and 'trifles' left for them were untouched. Hunter wrote that they 'frequently saw fires' in the woods as they sailed further up the Hawkesbury, and sometimes heard voices. 'We called them in their own manner, repeating the word *Co-wee*.' Eventually, two men responded to the whipping sound of these calls from the water, appearing at the river bank 'with much apparent familiarity and confidence'. The Europeans presented them with a hatchet and a duck, and were given a coil of fishing line in return. From their manner Hunter thought 'they had seen us before', even if the Europeans had not seen them.[7]

It was another ten months, well after the Eora came in to Sydney, before more sustained meetings occurred. The officers' great trek to solve the mystery of whether the two rivers, Hawkesbury and Nepean, were in fact one, included 'our natives' Coleby and Ballooderry. It is clear that the Eora men were also in strange and unfamiliar country, but they nevertheless successfully mediated the meetings with Boorooberongal man Bereewan around present-day Dural, and later, on the Hawkesbury, with Gombeeree, his son Yellomundy (both were renowned karadji or doctors), and his grandson Deeimba. Tench busily noted some similarities and differences: their foods were small animals and wild yams; the men had not lost a front tooth like the Eora. But what struck him most was the fact that these people used different words, yet they 'understood each other perfectly'. The locals related stories about wars and conflicts over women; the coastal men told them of the wonders of Sydney and Rose Hill, those rich sources of food. That night the Europeans and the Aboriginal men slept together round the campfire. The wakeful Tench watched Yellomundy in the firelight, cradling Deeimba in his arms, carefully moving the child before he turned in his sleep.[8]

Nevertheless, the passionate curiosity of the First Fleet officers and others about the Eora was less sustained for the inland peoples, especially beyond Parramatta.[9] While they wrote detailed accounts of Eora cultural mores, rituals and languages, and tried to fathom religious beliefs, gender relations or the meaning of the contests, their interest in the 'woods' tribes, as they called them, was more superficial. There are few written or painted portraits of individuals, fewer accounts of encounters, and very few images of their weapons and tools. The descriptions of their cultures, languages and lifestyles, even the names and countries of the different groups, were far more cursory. We know almost nothing of the women of the inland, apart from some compelling glimpses of them as victims of abduction and punitive raids, but also as mediators in peace talks. Nevertheless they were, once more, often at the centre of frontier struggles. We have few snatches of intimate conversation to learn from, to imagine with. This was partly because most of the inland groups assiduously avoided contact with whites for the first eighteen months, but also as because most of those who wrote those early, more intimate descriptions lived in Sydney, with the Eora, and only visited the distant places on the plain and the rivers sporadically. And I think their fascination and familiarity with the Eora gathered a momentum of its own: they became 'our natives'.

This unevenness had a profound effect on the history of Aboriginal Sydney. It meant that the coastal Eora became in a way the 'default' Sydney people, they dominate the narratives, while the scores of groups and hundreds of people who occupied the inland, even the fiercest warriors and the most digni-fied elders, remain more shadowy or intermittent figures. As Kohen pointed out some years ago, the Aboriginal people of the Cumberland Plain remained archaeologically invisible right up to the late 1970s because the existence of open sites of scattered stone artefacts marking the places where people camped and made tools was 'not even recognised'.[10] Since then, the patient and extensive work of historians and archaeologists in reconstituting the Aboriginal history of western Sydney has greatly redressed this imbalance. Yet we have scarcely any images of the inland peoples, and there are very few individuals we can 'know' in the way we 'know' Bennelong, for example—to the extent that we can know him. The spread of smallpox in 1789 and thereafter meant that some groups evidently disappeared entirely before the Europeans could even learn their names. What evidence we have suggests a similar disproportion in numbers of men and women as on the coast, similar competition for women, and reports of violent relations, so women were probably hit harder and more fatally by the epidemic here too.[11]

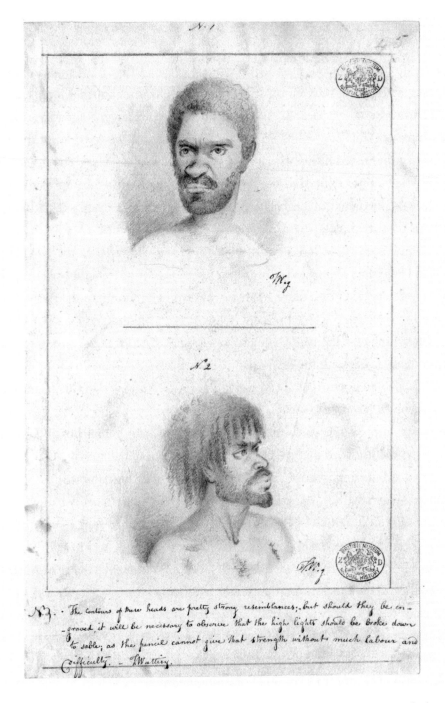

Two rare early portraits of 'Woods people'. Thomas Watling, 'Wear-ung commonly known by the name of Mr Long' and 'Karra-da who exchanged names with Captain Ball'. (Natural History Museum)

'THE NATIVES ARE OBLIGED TO LEAVE THAT PART OF THE COUNTRY': PARRAMATTA, 1788–91

Setting up a 'beachhead' port in Warrane was one thing. Putting the plan for subsistence farming into action was quite another. It meant that large tracts of land had to be taken, cleared, sown and defended. Strategies for race relations at Parramatta thus contrasted strikingly with those on the coast: once more the limits of enlightened humanism and 'soft colonisation' are clear. Here there were no heartfelt hopes expressed of 'living in amity', no gifts laid upon the sand, no drawn-out dance of negotiation and diplomacy, no desperate kidnapping raids to take men as envoys, 'no consultation or treaty and no talk of sharing and compensation'.[12] The establishment of the public farm at the head of the river in November 1788 was undisguised invasion, complete with well-organised military defences. Phillip first had an earthen-walled redoubt built above the flats where the river curved in a crescent below Rose Hill, and posted a detachment of soldiers to guard the new farm and its workers. The local Burramattagal were immediately faced with the redcoats and muskets they had no doubt heard about from the people downriver. There were no reported attacks on this farm. As the settlement grew with the success of the grain crops, 'it was no longer possible for the *Burramatta* people to camp on the Crescent . . . no longer possible to catch eels, fish, tortoises and platypus about the tidal limits'.[13]

The girl Boorong, who recovered from smallpox and came to live with the white people in Sydney, was from Burramatta. She and her family had witnessed the invasion first hand and then suffered the ravages of the smallpox epidemic. In October 1790, her father, Maugaron, came to Sydney to protest the loss of his people's lands to the governor, the first recorded formal protest in Australia. 'Indeed, if this man's information could be depended upon', wrote Phillip, 'the natives were very angry at so many people being sent to Rose Hill'. He acknowledged their dispossession quite frankly: 'Certain it is that wherever our colonists fix themselves, the natives are obliged to leave that part of the country'. But instead of attempts at compromise or amelioration one might expect from a governor so committed to peaceful relations, Phillip simply 'reinforced the detachment at that post'.[14] The policy of amity and kindness did not include sharing land with Aboriginal people, or protecting their food sources.

As we have seen, and as John Connor points out, the settlement at Sydney did not at first take much landspace from the Eora—while the foodstuffs lasted they could continue traditional food-gathering. Casualties were shocking but relatively small in number. The Eora avoided the Camp in this boundary country and the British for the main part felt secure because, as Phillip put it, 'they are perfectly sensible of the great superiority of our firearms'.[15] But on the plain, Phillip's early farms were clustered on river banks and on the pockets of fertile land and the chains of ponds, the same lands and waters Aboriginal people depended upon for sustenance. Maugaron's children—Boorong, Ballooderry, Yerranibe Goruey and Warraweer Wogul Mi—all went to live in Sydney with the white people. Two, possibly three of these children died young of disease or violence. Meanwhile Maugaron and his second wife Tadyera were forced from Parramatta. They moved east to Kissing Point, earlier the country of the Wallemedagal, now perhaps deserted because of smallpox. They named their newborn son Bidgee Bidgee for the river flats where they settled. It was here that Bennelong came to live with Boorong some years after his return from England, and where his own son was born.[16] But moving onto the lands of other people was not always possible, and would ignite more wars between different bands. Clan rivalries and survival strategies, later exploited ruthlessly by governors and settlers, would also shape the complex war that raged on the Cumberland Plain for the next 25 years.[17]

THE WHEEL OF COLONISATION

Collins concluded his first narrative in September 1796 with the happy news that 'after many untoward circumstances, and a considerable lapse of time, that friendly intercourse with the natives, which had been so earnestly desired, was at length established'.[18] Yet at precisely that time, settlers and Aboriginal people were at war, torturing, killing and mangling one another out on the Hawkes-bury. This strange phenomenon—peace and war simultaneously, in different places—would mark the expansion of the invaders across the continent. 'Peace' was always contingent on place rather than time, and, as we shall see, 'war' could be localised to a handful of farms on a single river reach.

Anthropologist Deborah Bird Rose, writing of the northern Australian frontier, has a marvellous—and suitably awesome—metaphor for the process by which Aboriginal country, long known, occupied and managed, was rendered 'empty', 'timeless' and 'wild' by colonisation. 'I suggest we imagine it', she writes, 'as a rolling Year Zero that is carried across the land cutting an ontological swathe between "timeless" land and "historicised" land'. We might think of this great wheel of colonisation, 'this moment of transfiguration', in terms of frontier violence too: rolling relentlessly into 'new' country, its heavy freight of dispossession, abduction and loss of food sources setting off new cycles of bloody attacks, which in turn triggered 'rituals of terror' from the Europeans. In one newly taken area after another, Aboriginal people disputed and disrupted this new version of time, place and ownership; they challenged the Europeans' conviction that colonisation was both inevitable and justified by larger historical processes.[19] But there was always that interwoven counter-theme: the one recorded only in fleeting glimpses, as if in the corner of our eyes—that 'middle ground', the world of relations and negotiations between settlers and Aboriginal people, of words, concepts and practices which crossed over, were grasped, of cultures which overlapped and sometimes ran together on common ground.

MAIZE WARS: PROSPECT AND TOONGABBIE, 1791–94

Phillip's instructions for laying out the small farms specified that he was to leave areas of crown land between each one. It appears to have been another strategy of social/spatial control—the convict settlers would form individual, isolated cells, each working their patch and discouraged from combination. But Phillip knew the threat of Aboriginal attack was real, and realised that his settlers would have to come together 'for mutual support' if they were to survive. So he soon abandoned the official plan, placed the farms next to one another and concentrated on clearing them as quickly as possible.[20]

Phillip also armed the ex-convict settlers. Muskets and ammunition were distributed among them in 1790, specifically for 'protection against the natives', although as Collins crossly noted, they were 'made a very different use of', and were (unsuccessfully) recalled. Collins later said settlers used them for hunting and 'committing depredations' and by 1796, Hunter was requesting more guns. The first had long vanished 'into the hands of worthless characters'.[21] We know the settlers at Prospect (its Aboriginal name was *Murrong*, meaning emu) were armed by mid-1791. No sooner had one of them almost finished his hut than he saw what looked like an army of black people materialise from the bush. They may have been travelling together in familiar country, they may have been curious, or they may have been planning to attack. The settler did not wait to find out— he fired off the musket in a panic. They responded by burning down his hut. Hearing the crack of the shot, a neighbour came running and fired his musket right into them. They ran off into the bush. When the news got to Parramatta, a party of soldiers marched out to Prospect and 'seeing about fifty, obliged them to disperse'. This may have been the same group of Aboriginal people, or it may not. After this incident, Phillip posted an officer and three soldiers at every new settlement, with orders to stay there until the land had been cleared 'so that the natives would find no shelter'.[22]

This early incident reveals some key factors of the coming war. The 'bush' was the retreat of Aboriginal people and therefore bushland became dangerous and 'hostile' to white settlers, especially those at the farthest boundaries. The use of fire as a weapon was new. Coastal Eora warriors had picked off enemies and wrongdoers with spears and clubs, but Phillip reported that they never set fire to corn. The inland peoples immediately torched the buildings and crops of the invaders with their firesticks. Meanwhile the settlers' instant resort to musket fire was common; guns remained the backbone of the colonial project. The reliance on the military to back them up continued too: as John Connor writes, 'mostly settlers expected colonial garrisons to help them'.[23] Military reprisal raids would become another pattern in this war, with severe and tragic results.

While the soldiers guarded the farms in that first year there were no further reports of attacks. Most likely the various bands and clans were considering and talking about how to respond to the invaders, and how to maintain and impose the Law. By May 1792, and probably well before, a new tactic emerged: the maize raids. The crop most of the poorer farmers favoured was also the most portable, and most easily eaten and stored. The ripening of the maize in autumn each year marked 'a prelude to barbarity', new cycles of hostilities as groups of women, men and children 'drew together round the settlers' farms and round the public grounds' and carried off the cobs in nets and blankets. The maize raids combined attack and resistance with food-gathering—and the way the

Aboriginal bands did it suggests they regarded the produce of their country as rightfully theirs, just as the Eora had come forward to claim their fish from the nets. Ironically, stockpiles of settler-grown maize at the campsites also allowed more constant attacks and raids, because people were freed from the everyday necessity of gathering food. Maize nourished the earliest raids and attacks, just as flour and wheat would in later decades.[24]

By 1792, too, the settlers knew they were subject to Aboriginal payback laws. A white man saw a raiding party emerge from a hut, dressed in clothes and carrying nets full of corn. He shot at them. In the blind blast and their panicked retreat, he wasn't sure if anyone had been hit, but when a convict well-sinker was killed on the road to Prospect soon after, they knew it was payback. They found him with 30 spear wounds in his body and his teeth knocked out.[25] For settlers the time between these killings must have been unnerving. What was it like knowing sooner or later someone would pay, an eye for an eye? They knew payback had no time limits. Was horror and hatred laced through with relief when the well-sinker's body was found? To know that the thing was at least over with?

This attack on the road also marked a new stage in hostilities: if redcoats and guns guarded farms and settlements, people moving about on foot along the tracks between them were vulnerable, and unarmed convicts most of all. Throughout 1793 and early 1794, men and women were attacked, wounded and robbed on the roads to Prospect and Toongabbie in particular. They appear to have started travelling in groups for protection by the end of 1793, but the attacks continued. Small armed parties had been sent in pursuit to 'spray them with shot' but were reportedly 'careful not to take a life'.[26]

This litany of reported attacks eclipses other cross-cultural contacts and emerging relationships which must have occurred, just as they did in Sydney. On his Tipperary farm near Parramatta, Irishman Lieutenant Cummings was learning local Aboriginal languages from people who were still camped there, listening with quickening interest to stories they told about a herd of wild cattle somewhere to the south.[27] Significantly, one report claimed the attack-ers of a group of settlers on the road to Toongabbie were 'strangers who seldom come among us'. This suggests local Aboriginal people *were* known, that they had 'come among' them. And they were sure those who assaulted and robbed women walking to their Prospect farms had 'sometimes come to Sydney'.[28] (One wonders whether these attacks were payback for attacks on Aboriginal women.) The frontier was porous, the 'enemy' was familiar, and moved amongst them. It was already becoming necessary to find ways of categorising them, twinning words like 'hostile' and 'friendly', 'strangers' and 'known'.

By April 1794 the maize raids were so frequent and extensive that armed watchmen were posted to guard the ripening green-and-gold fields at the Toongabbie Farm. One group of raiders was so persistent, they returned immediately after being 'driven off' and continued gathering. The incensed watchmen, as they reported later, 'pursued them for several miles', where they said the two sides fought and three warriors were killed. Back in Sydney the watchmen boasted of the glories of this 'battle of Toongabbie', as it became known. And as they knew they would be doubted, they brought proof back with them: the severed head of one of the slain men.[29]

The bloody, hacked head did the trick: the watchmen were believed. This is the first recorded account of a non-military reprisal party—probably made up of convicts—since that ill-fated convict posse marched out of the Brickfields in 1789. This time, however, their actions were applauded. The warrior's staring head even overcame the strange fact that none of them had 'sustained the slightest injury' in this 'battle', though they claimed the Aboriginal people fought 'desperately'. Another piece of evidence throws a shadow on their story. In 1804 a sixteen-year-old Aboriginal boy (re)named James died of dysentery in Sydney. The *Gazette* claimed that James was 'rescued from barbarism' by George Bath when his parents were shot at Toongabbie. Bath was a convict who had arrived in 1791 and may have been one of the Toongabbie watchmen.[30] Given their lack of injuries, and the presence of this child, there is a more likely scenario for the 'battle': the watchmen, rather than bravely fighting warriors in an even contest, had located a campsite, stolen up at night or in the early morning, attacked people as they slept, decapitated one man and carried off at least one child. I am speculating in this way because this kind of attack became the common pattern on the Cumberland Plain, and evidently throughout the nineteenth century. Since the warriors were so fleet-footed, and often appear to have been tipped off, they could usually evade their pursuers. Surprising sleeping people at campsites was practically the only way whites could actually kill Aboriginal people. But it was a blind, blunt and indiscriminate way of 'fighting', for it necessarily involved blasting into the darkness at the whole group, including the old people, women and children. Such attacks and killings must have seemed shocking and wild, beyond comprehension to Aboriginal survivors. Early chroniclers often noted how deeply and soundly Aboriginal people slept. The yappy little dogs they had adopted from the invaders became still more important.[31]

This was also the first recorded decapitation of an Aboriginal person. News about that must have travelled fast too. The Eora certainly mutilated bodies in their attacks, but there is no report of them severing parts until eighteen months after the 'Battle of Toongabbie', when the killers of the young Aboriginal girl in the Domain cut off her arms. Similar acts followed. It seems likely that the practice of dismemberment crossed over from Europeans to Aboriginal people. It is ironic, then, that in later years travellers invented grinning, ghoulish tales in which it was the 'savages' who cut off people's heads and made 'presents' of them.[32]

PAYBACK ON THE HAWKESBURY, 1794–99

The Hawkesbury River region today still boasts a marvellous collection of timber-slab barns, rugged vernacular monuments to pioneer innovation and know-how. They were built literally of slabs of hardwood, split from local trees, usually set vertically in grooved floorplates and lapped up against one another. As the timber dried and shrank, cracks opened between the slabs, letting slits of light fall into the dim interiors.

A barn like this may have stood on Constable Edward Powell's farm, which he had bought from Michael Doyle at what is now Cornwallis, on the river flats where the Hawkesbury twists sharply just north of the Green Hills (Windsor). One night in September 1799, a group of Hawkesbury men, led by Constable Powell, pushed three Aboriginal boys into a barn, probably on Powell's farm. The boys' hands were tied behind their backs. As Powell aimed his musket, one of them managed to break away, run for the river and, even with his arms pinioned, swim across to safety. But the other boys—the younger was about thirteen—

were murdered by the white men, stabbed and hacked with a cutlass, one nearly decapitated, the other finished off with a musket shot. Their young bodies were dragged out and buried in the garden.[33]

How do we explain such brutality? Is it possible to explain it? Is there any logical explanation, any way of grasping it, making it part of the 'known'? Or are sickening acts like this somehow beyond the pale, hanging repellent, unexplainable, in a separate dimension to history?[34] In her novel *The Secret River*, Kate Grenville seems to attribute such atrocities to innate personal evil. Her character Smasher Sullivan, for example, all alone on his isolated river reach, is free to kill, mutilate, imprison and rape Aboriginal people as he pleases (a rather unlikely scenario, given the swift retribution meted out by the warriors!). Meanwhile 'good', 'humane' settlers are equally free to make happier relations with them. In histories, the murders of these boys are usually mentioned briefly and explained within the general rubric of the Europeans' brutality and their ruthless attacks upon defenceless Aboriginal people on the frontier. They are unsurprising, just another depressing story to add to a vast and damning litany.[35]

The verdict from the elite back in Sydney at the time was similar: the violence was the inevitable result of the depravity and brutality of the lawless ex-convict settlers. Collins had predicted as much five years before, when violence broke out a few months after Ruse and his band took the river flats below the Green Hills in 1794. Grimly recounting those first attacks—settlers and servants left for dead, reprisal parties of settlers shooting Aboriginal people in return, a boy suspected of being a spy tortured and killed—Collins concluded that the settlers had brought it upon themselves 'through their own misconduct'.[36] What else could be expected of a place settled beyond official surveillance and control, where settlers 'finding themselves freed from bondage, instantly conceived they were above all restriction'? Collins presented the Hawkesbury frontier as utterly lawless, a zone of madness and mayhem, where people committed atrocities for no other reason than their own savage inclinations, their utter lack of morality and self-control. Was it violence without reason or meaning, without history? I want to argue, with Inga Clendinnen, that it is possible to 'stare the Medusa down' by *historicising* the murders of the boys in 1799, not in order to justify or excuse them, but to understand how such a thing could have happened. To do this we need to carefully reconstruct, as best we can, the context, the place and the action: to retrace journeys and listen carefully to what was said.

As we have seen, most of the white settlers who went out to the Hawkesbury from 1794 onwards were ex-convicts, with a few ex-soldiers or sailors. Since convicts

Native yam—Dioscorea transversa. *(Photo: M. Fagg)*

and sailors had suffered the brunt of Eora attacks closer to the coast, these sorts of people would have been well aware of the Aboriginal system of payback. Meanwhile, the land they took was bound to be contested. The river and the lagoons were rich in fish, birds and edible plants; precisely the same areas which provided the Aboriginal people with most of their foods, their campsites and their great gathering places. Archaeological evidence, the thicker scatters of artefacts, strongly suggests that the rivers and creeks were the locus of the densest Aboriginal population. Hunter had seen the river banks churned up by the digging sticks of Aboriginal women harvesting the nutritious tubers, including *Dioscorea transversa*, the native yam, which were a staple. The rivers also provided starchy edible tubers and floating nardoo fern (*Marsilea*), besides fish, freshwater mussels and turtles; donkey orchids and chocolate lilies grew in the river-flat forests.[37]

It would have been some time before the local people felt the full brunt of their dispossession. As Henry Reynolds wrote some years ago: 'If blacks often did not react to the initial invasion of their country it was because they were not aware it had taken place . . . the mere presence of Europeans . . . could not uproot certainties so deeply implanted in Aboriginal custom and consciousness'. Aboriginal people did not realise their land had been taken, and many continued to refuse to accept the idea. Denis Byrne, writing of the Biripi of the Manning Valley on the New South Wales north coast, thinks dispossession there may not have been truly understood until 'wire fences fixed the grid onto the face of the land'.[38] There were no fences on the small Hawkesbury farms in the 1790s.

In the meantime, there had evidently been a great deal of coming together. This was illustrated in reverse when in 1796 Hunter ordered settlers to stop 'allowing natives to lurk about their farms'. Collins, blaming the Green Hills settlers once more for their own problems, elaborated:

there could not be a doubt that if they [the Aboriginal people] had never met with the shelter that some had afforded them, they would not at this time have furnished so much complaint. Those who had lived with settlers had tasted the sweets of a different mode of living, and willing their friends and companions should partake, either stole from those with whom they were living, or communicated favourable opportunities from other settlers.

Settlers had foolishly invited Aboriginal people into their homes, shared food with them, given them shelter.[39] Plagued by chronic labour shortages, they persuaded some Aboriginal people to work for them on the farms, too—they were said to be 'extremely useful', hoeing the earth more efficiently than the convict workers. But later accounts claim settlers did not pay them fairly or at all, a likely source of conflict. When Aboriginal people then refused to work, they were labelled as lazy or 'unable to adapt'. Margaret Catchpole, by now grown accustomed to their nakedness and their visits, wrote that they 'will not work very little—they say the white man workt and the Black man patter—the word patter is eat'. Giving corn for 'patter' was a common way of keeping on good terms, hopeful insurance against attack. It is also very likely that settlers introduced Aboriginal people to the rough, sociable and exciting pleasures of their popular culture, and perhaps attended contests and corroborees themselves. Songs, stories and words must have crossed. Men went out hunting together.[40]

From April 1794 there were also killings. Any number of incidents may have sparked them: drunken fights, failures to pay Aboriginal workers, settlers refusing Aboriginal people access to land and the river, shooting at them, thefts of maize and clothing, thefts of artefacts and wild food, the appropriation and

S.T. Gill, 'Interior of settlers hut' (1845), suggests Aboriginal people commonly shared domestic spaces with settlers. (National Library of Australia)

destruction of the river-flat yam beds. Given that the white male–female ratio here was even more distorted than in Sydney, competition for Aboriginal women must have been fierce and assaults and abductions common. 'Are not the settlers or their men in the habits of taking the women from the natives', the court asked a witness in 1799, 'and . . . the native men . . . prevented taking them away through fear of their firearms?' [41]

Settlers also habitually stole Aboriginal children during raids 'after the flight of the parents'. Those parents came to the farmhouses later with 'earnest entreaties . . . for their return' but the settlers ignored them. This had happened in Sydney Harbour from at least September 1788, and at Toongabbie and Parramatta as well. [42] Often the whites later said the children were 'orphans' whom they 'rescued' from the bush. The infants were usually about two or three—old enough to survive without their mothers, but considered young enough to be successfully brought up within white society. Some of the white couples seem to have been childless themselves; others were perhaps keen on having such an exotic curiosity in their homes. The children, suitably Europeanised, would provide useful labour when they grew up too. Daniel Moowattin, George Caley's young collector and companion, was born at Parramatta about 1791, and had been taken and raised by 'the notorious convict informer, gaoler, flogger and hangman Richard Partridge alias Rice'. [43] There may have been child-hunger too. In 1800, a quarter of the Hawkesbury settlers, probably older couples, had no children. The childless Thomas and Mary Rickerby adopted their mixed-descent baby boy, John Pilot Rickerby, in about 1799 or 1800, even though his mother was still alive. He had been 'found in the woods' beside her—she was half-dead of hatchet wounds. When this child died in 1806, all the local settlers' children, dressed in white, followed his coffin to the Green Hills burial ground. The commonness of Aboriginal child-taking was expressed in the orders of the first detachment of soldiers sent out to the Hawkesbury in 1795: they were to 'destroy the natives wherever they were met with after their being guilty of Outrages *except such native children as were domesticated among the Settlers*'. [44] Private Henry Lamb was most likely among those soldiers, scooping up a little girl on one of the raids. A generation of black children was growing up in white households.

By May 1795 the situation had deteriorated and the Hawkesbury was said to be in a state of 'open war'. After attacks began on riverboats, and the spearing and terrible, slow death of free settler Thomas Webb, Acting Governor Paterson sent out the soldiers. This time the orders were not mitigated by a limit on numbers to be taken, or the avoidance of harming women and children. The soldiers were to 'destroy as many as possible' and to erect gibbets from which to hang black bodies. As Deborah Bird Rose points out, one of the deep contradictions of the frontier was that savagery was considered essential to the path of 'civilisation'. Some seven or eight warriors were reportedly killed, but strangely they vanished before they could be counted, or strung up. A baby was wounded in his mother's arms and later died, his mother was shot in the shoulder: it sounds like another dawn raid on a camp. Some women and a crippled man were captured and taken to Sydney. These attacks further inflamed the conflicts and led to equally horrific payback attacks upon settlers and their children. After that, soldiers were stationed permanently on the river and around the farms (not that these settlers deserved it, remarked Collins).[45]

Despite all this, there was no let-up in the taking of land and the spread of the farms. As settlers pushed further north, Aboriginal resistance intensified. Spread out on isolated farms, the settlers were vulnerable. Judge Atkins lamented that they had not been settled 'in villages, and their farms radiated, as from a centre'. When ex-soldiers took the narrow strip of fertile land along the west side of the isolated Sackville Reach in 1795, the Aboriginal people seized the topographic advantage, attacking from the high ridge looming hard by the flats with such fury that they successfully drove the settlers out. Once more a reprisal party marched out, killing four men and a woman, wounding a child and taking prisoners. By March the following year, there were reports of 'fresh outrages' in this area. A defiant warrior stood high on Portland Rock and menaced a schooner with his spears. Governor Hunter visited the evacuated area in January 1797 in order to learn from the land. Like Phillip before him, he was forced to take the deadly politics of geography and demography into account, trying to work out if it could 'admit such a number of settlers . . . for the purpose of mutual protection'. This side of Sackville Reach, though the soil was excellent, was 'much too narrow'. It failed the test—for the moment.[46]

But the problem of 'settlers coming together for mutual protection' was not only a geographic one. As we have seen, they refused to leave their farms and live together in villages, and as Alan Atkinson observes, the Hawkesbury settlers had to be *ordered* to combine as a group, for mutual benefits and governance. Perhaps they did lack a sense of common purpose, civic responsibility and care for one another; but by now there were probably other webs of allegiance at work too. Many settlers had clearly formed relationships with Aboriginal people, knew the different groups and who was related to whom, and wanted to maintain, if not friendly, then at least safe relations with them. In this 'nervous landscape', it sometimes may have been best to turn a blind eye to attacks which did not affect you, your family, your farm. Green Hills Chief Constable Thomas Rickerby was asked whether he was aware that 'after the natives had committed depredations and even murders . . . they have been received into the houses of the settlers?' He agreed that it was true. In this war, the settlers were not a monolithic, united group any more than the Aboriginal people.[47]

From the relative safety of Sydney, Collins was convinced the Hawkesbury was literally a lawless place, lacking both external regulation of courts and justice, and the internal laws of personal morality, enlightened attitudes and self-discipline. But there is strong evidence that by at least 1799, there *was* a legal system in operation there with regard to race relations: Aboriginal Law. What is more, indications are that settlers acted as though they understood the laws of payback, and responded in kind. Ironically, the evidence for this, and glimpses of the complicated world of personal, communal and interracial networks in which it operated, are recorded in the transcription of the trial of the five men who killed the Aboriginal boys in 1799.[48]

Let us begin by restoring names to the dead, as best we can. Alas, their full tribal names were not recorded, but the settlers knew the older boy as Jemmy—he was about fifteen or sixteen; the younger was called 'Little Geo'. Or that is how the court clerk wrote it: most likely, scribbling quickly, he meant 'George'; but it is possible his name sounded like 'Djo' or 'Joe'. 'Little' often meant the boy's father or older brother had adopted the same name.

Collins' description of Jemmy and Little George as 'unoffending lads' was not quite accurate. Neither of them were children, despite their age. They carried the spears, womeras and waddies of initiated men, and Jemmy was said to have a wife. They wore the jackets which Aboriginal warriors appear to have adopted as a sort of uniform. In Aboriginal society, as among the European lower orders, there was not such a gulf between childhood and adulthood as there is today. And since all initiated men were warriors, the boys behaved as warriors. They were reported to have raided farms for corn and, as part of larger groups, they had speared white men in an attack on a farm at Toongabbie in 1797.[49]

As in Sydney, though, children and young people were also the ones who crossed the racial boundaries most often, carrying news, information, words and goods back and forth. Jemmy and Little George were certainly well known, for they had 'been in the habit of being much with the settlers', and moved as easily and openly on the farms and tracks as they did in the bush. Collins claimed that they were living with Edward Powell, local constable and farmer, and his neighbours on Argyle Reach, as it was later called, at the time of the murders. But they also maintained their tribal connections. Jemmy was the brother of Terribandy, one of a group of warriors including Major White, Charley and Nabbin, well known for their attacks on farms and settlers. The boys were often seen with these older warriors. Other key figures like Yelloway (perhaps this was the warrior Yaragowhy mentioned later) and Major Worgan (who must have exchanged names with George Worgan) were also well known among the settlers, and seemed to know a lot about Terribandy and his group's movements and motivations too.[50]

Three weeks before the murder of the boys, there had been two other brutal killings. Thomas Hoskisson and John Wimbow were out hunting in the mountains, west of the river. This was emphatically Aboriginal country, for while they had a camp 'at the river and the creek' (perhaps the flat circle of ground between South Creek and the river), they were also known to 'come down from the mountains' and to retreat there after attacking settlers. But Hoskisson seems to have felt fairly confident in their country. He knew them personally and had always treated Aboriginal people with generosity and friendliness.

Towards evening, the two hunters met up with Major White, Nabbin and Terribandy as 'friends in the woods'. The boys may have been there too. There was a friendly exchange about hunting pheasants (perhaps lyrebirds or other native gamebirds) and the warriors invited the whites to camp with them. They built fires, shared food, no doubt talked and told stories, perhaps sang songs, and agreed to continue the hunt together in the morning. This was not at all unusual: from the earliest years Aboriginal and European men had gone out hunting together, and evidently enjoyed one another's company. But that night, after the white men lay down under their blankets and slept, the black men carefully removed their muskets, and drove spears into their bodies. They used 'davels' or *doulls*, the short spears used in ritual killings. The bodies were stripped, mutilated and covered roughly.[51]

When the news got back to the settlement—and it must have come back with Aboriginal people—a party of soldiers and settlers formed up and marched out to find and bury the bodies. Among the settlers were the dead men's neighbours— Edward Powell, Jonas Archer, James Metcalf, Simon Freebody. I suspect they had

Argyle Reach, Hawkesbury River, showing the farms of David White, Simon Freebody, Michael Doyle—who sold to Edward Powell—Jonas and Mary Archer and Thomas Rickerby. (Kate Nolan)

Aboriginal guides too, since locating the bodies in the bush high on 'the second ridge of the mountains' would have been difficult without them. When they found the bodies they were aghast. The dead men's clothing, provisions, blankets and muskets were gone. Their badly mutilated bodies lay naked, 'covered by wood'.[52]

Lieutenant Hobby, local commander, ordered the soldiers marching up the mountains to shoot any native they saw on sight. As we have seen, such orders were routinely given to soldiers on reprisal marches since the first detachment had arrived on the Hawkesbury in 1795. But Hobby was not sure if the settlers who went to find and bury their neighbours thought this order applied to them, nor whether they realised it was only for the duration of that expedition. The settlers said they were not confused at all: Jonas Archer told the court he understood the orders were 'to kill any natives the party could meet', adding 'and that was my intention'.[53]

The settlers, as they always did, asked other Aboriginal people why the men had been killed. Yelloway told Jonas Archer the story in detail, and seems to have suggested they were killed for their provisions. But Archer told the court the more likely reason: John Wimbow had Terribandy's daughter 'living with him'. Archer insisted to the court that she was not 'forcibly detained', that 'she might have left him had she chaused'; but these words suggest she had not chosen, that she had little choice in the matter.[54]

Archer now knew who the killers were. He waited three weeks before commencing what appears to be a deliberate process of avenging the deaths. When Jemmy, the brother of Terribandy, visited Archer's farm, Archer told him that Major White had Hoskisson's firelock, and asked the boy to retrieve it. Off went Jemmy obligingly to fetch it. Archer went straight to Hoskisson's widow, Sarah, and told her the gun would soon be returned to her. Jemmy, Little George and a third boy instead brought the gun to James Metcalf, who was working on Robert Forrester's farm nearby. Metcalf led the three of them into the farmhouse there, much to the alarm of Forrester's wife, Isabella Ramsay. The boys were armed, and one of them was wearing Metcalf's jacket. When the jacket was removed, a hatchet fell from the sleeve. Another man, John Pearson, a servant or lodger of Isabella Ramsay's, asked them: who killed Hoskisson and Wimbow? Why? The boys named the killers once more: Major White and

Jemmy's brother, Terribandy. They claimed the motivation was the theft of their provisions, avoiding the perhaps more explosive issue of Terribandy's daughter.

The news flew around the farms and more and more settlers and convict servants arrived at Forrester's house 'to see the natives', just as they would have gathered for a court hearing; or a hanging. The mood must have been tight as a bowstring, the room full of sweat. Constable Powell arrived among the crowd from his farm. He was blunt. When Jemmy got up for water, he stopped him: 'You shall have no water here you have killed a Good fellow and you shall not live long'. Then William Butler came in carrying a 'bright cutlass' and bellowing the language of the courts and the gallows:

> Where are these natives leave them to me I'll soon settle them, what sentence shall we pass on these blackfellows. I will pass sentence myself. They shall be hanged.

Metcalf, who seems to have known the boys, brought them water and tried to intervene, to redirect the retribution towards the real killers: 'We will not kill them, we will carry them out as the means of finding the natives who killed Hoskisson.'[55]

But by now Powell had spoken with the widow Sarah Hoskisson, and she had made her decision—the boys must die. In the British system, the individual guilty of the crime expiates it; guilt and sentence are decided by jury and judge. In Aboriginal Law the victim or their relatives were consulted, and the relatives and friends of the guilty could pay the price, including children. Powell also assured the assembled crowd that it was 'the Governors and Commanding Officers orders that the natives should be killed wherever they could be met'. But this was gloss. They were not marching in enemy territory, watching for foe among the trees, but holding a sort of rough trial in Isabella Ramsay's farmhouse. And the boys were not anonymous enemies. The settlers had probably seen them grow up. They were named, known, they had shared their houses, and, even since the killings, they 'lived in habits of friendly Intercourse with the Settlers'. But, as in Aboriginal society, and as in Wimbow's and Hoskisson's case, familiarity and friendship were suspended where payback laws were concerned.[56]

And so the boys' hands were tied and ropes put about their necks and they were led out of the house for execution. The timid were ordered to get out of the way, else they'd be shot; and they did, they melted away, went to hide, stopped their ears. Isabella Ramsay and John Pearson crept off to bed. All of them heard two musket shots. David White said he could hear the boys crying out from his farm half a mile further north. He went to Hoskisson's place to investigate, and waited there. Soon Sarah Hoskisson, Simon Freebody and another ex-convict, William Timms, returned. Freebody told him what had happened: Timms held one boy while Metcalf shot him. Freebody killed the second boy with the cutlass. Powell had shot at the third, but 'let him escape': the boy who swam the river, hands still tied. The widow Sarah Hoskisson was most likely there in the barn, too, watching, witnessing.[57]

But not everyone accepted this sort of justice. Mary Archer, the wife of Jonas, was disturbed enough by the killings to hurry to Chief Constable Thomas Rickerby the next morning. Rickerby and some assistants went up to Powell's farm, only two along from his own, and close to Archer's, and found some of the killers there in the house. *What murders?* they said, feigning ignorance. Constable Powell arrived, and his response was the same. But Rickerby persisted with his questions. Soon he found the rough grave and the bodies were exhumed. By this time Lieutenant Hobby and Robert Braithwaite, gentleman farmer on Rickerbys Creek, had also arrived. Seeing the faces and throats slashed, the ball ripped through the breast, Braithwaite remonstrated with the killers: 'It was a very cruel way of Killing them even if they had been detected in Committing any act of Depredation'. But the killers were having none of it: they spat out defiantly: 'if you seen the bodies of Wimbolt and Hodgekinson you would have not thought it so inhuman'. Rickerby immediately took five men into custody. In October 1799, Edward Powell, James Metcalf, William Timms, William Butler and Simon Freebody stood trial in Sydney for the murder of the two boys.[58]

It is clear that these men committed this terrible crime upon boys who were conscious, bound and helpless. Michael Flynn calls it the action of a 'lynch mob'.[59] Nevertheless, it was not a wild, irrational or impetuous act: there had been trickery in getting the boys to the house, a process of establishing 'guilt' by association, consultation with the injured relative, communal 'trial' and an execution, which mirrored and mimicked Aboriginal practice. In the process, too, Aboriginal people were guides and informants. And Major White, after all, gave up the gun.

We might ask why these people, including a constable appointed to enforce British law, did not resort to their own legal system in this case, as they did for crimes committed among themselves? I suspect the Aboriginal concepts of vengeance and communal guilt there struck deep resonances among them: the sort of justice that was 'felt' rather than 'argued'. There were cultural parallels with the practice of British law in the public expiation of the crime, and the sense of urgency about setting wrongs to right.[60]

But the main reason was that British law was ineffective in dealing with violence, attacks and killings between blacks and whites because of the ambiguous legal standing of Aboriginal people, especially in frontier zones. As we have seen, Aboriginal people were theoretically British subjects, but because they were not Christian, they could not swear an oath or give evidence in court; nor could they be tried.[61] The military on the ground were themselves confused about what action they were supposed to take. 'I wish to be informed after this attack on my life how I am in future to act', Sergeant Goodall told the court after he was speared in the back, chased and left for dead. Governor Hunter himself did not know how to deal with Aboriginal wrongdoers. When Lieutenant Hobby sent the warrior Charley down to Sydney for spearing Sergeant Goodall just before the murders in the mountains, Hunter was irritated and annoyed. He believed he could not 'punish the native in Cool blood' because the 'savage' Charley would have no comprehension of why it was being done. Charley was sent to Lieutenant Cummings at Parramatta, while Corporal Farrell and Private Henry Lamb were ordered back to the Hawkesbury with a curt message: Hobby was to 'deal with such miscreants on the spot', or failing that, 'as soon as they can be catched'. In other words, Hunter could not, and did not want to, deal with the messy business of retaliation and punishment in the civilised region of Sydney. The Hawkesbury was under de facto military rule, a different legal territory, a frontier war zone where British laws—and legal uncertainties like the status of Aboriginal people—were suspended, where reprisals and killings were permitted—during military raids. Hobby had the discretion to punish Aboriginal miscreants as he saw fit, and he was told to use it and not bother Hunter again.[62] It was this special status, this suspension of British law at the farthest outposts, that the accused settlers appropriated as their defence in court. They knew payback Law would never be accepted.

But this legal uncertainty worked both ways. Although the five white killers were found guilty, neither court nor governor knew what sentence could be passed on them either, again because the legal status of Aboriginal people was unclear. In the end Hunter sent the papers to London for a judgement. The response arrived two years later: they were all pardoned.[63] In the meantime, the five men were immediately set free on bail and returned to their farms. David Collins was sure this would enrage the Hawkesbury Aboriginal people and lead to further violence: they would not understand the legalistic confusions, and would see only injustice and betrayal. But there were no immediate reprisals. In fact the Hawkesbury was reportedly quiet for the next five years.[64]

Edward Powell was removed from the constabulary, but he went on to a prosperous career in hotels, farming and livestock. In October 1809, ten years almost to the day since the trial, a party of Aboriginal people arrived on his farm at Liberty Plains and drove away all his sheep. Over the hills and far away they went, down to the wilds of the Cooks River, where most of the sheep were killed, their wool singed off and their carcasses left rotting for Powell to find. Their raiders' leader was said to be Tedbury, the son of the warrior Pemulwuy, who had waged war on another front on the Cumberland Plain.[65]

PEMULWUY'S WAR

The awful deaths of Jemmy and Little George are recorded in detail because their killers stood trial. They are at least historically recoverable; we can explore and meditate upon them. By contrast, the death of the most famous resistance fighter of the early colonial period, Pemulwuy, is still mysterious. It floats as an 'event' in early 1802, but unanchored by place, or the people involved, or the immediate chain of events which led to it. Somewhere in London, possibly in the Hunterian Museum at the Royal College of Surgeons, Pemulwuy's head may still float too, set adrift from kin and country, and history.[66]

Governor King declared Pemulwuy an outlaw in 1801, encouraged both whites and blacks to hunt him, and offered a reward for him, dead or alive. When he was shot, therefore, there were no arrests, and no trial recording his last movements, or how he came by his death. Those who wrote of Pemulwuy's demise were vague, even blasé, as though his death had been inevitable, in fact long overdue.

Pemulwuy had been well known among settlers since he speared John McIntyre in 1790. His portrait shows a powerfully built, muscular man leaning from a nowie. He was said to have been marked by a 'speck in his eye'; Phillip thought he had lost an eye. He was a Bidgigal man, whose country stretched up along the Georges River and Salt Pan Creek from Botany Bay towards Prospect. Like the peoples of the other rivers and creeks, the Bidgigal were known as a 'woods tribe', an inland group, rather than Eora, the 'water tribes' of the coast. While so many Eora names and places were associated with water and coastal creatures, Pemulwuy's name meant 'earth'. His distinctive death spear was barbed with bits of sharp red silcrete from the inland quarries of the Cumberland Plain.[67]

S.J. Neele, 'Pimbly Native of New Holland 1804'. A rather strange portrait of Pemulwuy, a man of a 'woods tribe', shown afloat in a canoe, holding one paddle as though about to strike something. Nevertheless 'the resemblance is thought to be striking by those who have seen him'. James Grant described him as 'a chief, a sort of troublesome fellow'. By the time this picture was published, Pemulwuy was dead. (From James Grant, Narrative of a Voyage of Discovery, *Mitchell Library, State Library of New South Wales)*

At some time in the seven years after McIntyre was dealt with, there must have been a deep shift in Pemulwuy's thinking about the British invaders. McIntyre had most likely been a victim of payback: he was treated as subject to Aboriginal Law. But by at least 1797, it seems that Pemulwuy was among those warriors who no longer considered payback Law appropriate for the whites. In the relentless spread of settlement, the abduction of women and children, the taking of land and the failure of most to obey the Law, it was clear that the Berewalgal really were strangers, aliens outside the Law. Pemulwuy began a campaign to drive them out, using raids, fire and attacks. This war interwove two very different motives—payback and defence of country—underpinned by two different philosophies. One included whites in the Aboriginal legal system—the other saw them as aliens and invaders.

From at least autumn 1797, when the maize was ripening, Pemulwuy and his men raided the older farms in the Parramatta area—the big Toongabbie Farm, and the farms at the Northern Boundary, where a man and a woman were robbed and killed. It seems they attacked and robbed soldiers too, taking musket balls and 'other things'. The settlers responded by forming a punitive party, which hunted for the gang right through the night. Eventually they found their camp in the bush, strewn with maize and musket balls, and pursued the fleeing warriors all the way back to the outskirts of Parramatta. But they could never catch them, so the exhausted settlers gave up the chase and went into the town to rest.[68]

Then an extraordinary thing happened. An hour later, 100 Aboriginal warriors headed by Pemulwuy marched into the town to take them on. Pemulwuy was 'in a great rage', shouting at the assembled crowd and military about 'the coercive measures taken by settlers and soldiers to hunt them down like wild animals' and threatening to spear anyone who dared approach him. Soldiers ordered to seize him moved forward; he hurled a spear at one of them and was immediately blasted with buckshot. More spears whistled at the soldiers, the muskets opened fire and at least five warriors fell in the streets of Parramatta. Local people recalling the Battle of Parramatta many decades later claimed 50 warriors had been shot; and in 1899 a local historian claimed that Pemulwuy's warriors had 'marched almost in rows as if in imitation of a detachment of soldiers'.[69]

It's a compelling image, a 'high noon' confrontation: 100 black warriors with their spears, womeras and clubs, advancing in ranks unnervingly like those of the redcoats, Pemulwuy shouting defiantly at their head, the white townsfolk perhaps frozen, spellbound by the sight. It is possible that memory reshaped the event to better fit a 'battle' scenario; but we should not dismiss this evidence completely, for such things are known to have happened. At Battle Mountain in Queensland's Gulf country in 1884, 600 Kalkatunga warriors waiting to ambush their opponents suddenly formed rows like the soldiers, and were mown down by the carbines.[70] The Bidgigal, who were developing entirely new ways of fighting, a new kind of war, may have observed and mimicked the formations of soldiers.

By now, too, the lines between black and white were still more blurred. The authorities in the towns knew that the raids were not carried out exclusively by Aboriginal people. A number of convicts were known to have joined them, including that first cross-cultural traveller John Wilson and his associate, William Knight. They were thought to have been involved in driving the soldier-settlers from Sackville Reach in 1795, and were held responsible for that ultimately traitorous act: telling the warriors about the limitations of muskets.[71] By the time of Pemulwuy's renewed raids the following year, there were more renegades: John Jeweson, Joseph Saunders and Moses Williams had crossed over. Rumours that Irish convicts were living off the wild cattle at the Cowpastures were circulating too, and a military party led by Henry Hacking found short spears, tipped with the leg-bones of kangaroos 'supposed for stabbing calves'. Were the Muringong of the Cowpastures killing this new kind of food? Or were Irish convicts, said to be 'nearly as wild themselves as the cattle', using Aboriginal technology to feast on young beef?[72]

Pemulwuy, his head and body shot up with lead, was carted into Parramatta hospital and expected to die, the fetter round his ankle a token precaution. Within days, he rose up and escaped. A month later Hunter saw him at Botany Bay, fetter still about his leg. Was the governor still angry with him? came the polite question, as it always seemed to after the outbreak of hostilities. Hunter replied that he was not angry, and Pemulwuy seemed pleased.[73] By April the attacks had started again: raids, fires, robberies and assaults on the farms orbiting Parramatta, especially the settlers at Lane Cove. A year later the campaign spread to the farms at Georges River (present-day Bankstown), in Pemulwuy's own country. Hunter threatened to hang a black man in chains to deter them—that old gruesome dance of dangling corpse the British resorted to wherever they went in the world—but the offender had to be caught in the act. George Caley described it as intermittent war: 'At times nothing was heard of them; then all was silence. When they appeared again, then there was a hue and cry.'[74] One weapon in this war, then, was the terror of uncertainty, of silence, of not knowing who would be struck, or when, or where.

By now Pemulwuy had acquired an extraordinary reputation for super-natural powers: he was the first of a long line of Aboriginal heroes believed by his people—and probably by some whites as well—to be immune to gunfire.[75] He was reportedly killed by 'Black Caesar', the Madagascan convict-turned-bushranger, in 1795, only to reappear soon after. He survived the soldiers' guns at the Battle of Parramatta, and outwitted them all by escaping again. For the British authorities, whose power rested on guns, there could hardly have been a more maddening claim. 'From this fancied security', scoffed Collins, 'he was said to have been at the head of every party that attacked the maize grounds'.[76] It became increasingly urgent to prove the legend false, to demonstrate, logically and rationally, that Pemulwuy was just a man.

Pemulwuy's attacks continued through 1801 around Parramatta, Prospect and Georges River. Crops were set ablaze and now the growing flocks of sheep were targets too. The Europeans were told in no uncertain terms that the warriors would 'kill all the white men they meet'. Margaret Catchpole wrote of terrible atrocities, and more amputations:

> the Blacks the natives of this place killed and wounded 8 men and women and Children—1 man they cut off his arms half way up and broke the bones that they left on very much and cut their legs off up to their knees an the poor man was carried into the hospital alive—but the Governor have sent men out after them to shot every 1 they find . . .[77]

These were more than a series of stray skirmishes. This was a serious war, and the response was serious. In May 1801 Governor King ordered that all Aboriginal people be 'driven back from settlers' habitations by firing on them'.

The only exceptions were the Sydney Tribe and those on 'Parramatta Road'—which would have included Bennelong's group at Kissing Point, and also the people camped with Lieutenant Cummings outside Parramatta. This order meant settlers could virtually shoot Aboriginal people at will; but it also meant they were *forbidden* to have Aboriginal people on their farms and in their houses. Relationships were suspended: settlers lost the labour, help, protection and companionship of Aboriginal people, the fish, honey and other foods they brought; and Aboriginal people in turn lost the food, tobacco, clothing and shelter settlers gave them.[78]

Once more, the situation on the ground was complex, for ties of mutual dependence and friendship crossed racial lines. When the Reverend Samuel Marsden ordered Parramatta's convict servants to join soldiers on reprisal raids, George Caley's servant refused to go. This man got on well with the Parramatta Aboriginal people and would not join the hunt 'to apprehend the natives by force in the night'—that is, to carry out surprise raids on camps. Marsden instantly had the man gaoled, and an inevitably apoplectic Caley defended him vehemently. 'It will not do for me to fall out with them', he told Banks, for he depended on Aborigines for his collection work. These were words which a number of settlers might have echoed. Marsden appears to have been characteristically ruthless, for Caley claimed he dismissed botanising as a 'nonsensical pursuit' and declared 'there never would be any good done until there was a clear riddance of the natives'. A land emptied of Aboriginal people: an empty land, waiting for flocks and herds.[79]

Michael Flynn makes the important point that the language used to describe Aboriginal attacks echoed that used for Irish rebellions—they were both described as 'outrages', a word with 'political overtones, meaning terrorist attack'.[80] Governor King appears to have quickly realised that reprisal raids were either ineffective or, if campsites were found, counterproductive because they resulted in horrific payback. Borrowing from the tactics used with Irish rebels, he developed a new strategy: identify and remove the leaders. This was much more successful, and it was used repeatedly until the end of the war on the Cumberland Plain. But for it to be effective, both Aboriginal and settler cooperation was essential.

Pemulwuy was outlawed in November 1801, along with the white bandits William Knight and Thomas Thrush. Rewards were offered: for convicts, freedom; for the free, 20 gallons of rum and two suits of clothing. Meanwhile Aboriginal people at Sydney and the Hawkesbury disassociated themselves from Pemulwuy's activities. Some said he forced them to join his raids. They were still banned from the farms and townships. King gave them an ultimatum: if they gave up Pemulwuy 'they should be re-admitted to our friendship'. Within seven months of being outlawed, Pemulwuy was dead, shot by 'two settlers'. His head was cut off, brought back to Sydney, placed in a jar of spirits and sent aboard the *Speedy* to Sir Joseph Banks. King alleged that the Aboriginal people themselves had requested that his head be 'carried to the governor', as 'he was the cause of all that had happened'. He wrote of their 'joy' when the banishment order was lifted, and they returned to the towns and settlements in a second 'coming in'. 'I have every hope . . . that we shall continue on good terms with them'. He was not the first governor to believe he had finally achieved peace, nor would he be the last.[81]

But who killed Pemulwuy? How did they find the warrior who had so often escaped, who survived musket balls? King's report seems deliberately vague, giving few details, though he did acknowledge later that Pemulwuy had been a 'brave and independent character'. Other accounts, like those of David Dickenson Mann and George Suttor, were similarly perfunctory. Mann, however, included this odd phrase: the deed was 'soon accomplished by artifice'. A few years later, the *Sydney Gazette* described the cooperation of the Aboriginal people in Pemulwuy's death as treachery: it even claimed that the 'natives' themselves had 'carried out the assassination'. Research published in 2003 by historian Keith Vincent Smith suggested that the killer was Henry Hacking, who had arrived as the Quartermaster of the *Sirius* in 1788. Hacking became the *Sirius*'s game-shooter and was likely responsible for the first reported shooting of Aboriginal people in September 1789, so this identification seemed highly plausible. But since then, forensic research into the mystery has revealed that Hacking could not have been the killer. Doug Kohlhoff concludes that Governor King's original report, that Pemulwuy was executed by two settlers, is most likely correct. After all, settlers were the ones who suffered the brunt of Pemulwuy's attacks and would have been familiar with the country. Kohlhoff suggests that King did not name the settlers because he did not want to make heroes of them. There were no reports of revenge attacks on perpetrators after Pemulwuy's death. Perhaps there was 'artifice': unwritten arrangements between settlers and other Aboriginal people, negotiations and deals concerning the location, ambush and killing of Pemulwuy.[82]

THE HAWKESBURY, 1804–05: DIPLOMACY, ALLEGIANCES AND CROSSING OVER

Governor King learned some valuable lessons from the campaign against Pemulwuy. He discovered the effectiveness of banishing Aboriginal people from the farms and towns; and he realised that it was possible to exploit tribal differences and rivalries. Playing off the clans and bands against one another had another important effect: it discouraged mass attacks by cooperating clans, something that terrified settlers. King and Marsden used these tactics ever more forcefully and successfully over the next three years, mainly with the aim of removing resistance leaders. They also attempted to negotiate directly with tribal elders. But the wheel of colonisation rolled on, so the war on the Cumberland Plain re-ignited as settlers moved into new country. The 'peace' of 1802 soon dissolved as another generation of warriors led more desperate campaigns to drive settlers out of their land, and soldiers and settlers continued to march out on reprisal raids. But conflict was not restricted to those distant out-settlements—it flared defiantly in the longer-settled districts around Sydney too, where young Aboriginal men took on the tactics and mannerisms of bushrangers. There was no neatly patterned sequence of war and peace: they were cyclical, partial and contingent.

The lull in hostilities after 1802 was broken as the corn ripened in 1804. The main locus of conflict had now shifted north to the lower Hawkesbury: for 'among the reaches about Portland Head their ravages have been felt with much greater severity than elsewhere'. The farms abandoned in 1796 were retaken in 1803. Matthew Everingham, his wife and servant were speared on Sackville Reach in late May 1804 and their house and outhouses burnt to the ground. The attackers were said to be the 'wild' people from the north side of the river around Portland Head. We do not know their traditional clan or band names, but they became known, and feared, as the 'Branch natives'. 'The Branch' was the settlers' name for both the Colo and the Macdonald rivers.[83] Parties of settlers marched out to the mountains bent on retaliation after the attack on the Everinghams and others, but they were ambushed by 300 black men waiting for them on a ridge. When they tried to fire at them, a volley of spears rained down from the heights and they ran for their lives.[84]

Some of the Richmond Aboriginal people, whether from traditional enmity, or for their own security, or both, decided to distance themselves from these 'Branch natives'. They told a local farmer that they wanted to settle upon his farm, under his protection. The very next day, soldiers shot and killed Nabbin and Major White, described as 'two of the most violent and ferocious'. Marsden and the local magistrate Surgeon Arndell sent for the local elders, Yellomundy and Yaragowhy, and asked them to use their influence to stop further attacks. The elders left 'loaded up with food and clothes'. The Europeans continued to use material things to make peace.[85]

Further downriver, settler William Knight on Bostons (later Cumberland) Reach was unconvinced by the diplomatic strategies. Sometime after the attacks there, he sent a petition to King asking permission to shoot Aboriginal people on sight. At the bottom he forged the signatures of his neighbours. Presumably Knight knew they would not sign such a petition—perhaps his was the only voice calling for such action. In any case, he must have bungled the job, because the forgery was soon discovered and he went to gaol for a few days. He sold his farm soon after.[86] But King took the opportunity to summon representatives of the 'Branch' natives down from the Colo River: to ask them face to face why they attacked settlers.

And so three nameless elders travelled, probably to Parramatta, to put their case to the governor. When settlers' parties demanded to know why they were being attacked, the usual response from warriors was a direct and defiant assurance that they would 'kill all the white men'. But in this formal exchange with King, presumably in one of the rooms of Government House, the elders' message was quite clear:

> they did not like to be driven from the few places that were left on the banks of the river, where alone they could procure food; that they had gone down the river as the white men took possession of the banks; if they

went across the white men's ground the settlers fired upon them and were angry, that if they could retain some places on the lower part of the river they should be satisfied and not trouble the white men . . .

Driven from the river: it was an echo of Maugaron's protest from another river, fifteen years before. The core issue here was land: the precious strips and flats of riverside land which provided food, land where there was access to the river and the lagoons, land as familiar as one's own body. King wrote to Hobart that he could see the justice in this. He said he promised them 'no more settlements would be made lower down the river'.[87]

The problem was that most of the rich land was already granted, and there were very likely people on land without grants as well, holding merely by occupation, by 'naked possession'. In September 1804 King had sent the pinnace *Ann* to examine the land along the river from Portland Head to Mullet (now Dangar) Island; however, he does appear to have kept his promise to grant no more land in this area.[88]

Here is a little chink for counterfactual history: what if Governor Macquarie could have kept King's promise? Could settlers and Aboriginal people have lived in reasonable peace? Could those in authority on either side have kept their people from committing further incursions and attacks? Could there have been a system of justice which satisfied both?

There were more killings and burnings in the autumn of 1805. In the barrage of staccato reports, with the time lag between events and their reporting, it is difficult to tell whether these attacks aimed to drive back settlers (characterised by corn raids, spearing and setting fire to buildings and crops), or were payback killings (characterised by trickery, spearing and mutilation), or both types of attacks on different settlers. The killing of ex-soldier John Llewellyn and the near-death of his servant at the hands of the soon-to-be-infamous warrior Branch Jack was preceded by a friendly sharing of food in a field. On the same day, Feen Adlam and his servant were burned to death in their hut further downriver by the same party, 'their limbs severed and wantonly scattered'. Were these men the victims of frontier warfare, or of payback for their own or their associates' crimes? The *Gazette* insisted there were no grievances, because 'crimes against them were always investigated'. King stressed that the settlers had given the Aboriginal people 'corn and many other comforts to keep on good terms with them'. Armed boats were sent out from the Green Hills to patrol the river banks and a military party posted to the Branch. When the houses of the Lambs and the Youlers on Sackville Reach burnt down in July, everyone thought the Branch tribe had struck again.[89]

Meanwhile there were quite different types of attacks on stock farms to the west and south-west of Parramatta, probably led by Tedbury, the son of Pemulwuy. The warriors involved in these raids reportedly numbered between 300 and 400. These numbers mean there must have been a high degree of organisation and coordination between different tribes, or, as the *Gazette* worriedly recognised, 'systematic operations' and a 'pre-concerted plan'. At Macarthur's stock farm at Cabramatta, two stockmen were killed in a raid in which Tedbury's people were joined by 'strangers from the inland'. The settler party which set out in pursuit marched in 'heavy weather' and eventually found them gathered on the opposite side of a raging creek. They shouted the old question across the din of the torrent: 'Why do you attack the white men?' The warriors bellowed back that they would continue to attack whenever they could. Their English was good, commented the *Gazette*, and they were not afraid of guns.[90]

Attacks in areas which the Europeans considered 'settled', where the Aboriginal people were, in Margaret Catchpole's words, 'gittin civil', were perhaps the most difficult for the Europeans to deal with. We need to look carefully at words here. Increasingly, official reports tended to describe Aboriginal people as either 'domesticated' and 'quiet', or 'wild' and 'savage'. This parallels their language for animals—for example cattle, horses or dogs—and I think it betrays similar thinking. They wrote with an assumed trajectory in mind: Aboriginal people would naturally be 'tamed' or 'domesticated' through contact with superior European civilisation. Speaking English, wearing clothes, eating settler food, and most importantly, ceasing their attacks and becoming 'docile', were signs of the shift from the 'savage' to the 'civil' state, a shift which was natural, expected, inevitable.[91]

This process was only supposed to move one way—from the Europeans to the Aboriginal people; when it moved the other way, as when the convicts joined the tribes, observers were horrified.[92] When Aboriginal warriors wore jackets (and nothing else), ate stolen corn and informed them in perfect English that they wanted to kill them all, they were totally confounded. So when Aboriginal people who were considered 'friendly' and 'trustworthy' retracted cooperation, refused to submit, protested ill treatment, used payback to right wrongs, or resumed the raids and attacks to repel settlers when promises were broken, the whites were appalled and bewildered, and condemned them as intractable 'savages', so unchangeable as to be less than human.[93] But the concepts of 'wild' and 'domesticated', rooted so deeply in the European ways of thinking, failed to recognise the impacts of dispossession, let alone the complex politics of tribal law, inter-tribal relationships and allegiances; it was in short a way of thinking that failed to recognise the humanity of Aboriginal people.

On the Hawkesbury, Yellomundy and Yaragowhy, supposedly bought off with gifts of food and clothing, were obviously considered 'friendly' allies. The warrior Charley, once 'a great savage', must have been thought thoroughly 'tame' by 1805 too. He was probably the sailor whose name D.D. Mann could not recall, and he had even started farming, for he had a 'small spot of ground in cultivation . . . and patiently awaited the maturity of its produce'. Charley 'enjoyed the settlers' friendship' and they knew him well.[94] Both he and Yaragowhy appear to have been of the Branch tribe. So when King sent out detachments of soldiers to hunt the Branch warriors after yet another spate of autumn attacks and atrocities, the white men of the Green Hills thought they could rely on Yaragowhy and Charley.

As usual, the Aboriginal warriors were able to move quickly and lightly, easily evading the soldiers crashing after them. Andrew Thompson organised a party of settlers to join the hunt. The rains had begun, so the party hefted a boat on their shoulders to cross the swollen creeks and the river. They headed west towards the mountains, where they knew the camps of the Branch tribe were. But when they found the campsite on the opposite shore, it was deserted. They knew then that Yaragowhy, whom they had 'left behind under strict assurances of friendship' had taken a short-cut from the Green Hills, swum or canoed across the river, and raced through the bush to warn them.[95]

That probably would have been the end of that campaign, except two unnamed Richmond warriors then agreed to assist the party. Armed with guns, these men skilfully guided the whites away from a decoy fire and straight to a camp 'near the mountains' where the Branch men were making and stockpiling spears—the whites thought several thousand of them, 'frightfully jagged'. Among the seven or eight people killed by the blasts of the muskets was Yaragowhy, said to be dressed in the clothes of the settler dead. The Richmond guides then stopped the party from following retreating Branch men—they would have marched straight into another ambush, for the warriors once more climbed a ridge and were ready to 'hurl stupendous rocks upon their heads'. A guard was left behind to protect Sergeant Aicken, the only farmer on the mountain side of the river, from retributive attacks. When a furious young black man strode into the house demanding to see Aicken's weapons and threatening to search the house, they burst from the other room and shot him dead. It was Charley, 'well known, and little suspected'.[96]

Charley and Yaragowhy, though they mixed with white people, had clearly not renounced their tribal loyalties. But when the reprisal party forced their allegiances, their actions were interpreted by the whites as evidence of treachery and immutable savagery. Corn patch or no, opined the *Gazette*, Charley could not 'refrain from his barbarous habits'. As for the Aboriginal guides, who were obviously the key to the successful strike, they probably considered it a raid on traditional rivals and enemies rather than a win for civilisation and loyalty to the whitefellas. All they wanted, they said, 'was to each seize a wife from the opposing side'. They saw it as a raid to take women.[97]

This is another little clue, a glimpse, dropped casually into the reports: the Richmond men knew there would be women at this camp. The 'battle' scene is transformed—the image of a large group of warriors making thousands of spears dissolves to reveal a camp of men, women and children. Apart from Yaragowhy, the dead were not identified, so we don't know who else was killed. And we don't know if the Richmond men managed to carry off Branch tribe women; or whether soldiers and settlers snatched women and infants too and took them back to the Green Hills.

BANISHMENT, RECONCILIATION AND THE THIRD 'COMING IN', 1805

Faced with constant attacks on both farmers and stock on the Hawkesbury and South Creek, and also repeated raids on the government stock farm at Seven Hills,

King reintroduced the strategy that had successfully eliminated Pemulwuy: he again banished Aboriginal people from the farms and towns 'until the murderers are given up'. Significantly, his order spent a good many words insisting that *settlers* must cooperate:

> And that this Order may be carried into its full effect, the settlers are required to assist each other in repelling those visits; and if any settler . . . harbours any natives, he will be prosecuted for the breach of the Public order . . .[98]

This strategy turned on existing social relations. It would have been meaningless if Aboriginal people were not already living within the settler landscapes, if they did not already have relationships with settlers. King could not banish people who were not there. It must also have been to some extent a relationship of dependence, for the order had the politics of food at its heart. Aboriginal people often still lived in their own country, but the farms meant they had lost access to the richest grounds and their traditional foods, and now relied on settlers for bread, maize and meat. King's reports made frequent mention of this. Some Aboriginal people were already living on or close to the larger farms and estates, such as those of Lieutenant Cummings near Parramatta, Joseph Holt at Cox's Brush Farm, and probably Archibald Bell at Belmont. But King's order meant this food supply was literally cut off: Aboriginal people were not permitted to approach farms, and settlers were forbidden to give them food.

Why did King have to be so explicit about settlers cooperating? Why did settlers, for whose protection this order was issued, have to be threatened with prosecution? Read in reverse, it strongly suggests that settlers *would* 'harbour', or protect and hide, Aboriginal people on their farms, and King knew it. Again, the enemies in this war did not fall neatly along racial lines. This order aimed not only to force Aboriginal people to betray their warrior leaders, but also to force them apart from settlers.

King did not have to wait long. A few days later, Aboriginal people of Prospect, Parramatta and the Cowpastures asked Samuel Marsden to attend a conference 'with a view to opening the way to reconciliation'. A complex dance of diplomacy and negotiation followed, brokered by Aboriginal women with the assistance of a Prospect settler, Jonathon (also called John) Kennedy. When Marsden arrived at the appointed place, the women told him that the men were in conference and would be calling on him when they were ready. And they did: escorted by Kennedy, they went to Parramatta to talk, and Marsden agreed to another meeting. Accompanied by a detachment of soldiers, he returned to Prospect the next day. Twenty people came forward to negotiate while 'prodigious numbers' watched and waited in the surrounding bush.[99]

Marsden was tough: there would be no deal without the surrender of the killers' names. Gradually they were given up. But then the minister added another clause: they would have to help apprehend the killers too. The Aborigines protested and refused, but Marsden was uncompromising. Finally one man stepped forward, then another. Immediately a white guide, John Warby of Prospect, and six soldiers left the meeting ground to begin the hunt. Two days later settlers were ordered not to molest these Aboriginal people—a notice published in the *Gazette* said they were 'sit down at the Brush between Prospect and George's River'. Once Aboriginal people had avoided the dense brush forest; now it was their refuge. For the time being, they were safe.[100]

Those named at Prospect that day were Talboon, Corriangee and Doollonn, who were 'Mountain natives' (possibly Gandangarra); Moonaning and Doongial of the Branch tribe, and Boondudullock of Richmond Hill. None of them were from the same tribes as the informants, and so far scholars have not found their names elsewhere in the records. They may have been the tribal names of warriors the settlers knew by nicknames, like Branch Jack and Musquito. Perhaps Boondudullock was the proper name of Bulldog. In the criss-crossed webs of settler and Aboriginal society it is also possible that old tribal scores were being settled. Two weeks later, John Warby was still in the mountains on the trail of a 'chief delinquent'. But when he was found, it was the Aboriginal guide from Richmond who 'burst into a transport of rage . . . and shot him'.[101]

In the weeks following the Prospect meeting, too, there were more attacks and raids by leaders Tedbury, Branch Jack, Bulldog and Musquito, also called Bush Muschetta, a man from Broken Bay. But soldiers, constables and settlers were also having more success in tracking and arresting them. Tedbury was taken in a raid in the forests at Pennant Hills, and forced to give up more killers' names. He led them to caches of stolen goods and a murder weapon hidden in the rough country at North Rocks. Musquito and Bulldog were arrested in late June after other Aboriginal people were released from gaol on the promise of giving them up.[102] Again, there were probably tribal hostilities at work here, and King and Marsden were exploiting them. With these men in custody, the Europeans wondered, once more, whether Aboriginal people could be tried under British law, and decided, once more, that they could not. King was convinced that British justice would make no sense to people who were ignorant, heathen savages and whose laws revolved around payback. He decided to transport Musquito and Bulldog to Norfolk Island. Tedbury was released and returned to his people.[103]

As Michael Flynn observes, it seems clear from those negotiations at Prospect in May 1805 that 'the clans desperately needed the right to approach the towns and farms of the settlers to obtain food'. The ban also meant that tobacco and alcohol were unavailable, and that moving about safely was difficult, so sacred, ritual and teaching places within the settled areas were impossible to visit. Contests could not be held in Sydney. The new way of life Aboriginal people had forged was suspended, and they needed to resume it. It was another month before they were allowed to return to the Sydney and Parramatta districts, and the ban was not lifted completely until 7 July 1805, just after Musquito and Bulldog were captured. That week, Aboriginal people thronged the roads from the Hawkesbury, the Nepean, from the Cowpastures, Prospect and Georges River, converging on Parramatta. Like the Eora in Sydney fifteen years before, they were 'coming in' for a third time, to meet the governor for reconciliation. A few days later, a great ritual contest was held at Farm Cove, celebrating the return to Aboriginal Sydney.[104]

But away on the Hawkesbury and Broken Bay, the 'Branch Natives', in their 'implacable spirit', continued the fight. Branch Jack made a last assault on a boat in Broken Bay in September. Off Mangrove Point, the Aboriginal people had been welcomed on board and given presents, but that night Branch Jack, along with Woglomigh and Branch warriors, returned to the moored boat and crept aboard in the darkness. The master, old John Pendergrass, heard them whispering, gave the alarm and a salt-boiler grabbed a musket. Woglomigh was shot dead, and Branch Jack staggered back to his father on the shoreline, shot in the head by men he knew well. The rest of the gang 'begged quarter' and their jagged spears were destroyed—but they still tried to lure the boat's people ashore with the promise of a haul of stolen jackets.[105]

In December the wheat fields were again set ablaze. The settlers, confounded as ever about the cause, summoned the elders once more for talks. The *Gazette* reported this exchange: the tribe had no grievances, they admitted their crimes and 'promised to desist'. The Branch elders had decided to call a halt to the raids. They kept their word. For perhaps a year, there were no further attacks reported.[106]

Four years later, back along the Parramatta Road and surrounding farms, Tedbury, forgiven and released, also resumed his raids. Sometimes he was seen with Bondel (Bundle), the former sailor and future Cowpastures 'chief'. But now the gangs appeared to have taken up the ways of the white bushrangers and banditti. Sometimes they menaced and attacked people on the farms, both men and women, other times robbing carts, houses, people walking the roads, even travellers on horseback. They probably adopted the devil-may-care swagger of bushrangers too. Earlier, some soldiers who 'fell in with a horde of natives' at the Flats (Homebush) heard this bold salutation, in perfect English: 'Who comes there, white men I believe!' But when the warriors caught sight of the redcoats and muskets, they fled.[107]

In February 1811, Tedbury was shot dead by Edward Luttrell junior. Luttrell, the son of Surgeon Edward Luttrell, was arrested and gaoled for the killing, but was acquitted and released shortly after. The Luttrell sons continued to have violent relations with Aboriginal people—Hardy describes them as 'wild and uncontrolled'. Robert Luttrell was killed by blows of a waddy during a fight with Mulgowie men on the Hawkesbury in 1811. Was this Aboriginal Law, payback for Tedbury's death? These were not Tedbury's people, and it happened far from his country, so this seems very unlikely. What followed, however, hints at another extraordinary shift in legal thinking and practice. An inquest was held, and the Aboriginal people, instead of disappearing into the bush, 'waited nervously at Windsor' for the outcome. Mulgowie elder and spokesman, Mara Mara, promised the man responsible would be given up if the jury decided it was murder. It seems Aboriginal people not only understood the British legal system but were prepared to abide by it. But sensibilities had crossed both ways: the inquest jury discovered that Robert Luttrell had broken spears and violently attempted to abduct an Aboriginal woman. The death was explainable in Aboriginal terms; it was not judged to be murder.[108]

TROUBLE IN THE SOUTH, 1814

Among the first people to greet the newly arrived Lachlan Macquarie as he sailed through the Heads on 28 December 1809 was an Aboriginal man. He was on the pilot boat meeting the *Dromedary*. This waterborne greeting suggests that the man was Bungaree, whom Macquarie came to regard as the 'chief' of Sydney's Aboriginal people. A few days later, the Aboriginal people of the Sydney region, 'from the Hawkesbury and many miles round' converged once more on Sydney for a great contest to 'honour the new Governor'.[109] In grand spectacle and public rituals and gestures, Macquarie and the Aboriginal people understood one another perfectly.

The new governor included the Aboriginal people in his first proclamations, along with the other ranks: if they 'come in the Way in a peaceable manner' they were not to be 'molested in their persons or Property'. After all that had happened over the past two decades, Macquarie's initial policy echoed Phillip's: he wanted 'to conciliate them as much as possible to our Government and Manners' using 'Kindness and Attention'.[110]

Macquarie arrived in a period of relatively peaceful relations, although violent assaults were still made on convicts attempting to escape overland from the penal settlement at Newcastle. But by 1814 Macquarie believed the Aboriginal people, although only just 'emerged from the remotest State of rude and Uncivilised Nature', were nevertheless 'honestly Inclined, and perfectly devoid of . . . designing Trick and Treachery'. They needed only gentleness and kindness to help them along their long road to civilisation. Others observed that the numbers visiting Sydney had 'fallen off', that 'intimacy had subsided'. Many of the older generation were dead, and it was thought that the younger, having witnessed so much terror and violence, were more timid and less encouraged to 'come among us'.[111]

It must have been a shock, then, when violence erupted on the colony's south-western frontier, near present-day Appin, in early May 1814. The *Gazette* lamented the sudden rupture in the 'tranquillity and good understanding that for the last 5 or 6 years has subsisted'. Three armed soldiers from the Veteran Company saw a group of Aboriginal people raiding a maize field. The soldiers ordered them off, but they refused to leave, 'making use of every term of provocation and defiance' and 'menacing with their spears'. The soldiers fired on them, and a boy was killed. Before they could reload their muskets they were driven off in a hail of spears. Private Isaac Eustace was hit while the other two ran for their lives.[112]

The altercation in the maize field set off the next phase in the frontier wars, a chain of revenge attacks and atrocities. Private Eustace's body was found 'mangled', with one of his hands cut off. A revenge party marched out and killed an Aboriginal woman and three children, whereupon William Baker, Elizabeth Macarthur's stock-keeper and his wife Mary Sullivan, as well as the children of James Daley at Bringelly, were killed in return. Towards the end of May settlers were terrified by rumours of a planned attack, 'when the moon shall become as large as the sun', by the combined forces of the 'mountain tribes' and the hostile and feared people of Jervis Bay on the coast. With the next full moon looming, women and children were evacuated from the farms and the remaining men banded together to watch for attack. That night—3 June 1814—must have passed excruciatingly slowly. Nothing happened. The warriors either thought better of it, or they were masters of the art of bluff.[113]

Had the violence really flared suddenly from nothing, out of years of peace and good relations? Macquarie asked the same question. He commissioned an inquiry by the magistrates which returned the verdict that 'the first personal Attacks were made on the Part of the Settlers and of their Servants'. As we shall see, those 'servants' are particularly important in this story. Moreover, these maize raids were carried out in a 'manner very different to their former habits'. This suggests that similar food supply arrangements had been made here as elsewhere, but also that the oncoming drought had caused food shortages. Even so, the raids had not been carried on to an 'alarming extent, or even in serious Prejudice to any one individual settler'.[114] Macquarie also learned that 'idle and indisposed Europeans' had 'taken liberties with their women', and of the circumstances surrounding the deaths of the woman and children, and the settler victims. 'Having had their Revenge in the way they always Seek it', he concluded, 'I am not at all apprehensive of their making any further attacks'. Macquarie understood payback Law.[115]

Characteristically Macquarie himself went out to talk with the Cowpastures (Muringong) tribe and 'other natives of the interior': another significant meeting, unlocated, mentioned in passing. He told them that they must 'desist from all Acts of Depredation or Violence', to which their blunt reply was that if they were not 'shot at or wantonly attacked', they would not retaliate. Macquarie reminded the white colonists that Aboriginal people were protected by British laws, and that they were forbidden to take the law into their own hands. He continued with a sermon on the history of broader colonial race relations:

> . . . it must be evident that no deep rooted prejudice exists in their Minds against British Subjects or white Men; indeed the free and kindly Intercourses that have subsisted between them from the Foundation of the Colony (now upwards of 26 years) to the present Time, with the exception of a few slight interruptions, prove beyond a Doubt that the Natives have no other Principle of Hostility to the Settlers than what arises from such causal Circumstances as the present may be attributed to.[116]

I suspect Macquarie's historical revisionism elicited guffaws of disbelief from those who remembered the Battle of Toongabbie, the campaigns of Pemulwuy, or who had been driven off the lower Hawkesbury by the Branch warriors. But in Macquarie's scheme, British sovereignty extended across the entire territory, embracing black and white alike. It could not countenance 'deep rooted prejudice', a fundamental Aboriginal hostility to settlers which challenged the rightful settlement of the colony, and the natural historical progression from wilderness and savagery to 'civilisation'. So the raids, the attacks, the deaths and negotiations since Phillip's time were reduced to 'a few slight interruptions', while the present conflict could be resolved within British law.

Continued violence and hostilities in the south soon disrupted this soothing scheme. A few days before this proclamation was published, the men who killed the Aboriginal woman and children were speared to death on William Broughton's farm at Appin. On 21 July Macquarie ordered out his first reprisal party to hunt for the killers of these men and the earlier victims. The party was made up of armed civilians from the Campbelltown area guided by 'friendly natives' of the Cowpastures. Their targets were five Gandangarra, people of the mountains. After three weeks of tramping the country, this party returned, seemingly empty-handed.[117]

SETTLERS, SERVANTS AND ABORIGINAL PEOPLE

There are hints—vague outlines and small clues—of the world beyond these bare bones of names and dates, attacks and counter-attacks, black and white. A far more complex and mutable social landscape was emerging once more on this new frontier. From 1809, floods in the older riverside areas had forced settlement into the forest grounds in the new country south of Liverpool and Cabra-matta, around Camden and Campbelltown, west to the bushrangers' haunts on the Nepean around Mulgoa and Bringelly. The rising elite with their growing interest in sheep and cattle took vast tracts, hundreds of acres of undulating open woodlands: the Coxs at Mulgoa; John Blaxland's huge Luddenham, on the deep bend in the Nepean where it joins the Warragamba River; D'Arcy Wentworth and J.T. Campbell at Bringelly; and Surveyor General John Oxley's Kirkham estate at Narellan. All of these estates had Nepean River frontages, a great advantage, but one which made them vulnerable too. Most of these landholders were absentee owners and were using this land as stock farms. The real occupiers of the new 'estates' were their workers, a population of overseers, stockmen and labourers. Most were convicts and ex-convicts. A few brought wives with them. The buildings were rough slab-and-bark huts and outbuildings, the rafters tied with greenhide: the gracious colonial homesteads and lovely gardens we associate with this area today were still some years off.[118]

The other settlers in this area were the smaller farmers, the humblest still allotted 30-acre blocks fanned out along the creeks and bordering the large estates. They were a mixture of free arrivals, native born and emancipists, and the society they made was quite different from those of the large estates. Around Appin, where the trouble had erupted, the settlers were generally old hands— they had been in the colony for many years, and a number of families had intermarried. The largest landholder here was William Broughton, the Acting Commissary, who acquired 1000-acre Lachlan Vale in 1811. Broughton's wife, the widow Elizabeth Simpson, held another large grant adjoining to the north, and her brother John (or Jonathon) Kennedy lived on Teston Farm just to the west. John Kennedy married Caroline Catapodi (or Best), the stepdaughter of the emancipist William Sykes, their neighbour to the south. And John Kennedy's and Elizabeth Broughton's aunt, Elizabeth Kennedy, had married Andrew Hume, the Superintendent of Convicts, in 1796. The Humes were on a 100-acre farm back along the road to Campbelltown. The settlers around Appin seem to have all been in-laws, aunts and nieces, uncles and nephews.[119]

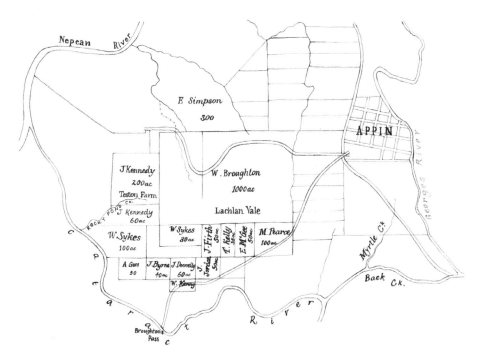

The farms and estates at Appin: the Broughtons' Lachlan Vale lies at the centre of a constellation of farms occupied by the interrelated Sykes, Kennedy, Byrne and Simpson families. The Cataract River flows on the southern side, the Georges River on the east and the Nepean on the west. (Kate Nolan)

This particular web of settler families was thrown across the tongue of land reaching down between the Georges and Nepean rivers to the dead-end gorges of the Cataract River. The rivers here have cut deep into the bones of the country. Some of the farms were seamed by deep rocky creek gullies too, but otherwise the land here is flat or undulating, rolling beautifully into a range of hills to the south of Lachlan Vale. The country was also occupied by the Muringong, by then known as the Cowpastures tribe, the people who first encountered the escaped cattle. Muringong warriors were impressive, their physique later described as 'most remarkable . . . rather short, but stocky, strong and superbly built', their bodypaint magnifying 'their martial attitude and . . . bellicose stance'.[120] The Norongerragal were the people of the Minto–Holsworthy area, and further north-west were the Mulgowie (later the Mulgoa tribe), named for the black swans of the rivers and lagoons, whose country extended along the Nepean south from around Castlereagh. The names of other groups have been lost. Today these peoples are known as Dharawal, the name of the language they spoke.[121]

From at least 1814, these districts were also visited by the Gandangarra (the Reverend Samuel Hassall spelt it Cundenorah) of the mountains. They were said to come down in the autumn months to raid the corn fields, though perhaps seasonal visits had been part of traditional movements too. Described as tall, lighter-skinned and good-looking, the Gandangarra were considered 'a much more hardy and athletic race'. They wore their hair 'tied in a bunch behind'. Early explorers of the region had quickly learned of the deep enmity between the Gandangarra and the Muringong, the peoples of the mountain and the plains. Caley said the Gandangarra were 'greatly dreaded and reverenced' by the people of the Cowpastures. By 1814 they were also depicted as the new 'myall' or wild strangers, fierce and warlike, while the local tribes were considered 'friendly' and helpful.[122]

Indications are that the settlers here already had long-established relationships with Aboriginal people. John (or Jonathon) Kennedy certainly did. By 1805 he was the Prospect settler who assisted the Aboriginal people of Prospect and Parramatta during their reconciliation negotiations. He must have met envoys from the Cowpastures tribe at that time too. His step-nephew William Byrne later wrote that he had 'partly brought up' an Aboriginal boy, Moudonigi, while next door, his mother-in-law Sarah Sykes was well regarded by the Aboriginal people, as she always gave the local people bread.[123] As we shall see, other locals, including ex-surgeon Charles Throsby of Glenfield, Andrew Hume, and his son, the celebrated explorer Hamilton Hume, had familiar and longstanding associations with Aboriginal people too. Throsby's trusted friend and guide Toodwit was known as Broughton, after William Broughton. Throsby himself was noted as a 'persistent critic' of the harsh and brutal treatment Aboriginal people suffered at the hands of settlers.[124]

Then there were settlers who were also bushmen and guides, like John Warby and John 'Bush' Jackson, natural successors of men like the early gamekeepers, and bushmen John Wilson and 'Black Caesar'. Rose calls them the 'outriders of civilisation'. Warby, Jackson and others were likewise on familiar terms with Aboriginal people. But they were not renegades and bandits—their connections and knowledge of country made them useful men, essential for exploratory trips and reprisal parties alike. John Warby, an ex-convict who had arrived in 1792, first farmed at Prospect with his wife, Sarah Bentley. His colonial career was tied to the lands to the south, with Aboriginal people and with cattle. The Warbys' Prospect farm was the starting point for all the expeditions travelling down to see the wonderful wild cattle, and Warby guided the parties. From 1802 he was also a herdsman down at the Cowpastures, guarding the cattle against raiders. Carol Liston writes that 'much of his knowledge of the district came from his friendship with the Dharawal', and he would also have met Gandangarra people when he guided George Caley's expedition to the Cowpastures in 1804. He went with Aboriginal guides and soldiers in pursuit of the outlawed Aboriginal men named during the 1805 reconciliation. By 1809 he had acquired a new grant at Airds, in the country of Aboriginal people whom he probably knew personally. He and 'Bush' Jackson, along with local Aboriginal men, led the unsuccessful 1814 reprisal party against the Gandangarra killers. Men like Warby, perhaps more than most, walked that complex, strange and often contradictory 'middle ground' between British authority and overlapping Aboriginal laws, alliances and rivalries.[125]

We need to look again at those 1814 attacks at Appin in the light of this social landscape. The smaller settler families—the Kennedys, the Sykes—were living on their own farms, while the larger Lachlan Vale was occupied by William Broughton's servants. One of William Sykes' stepsons recalled many decades later that the 'old soldier' who had shot the boy in the maize field in 1814 and been speared in return, was 'a servant on the Broughton Estate'.[126] So the soldiers' presence and the attack were not accidental. It is likely that Broughton arranged for armed veterans to patrol the place. After Eustace's body was found, it was Broughton's servants who 'went into Campbelltown and brought out a party of settlers'. The reality of what happened that night explains the fury of the subsequent killings. Charles Throsby, through patient questioning and cross-checking among his Aboriginal friends, discovered that the white party had gone into an Aboriginal camp at night, when people were asleep, and started shooting. Then

> . . . the people, not content with shooting at them in the most treacherous manner in the dark, but actually cut the woman's arm off and stripped the scalp of her skull over her eyes, and on going up to them and finding one of the children only wounded, one of the fellows deliberately beat the infants brains out with the butt of his musket.

Throsby found out who the victims were too: they were the wife and two children of Bitugally, and a child of Yellooming, both believed to be Gandangarra men. He continued in disgust: 'The whole of the bodies were then left in that state by the (brave) party unburied as an example for the savages to view the following morning'.[127]

But the bodies did not lie there for long. They were buried by John Kennedy in a corner of Teston Farm. Kennedy fenced off the graves properly and local Aboriginal elders say they are still there today, crowned with blackberries. These burials strongly suggest not only a bond between Kennedy and the Gandangarra people, but that the camp where this attack took place was somewhere nearby, or on the farm itself. Teston Farm and the gorge-locked land south of Appin may have been a retreat, a place of security for the Gandangarra as well as other Aboriginal peoples.[128]

Broughton's Lachlan Vale was the scene of payback in June. The killers, John Price and Dennis Newingham, had been identified and were singled out. They did not even see the warriors until they were 20 metres away. One fell 'covered in spear wounds', the other 'defended himself to the last extremity' until he died. The other servants spread all around the estate were startled to hear the warriors' great shout after the deed was done.[129]

CANDIDATES FOR CIVILISATION

Macquarie was also thinking about how to 'reconcile the natives' after the violence and killings at Appin. His solutions were remote from personal justice and alliances, from geography, hunger and payback: they revolved around the transformation of the Aboriginal people through Christianisation, education and small-farming. Schools and farms were intended as some compensation for the loss of 'the Natural advantages they previously derived from the animal and Other Productions', their native foods. They were also intended to hurry history along: for the Aboriginal people were considered to be already on a grand march from savagery to civilisation.[130]

The first 'candidates for civilisation' were the children. From August 1814, after the violence had abated, Macquarie began making plans for a Native Institution, a school where Aboriginal children, removed from their own people, would be cared for and instructed in Christianity, reading, writing and useful skills. He had been inspired by a suggestion from missionary William Shelley some months earlier. Shelley's letter argued persuasively against prevailing beliefs: he was certain Aboriginal children could learn to read and write and become 'useful'. But it was perceptive at a deeper level. Shelley was one of the few people who took the long view of race relations. He could see that the earlier attempts to 'conciliate' and 'civilise' the Aboriginal people by dressing them up in fine clothes, providing them with food and so on, was in the long run cruel folly, because they did not provide a 'useful' or respected role for Aboriginal people in white society. 'Where is the human being', he asked, 'who would be pleased to live at a Gentleman's table, and wear his Clothes, without having any prospect in view but food and Clothes, while he remained useless and despised in the Society in which he lived?'[131]

Then Shelley touched upon something still more fundamental: the fact that Aboriginal children brought up in white society had no hope of finding a partner, a mate, and thus no prospect of marriage:

A Solitary individual, either Woman or Man, educated from infancy, even well, among Europeans, would in general, when they grow up, be rejected by the other Sex of Europeans, and must go into the Bush for a companion.

The fact that Aboriginal children, taken as infants and raised in white households, so often returned to their own people once they reached puberty had long been remarked upon, and was seen as more evidence of Aboriginal inability to become 'civilised'.[132] But the penny dropped with Shelley. The fact was, he argued, no matter how well educated or 'civilised' an Aboriginal person became, they were still Aboriginal. He considered interracial marriage impossible; it simply could not be countenanced. 'No European woman would marry a *Native*, unless some abandoned profligate', he wrote firmly, and 'the same may be said of Native Women received for a time among Europeans'. The imagined spectre of Bennelong, cosseted by Europeans, supposedly spurned by women of both races, was powerfully at work here. Shelley may also have been struck by the words of an Aboriginal sailor returning to Sydney on the brig *James Hayes* in 1814, published in the *Gazette*. When asked why he was going back to his people, he retorted 'Will you keep me company? . . . Will any white man or woman keep me company? . . . No white women will have me; then why wish me to keep away from my own people?' Remember, too, the young girl brought up by the Lambs, a stranger to her own people, talking to the Aboriginal boy on the river before she burned the farmhouse down.[133] And Moowattin, the good-natured youth who had been brought up in white society and been of such help to George Caley. He visited England, lived the high life, dressed 'in the pink of fashion', but on his return was reduced to labouring on a settler's farm at Pennant Hills. He raped a young white woman at Parramatta in 1816 and became the first Aboriginal person to be tried in a British court. Aboriginal warriors who had killed settlers were deported or set free. But Daniel Moowattin, having been raised from infancy in

European society, was considered to know the difference between good and evil. He was found guilty and hanged in 1816.[134]

The Native Institution was a radical and thoroughgoing experiment in assimilating Aboriginal children so that their future within white society was possible and acceptable (to whites). The boys and girls would be trained in useful skills, so they could join the labour force, and they would find suitable partners among one another. So this plan went well beyond their childhood years—every aspect of their lives would be controlled and directed. The children were to be taken while still young, remoulded as literate Christians, then suitably married off and set up on small acreages, still under the supervision of white managers. There were marriages between some who came of age at St John's Parramatta— among them Maria, daughter of Yellomundy, to Dicky, son of Bennelong—and then a farming settlement was established out on the Richmond Road for the newlyweds and others to whom Macquarie returned small fragments of country. Soon more black farmers came to join them, and the place became known as the Blacks Town, from which the modern suburb of Blacktown, further east, took its name. Macquarie held out the inducements of free tools, seeds, clothing, and victuals for six months to prospective Aboriginal settlers. It was the very same scheme as had been originally devised to reform the convicts.[135]

The school at Parramatta became one of the governor's pet projects. A board was established and met regularly, a set of rules and regulations was drawn up and published in December 1814. A house and a large block of land were purchased in Parramatta, William and Elizabeth Shelley were installed as managers, clothing, food, equipment and tools were bought. There was only one thing missing: children. Shelley already had four Aboriginal children with him when he wrote to Macquarie in April, but no more appeared. Macquarie set about devising a recruitment strategy, and his solution was characteristi- cally spectacular: he would hold a grand feast at Parramatta, now the centre of cross-cultural meetings and negotiations, for all the Aboriginal people of the colony. He set a date of 28 December, 'the day after the full moon'. Full moon time was corroboree time. This feast set a precedent which continued for over two decades, for it was adopted by Aboriginal people themselves as a great meeting of all the tribes, a modern corroboree, and thus became a significant annual event in its own right. In 1814, however, its purpose was to persuade Aboriginal people to give up their children. Only around 60 people turned up in the Parramatta marketplace to hear about the advantages of sending their children to the new school. Many others hung back, despite the lure of roast beef, potatoes and grog, fearing the 'colonists' intentions'. It was said that the distant clans stayed away because they were afraid their children would be taken by force.[136]

By the end of that first feast, four more children had been relinquished to the school as 'candidates for civilisation'. It is unclear whether their parents understood Macquarie's fourteenth regulation: once a child was in the institution, he or she could never be reclaimed. The girls and boys were not to be 'discharged' until they were fourteen and sixteen respectively. Aboriginal parents stood in the streets of Parramatta, peering through the spaced paling fence Shelley had built especially so they could 'watch their children at work and play'. Presumably the children saw them too. For some the misery of separation and the alien world of routines, clothing, scripture, cleanliness and work were unbearable. Children escaped from the school by squeezing through the fence and returned to their people. Six months later there were only five children left, including Maria, who was so fluent in English she acted as an inquest court translator even before coming to the school. (Artist and Coroner William Lewin said her English was 'nearly equal to his own'.) Despite the inducements and rewards Macquarie apparently offered parents, Shelley wrote disappointedly that 'The natives are remarkably backward to give up their children'. Their attachment to their children was seen as savage stupidity. Macquarie's experiment was looking like an expensive folly.[137]

Macquarie also implemented other schemes to 'civilise' Aboriginal adults through farming. These naked people could be taught how to become true possessors of the soil. King had apparently arranged for Charley to farm on the Hawkesbury, but Macquarie was the first governor to officially grant parcels of land back to Aboriginal people. Although most soon lapsed, were retracted or regranted to whites, they do signal the beginning of an important, longer history: the steady reacquisition of land by Aboriginal people through reserves, grants and purchase over the nineteenth century.[138]

In Sydney, Bungaree had become 'Macquarie's favourite', the main contact and negotiator between the governor and the Sydney Aboriginal people. Macquarie decided to formalise Bungaree's leadership and set him and his people up on a new farm at Georges Head on Port Jackson, the country of the Borogegal. Naturally the inaugural ceremony in January 1815 was a splendid affair, involving a large party of ladies and gentlemen boating down the harbour to this picturesque place. The Aboriginal people received slop clothing, tools and food, and, best of all, a new fishing boat. Bungaree himself was ceremonially presented with a gorget, an engraved metal breastplate declaring him 'Chief of the Broken Bay Tribe'. It was a curious title considering that Bungaree was now so closely associated with Sydney. Small rectangular huts were built for them, just as they had been built for the first convict settlers. Now appropriately skilled convicts were sent to Georges Head to teach them farming.[139]

It was another transformation strategy: settled in their neat cabins in 'that very pretty place', and set to industriously farming, Bungaree's people would cease their 'roaming' and enjoy a reliable food supply. They would also serve as a model for others to follow: this is how it's done, this is how to be a 'civilised' Aborigine. There were practical advantages as well: Georges Head was far enough away from Sydney to discourage Aboriginal people from visiting the town. In effect this was also the first official attempt to remove Aboriginal people from the urban environment, reversing Phillip's relentless attempts to bring them in. The farm would separate them from the evils of town life too.

CONFLICT AND MASSACRE, 1815–16

The Native Institution at Parramatta and the farm at Georges Head were intended as models for the future, and to demonstrate the good and peaceable intentions of the British towards all Aboriginal people. They were supposed to 'ameliorate' the conditions of a people who were in 'a wretched state' because they had been dispossessed, and to stave off further outbreaks of violence and warfare. In the context of the reality of frontier dispossession, violent conflict over food, women and labour, as well as the complexity of intertribal politics, Macquarie's grand gestures seem surreal: they involved such small and select numbers of Aboriginal people, and were so far from the contested country, and so unlikely to appeal. As we shall see, it was the annual Parramatta Feasts, originally devised to secure children for the school, which played a crucial role instead.

Fatal conflict broke out at Bringelly at the end of February 1816. Here the large estates fronted the Nepean to the east, while the west was still wild, marshy and rocky—perfect country from which to launch lightning raids. Thirty or 40 Aboriginal people descended upon the huts on G.T. Palmer's farm and stole his servants' possessions. Outraged servants and stock-keepers from the surrounding farms formed an armed party and marched over the river in pursuit the next day—only in order to 'recover their goods', they said later. Struggling through the swamps on the opposite bank, they walked straight into an ambush. The warriors closed in on them, wrenched away their muskets and 'commenced a terrible attack', firing the muskets and showering them with spears. Four white men were killed and another was speared in the back. The rest were chased back over the river to Captain Fowler's farm.[140]

The warriors were not satisfied: the next day Fowler's farm was attacked by a party of 60 men. Mrs Wright, the resident farmer's wife, and a male servant climbed into the loft of the house where they cowered in terror as spears pierced the roof above them and the bark ceiling below. In desperation, the man flung open a dormer window to beg for their lives. Outside among the raiders they saw someone they thought they knew: David Budbury. They appealed to him and he called back that 'they should not be killed this time'. The warriors gathered up everything they could carry from the house, and called out 'Goodbye!' as they headed back over the river.[141]

Aboriginal raiders who spoke English and knew how to use guns: once more, this does not sound like a raid by 'wild' mountain people from beyond the line of settlement. And there was the man they knew, David Budbury, who evidently knew them. Could this have been the same 'friendly' Budbury of the Muringong (Cowpastures tribe), John Warby's friend and associate, who assisted official parties and explorers, who had greeted Governor Macquarie? It seems unlikely: Charles Throsby, with whom Budbury took refuge, publicly denied it, saying the terrified man was mistaken.[142] Nevertheless David Budbury, whoever he was, responded to their call, he had shouted up to the roof in English. Throsby himself offered a possible explanation in a letter to Chief Police Magistrate D'Arcy Wentworth shortly after this attack. He warned him about the camp on the flat opposite the Bringelly farms (including Wentworth's own) where the rocky country offered 'so many retreats'. Any party sent after them 'ought to act with caution, those natives who have been brought up among the white people being extremely cunning'. Throsby was saying there *were* 'domesticated natives' among them, boys who had been brought up on the farms with the settlers, boys who knew the whites' ways—and their weaknesses. This would explain why some knew how to use guns, spoke perfect English, and behaved with swaggering audacity.[143]

A week later the Gandangarra and their allies struck again just to the south at Camden. The news flew round the district: they had attacked the Macarthur estate, killed three of the men and were heading for Oxley's Kirkham across the Nepean. Once more women and children were evacuated and resident settlers, including the Reverend Samuel Hassall, were rallied by the local magistrate Robert Lowe. They formed a posse of about 40, armed with a motley collection of muskets, pistols, pikes and pitchforks. Budbury was among the 'friendly natives' who guided the party, and he acted as interpreter. The settlers were warned that the Gandangarra would 'show fight' but it seems they were led straight to the great 'pirpundicular rock', as Hassall recounted to his brother, north-west of upper Camden where the Gandangarra were waiting. It was another ambush from high ground, the same tactic used by the Branch tribe a decade before. When Budbury shouted at them—and one wonders what he said—the warriors 'immediately began to dance in a manner daring our approach', a furious dance of warning and defiance. They had new tactics to evade musket balls too: every time they saw the guns presented for firing, they dropped down to the ground, 'and then get up and dance'. In between dropping and dancing, they hurled spears and stones 'in great abundance' upon the heads of the whites below. The settler party fell into panicked disarray and fled, Hassall told his brother:

> ... in such a manner that il wonder a great number of us was not killed, some even threw off their shoes to enable them to run fast, others being weak and feeble rowled down the hill, the natives still pressing hard.[144]

They were chased up and down hills so steep Hassall could scarcely keep up, even though he was on horseback. Men feared going back to their farms, terrified of finding their wives and children speared to death. Women were worried sick about their husbands: 'One said she would not go till her husband whent with her', wrote Hassall, 'or she would die with him'. The men kept watch, some patrolling the tracks between Kirkham and the Hassalls' Macquarie Grove all through the night. But everything had gone eerily quiet.

These attacks by the Gandangarra and whoever had joined them reveal sophisticated and effective war strategies. The reported number of white victims wasn't high but the toll on settler psyche was devastating. Their reprisal parties were completely outmanoeuvred and routed. But, as David Roberts points out, these stories were published to encourage governments to send out soldiers. We have no available evidence about the settlers' attacks on Aboriginal people, though there must have been ongoing violence and abductions, and more victims: these events are lost. By the end of the month there were more dreadful settler casualties: on the Nepean at present-day Yarramundi, Maria Lewis and her male servant were killed—she was decapitated and the man's body was 'mangled'.[145]

Macquarie, like Phillip in 1790, had heard enough. Kindness and encouragement, and all his benevolent gestures and gifts, had been spurned. It was time to bring down the true power of British military might upon these naked savages. Rumbles of a planned offensive reached Charles Throsby at Glenfield, and he penned the worried letter to Wentworth in which he insisted on the innocence of the Gandangarra men Macquarie had outlawed—Bitugally and Yellooming. Besides, he wrote, 'all the friendly natives' had now left the hostile camp opposite the Bringelly farms. According to Throsby, friends and enemies were clearly demarcated, and his Glenfield estate was a retreat for the innocent. What he feared was the stupidity and brutality of 'the ignorant part of the white people' who could not tell one Aboriginal person from another, and who were baying for revenge after the deaths of Palmer's workers a month earlier. It was their indiscriminate attacks which would unleash more violence and put more white people at risk.[146] His words proved to be prophetic, though the 'ignorant' lower orders were not the perpetrators.

Throsby's letter also contains clues to an undertow of local alliances which must have eroded clear distinctions between friends and enemies. He reported that the guides John Warby and Bush Jackson had come to Glenfield looking for the Aboriginal men there, but found they were out fishing with D'Arcy Wentworth's son John. Warby and Jackson were serious: they soon returned and took Budbury 'and the others' (probably Bundle, previously known as Bondel) away to talk. Whatever the white men said terrified them; they came back 'under a considerable impression of fear'. Throsby tried to calm them down and reassure them they were safe, and sat down to write to Wentworth. But what had been said? I think Warby and Jackson already had their orders: they were to guide a massive military offensive against all the Aboriginal people of the Sydney region. They clearly impressed the Aboriginal men with the seriousness and danger of the situation: Budbury and Bundle must join the military party to hunt other Aboriginal people, otherwise they themselves became targets. Or at least they must be *seen* to be joining the party.

Meanwhile, 30 kilometres to the south, Gandangarra men including Bitugally and Yellooming had moved onto John Kennedy's Teston Farm at Appin, where their kin were buried. Perhaps they had got wind of what was about to happen too. But as we shall see, the warriors were there not only as refugees, but to protect the Appin farms from hostile attack. Was this the real reason for Throsby's Aboriginal guests at Glenfield too? How many of the settlers had made arrangements like this with Aboriginal warriors to protect them against the raids and attacks of others?

On 10 April 1816 Macquarie sent out three detachments of soldiers, each commanded by an officer, and accompanied by Aboriginal guides to comb the entire colony. They were ordered to track down, capture or kill all Aboriginal people, with no distinction between 'friendly' and 'hostile', although they carried lists of particular men who were wanted as killers. Macquarie ordered the bodies of the slain hung up in the trees 'in order to strike the greater terror into the survivors'. He wanted the hostile people gone, 'driven across the mountains'. Whereas Phillip had specifically excluded women and children from attack in 1790, now their deaths were considered unavoidable. They were to be buried 'where they fell'. But Macquarie had the severely under-enrolled Native

Institution on his mind too. He also ordered the officers to bring in twelve boys and six girls, but 'only fine, healthy and good-looking children'. The school was to be a showpiece after all. Ugly children would not do.[147]

And so a 'tremendous procession' marched once more out of Sydney. Captain Schaw and his men peeled off to the Hawkesbury, Lieutenant Dawe headed south to the Cowpastures and Captain Wallis trooped down to the furthest districts of Airds and Appin. Each detachment had both European and Aboriginal guides. Lieutenant Dawe had Bush Jackson with him, Wallis had John Warby, as well as Bundle and Budbury. Led by Aboriginal guides Bidgee Bidgee and Harry, Schaw's men marched up and down the Hawkesbury and Grose rivers and up to Kurrajong for days following false tip-offs and a trail of hit-and-run raids without seeing a single Aboriginal person, let alone taking any prisoners. Meanwhile down at the Cowpastures, Lieutenant Dawe, led by Tindale, the 'Chief of the Cowpastures Tribe', was similarly unsuccessful. He did locate the large camp of 70 huts north of Bents Basin—this was the 'hostile' camp opposite the Bringelly farms—but he was taken there by a white stock-keeper from the Macarthur estate. Moreover, the people there had been warned, and the camp was deserted. However, another tip-off from a stock-keeper did result in a dawn raid on a large camp on the Macarthur estate itself—two men were shot dead and a boy was taken prisoner.[148]

Already, we can see the operational problems: the fixed grid of the British military raid was forced over slippery, complex local networks, the chains of affiliation, arrangements for 'personal justice' and the superior local knowledge of both country and Aboriginal camps and movements. The black and white guides were supposed to loyally guide: instead they seem to lead the soldiers away from camps, or on wild goose chases, or they professed ignorance of the country they were marching over, which in the case of Harry and Bidgee Bidgee was probably true. Conversely some locals—mostly stockmen and convict servants, who perhaps had most reason to want revenge—were only too willing to assist with useful information. Yet others were clearly trying to decoy the soldiers. But which voices in this cacophony were telling the truth and which were deliberately deceiving? Who was in league with whom? For weeks the soldiers marched from one farm to another, chasing phantom sightings.

Eventually officers resorted to climbing the highest hills at night to watch for 'smokes' or the glow from campfires, their only hope of locating the camps.[149] Although this was supposed to be war, the surprise attack on camps of sleeping people was the only realistic strategy, as it had been since the beginning.

Captain Wallis marched his men south from Liverpool and was just as frustrated by his guides. Warby soon let it be known that he could not be responsible for Budbury and Bundle, and sure enough, they vanished one night when Warby was supposed to be watching them. Wallis was furious and berated the man, to no avail. A few days later Warby himself decided he could not continue and disappeared. He claimed that if Aboriginal people caught sight of him, they would suspect something, and this would jeopardise the operation.[150] Since the military raids must have already been common knowledge, this explanation makes very little sense. I suspect Warby either could not bring himself to betray his Aboriginal associates, or feared some terrible retribution from them.

Wallis' information on the whereabouts of Aboriginal groups kept pointing to Lachlan Vale, the Broughton farm at Appin, and his contingent arrived there on 12 April. He went over to the Kennedy farm next door, and after reassuring the nervous John Kennedy and Hamilton Hume that the Aboriginal men there would not be harmed, realised that two of them were outlaws on his wanted list— Bitugally and Yellooming. Kennedy and Hume said they were there to protect the farms and lied frantically to protect them. Hume alleged he had seen with his own eyes the governor remove the names from the list, and offered to ride to Sydney with them to intercede with the governor. Wallis was swayed. His orders were to make no distinction between 'hostile' and 'friendly', yet earlier he had not pursued Aborigines at Botany Bay after reports that they were 'friendly'. Now, on Teston Farm, he did not arrest men he was assured were 'friendly' and 'innocent'. He sent off to Sydney for instructions. Meanwhile more reports came in from settlers: there was an encampment on Kenny's 30-acre farm just to the south. Off marched the soldiers, only to find the Aboriginal people had 'retired o'er the rocks of the George's River'—this was in fact the steep-sided Cataract River just east of Broughtons Pass. Wallis missed them even though he had 'taken a circuit in the hopes of surprising them'. Evidently he knew the geography of this part of the world.[151]

Two weeks after his party had left Sydney, Wallis still had no result. Yet another report came in: they were gathered 'in force' at William Redfern's farm at Minto, some 30 kilometres to the north. The detachment marched back up the road to Campbelltown after them, and once more it proved to be a ruse. Wallis was furious with the informant, an overseer named Macallister, whom he thought must have acted through 'personal fears or a wish to succour the natives'. He wished he could punish the man.

Another message arrived with a servant. There was an Aboriginal group camped again at Lachlan Vale, and a convict called Thomas Noble could lead them to the place. The soldiers must have been tired, frustrated and edgy by this stage. Nevertheless at one o'clock on the moonlit morning of 17 April, they marched back down to Appin. Noble kept his word and led them to the campsite. There was no-one there, but the fires were still burning. Knowing they could not have gone far, a few of the soldiers searched the bush to the west. Someone heard the cry of a child. Wallis immediately 'formed line rank entire' and the soldiers 'pushed through a thick brush' towards that cry. They were also heading directly towards 'the precipitous banks of a deep rocky creek', the gorge of the Cataract River, 60 metres deep. The line of men pushed on, the dogs set up a frantic barking. As the soldiers opened fire on them, the Aboriginal people 'fled over the cliffs' and were smashed to death in the gorge. Others were wounded or shot dead. The soldiers secured only two women and three children—the rest had escaped or were so badly injured, 'death would . . . be a blessing'. They counted fourteen bodies 'in different directions' including that of an old man, Balgin, and more women and children. As always, old people, women and children were the most vulnerable in these dawn raids on camps.[152]

Wallis decided their bodies were too difficult to recover for burial, but it seems those of two warriors, Durelle and Cannabayagal, were worth the trouble. They were hauled up, and Wallis ordered Lieutenant Parker to cart them away, to be 'hanged in a conspicuous part of a range of hills near Mr Broughtons'. The spot was later remembered by William Byrne as 'McGee's Hill'. Edward McGee's grant bordered Lachlan Vale to the south, and there is a hill which stands a little higher than the others along that rolling green range. If this was the place, the soldier must have carried or dragged the warriors' bodies back through the brush

'A range of hills near Mr Broughton's'. Edward McGee's grant and the highest hill in this range are just to the south (right) of this view. (Photo: G. Karskens, 2007)

and the cleared ground over 2 or 3 kilometres in order to hoist them up in the trees on the hilltop there.[153]

The soldiers thought they had seen a familiar figure among those who managed to escape the massacre: Budbury. They waited to ambush him and the others at a pass over the river—probably Broughtons Pass just to the south. It may be that Budbury had left Wallis' party to warn these people. There are also hints that, rather than clear-cut enmity, there had been some association between the local and the mountain peoples, for Durelle is said to have been a Dharawal-speaker, and Cannabayagal was a well-known Gandangarra warrior and leader from the Burragorang Valley.[154]

Meanwhile, Macquarie had ordered the arrest of Bitugally and Yellooming. Their former protector John Kennedy was now extremely keen to cooperate with Captain Wallis. He provided ropes to bind the two men, along with the women and children who survived the massacre, and a cart to take them to Sydney. Kennedy and William Sykes now feared Aboriginal retribution and begged Wallis to leave soldiers behind to protect them, and he did.[155]

Back in Sydney, the massacre was reported in vague and muffled tones. Macquarie's proclamation in the *Gazette* on 4 May was long-winded but said only that 'several Natives have been unavoidably killed and wounded'. They themselves were to blame because they had not 'surrendered themselves on being called to do so'. As for the unnamed, unnumbered Appin victims, who had not had a chance to surrender, their deaths had been 'unavoidable' too, but would hopefully be useful in deterring further 'outrages':

And although . . . some few innocent Men, Women and Children may have fallen in these Conflicts, yet it is to be earnestly hoped that this unavoidable Result, and the Severity which has attended it, will eventually strike Terror amongst the surviving Tribes and deter them from further Commission of such sanguinary Outrages and Barbarities.

In Macquarie's report to Bathurst in England, he added the fiction that the Aboriginal people on Broughton's land had 'resisted' the soldiers and failed to mention that the five prisoners were women and children:

. . . the occurrence of most importance . . . was under Captain Wallis's direction, who, having Surprized One of the Native Encampments and meeting with some resistance, killed 14 of them and made 5 Prisoners; among the killed there is every reason to believe that Two of the most ferocious and Sanguinary of the Natives were included.

All the participants of the military operation, even Warby, Budbury and Bundle, were handsomely rewarded in spirits, shoes, cash, clothing, blankets, food and tobacco.[156]

Captain James Wallis, an officer generally known as 'brave, efficient, religious and humane', wrote the only official report on what really happened at Appin. There was nothing triumphant in it. He said that the massacre had been a 'melancholy but necessary duty', and he deeply regretted the deaths of the old man, the women and children. Nevertheless, there is a subtle attempt here to deflect blame for the deaths of innocents: the 'natives' after all had thrown *themselves* into the ravine in panic, an unfortunate occurrence, but not the direct doing of his soldiers. But given Wallis' knowledge of the local topography, I think he knew that the deep gorge lay beyond that brush, and that the Aboriginal people, including the child whose cry betrayed them, were trapped between the precipice and the advancing soldiers. He would have known they had little choice but to be shot or driven over.[157]

There is one other eyewitness report: almost ninety years later, William Byrne's recollections of the massacre, which happened when he was eight, were written down and published. Byrne was rather more laconic and frank: 'The Government then sent up a detachment of soldier', he said, 'who ran a portion of them into a drive, shot sixteen of them, and hanged three on McGee's Hill'. A *drive*: that old nineteenth-century word, used for mobs of cattle and sheep, but also for rounding up, chasing, capturing and killing Aboriginal people.[158]

In later years, legends of Aboriginal people driven over high cliffs to their deaths became part of oral tradition in many other country towns. As historians diligently investigating these stories have found, there is often no other evidence to verify them, but they do serve to explain the absence of Aboriginal people in settler landscapes. The single horrific event of 'the drive', often tied to local landmarks like cliffs, bluffs and gorges, both telescopes and obscures the long and complex history of frontier conflict—as well as the fact that Aboriginal people occasionally drove the settlers back. The Appin massacre may be their foundational story.[159]

William Byrne added some gruesome details to his telling of the massacre. After the three bodies had been strung up, he said, 'they . . . cut off the heads and brought them to Sydney, where the Government paid 30s and a gallon of rum each for them'. Was this a case of unreliable local lore, of Byrne sensationalising his story with horrifying details of the olden days? After all, Wallis' official report mentioned only two bodies and said nothing of decapitation. In fact, Byrne's account was accurate, while Wallis' was veiled with silences. In 1991, the National Museum of Australia in Canberra received three skulls. They had been held in the Anatomy Department at the University of Edinburgh for the previous 175 years. One is labelled 'G10 Carnamabygal': it is the skull of the Gandangarra leader Cannabayagal, killed at the Appin massacre. This skull, along with the two others, had been given to the university by a royal navy surgeon, who had received them from Lieutenant Parker. The bone still bears 'clear cut marks' where Parker or one of his soldiers severed the heads from the bodies, probably on McGee's Hill. As curator Mike Pickering points out, it is very likely that the other two skulls (G9 'Skull of a chief', and G11, the skull of a woman 'from the Cowpastures Tribe') are also massacre victims, probably Durelle and an unnamed woman. Silent yet eloquent, like the other remains of Aboriginal people making the long journeys home they serve 'as a reminder that the events of the past echo to the present'.[160]

PAYBACK AND RECONCILIATION

The Appin massacre is often said to have marked the end of hostilities on the Cumberland Plain—a painful, cathartic event which nevertheless brought peace. In fact, it unleashed another spate of violence and killings. Macquarie's military offensive resulted in at least fifteen deaths, but failed to remove the resistance leaders. In June settlers at the Kurrajong Brush on the steeply rising foothills of the Blue Mountains were attacked with such ferocity that by the end of the month Joseph Hobson was the only one left 'on that line of farms'. On 7 July 1816 he too was killed, speared through the heart, head split open, body mangled. In August the attacks on Cox's Mulgoa farm were renewed too. A shepherd was found dead and mutilated, and in an echo of Appin, 200 'very fine sheep' were hurled down an 'immense precipice'. The *Gazette* reported an old nightmare in this new phase of war: 'they now carry the appearance of an extensive combination in which all but a few who remain harmless in the settlements are united in the determination to do all the harm they can'. Over the next seven months at least, Macquarie and Windsor magistrate William Cox responded in kind, unofficially sending out parties of settlers and police to comb the Nepean and Hawkesbury, hunting and killing Aboriginal people.[161]

Besides the ongoing raids, Macquarie also reverted to King's successful strategy of banishment. This time, armed warriors were forbidden to approach within a mile of any town or farm, and no more than six Aboriginal people, even unarmed, could 'loiter' on any farm. Since men always carried spears and clubs, and Aboriginal family groups usually numbered more than six, this was virtual banishment. Lists of wanted men were published in the following weeks. Once more, settlers were forbidden to 'harbour or conceal' any of them, and they were banned from 'providing Aid or Provisions' to friendly Aborigines unless they gave up the outlaws. Again, banishment and the withholding of food proved effective weapons.[162] Gradually, some of the warriors were killed, or captured, arrested, sentenced and exiled. Every returning party also brought back Aboriginal children, some of them of mixed descent, for Macquarie's school. Only four children, two boys and two girls, had been captured during the April military raids, and the boys soon ran away. Now the school was finally filling up. It did become one of Macquarie's showpieces. Official guests and ship's officers were invited to see the children; obedient, orderly, reciting their prayers, their black faces contrasting strikingly with their white clothes.[163]

In November Macquarie declared an amnesty for the rest of the wanted warriors, on condition that they gave themselves up before 28 December 1816, the proposed date of the 'General Friendly Meeting of the Natives' at Parramatta. It is unclear whether any of the named outlaws actually did give themselves up by the specified date (one, Narrang Jack, did so a few months later) but the Annual Meeting at the end of 1816 was a great success.[164] Nearly 180 Aboriginal people appeared in the Parramatta marketplace and were seated according to their tribes behind their 'chiefs'—spatial arrangements mimicking those of the contests. Macquarie himself moved around the circle, speaking with each group in turn. Then came the investitures: 'chiefs' were ceremonially presented with breastplates, while two of the 'guides' from the military raid, Tindale and Harry, were promised 'Reward of Merit' breastplates. The children from the Native Institution were paraded around the circle and showed off their new skills in reading. Some of the Aboriginal women wept to see them. More children were surrendered, among them four-year-old Dicky, the 'son of the memorable Benni-long'. The official party then left to dine at Government House 'amidst long and recurring shouts of acclamation' from the assembled Aboriginal people, and the platters of roast beef and potatoes, baskets of bread and buckets of grog were dragged out for the great feast to begin. It was, the *Gazette* reported, 'a delighted congress' full of 'general festivity and good humour'.[165]

The long war on the Cumberland Plain was over. Macquarie declared that peace had been achieved at last. In February 1822, as he and Elizabeth sailed through the Heads, war broke out on a new frontier, the Bathurst Plains, over the mountains to the west.[166]

———•◦•———

The war, atrocities and hard-won truces of those first 28 years were etched deep into the memories of settlers and Aboriginal people alike. The stories emerged, like the tips of icebergs, in local talk and memory, and when old hands were asked about the past. They were told in snippets and glimpses when white colonists grew old, were proudly named pioneers and asked to record their stories for future generations; and when Aboriginal people grew old, were mournfully named 'the last of their tribe' and asked for last memories of a 'dying race'.

But the stories told by Cook and Banks cast long shadows. Their opinions on the Aboriginal people of New South Wales continued to shape the assumptions of rising numbers of immigrants, many of whom published popular accounts of their colonial adventures. Mostly they saw what they expected to see. Late in 1839, Louisa Anne Meredith, sharp-eyed and witty observer of colonial society, who had been in the colony a few months, assured her readers that the Aborigines were a harmless, wandering people 'without attachment' to particular places. They could simply be moved further out into neutral space which belonged to no-one. Besides, wrote Mrs Meredith brightly, '. . . in the cruel annals of colonization, I believe that of New South Wales to be the least objectionable. For the most part it has been peacefully effected.'[167] And so history was made.

Chapter 14

———◆•◆———

AFTERMATH

RETURNING TO BOTANY BAY

In January 1788, the Kameygal first watched the Berewalgal wade ashore in Yarra Bay just west of Bumborah Point on Botany Bay. Sixty years later, Aboriginal people were still living there. The swampy little creek where the strangers were directed when they asked for water still flowed out into the bay; by then it was called Bunnerong Creek. By 1832 an Aboriginal man had been granted a 10-acre lease beside this creek—he already lived there in a hut he had built. His name was Mahroot, he was the son of Meroot and Grang-Grang who were well known and long remembered, and this was his traditional country. Mahroot made his living from fishing the waters of Botany Bay. When he grew old he went to live in a gunyah in the grounds of the Sir Joseph Banks Hotel at Botany. He died there in 1854.[1]

Yarra Bay and the surrounding area remained an isolated place for decades. It was Sydney's 'backyard', where quarantine hospitals, jails, cemeteries and reserves were established to receive the people cast out by the city: the infectious sick, the criminal, the dead; and the Aboriginal people, who made their place in Sydney at La Perouse from the 1880s. Bunnerong Creek was still flowing in the 1930s, but since then land reclamation has obliterated it, along with the shoreline, the swamps, the beach and Mahroot's land. The place where Cook's people

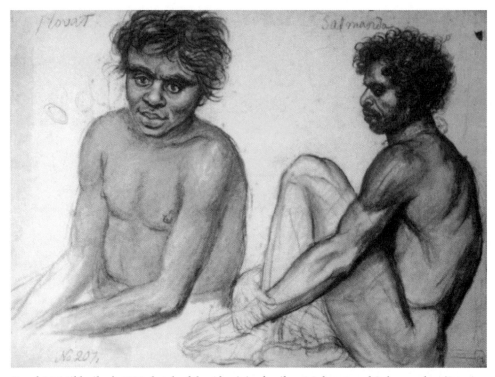

Pavel N. Mikhailov's 1820 sketch of the Aboriginal sailors Mahroot and Salamander. (Russian State Museum)

first met the Gweagal at Kurnell in 1770 has recently been renamed the Meeting Place, within Botany National Park. But, as far as I can make out, the site where that first encounter between Phillip and the Kameygal took place in 1788 now lies below the Port Botany Bus Depot.[2]

INVENTING THE 'REAL ABORIGINE'

By the late 1820s most Europeans could see only two kinds of Aboriginal people—if they saw them at all. In the towns and settled areas they were degraded paupers, hopeless people, great fodder for popular caricatures, and allegedly fast dying out.[3] Then there were those still living in a 'pure state of nature' in the bush, also to be pitied for their savage state, but at least uncorrupted by European ways. Surveyor William Romaine Govett, writing his 'Sketches of New South Wales' for the Christian publication *The Saturday Magazine* in 1836, summarised their predicament like this:

... the numerous tribes who, but a few years ago, were seen to dwell in the neighbourhood of Sydney area already gone! ... It was not ... either force or oppression that destroyed them, but it was corruption, the debasement, the brutality and the profligacy which was introduced among them; it was in short because they had imbibed from us our most destructive vices, and had lost what was good among their own customs. Nothing, indeed, could be more pitiable than the sight of these wretched creatures, half-naked, half-starved and half-drunk, straggling, squalling and jabbering daily through the streets of Sydney.[4]

If Europeans had earlier assumed that Aboriginal people would be uplifted and brought from darkness into light by 'civilisation', now the opposite was thought to be undeniable. Civilisation would corrupt and eventually wipe out Aboriginal people. This way of thinking recalls, once more, Deborah Bird Rose's relentless wheel of colonisation, crushing Aboriginal people who were unable to adapt, leaving only cultureless outcasts in its wake, people unable to fit in with history and fated to die out. Govett continued his exposition:

but it is not from these that the real, natural character of the Australian savage is to be drawn ... in order to see these blacks in their natural state, we must dive into the interior of the country, where we can behold them uncomplicated, uncivilised, untainted, unspoiled.

By the 1830s the 'real Aborigine' had been invented. You had to go 'upcountry', beyond the boundaries, to see them, and the further you moved from 'civil-isation' the more 'genuine' they became, until you reached those who were 'perfectly original; the same, probably, now as they were from the beginning', for 'no signs or symptoms of improvement, or invention, appear to have ever existed amongst them'.[5]

MAHROOT AND THE QUESTION OF ABORIGINAL 'DISAPPEARANCE'

What, then, shall we do with Mahroot, who was also known as the Boatswain or Bosun? Where does he fit in this dual scheme of things? He was born Kameygal, around Cooks River on Botany Bay in about 1796, and as a boy appears to have avoided the male initiation ceremony and went to live in Sydney. Teeth intact and chest unscarred, he became an experienced sailor, spent his wages in the pubs with shipmates, and later joined the hardworking whaling crews sailing south. We know he wore a jacket and trousers and liked a drink now and then. Sailors generally liked to dress well, often flamboyantly. Perhaps Mahroot did too. He may well have looked like the people in some astonishingly detailed drawings by P.H.F. Phelps of the Cabrogal at Liverpool in the 1840s. By then they were known as the Cabramatta tribe and some of them came to live in old Bidgigal country in Botany Bay, near Mahroot. The men dressed like 'fops' in tight pants and short jackets or lapelled blouses, lounged stylishly and smoked clay pipes. But they still wore their hair Botany Bay-style, gummed and dreadlocked like the 'thrums of a mop'.[6]

P.H.F. Phelps, 'Australian Aborigines, Cabramatta Tribe', 1840s, with the names of these people included below the picture. While many of Phelps' other sketches lampooned, caricatured and sensationalised Aboriginal people—possibly they were meant for a book of cartoons—here the images seem more convincing, for these are portraits of real, known people. Most of the women had been at the Native Institution as girls. (Mitchell Library, State Library of New South Wales)

By 1845 Mahroot had tried a little farming on the lease Bourke had granted him, but he was now a fisherman. He had also built huts on his land and was landlord to five tenants. At the same time, he was living with the remaining members of his own clan in his traditional country, knew its boundaries, spoke the traditional language as well as English and could understand the Cabrogal people (he called them 'Cobrakalls'), the group from Liverpool/Cabramatta who had moved down the Georges River to settle at Botany Bay. Mahroot, who spanned two worlds and then returned to his country, explodes the degraded outcast/uncorrupted savage binary. Like Bennelong and Bungaree before him, and like so many after, he was brilliantly adaptable. He had made a living within white society and then a life alongside it which maintained key strands of traditional life: country, hunting and fishing, kin, language. He was also one of the few Aboriginal people of the early colonial period whose voice we can 'hear', talking about the great changes since the whites arrived, and of how Aboriginal people were coping, what they did and did not do, what they believed and did not believe.[7]

Predictions and explanations for the disappearance of Sydney's Aboriginal people began in the late 1790s. Collins thought that their thin population was a result of their 'continually living in a state of warfare'. The demise of the race was confidently asserted in the *Gazette* in 1803—the warriors would all kill each other in the contests. The 'disappearance of the kangaroo' and loss of the men's hunting grounds through the 'clearance of the immense forests' were common reasons given in the Macquarie period. Some said this gave them 'a claim upon the consideration of the British settler'.[8]

But some, rare, observers saw that it was about more than the destruction of hunting grounds. They spoke and wrote eloquently of dispossession, of the deeply felt grievances and sense of loss among Aboriginal people. Here is Archbishop John Bede Polding, speaking frankly to a sceptical parliamentary committee in 1845 of the fundamental injustice of dispossession:

My opinion may be very different from that entertained by a greater part of the community. In the first place . . . there is established in the mind of the black population a sentiment that the whites are essentially unjust . . . that is the leading idea, founded on the whites coming to take possession of their lands, without giving them what they deemed an equivalent; of course they argue, not according to our views, but according to their own; to trespass upon the hunting ground of another tribe is deemed by them a case of war; and . . . must necessarily be considered by them an act of spontaneous injustice. I conceive that these principles will apply to the whites coming to this country; the Aborigines will demand 'what right have you to come here? We have not asked you to come, and you take away our lands, you drive away our means of subsistence'.[9]

He was right: 'the greater part of the community' did think very differently. Such observations were largely drowned out by a cacophony of explanations which for the main part excused Europeans and blamed the Aboriginal people themselves for their demise. Many agreed with William Govett: 'our destructive vices' were the cause, or, more particularly, 'the degraded beings who were banished to their shores', those evil convicts. They believed that the Aboriginal people had no resistance to 'vice'; they were naturally predisposed to degradation, particularly drunkenness. Moral disease paralleled physical illnesses and deterioration: the strong, stable, active bodies admired by the early officers were now 'wasted away and scar-covered', plagued by 'lingering catarrhs . . . large gangrenous sores and syphilitic ulcers'. Aboriginal women were also blamed for what was, after all, really considered race suicide. Their promiscuity had resulted in venereal disease and sterility. Some observers, trawling back through Collins' and Tench's readily available accounts, extrapolated from single incidents or snippets, and declared they killed babies by burying them alive, or deliberately brought on abortions.[10]

By 1845 the Sydney Aboriginal population, in places where they could be seen and counted, appeared to be in serious decline. The issue was considered of sufficient importance to warrant a parliamentary inquiry.[11] Mahroot was called in from Botany Bay to give evidence, and he came to Macquarie Street, where a new wing had been tacked on to the old Rum Hospital for the Legislative Council. The gentlemen of the committee bombarded him with questions: why had the Aboriginal birth rate fallen? Was it not because of the women's promiscuity? Because they practised infanticide? Why did the 'natives' seem to be dying out?

Was it not because the men were addicted to alcohol? And what of the civilisation process? Were there signs that they were Christians yet? Did they believe in God? Mahroot was at once historian, anthropologist, cultural ambassador, adviser on social problems and representative of all the peoples of the Sydney region. The loaded questions rained down, they were frenetic, sometimes badgering; his answers were calm, mild and pragmatic. He agreed that alcohol was a severe problem, that Sydney was a bad place for Aboriginal people, and suggested that they would be better off, safer, down at Botany Bay. He firmly and repeatedly denied the charge of infanticide. Sometimes he did not answer at all.[12]

The pioneer historian of Aboriginal Sydney, Keith Willey, seems rather disappointed with Mahroot, concluding that he was a victim of colonisation, his tone one of fatalism and 'hopeless resignation'.[13] Perhaps Willey wanted him to be angry, to say: you took our land, you gave us diseases, you raped and killed us, you took our women and children. But Mahroot chose not to say these things. He discussed current problems, including the ravages of alcohol and town life, and practical ways to help his people. And he tried to open a window onto something deeper.

'BOY JUST THE SAME AS YOU CALL THE DEVIL'

Pursuing the question of Christianisation, the committee wanted to know whether Mahroot's parents had believed there was a God; that is, whether Aborigines had a religion before colonisation. He replied simply that 'they believed there was something over them'. Ignoring the 'something' and hearing 'being', they asked, what did they call him? To which Mahroot responded: 'Boy just the same as you call the devil'. The interview then became increasingly perplexing, as the committee tried to pin down exactly who this Boy was, and Mahroot tried to answer in ways they would understand, or was evasive where he evidently felt he could not explain:

> Was that a good or bad being? *That is his name, just the same as you call the devil.*
> You know the devil is very wicked, and lived in a place where people will be punished. Is Boy very bad or very good? *He was very good.*

What does he do to the black fellows? *They say he will take black fellows away to where he lived . . .*
Is there any other person over them besides Boy? *Only Boy.*
What does Boy do, you say he takes black fellows away? *That is what they say.*
What is the meaning of Boy in your language? *The devil.*

The devil? What then was 'devil devil'? they asked. Mahroot explained: devil devil was 'all over small pox like', the evil sorcery of smallpox epidemics. Some of the committee members knew that 'boy' (*bo-y*, *Bò-ye*) was the Eora word for 'dead'. They got Mahroot to admit this too. But further inquiry seemed fruitless, so they moved on to 'who created the world?'[14]

As an uninitiated man, Mahroot may never have learned sacred knowledge. But I think he was perhaps expressing something of the overarching ontology of his parents' generation, of Grang-Grang and Old Meroot, Bennelong and Boorong, of Coleby and Daringa, the generation who witnessed their world so utterly changed by smallpox, and by the unrolling impacts of invasion. For 'Bò-ye' did not just mean 'dead'; it could also mean 'ghost', an apparition or spirit, something wider, larger, more pervasive than individual death, or the state of being dead.[15] Mahroot tried to explain by equating Boy with the Devil, which only seemed to alarm the gentlemen. Given the Aboriginal taboo surrounding death and the avoidance of naming the dead, this must have been a very difficult conversation for both sides.[16]

Mahroot told the committee he believed in God (whatever his beliefs, it must have seemed the wisest course in the circumstances) and spoke of Boy only in the past tense. But he said his people had once numbered 400. Now, just under 60 years after the British came ashore in Yarra Bay, there were only four, himself and three women. Mahroot had grown up with Boy too, Boy had been 'over' his country. As Tony Swain points out, death and dispossession were the 'ethnographic context', the words we cannot forget when tracing survival and resilience, the ongoing condition from which they had to create new lives, new ways of understanding the world, new ways of living with the invaders.[17]

Mahroot became a 'last of the Sydney tribe', yet another Aboriginal person with whom to end the story. In one sense it is true: Mahroot was very likely the last of his particular group, the Kameygal, the people of the north side of Botany Bay. Their disappearance was echoed in the diminishing numbers counted each year in the places where the re-formed bands still camped—Kissing Point, Concord, Duck River, Parramatta, Prospect, Eastern Creek, Richmond, Liverpool, Camden. Boy overspread their countries, some would say he still does.

Yet it was also untrue. Mahroot was not the last of the Sydney people, there was no 'last of the Sydney tribe', however many people we find so named in the annals of colonisation. Aboriginal people never died out or disappeared from the region, and throughout the nineteenth century the city also drew new peoples, whether curious, or seeking adventure, or arrested in raids, or displaced from traditional country. We have arrived at the crux, the contradiction of disappearance and survival, impoverishment and resilience. What does 'survival' mean in this context? As Kevin Gilbert wrote forcefully in 1990, the legacies of dispossession cannot simply be consigned to the past: 'Does it not live on in the mind of the victim? Does it not continue to scar and affect his thinking? Deny it, but it still exists.'[18] Complacency has no place in this history; survival here as elsewhere was hard won, a bitter sort of triumph, marred by ongoing marginalisation, stigma and poverty, and overshadowed by loss, by Boy.

'BOONGAREE IS IDENTIFIED WITH SYDNEY'

How did Aboriginal people seem to disappear, and yet remain at the same time?

In the aftermath of war and reconciliation, they continued to find ways to live with or alongside the settlers which were compatible with their own cultures. But as we shall see, settler culture was changing too. The growing numbers of free arrivals, many of them cashed-up, land-hungry and ambitious for themselves and their children, brought new expectations and ideas about what sort of colony, and what sort of city, this should be. The new urban lifeways developed by Sydney's Aboriginal people soon became old ways.

In Sydney, Bungaree continued to be a leader and elder to his people, 'generally loved' for his kindness, gentleness and generosity. He remained a celebrated and much-portrayed local identity, welcoming every new ship to his country, as well as Aboriginal people visiting from other districts. The land he and his people had regained at Georges Head became known as Bungaree's Farm, still marked as such on maps in 1841. Most observers were cynical about Macquarie's experiment in Aboriginal small-farming—some wrote it off immediately. They did make a start clearing and planting there, but soon went back to their customary fishing, and to their camp closer to Sydney. By the 1820s the farm was covered in peach trees and Bungaree still earned money by selling the peaches.[19]

The Macquaries were undeterred, however. Elizabeth appears to have been the instigator of an attempt to establish another 'Black town' on another romantic harbour foreshore—this time Currajin, or Elizabeth Bay. Again, huts were built in neat rows and convict overseers sent to help. A road was built down the slopes from South Head Road and the place became something of a tourist attraction, with ladies and gentlemen driving down in carriages to see the black farmers and their picturesque little cottages. The Aboriginal people liked this place very much: it was reportedly 'very much frequented and delighted in by the Sydney Blacks'. Their traditional 'great camping grounds' in Woolloomooloo Bay and Rushcutters Bay were close by too.[20] But if Georges Head was too far from Sydney, Elizabeth Bay was too close. The settlement was apparently the target of vandals and harassers. Some years later the Reverend William Cowper recalled that 'this place was too near to Sydney for while there was none to protect the property, there were many to destroy'.[21]

Edward Mason, 'Elizabeth Bay with bark huts for the natives', showing the neat huts set out in rows much like the earliest huts were for the convicts. A looped carriageway was built down the slopes so ladies and gentlemen could view the Aboriginal settlement. (Mitchell Library, State Library of New South Wales)

They were soon dispossessed of this promised land a second time. Newly arrived colonists brought a new aspiration to Sydney: the desire for fashionable suburban living. They wanted elegant detached villas in idyllic gardens with water views, separate from the city, but close to it too. Within a few years, Elizabeth Bay was hot property. Governor Darling gave it away in a 54-acre lot to his new Colonial Secretary, Alexander Macleay, who proceeded to remodel it as elegant gardens for a classical dream house he could not afford. The claims of the Aboriginal people were ignored, though Macleay took some interest in their welfare. Soon the ridge between those two key Eora places, Woolloomooloo and Currajin/Elizabeth Bay, was studded with more ostentatious mansions, and Australia's first suburb was born.[22]

By the late 1820s Bungaree was getting old, and he was ailing. He seems to have frequented the Domain more—instead of attending the annual big feast at Parramatta in 1828, he was seen sitting quietly by a fire above Bennelong Point. In the following winter, walkers saw him in the Domain early one morning, utterly naked except for his cocked hat with its red feather, his whole body trembling as he leant on a staff. The *Gazette* declared firmly that 'Boongaree is identified with

Enduring landscape: a sandstone overhang at Elizabeth Bay photographed in 1858 which was very likely used as a shelter by Aboriginal people both before and after 1788, probably up to around 1830. The cave became a picturesque feature in the Macleays' famous garden and still stands in Arthur McElhone Reserve. (Mitchell Library, State Library of New South Wales)

Sydney', and demanded something be done to help him. He was placed in the hospital but soon left, and when Catholic priest Father Therry was charged with his care, his family and friends rescued him from the presbytery and took him back to Elizabeth Bay. Clearly they still occupied their ground there, even while the Macleays were busily refashioning the landscape. Bungaree died on Garden Island on 24 November 1830, surrounded by his people. He was buried beside his first wife at Pannerong, Rose Bay.[23]

The cover of J.S. Prout's Sydney Illustrated *(1842) featured John Rae's drawing of the Sydney Tribe gathered at the base of what looks like one of the rockfaces in the Domain. Unlike many of the caricatures of the period, these people are depicted as good-natured and picturesque rather than debased and subhuman. Sydneysiders would probably have been able to identify well-known individuals. Strangely, Aboriginal people are not mentioned elsewhere in this publication. (National Library of Australia)*

Some of Bungaree's group, including his widow Cora Gooseberry, sons Young Bungaree and Bowen (Boin) Bungaree, Jacky Jacky, and the well-liked and highly regarded William Worrall (also known as Warrah Warrah), stayed on in Sydney. The whites saw them as fringe-dwellers, sitting by the wharf, roaming the streets, selling fish and oysters, giving boomerang-throwing demonstrations, still addressing people with grandiose greetings and polite but insistent requests for money. At night they continued to camp in the Governor's Domain. Painters still included Aboriginal people in their pictures of Sydney.[24]

Some, like Cora Gooseberry and Warrah Warrah, had long-time friends among the townsfolk. Cora sometimes camped with others near Camp Cove, but when she was in town she slept in the kitchen of Edward Borton's hotel in Castlereagh Street, where she died in 1852. She was buried in the Devonshire Street cemetery, her grave marked with a simple, handsome headstone erected by two more friends. It named her 'Gooseberry Queen of the Sydney Tribe of Aborigines'.[25] When Warrah Warrah grew old he developed a disease that left his legs paralysed. Perhaps it was a legacy of childhood smallpox. The once good-natured man became 'irritable' and a 'terror to children', and when he could no longer walk, he left Sydney and set up a camp on the South Head Road at

Charles Rodius' 'View from Government Domain' shows Aboriginal men in European-style pants spearing fish in the waters of Woolloomooloo Bay below the Domain in 1833. There appear to be women and children sitting on the shoreline. (Mitchell Library, State Library of New South Wales)

Rose Bay. William Charles Wentworth paid for food to be supplied to him. The townsfolk called him Ricketty Dick and travellers threw sixpences when they passed by his gunyah. Artists painted him, and notable silversmiths used his profile on medallions and restored his crippled body to youth and vigour in silver statuettes. He died on 11 June 1863. By 1886 he was remembered as 'the last aboriginal king'.[26]

There were other Aboriginal people in Sydney as well, and some Torres Strait Islanders, street people, blow-ins from distant places, sailors returned on the ships. Drinking was as popular with them as it was with the whites in Sydney town, but some of them suffered more from exposure, sleeping rough on cold

Charles Rodius, 'Gooseberry One Eyed Poll wife of King Bongarry', c1844. Gooseberry is sketched in European dress with her pipe. (Mitchell Library, State Library of New South Wales)

nights in country picked clean of firewood. Mahroot told the 1845 committee that they 'have no firewood here, and they lay about the Race Course in the cold when they have got a glass in their heads'. Hyde Park, proclaimed 35 years before, was now fenced in and partitioned off for cricket grounds. Yet ageing Aboriginal warriors were still returning to their old contest ground.[27]

Farm Cove, where contests and initiations had been held, became part of the Botanic Gardens. Meanwhile, much of the more distant Georges Head settlement appears to have become a reserve by 1841 but was resumed, along with other headlands, as a military reserve from 1854. A bit of the track which once led to Bungaree's farm still runs up from Chowder Bay there.[28] The Kirribilli camp

Charles Rodius, 'Ricketty Dick, Broken Bay Tribe', c1844. (Mitchell Library, State Library of New South Wales)

Warrah Warrah's crippled body was restored to beauty and strength in Julius Hogarth's fine figurine. His silver arm holds a golden boomerang and he strides on an ebony base. The figurine was made in about 1855 and exhibited in Paris in that year. (Powerhouse Museum)

where Bungaree's people met the people from the French and Russian ships in the 1820s became the site of the gingerbread-gothic Kirribilli House, built by a merchant in the 1850s, now the Sydney residence of the Australian Prime Minister.[29]

'THE SAME COMPLEXION AS YOURSELVES': SYDNEY AS A WHITE CITY

Newcomers like settler and public servant George Boyes, who arrived in 1824, could scarcely see Aboriginal people as human:

> On our first landing I had proceeded but a very little way up the street before I stopped to examine a group of Natives who had taken their station upon a green spot just opposite the regular landing place. At first glance an irresistible conviction . . . passed through my mind, that there could be little or nothing human in the creatures before me. They were standing, sitting and lying about a fire . . . Some were gnawing bones . . . others were smoking out of short pipes and the rest gazed vacantly upon me or their fellows.[30]

Boyes wrote of them as a spectacle of savage degeneracy, an unbearable contrast to the glories of the young city. He was echoed by so many others. And there was more than indifference in these appalled first-glance summations: the Aboriginal people were increasingly considered to be out of place in Sydney. Phillip had sought to include them in the town, incorporate them into settler society, and they had indeed forged urban ways of life, and made a particular place in the town. But this new Sydney, the one ushered in by the Macquaries, reversed all that. During the 1830s and 1840s, Sydney's emerging middle class was desperately striving for gentility and respectability. They felt the eyes of the empire upon them. They were utterly obsessed with the morality of women and practically hysterical in their avoidance of anyone tainted by convictism.[31] The naked 'original lords of the soil' were a blight on Sydney too, they were an embarrassment, relics of the colony's unrespectable origins; their time had passed, yet they would not go away.

Sydney was also being reconceived more broadly as 'white' space in this period: racial distinction was hardening into a blunter and cruder order, an imagined binary of 'white' and all other peoples. If the *Gazette* could confidently assert in 1829 that Bungaree was 'identified with Sydney', colonists in later years were increasingly concerned to present themselves, their city and their colony, as British and white. The Reverend Ralph Mansfield, evidently disturbed that his relatives back home assumed his family lived among, indeed were becoming, 'black people', was defensive in his assurances:

> I have no doubt you are like many more in Old England in your notions of these colonies. You seem to think we are quite different, and are surrounded by black people. No more than you are in L[iver]pool. Nay, I am sure you see more coloured people in your streets, East and West Indians, &c., than we see in the streets of Sydney. The Anglo-Australians,—your Cousins for instance,—are just of the same complexion as yourselves, and in all other respects are perfectly English.[32]

In fact, more English than the English. It was a claim that would have a long life.

'INVISIBLE' PEOPLE

As their camping grounds by the bays were given to wealthy immigrants, their bora rings and contest grounds taken for parks and racecourses, and their bodies considered offensive in the urban environment, many Aboriginal people were displaced once more. They retreated to places which were shunned by settlers, to public lands, commons and other reserves, to bushland beyond the reach of roads and carriages, where they could still hunt and gather food and camp in the old way, and sell fish and timber in the towns when they needed to.[33]

They were doubly invisible. By retreating or being forced to the fringe areas, seeking safety, refuge and sustenance under the cover of the remaining bushland, they literally disappeared from sight. But they dropped out of mainstream historical consciousness too. Accounts of the colony turned on the 'wealth and progress' model, in which Aboriginal people, along with convicts, were relegated to a sort of 'prehistory', a past Sydney was rapidly leaving behind. They had no part of the action and were best forgotten. Politicians mostly ignored them, except when using their plight to attack their own opponents.[34]

Nonetheless, they were there, their presence glimpsed in peripheral vision, mentioned in newspaper snippets, travellers' tales, seen in names on old maps, faces in photographs, in the reminiscences of old people, in local and family lore.

Mahroot and his people, and the Cabrogal, continued to live on Botany Bay and the Cooks River well into the 1850s. The vast Lachlan and Botany swamps just to the north, rich in fish, birds and other animals, were generally avoided by settlers and the first land grants were not made in the area until the 1820s. Development was slow and the major clearing, drainage and industries which would destroy the wetlands and eventually irreversibly pollute the waterways were still many decades off. Obed West recalled troupes of people, carrying nowie over their heads, heading down to Bondi, Coogee and Maroubra to fish in the 1830s. At Camp Cove inside South Head in 1845, the artist George French Angas was mesmerised by the sight of men spearing fish by torchlight, by their 'wonderful dexterity' and the ethereal scene 'of lights upon the gently undulating surface of the water'.[35]

In some places this kind of occupation reached well into the twentieth century. An unofficial camp of 'political activists and refugees' grew up on Salt Pan Creek, which flows into the Georges River, in the late 1920s and the Depression years of the 1930s.[36] Historians Peter Read and Denis Foley, a Guringai elder, tell of places around Manly, Forty Baskets Beach, and on Deep Creek near Narrabeen, where people still camped in the 1950s. The camp on Deep Creek only became 'visible' when the Wakehurst Parkway tore through nearby in the mid-1950s. The shacks were soon demolished, the people dispersed.[37]

Out on the plain, the rivers and the mountains, the Gandangarra were evidently able to maintain traditional lifeways for longer than other groups— their rugged country repelled settlers too. They were still firing their mountain lands in the early 1820s, smoke billowing out over the farms on the flats below.[38] Meanwhile, down on the river, Aboriginal people camped near Windsor, at the junction of East and South creeks, and found work on the farms. By the early 1850s local parsons were reporting that they were 'not aware that there is a single one left in the parish' and 'we see no blacks here now'.[39] Yet they were there. Aboriginal people continued to live around Sackville Reach over the course of the nineteenth century, and in 1889 a small reserve was officially declared for them a few more bends down the river, on the western banks of the isolated Cumberland Reach. A refuge and a delight, the Sackville reserve stood opposite the farm of William Knight, the settler, long gone, who had wanted permission to shoot them on sight in 1803. In succeeding decades, relations were good, even kindly and respectful, but integration through partnering, marriage and children waxed and waned. There had been early unions and mixed-descent children, but by the 1840s there was little official evidence of intermarriage and family formation between the 'white labouring population' and the Aboriginal people. There must have been some intimacy, though, because by the 1880s some of the Sackville people were also descended from local settler families, like the Everinghams, though evidently few were acknowledged by their white relatives.[40]

The Sackville reserve was closed in 1943 when Andrew Barber died. He was the last member of the community, a gentle man, well known among the white folk, 'in his glory when with children'. A memorial to the lost tribes of the Hawkesbury was raised on the site in 1952 by philanthropist and historian P.W. Gledhill and friends, a straight sandstone obelisk set in the shadow of an

Obelisk memorial to the 'lost' Hawkesbury tribes, on the site of the old Sackville Reserve, Hawkesbury River. (Photo: G. Karskens, 2007)

enormous tangled fig tree. But it too was forgotten, and slowly disappeared beneath an enveloping blanket of lantana. When it was rediscovered during a clean-up in 1973 nobody could remember anything about it. History had to be retraced, rediscovered once more.

Meanwhile the sons and daughters of the Sackville people had moved out and made new lives in the suburbs.[41]

'SITTING DOWN ON AN ENGLISH SETTLER'S FARM'

There was another, more visible way for Aboriginal people to remain in their country: by 'sitting down' on the large estates. Surveyor Govett observed in the 1830s that the settlers often encouraged Aboriginal families to stay on their estates 'to keep [away] strange blacks who might otherwise make dangerous incursions', just as the Kennedys had done at Appin in the 1810s.[42]

This is the history of shared country, of overlaid possession. It seems to have been in operation close to Sydney, for Bungaree's Kirribilli camp ('this is my shore') was on land granted to Robert Ryan of the Marines and New South Wales Corps in 1800. Bungaree and his people occupied Elizabeth Bay at the same time the Macleays were rejoicing in their emerging new garden there. At Parramatta, Aboriginal people had camped on Lieutenant Cummings' estate from the 1790s, and the Richmond band came to live on Archibald Bell's Belmont, on that old landmark, Richmond Hill.[43]

Some were workers as well as protectors. William Cox's Mulgoa estate on the Nepean, once the site of such determined and bloody attack, became the home of the Mulgowie, who became known as the 'Mulgoa tribe'. Cox discovered that if they were fed well, rather than fobbed off with 'a small piece of tobacco and a drink of sour milk', they worked as well as anyone else.[44] On Robert Lethbridge's huge Flushcombe estate, near present-day Blacktown, they still gave impressive tree-climbing demonstrations for visitors in 1829, but they worked here too, for the Reverend John Betts was 'pleased with the manner they fell the trees'.[45]

Betts also attended a corroboree on the Marsden estate at Mamre near St Marys in 1830. Corroborees with more than 100 people attending were still being held at the Macarthurs' Camden up to the 1850s. The white spectators enjoyed the 'figure dances' performed to 'wild cadences' by moonlight and myriad flickering fires. The Cowpastures tribe led by Budbury had gone to live on a part of the estate especially marked out for them. Budbury had long been known as 'Mr Macarthur's Budbury'. John Macarthur also commanded the Aboriginal people at Camden to attend church and 'occasionally used them as a bodyguard, liveried in crimson, red and yellow and carrying spears'. His daughter Elizabeth, watching carefully, considered them 'very intelligent and not obtrusive . . . their carriage is very graceful, and perhaps they possess more native politeness than is found among any people'.[46]

The artist Augustus Earle was another European who saw more deeply than the vast majority of his contemporaries. His painting 'A Native Family of New South Wales Sitting Down on an English Settler's Farm' shows Aboriginal people living in this way: on farms and estates which overlaid country they still considered to be their own. A family—mother, father, small child and baby—are 'sitting down' around a smouldering firestick with their three skinny dogs. Beyond is one of those Indian-verandahed homesteads the settlers were so fond of building. This one is very likely Erskine Park, on the Western Road, the estate of Lieutenant Colonel James Erskine and his wife Sarah. (Erskine had served as president of the Native Institution and helped found the Society for Christian Knowledge among the Aborigines.)[47] Earle depicts this Aboriginal family convincingly. The woman, baby in arms, is wrapped in a blanket. She is the one who makes eye contact, smiling slightly, shyly. The man sits cross-legged and has his back turned to us. Like many Aboriginal men of the time, he wears a jacket sans trousers and smokes a clay pipe. He seems to be busy doing something, thinking about something, and takes no notice of the artist, or indeed of the settler, all dressed up in top hat and tails, arms folded, watching from the verandah. The settler's red-gowned wife stands behind her husband, peering. I can't help thinking that Earle is poking a little gentle fun at this couple: they look like they are wondering why on *earth* the artist is painting the 'natives' sitting in the dirt and not them? Earle's Aboriginal family fills the picture, they are solid, grounded, *visible*, they have a certain self-contained air. Is it resignation and hopelessness, a 'pictorial narrative . . . of dispossession and impending catastrophe'

Earle conveys here?[48] Or endurance, patience and dignity? The settlers are, by contrast, small, slightly nervous and ephemeral: they are ghosts, you can see right through them to the country beyond.

EPILOGUE

---◆---

We need to have our sites in order to teach the kids, a picture's not the same,
just talking about it's not the same. How are we going to teach the kids
without our places?
AUNTY EDNA WATSON, DARUG ELDER AND ARTIST, 1999[1]

In 1999 I searched for Aboriginal sites in Kellyville, the place Aunty Edna Watson and I talked about earlier that year. The rock-shelters, grinding grooves, charcoal drawings and middens, hidden and unnoticed along the bush creeks, had been identified and recorded by a dedicated explorer in the 1960s, and again by a professional archaeologist in 1989.[2] But I was too late. They had disappeared in the turmoil of bulldozed earth and wrecked creeks that ran brown and clouded with earth from the thousands of new building sites of the North West Sector land release. The lightness, the subtlety and vulnerability of the Aboriginal sites in the face of those big machines was clear, and overwhelming. Despite the extensive heritage surveys and conservation plans, Kellyville, long-time urban fringelands, was chaotic country-in-transition. It was for the main part *tabula rasa* too.

At Castle Hill nearby, though, local memory and blessed accident saved the site of the Castle Hill Farm from development. From the 1940s, stands of silvery blue gums grew back along the surrounding creeks and lanes, where you may still see them in their 'glimmering groves'. After the orange trees of the old orchards disappeared, the site lay undisturbed, mantled by dense thickets of blackberries and lantana. In the upsurge of interest in Australian and pioneer history in the 1970s, local groups began agitating for its preservation. They fought development that crept right up to its boundaries and campaigned for funds for a new park on the site: Castle Hill Heritage Park. In 1997, 17.09 hectares of the old farm were granted to Baulkham Hills Shire Council, and an additional area, the original entranceway, was purchased by the council in 2001. Astonishingly, you can still see the outlines of the landscape sketched in that early anonymous watercolour of 1803 depicting Castle Hill Farm explored in Chapter 9: the rise and fall of the slopes, the seams of little creeks, the early track solidified in the modern roadway. In 2006 archaeologists finally located the foundations of the convict barracks, 203 years after they were first laid: roughset fieldstones, robbed out, fragile, crushed, fractured by ploughs and roots, but still there, and brought to light once more.[3]

The bicentennial of the Castle Hill rebellion was remembered too. In March 2004 thousands of spectators turned up to see the re-enactment of the rebellion, held at Rouse Hill Regional Park, close to the site of the original event. The participants were dressed and armed as authentically as possible and some of the rebels and soldiers were played by their respective descendants. The 'battle' was reported nationally on television that evening, and was later explored in an episode of the ABC's history series *Rewind*. What was the rebellion about? the reporter asked the spectators. Some said confidently that the Irish convicts were 'putting political issues on the agenda', including democracy and religious and cultural freedoms. The Irishman who played leader Philip Cunningham, thankfully spared his ancestor's grisly fate, was not so sure. He paused awhile and then, looking straight into the camera, replied simply: 'He just wanted freedom. I think that's all he wanted'.[4]

Yet other historical memorials in this region reveal deep and puzzling amnesia. In newly created William Harvey Reserve, an artist has created a landscape history installation. Each succeeding stone plinth is engraved with a word; together they tell a bloodless, inevitable but really rather dull story of colonisation, moving smoothly from empty land through farms to the suburbs:

The COLONY

Forest

Land grants

Land clearing

Agriculture

Hobby farms

Housing

I read these words with friends, local historians who have spent many years researching and writing about the public farm at Castle Hill, the massacre of Vinegar Hill, and local Aboriginal history. In this same reserve, those mysterious graves I first saw in the paddock in 1989 still stand, though the Georgian-style headstone now bears a spray-painted tag. Downhill, the surviving rock-shelter still overlooks Caddies Creek.

———•◦•———

Sydney once had hundreds of creeks, nourishing veins winding for kilometres over the plain, cascading over falls, studded with massive sandstone overhangs and outcrops, feeding rivers and animals and peoples. Some flow on, full of eels and carp, it is true, waters generally polluted, banks often thick with tangled privet, lantana, blackberries. Many others are now lost. One by one, they were denuded and polluted and became 'nuisances'. Then they were covered over or filled in, or redirected into concrete or brick canals, mere drains, bereft of vegetation, the unremarkable *terrain vague* of suburban Sydney.

Invisible streams slip easily from memory. But there is one exception: Sydneysiders have never quite forgotten their foundational stream, the Tank Stream. Art installations in the footpaths in Pitt Street quietly remind city workers and shoppers of what lies beneath: narrow strips of pulsating blue lights track the water's course below the surface of the city. Underground tours of the Tank Stream are held several times a year too. These are so popular, places in them are now awarded by lottery. In 2007, the *Sydney Morning Herald* ran a major story excitedly proposing the resurrection of the Tank Stream: such a project had been achieved with great success in Seoul, where the 'much-loved' Cheonggyecheon Stream was brought back to light, and to life. Sydney too should have its stream flowing once more through its heart.[5] Why not go further? Why not reinstate Phillip's corridor forest? Imagine it! Business meetings held high above a stream of pure waters running once more among spotted gums and pink-trunked angophoras, the birds swooping and chattering among the skyscrapers.

Lost landscapes have haunted succeeding generations ever since the settlers began lamenting the thickening of the parklike woodlands and the disappearance of birds and animals. Old settlers and early local historians reflected in disbelief upon the vanishment of once endless tall, dark forests, all gone for building and fencewood and firewood. Creeks and swimming holes and bushland remembered from childhood seem to grow more distinct in the memory with passing years. The stream below the bitumen and concrete whispers in the city's subconscious of that other, long history: the one about wonder, admiration, sensual pleasures, and yearning.

———·•·———

As you drive into the Hawkesbury towns of Windsor, Richmond, Wilberforce and Pitt Town, signs welcome you, proudly announcing that each is 'A Macquarie Town'. They are indeed four of the five towns Lachlan Macquarie proclaimed in 1810, so the association with Macquarie, self-styled 'father of Australia', is an important historical claim, a claim to legitimate origins, perhaps the most important one these towns make.

The Macquaries did improve and embellish the colony of New South Wales and they introduced a number of admirable and enlightened policies. Yet I cannot help thinking of those first farmers, James Ruse and Elizabeth Parry and their friends, and the way their audacious venture, their fifteen years of making river farms and families, their town of Green Hills, seem so effectively eclipsed by that single sweep of the vice-regal hand, the few lines scrawled in a journal. Can convicts who moved beyond the pale be founding fathers and mothers? Can we acknowledge the stories of places in ways other than through official gestures and particular dates? How would those welcome signs be worded?

———·•·———

It is hard to avoid the fact that those in power in early Sydney—the governors, the elite, the wealthy—were rather good at ensuring their own histories and material cultures would endure, that they would be remembered as the makers of early Sydney. As Denis Byrne notes, the material culture of power—not only stately homes, but places of authority and law like courthouses, churches, gaols, public buildings—is impressive and substantial. The buildings sit heavily in the landscape, they demand to be noticed, they are the obvious candidates for heritage protection.[6]

But the great lesson of early Sydney is that it was not made by those in authority, the wealthy and powerful, alone, and so the 'heavy' buildings only tell part of the story. The country was replete with lighter signatures: the camps of Aboriginal people, bushrangers and escapees, the bora rings and racecourses on the flats, rock-shelters and grinding grooves by the creeks, the tracks snaking through the town and bush, the rock faces peppered with pick marks which trace out the lines of old roads, the trees scarred for shields, canoes and toeholds, or scarred to mark journeys and surveys, the great smoking graveyards of tree stumps left after clearing, the stumps left by the timbergetters in the high forests, the bright green maize fields, the churned yam beds, the birthing places and burial grounds.

Time, weather, vegetation and building development seem to be in league with traditional ideas of who matters in history and heritage. The lighter signatures of Sydney's unofficial history are far more easily eroded away, leaving behind the harder, more substantial buildings. The big house may survive, but the servants' quarters, the workers' huts, the detached kitchens and other outhouses, the Aboriginal people's camps and gunyahs, the material culture of the people upon whom the big house was dependent, usually disappears. This process has tended to mask the histories and original meanings of places: masters with no servants, gardens with no gardeners, flocks with no shepherds. Imagine the famous picture of Parramatta in 1796, for example, without the orderly, subservient rows of convicts' huts in the foreground. Old Government House stands in splendid isolation in its parklands, severed from the political, social and symbolic meanings of Phillip's original townscape, an empty vessel for quite different imaginings about colonial life.

But all is not lost! Despite this deep unevenness in the historical landscape, and in our ways of seeing heritage, the *histories* of places are recoverable. We can reconnect places with their pasts, conjure the lost landscapes, structures and peoples, tell true stories of the struggles over contested ground, of the strategies to control and subdue, of quiet subversion and outright rebellion, of evasions and accommodations, of landscapes transformed beyond recognition.

Another great lesson of early Sydney is that city, towns, estates, farms were also *shared* landscapes. The Aboriginal history of Sydney has revealed the lost geography of Aboriginal places in the early town. Aboriginal heritage significance is not quarantined in 'prehistory', in Sydney 'before time', it is entangled with 'settler' heritage. It lies within Hyde Park, the famous contest ground, inside the early street alignments and the surviving early houses, on Goat Island and Pinchgut. It lies within those much-revered jewels in the heritage crown, the settlers' stately mansions and rural estates: Kirribilli House, Elizabeth Bay House, Brush Farm at Eastwood, Elizabeth Farm at Parramatta, Mamre at St Marys, Glenfield Farm at Casula, Camden House, and many others, extant or vanished. These places were not only predicated on dispossession, they had ongoing Aboriginal histories too.[7]

Places and things are incomparable teaching tools, just as Aunty Edna Watson says. So all of these are places where important lessons could be taught; cross-cultural stories about those early years of co-existence, about intimacy and enmity, adaptation and continuity, dispossession and reparation, contempt and respect. But we would first have to abandon narratives about the settlers' transformation of 'empty' wasteland into something useful, beautiful and civilised ('Forest, land grants, land clearing, agriculture . . .'). We would have to rethink those old ways of telling landscape history which seem to validate dispossession as 'inevitable', as history's 'proper' course. In 1831, for example, the creation of the Macleays' fabulous garden at Elizabeth Bay was used to justify the second dispossession of Aboriginal people there, for it had transformed 'stunted and unsightly bushes' into 'a spacious garden . . . tributary to the taste and advantage of civilised man'. Alexander Macleay 'deserved the boon, and has well repaid it'.[8] This, after all, is the oldest fiction about land in European Australia: the belief that the way people used land, the kind of labour they invested in it, underpins claims to rightful possession and who really belongs.

For Aboriginal people, the preservation of traditional sites and places presents a double bind. The lighter, subtler sites—artefact scatters, shell middens, scarred trees, grinding grooves, rock carvings—represent teaching places and 'title to country'. But they are hard to monitor and, despite the nominal protection of all Aboriginal sites under the National Parks and Wildlife Amendment Act of 1969, very few are saved if they stand in the way of development projects. They do not seem 'heavy' enough, they have insufficient gravitas to challenge new housing estates or freeways or factories. Local Aboriginal groups often have to fight each battle as though it was the first one. This is one reason a close association has grown between Aboriginal sites and national parks, where development is excluded and preservation is assumed. But the implication is that Aboriginal culture properly belongs in the 'natural environment' and not in the city or suburbs.[9]

Bull Cave, on the slope above a creek near Campbelltown. (Photo: G. Karskens, 2007)

On the other hand, those Aboriginal sites which are large and impressive are better kept secret, for they attract souvenir hunters and vandals. The Bull Cave near Campbelltown is where Muringong artists drew those renegade Afrikaner cattle snorting and bellowing on their open, rolling country. There are white handprint stencils too, insistent testimony to prior occupation. The cave was caged with strong steel mesh in 1982 to protect it from vandalism. Set above a small creek, it looks eerie and slightly menacing, like a half-blind eye, staring out from its rocky slope. As photographer Jon Rhodes writes, devices like cages, chains, railings, walls, boardwalks preserve places, but they also destroy their spiritual meaning and any possibility of future use.[10]

As in so many other places, Aboriginal title to country through the Bull Cave has been furiously challenged. In 1993 someone cut through the strong bars of the cage and scrawled over the bulls in flaming orange paint: 'THIS IS BULLshit', 'fuck off', adding for good measure a goofy face, and a cock-and-balls drawing just a little larger than the bull's impressive appendage. They even spray-painted stencils of their own hands, scoffing orange beside the ghostly white: we can do that, anyone can do that, you are nothing special, you have no claim. This is not 'mindless' vandalism: it's too pointed, too deliberate, too articulate.[11]

Yet the bull endures. Look closely. Below the belligerent words, you can still see the cloven feet, the swishy tail, the blunt unhorned head, the broad back drawn into a fold on the cave wall.

———•·•———

Still, in Sydney's local places, there are smaller things, words, gestures and monuments, signalling a sea change in attitudes and interest, minds and hearts. The Museum of Sydney on the site of the first Government House remembers the original people of Sydney in Cadigal Place, a quiet and reflective space. Many local councils have commissioned histories of Aboriginal Sydney, and websites which heighten both public knowledge and acknowledgement. At Gough Whitlam Park in Earlwood there is a mosaic memorial honouring the Bidgigal people, with portraits of Pemulwuy and Tedbury.[12] At Watsons Bay, the paving stones near Camp Cove have Eora words and English translations etched into them: 'bara FISH HOOK', 'garradjun BARK FISHING LINE'. Inside Bridgewater, the new

'garradjun BARK FISHING LINE', *paving stone near Camp Cove, Watsons Bay.*
(Photo: G. Karskens, 2008)

master-planned housing estate near Camden, five venerable scarred trees are preserved and carefully maintained (they have their own management plan). Books like Melinda Hinkson's *Aboriginal Sydney: A Guide* present inventories, histories and descriptions of Aboriginal places in the city, from the Dreaming to the streets of Redfern.[13]

Southwards of Sydney, the country around Appin is still mostly open farmland, level paddocks between the gently folded ranges of hills. This is dam country now too, for one by one the wild rivers—Cataract, Cordeaux, Avon, Wollondilly, Woronora, Nepean, Warragamba—were walled off and stopped up for water storage to service the ever-growing city. Dense bushland still shrouds the dramatic gape of the Cataract Gorge where the Appin massacre took place in 1816. A few kilometres away, new housing estates are rising on the old farmlands: 65 kilometres from Sydney Cove, the metropolis has arrived. Local memory is uneven here. The story of the massacre is apparently not widely known among the general populace. But since 2000, people from both the non-Aboriginal and Aboriginal communities of the region have come together every year on 17 April for a service to remember the Appin dead.[14] A memorial has been erected at Cataract Dam, where the huge curved wall unites the sides of the rugged gorge downstream from the massacre site. A simply worded plaque, set in a single block of rough-hewn sandstone, says this:

The Massacre of men, women and children
of the Dharawal Nation occurred near here
on 17th April, 1816.
Fourteen were counted this day, but the real
number will never be known. We acknowledge
the impact this had and continues to have
on the Aboriginal people of this land.
We are deeply sorry.
We will remember them.

The pent-up waters of the Cataract dance and glitter behind the dam wall. Deep in the rocky gorge below, the river flows on.

ABBREVIATIONS

AJCP	Australian Joint Copying Project
BT	Bonwick Transcripts (of the Appendices to the Bigge Report, 1819–21)
CSC	Colonial Secretary's Correspondence
facs. ed.	facsimile edition
f.p.	first published
HRA	*Historical Records of Australia*
HRNSW	*Historical Records of New South Wales*
ML	Mitchell Library, State Library of New South Wales, Sydney
MS	manuscript
n.d.	no date
pers. com.	personal communication
SG	*Sydney Gazette*
SRNSW	State Records of New South Wales

NOTES

INTRODUCTION

1. See Daly and Pritchard, 'Sydney: Australia's financial and corporate capital'; McNeill et al., 'Sydney/global/city'.

2. 'Fidget wheels', Kenneth Slessor, 'Five Bells', *Selected Poems*.

3. See Byrne, 'Nervous landscapes'.

4. Smith, 'History and the collector'.

5. Gutman, *Work, Culture and Society*, ix.

6. Geertz, 'Thick description', 6ff.

7. Hirst, *Convict Society*, 69; cf. Boyce, *Van Diemen's Land*.

8. Hughes, *Fatal Shore*, chap. 4; Clark, *History of Australia* 1, parts 3 and 4; Summers, *Damned Whores*, chap. 8; Aplin, *A Difficult Infant*, preface; Clendinnen, *Dancing*, 88–9; Birmingham, *Leviathan*, 79, 156ff.; Davison, 'From urban gaol to bourgeois suburb'; see also mini-series *Mary Bryant* and film *The Floating Brothel*. For discussion see Frost, *Botany Bay Mirages*, introduction.

9. Freeland, *Architecture in Australia*, chaps 2 and 3.

10. *Blackwoods Magazine*, November 1827, in Neville, 'Eager curiosity', 7.

11. Pryke, 'Old Sydney Town' (thesis).

12. Karskens, 'Banished and reclaimed', 27; Griffiths, *Hunters and Collectors*, 115.

13. Here I am referring to convicts and ex-convicts. See A.J. Gray, 'Social life at Sydney Cove'; Karskens, *The Rocks*; Karskens, *Inside the Rocks*, chaps 1 and 2; Elliot, 'Was there a convict dandy?'; Hainsworth, *The Sydney Traders*; Parsons, 'The commercialisation of honour'; Aplin and Parsons, 'Maritime trade'; Hirst, *Convict Society*, 57–69, 82ff., 94; Waterhouse, *Private Pleasures*, chap. 1.

14. Karskens, 'The dialogue of townscape'.

15. 'Naked possession': see Government and General Order, *SG* 7 May 1823.

16. For further discussion see Rowse, 'Transforming the notion of the urban Aborigine'; Creamer, 'Aboriginality in New South Wales'.

17   See for example Rowse, 'Transforming the notion'; Creamer, 'Aboriginality'; Goodall, *Invasion to Embassy*; Foley and Maynard, *Repossession of Our Spirit*; Plater, *Other Boundaries*; Smith, *King Bungaree*; Smith, *Bennelong*; Kohen, *The Darug and their Neighbours*; Broome, *Aboriginal Victorians*; and Angela Martin's novel *Beyond Duck River* (2001). For an excellent historiographical overview, see Brock, 'Skirmishes in Aboriginal history'.

18   Griffiths, *Hunters and Collectors*, chap. 5.

19   Clendinnen, *Dancing*, 92, 285.

20   Grenville, *Searching*, 13, 147–8; Grenville, 'History and fiction'; Grenville, 'The novelist as barbarian'.

21   Grenville, *Searching*, 124, 162. *The Secret River* falls within a long and well-established literary tradition of historical fiction-writing about the early colony, beginning with John Lang's *The Forger's Wife* (1855) and Louisa Atkinson's *Gertrude The Emigrant: A Tale of Colonial Life* (1857) and including M. Barnard Eldershaw's *A House is Built* (1929), Eleanor Dark's *The Timeless Land* trilogy (1941, 1948, 1953), Thomas Keneally's *Bring Larks and Heroes* (1967) and most recently Roger McDonald's *The Ballad of Desmond Kale*, 2005.

22   Maral, 'Making history real'.

23   Cf. Ryan, 'Waterloo Creek', 43.

24   Dolores Hayden, *The Power of Place*, 18. See also Lippard, *The Lure of the Local*.

25   White, *The Middle Ground*.

26   *The (Sydney) Magazine*, May 2007. Performance scholar Gay McAuley believes that places literally store memories, but that performance, not history, unlocks those memories, see 'Remembering and Forgetting'; see also Read, *Haunted Earth*.

27   The story of the rushcutters' murders was first (incorrectly) located at Rushcutters Bay by Obed West, *Memoirs of Obed West*.

28   Clendinnen, 'The history question', 20–1, 24.

29   Cf. Byrne, *Surface Collection*.

30   See for example Tina Jackson et al., 'Our place—what makes it special'; Australian Heritage Commission, *Places in the Heart*; Johnson, *What is Social Value?*

31   Read, *Belonging*.

32   Walton, *Storied Land*.

33   Australian Heritage Commission, *Places in the Heart*.

CHAPTER 1   DEEP TIME AND HUMAN HISTORY

1   Birmingham, *Leviathan*, 127; see Monash University, http://sahultime.monash.edu/explore.html; pers. com. Bob Salt, April 2008.

2   West, *Old and New Sydney*; Cumming, 'Chimneys and change'.

3   This story is most engagingly told by Flannery, *Birth of Sydney*, 8–17; see also White, *Greening of Gondwana*; Benson and Howell, *Taken For Granted*, chap. 1; Johnson, *Geology of Australia*, 126.

4   Benson and Howell, *Taken for Granted*, 7.

5   Griffiths, *Forests of Ash*, 1.

6   Flannery, *Birth of Sydney*, 15; Benson and Howell, *Taken For Granted*, 17 and chap. 3.

7   Pers. com. Frances Bodkin, Sydney, 2001. See also Colley, *Uncovering Australia*, viii.

8   Thomas, *Artificial Horizon*, 157. For other stories about the creation of the east coast environment, see Peter Turbet, *Aborigines of the Sydney District*, chap. 12.

9   The legend was first transcribed by pioneer ethnologist and linguist R.H. Matthews in about 1900; his informant was from the Burragorang Valley, see Matthews, 'Some mythology of the Gundungurra tribe'; retold in Thomas, *Artificial Horizon*, 91–3.

10   Flood, *Rock Art*, 284–5, 306; McCarthy, 'Aboriginal cave art', 97–103.

11   Attenbrow, *Sydney's Aboriginal Past*, 38–9, 152–9; pers. com. Val Attenbrow email 2 September 2004; Stockton and Holland, 'Cultural sites . . . in the Blue Mountains'; Nanson et al., 'Alluvial evidence', 233–58.

12   Attenbrow, *Sydney's Aboriginal Past*, 38–9, 152–9.

13   Flannery, *Future Eaters*, 81.

14   ENSO story, see Birmingham, *Leviathan*, 156ff.

15   Worgan, Letter and journal, 32; McLoughlin, 'Seasons of burning'; Gammage, *Australia Under Aboriginal Management*. Horton, *Pure State of Nature*, argues that Aboriginal firestick management is a myth. For description of dense forests, or 'brush', see Atkinson, *Account of Agriculture*, 21–4.

16   Benson and Howell, *Taken for Granted*, 15; Kohen, *Aboriginal Environmental Impacts*, chap. 4.

17   Attenbrow, *Sydney's Aboriginal Past*, 153; pers. com. Val Attenbrow, email 3 September 2004; cf. Twidale and Campbell, *Australian Landforms*, re glaciation, 208, 220.

18   Bodkin, 'Boora Birra'; Attenbrow, *Sydney's Aboriginal Past*, 17–21, 37–40.

19   Dawes, Collins and Phillip, Vocabulary; Keith Vincent Smith says 'cadi' also means grass tree (*Xanthorrhoea* species), from which spear shafts were made: Smith, *Eora*, exhibition, Image 20.

CHAPTER 2   ENCOUNTERS IN EORA COUNTRY

1   Burnum Burnum in Stanbury and Clegg, *Field Guide to Aboriginal Rock Engravings*, introduction and 9, 54–6, 57–9, 115; Mulvaney and Kamminga, *Prehistory of Australia*, 284.

2   I am using the word Eora because this is the coastal Aboriginal word in Sydney used for 'people'. It is unlikely to be a tribal or language name. The word the inland groups used for 'people' was later recorded as 'koori'. See discussion in Attenbrow, *Sydney's Aboriginal Past*, 35–6; Troy, *The Sydney Language*, 9; Tuckerman, 'No 189: Hawkesbury River'.

3   Stanbury and Clegg, *Field Guide to Aboriginal Rock Engravings*, 25–7, 32–3; Attenbrow, *Sydney's Aboriginal Past*, 48–53 and see map, plate 12. See also Myers, 'The third city'.

4   Maroubra, *Mooroobra*, place or name of clan and of a well-known individual; Turrumurra, *Tarranburra*; Lane Cove River, *Darramarragal*, people of Lane Cove River, see Attenbrow, *Sydney's Aboriginal Past*, 24, 32; Kohen, *The Darug and their Neighbours*, 224; Bondi, *boondi*, noise made by waves breaking; Bunnerong, *bunnerung*; blood, original name of Rose Bay; Patonga, *patanga*, oyster, see Kohen, *The Darug*, 210, 211, 222.

5   Jones, 'Ordering the landscape', 185; Tench, *Narrative*, 38.

6   See Collins, *Account*, 1, 7; Frost, 'New South Wales as *terra nullius*'.

7   Frost, 'New South Wales as *terra nullius*'; Nugent, *Botany Bay*, 10.

8   Parkinson, 'Journal of a Voyage', in Smith, *Documents on Art and Taste*, 7. 'Warra warra' is often assumed to mean 'go away', as it probably did, but it was also an exclamation meaning 'now, recently'. Stanner thought it may have been 'no more than a conventional response to anything startlingly new', see 'History of indifference', 5.

9   Banks, *Endeavour Journal*, 54–5.

10 Smith, *Eora*, exhibition, image 137; Nugent, *Botany Bay*, 11–14.

11 See Pyne, *Burning Bush*, 136ff.

12 Frost, 'New South Wales as *terra nullius*', 519–21, Cook's famous words 'in the pure state of nature' cited 520; on Banks' assertion, see Williams, 'Far happier', 511.

13 Fitzmaurice, 'Genealogy of *Terra Nullius*', 5; McGrath, *Contested Ground*, 13, 71.

14 See Mulvaney and Kamminga, *Prehistory of Australia*; Swain, *Place for Strangers*; Kohen, *The Darug*, 6; re Lake Condah and similar sites, Kohen, *Aboriginal Environmental Impacts*, 95–7; Flood, *Archaeology of the Dreamtime*, 205–8; *The Age*, 13 March 2003.

15 Collins, *Account* 1, 558; Attenbrow, *Sydney's Aboriginal Past*, 22–8; Turbet, *Aborigines of the Sydney District*, 21, 28, 75; Tench, *Complete Account*, 285.

16 Attenbrow, *Sydney's Aboriginal Past*, 57–60, 29; Turbet, *Aborigines of the Sydney District*, 18–19.

17 Collins, *Account* 1, 551–2; Worgan, Letter and journal, 9; Phillip (in Hunter), *Journal*, 342; Bradley, Journal, 62; Hunter, *Historical Journal*, 41.

18 Tench, *Narrative*, 51; Collins, *Account* 1, 609. However, the inland Darug Language is sufficiently similar to the coastal Sydney Language that they are considered dialects of the same language, see Troy, *The Sydney Language*, 6, 11; pers. com. James Wafer and Jasmine Seymour.

19 For some decades now, archaeologists, anthropologists and some Aboriginal groups have argued over the exact boundaries of the clans' territories, and about the language and cultural commonalities and differences between the coastal and inland peoples. These deliberations have powerful implications in modern identity, allegiance and land claims. Yet despite intense scrutiny, the hard boundaries and clear divisions are elusive and probably always will be. See Ross, 'Tribal and linguistic boundaries'; Kohen and Lampert, 'Hunters and fishers'.

20 Banks, *Endeavour Journal*, 55; Collins, *Account* 1, 557; Jane Maria Cox, Reminiscences.

21 Phillip (in Hunter), *Journal*, 338–9; Collins, *Account* 1, 552–3; Tench, *Complete Account*, 277; Smith, *Bennelong*, 131; Turbet, *Aborigines of the Sydney District*, 74.

22 Illert, *Mayran Clan*; Turbet, *Aborigines of the Sydney District*, 102. Turbet wonders whether Mile-gun was in fact *Mail-kan*, the wife of the spirit Koen spoken of by the people of Lake Macquarie in the 1830s. Mail-kan could kidnap people and 'carry them off under the earth in a net bag', never to return. Koen was thought to be the same being as the Sky Hero Daramulan.

23 Worgan, Letter and journal, 11; Bradley, Journal, 133; Tench, *Complete Account*, 284; for photographs of the hooks and how they were made, see Attenbrow, *Sydney's Aboriginal Past*, 98, 118; Attenbrow and Steele argue that the Eora probably also netted fish in the shallows and built fish traps from stone and brush, see 'Fishing in Port Jackson'.

24 Attenbrow, *Sydney's Aboriginal Past*, 98ff., 118, 157; Lampert, 'Aboriginal life around Port Jackson', 43.

25 See Attenbrow, *Sydney's Aboriginal Past*, 101; Kohen, *Aboriginal Environmental Impacts*, 82–3; Mulvaney and Kamminga, *Prehistory of Australia*, 252–3, 291–3.

26 Phillip (in Hunter), *Journal*, 344–6; Bradley, Journal, 170; Collins, *Account* 1, 586; Kohen, *The Darug*, 23–30; Kohen and Lampert, 'Hunters and fishers', 355–6; Attenbrow, *Sydney's Aboriginal Past*, chap. 7, 63, 122–4; Lampert, 'Aboriginal life', 50–3.

27 McBryde, 'To establish a commerce', 172–4; Turbet, *Aborigines of the Sydney District*, 23–5, 42, 47; Attenbrow, *Sydney's Aboriginal Past*, 122–4.

28 Attenbrow, *Sydney's Aboriginal Past*, 53–4; Tench, *Complete Account*, 226–33; Phillip (in Hunter), *Journal*, 326; Turbet, *Aborigines of the Sydney District*, 47.

29 Attenbrow, *Sydney's Aboriginal Past*, 53, 93–4, 137–8; Tench, *Narrative*, 51; Tench, *Complete Account*, 226; Bradley, Journal, 121; Clendinnen, *Dancing*, 165 and loc. cit.

30 Collins, *Account* 1, 5.

31 Edwards, 'Footsteps that went before', 90–1.

32 ibid. Angas, *Savage Life*, 202, 273; Stanbury and Clegg, *A Field Guide to Aboriginal Rock Engravings*, 129. Gulaga (Mt Dromedary) on the New South Wales south coast is a 'mother, a women's mountain . . . a source of all life', see *Sydney Morning Herald*, 7–8 June 2003; Jacobs, 'Women talking up big'; Bell, *Daughters of the Dreaming*.

33 Attenbrow, *Sydney's Aboriginal Past*, list, 26; interview with Frances Bodkin, 11 May 2001, and Bodkin, 'Boora Birra'.

34 Myers, 'The third city'; Meredith, *Notes and Sketches*, 48; Flannery, *Birth of Sydney*, 20; Bowdler, 'Hook, line and dilly bag', 256.

35 Hunter, *Historical Journal*, 96, 107; White, *Journal*, 136; Bradley, Journal, 116.

36 Smith in O'Loughlin, 'Art find lifts veil'; Turbet, *Aborigines of the Sydney District*, 15–16; Kohen and Lampert, 'Hunters and fishers', 361–2; Attenbrow, *Sydney's Aboriginal Past*, 54–5; Bradley, Journal, 116; Collins, *Account* 1, 555; ants' eggs were collected as food, Attenbrow, *Sydney's Aboriginal Past*, 76.

37 Turbet, *Aborigines of the Sydney District*, 15–16; Attenbrow, *Sydney's Aboriginal Past*, 42, 90, 92–3, 113; Benson and Howell, *Taken for Granted*, 15.

38 Hunter, *Historical Journal*, 55; Worgan, Letter and journal, 32.

39 Hunter, *Historical Journal*, 43.

40 Worgan, Letter and journal, 32; McLoughlin, 'Seasons of burning', 393–404; Gammage, *Australia Under Aboriginal Management*; Attenbrow, *Sydney's Aboriginal Past*, 42, 152–9. For a summary of the debate over Aboriginal 'firestick farming', see Kohen, *Aboriginal Environmental Impacts*, chap. 4.

41 Atkinson, *Europeans*, 181.

42 Banks, *Endeavour Journal*, 54, 58–9; Nugent, *Botany Bay*, 9.

43 Kohen, *Darug*, word list 239; Dawes, word list in Flannery, *Birth of Sydney*, 112; evidence of Mahroot, NSW Parliament, *Report . . . on the Condition of the Aborigines*, 5; picture of ships with billowed 'wings' see Clegg and Ghantous, 'Rock-painting', 262. Eleanor Dark in her famous novel *The Timeless Land* used *Bereewolgal* as the name for the Europeans: see her annotated copy, 182, Varuna Collection, Katoomba, NSW.

44   Swain, *A Place for Strangers*, 114ff.

45   Hunter, *Historical Journal*, 28.

46   King, Private Journal, 18 January 1788; Bradley, Journal, 59.

47   King, Private Journal, 18 January 1788; David Blackburn to Richard Knight, cited in Jones, *Ochre and Rust*, 23; McBryde, 'To establish a commerce', 169–70, 174ff.; Smith, *Bennelong*, chap. 20; Phillip in Stanner, 'History of indifference', 3; Atkinson, *Europeans*, 146.

48   King, Private Journal, 20 January 1788; Phillip's Instructions, 27 April 1787, *HRA* 1, 13–14; Clendinnen, *Dancing*, 26, 122, 124.

49   Worgan, Letter and journal, 18, cited in Stanner, 'History of indifference', 7–8.

50   Bradley, Journal, 67, 68; Hunter, *Historical Journal*, 37; Worgan, Letter and journal 3, 6.

51   Clendinnen, *Dancing*, loc. cit., quotes 181, 5.

52   White, *Journal*, 111; Bradley, Journal, 66.

53   Hunter, *Historical Journal*, 39; Tench, *Narrative*, 37, 50; White, *Journal*, 111; Worgan, Letter and journal, 3.

54   White, *Journal*, 153, 165; Worgan, Letter and journal, 18; Bradley, Journal, 125–6.

55   Worgan, Letter and journal, 32; Collins, *Account* 1, 458; see also Bradley, Journal, 127–8.

56   Anonymous word list, c1790–91, in Smith, *Bennelong*, 24.

57   Coleman, 'Inscrutable history', 203.

58   Coleman, ibid.; see also Coleman, *Romantic Colonization*, 164–6; Thomas, *Possessions*, 38; Morrissey, 'Dancing with shadows'.

59   Collins, *Account* 1, 5; Tench, *Narrative*, 46.

60   Collins, *Account* 1, 3; see also Hunter, *Historical Journal*, 41.

61   Tench, *Narrative*, 34; Bradley, Journal, 61.

62   Collins, *Account* 1, 3; Hunter, *Historical Journal*, 37, 38.

63   Hunter, *Historical Journal*, 37; Curby, *Manly*, 9–10.

64   Bradley, Journal, 60, 63; Worgan, Letter and journal, 4, 9.

65   King, Private Journal, 20 January 1788; Bradley, Journal, 60; *barin*, see Collins, *Account* 1, 562; White, *Journal*, 160; Attenbrow, *Sydney's Aboriginal Past*, 109; Smith, *Bennelong*, 140.

66   Worgan, Letter and journal, 10.

67   Bradley, Journal, 67, 77.

68   Hunter, *Historical Journal*, 39–40; Tench, *Narrative*, 49; Bradley, Journal, 72–3; Worgan, Letter and journal, 4; see also White, *Journal*, 160; Curby, *Manly*, 20–2; 'Eve's Cove' (Manly Cove) was inscribed on the earliest known map of Port Jackson, an anonymous copy of Hunter's *Chart of Port Jackson, New South Wales, Survey'd Feby 1788* (Watling Collection LS3), see Smith and Wheeler, *Art of the First Fleet*, 73.

69   Bradley, Journal, 70, 87, cited in Curby, *Manly*, 20, 22.

70   Southwell, Diary; Tench, *Narrative*, 38; Collins, *Account* 1, 5.

71   See for example Raper, 'Chart of Port Jackson', 1788.

72   Flannery, *Birth of Sydney*, 20.

73   Pers. com. Doug Benson, Senior Plant Ecologist, Royal Botanic Gardens, email 5 August 2005.

74   Hunter, *Historical Journal*, 29.

75   Nagle, *Nagle Journal*, 94; Phillip, *Voyage*, 40; see also Tench, *Narrative*, 65; Clark, Journal, 10 February 1788.

76   Benson and Howell, *Taken for Granted*, 42–5; pers. com. Doug Benson, Senior Plant Ecologist, Royal Botanic Gardens, email 5 August 2005. The question of Sydney Cove's original vegetation has intrigued botanists since the late nineteenth century, when Joseph Maiden, Director of the Botanic Gardens, recorded the surviving vegetation of the outer Domain.

77   MacPhail, 'Blackwattle Creek Catchment'; MacPhail, 'Pollen analysis . . . Broadway, Sydney . . . Middle to Late Holocene'; MacPhail, 'Pollen analysis . . . Broadway, Sydney . . . Late Pleistocene'.

78   ibid. and pers. com. Mike MacPhail, emails 5 and 9 August 2005.

79   For a succinct overview of known Aboriginal sites in the Sydney city area, see Dallas, 'Aboriginal Context', 11–23; Godden Mackay Logan, 'Angel Place Project', 1 and 3.

80   Dallas, loc cit. The absence contrasts with the sites from other coastal areas, and from the Cumberland Plain, see Attenbrow, *Sydney's Aboriginal Past*, loc. cit., especially 49–53; MacDonald et al., 'The Rouse Hill Infrastructure Project', 260–93.

81   King (in Hunter), *Journal*, 275.

CHAPTER 3   THE CAMP, THE CANVAS

1   Collins, *Account* 1, 5, 9, 15; Tench, *Narrative*, 39; Smyth, 8 March 1788, cited in Emmett, *Fleeting Encounters*, 74; Phillip to Sydney, 15 May 1788, *HRNSW* 1, 133.

2   White, *Journal*, 112.

3   See Frost, *Botany Bay Mirages*, 87–97.

4   Phillip to Sydney, 15 May 1788, *HRNSW* 1, 133; see also White, *Journal*, 112.

5   Smyth, Journal, *HRNSW* 2, 392.

6   Lord Sydney to the British Treasury, 18 August 1786, in Frost, *Botany Bay Mirages*, 46; see commentaries on conditions of the gaols in Clark (ed.), *Select Documents*, 18–23.

7   See 'Heads of A Plan', August 1786, in Frost, *Botany Bay Mirages*, 44–5; Blainey, *Tyranny of Distance*, 24ff.

8   Abbott, 'Expected cost of the Botany Bay Scheme', 153–4.

9   Complete list of the First Fleet stores, see Frost, *Botany Bay Mirages*, chap. 6.

10   See Butlin, *Australian Monetary System*, 12–13; Parsons, 'Commercialisation of honour', 107–8; Fletcher, *Landed Enterprise*, 6–7.

11   Instructions to Phillip, Hunter, Bligh and Macquarie, cited and discussed in Fletcher, *Landed Enterprise*, 6; see also Bonyhady, *Colonial Earth*, chap. 2.

12   Aplin and Parsons, 'Maritime trade', 156.

13   Linebaugh and Rediker, *Many Headed Hydra*, 49 and loc. cit.; Linebaugh, *The London Hanged*.

14   See McKendrick et al., *Birth of a Consumer Society*; McKendrick, 'Home demand'; Karskens, *The Rocks*, 11, 206–7; Karskens, *Inside the Rocks*, chaps 1 and 2.

15   Phillip's address to the convicts, in Worgan, Letter and journal, 22; Fletcher, *Landed Enterprise*, chap. 1; Tench, *Narrative*, 12; Keneally calls it the 'Sydney Experiment', *Commonwealth of Thieves*, 63.

16   Karskens, *Inside the Rocks*, 70; Cowan, *Wattle & Daub*, 9–10.

17   For an excellent summary of the debate over the founding of the colony and analysis of the costs of the project, see Abbott, 'Expected cost of the Botany Bay Scheme'.

18   Tench, *Narrative*, 28.

19   Tench, *Narrative*, 31, 38.

20   Collins, *Account* 1, 6.

21   See Tench's musings on these divergent destinies, *Narrative*, 74ff.

22   Coltheart, 'Landscape of public works', 160–73; Smith, *European Vision*, 178–9. The medallion was designed by Henry Webber. Copies are held in the Mitchell Library, and in the Wedgwood Museum, Barlaston, Staffordshire.

23   The poem and an engraving of the medallion were reproduced as the frontispiece of Phillip's *Voyage of Governor Phillip*.

24   Nicholas and Nicholas, *Charles Darwin*, 53–7, 84.

25   Dixon, *Course of Empire*, 16–17; Bird, 'The settling of the English', 26–7.

26   Dixon, ibid.

27   See maps and paintings in McCormick, *First Views*, 37–45.

28   Attenbrow, *Sydney's Aboriginal Past*, 11; Johnson, 'Showdown in the Pacific', 114–27; Dawes to Maskelyne, 10 July 1788, in McAfee, *Dawes' Meteorological Journal*, 11.

29   Bridges, *Foundations of Identity*, 14; Tench, *Narrative*, 57; Proudfoot argues convincingly that Phillip was inspired by the great port cities worldwide, where main squares were commonly placed next to harbours, and particularly by Greenwich where he and several of his officers had been educated. See Proudfoot, 'Fixing the settlement', 56–7. For the traditional view of Phillip's plan as a 'vision thwarted' by greed and laxity, see Freeland, *Architecture in Australia*, 19–20.

30   Atkinson, 'Taking possession', 74–5.

31   Collins, *Account* 1, 5; Phillip to Sydney, 9 July 1788, *HRNSW* 1, 46.

32   Bonyhady, *Colonial Earth*, 46–7; Bridges, *Foundations of Identity*, 15–18; McCormick, *First Views*; Proudfoot et al., *First Government House*, 44ff.

33   McCormick, *First Views*, 72–3, 76–7; Collins, cited in Bridges, *Foundations of Identity*, 33; Broadbent, *Francis Greenway*, 54–5; Collins, *Account* 1, 231. The new burial ground 'on Captain Shea's farm' became the Old Sydney Burial Ground and was later the site for Sydney Town Hall.

34   Tench, *Narrative*, 57; Hunter, *Historical Journal*, 50; Worgan, Letter and journal, 28; Thompson, 'Journal', 794; Grant (Cramer), *Beauteous, Wicked Place*, 42; Catchpole to Mrs Cobbold, 21 January 1802; Bridges, *Foundations of Identity*, 31. For detailed descriptions of early building methods see Freeland, *Architecture in Australia*, 10ff.; Cowan, *Wattle & Daub*, chap. 1.

35   Bradley, Journal, 75.

36   Frost, *Botany Bay Mirages*, 217–19; Collins, *Account* 1, 15; Tench, *Complete Account*, 136; Kass et al., *Parramatta*, 9–14; Phillip (in Hunter), *Journal*, 300.

37 Girouard, *Cities and People*, 35ff. and 69ff.; Mrozowski, 'Landscapes of inequality', 29.

38 Karskens, 'Engaging artefacts'; Karskens, *Inside the Rocks*, chaps 1 and 2; Gray, 'Social life at Sydney Cove', 384–7.

39 Murray and Crook, 'Archaeology of the Modern City Database', item nos 26935, 26939, 39215, and 60609 a tea bowl/cup found in the well of convict butcher, George Cribb. See also Wilson, 'Ceramics . . . Artefact Report', 333 and catalogue entries. Pers. com. Dr Penny Crook, Department of Archaeology, La Trobe University, email 3 February 2006, and Dr Wayne Johnson, Sydney Harbour Foreshore Authority, February 2006.

40 Government and General Order, *SG* 7 May 1823; Karskens, 'Dialogue of townscape'; Karskens, *Inside the Rocks*, chap. 1.

41 Worgan, Letter and journal, 35.

42 Karskens, 'Dialogue of townscape', 106–7; Karskens, *The Rocks*, chaps 10 and 11, 150–1; Waterhouse, *Private Pleasures*, chap. 1; Jordan, *The Convict Theatres*, chap. 3.

43 Johnson to Fricker, 15 November 1788; Jordan, *The Convict Theatres*, chap. 3.

44 Phillip (in Hunter), *Journal*, 373; Karskens, *Inside the Rocks*, 42; Hirst, *Convict Society*, loc. cit.

45 Tench, *Complete Account*, 259; Collins, *Account* 1, 455; Fitzgerald and Hearn point out that the enlisted men were 'not unlike the convicts they had been sent to guard'—they too were drawn from the ranks of the labourers and unemployed, see Fitzgerald and Hearn, *Bligh, Macarthur*, 24–5, quote 27.

46 Collins, *Account* 1, 237.

47 Phillip to Grenville, 17 June 1790, *HRA* 1, 182, 198; Phillip (in Hunter), *Journal*, 303; Tench, *Complete Account*, 195; Collins, *Account* 1, 132; Kass et al., *Parramatta*, 22–4; Bridges, *Foundations of Identity*, chap. 4.

48 Freeland, *Architecture in Australia*, 19; Kass et al., *Parramatta*, 23–4.

49 Clark, *History of Australia* 1, 73; Keneally, *Commonwealth of Thieves*, 41–2.

50 Newman and Pevsner, *Buildings of England: Dorset*, 292–4; Darley, *Villages of Vision*, 35–7; Fookes, *Milton Abbas, Dorset*.

51 Darley, *The Idea of the Village*, 3–4, 8; Johnson, 'The Phillip Towns' (thesis), 47–53.

52 A Soldier's Letter, 13 December 1794, *HRNSW* 2, 817.

53 Re slave housing, see Vlach, *Back of the Big House*. At Mulberry plantation in South Carolina, Thomas Broughton built small thatched houses for his slaves in two rows below the great house, a vista that was made famous by Thomas Coram's painting c1800, see Vlach, *The Planter's Prospect*, 2002; re symbolism of such architecture in eighteenth-century Virginia, see Isaac, *Transformation of Virginia*, 36.

54 Vlach, *Back of the Big House*, 164.

55 Tench, *Complete Account*, 258–9; Collins, *Account* 1, 212.

56 Collins, *Account* 1, 237; newly arrived convicts were still sent to Parramatta in 1797, see Collins, *Account* 2, 39.

57 Phillip (in Hunter), *Journal*, 300; Collins, *Account* 2, 309.

CHAPTER 4 'FOOD FROM A COMMON INDUSTRY'

1   Governor Phillip's Instructions, 25 April 1787, *HRA* 1, 11.
2   ibid., 13. The link between organised public farming and penology would be revived in the twentieth century, when prison farms and afforestation camps sought once more to reform both fallen men and wastelands: Benedict Taylor, 'Cultivating Reform', PhD in progress, School of History, UNSW.
3   Fletcher, *Landed Enterprise*, chap. 2, quote 41.
4   Collins, *Account* 2, 204.
5   Campbell, 'Rose Hill government farm', 357; Jervis, *Cradle City*, 11.
6   Anon. (A gentleman), Letter from Toongabbie, 30 November 1792, *HRNSW* 2, 807.
7   Tench, *Complete Account*, 249–50; Fletcher, *Landed Enterprise*, 27ff.
8   McClymont, 'Toongabbie'; Johnson, 'The Phillip Towns', 266, 369; Collins, *Account* 1, 413.
9   McClymont, 'Toongabbie', 7; see also Collins, *Account* 1, 402—a 'jail gang' was also ordered to be established at Toongabbie 'for the employment and punishment of all bad and suspicious characters', December 1794.
10   Collins, *Account* 1, 212–13.
11   Karskens, *Holroyd*, 23–4; Collins, *Account* 1, 343, 349.
12   Collins, *Account* 1, 403, 414; Fletcher, *Landed Enterprise*, 31.
13   Fletcher, 'Small scale farming', 3; Fletcher, *Landed Enterprise*, 7.
14   Collins, *Account* 1, 386.
15   Hunter to Portland, 10 June 1797, *HRA* 2, 18; Hunter to Portland, 20 March 1800, *HRA* 2, 475; Fletcher, 'Small scale farming', 6–7; Fletcher, *Landed Enterprise*, 7.
16   Fletcher, *Landed Enterprise*, 8.
17   Fletcher, *Landed Enterprise*, 30–1, 37; Baskerville, 'The Hawkesbury commons', 58–9. King's commons and reserves totalled over 105,823 acres; McLoughlin, 'Landed peasantry', note 11, 146; Hawkins, 'Timbergetting in the Bluegum High Forest', 40–1.
18   Hawkins et al., *Castle Hill and its Government Farm*; Péron, *Voyage*, 307.
19   Wilson, 'Castle Hill Heritage Park', 70–1, 99–100; pers. com. Graham Wilson, 30 April 2007.
20   McClymont, 'Toongabbie', 9; Hills District Historical Society, *Beginnings of the Hills District*, 11–30; Hawkins et al., *Castle Hill and its Government Farm*, 10–11.
21   Collins, *Account* 1, 317; Coupe, *Concord*, 44–5; Hawkins, 'Timbergetting in the Bluegum High Forest', 15; see Prieur, *Notes*; Ducharme, *Journal*; Lepailleur, *Land of a Thousand Sorrows*; Petrie, 'The French-Canadian convict experience', 167–83.
22   Campbell, 'Early history of Sydney University', 274–93; McKern, 'State industrial activities', 30. For location of Grose Farm, see Bemi, 'Plan of Laing's Clear', 1838.
23   Stacker, *Chained to the Soil*, chaps 1 and 2; Fletcher, *Landed Enterprise*, 10; *SG* 13 November 1823, cited in Stacker, 29.
24   Stacker, *Chained to the Soil*, chap. 3; the convict theatre, see Stacker, 43; Jordan, *Convict Theatres*, 153–8; Bougainville (Riviere), *Governor's Noble Guest*, 102–3; Waterhouse, *Private Pleasures*, 25.
25   Stacker, *Chained to the Soil*, chap. 4.
26   Robinson, 'Land', 97–8. The grant to the Orphan Schools at Fairfield/Cabramatta

totalled 12,300 acres, see George, *Fairfield*, 13; see also Grose, 'What happened to the Clergy Reserves'.

27 Coupe, *Concord*, 62–4.

28 Ryde City Council, 'Parks and park name history: Field of Mars Reserve'; McLoughlin, *An Island of Bush*; NSW National Parks and Wildlife Service, 'Scheyville National Park', 10–23. The Hawkesbury commons were revoked and enclosed for many other purposes as well, including an agricultural college and the RAAF base at Richmond, small selectors' blocks for farming schemes, labour settlement schemes: see Baskerville, 'The Hawkesbury commons', 63–5.

29 Ashton and Blackmore, *Centennial Park*, 15–21.

30 Hawkins, *Convict Timbergetters of Pennant Hills*, chap. 6.

31 Dyer (ed.), *Slavery and Famine*, 1794; Coleman, *Romantic Colonization*, 10; see also Thompson, 'Journal', 795–6.

32 Sidney, *Three Colonies of Australia*, 41.

33 Stacker, *Chained to the Soil*, xii; pers. com. James Broadbent, 2005, 2008.

34 These are said to be the words of Joseph ('Smasher') Smith to Caroline Chisholm in 1845, published in Sidney, *Three Colonies*, cited in Hutton Neve, *Forgotten Valley*, 34, and many other works. However, this passage did not appear in Chisholm's own booklet *Comfort for the Poor*. 'Smasher' Smith was so named because he was outspoken and did not suffer fools gladly, though he was considered conscientious and hardworking by his neighbours. Grenville presumably appropriated the nickname for her appalling character Smasher Sullivan in *The Secret River*.

35 Tick, 'Samuel Sidney'; Hughes, *Fatal Shore*, 107–8, 187–8.

36 Kelly, 'Jerilderie Letter', 131.

37 Hirst, *Convict Society*, 87.

38 Bruce, Life of a Greenwich Pensioner, 7–8; Gilberthorpe, Memorial, 1810, in Hardy, *Early Hawkesbury Settlers*, 125.

39 Catchpole, Letter to Dr Stebbens, 21 January 1802.

40 Tucker, *Ralph Rashleigh*, 76; Holt (O'Shaughnessy), *A Rum Story*, 40; song 'Van Diemen's Land', in Maxwell-Stewart and Duffield, 'Skin deep devotions', 118.

41 Pendergrass, Memorial, 1825; Jewell to his brother, May 1820.

42 Ducharme, *Journal*, 31. Petrie points out that the Patriotes' accounts of their experiences at Longbottom and in Sydney as tyranny and slavery, and unjust and unfair punishment, are not borne out by their actual experience at Longbottom, or their treatment by the colonial government; see 'The French-Canadian convict experience'.

43 Maxwell-Stewart and Duffield, 'Skin deep devotions', 118; Phillip's Instructions, 25 April 1787, *HRA* 1, 12.

44 Tench, *Complete Account*, 253; McCormick, *First Views*, Plate 11 (45), Plate 17 (51); Hawkins, 'Timbergetting in the Bluegum High Forest', 14.

45 Collins, *Account* 1, 200.

46 Karskens, 'Spirit of emigration'; Sargeant, *Toongabbie Story*, 95.

CHAPTER 5   SEEDING AND BREEDING

1   Collins, *Account* 1, 38, 54, 153; Attenbrow, *Sydney's Aboriginal Past*, 63.

2   Ruse was convicted in 1782 at Bodmin, and Bryant in 1784 in Launceston; Collins, *Account* 1, 155–7; Hirst, *Great Convict Escapes*, 19. Interestingly the famous escape story was and remained focused on Mary Bryant rather than William. It has been revived recently, with two popular books, see King, *Mary Bryant*, and Erickson, *The Girl from Botany Bay*, and a television mini-series *Mary Bryant* in which 'Mary' looks suspiciously like the young woman in Vermeer's famous painting 'Girl with a Pearl Earring', also currently enjoying a revival of interest.

3   Keneally, *Commonwealth of Thieves*, 297, 435; Fletcher, 'Ruse, James (1760–1837)'.

4   Phillip (in Hunter), *Journal*, 300–1, 351; Tench, *Complete Account*, 197–8; Collins, *Account* 1, 92–3; White, *Journal*, 128. The bearded wheat 'differing much from the English' was from the Cape, and was not very successful: Collins, *Account* 1, 442.

5   Phillip wrote of Ruse: 'Others may prove more intelligent, though they cannot well be more industrious', see *Journal* (in Hunter), 301; Tench, *Complete Account*, 197–8.

6   Tench, *Complete Account*, 197–8, 256; Collins, *Account* 1, 158, 225; Fletcher, 'James Ruse'; Cowell and Best, *Where First Fleeters Lie*, 126–30; Aveling, 'Imagining New South Wales', 1–12. For the location of Ruse's grant see Campbell, 'Rose Hill government farm', 356. The farm was bounded on the north side by Clay Cliff Creek.

7   Charles Williams' story is told with an ethnographic eye in Atkinson, *Europeans*, 168–71.

8   Collins, *Account* 1, 340; Tench, *Complete Account*, 250–9; Atkins, Journal, 21; Phillip also sent David Burton on an inspection tour of the farms in 1792, see Burton's report, enclosure no. 1, Phillip to Dundas, 19 March 1792, *HRA* 1, 341.

9   Maxwell-Stewart, *Closing the Gates of Hell*, 146; Fletcher, *Landed Enterprise*, 14–15, 21.

10   Waterhouse, *Vision Splendid*; Powell, 'Snakes and cannons'.

11   Fletcher, *Landed Enterprise*, 58.

12   Morris and Britten, 'Colonial cultural landscapes'. Some examples of these surviving homesteads include Charles Throsby's Glenfield at Casula, Denbigh at Cobbity, Mulgoa Cottage at Mulgoa, Denham Park near Campbelltown.

13   Karskens, 'Water dreams, earthen histories'; Kingston, *Early Slab Buildings*; Proudfoot, *Exploring Sydney's West*; Jack, *Exploring the Hawkesbury*; Hutton Neve, *Forgotten Valley*.

14   Collins, *Account* 1, 264; Cowell and Best, *Where First Fleeters Lie*, 126–30.

15   William Harvey Reserve, which has now been extensively landscaped with paths and native plants; site visits, 1989, 1999, 2005; Varman, 'Early Settlement Site'; Attenbrow, *Sydney's Aboriginal Past*, 24.

16   Kass et al., *Parramatta*, Part 1; Purtell, *Mosquito Fleet*, chap. 1; Rosen, *Bankstown*; Cunningham, *Blue Mountains Rediscovered*, chap. 5. For useful summaries of exploration and the location of arable land, see Robinson, 'Land', 95–6.

17   Phillip (in Hunter), *Journal*, 360–1, 340; Rolls, 'More a new planet', 174.

18   Tench, *Complete Account*, 225, 256; Meredith, *Notes and Sketches*, 158.

19   Hawarth, 'Shaping of Sydney'; Perry, *Australia's First Frontier*, 18ff.; McLoughlin,

'Landed peasantry', 125–7, and see excellent maps figs 7.1 and 7.2; Fletcher, 'Agriculture', 208.

20 Rolls, 'More a new planet', 161.

21 White, *Journal*, 124; Tench, *Complete Account*, 175, 263; Phillip to Sydney, 15 May 1788, *HRA* 1, 29: Phillip wrote, 'I did not doubt but that a large river would be found'. Phillip's Instructions included orders to carry out the soil survey, 15, as noted in Robinson, 'Land', 92. Campbell reports that over 130 soil samples were taken and tested: Campbell, 'The dawn of rural settlement', 84.

22 Hunter, *Historical Journal*, 105; Tench, *Complete Account*, 153; Phillip (in Hunter), *Journal*, 348; Dash, 'Phillip's exploration of the Hawkesbury River', 11–30.

23 Hawarth, 'Shaping of Sydney', 49; Tench, *Narrative*, 35; Fitzgerald, *Rising Damp*, 29, 32; see entry for Chinese Market Gardens, La Perouse, on the State Heritage Register.

24 Worgan, Letter and journal, 27; Fletcher, *Landed Enterprise*, 42; Hunter, *Historical Journal*, 95; Frost, *Botany Bay Mirages*, 95.

25 Collins, *Account* 1, 555; Harris, Letter, 21 March 1791; *SG* 21 August 1803; 'A soldier's letter', 13 December 1794, *HRNSW* 2, 816.

26 Phillip to Sydney, 28 September 1788, *HRNSW* 1, 190; Tench, *Complete Account*, 264, cited in Frost, *Botany Bay Mirages*, 211–23, see also 91; Karskens, *Inside the Rocks*, 33, 63.

27 Jervis, *Cradle City*, 4, 10–11.

28 For a summary of soils and their exhaustion, see Perry, *Australia's First Frontier*, 8ff.; see McIntyre, 'Between the wines of Madeira'; McIntyre, 'Not rich and not British'.

29 Marsden to Stokes, 16 September 1795.

30 Fletcher, *Landed Enterprise*, 12ff.

31 McLoughlin, 'Landed peasantry', 132; Fletcher, *Landed Enterprise*, 6.

32 Phillip's Instructions, 25 April 1787, *HRA* 1, 14–15; Keneally, *Commonwealth of Thieves*, 63.

33 Phillip's Instructions, op. cit., 12; Dunsdorfs, *Australian Wheat-Growing Industry*, 20; Robinson, 'Land', 92–4.

34 Fletcher, *Landed Enterprise*, 21–2; Yelling, *Common Field and Enclosure*; for an intimate account of the impact of the poaching laws on ordinary people, see Seal, *These Few Lines*; Phillip's Instructions re land grants, enclosure in Grenville to Phillip, 22 August 1789, *HRA* 1, 127, cf. Macquarie's Instructions, 1809, *HRA* 7, 196.

35 Linebaugh and Rediker, *Many Headed Hydra*, 49 and loc. cit.; see also Atkinson, *Europeans*, 171.

36 Atkinson, *Europeans*, 113–14, 203–4; see also his discussion of the visions for the colony, 67ff., 171; Rediker, 'How to Escape Bondage'; Aveling, 'Imagining New South Wales'.

37 Mann, *Present Picture*, 36–7.

38 Hirst, *Convict Society*, chaps 1 and 4.

39 Collins, *Account* 1, 320.

40 Hirst, *Great Convict Escapes*, 19.

41 Collins, *Account* 1, 249; for list of settlers see Campbell, 'Dawn of rural settlement', 96–7.

42 Ross, *Everingham Letterbook*, 35; Grose to Dundas, 9 January 1794, *HRA* 1, 414; Collins, *Account* 1, 243–4.

43 Phillip (in Hunter), *Journal*, 340.

44 NSW Legislative Assembly, *Progress Report . . . on the Field of Mars Common*, 6, 125.

45 See Campbell, 'Dawn of rural settlement', 85ff.; McLoughlin, 'Landed peasantry', 120–2; Jeans, *Historical Geography*, 81; the present-day location of the Ponds farms is shown in Ross, *Matthew Everingham*, 61.

46 Collins, *Account* 1, 249.

47 Coupe, *Concord*, 21, 24ff.; the name 'Liberty Plains' was recently resurrected for a new housing estate—Liberty Grove.

48 Caley, 'A short account', 294; see picture of slab house built for George Suttor c1801, in Carr et al., *Heritage Tour of the Hills District*, 8; see Hawkins, *Convict Timbergetters*, 19, for a detailed description of government huts for convicts in the 1810s.

49 Bradley, Journal, 232; lists of tools reproduced in Frost, *Botany Bay Mirages*, 132–3; Hawkins et al., *Castle Hill and its Government Farm*, 23.

50 Holt eventually did have his men work with hoes, and gave the more recalcitrant the heaviest and more cumbersome ones, which he called his 'private flogger', see Holt (O'Shaughnessy), *Rum Story*, 52, 66; Grant (Cramer), *Beauteous, Wicked Place*, 102, see also 100, 101.

51 Ryan, *Reminiscences*, 9; Cunningham, *Two Years* 1, 118; Caley, 'A short account', 293; see also Anon., A Letter from Sydney, 1792, *HRNSW* II, 808; Raby, *Making Rural Australia*, 36–7; Dunsdorf, *Australian Wheat-Growing Industry*, 12–14; Jeans, *Historical Geography*, 87–9; Fletcher, 'Agriculture', 214–15; Atkinson, *Camden*, 29.

52 See for example Jeans, Fletcher, ibid.; Murray and White, *Dharug and Dungaree*, 53–63; Caley, ibid., 292.

53 Caley, ibid.; Atkinson, *An Account*, 18, 48–51; Cunningham, *Two Years*; Bowd, *Macquarie Country*, 7–8; Raby, *Making Rural Australia*, 40–8. Compare with later methods introduced at Camden in the 1840s–60s, Atkinson, *Camden*, 79ff. For an exploration of the powerful influence of these themes in literature and art, see Dixon, *Course of Empire*, 1–2, 43–5, 58.

54 Collins, *Account* 1, 284, 365, 442; Gipps to Marquess of Normanby, 11 January 1840, *HRA* 20, 475–6. Maize was considered an inferior grain, though, and while the production of other crops and meat increased remarkably between 1810 and 1820, the value of the maize crop declined; Raby, *Making Rural Australia*, 18, 40, 52–71; Dunsdorf, *Australian Wheat-Growing Industry*, 15; Tench, *Complete Account*, 263; Butlin, *Forming a Colonial Economy*, 180.

55 See Bunn, 'Weeds', entry for capeweed and others; Collins, *Account* 1, 466–7; Caley, 'A short account', 292–3.

56 Howe, *New South Wales Pocket Almanack*; Atkinson, *An Account*, 48–51; Raby, *Making Rural Australia*, 48–52.

57 Collins, *Account* 1, 249; Phillip issued a total of 80 grants but eight were cancelled, and there must have been more abandonments, cf. Fletcher, *Landed Enterprise*, 47, 58.

58 Collins, *Account* 1, 320, 340; Fletcher, 'Grose, Paterson and the settlement of the Hawkesbury', 342–3.

59 Fletcher, ibid.; Bowd, *Macquarie Country*, 5ff.

60 Robinson, 'Land', 93.

61 Hunter, *Historical Journal*, 106; Phillip (in Hunter), *Journal*, 301; Tench, *Complete Account*, 226, 234.

62 Collins, *Account* 1, 320, 340; Fletcher, 'Grose, Paterson and the settlement of the Hawkesbury', 342–3.

63 Atkinson, *Europeans*, 248; see also Karskens, 'Spirit of emigration', 16–17; Pleij, *Dreaming of Cockaigne*.

64 Atkins, Journal, November 1792; Collins, *Account* 1, 371; Ryan, *Reminiscences*, 36; Calaby, 'The natural history drawings', 192, 195.

65 Britton and Morris, 'Castlereagh Cultural Landscape Study', 75–80; see *Penrith Press* 2, 7 January, 9, 16 May 2003, 21 December 2004, 14 October 2005, 17 January 2006; *Sydney Morning Herald*, 4 February 2003, 22 September 2004, 5, 6 October 2006.

66 Atkinson, *Europeans*, 199; Hardy, *Early Hawkesbury Settlers*, 11, and see biographical entries 53–220; Barkley and Nichols, *Hawkesbury*, 13; Parsons, 'Soldiers and specialisation', 12.

67 Fletcher, 'Grose, Paterson', 343; Grose to Dundas, 5 July 1794, *HRA* 1, 479.

68 Collins, *Account* 1, 406–7; 'A Soldier's Letter', 13 December 1794, *HRNSW* II, 817; Catchpole to Mrs Cobbold, 21 January 1802; Holt (O'Shaughnessy), *Rum Story*, 56.

69 Collins, *Account* 1, 413; Hardy, *Early Hawkesbury Settlers*, 14; Fletcher, 'Small scale farming', 4; Fletcher, 'Grose, Paterson', 345–6; Fletcher, 'Agriculture', 195. The fertility of the soils was celebrated in W.C. Wentworth's poem 'Australasia', see Dixon, *Course of Empire*, 133–4.

70 Bowd, *Macquarie Country*, 56; Parsons, 'Soldiers and specialisation', 12; Collins, *Account* 1, 406; Hardy, *Early Hawkesbury Settlers*, 13.

71 Fletcher, 'Grose, Paterson', 346–7; Fletcher, *Landed Enterprise*, 47–8; Hunter to Portland, 12 November 1796, *HRA* 1, 667; Ross, *A Hawkesbury Story*, tracks the expansion up the rivers of the first three settler generations; see also Croucher, *Years of Hardship*.

72 Collins, *Account* 2, 20, 32, 39, 224.

73 Collins, *Account* 1, 415, 541; Péron, *Voyage*, 307; Wentworth, *Statistical, Historical and Political Description*, 65–8.

74 Hardy, *Early Hawkesbury Settlers*, 12–13; Hutton Neve, *Forgotten Valley*, chaps 1 and 2.

75 Purtell, *Mosquito Fleet*, 37; Hardy, *Early Hawkesbury Settlers*, 17; Jack, 'Early boat building', 37.

76 Bowd, *Macquarie Country*, chap. 5; Jack, 'Early boat building', 53 and loc. cit.; see also Hawkins, 'Timbergetting in the Bluegum High Forest', 33.

77 Bowd, *Macquarie Country*, 79; Ross, *Hawkesbury Story*, 45, 47, 50, 95ff., 111–12.

78 'Took' and 'took up', see Grenville's discussion in *Searching for the Secret River*, 28–9.

79 Collins, *Account* 1, 338–9, see also 54 and vol. 2, 18; Hunter grumbled that 'the worst characters have unfortunately been placed at the greatest distance from the head quarters', Hunter to Portland, 20 June 1797, *HRA* 2, 23.

80 Bowd, *Macquarie Country*, 49; Berzins, *Coming of the Strangers*, 78, 95; Day, *Smugglers and Sailors*, 4.

81 Campbell, 'The use and abuse of stimulants', 74.

82 Collins, *Account* 1, 25, 160, 260, 272.

83 Campbell, 'The use and abuse of stimulants', 87–8, 97; Collins, *Account* 1, 449; *SG* 3 March 1805.

84 Collins, *Account* 1, 411; Minton v Richards and Richards v Minton, March/April 1818, 385ff.

85 See for example, Collins, *Account* 1, 284, 287, 414, 434; R v Hunt (murder of Stephen Smith on the Nepean) 20 February 1812, 81–99; R v William Swift and Daniel Grogan (murder of Maria Minton) 20 March 1821, 138–60. See also Atkinson, *Europeans*, 199.

86 Tench, *Complete Account*, 249–50; Hunter to King, 4 June 1798, *HRA* 2, 155; see also Collins, *Account*, 1, 227, and discussion in Karskens, *The Rocks*, 162–3.

87 Huntington, *My Mother Reread Me*, 54; Collins, *Account* 1, 427.

88 Ryan, *Reminiscences*, 116; Bowd, *Macquarie Country*, chap. 19, cockfighting 153; *Bell's Life in Sydney*, 4, 11, 25 January, 13, 27 September 1845, 6 March 1847.

89 Ryan, *Reminiscences*, 114–18.

90 Hardy, *Early Hawkesbury Settlers*, 13, 15, 206; Atkinson, *Europeans*, 179ff.; Collins, *Account* 1, 400.

91 Marsden to Mrs Stokes, 26 October 1795; Bowd, *Macquarie Country*, 66–7, 78–9. The Rev. Henry Fulton, transported with the Irish rebels of 1798, preached at the Green Hills 'briefly' in 1800 before settling in Castlereagh and founding his famous school, where he endowed the rising generation of 'Cornstalks' with a precious classical education. Hardy, *Early Hawkesbury Settlers*, 15.

92 Hunter to Portland, *HRA* 2, 23; also part quoted in Atkinson, *Europeans*, 171; Collins, *Account* 2, 69, 133.

93 The others were Richmond, Castlereagh, Wilberforce and Pitt Town. Governor Macquarie's Instructions, 1809, *HRA* 7, 196; Proudfoot, 'Opening towns', 61, 65–7, and see Macquarie, Journal; Macquarie to the Secretary of State for Colonies, 4 April 1817, ML MMS 1191, vol. 2, no. 18, 246–8; Hardy, *Early Hawkesbury Settlers*, 37; Robinson, 'Land', 101.

94 Macquarie to Secretary of State for the Colonies, ibid.; Bowd, *Macquarie Country*, 83–4; Hardy, *Early Hawkesbury Settlers*, 45.

95 Tollard, *Years of Endeavour*; Rosen, *Bankstown*, 24–5.

96 Silver, *Battle of Vinegar Hill*, chap. 3 and 73–103.

97 See Bruce, Life of a Greenwich Pensioner; Collins, *Account* 1, 400, 473, 474; *SG* 10 July 1803, 26 February, 21 October 1804, 19 January, 2 March, 24 August, 2 November 1806, 24 November 1810 (harvest), and see the numerous reports on individual absconders and bushrangers 1803–10; Bowd, *Macquarie Country*, chap. 8; Murray and White, *Dharug and Dungaree*, 218–30.

98 Hunter to an unknown person, 16 October 1795, *HRNSW* 2, 1819; Collins, *Account* 1, 375.

99   Collins, *Account* 2, 203, 272–3. An 'insect . . . known to overspread a field of corn in the course of one night and totally destroy it' was reported in 1792 (*HRNSW* 2, 799), though this could have been a locust. Tench reported in December 1791 that the 'people at Prospect complain sadly of a destructive grub which destroys the young plants of maize. Many of the settlers have been obliged to plant twice, nay thrice, on the same land from the depredations of these reptiles . . .', *Complete Account*, 254.

100 Hunter to Portland, 1 May 1799, *HRA* 2, 351; Collins, *Account* 2, 139, 140, 195; *SG* 5 March 1803; Fletcher, 'Agriculture', 195ff.

101 Hunter to Portland, ibid., 354–5, see also 738, note 188; Collins, *Account* 2, 200. The catchment of the Hawkesbury–Nepean occupies 69,930 square kilometres; Bowd, *Macquarie Country*, 11.

102 Paterson to Dundas, 16 September 1795, *HRA* 1, 529; Hardy, *Early Hawkesbury Settlers*, 19.

103 Hunter to Portland, 26 March 1800, *HRA* 2, 474; Fletcher, 'Agriculture', 195ff., 204; Fletcher, *Landed Enterprise*, 54ff., 59–60; Hawkesbury Historical Society, 'Flood Levels of the Hawkesbury'.

104 Catchpole to W. Howes, 8 October 1806.

105 Petition of James Ward re floods, January 1801, with Report of Charles Grimes, January 1801, 363–9a.

106 'By 1821 only 34.9% of 1226 original emancipist grantees to that date were still on their land. However . . . there were 1243 former convicts farming at this time on rented or purchased land . . .', McLoughlin, 'Landed peasantry', 132; see also Fletcher, 'Small scale farming', 14; Fletcher, *Landed Enterprise*, 55.

107 Collins, *Account* 2, 133. Forty years later, rural housing was still poor and slovenly, see Meredith, *Notes and Sketches*, 60.

108 Arnold to his brother, 18 March 1810, 5–11, also in Purtell, *Mosquito Fleet*, 1, and Martin, *A New Land*, 76.

109 Fletcher, *Landed Enterprise*, 50.

110 Robinson, 'Land', 91; Fletcher, *Landed Enterprise*, 12; Dunsdorf, *Australian Wheat-Growing Industry*, 7; McLoughlin, 'Landed peasantry', 127; Rosen, *Bankstown*, 24.

111 Huntington, *My Mother Reread Me*, 62, 74. Ruse sold Marsden the Bankstown grant in 1821 and the Riverstone grant in 1823.

112 Grenville, *Secret River*, 106; Ralph Hawkins, 'Solomon Wiseman', 9.

113 Fletcher, 'Small scale farming', 16; Karskens, *The Rocks*, chap. 18; Parsons, 'Wiseman, Solomon, 1777–1838'; Karskens, 'Deference, defiance and diligence', 17–28; Ross, *Hawkesbury Story*, 22.

114 Karskens, 'The Grandest Improvement' (thesis).

115 Hardy, *Early Hawkesbury Settlers*, 206–7.

116 Walsh, 'Reibey, Mary (1777–1855)'; Irvine (ed.), *Dear Cousin*; Irvine, *Mary Reibey*.

117 Nix, *Glimpses of Glenhaven*, 13; Karskens, *Inside the Rocks*, 40.

118 Fletcher, 'Agriculture', 210–11.

119 Campbell, 'Dawn of rural settlement', note, 92; Dyster, *Servant and Master*, 14–15; McCormick, *First Views*, 165; Mann, *Present Picture*, 62; Broadbent, *Australian Colonial House*, 314; National Trust of Australia (NSW), 'Places to visit: Experiment Farm'.

120 Phillip's Instructions re Land Grants, 20 August 1789, encl. in Grenville to Phillip, 22 August 1789, *HRA* 1, 124–5; Bradley, Journal, 13 March 1788, 95; Collins, *Account* 1, 266–8; Fletcher, *Landed Enterprise*, 10–12, 57. Fletcher shows that the process by which the British decision was made to grant land to the officers was most unusual— perhaps underscoring the unusual nature of the colony, or a 'surreptitious' decision on Dundas' part; see also McLoughlin, 'Landed peasantry', 129–31. The patchwork of grants is shown on Burrowes' 1840 map 'Petersham' and in Campbell, 'Dawn of rural settlement', 120–1.

121 McLoughlin, 'Landed peasantry', 136; Dyster, *Servant and Master*, 13. Farmhouses with jerkinhead roofs survive at Castlereagh (Hadley Park), Cattai (Macquarie Retreat, Caddie Park) and Ebenezer (Stannix Park); Broadbent, *Australian Colonial House*, 19, 23, 25, 103–9.

122 Johnson, letters to Henry Fricker, 1788–89; Tench, *Complete Account*, 193; Madden and Muir, *Canterbury Farm*, 1–6.

123 Marsden to Mrs Stokes, 8–9 August 1794, 26 October 1795; to Mr Stokes, 26 November 1811, ML MSS 719; McLoughlin, 'Landed peasantry', 136, 139; Dyster, *Servant and Master*, 21–2; Yarwood, 'Marsden, Samuel (1765–1838)'.

124 Marsden added 1600 acres to his holdings through purchase; Dyster, *Servant and Master*, 16–17, 22; Macquarie, 'Journal of a tour of inspection . . . 1810'.

125 Wood, *History of Bankstown*, map, 49; Peters, *Bankstown's Northern Suburbs*, 5; Fitzgerald and Hearn, *Bligh, Macarthur*, 70.

126 Phillip (in Hunter), *Journal*, 302–3; Butlin, *Forming a Colonial Economy*, 44; by 1792 Collins had decided that sailors and soldiers also made poor settlers who soon gave up, *Account* 1, 234–5.

127 Phillip's Instructions re Land Grants, 20 August 1789, *HRA* 1, 125–6; Fletcher, *Landed Enterprise*, 16ff.

128 Collins, *Account* 1, 267; Collins says a group of Quakers was also supposed to arrive on the *Bellona*, but they decided not to come after the colony had been 'misrepresented to them', 262; McMartin, 'Rose, Thomas (1754?–1833)'.

129 Auburn Municipal Council, *Liberty Plains*, 22. Compare with the portrayal of the settler experience in David Malouf's novel *Remembering Babylon*, for example.

130 Scott, 'The Hall estate or "firm"', 81.

131 *SG* 20 May 1804.

132 Suttor, *Memoirs*, 43; see also Suttor's long hysterical letter to Banks, 10 March 1804, complaining of settlers being plagued by the Irish rebels.

133 Hall, Journal; Bowd, 'Settling in', in Warner, *Over-Halling the Colony*, 67–70.

134 Hardy, *Early Hawkesbury Settlers*, 15, 20–1.

135 For a detailed account of the complex alliances and enmities during Bligh's administration, see Hardy, ibid., 20ff.

136 Ross, *Matthew Everingham*, 74; Bowd, *Macquarie Country*, 78–9; Atkinson, *Europeans*, 217; Hardy, *Early Hawkesbury Settlers*, 21–2.

137 Warner, *Over-Halling the Colony*, 28, 62, 66. See also the numerous other family and local histories, particularly for the Hawkesbury–Nepean.

138 Fletcher, *Landed Enterprise*, 16ff.; Dunsdorf, *Australian Wheat-Growing Industry*, 10, 40, 46; McLoughlin, 'Landed peasantry', 131–2; Suttor, *Memoirs*, 41, 44, 58.

139 Conway, 'Riley, Alexander (1778?–1833)'; Dixon, *Course of Empire*, 72.

140 Dyster, *Servant and Master*, 17–18; 'The Blaxlands', exhibition, Mitchell Library, 2007.

141 Dyster, *Servant and Master*, 28 and loc. cit.; Madden and Muir, *Canterbury Farm*, 5–7.

142 Waterhouse, *Private Pleasures*, 15.

143 ibid., 15–17; Ryan, *Reminiscences*, 36–7.

144 See for example Worgan, Letter and journal, 19 May 1788; Cunningham, *Blue Mountains Rediscovered*, 157; Waterhouse, *Private Pleasures*, 11–17; Fletcher, *Landed Enterprise*, 10; Karskens, *The Rocks*, 76–8; White, *Journal*, biographical introduction, 28; Hardy, *Early Hawkesbury Settlers*, 23, 54. Rummers were robust stemmed glasses which made a satisfying report when slammed on the table. Hyacinthe de Bougainville included hilarious accounts of the horses lent to him and his party by their colonial friends: the French visitors were often thrown from these rather spirited creatures—see diary entries in *Governor's Noble Guest*.

145 Broadbent et al., *India, China, Australia*, 16, 19, 96ff.

146 Macarthur (de Falbe), *My Dear Miss Macarthur*, 15; see also Dyster, *Servant and Master*, 14–15.

147 Atkins, Journal, 15 March 1794, 167; Cavanilles (in King), *Secret History of the Convict Colony*, 155; Péron, *Voyage*, 280–1; Cunningham, *Two Years*, 52–4.

148 Parsons, 'Commercialisation of honour', 108–9; Dunsdorf, *Australian Wheat-Growing Industry*, 39–40; Fletcher, 'Agriculture', 197; Fletcher, *Landed Enterprise*, 45, 57, 70; Hardy, *Early Hawkesbury Settlers*, 23; Collins, *Account* 1, 432.

149 Bowd, 'Settling In', in Warner, *Over-Halling the Colony*, 69; Parsons, 'Commercialisation of honour', 112; Butlin, *Forming a Colonial Economy*, 173–4; Fletcher, 'Agriculture', 206; Ritchie, *Punishment and Profit*, Appendix V, 265–94.

150 Dyster, *Servant and Master*, 26–8; Parsons, 'Commercialisation of honour', 111; Robinson, 'Land', 88.

151 Fletcher, 'Small scale farming', 10–13; Fletcher, 'Agriculture', 201–3, 204.

152 Dyster, *Servant and Master*, 13–15, 17–19; Broadbent, *Australian Colonial House*, 96ff., 109, 113–18.

153 Fletcher, 'Agriculture', 191, 201; Fletcher, *Landed Enterprise*, 80; Fletcher 'Small scale farming', 1, 20–1; Dunsdorf, *Australian Wheat-Growing Industry*, 46. The emancipists made up between 69 and 80 per cent of the colony's farmers. See also McLoughlin, 'Landed peasantry', 135.

154 Catchpole to William Howes, 2 September 1811.

155 Robinson, 'Land', 87–8. The population of the Sydney district in 1813 was 5356, compared to 6436 elsewhere in the colony.

156 Fletcher, *Landed Enterprise*, 44; see shipping notices and advertisements in early issues of *SG*.

157 Dyster, *Servant and Master*, 27; Jeans, *Historical Geography*, 85ff.; Hawkins, 'Timbergetting in the Bluegum High Forest'; Ritchie, 'Red cedar timber industry', 43–4.

158 Butlin, *Forming a Colonial Economy*, 152–3; see also Cronon, *Nature's Metropolis*.

159 Bigge, in Dunsdorf, *Australian Wheat-Growing Industry*, 32; Karskens, *The Rocks*, 54–5.

160 *SG* 26 June 1803, 1 July 1804, 8 May 1803, 25 December 1803.

161 *SG* 12 August 1804.

162 Interestingly, kangaroo moccasins worn by the 1820s were made in Sydney by Crane, see Ross, *A Hawkesbury Story*, 26.

163 Robert Howe, Diary, 9.

164 Mathew (Harvard), 'Mrs Felton Mathew's Journal', 240, also 242; also in Ross, *A Hawkesbury Story*, 42, 75.

165 These local and family histories have been told in extraordinarily fine-grained detail in works such as Ross, *A Hawkesbury Story*; Warner, *Over-Halling the Colony*; Croucher, *Years of Hardship*; see also Freame, 'Reminiscences of a district veteran'; Freame, 'Michael Long'; Jack, 'The Future', in Jack (ed.), *A Colonial Scene*, 51–6; Jack, 'Early boat-building'; Holland, *Growing Up on the Hawkesbury*.

166 Holok, 'Evolution of an exhibition', 14–15.

167 Ruse, Petition, 1810; *Australian* 15 June 1827; *SG* 20 June 1827, in Huntington, *My Mother Reread Me*, 77–8.

168 T.D. Mutch, Index to Births, Deaths and Marriages, entries for James Ruse and Elizabeth Parry and their children, ML; Huntington, ibid., 79ff.; Fletcher, 'Ruse, James (1760–1837)'.

169 Huntington, *My Mother Reread Me*, 79–80. The headstones of Ruse and Parry stood in St John's Cemetery at Campbelltown until 1994 when vandalism forced their removal to the Campbelltown and Airds Historical Society Museum, pers. com. Jackie Green, email 27 March 2008.

CHAPTER 6   VIEWS FROM FLAGSTAFF HILL

1   Pickett and Lomb, *Observer and Observed*; McCormick, *First Views*, pictures 1800–10; Observatory Park Trustees Letter Book and Minutes of Meetings, 1876–95, SRNSW.

2   McCormick, *First Views*, plates 9, 20, 21, 26, 27, 38, 39, 76, 77, 79, 80, 87, 96, 106, 177, 179, 181, 184, 205, showing views to South Head, the flagstaff and tower from c1790 to 1822; Tench, *Complete Account*, 169, 191, 245; *Heads of the People*, 13 November 1847 cited in Pickett and Lomb, *Observer and Observed*, 18.

3   Hunter, *Historical Journal*, 117; Phillip (in Hunter), *Journal*, 305, 312; Bradley, Journal, 98, 106, 118 and see also 186, 286. Bradley noted that the column could be seen 6 leagues out to sea, but still worried that it might be missed; Tench, *Complete Account*, 162, 178.

4   Noah, *Voyage*; Collins, *Account* 1, 147; Smith, *King Bungaree*, Part 2.

5   Collins, *Account* 1, 15; Smith and Wheeler, *Art of the First Fleet*, 74. Surveys of Botany Bay and Broken Bay were carried out soon after—in August 1788 and September 1789; see also Bradley's detailed description of the harbour for the benefit of shipping, Journal, 77.

6   See Bradley's detailed description of the harbour, Journal, 77.

NOTES

7   See McCormick, *First Views*, plates 3 and 4.

8   Tench, *Complete Account*, 224.

9   Linebaugh and Rediker, *Many Headed Hydra*, chap. 5; Rodger, *The Wooden World*; Dening, *Mr Bligh's Bad Language*, 81, 85ff.; Clendinnen, *Dancing*, 186–9.

10 Collins, *Account* 2, 44, 47; Hawkins, 'Timbergetting in the Blue Gum High Forest', 17–18. By the time Governor John Hunter arrived, it was the NSW Corps which offended naval notions of discipline. 'Accustomed to shipboard discipline which he expected to see …' Hunter found 'an entrenched and mutinous soldiery', see Fitzgerald and Hearn, *Bligh, Macarthur*, 37.

11 Gray, 'Social life at Sydney Cove', 381; Bradley, Journal, 2 May 1788, 104–5; Worgan, Letter and journal, 15, 22; Tench, *Narrative*, 44. Linebaugh names this 'thanatocracy', rule by terror and death, see *London Hanged*, 50, 53–4.

12 Karskens, 'Spirit of emigration'; Atkinson, *Europeans*, 57, 113.

13 McLoughlin, 'Estuarine wetland distribution'; *SG* 10 April 1803, 9, 30 August 1807, 30 June 1810 and see stories and advertisements on market days.

14 For a more detailed account, see Karskens, *The Rocks*, chap. 16.

15 Karskens, 'Spirit of emigration'; Gibson, 'Ocean settlements'; Bigge, *Report . . . on the Colony of New South Wales*, 33–4, 47.

16 See 'Plan of the town and suburbs of Sydney, August 1822', in Ashton and Waterson, *Sydney Takes Shape*, 19.

17 Walsh, 'Geography of manufacturing', 22–31, map, 29.

18 Péron, *Voyage*, 275–6; Karskens, 'Death was in his face'; Karskens, *The Rocks*, 47; Collins, *Account* 1, 231.

19 Péron, *Voyage*, 275; Karskens, *The Rocks*, 47.

20 In 1808 only 120 out of the roughly 300 soldiers lived in the barracks, see McMahon, 'Not a rum rebellion', 128; McCormick, *First Views*, plates 19, 29, 42, 43, 156; Broadbent, *Francis Greenway*, 54–5.

21 Collins, *Account* 2, 310; McCormick, *First Views*, plates 15, 53, 55, 56, 83, 94, 105, 155; Kerr and Broadbent, *Gothick Taste*, 37–8; Broadbent and Hughes, *Age of Macquarie*, 4. The church was demolished in 1857.

22 McCormick, *First Views*, 292–3 and see series of pictures; Ashton and Waterson, *Sydney Takes Shape*, 14, 15; *SG* 5 June, 3 July, 11 December 1803, 21 April 1805, 23 November 1806, 8 February 1807, 30 July 1809.

23 McCormick, *First Views*, 109, 110–11, 119 and series of plates; Atkinson, *Europeans*, 268–9; Proudfoot et al., *First Government House*, 86–7.

24 Bonyhady, *Colonial Earth*, 46–7; Clendinnen, *Dancing*, 137–8; Smith, *Bennelong*, 67; Collins, *Account* 1, 433.

25 McLoughlin, 'Shaping Sydney Harbour', 186–7; Campbell, 'Valley of the Tank Stream', 69.

26 Kerr and Falkus, *Sydney Cove to Duntroon*, 33–7; Hughes, *Demolished Houses*, 38; see also Steven, *Merchant Campbell*.

27 Irving, 'Georgian Australia', 44–8; Hainsworth, *Sydney Traders*, loc. cit., see pictures after 72; Rowland, 'Simeon Lord'.

28 Bonyhady, *Colonial Earth*, 46–9.

29 Karskens, *Inside the Rocks*, chap. 2; Butlin, *Australian Monetary System*, chap. 2; quote from Day, *Smugglers and Sailors*, 6.

30 Karskens, *The Rocks*, 20, 46.

31 They included John Macarthur, William Paterson and Thomas Laycock as well as Joseph Foveaux, George Johnston, Thomas Rowley, Surgeon John Harris and the commissaries John Palmer and James Williamson.

32 Paine (Knight and Frost), *Journal of Daniel Paine*, 23.

33 Hainsworth, *Builders and Adventurers*, 74–5; Parsons, 'Commercialisation of honour', 111; Dow, *Samuel Terry*.

34 Fitzgerald and Hearn, *Bligh, Macarthur*, 61.

35 Atkinson, 'John Macarthur'; Griffiths, 'Past silences'; Dow, *Samuel Terry*, 59–60.

36 Collins, *Account* 1, 121; Griffiths, 'Past silences'; Péron, *Voyage*, in Aplin and Parsons, 'Maritime trade', 162.

37 Frost, 'The growth of settlement', 131; Collins, *Account* 2, 279; Lisle, 'Rum beginnings'; Suttor, Sketch of Events, 2; Nicholas and Nicholas, *Charles Darwin*, 78.

38 Hainsworth, *Sydney Traders*, 82–5, 128–56.

39 Frost, *Global Reach*, 241, 308–9, 317; Day, *Smugglers and Sailors*, 10, 35–45; Aplin and Parsons, 'Maritime trade', 151–6; Kelly, *Anchored in a Small Cove*, 44–5; Hainsworth, *Builders and Adventurers*, 99–107; Griffiths, *Slicing the Silence*, 54–7.

40 Aplin and Parsons, 'Maritime Trade', 156; Bolton, *Spoils and Spoilers*, 51.

41 Anon., Letter from a Female Convict, 14 November 1788, HRNSW II, Appendix, 746–7.

42 Catchpole to W. Howes, 8 October 1806; see McKendrick et al., *Birth of a Consumer Society*; Johnson, *Housing Culture*; Johnson, *Archaeology of Capitalism*.

43 Noah, *Voyage*, 70; Karskens, *Inside the Rocks*, 69–72.

44 Most recently, Grenville, *The Secret River*, 3–6, 75ff.

45 Frost, 'Going Away, Coming Home', 21.

46 Noah, *Voyage*; Catchpole to Mrs Cobbold, 21 January 1802.

47 Linebaugh and Rediker, *Many Headed Hydra*; Atkinson, 'Four patterns of convict protest'.

48 Walsh, 'The geography of manufacturing', 26–9; Varley, 'Australian clays', 218–21; Karskens, *Inside the Rocks*, 43–5, 70–1; Frith, 'From tanning to planning', 49–50.

49 *SG* 20 November 1803.

50 Karskens, *Inside the Rocks*, 31–4, 50–6; Karskens, *The Rocks*, 32–3; Freeland, *Architecture in Australia*, 11–12; Irving, 'Georgian Australia', 44; Bridges, *Foundations of Identity*, 27–31; compare with Stephen Mrozowski, 'Landscapes of inequality', 79ff.

51 Blair, 'Newspapers and their Readers in early Australia' (thesis).

52 Bridges, *Foundations of Identity*, 36, 45–7; Fitzgerald and Keating, *Millers Point*, 24.

53 *SG* 5 February, 23 September, 25 November, 1804, 9 October 1808, 19 November 1809, 29 December 1810; Foveaux to Macquarie, 27 February 1810, HRNSW 7, 297.

54 Pye, *Maximum City*, esp. 56–7; Blumin, *Emergence of the Middle Class*, 20ff.; Jackson, *Crabgrass Frontier*, 12–19.

55 Girouard, *Cities and People*, chaps 1–4, esp. 35ff., 69ff.; Jackson, ibid.; Davison, 'The

first suburban nation?' and 'Past and future of the Australian suburb'; cf. Girouard: 'Separate buildings, each on its own little plot, have always been the usual arrangement in any new settlement', 70.

56   Morehead, *My Recollection*; Coghill, *Diary*; Kean to Mrs Horace Twiss; earlier, Spanish visitor Cavanilles wrote similarly of Parramatta, see King, *Secret History*, 155.

57   Johnston, Evidence at trial, 1811, cited in Bonyhady, *Colonial Earth*, 63.

58   Campbell to King, 23 February 1803, *HRA* 4, 127–9; Foveaux to Castlereagh, 20 February 1810, *HRNSW* 7, 41. Grose and Paterson also recognised that convicts 'had at least some rights to the land on which they had built their huts', see Bonyhady, *Colonial Earth*, 47.

59   Hunter to Portland, 12 November 1796, *HRA* 1, 676; Government and General Orders, 9 November 1796, *HRA* 1, 701.

60   Karskens, 'Dialogue of townscape', 104–5; Bonyhady, *Colonial Earth*, 5–6.

61   King to Portland, 10 March 1801, *HRA* 2, 8.

62   *SG* 16 October 1803; Karskens, 'Dialogue of townscape', 105; Atkinson, 'Taking possession', 81–2.

63   Atkinson, ibid.; Parsons, 'Commercialisation of honour', 112–14; Fitzgerald and Hearn, *Bligh, Macarthur*, 51–2; Aplin and Parsons, 'Maritime trade', 157; Frost, *Global Reach*, 308–9.

64   Fletcher, *Landed Enterprise*, 29, 31, 36, 37, 81; Hardy, *Early Hawkesbury Settlers*, 20; though contrast with Abbott, 'Governor King's administration'.

65   See Dening, *Mr Bligh's Bad Language*; Karskens, 'Spirit of emigration', 14–15; Fitzgerald and Hearn, *Bligh, Macarthur*, 11.

66   Fitzgerald and Hearn, *Bligh, Macarthur*, 20, 71–3, 82–3, 93, 96.

67   Atkinson, 'Taking possession', 76; Bonyhady, *Colonial Earth*, 43, 64–5.

68   Bonyhady, *Colonial Earth*, 53–60; Ellis, *John Macarthur*, 300; Fitzgerald and Hearn, *Bligh, Macarthur*, 79, 92; Alan Atkinson, 'Taking possession', 84–6.

69   Hardy, *Early Hawkesbury Settlers*, 30.

70   Fitzgerald and Hearn, *Bligh, Macarthur*, 101–4; Caley, 'A Short Account', 687; Anon., 'William Bligh's chickens'.

71   John Macarthur, January 1808, in Fitzgerald and Hearn, *Bligh, Macarthur*, 99; Bonyhady, *Colonial Earth*, 43–4, 60–5. Macarthur's campaign and rhetoric was most likely also underpinned by the ideas of Jeremy Bentham, who argued that the governors of New South Wales had no legal power over the free settlers and emancipists; see Atkinson, 'Jeremy Bentham and the Rum Rebellion'.

72   Fitzgerald and Hearn, *Bligh, Macarthur*, 92.

73   The number of houses/households in Sydney in 1808 is unclear, but by 1804 there were already 678 (see *SG* 15 April 1804). Meehan's 1807 map, commissioned by Bligh, recorded a total of 99 leases. Since there must have been more houses built in the intervening years, the leaseholders made up less than one-seventh of householders. Meehan's map shows that the permissive occupations (blacked-in) were far more extensive; see James Meehan, 'Plan of the Town of Sydney', 1807. By 1820, the proportion of leaseholders in Sydney and Parramatta was one-fifth of householders, see Bigge, *Report . . . on the State of Agriculture and Trade*, 42.

CHAPTER 7   LANDSCAPE ARTISTS: THE MACQUARIES IN SYDNEY

1   Callaway, *Visual Ephemera*, 4 and chap. 2.

2   *SG* 21 January 1810; Dunlop, 'Blaxcell, Garnham (1778–1817)'.

3   Freeland, *Architecture in Australia*, 29. Compare with Scott, *Short History of Australia*, 'The last of the tyrants', 99ff.

4   ibid.; see also Broadbent and Hughes, *Age of Macquarie*, esp. 157.

5   Broadbent, 'Macquarie's Domain', 4. The batteries on Dawes and Bennelong points are now the sites of two great Sydney icons: Dawes Point now lies under the roar and deep shadow of the Sydney Harbour Bridge, and Bennelong Point, once an island, now bears the ponderous weight of the Sydney Opera House.

6   Karskens, *The Rocks*, 158; Proudfoot, 'Fixing the settlement', 66 and fig. 3.6; Kelly, *Anchored in a Small Cove*, 99–101.

7   St Philip's: Kerr and Broadbent, *Gothick Taste*, 135–6. First and second Government houses: Proudfoot et al., *First Government House*, 121–32; Kerr and Broadbent, *Gothick Taste*, 91, 94–5. Merchants' houses: Hainsworth, *The Sydney Traders*, plate following 72; Hughes (ed.), *Demolished Houses of Sydney*, 38. Fort Phillip: King to Hobart 14 August 1804, *HRA* 5, 2; Karskens, *The Rocks*, 63.

8   See Macquarie, Journals; Dixon, *Course of Empire*, chap. 4.

9   Macquarie to Bathurst, 10 September 1822, *HRA* 10, 671–2.

10   Macquarie to Castlereagh, 8 March 1810, *HRA* 7, 222ff. Some public buildings were in need of replacement, Macquarie to Liverpool 9 November 1812, *HRA* 7, 528; Fletcher, *Landed Enterprise*, 117.

11   Broadbent and Hughes, *Age of Macquarie*, 1–2; Ellis, *Lachlan Macquarie*; Atkinson, *Europeans*, 317, 326.

12   Castlereagh to Macquarie, 14 May 1809, *HRA* 7, 80–5.

13   Elizabeth Macquarie, Diary, in Ellis, *Lachlan Macquarie*, 171; an engraving of Ultimo c1812 is reproduced in McCormick, *First Views*, plate 129.

14   These were recurring visions of Europeans first sailing into Port Jackson; see Southwell, Diary, as discussed in Kerr and Broadbent, *Gothick Taste*, 93.

15   Kerr and Broadbent, *Gothick Taste*, 11–16, quote from the Reverend William Gilpin, cited 12; Atkinson, *Europeans*, 317–18.

16   Coltheart, 'Landscape of public works', 160; Broadbent, 'Building in the colony', 163, 168–9; Broadbent and Hughes, *Francis Greenway*, 6; Proudfoot, 'Opening towns', 60ff.

17   Castlereagh to Macquarie, 14 May 1809, *HRA* 7, 82.

18   See series of memorials to Macquarie in CSC 1810, SRNSW and microfiche copies, ML; Atkinson, 'Taking possession', 85–7; similarly he reviewed all the grants of land made in the period 1808–09—Fletcher estimates that 86 per cent of these were also ratified; see Fletcher, *Landed Enterprise*, 117.

19   See Commissioner of Claims, Memorials Forwarded, 1832–42, and Reports, c1835–55, 2/1752–75; Fletcher, *Ralph Darling*, 175.

20   Castlereagh to Macquarie, 14 May 1809, *HRA* 7, 82–5; Governor Macquarie's Commission and Instructions, 1810, *HRA* 7, 183–97; Fletcher, *Landed Enterprise*, chap. 6.

21   ibid.

22   Asked for such records by Commissioner Bigge, Surveyor James Meehan replied, 'I kept none'. Bigge, *Report*, Appendix, BT Box 5, 2224.

23   *SG* 11 August, 6, 27 October 1810; Proudfoot, 'Opening towns', 61; Freeland, *Architecture in Australia*, 30.

24   Broadbent, 'Building in the colony', 166–7; Broadbent, *Australian Colonial House*, chap. 3.

25   For the saga of the judge advocate's house, see Broadbent, *Australian Colonial House*, 33–41.

26   Bigge, *Report . . . on the Judicial Establishments*, 70, 62; and *Report*, Appendix, Evidence of James Meehan, BT Box 5, 2237.

27   Karskens, *Inside the Rocks*, 28–34, 75; Karskens, *The Rocks*, 4, 28, 32–3; cf. Meehan, 'Plan of the Town', 1807; Harper, 'Plan of the Allotments', 1823, and section maps by Russell, 1835.

28   Broadbent, 'Building in the colony', 164–5; Freeland, *Architecture in Australia*, 32–3.

29   Collins, *Account* 2, 310; Broadbent and Kerr, *Gothick Taste*, 32, 38–40. Elizabeth Macquarie's watercolours of St John's reproduced in Kass et al., *Parramatta*, facing 47 and see 81–2; see also paintings by Watts and Lewin, facing 78; and McCormick, *First Views*, plate 220.

30   Broadbent and Hughes, *Francis Greenway*, 5–10.

31   Cited in ibid., 9.

32   ibid., 9–10 and note 25.

33   ibid., 8, 11–12; Freeland, *Architecture in Australia*, 35.

34   Broadbent and Hughes, *Francis Greenway*, 11–12, 15–16, 48.

35   See ibid.; Broadbent, 'Building in the colony'; Oppenheim, *Fragile Forts*, 20; Karskens, 'The house on the hill', 125–6.

36   Wrigley, 'Urban growth and agricultural change', 42, 78; Borsay, 'The English urban renaissance', 175; quote, R. Porter, 'Science, provincial culture and public opinion', 252.

37   Borsay, 'From Bath to Poundbury'; Borsay, 'Health and leisure resorts'.

38   Broadbent, 'Macquarie's domain', 4; Broadbent, 'Building in the town', 167–8; Kerr and Broadbent, *Gothick Taste*, 40–4; Broadbent and Hughes, *Francis Greenway*, 53–4, 81. The pigeon house is thought to have been designed for and built in the Domain at Parramatta, but a similar structure appears in Sophia Campbell's 'Sydney in all its Glory' (c1817) in the Domain at Sydney.

39   Broadbent and Hughes, *Francis Greenway*, 53; Broadbent, 'Building in the colony', 162; Lighthouses of Australia Inc., 'Macquarie Lighthouse'.

40   ibid. The lighthouse was demolished and replaced with an almost exact copy designed by James Barnett in 1883; Joseph Lycett, 'East view of Sydney . . . 1819 . . . taken from the Macquarie Tower' and 'Distant View of Sydney, from the Light House at South Head . . .' c1822, in McCormick, *First Views*, plates 207 and 208. See later paintings of the lighthouse and South Head by artists including Augustus Earle (c1825), Jean Baptiste Armout (1833), Robert Russell (1836), Conrad Martens (1850), Samuel Elyard (1864) and Charles Cousen (c1874), in the National Library of Australia.

41   Waterhouse, *Private Pleasures*, 17–18; Proudfoot, 'Hyde Park Sydney', 5, 9–19.

42   Proudfoot, ibid.; Oldfield, 'A Walk through Sydney in 1828', 318; compare with analysis of Worcester parks and working people's struggle to retain them for their own uses in Rosenzweig, *Eight Hours for What We Will*, chap. 5, 127–41. See also the many pictures of 'darling Hyde Park' in the State Library of NSW, especially the series by John Rae in the 1840s.

43   Walsh, 'Geography of manufacturing', 34.

44   Wilson, *Discovering the Domain*, 22–3; Proudfoot et al., *First Government House*, 102–4; Ellis, *Lachlan Macquarie*, 340ff.; Bridges, *Foundations of Identity*, 61–2; Gilbert, *Royal Botanic Gardens*, 37; Cartwright, 'Map of Governor's Desmesne'.

45   *SG* 11 August 1810; Proudfoot, 'Opening towns', 61.

46   Cox, Reminiscences; Parsons, 'Brooks, Richard (1765?–1833)'; Liston, *Campbelltown*, 12–13.

47   Cox, ibid.; Broadbent, *Francis Greenway*, 12; Broadbent, *Australian Colonial House*, 87–8; Fletcher, 'Harris, John (1754–1838)'.

48   Dyster, *Servant and Master*, 32, 80; George Johnston to Captain Piper, 28 December 1804.

49   Cox, Reminiscences.

50   Barnard, 'Piper, John (1773–1851); Waterhouse, *Private Pleasures*, 13–14; Liston, 'Colonial society', 20–3, 31. See also Evidence of Archibald Bell, c1819, Bigge, *Report*, Appendix, BT Box 5, 2045.

51   Liston, *Campbelltown*, 45; Cox, Reminiscences; Hirst, *Convict Society*, 46.

52   Dyster, 'Bungling a Courthouse', case of Edward Cureton and his servants, 6.

53   Dyster, *Servant and Master*, chap. 9 and 162.

54   Walsh, 'Geography of manufacturing', 31, 32; Cumming, 'Chimneys and change', 32.

55   Karskens, *The Rocks*, 134, 46.

56   For a detailed account see Dyster, 'Bungling a courthouse'.

57   Evidence of Major Druitt, Bigge, *Report*, Appendix, BT Box 1, 4, 17; Karskens, *Inside the Rocks*, 31–3, 50–3.

58   Macquarie, Public Notice, 3 January 1810.

59   Hirst, *Convict Society*, 88; Fletcher, *Ralph Darling: A Governor Maligned*, 103ff.

60   Karskens, 'Spirit of emigration', 27–9.

61   Karskens, *The Rocks*, chap. 7; Waterhouse, *Private Pleasures*, 17–19, 36–9; Evidence of D'Arcy Wentworth, Bigge, *Report*, Appendix, 1819, BT Box 2, 576, 579; Trial of James McAllister, 3 January 1822, 306.

62   Karskens, *The Rocks*, 115; *SG* 14 June 1807; Bonwick, *Australia's First Preacher*, 126–7; Collins, *Account* 2, 216; Catherine Cotton, Petition, January 1810; *SG* 28 May 1809; West (Marriot), *Memoirs*, 30.

63   Ellis, *Lachlan Macquarie*, 340–1; Evidence of Major Druitt, 27 October 1819, Bigge, *Report*, Appendix, BT Box 1, 8, 16; Evidence of Henry Cowper, 16 November 1819, BT Box 6, 2371; Broadbent, 'Macquarie's domain', 3–4.

64   Evidence of Mr Murray, Bigge, *Report*, Appendix, BT Box 1, 629; evidence of D'Arcy Wentworth, 1819, BT Box 2, 601; papers re abduction of Emma Crook, 31ff.

65   Bigge, *Report . . . on the Judicial Establishments*, 75–80; Evidence of D'Arcy Wentworth,

1819 *Report*, Appendix, BT Box 2, 601; evidence of Mr Murray and Thomas Hughes, BT Box 2, 646, 656; Ellis, *Lachlan Macquarie*, 341–3.

66 Bigge, *Report . . . on the Judicial Establishments*, 75–80.

67 ibid., 76.

68 See Kerr and Falkus, *Sydney Cove to Duntroon*, 34; pictures and commentary 8–9, 30; Kerr (ed.), *Heritage*, entry for Sophia Campbell; McCormick, *First Views*, Plate 160 and p. 320; Gray, 'Close, Edward Charles'; pers. com. Richard Neville, Mitchell Librarian, November 2009.

69 For example Lycett, 'Convict Barracks', 1820, though compare with the series of 1836 lithographs by J.G. Austin & Co. (held in the National Gallery of Australia and Mitchell Library) which depict working people in the streets outside.

70 Evidence of Henry Cowper, 16 November 1819, Bigge, *Report*, Appendix, BT Box 6, 2323–30.

71 *SG* 8 June 1817.

72 *SG* 6 April 1816; evidence of James Bean (carpenter) c1819, Bigge, *Report*, Appendix, BT Box 6, 2527.

73 As well, women caught having sex were sent to the Factory or to Newcastle, and men were flogged in the hospital yard and put in solitary cells. Evidence of Henry Cowper and William Johnstone c1819, Bigge, *Report*, Appendix, BT Box 6, 2322–71, 2417–21. Jalap was a purgative; tincture probably referred to tincture of iodine; calomel was mercury chloride, a purgative; laudanum was an opium-based painkiller.

74 Evidence of John Clarisey, James Hunter (Surgeon R.N.), William Redfern, D'Arcy Wentworth, c1819, Bigge, *Report*, Appendix, BT Box 6, 2389, 2480–1, 2491, 2497, 2517–18.

75 Evidence of Henry Cowper, 1821, Bigge, *Report*, Appendix, BT Box 6, 2455; Inquest on James Church, 10 August 1822, 315; Karskens, 'Death was in his face'.

76 Evidence of Henry Cowper 16 November 1819, Bigge, *Report*, Appendix, BT Box 6, 2371.

77 Evidence of Henry Cowper, D'Arcy Wentworth and Mr Bowman, 1821, Bigge, *Report*, Appendix, BT Box 6, 2454–5, 2525, 2646; Karskens, 'Death was in his face'.

78 Eddy, 'Empire and politics', 45.

79 Hirst, *Convict society*, 40–1.

80 *SG* 17 July 1819; see Higginbotham, 'The workhouse'.

81 Hirst, *Convict Society*, 41–2; Broadbent, *Francis Greenway*, 56–7; Macquarie, Journal, 45.

82 Evidence of Major Druitt, Bigge, *Report*, Appendix, BT Box 1, 17.

83 Dyster, 'Bungling a courthouse', 6; Evidence of Major Druitt and William Hutchinson, 1819, Bigge, *Report*, Appendix, BT Box 1, 26, 93, 151; evidence of Christopher Tattersall, 5 August 1820, Box 6, 2451–2; Greenway to Druitt 14 August 1819, BT Box 19, 2875–8.

84 Historic Houses Trust, *Hyde Park Barracks Museum Guidebook*, 37; Historic Houses Trust of NSW, *Hyde Park Barracks Museum Guidebook*, Draft copy, 2003, copy courtesy John Petersen.

85 Inquest on Matthew Hyard, 31 July 1820, 315.

86 Evidence of Major Druitt, 27 October 1819, Bigge, *Report*, Appendix, BT Box 1, 4, 17, 29; evidence of Thomas Messling 27 May 1821, BT Box 1, 145 and D'Arcy Wentworth, BT Box 2, 576; Karskens, 'Resurrecting Chapman', 8–21.

87 Hainsworth, *Sydney Traders*, chap. 6; Fletcher, *Landed Enterprise*, 112; Perry, *Australia's First Frontier*, 29–32; Liston, 'Colonial society'; Proudfoot, 'Opening towns', 64; Hirst, *Convict Society*, 154–6; Liston, *Campbelltown*, 21–3.

88 Fletcher, *Landed Enterprise*, 122.

89 Magistrate's Report on the State of the Gaol, 7 July 1821; Bigge, *Report ... on the Colony*, 50–1, 71; Data on condition and size of the gaol, Bigge, *Report*, Appendix, BT Box 27, 6502; evidence of George Panton, c1819, BT Box 9; Steven, 'Public credit and private confidence', 55–6.

90 Ellis, *Lachlan Macquarie*, 506–9; Callaway, *Visual Ephemera*, 14.

91 Fletcher, *Landed Enterprise*, 133; Hirst, *Convict Society*, 63, 87, 111.

92 John Pendergrass, Memorial, 18 January 1825; Karskens, 'Declining life'; Hirst, *Convict Society*, 130.

93 Fletcher, *Landed Enterprise*, 166–8, 187; Hirst, *Convict Society*, 87–8; Bigge, *Report ... on the Judicial Establishments*, 76–7.

94 Karskens, 'Spirit of emigration'; Bigge, *Report ... on the Colony*, Section III, 21–52; Broadbent, *Francis Greenway*, 44.

95 Ellis, *Lachlan Macquarie*, 508–9.

96 ibid., 520.

97 ibid, 520–2; Liston, 'Colonial society', 27–8.

98 Wilson, *Old Colonial Architecture*.

99 Dyster, *Servant and Master*, 80, 162–3; Broadbent, 'Building the colony', 171; Irving, 'Georgian Australia', 62; Barnard, 'Piper, John (1773–1851)'.

100 Dyster, *Servant and Master*, 24–8; Fitzgerald and Golder, *Pyrmont and Ultimo*, 18, 20, 60, 75; Broadbent, *Francis Greenway*, 83–4.

101 Broadbent, *Francis Greenway*, 5, 29–30.

102 McCormick, *First Views*, plates 164–72; Meagher, *Painted Panorama*, 48.

103 Callaway, *Visual Ephemera*, 139–41; see also Neville, *Rage for Curiosity*, 76–7.

104 Bigge to Macquarie, 6 June 1820, Bigge, *Report*, Appendix, BT Box 24, 4970; Hirst, *Convict Society*, 87.

105 Bigge, *Report ... on the Colony*, Section III, 21–52; Section VIII, 155–76; Dyster, 'Bungling a courthouse', 8–9; Hirst, *Convict Society*, 88; Fletcher, *Landed Enterprise*, 187–8; Karskens, 'Defiance, deference and diligence'.

CHAPTER 8 THE FACE OF THE COUNTRY

1 Young, *Environmental Change*, 1–2; Hughes, *Fatal Shore*, 94; Hetherington and Doherty (eds), *World Upside Down*, 3–4, 21; see also MacDonald, 'By whom and for whom?', 28; Freeland, *Architecture in Australia*, 10; Grenville, *The Secret River*, 3–6, 77–81; Bickel, *Australia's First Lady*, 30–1; Urquhart, *New Native Garden*, 10–11.

2 Bolton, *Spoils and Spoilers*, 17; Hetherington and Doherty (eds), *World Upside Down*, 3–4, 21; Hancock, *Australia*, 33, discussed in Bolton, *Spoils and Spoilers*, 38 and Bonyhady, *Colonial Earth*, 160ff.; MacDonald, 'By whom and for whom?', 27; Hughes, *Fatal Shore*, 93; Powell, *Environmental Management*, 13; Berzins, *Coming of the Strangers*, 48.

3 Franklin, *Animal Nation*, 4, 14, chap. 2; Bolton, *Spoils and Spoilers*, 17 and loc. cit.;

Berzins, *Coming of the Strangers*, 54–5; Smith, *Documents on Art and Taste*, 128–9; Rosen, *Losing Ground*, introduction, chap. 2; Lines, *Taming the Great South Land*, chap. 3; Read, *Belonging*; see Bonyhady's succinct overview of the historiography, *Colonial Earth*, introduction.

4   Two early references to 'inversion' are Watling, *Letters from an Exile*, 23; Noah, *Voyage to Sydney*, 75; cf. Hetherington and Doherty (eds), *World Upside Down*, 3–4, 21; Martin, *New Land*, 113; Martin (1838) in Powell, *Environmental Management*, 13–14; Westall in Findlay, *Arcadian Quest*, chap. 1; Felton and Sarah Mathew, Diaries; Hall, *Wasteland to World Heritage*, 75; Bonyhady, *Colonial Earth*, 72.

5   Worgan, Letter and journal, 5, see also description of coastline between Botany Bay and Broken Bay; Southwell, Journal, *HRNSW* II, 666; Elizabeth Macarthur to Miss Kingdon, 7 March 1791, *HRNSW* II, 501; Smith, *European Vision*, 180–1.

6   Tench, *Narrative*, 65; Rolls, 'More a new planet', 161ff.

7   Atkins, Journal, 16 April 1792.

8   Tench, *Complete Account*, 237.

9   Gergis et al., 'The influence of climate', 502–3; A Soldier's Letter, 13 December 1794, *HRNSW* II, 817.

10   Rolls, 'More a new planet', 162.

11   Ireland, 'Absence of ghosts'; Malouf, *Remembering Babylon*, 110; Smith, *Documents On Art and Taste*, chap. 5.

12   Tench, *Complete Account*, 155, 215; White, *Journal*, 110; Anon., Letter from Sydney, 24 March 1791, *HRNSW* II, 777; Watling, *Letters from an Exile*, 23; Frost, *Botany Bay Mirages*, chap. 4; Williams and Frost, 'New South Wales', 169.

13   Jones, *Ochre and Rust*, 33.

14   Worgan, Letter and journal, 28.

15   Chisholm, Editor's Introduction to White, *Journal*, 11; Major Grose, letter, February 1793, in Tench (Fitzhardinge), *Complete Account*, notes, 301.

16   Collins, *Account* 1, 375.

17   Phillip to Dundas 19 March 1792, *HRA* 1, 340–1; Collins, ibid.

18   Smith, *European Vision*, 181–5; Neville, *Rage for Curiosity*, 65; Martin, *A New Land*, 110–12; Smith, *Documents on Art and Taste*, 3.

19   Neville, *Rage for Curiosity*, 12–13; Smith, 'The artwork', 217; Watling, *Letters*, 23, 25; English painter Westall did in fact 'select and combine', see Findlay, *Arcadian Quest*, 19–32; re 'deceitfulness' see also Worgan, Letter and journal, 6; Elizabeth Macarthur to Miss Kingdon, 7 March 1791, *HRNSW* II, 500; Scott, Letter to his mother, 1801.

20   Watling, *Letters*, 24, 25; see also his lavish descriptions of animals.

21   Smith, *Documents in Art and Taste*, 3.

22   Watling, *Letters*, 42–4.

23   Aplin, 'People in an alien landscape', describes both despair and delight, 27–31; Berzins, *Coming of the Strangers*, describes initial enchantment giving way to 'disillusion and disappointment', 44.

24   Johnson to Fricker; Hunter, *Historical Journal*, 49; Clark, Journal, 27 January, 16 February 1788; White, *Journal*, 121.

25 Hall, reviewing the settlers' responses, decided they were 'ambivalent', *Wasteland to World Heritage*, 76.

26 Gergis et al., 'The influence of climate', 486, 488.

27 See Price, 'Thirteen Ways of Seeing nature in LA'.

28 Seddon, 'Evolution of perceptual attitudes', 10–11.

29 Bonyhady, *Colonial Earth*, introduction, chaps 1 and 2; Powell, *Environmental Management*, 18–20.

30 Tench, *Narrative*, 66.

31 Seddon, 'Evolution of perceptual attitudes', 11.

32 Elizabeth Macarthur to Miss Kingdon, 7 March 1791, *HRNSW* II, 501.

33 Williams and Frost, 'New South Wales', 161–8.

34 Worgan, Letter and journal, 9; White, *Journal*, 113.

35 Worgan, Letter and journal, 6; Hunter, *Historical Journal*, 53.

36 Tench, *Complete Account*, 215.

37 Hancock, *Australia*, 33; Berzins, *Coming of the Strangers*, 54, 56.

38 Watling, *Letters from an Exile*, 9; Worgan, Letter and journal, 7; White, *Journal*, 145.

39 Worgan, Letter and journal, 7; White, *Journal*, 145.

40 Bonyhady, *Colonial Earth*, 79.

41 Harris, Letter, 20 March 1791; Bradley, Journal, 144; Hunter, *Historical Journal*, 19; White, *Journal*, 133.

42 Bradley, Journal, 232–3; Jack, 'Early boat building', 53.

43 Paine, *Journal*, 38; Hawkins, *Timbergetters of Pennant Hills*, 29; Bolton, *Spoils and Spoilers*, 38; see also Bigge, List of Prevailing Timber Trees of New South Wales, 1819; Martin, *A New Land*, 9–10; Berzins, *Coming of the Strangers*, 57.

44 Harris, Letter, 20 March 1791; Worgan, Letter and journal, 7; Tench, *Narrative*, 71.

45 Karskens, *Inside the Rocks*, 31, 40, 53, 57, 60–1; Deirmendjian, *Sydney Sandstone*.

46 Tench, *Narrative*, 58; Worgan, Letter and journal, 28.

47 Worgan, Letter and journal, 29; Elizabeth Macarthur to Miss Kingdon, 1 September 1795, in Onslow, *The Macarthurs*, 48.

48 Bonyhady, *Colonial Earth*, 77–9; Bonyhady, *Images in Opposition*, 44–6.

49 See for example Karskens, *Holroyd*, 69–74; Coupe, *Concord*, 101–8.

50 Bonyhady, *Colonial Earth*, introduction, chaps 1, 2; see also Powell, *Environmental Management*, 18–20; Collins, *Account* 1, 158.

51 Collins, *Account* 1, 24; see McCormick, *First Views*, plates 5, 8, 19, 29, 35.

52 Government and General Order, 25 January 1796, enclosure in Hunter to Portland, 12 November 1796, *HRA* 2, 686; Bonyhady, *Colonial Earth*, 5, 10; *SG* 7 August, 16 October, 4, 18 December 1803.

53 *SG* 11 February, 11 August, 15 September 1810; de Vries-Evans, *Historic Sydney*, 88–9.

54 Hunter, Government and General Order of 8 December 1795, *HRNSW* II, 341; King, Government and General Order, 4 October 1805, *HRNSW* V, 230–1; *SG* 18 December 1803; Rosen, *Losing Ground*, 30–3.

55 Rosen, *Losing Ground*, 72–3.

56 Bonyhady, *Colonial Earth*, 5; see also Horton, *Pure State of Nature*, 85; Hutton and

Connors, *Australian Environmental Movement*, 197, 29; Bolton, *Spoils and Spoilers*, loc. cit.

57 Baskerville, 'The Hawkesbury commons'.

58 Anon., A Letter from Sydney, 29 October 1791, *HRNSW* II, 787. Tench and Clark both commented upon Phillip's wide-ranging powers, *Narrative*, 42; Journal, 7 February 1788.

59 Palmer to Joyce, 15 December 1794, Letters and notes, and in White, *Journal*, 15.

60 Grant (Cramer), *Beauteous, Wicked Place*, 35, 37, 41, 43, 45, 61, 85, 99.

61 ibid., 6–7, and loc. cit.

62 ibid., 29, 31, 55, 100; Atkinson, *Europeans*, 209, 262.

63 Grant (Cramer), *Beauteous, Wicked Place*, 28, 69–72, 105, 121.

64 ibid., 102, 130–2.

65 ibid., chap. 10.

66 ibid., 97–8, 165, 178ff., 200; King to Hobart, 30 October 1802, *HRA*, 4, 869–70.

67 Calaby, 'The natural history drawings', 140.

68 Byrne, 'The Ethos of Return', 75.

69 Calaby, 'The natural history drawings', 141–2; Benson and Howell, *Taken for Granted*, 28–9; Martin, *A New Land*, 84.

70 Neville, 'Eager curiosity', 7–12; Neville, *Rage for Curiosity*, 17–20; White, *Journal*, 14 and note 263; Williams and Frost, 'New South Wales', 177–8; Caley (Currey), *Reflections on the Colony*, loc. cit.

71 White, *Journal*, 158; Worgan, Letter and journal, 8; Williams and Frost, 'New South Wales', 174, 177; Caley (Currey), *Reflections*, 63; see also Phillip to Sydney, 15 May 1788, *HRA* 1, 23–4.

72 Smith, 'The artwork', 217, 220.

73 Catchpole to Mrs Cobbold, 18 October 1807.

74 Samuel Marsden to Mrs Stokes, 3 December 1796, 22 February 1800, Marsden family, Letters.

75 Macarthur in Neville, *Rage for Curiosity*, 20; Cunningham, *Two Years*, 161.

76 Neville, *Rage for Curiosity*, 28.

77 ibid., 32; Caley (Currey), *Reflections*, 71.

78 Currey, introduction in Caley, *Reflections*, x; and 26, 28, 94, 100, 148.

79 Caley (Currey), *Reflections*, 1–5, 22.

80 ibid., 39, 42, 65, 67–9, 175, 176, 178; Péron, *Voyage*, 283.

81 Caley (Currey), *Reflections*, 173.

82 ibid., 41, 46, 49, 174, 177–8; Bruce, Life of a Greenwich Pensioner, 17.

83 Caley (Currey), *Reflections*, 15, 42, 54, 100, 114–17, 178; Cunningham, *Blue Mountains Rediscovered*.

84 Caley, 'A Short Account'; Caley (Currey), *Reflections*, 190–1; Caley to Banks, 11 March 1814, in Martin, *A New Land*, 86.

85 Caley to Banks, 4 February, 11 March 1814, in Martin, *A New Land*, 86.

86 Caley (Currey), *Reflections*, 195ff., 204–5; see also Else Mitchell, 'George Caley'. Some of Caley's work was incorporated into Robert Brown's monumental collection. His

explorations were not lauded as breaking new ground, and the names he bestowed upon places were soon forgotten.

87 Fowell, letter to John Fowell, 12 July 1788; Watling, 'Leaf-tailed gecko', in Smith and Wheeler, *Art of the First Fleet*, 154, and see paintings from the Watling Collection.

88 Smith, 'The artwork' 203ff.; Thompson, 'First Fleet treasure trove'.

89 Smith, 'The artwork', 213, 214.

90 See Hunter, 'Birds and Flowers of New South Wales', sketchbook.

91 Smith, *Documents on Art and Taste*, 17.

92 Neville, *Rage for Curiosity*, 32–3; Grant (Cramer), *Beauteous, Wicked Place*, 76–9.

93 Neville, *Rage for Curiosity*, 33–6, 77–80; Smith, *Documents on Art and Taste*, 17–18.

94 Lewin to Drury, 7 March 1803, in Smith, *Documents on Art and Taste*, 18–20.

95 Neville, *Rage for Curiosity*, 32.

96 Calaby, 'The natural history drawings', 142–4; Hay, *Gum*, 35–4.

97 Spooner, 'History of gardening'; Tench, *Complete Account*, 247; Karskens, *The Rocks*, 18, 32, 220–1.

98 Péron, *Voyage*, 273, 275.

99 Caley (Currey), *Reflections*, 24ff.; Fox, *Clearings*, xv; Samuel and Eliza Marsden to Mrs Stokes, 13 December 1794, 1 May 1796, 3 December 1796; Grant (Cramer), *Beauteous, Wicked Place*, 15; Grant also proposed to plant orange pips and give the fruit to his friend and patron Mr Williamson, 35.

100 Hunter, *Historical Journal*, 133; Johnston to Piper, 12 April 1804, 28 December 1804; Dyster, *Servant and Master*, 27.

101 Grant (Cramer), *Beauteous, Wicked Place*, 79, 84; Meredith, *Notes and Sketches*, 133.

102 Grant (Cramer), *Beauteous, Wicked Place*, 42 and note 1; Catchpole to Mrs Cobbold, 21 January 1802; Mann, *Present Picture*, 51; Cunningham, *Two Years*, 31; Meredith, *Notes and Sketches*, 157.

103 Caley (Currey), *Reflections*, 81, 171; Grant (Cramer), *Beauteous, Wicked Place*, 42; Arnold to his brother, 18 March 1810; Péron, *Voyage*, 305; Kohen, *Aboriginal Environmental Impacts*, 98; Low, *New Nature*, 20.

104 Bolton, *Spoils and Spoilers*, 86–7; Benson and Howell, *Taken for Granted*, 38; Low, *New Nature*, 91ff.

105 Tench, *Narrative*, 49; White, *Journal*, 151; Hunter, *Historical Journal*, 47; Rolls, *From Forest to Sea*, 51.

106 See Atkinson, *History and the love of places*, 14–17; Phillip (in Hunter), *Journal*, 337, 361; Catchpole to Mrs Cobbold, 21 January 1802; Cunningham, *Two Years*, 159–60; Meredith, *Notes and Sketches*, 61, 133.

107 Tench, *Complete Account*, 270; Collins, *Account* 1, 58; Hunter, *Historical Journal*, 95; Flannery, 'Beautiful Lies', 21.

108 Worgan, Letter and journal, 13; Calaby, 'The natural history drawings', 158–9.

109 Caley, in Low, *New Nature*, 7; Cunningham, *Two Years* 1, 113–14.

110 Collins, *Account* 1, 460.

111 NSW Dept of Environment and Climate Change, 'Threatened Species in New South Wales'; Australian Museum, 'Eastern Quoll, *Dasyurus viverrinus*'.

112 See paintings and captions in Calaby, 'The natural history drawings', 170–97; NSW National Parks and Wildlife Service, 'Turquoise parrot—threatened species information', 2; Ryan, *Reminiscences*, 36.

113 Benson and Howell, 'Cumberland Plain Woodland ecology', 644.

114 NSW Legislative Assembly, *Progress Report . . . on the Field of Mars Common*, 1337, 52. The forest history at Granville was different. There the forest survived until the firewood contractors moved in, see Fowlie, *Granville*, 27.

115 Arnold to his brother, 25 February 1810, in Martin, *A New Land*, 87; Mitchell, *Journal of an Expedition*, 412, 413; Attenbrow, *Sydney's Aboriginal Past*, 42, 152–9; see also Kartzoff, *Nature and a City*, chap. II; Adamson and Fox, 'Change in Australasian Vegetation', 135–8. For a summary of the debate over Aboriginal fire management, see Kohen, *Aboriginal Environmental Impacts*, chap. 4.

116 Tench, *Complete Account*, 264; Smith, 'The burning bush'; Cunningham, 'Fire history of the Blue Mountains'; McLoughlin, 'Seasons of burning'.

117 Southwell, Diary, 275; see also Harris on yellow gum as remedy for 'chronic fluxes', Harris, Letter, 20 March 1791.

118 Collins, *Account* 1, 7; Tench, *Narrative*, 56; Phillip (in Hunter), *Journal*, 318; Worgan, Letter and journal, 5, 14. See also Phillip to Sydney, 15 May 1788, *HRA* 1, 16–32; Bradley, Journal, 135; Anon., Letter from a Female Convict, 14 November 1788, *HRNSW* II, Appendix, 746–7; Frost, *Botany Bay Mirages*, 211–23. Most of these plants have been identified by Tim Low, see 'Foods of the First Fleet'.

119 Worgan, Letter and journal, 14; Hunter, *Historical Journal*, 46, 48; Tench, *Narrative*, 69; Tench, *Complete Account*, 67; White disagreed about the kangaroo, *Journal*, 149; Péron, *Voyage*, 278–9; Newling, 'Foodways Unfettered', 29–34; Frost, *Global Reach*, 239–40.

120 Letter by a Surgeon's Mate [Lowe], 1790, *HRNSW* II, 771; Tench, *Narrative*, 79; Tench, *Complete Account*, 267; Hunter, *Historical Journal*, 53, 94; Frost, *Botany Bay Mirages*, 211–23; Gandevia and Cobley, 'Mortality at Sydney Cove'; see also Newling, 'Foodways Unfettered', 37ff.

121 Cf. Low, 'Foods of the First Fleet', and discussion in Newling, 'Foodways Unfettered', 37ff.

122 Phillip (in Hunter), *Journal*, 348; Collins, *Account* 1, 192–3; cf. Hirst, *Convict Society*, 29, 47ff.; Boyce, *Van Diemen's Land*, 49–51.

123 Gergis et al., 'The influence of climate', 486, 488; Berzins, *Coming of the Strangers*, 45; Clark to Ross, 10 July 1788; White, *Journal*, 114; Bradley, Journal, 80; Worgan, Letter and journal, 14; Phillip (in Hunter), *Journal*, 336–7.

124 Atkins, Journal, 4, 5, 7 December 1792.

125 Péron, *Voyage*, 306.

126 Atkins, Journal, 12, 13 April 1792.

127 Williams, 'Far happier', 510; Anderson, *Cultivation of Whiteness*, 14–16.

128 Collins, *Account* 1, 366; see also Bradley, Journal, 145.

129 Tench, *Narrative*, 69, 79; Tench, *Complete Account*, 267; Palmer, letter, 16 September 1795, cited in Paine, *Journal of Daniel Paine* (Knight and Frost), xiii; Péron, *Voyage*, 277–8.

130 Tench, *Narrative*, 69; *Complete Account*, 266–7.

131 Worgan, Letter and journal, 29–30.

132 Arnold to his brother, 25 February 1810, in Martin, *A New Land*, 88; 'A Gentleman', *A Month in the Bush*, 30; see Cunningham, *Blue Mountains Rediscovered*, 157–8.

133 See Govett, 'Sketches of New South Wales', 1 April 1837, 128; Waterhouse, *Private Pleasures*.

CHAPTER 9 NEFARIOUS GEOGRAPHIES

1 Hancock, *Australia*, 33.

2 Birmingham, *Leviathan*, 146; Berzins, *Coming of the Strangers*, 78, 95; see also Day, *Smugglers and Sailors*, 4.

3 For provenance of the painting see Whittaker, 'Mrs Paterson's keepsakes', quote 147; Gapps, 'Convict Clothing in 1804 Sydney'.

4 See Silver, *Battle of Vinegar Hill*, 104.

5 This is a symbolic depiction: Johnston and Humes were not hanged on the battle site itself.

6 Clark, *History of Australia* 1, 155, 171–4; Collins, *Account* 1, 69; see also O'Farrell, *Irish in Australia*, 23; Neville, *Rage for Curiosity*, 9; Neville, 'Eager curiosity', 7.

7 Neville, *Rage for Curiosity*, 9–10.

8 Atkinson, *Europeans*, 113–17; Anderson, 'Multiple border crossings'.

9 Rolls, 'Country and city', 22; Bolton, *Spoils and Spoilers*, 15.

10 Noah, *Voyage to Sydney*, 75. Botanist George Caley thought 'the lower order of settlers in NSW are led away by the idea that everything is the reverse in that country to what it is in England', cited in Neville, *Rage for Curiosity*, 18.

11 Everingham (Ross), *Letterbook*, 51, 52, 54–5.

12 Bruce, Life of a Greenwich Pensioner, 43–8.

13 Collins, *Account* 1, 5, 9, 15; Worgan, Letter and journal, 15; Tench, *Narrative*, 39 and note.

14 Worgan, Letter and journal, 20; Arthur Bowes Smyth in Emmett, *Fleeting Encounters*, 74; Phillip to Sydney, 15 May 1788, *HRNSW* I, ii, 133; Bradley, Journal, 82.

15 See Karskens, 'Spirit of emigration'; see series of early views, McCormick, *First Views*.

16 Collins, *Account* 1, 61; Southwell to Mrs Southwell, 14 April 1790, *HRNSW* II, 712.

17 Thompson, 'Cattle and Cattlemen' (thesis), 29–32; Thompson and Perkins, 'The Wild Cowpastures Revisited', 3–19.

18 Thompson, 'Cattle and Cattlemen', 28ff.; Cunningham, *Blue Mountains Revisited*, 72–3. Mount Taurus see map (1798) in Collins, *Account* 1, frontispiece.

19 Collins, *Account* 1, 94, 295.

20 Sydney Prehistory Group, *In Search of the Cobrakall*, 51–2, plates 18–20; Liston, *Campbelltown*, 3–4; Clegg and Ghantous, 'Rock-painting', 260–1; Kohen, *The Darug*, word list, 260. Perhaps the first part of 'gumbukgooluk' is related to 'jumbuck', which appears to have Aboriginal origins—see *Australian National Dictionary*.

21 King to Hobart, 1 March 1804, *HRA* 3, 462; Collins, *Account* 1, 436–7.

22 Collins, *Account* 2, 50; Liston, *Campbelltown*, 14–15.

23   Collins, *Account* 2, 86; Thompson, 'Cattle and Cattlemen', 45–6; Thompson and Perkins, 'The Wild Cowpastures'; see also Liston, *Campbelltown*, 3–4; Macarthur to King, 15 September 1800, in Rusden, *Curiosities of Colonisation*, 62–4.

24   Thompson, 'Cattle and Cattlemen', 36–55; Else Mitchell, 'The Wild Cattle'. Else Mitchell sighted descendants of the wild cattle c1939; Rolls, *A Million Wild Acres*, 22.

25   Cunningham, *Blue Mountains Rediscovered*, 58–61.

26   See biography of Wilson in Cunningham, *Blue Mountains Rediscovered*, chap. 4.

27   Cunningham, *Blue Mountains Rediscovered*, 78.

28   Noah, *Voyage*, 69.

29   Caley (Currey), *Reflections on the Colony*. Caley does not name his collectors apart from the Aboriginal youth, Moowattin.

30   Perkins and Thompson, 'Cattle theft', 289.

31   Bruce, Life of a Greenwich Pensioner, 14–36.

32   ibid., 36.

33   For a fuller discussion see Karskens, 'Spirit of emigration', 1–5.

34   These conclusions are based on a survey of escapes from New South Wales 1788–1810, see Karskens, 'Spirit of emigration'.

35   Anderson, 'Multiple border crossings', 1–22.

36   Phillip to Nepean, 22 August 1790, *HRA* 1, 207.

37   Bigge, *Report . . . on the Colony of New South Wales*, 33; MacFie, 'Dobbers and cobbers'.

38   Hirst, *Convict Society*, 133–4, 136; Silver, *Battle of Vinegar Hill*, chap. 3.

39   Holt (O'Shaughnessy), *Rum Story*, 79; evidence of Father James Harrold, 4 September 1800, Proceedings of Inquiry on the Irish Conspiracy, *HRA* 2, 575–6.

40   Macarthur to King, 15 September 1800, in Rusden, *Curiosities of Colonisation*, 62–4 and in Silver, *Battle of Vinegar Hill*, 29.

41   Silver, *Battle of Vinegar Hill*, chaps 4 and 5; Hirst, *Convict Society*, 133; Fletcher, *Landed Enterprise*, 37, 40; Hills District Historical Society, *Beginnings of the Hills District*, 11–27; King to Hobart, 30 October 1802, *HRA* 4, 871.

42   Silver, *Battle of Vinegar Hill*, 72–86; Suttor to Banks, 10 March 1804; King to Hobart, 12 March 1804, and enclosures 1–13, *HRA* 4, 563–79.

43   *SG* 11 March 1804; liberty tree, see Harden, 'Liberty caps and liberty trees'.

44   King to Hobart, 12 March 1804, *HRA* 4, 564; Silver, *Battle of Vinegar Hill*, 93–4.

45   Silver, *Battle of Vinegar Hill*, 102–3; Johnston to Paterson, 9 March 1804, sub-enclosure 5 in King to Hobart, ibid., 569–70.

46   Johnston, letter to Captain Piper, 12 April 1804.

47   See also Holt (O'Shaughnessy), *Rum Story*, 81; Silver, *Battle of Vinegar Hill*, 103–4.

48   Ryan, *Reminiscences*, 3; Karskens, 'Death was in his face'.

49   Ryan, *Reminiscences*, 3; since Ryan was born in 1818, this information must have been local lore; Warren et al., *Rouse Hill Village*, 5, 39–40; Symes, *Castle Hill Rebellion*, 32–40.

50   Grant to King, 1 May 1805, in Grant (Cramer), *Beauteous, Wicked Place*, 105.

51   Sargeant, *Toongabbie Story*, 28, 95.

52   For excellent analyses of this painting see Archaeological & Heritage Management Solutions, 'Castle Hill Heritage Park' and Wilson, 'Castle Hill Heritage Park'.

53   See Benson and Howell, *Taken for Granted*, facing 17.

54   Péron, *Voyage of Discovery*, 307–8.

55   Sarah and Felton Mathew (Jones), Diary, 18 March 1830.

56   Holt (O'Shaughnessy), *Rum Story*, 102; Curby, *Seven Miles from Sydney*, 40.

57   Holt (O'Shaughnessy), *Rum Story*, 102–4; *SG* 16 September 1804; Wilson and Pullen, *North Rocks*, 1–2, 5; see also Karskens, *Inside the Rocks*, 42.

58   Byrne, *Criminal Law*, 229–33.

59   See Rev. Richard Taylor in Rosen, *Bankstown*, 42; 'A Gentleman', *A Month in the Bush*, 10; Thompson and Perkins, 'The Wild Cowpastures', 16; Thompson, 'Cattle and Cattlemen', 19, 27.

60   Perkins and Thompson, 'Cattle theft', 291; Hutton Neve, *Forgotten Valley*, 105–7; Thompson, 'Cattle and Cattlemen', 124–6.

61   See Index to *SG*, ML; *SG* 10 December 1827; Perkins and Thompson, 'Cattle theft', 291.

62   Thompson, 'Cattle and Cattlemen', 136–42; Perkins and Thompson, 'Cattle Theft', 290–1, 297–8; Hirst, *Convict Society*, 148; Waterhouse, *Vision Splendid*, 80–2.

63   Gunn, 'Australian Bushranging Society', 60–1; McKinnon, 'Convict Bushrangers' (thesis), 7–33, 50–60.

64   *SG* 7 July 1805; Dangar Island Historical Society, *A Guide to Historic Dangar Island*.

65   *SG* 9 April 1827; McKinnon, 'Convict Bushrangers', 4.

66   Byrne, *Criminal Law*, 141.

67   Cf. Susan West, 'The role of the "bush" in 1860s bushranging', loc. cit. and 137; McKinnon, 'Convict Bushrangers', 61, 63.

68   Meredith, *Notes and Sketches*, 132.

69   Byrne, *Criminal Law*, table, 131.

70   Hawkins, 'Geary's Gang', 15–19; Kass et al., *Parramatta*, 107; Byrne, *Criminal Law*, 135ff.; Bowd, *Macquarie Country*, 43–4; West, 'The role of the "bush"', 136.

71   Bowd, *Macquarie Country*, 47.

72   Ryan, *Reminiscences*, 22; Murray and White, *Dharug and Dungaree*, 218–30; Camm and McQuilton (eds), *Australians: A Historical Atlas*, 212 and map.

73   Coupe, *Australian Bushrangers*, 51–8.

74   Hirst, *Convict Society*, 142ff.; McKinnon, 'Convict Bushrangers', 103–20; Boyd, *Macquarie Country*, chap. 8; see also West on 1860s bushrangers, 'Spiders', 2.

75   See Byrne, *Criminal Law*, table, 137 and discussion.

76   Byrne, *Criminal Law*, 134, 138; Bowd, *Macquarie Country*, 45–8.

77   Byrne, *Criminal Law*, 130, 132, 138; Murray and White, *Dharug and Dungaree*, 225–7; Hirst, *Convict Society*, 140.

78   Cunningham, *Blue Mountains Rediscovered*, 148–9; Karskens, 'Spirit of emigration', 34.

79   Goodall, 'Visions: Wild Places in the Suburbs'; Murray and White, *Dharug and Dungaree*, 222.

80   Edwards, 'History and Reminiscences', in Hawkins, 'Geary's Gang', 21.

81   Jamison in Byrne, *Criminal Law*, 129–30.

82   Meredith, *Notes and Sketches*, 129.

83   King to Hobart, 14 August 1804, 20 December 1804, encl. no. 5, *HRA* 5, 2, 178.

84   Kass et al., *Parramatta*, 106–7; Jeremy, *Cockatoo Island*, 2–4; Anon., Letter to Gledhill family, 1856.

85   *Australian* 7 October 1826; *Monitor* 13, 20 October 1826.

86   Beck, *Hope in Hell*, 15; Coupe, *Australian Bushrangers*, 58.

87   Bigge, *Report . . . on the Judicial Establishments*, 78–81; Bigge, *Report . . . on the State of Agriculture*, 54–5; Anderson, 'Multiple border crossings', 16; Karskens, 'Spirit of emigration'.

88   Karskens, 'Resurrecting Chapman', 11–13; Byrne, *Criminal Law*, 142–8; Hirst, *Convict Society*, 125.

CHAPTER 10   'A VERY BOUNTIFUL PLACE INDEED'

1   'A Gentleman', *A Month in the Bush*, 53.

2   Freeland, *Architecture in Australia*, 12–13 cf. chap. 3; Bridges, *Foundations of Identity*, 27–31 cf. chaps 8 and 9; see commentary in McCormick, *First Views*; Karskens, 'Dialogue of townscape', 90–6. Some of the early huts lasted for decades, see Karskens, *Inside the Rocks*, 51.

3   Aveling, 'Imagining New South Wales'.

4   Byrne, 'A colonial female economy'; Karskens, *The Rocks*, 220–1; Karskens, 'Dialogue of townscape', 100–1.

5   Karskens, *Inside the Rocks*, 50–3.

6   Hughes, *Fatal Shore*, 89.

7   Clark, *Short History*, 25; Aveling, 'Gender in early New South Wales', 32; Flannery, *The Birth of Sydney*, 1–2; FitzSimons, 'Place in time: the Rocks', 25.

8   Kociumbas, *Oxford History*, 18–19; Keneally, *Commonwealth of Thieves*, 121–2; Clendinnen, *Dancing*, 68, 153; Rees, *Floating Brothel*, 207, and 208 where the orgy is moved to 1787 and Arthur Bowes Smyth is grievously misquoted.

9   This was pointed out twenty years ago by Aveling in 'Gender in early New South Wales', 30–2; convicts were not issued grog until 4 June (King's Birthday), see Tench, *Narrative*, 60; Clark, Journal, 12 February 1788; Tench, *Narrative*, 39.

10   Clark, Journal, 6, 7, 9, 11, 12, 20 February 1788.

11   Tench, *Narrative*, 44.

12   Robinson, *Women of Botany Bay*; Perrot, *Tolerable Good Success*; Oxley, 'Packing her . . . bags'; Daniels, *Convict Women*; Atkinson, *Europeans*; Aveling, 'Gender in early New South Wales', 32, 34; Berzins, *Coming of the Strangers*, 102–6; Picton Phillips, 'Family matters'.

13   Aveling, 'Gender in early New South Wales', 36–7; Karskens, *The Rocks*, 71–9; see also Robinson, *Women of Botany Bay*.

14   Grant (Cramer), *Beauteous, Wicked Place*, 83, 108–13.

15   Michael Hayes to his sister Mary, 2 November 1802; Noah, *Voyage*, 71.

16   Atkinson, *Europeans*, 253–4; Holt (O'Shaughnessy), *Rum Story*, 79; Karskens, *Inside the Rocks*, 35–9; O'Farrell, *Irish in Australia*, 29–34.

17 Rees, *Floating Brothel*, 220–1.

18 Collins, *Account* 1, 154, 155–9; Tench, *Complete Account*, 145, 245; Hunter, *Historical Journal*, 94.

19 Fitzgerald and Hearn, *Bligh, Macarthur*, 124–5; Macquarie to Bathurst, 31 July 1813, *HRA* VIII, 4 cited in Fletcher, *Landed Enterprise*, 127.

20 Liston, 'Colonial society', 25; King (in Hunter), *Journal*, 232 and note, 425.

21 For discussion see Oxley, *Convict Maids*, 6–15; on feminist and women's history scholarship since the 1970s see Daniels, *Convict Women*, chap. 2, and 185–6.

22 Daniels, *Convict Women*, x, 32–3, 185, 213.

23 Irvine, *Mary Reibey*, 59; Spooner, 'History of gardening', 84; MacKellar, *Core of My Heart*, 10–12; Ireland, 'Absence of ghosts', 60–2; Lawson, 'Past Carin'', *Poetical Works*, 18–20.

24 Rees, *Floating Brothel*, chap. 2, 64; Heney, *Dear Fanny*, introduction; and see letters published in newspapers and republished in *HRNSW*; MacKellar, *Core of My Heart*, 7.

25 Letter from a Female Convict, 14 November 1788, *HRNSW* II, Appendix, 746–7; Anon. (*Lady Juliana* convict), Letter from Sydney, 24 November 1791, in Heney, *Dear Fanny*, 3.

26 Sarah Bird, Letter to her father, c1798, in Heney, *Dear Fanny*, 16–17.

27 Catchpole, Letters to Mr and Mrs Howes and Mrs Cobbold; quote, 21 January 1802.

28 Anon. (*Lady Juliana* convict), Letter from Sydney, 24 November 1791, in Heney, *Dear Fanny*, 3 and *HRNSW* II, 789; see Tench, *Complete Account*, 174.

29 Talbot, Letter to her patron, *HRNSW* II, 780; Catchpole to Mrs Cobbold, 21 January 1802; cf. Tench, *Complete Account*, 221.

30 Catchpole to Dr Stebbens, 21 January 1802; see also Hunter, *Historical Journal*, 139; Extract from a letter by a Surgeon's Mate [Lowe], 1790, *HRNSW* II, 771; Tench, *Complete Account*, 240.

31 Frost, *Botany Bay Mirages*, 214–23; Catchpole to W. Howes, 28 January 1807.

32 Collins, *Account* 2, 51; see also vol. 1, 346; Extract from a letter by a Surgeon's Mate [Lowe], *HRNSW* II, 771; cf. accounts of infancy and childhood in England, Stone, *The Family, Sex and Marriage*.

33 Holt (O'Shaughnessy), *Rum Story*, 72.

34 Péron, *Voyage of Discovery*, 277–8, 281–2.

35 Collins, *Account* 2, 120.

36 Aveling, 'Gender in early New South Wales', 38; Collins, *Account* 1, 72, 129.

37 Collins, *Account* 2, 120.

38 Karskens, *The Rocks*, 81–3; Picton Phillips includes baptismal records indicating that marriage became more common in the 1810s, 'Family matters', 129.

39 Karskens, *The Rocks*, 84–5; Aveling, 'Gender in early New South Wales', 35; Atkinson, *Europeans*, 134; Catchpole to W. Howes, 2 May 1803; Thompson, 'Journal', *HRNSW* II, 796.

40 Daniels, *Convict Women*, 52; Oxley, *Convict Maids*, 73–7; Oxley, 'Female convicts', 94–5; Catchpole to Dr Stebbens, 21 January 1802; Karskens, *The Rocks*, 9, 43–4.

41 Grimshaw et al., *Creating a Nation*, 49; Hirst, *Convict Society*, 17–19.

42 Grimshaw et al., *Creating a Nation*, 49; see also Alford, *Production or Reproduction*, 44.

43 Karskens, *The Rocks*, 35; Byrne, 'Convict women reconsidered'; Byrne, 'A colonial female economy'; see also Land Titles Office 'Old Registers'; and Picton Phillips, 'Family matters', 122–3 for a close reading of the original source of this interpretation.

44 Byrne, 'A colonial female economy'; Karskens, *The Rocks*, chap. 10.

45 Hunter to Portland, 18 November 1796, *HRA* 1, 707; Collins, *Account* 1, 194.

46 Karskens, *The Rocks*, chap. 11; Flynn, 'Silent Boundary', 26 (Lawler); Atkinson, *Europeans*, 134, 137, 144; Kercher, *Unruly Child*, 49–51; Karskens, *Inside the Rocks*, 44, 138–40; Dow, *Samuel Terry*, 59.

47 Noah, *Voyage*, 71.

48 Byrne, 'Convict women reconsidered'.

49 Inquest on Lydia Ragin, 9 March 1817, SRNSW, R2232,131ff.; *SG* 15 March 1817.

50 See also Karskens, *The Rocks*, 62; Catchpole to Mrs Cobbold, 21 January 1802; Byrne, *Criminal Law*, 112–16.

51 Atkinson, *Europeans*, 199–200; Kingston, *Glad, Confident Morning*, 114; Ward, *Australian Legend* and 'Australian Legend revisited'.

52 Mary Reibey to her aunt, in Irvine, *Dear Cousin*, 13, 14; Walsh, 'Reibey, Mary (1777–1855)'; Irvine, *Mary Reibey*.

53 Mary Reibey, probably to George Howe, 'Description of Thomas Reibey's Tomb'; *SG* 20 July 1811; Irvine, *Mary Reibey*, 101–3; Walsh, 'Reibey, Mary (1777–1855)'.

54 Mary Reibey to her cousin Alice Hope in Irvine, *Dear Cousin*, 15–16.

55 Irvine, *Dear Cousin*, 19ff.; *Census*, 1828; Walsh, 'Reibey, Mary (1777–1855)'.

56 Young, 'The Struggle for Class' (thesis), 137.

57 Reibey to her cousin Alice Hope, 12 August 1818, in Irvine, *Dear Cousin*, 16; cf. Liston, *Sarah Wentworth*.

58 Sharpe, *Pictorial History of Newtown*, 7, 9–10; Irvine, *Mary Reibey*, 75; Walsh, 'Reibey, Mary (1777–1855)'; Johnson and Sainty, *Sydney Burial Ground*, 16, 64.

59 Jane Atkinson (nee Reibey) to her cousin David Hope, 9 February 1825 in Irvine, *Dear Cousin*, 88.

60 Catchpole's spelling was extremely adventurous, often phonetic. While this gives a marvellous idea of the way she spoke, the words are often rather hard to decipher. In the interests of clarity I have used versions of her letters 'translated' into standard spelling, though I have tried to leave something of her accent and the rhythms of her sentences in these quotations. For her original letters, see ML A1508.

61 Catchpole to Mrs Cobbold, 21 January 1802, 18 October 1807 and 1 September 1811; Ryan, *Reminiscences*; Dowling, 'Reminiscences of the Late Judge Dowling', 188.

62 Catchpole to W. Howes, 20 December 1804; Tench, *Complete Account*, 73; Arnold, Journal, 1809, in Martin, *A New Land*, 88; Meredith, *Notes and Sketches*, 149.

63 Catchpole to Mrs Cobbold, 18 October 1807. Other colonists thought the climate had become milder because of clearing—see 'A Soldier's Letter', *HRNSW* II, 817.

64 Catchpole to W. Howes, 20 December 1804; to Mrs Cobbold, 8 October 1809.

65 Catchpole to W. Howes, 8 October 1806, 28 January 1807 and 2 September 1811.

66 Catchpole to W. Howes, 20 December 1804; 8 October 1806.

67 Catchpole to W. Howes, 8 October 1806, 2 September 1811; to Mrs Cobbold, 21 January 1802; Lynravn, 'Catchpole, Margaret (1762–1819)'.

68   Elizabeth Macarthur to Miss Kingdon, 7 March 1791, *HRNSW* II, 498; Elizabeth Macarthur to Mrs Veale, 18 March 1791, in Onslow, *Some Early Records of the Macarthurs*, 42.

69   Elizabeth Macarthur to Miss Kingdon, 7 March 1791, *HRNSW* II, 494–6; Elizabeth Paterson to her uncle, 3 October 1800, in Heney, *Dear Fanny*, 19.

70   Catchpole to W. Howes, 20 December 1804; Eliza Marsden to Mrs Stokes, 1 May 1796, Marsden Letters; see also Tench, *Complete Account*, 170.

71   Elizabeth Paterson to her uncle, 3 October 1800, in Heney, *Dear Fanny*, 19.

72   Eliza Marsden to Mrs Stokes, 13 December 1794, Marsden Letters; Mary Pitt to George Matcham Esq, 31 May 1801, in Matcham, Letters; Bowd, *Macquarie Country*, 135; Hardy, *Early Hawkesbury Settlers*, 182–3.

73   Atkinson, *Europeans*, chap. 12, 267–72; Bridges, *Foundation of Identity*, 41.

74   Elizabeth Paterson to her uncle, 3 October 1800, in Heney, *Dear Fanny*, 19; Atkinson, *Europeans*, 270–1; re convicts as parents see Karskens, *The Rocks*, chaps 12, 13; Robinson, *Hatch and Brood*.

75   Elizabeth Macarthur to Miss Kingdon, 7 March 1791, *HRNSW* II, 499, 501; Elizabeth Macarthur to Mrs Veale, 18 March 1791, and letter 18 November 1791, in Onslow, *Some Early Records of the Macarthurs*, 41, 42.

76   Elizabeth Macarthur to Miss Kingdon, 7 March 1791, *HRNSW* II, 498–9; Young, *Middle Class Culture*, 25–6, 72–8.

77   Catchpole to Dr Stebbens, 21 January 1802; Elizabeth Macarthur to Miss Kingdon, 7 March 1791, *HRNSW* II, 501.

78   Elizabeth Macarthur to Mrs Veale, 8 October 1789, in Onslow, *Some Early Records of the Macarthurs*, 2; Elizabeth Macarthur to Miss Kingdon, 7 March 1791, *HRNSW* II, 501.

79   Elizabeth Macarthur to Miss Kingdon, 7 March 1791, *HRNSW* II, 501.

80   Elizabeth and John Macarthur, letter, 23 August 1794, in Onslow, *Some Early Records of the Macarthurs*, 44–6; see also Marsden letters; Cox, Reminiscences.

81   Elizabeth and John Macarthur, letter, 23 August 1794, in Onslow, *Some Early Records of the Macarthurs*, 44–6; Atkinson, *Europeans*, 270; Atkinson, *History and the Love of Places*, 16–17; King to Camden, 20 July 1805, *HRA* 5, 510–11.

82   Conway, 'Macarthur, Elizabeth (1766–1850)'; Bickel, *Australia's First Lady*, 136–41; King, 'Lives in exile', 43–9; MacKellar, *Core of My Heart*; Waterhouse, *Vision Splendid*, 115–21; see also Macleay (Earnshaw and Hughes), *Fanny to William*.

83   West, 'The role of the "bush"', 137. See also Bremer, 'Pathless wilds'.

84   McPhee, *Joseph Lycett*, 163; Bonyhady, *Images in Opposition*, 44–5.

85   Elizabeth Macarthur to Miss Kingdon, 7 March 1791, *HRNSW* II, 501, 505.

86   ibid., 504.

87   Catchpole to W. Howes, 20 December 1804.

88   Catchpole to Dr Stebbens, 21 January 1802; Smith, *Aborigines of the Burragorang*, 27ff.; Holland, *Growing Up on the Hawkesbury*, 26–7.

CHAPTER 11   SOFT COLONY

1   Phillip (in Hunter), *Journal*, 359; Collins, *Account* 1, 328, 408; Lesson in Dyer, *French Explorers*, 168.

2   Phillip (in Hunter), *Journal*, 313.

3   Collins, *Account* 2, 4, 16. Perhaps this was the perpetrator of the murder Catherine Cotton referred to in 1810 when she complained no-one would work on her north shore land.

4   White, *Journal*, 115; Threlkeld, Annual Report, 1836; Clark and Clark, *The Islands*, 14.

5   Phillip's Instructions, 27 April 1787, *HRA* 1, 13–14; Tench, *Complete Account*, 53.

6   Collins, *Account* 1, 3, 41.

7   Doukakis, *The Aboriginal People*, 41–3.

8   Worgan, Letter and journal, 2, 3, 4, 12, 21; Tench, *Narrative*, 35, 37.

9   Smith, *Bennelong*, 17; Clendinnen, *Dancing*, 31–2; Nye, *Soft Power*; cf. Gosden's argument that 'colonialism is about material culture . . . colonialism is the particular grip that material culture gets on the bodies and minds of people', *Archaeology and Colonialism*, 1, 3.

10   Phillip cited in Stanner, 'History of indifference', 3; McBryde, 'To establish a commerce', 169–70, 174ff.; Smith, *Bennelong*, chap. 20; Atkinson, *Europeans*, 146.

11   Bradley, Journal, 66, 82–3, 99, 139; Southwell, Diary, 266.

12   Hunter, *Historical Journal*, 107; Collins, *Account* 1, 35; Worgan, Letter and journal, 12; Elizabeth Macarthur to Miss Kingdon, 7 March 1791, *HRNSW* II, 502; King, Private Journal, 20 January 1788; Tench, *Narrative*, 48; Smith, *Bennelong*, 152.

13   Smith, *Bennelong*, 69–70, 149–55; hatchets and jackets, Collins, *Account* 1, 16, 34, 52; Bradley, Journal, 83, 99, 139; Worgan, Letter and journal, 11, 12; White, *Journal*, 157; Phillip (in Hunter), *Journal*, 313; knives and glass, Phillip (in Hunter), *Journal*, 311; Attenbrow, *Sydney's Aboriginal Past*, 102–4, 124–5; dogs, Collins, *Account* 1, 555.

14   Tench, *Complete Account*, 47; White, *Journal*, 156; Hunter, *Historical Journal*, 42.

15   Tench, *Complete Account*, 281–2.

16   Collins, *Account* 1, 16.

17   Southwell, Diary, 266, 278; White, *Journal*, 115; Collins, *Account* 1, 24.

18   Phillip (in Hunter), *Journal*, 373, 374; Carter, 'Encounters', 18.

19   Nicholas (ed.), *Convict Workers*, 75–7; Karskens, *The Rocks*, 10, 11, 222.

20   Karskens, 'Spirit of emigration', 13; Karskens, *The Rocks*, 42–9, 62; Smith, *Bennelong*, 120; Worgan, Letter and journal, 12; Tench, *Complete Account*, 282.

21   Bradley, Journal, 61; Fowell, Letter to his father, 21 January 1788; Collins, *Account* 1, 37.

22   Phillip (in Hunter), *Journal*, 311; Bradley, Journal, 187; cf. Waterhouse, *Private Pleasures*, 15–16.

23   Collins, *Account* 1, 329, 587.

24   Karskens, *The Rocks*, 46–9; Foucault, *Discipline and Punish*, chap. 1.

25   Funeral of Boggara/Bagary, *SG* 27 November 1813; Collins, *Account* 1, 595–6; vol. 2, 16, 72; Richardson, *Death*, 7, 17; Tench, *Complete Account*, 216, 280; Noah, *Voyage*, 72; Holt (O'Shaughnessy), *Rum Story*, 68.

26   Noah, *Voyage*, 61; Collins, *Account* 1, 407; Clendinnen, *Dancing*, 92, 248.

27   Worgan, Letter and journal, 36; John Grant in Curby, *Seven Miles from Sydney*, 37; cf. Ward, *The Australian Legend*, 200–3; Urry, 'Savage Sportsmen', 62–3.

28   Karskens, *Inside the Rocks*, 26; Attenbrow, *Sydney's Aboriginal Past*, 124–5; foods, White, *Journal*, 137 and Collins, *Account* 1, 557; *SG* 26 June 1803; Mann, *Present Picture*, 54–5; Bruce, Life of a Greenwich Pensioner, 13.

29   Bradley, Journal, 134; Collins, *Account* 1, 407; Curby, *Seven Miles from Sydney*, 40, 52; Byrne, *Criminal Law*, 271; *Bell's Life*, 6 December 1845.

30   Troy, *The Sydney Language*, wordlists; Phillip (in Hunter), *Journal*, 325, 341, 344, loc. cit.; Dawes, Notebooks; Tench, *Complete Account*, 227.

31   Urry, 'Savage Sportsmen', 63; Donaldson, 'Hearing the first Australians', 79–80.

32   Collins, *Account* 1, 23–4, 30, 37, 26, 40; Bradley, Journal, 94, 102; Worgan, Letter and journal, 26, 30; White, *Journal*, 142; Smith, *Bennelong*, 23.

33   White, *Journal*, 132, 134; Worgan, Letter and journal, 33; Collins, *Account* 1, 16–17, 30–1; Tench, *Narrative*, 50; Bradley, Journal, 107, 111; Hunter, *Historical Journal*, 53–4 and note 39, 400; Smith, *Eora*, exhibition, believes the killing place may have been Pyrmont/Kameagang, image 40.

34   Bradley, Journal, 108, 109, 112; see also Worgan, Letter and journal, 33.

35   Collins, *Account* 1, 43; White, *Journal*, 165.

36   Bradley, Journal, 85, 95, 112, 119; Tench, *Complete Account*, 137; Hunter, *Historical Journal*, 56, 113; Clendinnen, *Dancing*, 93.

37   Bradley, Journal, 94, 186 (report of Black Caesar escaping 'through a very thick brush').

38   Bradley, Journal, 119; see also Hunter, *Historical Journal*, 43; see also Tench, *Complete Account*, 137.

39   White, *Journal*, 142.

40   Collins, *Account* 1, 15, 17; Tench, *Narrative*, 55; Bradley, Journal, 112; Fowell, Letter to his father.

41   Collins, *Account* 1, 23–4; Bradley, Journal, 94, 112.

42   Noah, *Voyage*, 72; Collins, *Account* 1, 596–7.

43   Southwell, Letter to Mrs Southwell, 712; Bradley, Journal, 85, 93–4, 177–8; Collins, *Account* 1, 16–17, 82; Worgan, Letter and journal, 26.

44   Collins, *Account* 1, 16. When Bennelong's wife Barangaroo complained that her fishing gear had been stolen, the governor and officers mysteriously knew of its whereabouts and returned it the following day. Tench, *Complete Account*, 135, 221 and see also Tench's urgent desire to possess a spear, 184.

45   White, *Journal*, 109.

46   Collins, *Account* 1, 16, quote 57; Stanner, 'History of indifference', 17.

47   Watling, *Letters*, 28; see also Noah, *Voyage*, 71.

48   Tench, *Complete Account*, 145; Bradley, Journal, 136; Collins, *Account* 1, 57; Hunter, *Historical Journal*, 112; Benson and Howell, *Taken for Granted*, 24, 149, 44.

49   Pers. com. Kate Peppercorn, Harvest Seeds and Native Plants, Terrey Hills, NSW, June 2008.

50   Tench, *Complete Account*, 144–5; Collins, *Account* 1, 57; White, *Journal*, 151, 154; Smith, *Eora*, exhibition, image 39.

51 Tench, *Complete Account*, 144–5; Collins, *Account* 1, 57–8.

52 NSW Environment Protection Authority, *New South Wales State of the Environment*, 1997, chap. 5; and 2003, chap. 1; see also Beale and Dayton, 'Sydney found to be consuming 35 times its share'; Jellie, 'Metropolis now'; Hogarth, 'I've seen the futures'; Angel, 'Emerald city?'

53 Phillip to Sydney, 15 May 1788, *HRA* 1, 23–4; Tench, *Narrative*, 59, 263.

54 Southwell, Diary, 262; Attenbrow, *Sydney's Aboriginal Past*, 66–7, 76–7, 82–3; Steele, 'Animal Bone and Shell', 154, 168, 172–3, 200–2; Karskens, *Inside the Rocks*, 66; Collins, *Account* 1, 43. Low points out that leafy vegetables like wild spinach (*Tetragonia tetragonioides*) are halophytes, plants that store salt in their tissues, and have to be boiled to make them palatable. The Eora had no such cooking methods or vessels, see Low, 'Foods of the First Fleet', 296.

55 Compare to Tench's musings on the way the Eora left the colonists alone, *Complete Account*, 40.

56 Collins, *Account* 1, 58.

57 ibid., 34; Bradley, Journal, 106, 107, 110, 118, 154; Worgan, Letter and journal, 32; White, *Journal*, 134; Hunter, *Historical Journal*, 55.

58 Tench, *Complete Account*, 269, 287; Attenbrow, *Sydney's Aboriginal Past*, 76. As Tony Swain writes, 'Only the most starry-eyed would ignore Aborigines' stories of hunger and shortage', *Place for Strangers*, 76.

59 Bradley, Journal, 61–2, 85–6, 105, 116, 181–2; Collins, *Account* 1, 16, 36, 42, 80, 86, 93–4; White, *Journal*, 110, 113; Tench, *Narrative*, 48; Clendinnen, *Dancing*, 54.

60 Collins, *Account* 1, 40; Bradley, Journal, 120, 126; White, *Journal*, 165.

61 White, *Journal*, 152–3; Collins, *Account* 1, 41.

62 Bradley, Journal, 95.

63 Southwell, seeing whalebone on the shoreline at Botany Bay in 1788, wondered how it got there, for it would be 'no use to them', Diary, 263; Bradley, Journal, 120; Phillip (in Hunter), *Journal*, 311–12; cf. Freycinet 1819 in Dyer, *French Explorers*, 68; Smith, *Bennelong*, 60; Attenbrow, *Sydney's Aboriginal Past*, 66.

64 Rowse, *White Flour, White Power*; Clendinnen calls it a 'fatal dependency', *Dancing*, 196.

65 Tench, *Complete Account*, 145; Collins, *Account* 1, 57–8.

66 Tench, *Complete Account*, 137.

67 ibid., 139; Collins, *Account* 1, 49; Bradley, Journal, 161; Hunter, *Historical Journal*, 92.

68 Clendinnen, *Dancing*, 25, 97; McBryde, *Guests of the Governor*, 7–9.

69 Tench, *Complete Account*, 139–43; Hunter, *Historical Journal*, 92–3; Collins, *Account* 1, 53.

70 Hunter, *Historical Journal*, 92–3.

71 Tench, *Complete Account*, 146–8; Hunter, *Historical Journal*, 93–4; Collins, *Account* 1, 65, 597; Bradley, Journal, 162.

72 Campbell, *Invisible Invaders*, 34–5. Smallpox also had complications and long-term effects, including pitted skin, bronchitis, secondary skin infections, bone defects, limb deformities and blindness.

73   Smith, *Bennelong*, 35.

74   Collins, *Account* 1, 597.

75   Tench, *Complete Account*, 147, 149; Collins, *Account* 1, 66; Hunter, *Historical Journal*, 94, 96.

76   King, Remarks and Journal—fair copy, 397; Bradley, Journal, 162. The question of culpability has a long and intense historiography. Tench wondered about the 'variolous matter' in the surgeons' chests, brought out in case of a shipboard outbreak, but he dismissed the idea that they were the source (*Complete Account*, 146). Butlin (*Our Original Aggression*) put the strongest argument for this material as the source of the epidemic and suggested it was deliberate. Watt in 'The colony's health' pointed out that the surgeons feared smallpox so much that if they had had variolous matter available, they would have used it to innoculate Arabanoo. Reynolds (*Question of Genocide*) examined the case for deliberate infection (and thus attempted genocide) from the presence of this matter, and the fact that Collins and Lieutenant Governor Ross would have been aware of the earlier use of smallpox against Native Americans at Fort Pitt in western Pennsylvania in 1763. Day (*Claiming a Continent*, 43) argued similarly for deliberate infection; Campbell argues that this variolous matter could not have remained potent after such a length of time or in these temperatures (*Invisible Invaders*, 62), but Reynolds counters that the experienced surgeons would have protected it and Mear ('Smallpox outbreak', 5–7) points out that such infective material could remain potent in both hot and cold conditions; Connor (*Australian Frontier Wars*, 29–30) also argues Day's claims are unsustainable; Ross, for example, was not stationed at Fort Pitt. Clendinnen gives little space to smallpox (it does not appear in the index) but points out that deliberate infection is inconsistent both with the officers' care of the sick and their 'bafflement' at its origins, *Dancing*, 99.

77   Collins, *Account* 1, 66, 597–8; Hunter, *Historical Journal*, 100, 107.

78   Collins, *Account* 1, 65; Rex Rienits, 'Biographical Introduction', in White, *Journal*, 19; Tench, *Complete Account*, 148; Hunter, *Historical Journal*, 94.

79   Collins, *Account* 1, 65, 596–7; Campbell, *Invisible Invaders*, 15–17; Read, 'Clio or Janus?'. Many government and non-government organisations today state that smallpox was introduced by the Europeans, for example National Museum of Australia, 'The scourge of smallpox'; Royal Botanic Gardens Sydney, 'Indigenous people of Sydney'; Aboriginal Housing Company, 'History'; NSW Board of Studies, 'Incidents between British and Koori people'.

80   Mulvaney and Kamminga, *Prehistory of Australia*, 416–19; Campbell, *Invisible Invaders*, chaps 4 and 5; Mear, 'Smallpox outbreak in Sydney'; compare with Butlin, *Our Original Aggression*. Connor suggests it may have been chickenpox, to which the Aboriginal people had no resistance, *Australian Frontier Wars*, 30. Compare to discussion of the epidemiology of measles in Goodall, 'Colonialism and catastrophe'.

81   Péron, *Voyage of Discovery*, 291; George Bowen cited in Kohen, *The Darug*, 78; see also Swain, *Place for Strangers*, 130 (sky-heroes linked with sending smallpox and other diseases).

82   Bradley, Journal, 162, 178; Collins, *Account* 1, 597, Hunter, *Historical Journal*, 93, 100.

83   Megaw, 'Excavation of . . . rock shelter', 25–30; Hiatt, 'Mystery at Port Hacking', 313–17; Cleland and Kiss, 'Notes and Comments', 432–3. Megaw mentioned that an earlier, unsystematic excavation at Little Jibbon Cove in the 1890s revealed the remains of an adult and four children, 38; Attenbrow, *Sydney's Aboriginal Past*, 141.

84   Collins, *Account* 1, 598; Tench, *Complete Account*, 285.

85   Bradley, Journal, 164; Phillip, (in Hunter), *Journal*, 328; Clarke, cited in Campbell, *Invisible Invaders*, 95, and 98–9; Kimber, 'The dynamic century', 94–6. Clendinnen also concludes that Eora men's violence towards women was part of 'traditional' behaviour, see *Dancing*, 159ff. Compare with post-smallpox responses in Wellington Valley, NSW, between 1829 and 1840, see Carey and Roberts, 'Smallpox and the Baiame Waganna'.

86   Tench, *Narrative*, 35; Collins, *Account* 1, 544; Bradley, Journal, 70–1.

87   Bradley, Journal, 164.

88   Hunter, *Historical Journal*, 96–8, 114; Bradley, Journal, 165, 171; cf. Clendinnen, *Dancing*, 42–3; Coleman, 'Inscrutable history', 208–9.

89   Bradley, Journal, 171, 172; Collins, *Account* 1, 86.

90   Collins, *Account* 1, 81; Bradley, Journal, 177.

91   Bradley, Journal, 182–3; Tench, *Complete Account*, 158; King, Remarks and Journal—fair copy, 392.

92   Bradley, Journal, 183; Collins, *Account* 1, 86–7; Hunter, *Historical Journal*, 115–16.

93   Collins, *Account* 1, 544–5; Tench, *Complete Account*, 285.

94   Smith, *Bennelong*, vii and pers. com. October 2007; Clendinnen, *Dancing*, 101. Coleman points out that Hunter and Bradley did not approve of Phillip's tactics and hotly rejects the suggestion that Bennelong had any agenda in his own capture, 'Inscrutable history', 211.

95   Bradley, Journal, 184, 185; Collins, *Account* 1, 86; Hunter, *Historical Journal*, 116.

96   Hunter, *Historical Journal*, 116; King, Remarks and Journal—fair copy, 395–6; Tench, *Complete Account*, 159–60, 167, 189; Bradley, Journal, 187.

97   Bradley, Journal, 83–4.

98   King, Remarks and Journal—fair copy, 393–4; Bradley, Journal, 187.

99   Bell, *Daughters of the Dreaming*, 18, see also 20.

100   Tench, *Complete Account*, 167; Collins, *Account* 1, 163; Hunter, *Historical Journal*, 139; Phillip (in Hunter), *Journal*, 311; Southwell, cited in Smith, *Bennelong*, 51.

101   Phillip thought he had gone to find Kurubarabulu, whom he later abducted, see *Journal* (in Hunter) 323; Tench, *Complete Account*, 177; Clendinnen, *Dancing*, 107.

102   Hunter, *Historical Journal*, 139; Phillip (in Hunter), *Journal*, 305–6, 308; Tench, *Complete Account*, 176–80.

103   Phillip (in Hunter), *Journal*, 307–8; Hunter, *Historical Journal*, 141; Collins, *Account* 1, 132–4; Tench, *Complete Account*, 176–80. Waterhouse, in Bradley, Journal, 229; wordlist, Kohen, *The Darug*, 240.

104   Waterhouse, in Bradley, *Journal*, 229; Collins, *Account* 1, 132–4.

105   Phillip (in Hunter), *Journal*, 308.

106   Stanner, 'History of indifference', 20; Smith, *Bennelong*, 57–9; Clendinnen, *Dancing*, 110–32.

107 Jones, *Ochre and Rust*, 42.

108 Phillip (in Hunter), *Journal*, 308–10.

CHAPTER 12   TAKING POSSESSION

1   Tench, *Complete Account*, 183, 200; Collins, *Account* 1, 133, 135.

2   Tench, *Complete Account*, 183–4; Phillip (in Hunter), *Journal*, 310–12.

3   Tench, *Complete Account*, 183–4; Phillip (in Hunter), *Journal*, 309–11; Collins, *Account* 1, 137; I would guess the other two figures, a woman and a man, might be Warraweer, Bennelong's sister, with whom he spent a lot of time, and perhaps her husband Gnunga Gnunga Murremurgan or 'Collins', the man who had earlier exchanged names with David Collins. Or it could be one of Bennelong's many male friends.

4   Tench, *Complete Account*, 188–9.

5   Hunter, *Historical Journal*, 139, 143; Tench, *Complete Account*, 192; Bradley, Journal, 26 February 1790; Smith, *European Vision*, 218–20.

6   Collins, *Account* 1, 209, 588; Phillip (in Hunter), *Journal*, 314, 316; Hunter, *Historical Journal*, 139; Dawes, Notebooks; Troy, 'The Sydney Language', 158 and loc. cit.

7   Watling, *Letters*, 27, 29; Smith, *European Vision*, 187; John Calaby, 'The natural history drawings', 167.

8   King, *The Secret History*, 83; Phillip (in Hunter), *Journal*, 311.

9   Collins, *Account* 1, 137, 142 compare with 554; Tench, *Complete Account*, 200; Phillip (in Hunter), *Journal*, 316; Thompson, Extracts from Journal, *HRNSW* 2, 797; Smith, *Bennelong*, 68–9.

10 Bradley, Journal, 231; Hunter, *Historical Journal*, 40, 143.

11 Clendinnen, *Dancing*, 141; Phillip (in Hunter), *Journal*, 319, 336, 339, 359.

12 Tench, *Complete Account*, 200.

13 Phillip (in Hunter), *Journal*, 314, 315; cf. Smith, *Bennelong*, 68–9.

14 Phillip (in Hunter), *Journal*, 332.

15 Tench, *Complete Account*, 200ff.; Collins, *Account* 1, 560; Phillip (in Hunter), *Journal*, 319–23.

16 Tench, *Complete Account*, 181ff., 200; Collins, *Account* 1, 34; for the wider impact of steel hatchets, see Broome, *Aboriginal Australians*, 63.

17 Collins, *Account* 1, 543, 600; Tench, *Complete Account*, 239; Phillip (in Hunter), *Journal*, 352.

18 Harris, Letter to unnamed correspondent, 20 March 1791, Harris Papers, ML A1597; George Thompson cited in Smith, *Bennelong*, 143; Phillip (in Hunter), *Journal*, 331.

19 Phillip (in Hunter), *Journal*, 314; Collins, *Account* 1, 544; Hunter, *Historical Journal*, 43.

20 Tench, *Complete Account*, 205–6; Phillip (in Hunter), *Journal*, 326–7; Kohen, *Darug, wordlist*, 240; for discussion of the country of the Bidgigals see Flynn, 'Holyroyd History', 14–15.

21 Tench, *Complete Account*, 207–9; Collins, *Account* 1, 143; Phillip (in Hunter), *Journal*, 328–9.

22 Collins, *Account* 1, 143–4; Attenbrow, *Sydney's Aboriginal Past*, 23–5; Smith, 'Moorooboora's daughter'.

23   Tench, *Complete Account*, 209–11; Clendinnen, *Dancing*, 173.

24   Tench, *Complete Account*, 212–15; Connor, *Australian Frontier Wars*, 32–3.

25   Stanner, 'History of indifference', 19–21; Clendinnen, *Dancing*, 172–81, quotes 174, 179.

26   Collins, *Account* 1, 144.

27   Both pictures in Watling Collection, British Museum of Natural History (Watling, 25 and 41); Smith, *Bennelong*, 90. The bodypaint in the portrait appears to be pale or white in reproductions, rather than red, but an examination of the original painting by curators confirmed that red paint was also applied to the picture (pers. com. Angela Thresher, General & Zoology Library, Natural History Museum, email, 16 August 2007); pers. com. Michael Flynn, 2014.

28   Clendinnen, *Dancing*, 237.

29   Collins, *Account* 1, 161; Tench, *Complete Account*, 282.

30   Collins, *Account* 1, 598; Smith, *Bennelong*, 88–9; Smith, *Eora*, exhibition, image 109.

31   Collins, *Account* 1, 144. Another clue to their dilemma is that Tench left out the fact that the second expedition did see some of the Botany Bay people. One of the soldiers, Private Easty, noted in his journal that the party went back to Botany Bay to camp overnight 'until 2 in the Morning of the 24 when we went Down the Beach for abougt 3 miles whaare we Saw Sevaral of the natives by their fires and then Marched Back', Memarandom, 122; compare with Phillip, 'they did not see a single inhabitant during the two days which they remained out' (in Hunter), *Journal*, 329. Evidently, this time Tench did not shoot.

32   Mander-Jones, 'Dawes, William (1762–1836)'; see also Coleman, 'Inscrutable history', 208.

33   Tench, *Complete Account*, 240; Phillip (in Hunter), *Journal*, 352.

34   Tench, *Complete Account*, 215–16; Collins, *Account* 1, 146–7; Phillip (in Hunter), *Journal*, 331.

35   Tench, *Complete Account*, 216; Phillip (in Hunter), *Journal*, 333–4, 337; Clendinnen, *Dancing*, 194–6.

36   Collins, *Account* 1, 147.

37   ibid.

38   King, *The Secret History*, 83; Tench, *Complete Account*, 188, 190, 291; Phillip (in Hunter), *Journal*, 313, 319, 323.

39   Clendinnen, *Dancing*, 136, 219–29.

40   White, *Journal*, 137, 161; Worgan, Letter and journal, 10.

41   Bradley, Journal, 179–80, see also 120.

42   Phillip (in Hunter), *Journal*, 311.

43   Tench, *Complete Account*, 184.

44   Collins, *Account* 1, 136.

45   Worgan, Letter and journal, 23; Bradley, Journal, 92. Interestingly, Bowdler noted a similar shift in types and size of fish caught after the introduction of the shell hook at Bass Point, south of Sydney, around 600 years ago. After women started using the hooks, catches of smaller fish (including rock cod, more easily line-caught) increased in proportion and those of larger fish (including wrasse and leatherjacket, more easily speared) decreased; 'Hook, line and dilly bag', 254–5.

46   Tench, *Narrative*, 48; *Complete Account*, 286.

47   Tench, *Complete Account*, 286; Worgan, Letter and journal, 9; Bradley's description differs slightly, Journal, 130.

48   Collins, *Account* 1, 557, 592–3; Bradley, *Journal*, 131.

49   Hunter, *Historical Journal*, 44; Tench, *Complete Account*, 286; Bradley, Journal, 131.

50   Collins, *Account* 1, 557; White, *Journal*, 149; Worgan, Letter and journal, 10; Tench, *Complete Account*, 286.

51   Collins, *Account* 1, 583; Hunter, *Historical Journal*, 44, 55.

52   Worgan, Letter and journal, 11; Southwell, Diary, 264; Dawes, Notebook; Tench, *Complete Account*, 189, 221, 283, 286; Bradley, Journal, 133; White, *Journal*, 159.

53   Collins, *Account* 1, 601.

54   Bowdler, 'Hook, line and dilly bag', 256; see also Colley, 'Engendering pre- and post-contact Australian archaeology'; McCarthy, 'The Lapstone Creek excavation'; McCarthy, 'Culture succession'; see Megaw, *Recent Archaeology*; Attenbrow, *Sydney's Aboriginal Past*, 101–2.

55   Walters, 'Fish hooks'; re Memil, see Collins, *Account* 1, 599.

56   Bell, *Daughters of the Dreaming*, 56; Clendinnen, *Dancing*, 152–3.

57   Bradley, Journal, 66, 105; Hunter, *Historical Journal*, 56.

58   Bradley, Journal, 66; White, *Journal*, 149.

59   White, *Journal*, 141.

60   Worgan, Letter and journal, 30; South Head was also called Burrawara.

61   Worgan, Letter and journal, 30.

62   Collins, *Account* 1, 113.

63   Phillip (in Hunter), *Journal*, 314, 349; Johnson to Fricker in Smith, *Bennelong*, 140.

64   Dawes, Notebook; Smith, *Bennelong*, 108ff.; I have found only two references to old women—Mawberry and the old possum-skin-clad woman who officiated at the post-initiation contest of 1795, Collins, *Account* 1, 584.

65   Dawes, Notebook; Tench, *Complete Account*, 276.

66   Troy, 'Role of Aboriginal women'; Collins, *Account* 1, 544, see also 136, 209; Dawes, Notebook.

67   Dawes, Notebook; see insightful readings of the notebook in Jones, *Ochre and Rust*, 46–7; and Coleman, *Romantic Colonization*, chap. 5.

68   Collins, *Account* 1, 153; Phillip (in Hunter), *Journal*, 338; Clendinnen, *Dancing*, 198.

69   Catchpole, Letter to Dr Stebbens, 21 January 1802; McGrath, 'White man's looking glass', 197.

70   Southwell to his mother, 7 September 1791, *HRNSW* II, 731; Collins, *Account* 1, 607.

71   Tench, *Complete Account*, 276, 290; Collins, *Account* 1, 559, 583; Phillip (in Hunter), *Journal*, 316, 319, 333, 339, 350.

72   Clendinnen, *Dancing*, 159–67, quote 165; Noah, *Voyage*, 72.

73   Tench, *Complete Account*, 160; Collins, *Account* 1, 299, 445.

74   Collins, *Account* 1, 587, 588, 591; Tench, *Complete Account*, 290; Phillip (in Hunter), *Journal*, 319; Clendinnen, *Dancing*, 161–2.

75 Collins, *Account* 1, 563; Tench, *Complete Account*, 289; Smith, *Bennelong*, 75; cf. Clendinnen, 159–67.

76 Collins, *Account* 1, 583.

77 ibid., 354, 362.

78 ibid., 590 (Collins spells it 'Collindium'); Phillip (in Hunter), *Journal*, 320–2, 350.

79 Collins, *Account* 1, 561; see also Grimshaw et al., *Creating a Nation*, 7–11.

80 Dawes, Notebook, and see discussion in Smith, *Bennelong*, 135; Phillip, (in Hunter), *Journal*, 360; Collins, *Account* 1, 561–2; McGrath takes Bennelong's statement that Barangaroo wanted to give birth at Government House literally, see 'Birthplaces', 9–11.

81 Clendinnen, *Dancing*, 216; Collins, *Account* 1, 545, 589, 606; Phillip (in Hunter), *Journal*, 353.

82 Collins, *Account* 1, 545, 563; Phillip (in Hunter), *Journal*, 336; Smith, *Eora*, exhibition, image 14. Interestingly, *bora* also means 'testicle' in the coastal Eora language.

83 Collins, *Account* 1, 564–83.

84 ibid., 581–2. The ritual of 'Erah-ba-diang' soon featured in the popular 'New South Wales; Or, Love in Botany Bay', performed by Jones' Royal Circus in London, see playbill, ML and Smith, *Eora*, exhibition, image 15.

85 Clendinnen, *Dancing*, 142, 153; Phillip (in Hunter), *Journal*, 334; Collins, *Account* 1, 560; Broome, *Aboriginal Australians*.

86 Collins, *Account* 1, 407, 424, 425–6; vol. 2, 300; Cunningham, *Blue Mountains Rediscovered*, 84.

87 Holt (O'Shaughnessy), *Rum Story*, 72; Kohen, *The Darug*, 92–131; Ward, *Australian Legend*, 201.

88 Inquest on Nanny Cabbage, 14 June 1817, Judge Advocate Reports of Coroner's Inquests, 1796–1820, 48286, Reel 2232, 97ff., SRNSW; research notes and advice courtesy of Keith Vincent Smith.

89 Collins, *Account* 1, 251, 439; McBryde, *Guests of the Governor*, 23; Smith, *Eora*, exhibition, images 50–2; Brook, 'The forlorn hope'; Hiatt, 'Bennelong and Omai'.

90 Collins, *Account* 1, 439–40, 469; Mann, *Present Picture*, 46–7.

91 Collins, *Account* 2, 7, 46; *SG* 9 January 1813; see also Mann, *Present Picture*, 46–7.

92 Collins, *Account* 2, 69; Smith, *Bennelong*, 44; Clendinnen, *Dancing*, 264ff.; Stanner, 'History of indifference', 17–18, 19.

93 Smith, *Wallumedegal*, 12–13, 25–7; Smith, 'Bennelong, ambassador of the Eora', 80–1; Kohen, *Darug*, 55; Collins, *Account* 2, 69; Dark, 'Bennelong (1764?–1813)'. Bennelong and Boorong may have had another son, Adam Clark, see Smith, *Eora*, exhibition, images 55, 64.

94 Collins, *Account* 2, 7; Smith, *Wallumedegal*, 26–8; Smith, *Eora*, exhibition, image 14; Turner, *Joseph Lycett*, 99–100.

95 Smith, 'Bennelong, ambassador of the Eora', 81.

96 Collins, *Account* 1, 275, 427, 433. The site of the first flagstaff and the tower is now Signal Hill Reserve, near Dunbar Head.

97 Clendinnen, *Dancing*, 258; Broome, *Aboriginal Australians*, 64–5; Rose, *Dingo*, 10, 15; but compare to Fels, *Good Men and True*.

98 Byrne, 'Segregated landscapes', 14.

99 Tench, *Complete Account*, 218; Collins, *Account* 1, 177, 228, 391; Bradley, Journal, 245.

100 Smith, *Bennelong*, 117–18; Smith, *King Bungaree*, 84, 116; Smith, 'Bundle (c1787–c1844)'; Jones, *Ochre and Rust*, 48.

101 Collins, *Account* 1, 299, 362, vol. 2, 54; *SG* 17 Mar 1805, see also 15 September 1805.

102 Collins, *Account* 2, 233; Smith, *King Bungaree*, chaps 3 and 4, 67–8; Jones, *Boomerang*, 106–7; Attenbrow, *Sydney's Aboriginal Past*, 95–6.

103 Flannery, *The Explorers*, 5–10; Warren Whitfield in Stephens, 'Admired by Macquarie but ignored for a sailing cat'; Hansen, 'Death dance', 27.

104 Dening, *Mr Bligh's Bad Language*, 24–8, 54–7, 76ff.; Karskens, *The Rocks*, 188–9; Collins, *Account* 1, 595; Bradley, Journal, 132; Flinders in Smith, *King Bungaree*, 62; Bradley, Journal, 132.

105 Mann, *Present Picture*, 47. Mann refers to another sailor who had 'a farm of four acres . . . planted with maize at Hawkesbury'; this was probably Charley, see Chapter 13.

106 Mann, *Present Picture*, 47.

107 Bellingshausen in Barratt, *The Russians*, 35–6; Bougainville (Riviere), *Governor's Noble Guest*, 173; Oldfield in Smith, *King Bungaree*, 141; Susan Lawrence writes of the Aboriginal men who joined the whaling crews in Tasmania, see *Whalers and Freemen*, 26.

108 Bougainville (Riviere), *Governor's Noble Guest*, 174; Bellingshausen in Barratt, *The Russians*, 34; Smith, *King Bungaree*, 103.

109 Tench, *Complete Account*, 239; Collins, *Account* 1, 141–2, 221, 223.

110 *SG* 26 March, 2 April 1809; 14 June 1807, 19 June 1803, 14, 21 June, 19, 26 July 1807, 30 April 1809; Karskens, *The Rocks*, 16–17, 188; committal of James McAllister, 3 January 1822.

111 Field, *Geographical Memoirs*, 435–6, also in Smith, *King Bungaree*, 117–18; see also Freycinet (1819) and Delessert (1845) in Dyer, *French Explorers*, 186–8.

112 Simonov in Barratt, *The Russians*, 49.

113 See sketch, Jules Lejeune, 'Indigenos de nouvelle hollande', reproduced in Smith, *King Bungaree*, 128; Swain, *A Place for Strangers*, chap. 3.

114 Bougainville (1825) cited in Dyer, *French Explorers*, 196; see also 'A Woodman', *SG* 21 August 1808; Field, *Geographical Memoirs*, 203–5.

115 Collins, *Account* 2, 34.

116 Grant (Cramer), *Beauteous, Wicked Place*, 38; Lesson in Dyer, *French Explorers*, 189, see also 180; Bellingshausen and Simonov in Barratt, *The Russians*, 43, 48–9; Boyes, *Diaries and Letters*, 193.

117 Oldfield, 'New Holland', 103, and in Smith, *King Bungaree*, 140; see also Bremer, 'Pathless wilds', 102–4.

118 Field, *Geographical Memoirs*, 225–6, and Oldfield in Smith, *King Bungaree*, 117, 140; Bougainville (Riviere), *Governor's Noble Guest*, 173.

119 Thompson, 'Journal', 797; Lesson in Dyer, *French Explorers*, 190; Arnold, Bellingshausen and Oldfield in Smith, *King Bungaree*, 73, 108, 109, 142; Bougainville (Riviere), *Governor's Noble Guest*, 174; Cunningham, *Two Years*, 185.

120 Tench, *Complete Account*, 225; Clendinnen, *Dancing*, 34.

121 Collins, *Account* 1, 297; Bellingshausen in Barratt, *The Russians*, 42.

122 Arnold in Smith, *King Bungaree*, 73; Smith, *Bennelong*, 120; see also Bellingshausen in Barratt, *The Russians*, 34.

123 Bellingshausen in Barratt, *The Russians*, 42. 'Bull' apparently entered the popular lexicon: Cunningham mentioned a stowaway 'bulling' a rum-cask and 'drinking the contents', *Two Years*, 287. Compare the silhouette portraits of well-known Aboriginal people by W.H. Fernyhough (1836) and William Nicholas (1840).

124 Phillip (in Hunter), *Journal*, 352, 357–8; Collins, *Account* 1, 165, 166, 175; Tench, *Complete Account*, 239.

125 Freycinet in Dyer, *French Explorers*, 187–8; Bellingshausen in Barratt, *The Russians*, 42–3; Cunningham, *Two Years*, 186; Kercher, *Unruly Child*, 3–4.

126 Bougainville (Riviere), *Governor's Noble Guest*, 70, 173–4; Holt (O'Shaughnessy), *Rum Story*, 69; Bellingshausen and Simonov in Barratt, *The Russians*, 39, 42, 48.

127 Arago, 1819, cited in Dyer, *French Explorers*, 71; Kohen, *Aboriginal Environmental Impacts*, 92; Urry, 'Savage Sportsmen'; *SG* 21 August 1808.

128 McCormick, *First Views*, plate 60, 94; Findlay, *Arcadian Quest*, 22–30; Urry, 'Savage Sportsmen', 58–60; McPhee (ed.), *Joseph Lycett*, 105, see also 121 and images 85–120.

129 Broadbent, *India, China, Australia*, 148–9; McCormick, *First Views*, 182–5; State Library of New South Wales, '[Chinese export ware punchbowl . . .]', Webcat entry.

130 Phillip (in Hunter), *Journal*, 359; Collins, *Account* 1, 343, see also 328–9, 408, 444–5, 584; vol. 2, 50, 66–8; Thompson, 'Journal', 798; Noah, *Voyage*, 72; *SG* 18 September, 2 October, 16 October 1803.

131 Lesson in Dyer, *French Explorers*, 168; the road Lesson referred to was South Head Road, which branched to Botany Bay at Darlinghurst Gaol, see series of maps 1802–31 in Ashton and Waterson, *Sydney Takes Shape*, and Govett, 'Sketches of New South Wales', 1 April 1837, 133; evidence of Mahroot, New South Wales Parliament, *Report . . . on the Condition of the Aborigines*, 6; Collins, *Account* 1, 328, 408; see also Morrison, *Aldine Centennial History*, 416.

132 Collins, *Account* 1, 589; vol. 2, 22–3, 66; *SG* 21 October 1804, 14 July, 10 November, 8, 15, 22, 29 December 1805, 12, 19 January, 2 February, 16, 23 March 1806, 23 December 1808.

133 Collins, *Account* 1, 425, 436; *SG* 31 March, 8, 15, 22, 29 December 1805, 12, 19 January, 2 February, 16, 23 March 1806, 23 December 1808, 15 January 1809.

134 Collins, *Account* 1, 328–9, 390, see also 55, 65–6.

135 ibid., 329, 588, 592.

136 ibid., 412, 425, 556, 586, 587; vol. 2, 13, 34, 124.

137 Collins, *Account* 2, 12; Clendinnen, *Dancing*, 62.

138 Smith, *European Vision*, 187; Neville, *Rage for Curiosity*, 45–6.

139 Smith, Journal, 21; Catchpole to Dr Stebbens, 21 January 1802; see also d'Urville in Dyer, *French Explorers*, 195; *SG* 29 December 1805.

140 Kercher, *Unruly Child*, 4–5; 'Aborigines were not granted the right to give unsworn testimony in criminal trials until 1876', Turnbull, *Sydney*, 42.

141 Collins, *Account* 2, 196; Ford, 'Traversing the frontiers'; Ford, 'Indigenous policy and

its historical occlusions'; Clendinnen, *Dancing*, 255–7; Kercher, *Unruly Child*, 9–10; Kercher, 'Recognition of indigenous legal autonomy'.

142 Clendinnen, *Dancing*, 261.

143 *SG* 2 October 1803.

144 *SG* 15 January 1809.

145 *SG* 16 October 1803; see also *SG* 23 December 1808.

146 *SG* 4 May 1816; see Ford, 'Traversing the Frontiers'.

147 Arago in Dyer, *French Explorers*, 195; see also Arago, *Narrative of a Voyage*, 172–7; Lesson in Dyer, *French Explorers*, 165.

148 Thrush, *Native Seattle*, introduction.

149 D'Urville in Dyer, *French Explorers*, 197; *SG* 2 October 1803; see also Collins, *Account* 2, 125.

150 D'Urville, *An Account* 1, 85–90; d'Urville and Lesson, cited in Dyer, *French Explorers*, 168–72; and Smith, *King Bungaree*, 170–3.

CHAPTER 13   WAR ON THE CUMBERLAND PLAIN

1 *SG* 2, 9, 30 June, 7 July 1805; see Cornelia Parish Map.

2 Caley, 'A Short Account', 299; Connor, *Australian Frontier Wars*, xi.

3 Griffiths, *Hunters and Collectors*, 109.

4 White, *Middle Ground*.

5 *SG* 7 July 1805; Kohen, *The Darug*, 93–102; Parry, 'Lock, Maria (c1805–1878)'; Tobin, *The Dharug Story*; Taylor, 'Henry Lamb'.

6 Tench, *Narrative*, 58; Tench, *Complete Account*, 153; Collins, *Account* 1, 171, 593; Bradley, Journal, 166–7; White, *Journal*, 123, 129, 130.

7 Hunter, *Historical Journal*, 101–3; Willmot, *Pemulwuy*, 28.

8 Tench, *Complete Account*, 225–33; Bradley, Journal, 168; Phillip (in Hunter), *Journal*, 341.

9 As Smith points out, Phillip and the officers did have contacts from the inland Aboriginal groups, including Boorong, Ballooderry and Warraweer Wogul Mi, see *Bennelong*, 62–3, 68, 121ff.

10 Kohen, 'Importance of archaeology to Aboriginal communities', 123–4.

11 Tench, *Complete Account*, 153; *SG* 24, 31 March 1805.

12 'Beachhead', see Connor, *Australian Frontier Wars*, 26; compare with Phillip (in Hunter), *Journal*, 299; Kohen et al., 'Uninvited guests', 16.

13 Kohen et al., 'Uninvited Guests', 18; Connor, *Australian Frontier Wars*; cf. Clendinnen, *Dancing*, 68.

14 Phillip (in Hunter), *Journal*, 312; Tench, *Complete Account*, 181.

15 Connor, *Australian Frontier Wars*, 26–7; Phillip (in Hunter), *Journal*, 299.

16 Smith, *Wallumedegal*, 12–13, 25–7; Smith, *Bennelong*, 138.

17 Cf. Broome, *Aboriginal Australians*, 59–60.

18 Collins, *Account* 1, 543.

19 Rose, 'The Year Zero', 19, 21, 28, 29.

20 Phillip to Grenville, 5 November 1791, *HRA* 1, 272; Phillip (in Hunter), *Journal*, 355–6; Collins, *Account* 1, 173; Prospect Parish Map.

21 Phillip (in Hunter), *Journal*, 355–6; Collins, *Account* 1, 450; Hunter to Portland, 3 March 1796, *HRA* 1, 554; Clendinnen, *Dancing*, 260.

22 Phillip (in Hunter), *Journal*, 299.

23 Connor, *Australian Frontier Wars*, xii, 17, 40.

24 Phillip (in Hunter), *Journal*, 299; Collins, *Account* 1, 342, 349, 364; Connor, *Australian Frontier Wars*, 40; Reynolds, *Other Side*, 51; *SG* 30 March 1816.

25 Collins, *Account* 1, 213.

26 ibid., 328, 340, 349.

27 Holt (O'Shaughnessy), *Rum Story*, 68; Smith, *Eora*, exhibition, image 67; Flynn, 'Holroyd History and the Silent Boundary', 49.

28 Collins, *Account* 1, 409.

29 ibid., 364; this head is probably the one referred to by Atkins, *Journal*, 15 April 1794. He said it was preserved 'as a present for Dr [John] Hunter'; see Kohen et al., 'Uninvited Guests', 31; Smith, 'The white headhunters'.

30 Collins, *Account* 1, 364; *SG* 2 December 1804.

31 Collins, *Account* 1, 555; Pedersen and Woorunmurra, *Jandamarra*, 145–6.

32 Arago, *Narrative*, 172; Arago in Dyer, *French Explorers*, 188–9; Phelps, 'A Present for One's Friends', sketch; Anon. 'Phelps, P.H.F.'; cf. Smith, *Bennelong*, 156ff.

33 Collins, *Account* 2, 281; see Saint Matthew Parish Map.

34 Clendinnen, *Reading the Holocaust*, 5, 7–8.

35 Grenville, *Secret River*; Turnbull, *Sydney*, 36; Kohen, *The Darug*, 63; Martin, *On Darug Land*, 71; Atkinson calls the murders 'a deliberate act of revenge', *Europeans*, 164–5.

36 Collins, *Account* 1, 364, 390, 394, 405, 407.

37 Hunter, *Historical Journal*, 104; Bradley, Journal, 168; Benson and Howell, *Taken for Granted*, 13–14; Howell, McDougall and Benson, *Riverside Plants*.

38 Reynolds, *Other Side*, 65; Byrne, 'Nervous landscapes', 175.

39 Hunter, Order, 22 February 1796, *HRA* 3, 25; Collins, *Account* 1, 458.

40 Collins, *Account* 1, 405; Archibald Bell in Brook and Kohen, *Parramatta Native Institution*, 21; Catchpole to W. Howes, 20 December 1804; *SG* 26 June 1803; Bellingshausen told a similar story about a large landholder, see Barratt, *The Russians*, 43–4.

41 R. v. Powell and others, Court of Criminal Judicature, 15–16 October 1799 [hereafter R. v. Powell], 13.

42 Bradley, Journal, 176.

43 Kohen et al., 'Uninvited Guests', 45.

44 Atkinson, *Europeans*, 200; *SG* 11 August 1805, 27 July 1806; R. v. Powell, evidence of Lieutenant Neil McKellar, 19 (my emphasis).

45 Collins, *Account* 1, 413, 416–17; see also Hunter's recognition of the Aboriginal people's considerable advantage and power, Hunter to Portland, 2 January 1800, *HRA* 4, 1; Connor, *Australian Frontier Wars*, 38.

46 Collins, *Account* 1, 444, 468; vol. 2, 15, see also 56; Judge Atkins to King, 8 July 1805, *HRNSW*, 653; Parry, '"Hanging no good"'; Wilberforce Parish Map.

47 Atkinson, *Europeans*, 232–3; Hunter, General Order, 22 February 1796, *HRA* 3, 25; R. v. Powell, evidence of Thomas Rickerby, 4.

48   R. v. Powell.

49   ibid., evidence of Jonas Archer, William Fuller, John Tarlington, 13, 14, 17–18; Collins, *Account* 2, 281–2; Connor, *Australian Frontier Wars*, 3.

50   Phillip (in Hunter), *Journal*, 341; Hunter to Portland, 2 January 1800, *HRA* 4, 1; R. v. Powell, loc. cit. Terribandy, it was whispered, had killed a white man on the Green Hills raceground. This dead man haunted the court proceedings too, his death even became an event by which they recollected dates, but he was never named and his death was not investigated.

51   R. v. Powell, evidence of Isabella Ramsay, Jonas Archer, 4, 12; Flynn, 'Winbow, John', *Second Fleet*, 619–20.

52   See Saint Matthew Parish Map; R. v. Powell, evidence of Jonas Archer, 12.

53   R. v. Powell, evidence of Lieutenant Hobby and Jonas Archer, 8, 9, 13.

54   R. v. Powell, evidence of Jonas Archer, Henry Baldwin 12, 13, 18–19.

55   R. v. Powell, evidence of Isabella Ramsay, 4–5.

56   R. v. Powell, evidence of Thomas Rickerby, 3.

57   R. v. Powell, evidence of Thomas Rickerby, Thomas Lambourne, John Pearson, David White, 2, 5–7, 11–12; Saint Matthew Parish Map.

58   R. v. Powell, evidence of Thomas Rickerby, Lieutenant Hobby, Robert Braithwaite, 2–3, 7, 10–11; Rickerby was granted his farm in 1794, Ryan, *Land Grants*, 33.

59   Flynn, 'Winbow, John', *Second Fleet*, 620.

60   Evidence of Polding, New South Wales Parliament, *Report . . . on the Condition of the Aborigines*, 6; Karskens, *The Rocks*, 47–9.

61   Kercher, *Unruly Child*, 4–5, 11–12.

62   R. v. Powell, evidence of Thomas Rickerby, Lieutenant Hobby, William Goodall, Peter Farrell, 3, 8–9, 14–15, 16; cf. Ford, 'Traversing the frontiers'.

63   Hunter to Portland, 2 January 1800, *HRA* 4, 1–3; Collins, *Account* 2, 282.

64   Collins, *Account* 2, 281; Flynn, 'Simon Freebody', *Second Fleet*, 279.

65   *SG* 15 October 1809.

66   Smith, *Eora*, exhibition, images 117–18; Smith, 'Australia's oldest murder mystery'; Kohen, 'Pemulwuy (c1750–1802)'.

67   Kohen, 'Pemulwuy (c1750–1802)'.

68   Collins, *Account* 2, 27, 35.

69   Collins, *Account* 2, 27–8; Heaton, *Australian Dictionary of Dates*, 4; Huntington, 'History of Parramatta', 25.

70   Flynn, 'Holroyd history and the silent boundary', 34; Swain, *Place for Strangers*, 230–1.

71   Collins, *Account* 1, 458; Hunter to Portland, 3 March 1796, *HRA* 1, 554.

72   Collins, *Account* 2, 86.

73   ibid., 27, 32.

74   ibid., 33, 101, 208; Caley, 'A Short Account', 299.

75   Pederson and Woorunmurra, *Jandamarra*, 9, 148.

76   Collins, *Account* 1, 444; vol. 2, 70.

77   Catchpole to Dr Stebbens, 21 January 1802.

78   King, Government and General Order 1 May 1801, *HRA* 4, 362; Caley, 'A Short Account', 299.

79 Caley (Currey), *Reflections on the Colony*, 49.

80 Flynn, 'Holroyd history and the silent boundary', 40.

81 King to Hobart, 30 October 1802, *HRA* 4, 867–8.

82 *SG* 24 June 1804; Smith, 'Australia's oldest murder mystery'; Kohen, 'Pemulwuy (c1750–1802)'; Kohlhoff, 'Did Henry Hacking shoot Pemulwuy?', 77–93.

83 *SG* 3 June 1804, see also 24 June 1804; Ross, *Matthew Everingham*, 83. Today Aboriginal people from this region are known by their language name Darkinjung, research carried out by Geoff Ford suggests that Darkinjung was spoken much further south than previously thought, pers. com. Dr Geoff Ford, 2008.

84 *SG* 17 June 1804.

85 *SG* 17 June, 1 July 1804.

86 King to Hobart, 20 December 1804, *HRA* 5, 512–3; Ross, *Hawkesbury Story*, 59; see Knight's farm on Cumberland Reach, Cornelia Parish Map.

87 King to Hobart, 20 December 1804, *HRA* 5, 512–13; Kohen et al., 'Uninvited Guests', 64.

88 Ross, *Matthew Everingham*, 85–6; Hutton Neve, *Forgotten Valley*, 28, 67; see Ryan, *Land Grants*.

89 King to Hobart, 30 April 1805, *HRNSW* 5, 598; *SG* 21, 28 April, 5 May, 2, 16, 30 June 1805.

90 *SG* 3 March, 28 April, 12 May, 9 June 1805.

91 'Domesticated': see King to Hobart, 30 October 1802, *HRA* 4, 867; Sheehan, *Savagism and Civility*, 2–3.

92 *SG* 15 October 1809.

93 Anderson, *Race and the Crisis of Humanism*.

94 *SG* 5 May 1805; Mann, *Present Picture*, 47.

95 *SG* 5, 12 May 1805; Connor, *Australian Frontier Wars*, 44.

96 *SG* 5, 12 May 1805; Connor, *Australian Frontier Wars*, 45.

97 *SG* 12 May 1805.

98 *SG* 5 May 1805.

99 ibid.; Flynn, 'Holroyd history and the silent boundary', 39–41.

100 *SG* 5 May 1805.

101 *SG* 19 May 1805.

102 *SG* 19 May, 30 June, 7 July, 11 August 1805; Parry, '"Hanging no good"'; Parry, 'Musquito (c1780–1825)'.

103 Atkins to King, 8 July 1805, *HRNSW* 5, 653; *SG* 4 August 1805.

104 Flynn, 'Holroyd history and the silent boundary', 40; King to Camden, 20 July 1805, *HRNSW* 5, 658–9; Government and General Order, *SG* 9 June, also 7 July, 14 July 1805.

105 *SG* 15 September 1805, also 5 May, 22 December 1805.

106 *SG* 22 December 1805.

107 *SG* 14 May, 10, 24 September, 1, 15 October 1809, 12 May 1805.

108 *SG* 24 February, 17 March 1810, 18 November 1811; Connor, *Australian Frontier Wars*, 44.

109 Huey in Kohen et al., 'Uninvited Guests', 78.

110   Proclamation, *SG* 7 January 1810.

111   Macquarie to Bathurst, 8 October 1814, *HRA* 8 368; *SG* 28 July 1810.

112   *SG* 14 May 1814.

113   *SG* 14 May, 4 June 1814; see also 7 May 1814, Government and General Orders, *SG* 18 June 1814.

114   Government and General Orders, *SG* 18 June 1814; Brook and Kohen, *Parramatta Native Institution*, 20–2.

115   Macquarie to Goulburn, 7 May 1814, *HRA* 8, 250–1.

116   Government and General Orders, *SG* 18 June 1814; see also the statement when the Native Institution was opened *SG* 10 December 1814: settlers 'never met with any serious or determined hostility from them'.

117   Liston, 'The Dharawal and Gandangara', 51; Connor, *Australian Frontier Wars*, 48.

118   Parish Maps for Bringelly, Mulgoa and Cook; for detailed description of the construction and interiors of these huts in the 1830s, see Mason (Kent and Townsend), *Joseph Mason*, 43–4; for gracious old homes see Wilson, *Old Colonial Architecture*, plates XVII, XXXIX, XL, XLV; Hughes, *Demolished Houses of Sydney*, 92–4; Proudfoot, *Colonial Buildings*.

119   Sykes, *The History of the Sykes Family in Australia*, 1–2; Flynn, *Settlers and Seditionists*, 83–4; Whittaker, *Appin*, 6; see Appin Parish Map, 1867.

120   D'Urville, *An Account*, 85.

121   Kohen, *The Darug*, 21; Attenbrow, *Sydney's Aboriginal Past*, 32–3.

122   *SG* 4 June 1814; Samuel Hassall to Thomas Hassall, 16 March 1816; Caley, *Reflections*, 178; Liston, *Campbelltown*, 1ff., 19–20; Cunningham, *Blue Mountains Rediscovered*, 101; Illert, *The Mayran Clan of the Gayn-d'hay-ungara*.

123   *SG* 24 June 1804; Flynn, 'Holroyd history and the silent boundary', 4, 40; Byrne, 'Old Memories', 105.

124   Campbell, 'Broughton (c1798–c1850)'; Parsons, 'Throsby, Charles (1777–1828)'; Liston, *Campbelltown*, 16–19.

125   *SG* 5 May 1805; Rose, 'The Year Zero'; Liston, *Campbelltown*, 14–15; see Index to the Colonial Secretary's Correspondence, 1788–1825.

126   Byrne, 'Old Memories', 105.

127   Throsby to Wentworth, 5 April 1816.

128   Byrne, 'Old Memories', 105; pers com. Glenda Chalker, Elder, Cubbitch Barta Native Title Corporation, September 2007.

129   *SG* 18 June 1814.

130   *SG* 10 December 1814; Rose, 'The Year Zero', 22, 23.

131   Shelley to Macquarie, 8 April 1814, *HRA*, 8, 370–1; for earlier similar reflections see 'Philanthropus' (Reverend Robert Cartwright), in *SG* 7, 14, 28 July, 4, 11 August, 8 September, 1810.

132   Brook and Kohen, *Parramatta Native Institution*, 54–7; cf. Collins, *Account 2*, 34; Field, *Geographical Memoirs*, 436.

133   *SG* 1 January 1814, 7 July 1805.

134   *SG*, 28 September, 12 October 1816; Smith, 'Moowattin, Daniel (c1791–1816)'; Kohen et al., 'Uninvited Guests', 54–60; Ford and Salter, 'From pluralism to territorial sovereignty'.

135 *SG* 4, 11 May 1816; Brook and Kohen, *Parramatta Native Institution*, 252.

136 *SG* 31 December 1814; Smith, *King Bungaree*, 76 (full moon); Brook and Kohen, *Parramatta Native Institution*, 66.

137 *SG* 10, 31 December 1814; Tobin, *The Dharug Story*; Brook and Kohen, *Parramatta Native Institution*, 66–9; Maria—see Inquest on Nanny Cabbage, research notes and advice courtesy of Keith Vincent Smith.

138 Goodall, *Invasion to Embassy*, chap. 4 and see maps 135, 138.

139 *SG* 4 February 1815; see also Macquarie's Proclamation, 4 May 1816; Smith, *King Bungaree*, 77–8.

140 See Bringelly Parish Map.

141 *SG* 9 March 1816; Bringelly Parish Map.

142 *SG* 16, 23 March 1816.

143 Throsby to Wentworth, 5 April 1816; cf. Reynolds, *Other Side*, 118–21.

144 Samuel Hassall to Thomas Hassall, 16 March 1816; Connor, *Australian Frontier Wars*, 47; see Cook Parish Map.

145 *SG* 30 March 1816; Roberts, 'Bell's Falls', 618.

146 Throsby to Wentworth, 5 April 1816.

147 Macquarie to Bathurst, 25 May 1816, *HRA* 9, 139 and note 36, 854; 'Instructions to Captain Schaw', CSC 4/1734, 149–68; Brook and Kohen, *Parramatta Native Institution*, 22–3.

148 Brook and Kohen, *Parramatta Native Institution*, 23–6.

149 ibid., 26; Connor, *Australian Frontier Wars*, 13.

150 Wallis, Journal and Report, 52, 54.

151 ibid., 52–4.

152 ibid., 54–7.

153 ibid., 57; Byrne, 'Old Memories', 105; Appin Parish Map; Department of Lands, Appin 9029–1S Topographic & Orthophoto map.

154 Liston, *Campbelltown*, 23.

155 Wallis, Journal and Report, 57; Byrne, 'Old Memories', 105.

156 Macquarie, Proclamation, *SG* 4, 11 May 1816; Macquarie to Bathurst, 8 June 1816, *HRA* 9, 139–40; Brook and Kohen, *Parramatta Native Institution*, 31.

157 Blunden's biography, 'Wallis, James (1785?–1858)', does not mention the Appin massacre; Wallis, Journal and Report; Byrne, 'Old Memories', 105.

158 Byrne, 'Old Memories', 105; Schlunke, *Bluff Rock*, 85; the massacre was remembered in the region for decades too—see Mason (Kent and Townsend), *Joseph Mason*, 139.

159 See Roberts, 'Bell's Falls'; Milliss, *Waterloo Creek*; Moore, 'Blackgin's Leap'; Blomfield, *Baal Belbora*; Schlunke, *Bluff Rock*; Wright, *Half a Lifetime*; Griffiths, 'Truth and Fiction'.

160 Pickering, 'Lost in time', 4–7; pers. com. Mike Pickering, Senior Curator, National Museum of Australia.

161 *SG* 29 June, 13 July, 31 August 1816; see early Kurrajong grants on Kurrajong Parish Map; see Cox's letters to Macquarie, 1816, Dixson Collection.

162 *SG* 4 May, 20 July, 3 August 1816.

163 Brook and Kohen, *Parramatta Native Institution*, 30–1, 69–70; see de Freycinet (1819) in Smith, *King Bungaree*, 99–100; Bellingshausen and Simonov (1820), in Barratt, *The Russians*, 44–6, 49.

164 *SG* 2 November 1816; Kohen et al., 'Uninvited Guests', 91.

165 *SG* 4 January 1817.

166 Macquarie to Bathurst, 4 April 1817, *HRA* 9, 342; Roberts, 'Bell's Falls', 618ff.

167 Meredith, *Notes and Sketches*, 12; see Stanner, 'History of indifference', 25.

CHAPTER 14   AFTERMATH

1 Smith, *Eora*, exhibition, image 126; Nugent, *Botany* Bay, 30, 57; West in Flannery, *Birth of Sydney*, 311; Balcombe, 'Sketch shewing . . . huts . . . belonging to Maroot'.

2 Botany Parish Map cf *UBD 2003 . . . Street Directory*, map 296; Nugent, *Botany Bay*, 65–70; National Parks and Wildlife Service, 'Meeting Place Precinct Master Plan'.

3 See for example the accounts of Jacques Arago in *Narrative of a Voyage*. Most of Arago's stories are highly sensationalised and seem to have little basis in truth. They were clearly written with the intention of both entertaining readers with lurid tales of 'darkest savagery', and in defiance of the older philosophical idea of the 'noble savage'.

4 Govett, 'Sketches of New South Wales', 28 May 1836, 202.

5 ibid.

6 Evidence of Mahroot, New South Wales Parliament, *Report . . . on the Condition of the Aborigines*, 1, 3; Smith, *Eora*, exhibition, images 119, 121; Anon., 'Phelps, P.H.F'; pers. com. Keith Vincent Smith 2007.

7 Evidence of Mahroot, New South Wales Parliament, *Report . . . on the Condition of the Aborigines*.

8 Collins, *Account* 2, 125; *SG* 2 October 1803; Arago citing Barron Field and John Oxley in Dyer, *French Explorers*, 180; *SG* 31 December 1816, Government and General Order, 10 December 1814.

9 Evidence of Polding, New South Wales Parliament, *Report . . . on the Condition of the Aborigines*, 6; see also Baudin in Dyer, *French Explorers*, 199–200; Bellingshausen in Barratt, *The Russians*, 43–4; Reynolds, *Whispering*, chap. 1.

10 Govett, 'Sketches of New South Wales', 22 May 1836, 202; La Place and Lesson in Dyer, *French Explorers*, 152, 179; cf. Collins, *Account* 2, 125; Cunningham, *Two Years*, 18, 61. The claim of infanticide was still in circulation among whites in the 1850s, see Brook, *Shut Out from the World*, 16.

11 Flynn, 'Place of Eels', section 16.

12 Evidence of Mahroot, New South Wales Parliament, *Report . . . on the Condition of the Aborigines*, 4.

13 Willey, *When the Sky Fell Down*, 217–19; cf. Goodall, *Invasion to Embassy*, 45.

14 Evidence of Mahroot, New South Wales Parliament, *Report . . . on the Condition of the Aborigines*, 3.

15 Troy, *The Sydney Language*, 38. The word appeared in the list in King's Journal.

16   Ferry, cited in Brook, *Shut Out from the World*, 4; Turbet, *Aborigines of the Sydney District*, 89; Attenbrow, *Sydney's Aboriginal Past*, 139.

17   Swain, *Place for Strangers*, 115.

18   Gilbert, cited in Morrissey, 'Dancing with shadows', 73.

19   Smith, *King Bungaree*, chaps 1 and 9; Arnold and Bellingshausen cited 78, 79; Bellingshausen in Barratt, *The Russians*, 44; Hansen, 'Death dance', 28.

20   Smith, *King Bungaree*, 118; West in Flannery, *Birth of Sydney*, 312.

21   Smith Hall in Smith, *King Bungaree*, 119; Cowper, Attempts made to ameliorate . . ., 1838.

22   Smith, *King Bungaree*, 119; Dyster, *Servant and Master*, 6–7, 35–8; Carlin, *Elizabeth Bay House*, 37–40; Broadbent, 'The push east'.

23   *Australian* 4 January 1828; *SG* 9 July 1829; Smith, *King Bungaree*, 142–3, 167.

24   Cunningham, *Two Years*, 188; Govett, 'Sketches of New South Wales', 4 June 1836, 217; Smith, *King Bungaree*, 145–6; Smith, *Eora*, exhibition, images 33, 89–95.

25   Smith, 'Gooseberry, Cora'; Smith, 'Morooboora's daughter'. 'Old Gooseberry' appears to be her European nickname; one of its old meanings was 'a third person' or chaperone, perhaps a reference to the trio formed with Bungaree and his first wife Matora. It was also a nickname for the devil, see Brewer, *Dictionary*. Her grave and headstone were moved to Bunnerong on Botany Bay when Central Railway Station was built in 1901; Nugent, *Botany Bay*, 57; Johnson and Sainty, *Sydney Burial Ground*, 385.

26   Czernis-Ryl, 'Early Australian silver statuette', 6–10; Dowling, 'Reminiscences of the late Judge Dowling', 55; Smith, *Eora*, exhibition, images 102, 104; another 'last King' and 'last of the Sydney Tribe' was Tamara, see image 29.

27   Evidence of Mahroot, New South Wales Parliament, *Report . . . on the Condition of the Aborigines*, 5; old sailor Willammanan died of exposure in Hyde Park in 1844, Smith, *Eora*, exhibition, image 114.

28   See Sydney Harbour Federation Trust, 'Management Plan, Mosman No. 2, Chowder Bay'; Souter, *Mosman*, 77–9.

29   Smith, *Eora*, exhibition, image 101; Karskens, 'The Gem of Port Jackson'.

30   Boyes, *Diaries and letters*, 192–3; see also Mathew, 'Stray leaves', 2 December 1829.

31   See Liston, *Sarah Wentworth*; Waterhouse, *Private Pleasures*, 12–13.

32   Mansfield to his nephew Ralph Mansfield, Sydney, 5 October 1855.

33   LaPlace (1831) and Delessert (1845) in Dyer, *French Explorers*, 179, 186. The displacement of Aboriginal people from the Cleveland Paddocks Reserve, now Prince Alfred Park, was reported in *Sydney Echo* 12 June 1890, cited in Smith, *Eora*, exhibition, image 36.

34   See Doukakis, *The Aboriginal People*, loc. cit.

35   Doran, 'The pre-European environmental landscape', and Cumming, 'Chimneys and change', in Karskens and Rogowsky, *Histories of Green Square*; West, *Old and New Sydney*, and in Smith, *Eora*, exhibition, image 140; Angas, *Savage Life and Scenes* 2, 200.

36   Goodall, *Invasion to Embassy*, 160, 169–71, 236.

37   Read, *Belonging*, 23–6, 206; see also Foley, *Repossession*.

38   Mansfield, Journal, extract, 17 November 1822; see also Darwin in Nicholas and Nicholas, *Charles Darwin*, 28–9.

39   Brook, *Shut Out from the World*, 16.

40   Kohen, *Darug and their Neighbours*, 92; Brook, *Shut Out from the World*, 42, 64–7 but see 11; Ross, *Hawkesbury Story*, 200–2; evidence of *Select Committee . . . on the condition of the Aborigines*, 33; cf. Taylor, *Unearthed*, 220–48.

41   Brook, *Shut Out from the World*, 12, 16, 60.

42   Govett, 'Sketches of New South Wales', 25 June 1836, 242.

43   Ryan, *Land Grants*, 20; Holt (O'Shaughnessy), *Rum Story*, 68, see also Flynn, 'Holroyd history and the silent boundary', 49; Kohen, *Darug and their Neighbours*, 68, 70.

44   *SG* 23 November 1826; Cunningham, *Two Years*, 185–6, 188.

45   Betts, Diary, 45, 78.

46   ibid., 78; Macarthur correspondence and journal in Liston, *Campbelltown*, 25; Liston, 'Dharawal and Gandangara', 57; Kohen, *Darug and their Neighbours*, 74.

47   MacMillan, 'Erskine, James (1765?–1825)'; see picture of Erskine Park in the background of Templar, 'Skeletine by Skeleton, July 1844'; Melville Parish Map; pers. com. Dr James Broadbent, architectural historian 2008.

48   Rosenthal, 'The extraordinary Mr Earle', 39.

EPILOGUE

1   Pers. com. Aunty Edna Watson, 22 October 1999.

2   Rosemary Taplin located and recorded many of these sites in Sydney's bushland areas during the 1960s, pers. com. Val Attenbrow; and see Dallas, Mackay and Karskens, 'Archaeological Study of the . . . Parklea Release Area', 18–27.

3   Pers. com. Graham Wilson 30 April 2007; Wilson, 'Castle Hill Heritage Park'; Carr et al., *Heritage Tour of the Hills District*, 31–2; Hawkins et al., *Castle Hill and its Government Farm*, 59–61.

4   ABC TV, *Rewind* series, 'Vinegar Hill'; Gapps, 'Mobile monuments'; pers. com. Dr Stephen Gapps, historian.

5   *Sydney Morning Herald*, 14 November 2007.

6   Byrne, 'Segregated landscapes', 13–14.

7   See also Byrne, 'Ethos of return', 79ff.

8   *SG* 28 May 1831; Carlin, *Elizabeth Bay House*, 2, 37–9.

9   Upton, 'A Darug discussion'; Byrne, 'Ethos of return', 73–4, 77, 78–9; Byrne et al., *Social Significance*, 21; pers. com. Mr Ross Evans, Aboriginal Development Officer, Wollondilly Shire Council, September 2007; Glenda Chalker, Elder, Cubbitch Barta Native Title Corporation, September 2007.

10   Miller, 'Bull Cave', 16–18; Sydney Prehistory Group, *In Search of the Cobrakall*, 51–2; Rhodes, *Cage of Ghosts*; Rhodes, 'Finding cages of ghosts'.

11   See also Thomas, *Artificial Horizon*, 274, 276–8, 287–90.

12   Canterbury City Council, 'Indigenous Mosaic'.

13 Wollondilly Shire Council, 'Scar Tree Plan of Management, Bridgewater Estate 2006'; Local Government and Shires Association, Cultural Award Nominations, 2007; Hinkson, *Aboriginal Sydney: A Guide.*

14 Pers. com. Sister Kerry McDermott, Winga Myamly Reconciliation Group, September 2007; Mr Ross Evans, Aboriginal Development Officer, Wollondilly Shire Council, September 2007.

ILLUSTRATIONS

COLOUR PLATES

Shoreline, Broken Bay, 2002. G. Karskens.

Fish Rock, Broken Bay, 2002. G. Karskens.

Port Jackson Painter, 'Method of Climbing Trees', n.d. Watling Collection, Natural History Museum.

Port Jackson Painter, 'A Native Woman and her Child', n.d. Watling Collection, Natural History Museum.

William Bradley, 'Broken Bay, New South Wales, March 1788'. Mitchell Library, State Library of New South Wales.

William Bradley, 'Sydney Cove, Port Jackson, 1788'. Mitchell Library, State Library of New South Wales.

George Raper, 'View of the East Side of Sidney Cove, Port Jackson; from the Anchorage. The Governor's House bearing S.b. E ½ E & the Flag Staff S.E b. E. ¼ E', c1789. Raper Collection, Natural History Museum.

Artist unknown, 'Port Jackson from the Entrance up to Sydney Cove taken in October 1788', detail. Watling Collection, Natural History Museum.

Francis Wheatley, 'Captain Arthur Phillip', 1786. Mitchell Library, State Library of New South Wales.

William M. Bennett, 'Portrait of Vice-Admiral John Hunter', c1812. National Library of Australia.

Artist unknown, [Philip Gidley King], c1800–05. Mitchell Library, State Library of New South Wales.

Alexander Huey, [Portrait of Rear Admiral William Bligh], 1814. National Library of Australia.

ILLUSTRATIONS

John Lewin, 'A view of the River Hawkesbury N. S. Wales', c1810. Dixson Galleries, State Library of New South Wales.

George William Evans (attrib.), 'Head of navigation Hawkesbury River', c1810. Mitchell Library, State Library of New South Wales.

Artist unknown, 'Sketch of the Inundation in the Neighbourhood of Windsor taken on Sunday the 2nd of June 1816'. Mitchell Library, State Library of New South Wales.

Richard Read junior (attrib.), [Reverend Samuel Marsden, 1833]. Mitchell Library, State Library of New South Wales.

Joseph Lycett, 'Raby, a farm belonging to Alexander Riley Esqr. New South Wales', 1826. National Library of Australia.

Port Jackson Painter, 'View of Entrance to Port Jackson, taken from the Boat', c1790. National Library of Australia.

Frederic Charles Terry (attrib.), 'St Phillips Church', c1855, folding tea-table with central roundel featuring St Phillips. Dixson Galleries, State Library of New South Wales.

Stanley Owen, 'George Street, Sydney from the Main Guard', 1847. Mitchell Library, State Library of New South Wales.

Artist unknown, [Miniature portrait of Simeon Lord], c1830. Mitchell Library, State Library of New South Wales.

John Eyre, 'New South Wales, View of Sydney from the West Side of the Cove No 2', c1808. Mitchell Library, State Library of New South Wales.

George Roberts, [Punchbowl Gloucester Street Sydney], c1830. Dixson Galleries, State Library of New South Wales.

Richard Read senior, [Lachlan Macquarie], 1822. Mitchell Library, State Library of New South Wales.

Artist unknown, [Elizabeth Macquarie], c1819. Mitchell Library, State Library of New South Wales.

Joseph Lycett, 'Convict Barracks Sydney N. S. Wales', c1820. Mitchell Library, State Library of New South Wales.

Richard Jones, 'Port Jackson Lighthouse', c1840. Mitchell Library, State Library of New South Wales.

Augustus Earle, 'South Head and lighthouse, Port Jackson N.S. Wales, with the approach of a southerly squall', c1825. National Library of Australia.

C. Cartwright, 'Map of the Governor's Desmesne', 1816. Mitchell Library, State Library of New South Wales.

Richard Read, 'Elizabeth Henrietta Villa', 1820. Mitchell Library, State Library of New South Wales.

Frederick Garling (attrib.), 'The domed salon, Henrietta Villa Point Piper, Sydney', n.d. Mitchell Library, State Library of New South Wales.

Edward Close, 'Sydney Barracks', 1817. National Library of Australia.

Edward Close, 'The Public Buildings in Macquarie Street from the road to Mrs Mc [Macquarie's] Chair', c1817. National Library of Australia.

Major James Taylor, [Panoramic views of Port Jackson] engraved by R. Havell & Sons, including 'The entrance of Port Jackson and part of the town of Sydney, New South Wales', 'The town of Sydney in New South Wales' and 'Part of the Harbour of Port Jackson, and the country between Sydney and the Blue Mountains, New South Wales', c1821. Mitchell Library, State Library of New South Wales.

Augustus Earle, 'Sydney Heads', c1825. National Library of Australia.

Augustus Earle, 'View of farm of J. Hassall, Cow Pastures', c1826. Mitchell Library, State Library of New South Wales.

George Raper, 'Bird & Flower of Port Jackson', [blue-faced honeyeater, native iris, *Patersonia* sp., and a sundew, *Drosera* sp.], n.d. Raper Collection, Natural History Museum.

John Hunter, 'Gomah (Murry)' [king parrot], n.d. National Library of Australia.

John Lewin, 'Dappled grey—Cryptophasa Irrorata', pre-publication plate from his *Prodromus Entomology*, 1803. Mitchell Library, State Library of New South Wales.

John Lewin, [Acacia], c1805. Mitchell Library, State Library of New South Wales.

Samuel Elyard, 'Johnston's Estate Annandale', 1877. Dixson Galleries, State Library of New South Wales.

Port Jackson Painter, 'Marsupials, Native names 'Mer-re-a-gan and Din-e-gow-a', n.d. Watling Collection, Natural History Museum.

Artist unknown, 'Major Johnston with Quartermaster Laycock One Serjeant and twenty-five Private of ye New South Wales Corps defeats two hundred and sixty six armed Rebels, 5th March 1804', [Convict uprising at Castle Hill], 1804. National Library of Australia.

Artist unknown, 'View of the establishment at Castle Hill', c1803. Mitchell Library, State Library of New South Wales.

Joseph Lycett, 'View upon the Nepean River at the Cow Pastures, New South Wales', 1825. National Library of Australia.

Augustus Earle, 'Skirmish between bushrangers and constables, Illawarra', 1827. National Library of Australia.

Port Jackson Painter, 'Ban nel lang meeting the governor by appointment after he was wounded by Wil le ma ring', c1790. Watling Collection, Natural History Museum.

George William Evans (attrib.), 'Sydney from the West side of the Cove', 1802. Mitchell Library, State Library of New South Wales.

Port Jackson Painter, 'Native named Ben-ne-long. As painted when angry after Botany Bay Colbee was wounded', 1790, Watling Collection, Natural History Museum.

Port Jackson Painter, 'Mr White, Harris & Laing with a party of soldiers visiting Botany Bay Colebee at that place when wounded near Botany Bay', c1790. Watling Collection, Natural History Museum.

ILLUSTRATIONS

Port Jackson Painter, 'Natives returned from fishing', 1790. Watling Collection, Natural History Museum.

William Bradley, 'Port Jackson from the South Head leading up to Sydney; Supply sailing in', 1788. Mitchell Library, State Library of New South Wales.

Augustus Earle, 'Portrait of Bungaree, a native of New South Wales', c1826. National Library of Australia.

Pellion, Alphonse (attrib.), 'Sauvages de la Nouvelle Galles du Sud [Tara et Peroa]', 1819. Mitchell Library, State Library of New South Wales.

Joseph Lycett, [Contest with spears, shields and clubs], c1817. National Library of Australia.

Augustus Earle, 'A View in Parramatta N. S. Wales looking East', c1826. Mitchell Library, State Library of New South Wales.

Augustus Earle, 'Natives of N. S. Wales as seen in the streets of Sydney', c1826. National Library of Australia.

Artist unknown, Punchbowl, made in China c1818. Mitchell Library, State Library of New South Wales.

Augustus Earle, 'The Annual meeting of the native tribes at Parramatta, New South Wales, the Governor meeting them', c1826. National Library of Australia.

Augustus Earle, 'A native family of New South Wales sitting down on English settlers farm', c1826. National Library of Australia.

Bull Cave, 2007. G. Karskens.

GREYSCALE ILLUSTRATIONS

ILLUSTRATIONS

ILLUSTRATIONS

ILLUSTRATIONS

BIBLIOGRAPHY

PRIMARY SOURCES—ARCHIVAL

Colonial Secretary's Papers

Cotton, Catherine, Petition, January 1810, 4/1822 no. 272, ML.

Crook, Emma, papers re abduction, 4/1743, 31ff., ML.

Gilberthorpe, Thomas, Memorial, 1810, 4/1723, 99, ML.

Macquarie, Lachlan, Public Notice, 3 January 1810, 4/1723, 17, ML.

Magistrate's Report on the State of the Gaol, 7 July 1821, and related correspondence, 4/1748, ML.

Pendergrass, John, Memorial, 18 January 1825, R6063, 4/1785, 41, ML.

Ruse, James, Petition, January 1810, 4/1822 no. 287, ML.

Ward, James, Petition for Assistance re floods and indebtedness, January 1801, with Report of Charles Grimes, January 1801, 2/8130, 363–9a, ML.

Commissioner of Claims

Memorials Forwarded, 1832–42, 2/1777–93, 2/1839–1842A, SRNSW.

Reports, c1835–55, 2/1752–75, SRNSW.

Coroner's Inquests

Inquest on James Church, 10 August 1822, Colonial Secretary's Papers, 4/1819, 315, ML.

Inquest on Matthew Hyard—died in the new convict barracks, 31 July 1820, Colonial Secretary's Papers, 4/1819, 315, ML.

Inquest on Nanny Cabbage, 14 June 1817, Judge Advocate Reports of Coroner's Inquests, 1796–1820, 2/8286, Reel 2232, 97ff., SRNSW.

Court of Criminal Judicature

McAllister, James, committal for assault, 3 January 1822, Reel 1976, 306, SRNSW.

Minton v. Richards and Richards v. Minton (rape of Mary Richards), March/April 1818, SZ782, 385ff., SRNSW.

BIBLIOGRAPHY

R. v. Hunt (murder of Stephen Smith on the Nepean) 20 February 1812, 5/1120, 81–99, SRNSW.

R. v. Powell and others, 15–16 October 1799, Minutes of Proceedings, SRNSW, X905, 323, 329–62; see *Decisions of the Superior Courts of New South Wales*, Division of Law, Macquarie University, <http://www.law.mq.edu.au/scnsw/html/R%20v%20Powell,%20 1799.htm>.

R. v. William Swift and Daniel Grogan (murder of Maria Minton), 20 March 1821, SZ794, 138–60, SRNSW.

Flagstaff Hill Reserve Trustees/Observatory Park Trustees
Minutes and related correspondence, 1875–1909, 2/679, SRNSW.

Land Titles Office
Index and Registers of Assignment 1800–1825 ('Old Registers'), ML A3609–A3620.

Unpublished manuscripts
Anon., Letter to members of the Gledhill family from a constable at Cockatoo Island, Sydney, NSW, 8 October 1856, ML Doc 2784.

Arnold, Surgeon Joseph, Letter to his brother, 18 March 1810, ML A1849–2.

Atkins, Richard, Journal 1792–1810, ML MSS 737.

Betts, Reverend John, Diary, 12 April 1829–16 August 1833, ML B782, online at <http://libapp.sl.nsw.gov.au/cgi-bin/spydus/TRN/PM/AUHDG/769/435463>.

Bigge, John Thomas, List of Prevailing Timber Trees of New South Wales, c1819, in Bigge, *Report* Appendix, BT Box 25, 5465–9, ML.

Bigge, John Thomas, *Report*, Appendices, Bonwick Transcripts, ML.

Bradley, William, Journal: A Voyage to New South Wales, December 1786–May 1792, compiled 1803, ML Safe 1/14, transcripts online at <http://image.sl.nsw.gov.au/Ebind/safe1_14/a138/a138000.html>.

Bruce, George [Druce, William], Life of a Greenwich Pensioner 1776–1817, ML MSS CY 196, A1618^{-1}, transcribed by Benedict Taylor, 2004.

Catchpole, Margaret, Letters to Mr and Mrs Howes, Mrs Cobbold and Dr Stebbens, ML A1508, transcripts online at <http://image.sl.nsw.gov.au/Ebind/a1508/a547/a547000.html>.

Clark, Ralph, Journal kept on the *Friendship* during a voyage to Botany Bay and Norfolk Island . . . 9 March 1787–31 December 1787, 1 January 1788–10 March 1788, Fair copy, probably compiled later, transcripts online at <http://image.sl.nsw.gov.au/Ebind/safe1_27/a262/a262000.html>.

Clark, Ralph, Letterbook, 3 April 1787–30 September 1791, ML C221, transcript online at <http://image.sl.nsw.gov.au/Ebind/c221/a1380/a1380000.html>.

Coghill, Elizabeth M., Diary, 1858–59, ML MSS 1886.

Cowper, Reverend William, Attempts made to ameliorate the Condition of the Aborigines of New South Wales 1814–1823, Memo re Aborigines in Sydney, Parramatta and Blacktown, 11 June 1838, Document 68a, Miscellaneous Correspondence Relating to Aborigines, SRNSW, NRS 13696 [5/1161] online at <http://www.law.mq.edu.au/scnsw/Correspondence/documents.html>.

Cox, Jane Maria, Reminiscences, 1813–80, ML A1603.

Cox, William, Letters to Governor Macquarie, 1816, in Sir William Dixson—Documents relating to Aboriginal Australians [Dixson Collection], 1816–53, ML DL Add 81, 177–94.

Dawes, Lieutenant William, Vocabulary of the language of N. S. Wales, in the neighbourhood of Sydney (Native and English) [Notebooks], ML 41645A and 41645ᴮ, FM4/3431.

Dawes, William, Collins, David and Phillip, Arthur, Vocabulary, c1788–91, ML FM4/3432, frames 795–817.

Easty, Private John, Book. A Memarandom of the Transa . . . of a Voiage from England to Botany Bay in the Scarborough Transport Gaptn Marshall Commander kept by me your humble Servan, ML DL Spencer 374, transcript online at <http://image.sl.nsw.gov.au/Ebind/dl_spencer374/a1145/a1145000.html>.

Fowell, Newton, Letter to his father, John Fowell, 12 July 1788, ML MSS 4895/1/18, online at <http://image.sl.nsw.gov.au/Ebind/mss4895/a616/a616000.html>.

Hall, George, Journal, 1801–04, ML A2585.

Harris, Surgeon John, Letter, 20 March 1791, ML CY A1597.

Hassall, Reverend Samuel, Letter to his brother Thomas Hassall, 16 March 1816, Hassall Correspondence, ML A1677⁻⁴ CT928, 619–27.

Hayes, Michael, Letters to his family, 1802–25, ML A3586.

Howe, Robert, Diary, 1 August 1822–4 April 1823, copied by A.C. Lawry with notes, ML ZB846–2.

Huey, Alexander, Journal of Alexander Huey, 1809–10, ML (Tyler Papers) M1663 (AJCP D3220).

Jewell, William Henry, Letter to his brother, May 1820, ML Doc 1042.

Johnson, Richard, Letters to Henry Fricker, 15 November 1788–89, ML Safe A21, Aj1, C232, partial transcript online at <http://image.sl.nsw.gov.au/Ebind/safe1_121/a1769/a1769000.html>.

Johnston, Major George, Letters to Captain Piper, 12 April 1804, 28 December 1804, Piper Papers, vol. 3, ML A256, 325–31, 623–5.

Kean, Ellen (Mrs Charles Kean, nee Free), to Mrs Horace Twiss, Sydney, 1 February 1864, ML Ak 24/4.

King, Philip Gidley, Private Journal, Vol. 1, 24 October 1786–12 January 1789, ML Safe 1/16, transcript online at <http://image.sl.nsw.gov.au/Ebind/safe1_16/a1296/a1296242.html>.

King, Philip Gidley, Fair copy of Remarks & Journal kept on the Expedition to form a Colony . . ., with additional information, 1786–December 1790; compiled 1790, ML C115, transcript online at <http://image.sl.nsw.gov.au/Ebind/c115/a1519/a1519000.html>.

Macquarie, Lachlan, Journal, ML A774, transcript online at <http://www.lib.mq.edu.au/digital/lema/documents.html>.

Macquarie, Lachlan, Journal of a tour of inspection commencing 6 November 1810, online at <http://www.lib.mq.edu.au/all/journeys/1810/1810.html>.

Mansfield, Reverend Ralph, extracts from Journal, 17 November 1822, in J.T. Bigge, *Report*, Appendix, Bonwick Transcripts, Box 52, 1306–13.

BIBLIOGRAPHY

Mansfield, Reverend Ralph, Letters 1819–55, National Library of Australia MS 2045.

Marsden family, Letters to John and Mary Stokes, 1794–1824, ML MSS 719.

Matcham, Charles Horatio Nelson, Letters 1831–39, ML Am166.

Mathew, Sarah, and Mathew, Felton, Diaries of Felton and Sarah Mathew, 1829–34, National Library of Australia, MS 15. Transcribed and edited by Bruce Jones as 'Stray Leaves from the Journal of a Wanderer in Australia' (written in first person of Felton Mathew), online at <http://www.users.bigpond.com/narrabeen/feltonmathew/>.

Morehead, Ellie, My Recollection—Being reminiscences of her life particularly in Sydney 1841–1870s, n.d. typescript, ML, Doc 867.

Mutch, T.D., Index to Births, Deaths and Marriages, ML Reference Shelf.

Palmer, Thomas Fyshe, Letters and notes, 1794–1862, ML M391.

Reibey, Mary, probably to George Howe, Description of Thomas Reibey's tomb, 1811, ML Ar27.

Scott, Robert, Letter to his mother, 16 August 1801, ML Doc 1109.

Smith, Samuel, Journal written by Samuel Smith Seaman who served on board the *Investigator*, Capt Flinders on a Voyage of Discovery in the South Seas, 26 May 1801– 7 October 1803, ML C222/CY581.

Southwell, Daniel, Diary, 1787–91, Bigge, *Report*, Appendix in Bonwick Transcript Box 57, ML, 244–85.

Suttor, George, Letter to Joseph Banks 10 March 1804, Banks Papers ML MSS A78–3 vol. 4, 150–2.

Suttor, George, Sketch of Events in NSW 1800–20, ML C783.

Threlkeld, Reverend Lancelot, Annual Report of the Mission to the Aborigines, Lake Macquarie, December 31 1836, Document 52, Miscellaneous Correspondence Relating to Aborigines, SRNSW, NRS 13696 [5/1161] online at <http://www.law.mq.edu.au/ scnsw/Correspondence/documents.htm>.

Throsby, Charles, Letter to D'Arcy Wentworth, 5 April 1816, Wentworth Papers, ML A752 CY699, 188.

Wallis, Captain James, Journal and Report, 10–17 April 1816, Colonial Secretary's Correspondence, 4/1735, 50–61, ML.

Worgan, George Bouchier, Letter written to his brother Richard Worgan, 12–18 June 1788. Includes journal fragment on a voyage to New South Wales with the First Fleet on board HMS *Sirius*, 20 January 1788–11 July 1788, ML C830 and transcript online at <http:// image.sl.nsw.gov.au/Ebind/c830/a1175/a1175000.html>.

PRIMARY SOURCES—PUBLISHED

Angas, George French, *Savage Life and Scenes in Australia and New Zealand being an Artist's Impression of Countries and People at the Antipodes*, 2 volumes, London, Smith, Elder & Co., 1847.

Anon., Letter from a Female Convict, Port Jackson 14 November 1788, in F.M. Bladen (ed.), *Historical Records of New South Wales*, Vol. II, Sydney, Government Printer, 1893, Appendix E, 746–7.

Arago, Jacques, *Narrative of a Voyage around the World in the Uranie and Physicienne Corvettes*, Amsterdam, N. Israel/New York De Capo Press, 1971 (f.p. 1823).

Atkinson, James, *An Account of the State of Agriculture and Grazing in New South Wales*, London, J. Cross, 1844.

Banks, Joseph, *The Endeavour Journal of Joseph Banks 1768–1771*, 2 volumes, edited by J.C. Beaglehole, Sydney, Trustees of the Public Library of New South Wales and Angus & Robertson, 1962.

Bellingshausen, F.G., Journal, March–April 1820, in Glynn Barratt, *The Russians in Port Jackson 1814–1822*, Canberra, Australian Institute of Aboriginal Studies, 1981, 34–46.

Bigge, John Thomas, *Report of the Commissioner of Inquiry on the Colony of New South Wales*, Adelaide, Library Board of South Australia, 1966 (f.p. London 1823).

Bigge, John Thomas, *Report of the Commissioner of Inquiry, on the Judicial Establishments of New South Wales*, Adelaide, Library Board of South Australia, 1966 (f.p. London 1823).

Bigge, John Thomas, *Report of the Commissioner of Inquiry on the State of Agriculture and Trade in the Colony of New South Wales*, Adelaide, Libraries Board of South Australia, 1966 (f.p. London 1823).

Bladen, F.M. (ed.), *Historical Records of New South Wales*, vols I–V, Sydney, Charles Potter, Government Printer, 1893.

Bougainville, Hyacinthe de, *The Governor's Noble Guest: Hyacinthe de Bougainville's Account of Port Jackson, 1825*, translated and edited by Marc Serge Riviere, Melbourne, Miegunyah Press, 1999.

Boyes, G.T.W.B., *The Diaries and Letters of G.T.W.B. Boyes Volume 1*, edited by Peter Chapman, Melbourne, Oxford University Press, 1985.

Byrne, William, 'Old Memories: General Reminiscences of Early Colonists—II', *Old Times*, May 1903, 105–8.

Caley, George, *Reflections on the Colony of New South Wales*, edited by J.E.B. Currey, Sydney, Landsdowne Press, 1966.

Caley, George, 'A Short Account relative to the proceedings in New South Wales from the year 1800 to 1803, with hints and critical remarks . . . addressed to Sir Joseph Banks', *Historical Records of New South Wales*, vol. 5, King 1803–05, 291–300.

Chisholm, Caroline, *Comfort for the Poor! Meat Three Times a Day!!*, London, John Oliver, 1847.

Clark, C.M.H. (ed.), *Select Documents in Australian History 1788–1850*, Sydney, Angus & Robertson, 1962.

Collins, David, *An Account of the English Colony in New South Wales*, 2 vols, facs. ed. Adelaide, Libraries Board of South Australia, 1971, (f.p. T. Cadell and W. Davies, London, 1798).

Cunningham, Peter, *Two Years in New South Wales*, edited by D.S. MacMillan, Sydney, Angus & Robertson, 1966 (f.p. 1827).

Dowling, Judge James Sheen, 'Reminiscences of the Late Judge Dowling', *Old Times*, June 1903, 183–92.

Ducharme, Léandre, *Journal of a Political Exile in Australia*, translated by George Mackaness, Sydney, D.S. Ford, 1944.

d'Urville, Jules Dumont, *An Account in Two Volumes of Two Voyages to the South Seas*, translated and edited by Helen Rosenman, Melbourne University Press, 1981 (f.p. Paris 1834).

Dyer, George (ed.), *Slavery and Famine, Punishment for Seditions: An Account of Miseries and Starvation at Botany Bay*, London, J. Ridgeway, 1794.

Everingham, Matthew, *The Everingham Letterbook*, edited by Valerie Ross, Sydney, Anvil Press, 1985.

Field, Barron, *Geographical Memoirs of New South Wales*, London, John Murray, 1828.

'A Gentleman', *A Month in the Bush of Australia*, London, J. Cross, 1838.

Govett, W.R., 'Sketches of New South Wales', *The Saturday Magazine*, Society for Promoting Christian Knowledge, vols VIII–XVII, 28 May 1836–17 June 1837.

Grant, John, *This Beauteous, Wicked Place: Letters and Journals of John Grant, Gentleman Convict*, edited by Yvonne Cramer, Canberra, National Library of Australia, 2000.

Grose, Major Francis, 'Letter from Sydney, 1792', *Gentleman's Magazine*, LXIII, February 1793, 176.

Heaton, J.H., *Australian Dictionary of Dates Containing History of Australia from 1542 to May, 1879*, f.p. Sydney, George Robertson, 1879, facs. ed. published as *The Bedside Book of Colonial Doings*, Sydney, Angus & Robertson, 1984.

Historical Records of Australia, see Watson, Frederick.

Historical Records of New South Wales, see Bladen, F.M.

Holt, Joseph, *A Rum Story: The Adventures of Joseph Holt Thirteen Years in New South Wales 1800–1812*, edited by Peter O'Shaughnessy, Sydney, Kangaroo Press, 1988.

Howe, George (compiler), *New South Wales Pocket Almanack and Colonial Remembrancer*, facs. ed. Sydney, Trustees of the Public Library of New South Wales, 1966 (f.p. 1806).

Hunter, John, *An Historical Journal of Events at Sydney and at Sea 1787–1792*, Sydney, Angus & Robertson, 1968 (f.p. 1793).

Kelly, Ned, 'The Jerilderie Letter', 1879, in Max Brown, *Australian Son*, Melbourne, Georgian House, 1948, Appendix II, 131–48; and online at <http://www.slv.vic.gov.au/collections/treasures/jerilderieletter1.html>.

King, Philip Gidley, *Lieutenant King's Journal* published in John Hunter, *An Historical Journal of Events at Sydney and at Sea 1787–1792*, Sydney, Angus & Robertson, 1968 (f.p. 1793), 196–298.

Lepailleur, François-Maurice, *Land of a Thousand Sorrows*, translated by F. Murray Greenwood, Melbourne University Press, 1980.

Macarthur, Emmeline, *My Dear Miss Macarthur: The Recollections of Emmeline Macarthur 1828–1911*, edited by Jane de Falbe, Sydney, Kangaroo Press, 1988.

Macleay, Frances Leonora, *Fanny to William: The letters of Frances Leonora Macleay 1812–1836*, edited by Beverley Earnshaw and Joy Hughes, Sydney, Historic Houses Trust of NSW and Macleay Museum, c1993.

Mann, David Dickenson, *The Present Picture of New South Wales 1811*, Sydney, John Ferguson, 1979 (f.p. London 1811).

Mason, Joseph, *Joseph Mason Assigned Convict 1831–1837*, edited by David Kent and Norma Townsend, Melbourne University Press, 1996.

Mathew, Sarah, 'Mrs Felton Mathew's Journal', edited by Olive Harvard, *Journal of the Royal Australian Historical Society*, vol. 29, part 2, 8–128, part 3, 162–95, part 4, 217–43, 1943.

Meredith, Louisa, *Notes and Sketches of New South Wales during a Residence in that Colony from 1839 to 1844*, London, John Murray, 1861 (f.p. 1849).

Mitchell, Sir Thomas Livingstone, *Journal of an Expedition into the Interior of Tropical Australia*, London, Longman, Brown, Green and Longmans, 1848.

Morrison, W. Frederic, *The Aldine Centennial History of New South Wales Illustrated*, Sydney, Aldine Publishing Company, 1888.

Nagle, Joseph, *The Nagle Journal: A Diary of the Life of Jacob Nagle, Sailor, from the Year 1775 to 1841*, New York, Weidenfeld & Nicholson, 1988.

New South Wales Legislative Assembly, *Progress Report from the Select Committee on the Field of Mars Common together with the Proceedings of the Committee and Minutes of Evidence*, in *Votes and Proceedings*, 1861/2, vol. 2, 1323–52 and vol. 5, 1–128.

New South Wales Parliament, *Report from the Select Committee on the Condition of the Aborigines with Appendix, Minutes of Evidence and Replies to a Circular Letter*, Sydney, Government Printing Office, 1845.

Noah, William, *Voyage to Sydney in the Ship Hillsborough 1798–99 and A Description of the Colony 1799*, Sydney, Library of Australian History, 1978.

Oldfield, Roger, 'New Holland', *The South Asian Register*, no. II, January 1828, 101–15.

Oldfield, Roger (ed.), *The South Asian Register*, Sydney, Arthur Hill, no. 1 (October 1827)–no. 4 (December 1828).

Oldfield, Roger, 'A Walk through Sydney in 1828', *The South Asian Register*, no. IV, December 1828, 319–30.

Paine, Daniel, *Journal of Daniel Paine 1794–1797*, edited by R.J.B. Knight and Alan Frost, Sydney, Library of Australian History, 1983.

Péron, M.F., *A Voyage of Discovery to the Southern Hemisphere, Performed by Order of Emperor Napoleon in the Years 1801, 1802, 1803, and 1804* (translated from French), London, Richard Phillips, 1809, facs. ed., Melbourne, March Walsh Publishing, 1975 (f.p. Paris 1807).

Phillip, Arthur, *The Voyage of Arthur Phillip to Botany Bay*, J. Stockdale, London 1789, facs. ed., Hutchinson, Sydney, 1982.

Prieur, François Xavier, *Notes of a Convict of 1838*, translated by George Mackaness, Sydney, Australian Historical Monographs, D.S. Ford, 1949.

Ryan, J.T. 'Toby', *Reminiscences of Australia*, Sydney, facs. ed., Nepean Family History Society, Penrith, 1982 (f.p. George Robertson and Company, c1880).

Sidney, Samuel, *The Three Colonies of Australia*, London, Ingram Cooke and Co., 1852.

Simonov, I.M., 'Journal, April–May, September–November 1820', in Glynn Barratt, *The Russians in Port Jackson 1814–1822*, Canberra, Australian Institute of Aboriginal Studies, 1981, 47–53.

Smyth, Arthur Bowes, 'Extracts from the Journal of Arthur Bowes Smyth . . . April, 1787, to 20th April, 1788', in F.M. Bladen (ed.), *Historical Records of New South Wales Volume II Grose and Patterson*, Sydney, Charles Potter, Government Printer, 1893, 389–94.

Southwell, Daniel, 'Letter to Mrs Southwell, Port Jackson, 14 April 1790', in F.M. Bladen (ed.), *Historical Records of New South Wales, Volume II, Grose and Paterson*, Sydney, Charles Potter, Government Printer, 1893, Appendix E, 661–734.

Suttor, George, *Memoirs of George Suttor, Banksian Collector (1774–1859)*, Australian Historical Monographs, Sydney, D.S. Ford, Printer, 1948.

Tench, Watkin, *A Narrative of the Expedition to Botany Bay* and *A Complete Account of the Settlement at Port Jackson*, published as *Sydney's First Four Years* edited by L.F. Fitzhardinge, Sydney, Library of Australian History, 1979 (f.p. 1789 and 1793).

Thompson, George, 'The Journal of George Thompson, who sailed in the *Royal Admiral*, May 1792 [extracts]', in F.M. Bladen (ed.), *Historical Records of New South Wales: Volume II, Grose and Paterson*, Sydney, Charles Potter, Government Printer, 1893, Appendix E, 793–9.

Watling, Thomas, *Letters from an Exile at Botany Bay to his Aunt in Dumfries*, ed. George Mackaness, Sydney, D.S. Ford, Printer, 1945 (f.p. 1794).

Watson, Frederick (ed.), *Historical Records of Australia*, Series 1, vols 1–10, Sydney, Library Committee of the Commonwealth Parliament, 1914–25.

Wentworth, W.C., *A Statistical, Historical and Political Description of The Colony of New South Wales, and its Dependent Settlements in Van Diemen's Land*, London, G. & W.B. Whittaker, 1819.

West, Obed, *Memoirs of Obed West: A Portrait of Early Sydney*, ed. Edward West Marriot, Bowral, NSW, Barcom Press, 1988 (f.p. *Sydney Morning Herald*, 1878).

West, Obed, *Old and New Sydney*, Sydney, Edward Horden and Sons, 1888 (f.p. *Sydney Morning Herald* 1878).

White, John, *Journal of a Voyage to New South Wales*, Sydney, Angus & Robertson, 1962 (f.p. 1790).

Fiction

Dark, Eleanor, *The Timeless Land*, London, Collins, 1941.

Grenville, Kate, *The Secret River*, Melbourne, Text, 2005.

King, Jonathon, *Mary Bryant: Her Life and Escape from Botany Bay*, Sydney, Simon & Schuster, 2004.

McDonald, Roger, *The Ballad of Desmond Kale*, Sydney, Vintage, 2005.

Malouf, David, *Remembering Babylon*, London, Chatto & Windus, 1993.

Martin, Angela, *Beyond Duck River*, Sydney, Hodder, 2001.

SECONDARY SOURCES

Published secondary sources (books, chapters, articles, reports)

Abbott, Graham, 'The expected cost of the Botany Bay Scheme', *Journal of the Royal Australian Historical Society*, vol. 81, part 2, 1995, 151–66.

Abbott, G.J., 'Governor King's administration', in G.J. Abbott and N.B. Nairn (eds), *Economic Growth in Australia 1788–1821*, 162–75.

Abbott, G.J. and Nairn, N.B. (eds), *Economic Growth in Australia 1788–1821*, Melbourne University Press, 1979 (f.p. 1969).

Aboriginal Housing Company, 'History', n.d. <http://www.ahc.org.au/history/history.html>.

Adamson, D.A. and Fox, M.D., 'Change in Australasian Vegetation since European settlement', in J.M.B. Smith (ed.), *A History of Australasian Vegetation*, Sydney, McGraw Hill, 1982.

Alford, Katrina, *Production or Reproduction: An Economic History of Women in Australia 1788–1850*, Melbourne, Oxford University Press, 1984.

Anderson, Clare, 'Multiple border crossings: "Convicts and Other Persons Escaped from Botany Bay and residing in Calcutta" ', *Journal of Australian Colonial History*, vol. 3, no. 2, October 2001, 1–22.

Anderson, Kay, *Race and the Crisis of Humanism*, London, Routledge, 2007.

Anderson, Warren, *The Cultivation of Whiteness: Science, Health and Racial Destiny in Australia*, Melbourne University Press, 2002.

Angel, Jeff, 'Emerald city? It's only pale green', *Sydney Morning Herald*, 3 July 2000.

Anon., 'Phelps, P.H.F.', *Dictionary of Australian Artists Online*, 2007, <http://www.daao.org.au/main/read/5083>.

Anon., 'William Bligh's chickens', *Push from the Bush*, no. 25, October 1987, 72–93.

Aplin, Graeme, 'People in an alien landscape', in Graeme Aplin (ed.), *A Difficult Infant: Sydney Before Macquarie*, 18–41.

—— (ed.), *A Difficult Infant: Sydney Before Macquarie*, Sydney, UNSW Press, 1988.

—— and Parsons, George, 'Maritime trade: shipping and the early colonial economy', in Graeme Aplin (ed.), *A Difficult Infant: Sydney Before Macquarie*, 1988, 148–63.

Ashton, Paul, and Blackmore, Kate, *Centennial Park: A History*, Sydney, UNSW Press, 1988.

Atkinson, Alan, 'Jeremy Bentham and the Rum Rebellion', *Journal of the Royal Australian Historical Society*, vol. 64, part 1, 1978, 1–13.

——, 'John Macarthur before Australia knew him', *Journal of Australian Studies*, no. 4, June 1979, 22–37.

——, 'Four patterns of convict protest', *Labour History*, no. 37, 1979, 28–50.

——, 'Taking possession: Sydney's first householders', in Graeme Aplin (ed.), *A Difficult Infant: Sydney Before Macquarie*, 1988, 72–90.

——, *Camden*, Melbourne, Oxford University Press, 1988.

——, 'The pioneers who left early', *The Push*, no. 29, 1991, 110–16.

——, *The Europeans in Australia: A History*, vol. 1, Melbourne, Oxford University Press, 1997.

——, *History and the love of places*, Armidale, N.S.W., University of New England, 1999.

Attenbrow, Val, *Sydney's Aboriginal Past: Investigating the Archaeological and Historical Records*, Sydney, UNSW Press, 2002.

—— and Steele, Dominic, 'Fishing in Port Jackson, New South Wales: more than met the eye?', *Antiquity*, vol. 69, 1995, 47–60.

Auburn Municipal Council, *Liberty Plains: A History of Auburn NSW*, Centenary Edition, Auburn, the Council, 1992.

Australian Heritage Commission, *Places in the Heart: Australians Writing About their Favourite Heritage Places*, Canberra, the Commission, 1998.

Australian Museum, 'Eastern Quoll, *Dasyurus viverrinus*', online at <http://www.livingharbour.net/mammals/quoll.htm>.

Australian National Dictionary see Ramson, W.S.

Aveling, Marian, 'Gender in early New South Wales society', *The Push from the Bush*, no. 24, April 1987, 31–41.

——, 'Imagining New South Wales as a gendered society 1783–1821', *Australian Historical Studies*, vol. 98, 1992, 1–12.

——, 'Bending the bars: convict women and the state', in Kay Saunders and Raymond Evans (eds), *Gender Relations in Australia: Domination and Negotiation*, Sydney, Harcourt Brace Jovanovich, 1992, 144–57.

Barkley, Jan and Nichols, Michelle, *Hawkesbury 1794–1994: The First 200 Years of the Second Colonisation*, Windsor NSW, Hawkesbury City Council, 1994.

Barnard, Marjorie, 'Piper, John (1773–1851)', *Australian Dictionary of Biography*, vol. 2, Melbourne University Press, 1967, 334–5.

Barratt, Glynn, *The Russians in Port Jackson 1814–1822*, Canberra, Australian Institute of Aboriginal Studies, 1981.

Baskerville, Bruce, 'The Hawkesbury commons: the beginnings of conservation and democracy in colonial New South Wales', *Journal of the Hawkesbury Historical Society*, no. 1, 2006, 57–66.

Beale, Bob and Dayton, Leigh, 'Sydney found to be consuming 35 times its share of resources', *Sydney Morning Herald*, 18 March 1996.

Beck, Deborah, *Hope in Hell: A History of Darlinghurst Gaol and the National Art School*, Sydney, Allen & Unwin, 2005.

Bell, Diane, *Daughters of the Dreaming*, Melbourne, Spinifex, 2002 (f.p. 1983).

Benson, Doug and Howell, Jocelyn, *Taken For Granted: The Bushland of Sydney and its Suburbs*, Sydney, Kangaroo Press, 1995.

——, 'Cumberland Plain Woodland ecology then and now: interpretation of and implications from the work of Robert Brown and others', *Cunninghamia*, vol. 7, no 4, 2002, 631–50.

Bertie, Charles H., 'Captain Cook and Botany Bay', *Journal of the Royal Australian Historical Society*, vol. 10, part 5, 1924, 231–78.

Berzins, Baiba, *The Coming of the Strangers: Life in Australia 1788–1822*, Sydney, Collins and State Library of New South Wales, 1988.

Bickel, Lennard, *Australia's First Lady: The Story of Elizabeth Macarthur*, Sydney, Allen & Unwin, 1996.

Bird, Delys, 'The settling of the English', in Bruce Bennett and Jennifer Strauss, *The Oxford Literary History of Australia*, Melbourne, Oxford University Press, 1998, 26–7.

Birmingham, John, *Leviathan: The Unauthorised Biography of Sydney*, Sydney, Random House, 1999.

Blainey, Geoffrey, *The Tyranny of Distance*, Melbourne, Sun Books, 1976 (f.p. 1967).

Blomfield, Geoffrey, *Baal Belbora: The End of the Dancing*, Alternative Publishing Cooperative, Sydney, 1981.

Blumin, Stuart, *The Emergence of the Middle Class: Social Experience in the American City 1760–1900*, New York, Cambridge University Press, 1989.

Blunden, 'Wallis, James (1785?–1858)', *Australian Dictionary of Biography*, vol. 2, Melbourne University Press, 1967, 568–9.

Bolton, Geoffrey, *Spoils and Spoilers: A History of Australians Shaping Their Environment*, Sydney, Allen & Unwin, 1992.

Bonwick, James, *Australia's First Preacher: The Reverend Richard Johnson*, London, Sampson Low, Maston & Co, 1898.

Bonyhady, Tim, *Images in Opposition: Australian Landscape Painting 1801–1890*, Melbourne, Oxford University Press, 1985.

——, *The Colonial Earth*, Melbourne, Miegunyah Press, 2000.

Borsay, Peter, 'The English urban renaissance: the development of provincial culture', in Peter Borsay (ed.), *The Eighteenth Century Town*, 1990, 159–87.

——, 'Health and leisure resorts 1700–1840', in P. Clark (ed.), *Cambridge Urban History of Britain*, vol. 2, 1540–1840, Cambridge University Press, 2000, 775–803.

——, 'From Bath to Poundbury: The rise, fall and rise of polite urban space 1700–2000', in Roger Leech and Adrian Green (eds), *Cities in the World 1500–2000*, London, Maney, 2006, 97–116.

—— (ed.), *The Eighteenth Century Town: A Reader in English Urban History 1688–1820*, London, Longman, 1990.

Bowd, D.G., *Macquarie Country: A History of the Hawkesbury*, Sydney, Library of Australian History, 1994.

——, 'Settling in', in Warner, *Over-Halling the Colony*, 1990, 67–70.

Bowdler, Sandra, 'Hook, line and dilly bag: an interpretation of an Australian coastal shell midden', *Mankind*, 10:4 (December 1976), 248–57.

Boyce, James, *Van Diemen's Land*, Melbourne, Black Inc. Books, 2008.

Bremer, Annette, 'Pathless wilds: white women, walking and colonial dis/order', *Australian Studies*, vol. 15, no. 1, Summer 2000, 95–110.

Brewer, E. Cobham, *Dictionary of Phrase and Fable*, 1894, online at <http://www.infoplease.com/dictionary.html>.

Bridges, Peter, *Foundations of Identity: Building Early Sydney 1788–1822*, Sydney, Hale & Iremonger, 1995.

Broadbent, James, 'The push east: Woolloomooloo Hill, the first suburb', in Max Kelly (ed.), *Sydney: City of Suburbs*, Sydney, UNSW Press, 1987, 12–29.

——, *Francis Greenway, Architect*, Sydney, Historic Houses Trust of NSW, 1997.

——, *The Australian Colonial House: Architecture and Society in New South Wales, 1788–1842*, Sydney, Hordern House and Historic Houses Trust of NSW, 1997.

——, 'Macquarie's domain', in James Broadbent and Joy Hughes (eds), *The Age of Macquarie*, 1992, 3–18.

——, 'Building in the colony', in James Broadbent and Joy Hughes (eds), *The Age of Macquarie*, 1992, 157–72.

—— and Hughes, Joy (eds), *The Age of Macquarie*, Melbourne University Press, 1992.

——, Rickard, Suzanne and Steven, Margaret, *India, China, Australia: Trade and Society 1788–1850*, Sydney, Historic Houses Trust of NSW, 2003.

Brock, Peggy, 'Skirmishes in Aboriginal history', *Aboriginal History*, vol. 28, 2004, 207–25.

Brook, Jack, *Shut Out from the World: The Hawkesbury Aborigines Reserve and Mission 1889–1946*, Berowra Heights, Deerubbin Press, 1994.

——, 'The forlorn hope: Bennelong and Yemmerrawannie go to England', *Australian Aboriginal Studies*, 2001, 1, 36–47.

—— and Kohen, James L., *The Parramatta Native Institution and the Black Town: A History*, Sydney, UNSW Press, 1991.

Broome, Richard, *Aboriginal Australians: Black Responses to White Dominance 1788–1994*, Sydney, Allen & Unwin, 1994 (f.p. 1982).

——, *Aboriginal Victorians: A History Since 1800*, Sydney, Allen & Unwin, 2005.

Bunn, Ken, 'Weeds of roadsides and grazing lands', 2004, online at <http://www.lhccrems. nsw.gov.au/weeds_cd/roadgraz.html>.

Butlin, Noel, *Our Original Aggression: Aboriginal Populations of Southeastern Australia, 1788–1850*, Sydney, George Allen & Unwin, 1983.

——, *Forming a Colonial Economy: Australia 1810–1850*, Melbourne, Cambridge University Press, 1994.

Butlin, S.J., *Foundations of the Australian Monetary System 1788–1851*, Sydney University Press, 1968 (f.p. 1953).

Byrne, Denis, 'The ethos of return: erasure and reinstatement of Aboriginal visibility in the Australian historical landscape', *Historical Archaeology*, vol. 37, no. 1, 2003, 73–86.

——, 'Nervous landscapes: race and space in Australia', *Journal of Social Archaeology*, vol. 3, no. 2, 2003, 169–93.

——, 'Segregated landscapes: the heritage of racial segregation in New South Wales', *Historic Environment—Islands of Vanishment*, vol. 17, no. 1, 2003, 14.

——, *Surface Collection: Archaeological Travels in Southeast Asia*, Lanham, Altamira Press, 2007.

——, Brayshaw, Helen and Ireland, Tracey, *Social Significance: A Discussion Paper*, Sydney, New South Wales National Parks and Wildlife Service, 2001.

Byrne, Paula J., *Criminal Law and Colonial Subject: New South Wales 1810–1830*, Melbourne, Cambridge University Press, 1993.

——, 'A colonial female economy', *Social History*, vol. 24, part 3, October 1999, 281–93.

——, 'Convict women reconsidered . . . and reconsidered', *History Australia*, vol. 2, no. 1, November 2004, online at <http://publications.epress.monash.edu/doi/full/10.2104/ ha040013>.

Calaby, John, 'The natural history drawings', in Bernard Smith and Alwyne Wheeler (eds), *The Art of the First Fleet and Other Early Australian Drawings*, 140–97.

Callaway, Anita, *Visual Ephemera: Theatrical Art in Nineteenth Century Australia*, Sydney, UNSW Press, 2000.

Camm, J.C.R. and McQuilton, John (eds), *Australia: A Historical Atlas*, Sydney, Fairfax, Syme & Weldon Associates, 1987.

Campbell, J.F., 'The valley of the Tank Stream', *Journal of the Royal Australian Historical Society*, vol. 10, 1924, 63–103.

——, 'The dawn of rural settlement in Australia, *Journal of the Royal Australian Historical Society*, vol. 11, part 2, 1925, 83–134.

——, 'Rose Hill government farm and the founding of Parramatta', *Journal of the Royal Australian Historical Society*, vol. 12, part 6, 1925, 353–80.

——, 'The early history of Sydney University grounds', *Journal of the Royal Australian Historical Society*, vol. 16, part 4, 1930, 274–93.

Campbell, Judy, *Invisible Invaders: Smallpox and Other Diseases in Aboriginal Australia 1780–1880*, Melbourne University Press, 2002.

Campbell, Keith, 'Broger' (c1800–1830)', *Australian Dictionary of Biography*, supplementary vol., Melbourne University Press, 2005, 48–9.

——, 'Broughton (c1798–c1850)', *Australian Dictionary of Biography*, supplementary Volume, Melbourne University Press, 2005, 48–9.

Campbell, Walter S., 'The use and abuse of stimulants in the early days of settlement in New South Wales', *Journal of the Royal Australian Historical Society*, vol. 18, 1932, 74–99.

Canterbury City Council, 'Indigenous mosaic', c2004, online at <http://www.canterbury.nsw.gov.au/www/html>/1251-indigenous-mosaic.asp>.

Carey, Hilary M. and Roberts, David, 'Smallpox and the Baiame Waganna of Wellington Valley, New South Wales, 1829–1840: the earliest nativist movement in Aboriginal Australia', *Ethnohistory*, vol. 49, no. 4, 2002, 821–69.

Carlin, Scott, *Elizabeth Bay House: A History and Guide*, Sydney, Historic Houses Trust of NSW, 2000.

Carr, Harry, Pullen, Noelene, Wilson, Pam and Clark, Bruce, *Heritage Tour of the Hills District, Castle Hill, NSW*, Hills District Historical Society, 1996.

Carter, Paul, 'Encounters', in Peter Emmett (ed.), *Fleeting Encounters: Pictures and Chronicles of the First Fleet*, 13–18.

Clark, C.M.H., *A History of Australia*, vol. 1, Melbourne University Press, 1974 (f.p. 1962).

Clark, Manning, *A Short History of Australia*, New York, Mentor Books, 1963.

Clark, Mary Shelley and Clark, Jack, *The Islands of Sydney Harbour*, Sydney, Kangaroo Press, 2000.

Clegg, John and Ghantous, Simon, 'Rock-painting of exotic animals in the Sydney Basin, New South Wales, Australia', *Before Farming*, vol. 1, no. 7, 2003, 257–66.

Cleland, J.B. and Kiss, Carol, 'Notes and Comments', *Mankind*, vol. 6, no. 9, June 1967, 432–3.

Clendinnen, Inga, *Reading the Holocaust*, Melbourne, Text, 1998.

——, *Dancing with Strangers*, Melbourne, Text, 2003.

——, 'The history question: who owns the past?', *Quarterly Essay*, Issue 23, 2006, 1–72.

Coleman, Deirdre, 'Inscrutable history or incurable romanticism? Inga Clendinnen's *Dancing with Strangers*', *Heat*, vol. 8, 2004, 201–13.

——, *Romantic Colonization and British Slavery*, Cambridge, Cambridge University Press, 2005.

Colley, Sarah, 'Engendering pre- and post-contact Australian archaeology: a theoretical challenge', in M. Casey, D. Donlan, J. Hope and S. Wellfare (eds), *Redefining Archaeology: Feminist Perspectives*, 1998, Canberra, ANU Publications, 9–12.

——, *Uncovering Australia: Archaeology, Indigenous People and the Public*, Sydney, Allen & Unwin, 2002.

Coltheart, Lenore, 'The landscape of public works', in Lenore Coltheart (ed.), *Significant Sites: History and Public Works in New South Wales*, 160–82.

——, (ed.), *Significant Sites: History and Public Works in New South Wales*, Sydney, Hale & Iremonger, 1989.

Connor, John, *The Australian Frontier Wars 1788–1838*, Sydney, UNSW Press, 2000.

Conway, Jill, 'Macarthur, Elizabeth (1766–1850)', *Australian Dictionary of Biography*, vol. 2, Melbourne University Press, 1967, 144–7.

——, 'Riley, Alexander (1778?–1833)', *Australian Dictionary of Biography*, vol. 2, Melbourne University Press, 1967, 379–81.

Coupe, Robert, *Australian Bushrangers*, Sydney, New Holland, 1998.

Coupe, Sheena, *Concord: A Centenary History*, Concord NSW, Concord Municipal Council, 1983.

Cowan, Henry J., *From Wattle & Daub to Concrete and Steel: The Engineering Heritage of Australia's Buildings*, Melbourne, Melbourne University Press, 1998.

Cowell, Joyce and Best, Roderick, *Where First Fleeters Lie*, Sydney, Fellowship of First Fleeters, 1989.

Creamer, Howard, 'Aboriginality in New South Wales: beyond the image of cultureless outcasts', in Jeremy R. Beckett (ed.), *Past and Present: The Construction of Aboriginality*, Canberra, Aboriginal Studies Press, 1988, 45–62.

Cronon, William, *Nature's Metropolis: Chicago and the Great West*, New York, W.W. Norton, 1992.

Croucher, Tom, *Years of Hardship: The Story of Catherine Edward, A Pioneer of Parramatta and the Hawkesbury*, Sydney, published by the author, 2002.

Cumming, Scott, 'Chimneys and change: Post-European environmental impact in Green Square', in Grace Karskens and Melita Rogowsky (eds), *Histories of Green Square*, 31–40.

Cunningham, Chris, *The Blue Mountains Rediscovered*, Sydney, Kangaroo Press, 1996.

——, 'Fire history of the Blue Mountains', in J. Powell (ed.), *The Improvers' Legacy: Environmental Studies of the Hawkesbury*, 1998, 39–48.

Curby, Pauline, *Seven Miles from Sydney: A History of Manly*, Sydney, Manly Council, 2001.

Czernis-Ryl, Eva, 'Early Australian silver statuette: a story of Julius Hogarth and Ricketty Dick', in *Australian Antiques & Fine Arts Dealers' Fair*, Sydney, James A. Johnson & Associates, 1996, 6–10.

Daly, Maurie and Pritchard, Bill, 'Sydney: Australia's financial and corporate capital', in John Connell (ed.), *Sydney: The Emergence of a World City*, Melbourne, Oxford University Press, 2000, 144–66.

Dangar Island Historical Society, *A Guide to Historic Dangar Island: Island Gem of the Hawkesbury*, Dangar Island, the Society, 2000.

Daniels, Kay, *Convict Women*, Sydney, Allen & Unwin, 1998.

Dark, Eleanor, 'Bennelong (1764?–1813)', *Australian Dictionary of Biography*, vol. 1, Melbourne University Press, 1966, 84–5.

Darley, Gillian, *The Idea of the Village*, exhibition catalogue, Arts Council of Great Britain, 1976.

——, *Villages of Vision*, London, Paladin, 1978.

Dash, Alan M., 'Phillip's exploration of the Hawkesbury River', in Jocelyn Powell and Lorraine Banks (eds), *Hawkesbury River History: Governor Phillip, Exploration and Early Settlement*, Wisemans Ferry, Dharug and Lower Hawkesbury Historical Society, 1990, 11–30.

Davison, Graeme, 'The first suburban nation?', *Journal of Urban History*, vol. 22, no. 1, 1995, 40–74.

——, 'The past and future of the Australian suburb', in Louise C. Johnson (ed.), *Suburban Dreaming: An Interdisciplinary Approach to Australian Cities*, Geelong, Deakin University Press, 1996, 99–113.

——, 'From urban gaol to bourgeois suburb: the transformation of neighborhood in early colonial Sydney', *Journal of Urban History*, vol. 32, no. 5, 2006, 741–60.

Day, David, *Smugglers and Sailors: A Customs History of Australia*, Canberra, Australian Government Printing Service, 1992.

——, *Claiming a Continent: A New History of Australia*, Sydney, HarperCollins, 2001 (f.p. 1996).

Deirmendjian, Gary, *Sydney Sandstone*, Sydney, Craftsman House, c2002.

Dening, Greg, *Mr Bligh's Bad Language: Power, Passion and Theatre on the Bounty*, Cambridge, Cambridge University Press, 1988.

de Vries-Evans, Susanna, *Historic Sydney as Seen by its Early Artists*, Sydney, Angus & Robertson, 1983.

Dixon, Robert, *The Course of Empire: Neo-Classical Culture in New South Wales 1788–1860*, Melbourne, Oxford University Press, 1986.

Donaldson, Ian and Donaldson, Tamsin (eds), *Seeing the First Australians*, Sydney, George Allen & Unwin, 1985.

Donaldson, Tamsin, 'Hearing the first Australians', in Ian Donaldson and Tamsin Donaldson (eds), *Seeing the First Australians*, Sydney, George Allen & Unwin, 1985, 76–91.

Doran, Jason, 'The pre-European environmental landscape of Green Square', in Grace Karskens and Melita Rogowsky (eds), *Histories of Green Square*, 23–30.

Doukakis, Anna, *The Aboriginal People, Parliament & 'Protection'*, Sydney, The Federation Press, 2006.

Dow, Gwyneth, *Samuel Terry: The Botany Bay Rothschild*, Sydney University Press, 1974.

Dunlop, E.W., 'Blaxcell, Garnham (1778–1817)', *Australian Dictionary of Biography 1788–1850*, vol. 1, Melbourne University Press, 1966, 115.

Dunsdorfs, Edgar, *The Australian Wheat-Growing Industry 1788–1948*, Melbourne, Cambridge University Press, 1956.

Dyer, Colin, *The French Explorers and the Aboriginal Australians*, St Lucia, University of Queensland Press, 2005.

Dyster, Barrie, *Servant and Master: Building and Running the Grand Houses of Sydney 1788–1850*, Sydney, UNSW Press, 1989.

——, 'Bungling a courthouse: convict workplace reform', *Journal of the Royal Australian Historical Society*, vol. 93, part 1, 2007, 1–21.

Eddy, John J., 'Empire and politics', in James Broadbent and Joy Hughes (eds), *The Age of Macquarie*, 35–47.

Edwards, Coral, 'Footsteps that went before', in Bill Bottomley (ed.), *By Force of Maul and Wedge: Talking About the Great North Road*, Kulnura, NSW, Wirrimbirra Workshop, 1996, 88–91.

Edwards, J.G., 'History and reminiscences', *Evening News*, 18–22 July 1921.

Elliot, Jane, 'Was there a convict dandy? Convict consumer interests in Sydney 1788–1815', *Australian Historical Studies*, vol. 26, no. 104, 1995, 373–92.

Ellis, M.H., *Lachlan Macquarie: His Life, Adventures and Times*, Sydney, Dymocks, 1947.

——, *John Macarthur*, Sydney, Angus & Robertson, 1955.

Else Mitchell, R., 'George Caley: his life and work', *Journal of the Royal Australian Historical Society*, vol. 25, part 4, 1939, 437–542.

——, 'The wild cattle of the Cowpastures', *Journal of the Royal Australian Historical Society*, vol. 25, part 2, 1940, 128–30.

Emmett, Peter, *Fleeting Encounters: Pictures and Chronicles of the First Fleet*, Sydney, Historic Houses Trust, 1995.

Erickson, Carolly, *The Girl from Botany Bay: The True Story of the Convict Mary Broad and her Extraordinary Escape*, Sydney, Macmillan, 2004.

Fels, Marie, *Good Men and True: the Aboriginal Police of the Port Phillip District 1837–1853*, Melbourne University Press, 1988.

Findlay, Elizabeth, *Arcadian Quest: William Westall's Australian Sketches*, Canberra, National Library of Australia, 1998.

Fitzgerald, Ross and Hearn, Mark, *Bligh, Macarthur and the Rum Rebellion*, Sydney, Kangaroo Press, 1988.

Fitzgerald, Shirley, *Rising Damp: Sydney 1870–1890*, Melbourne, Oxford University Press, 1987.

—— and Golder, Hilary, *Pyrmont and Ultimo: Under Siege*, Sydney, Hale & Iremonger, 1994.

—— and Keating, Chris, *Millers Point: The Urban Village*, Sydney, Hale & Iremonger, 1991.

Fitzmaurice, Andrew, 'The genealogy of *Terra Nullius*', *Australian Historical Studies*, vol. 38, no. 129, 1–15.

FitzSimons, Peter, 'Place in time: the Rocks', *The (Sydney) Magazine*, no. 25, May 2005, 25.

Flannery, Tim, *The Future Eaters: An Ecological History of the Australian Lands and People*, Sydney, Reed Books, 1994.

——, 'Beautiful lies: population and the environment in Australia', *Quarterly Essay*, Issue 9, 2003, 1–73.

—— (ed.), *The Explorers*, Melbourne, Text, 1998.

—— (ed.), *The Birth of Sydney*, Melbourne, Text, 1999.

Fletcher, Brian, 'The development of small scale farming in New South Wales under Governor Hunter', *Journal of the Royal Australian Historical Society*, vol. 50, part 1, 1964, 2–31.

——, 'Harris, John (1754–1838)', *Australian Dictionary of Biography*, vol. 1, Melbourne University Press, 1966, 519–20.

——, 'Grose, Paterson and the settlement of the Hawkesbury 1794–1795', *Journal of the Royal Australian Historical Society*, vol. 51, part 4, 1965, 341–9.

——, 'Ruse, James (1760–1837)', *Australian Dictionary of Biography*, vol. 2, Melbourne University Press, 1967, 404–5.

——, *Landed Enterprise and Penal Society: A History of Farming and Grazing in New South Wales before 1821*, Sydney University Press, 1976.

——, 'Agriculture', in G.J. Abbott and N.B. Nairn, *Economic Growth of Australia 1788–1821*, 1979, 191–218.

——, *Ralph Darling: A Governor Maligned*, Melbourne, Oxford University Press, 1984.

Flood, Josephine, *Archaeology of the Dreamtime*, Collins, Sydney, 1983.

——, *Rock Art of the Dreamtime*, Sydney, Angus & Robertson, 1997.

Flynn, Michael, *The Second Fleet: Britain's Grim Convict Armada of 1790*, Sydney, Library of Australian History, 1993.

——, *Settlers and Seditionists*, Sydney, Angela Lind, 1994.

Foley, Dennis and Maynard, Rickey, *Repossession of our Spirit: Traditional Owners of Northern Sydney*, Canberra, Aboriginal History Inc., Monograph no. 7, 2001.

Fookes, C.H.R., *Milton Abbas, Dorset*, Milton Abbas, 1999 (f.p. 1971).

Ford, Lisa, 'Traversing the frontiers of the history wars: the plurality of settler sovereignty in early New South Wales', Sydney, Macquarie Law Working Paper No. 2008-1, SSRN, <http://papers.ssrn.com/sol3/papers.cfm?abstract_id=1090381>.

——, 'Indigenous policy and its historical occlusions: the North American and global contexts of Australian settlement', *Australian Indigenous Law Review*, forthcoming, 2009.

—— and Salter, Brent, 'From pluralism to territorial sovereignty: the 1816 trial of Mowatty in the Superior Court of New South Wales', *Indigenous Law Journal*, forthcoming, 2009.

Foucault, Michel, *Discipline and Punish: The Birth of the Prison*, translated by Alan Sheridan, Harmondsworth, Penguin, 1977 (f.p. 1975).

Fowlie, Thomas, *The History of Granville 1919*, Granville, NSW, Granville Historical Society, 2001, MS 1919, ML A1492.

Fox, Paul, *Clearings: Six Colonial Gardeners and Their Landscapes*, Melbourne, Miegunyah Press, 2005.

Franklin, Adrian, *Animal Nation: The True Stories of Animals and Australia*, Sydney, UNSW Press, 2006.

Freame, William, 'Reminiscences of a district veteran', *Nepean Times*, 1912, republished by Penrith City Council, 1984.

——, 'Michael Long', *Nepean Times*, 27 February 1926.

Freeland, J.M., *Architecture in Australia: A History*, Melbourne, Penguin, 1982 (f.p. 1968).

Frith, Susannah, 'From tanning to planning: an industrial history of Green Square', in Grace Karskens and Melita Rogowsky (eds), *Histories of Green Square*, 49–54.

Frost, Alan, 'New South Wales as *terra nullius*: the British denial of Aboriginal land rights', *Australian Historical Studies*, vol. 19, no. 77, 1981, 513–23.

——, 'Going away, coming home', in John Hardy and Alan Frost (eds), *Studies from Terra Australis to Australia*, Canberra, Australian Academy for the Humanities, 1989, 219–32.

——, 'The growth of settlement', in Bernard Smith and Alwynne Wheeler (eds), *Art of the First Fleet and Other Early Australian Drawings*', 1988, 109–39.

——, *Botany Bay Mirages: Illusions of Australia's Convict Beginnings*, Melbourne University Press, 1995.

——, *The Global Reach of Empire*, Melbourne, Miegunyah Press, 2003.

Gammage, Bill, *Australia Under Aboriginal Management*, Fifteenth Barry Andrew Memorial Lecture, Canberra, UNSW Australian Defence Force Academy, 2002.

Gandevia, B. and Cobley, J., 'Mortality at Sydney Cove, 1788–1792', *Australia New Zealand Journal of Medicine*, vol. 4, 1974, 111–25.

BIBLIOGRAPHY

Gapps, Stephen, 'Convict clothing in 1804 Sydney', Battle of Vinegar Hill Reenactment 2004—Pamphlet No. 1, online at <http://www.battleofvinegarhill.com.au/register.htm>.

Gascoigne, John, *The Enlightenment and the Origins of European Australia*, Cambridge, Cambridge University Press, 2002.

Geertz, Clifford, 'Thick description: towards an interpretative theory of culture', in his *The Interpretation of Cultures*, London, Hutchinson, 1975.

George, Vance, *Fairfield: A History of the District*, Fairfield City Council, 1982.

Gergis, Joëlle, Garden, Don and Fenby, Clare, 'The influence of climate on the first European settlement of Australia: A comparison of weather journals, documentary data and Palaeoclimate Records 1788–1793', *Environmental History*, vol. 15, 2010, 485–507.

Gibson, Ross, 'Ocean settlements', *Meanjin*, vol. 53, no. 4, 1994, 665–77.

Gilbert, Kevin, *Aboriginal Sovereignty, Justice, the Law of the Land*, Canberra, Burrambinga Books, 1993, c1987.

Gilbert, Lionel, *The Royal Botanic Gardens, Sydney: A History 1816–1985*, Melbourne, Oxford University Press, 1986.

Girouard, Marc, *Cities and People: A Social and Architectural History*, New Haven, Yale University Press, 1985.

Goodall, Heather, 'Colonialism and catastrophe: contested memories of nuclear testing and measles epidemics at Ernabella', in Kate Darian-Smith and Paula Hamilton (eds), *Memory and History in Twentieth Century Australia*, Melbourne, Oxford University Press, 1994, 55–76.

——, *Invasion to Embassy: Land and Aboriginal Politics in New South Wales, 1770–1972*, Sydney, Allen & Unwin, 1996.

Gosden, Chris, *Archaeology and Colonialism: Cultural Contact from 5000 BC to the Present*, Cambridge, Cambridge University Press, 2004.

Gray, A.J., 'Social life at Sydney Cove in 1788–1789', *Journal of the Royal Australian Historical Society*, vol. 44, no. 6, 1958, 374–98.

Gray, Nancy, 'Close, Edward Charles (1790–1866)', *Australian Dictionary of Biography*, vol. 1, Melbourne University Press, 1966, 231–232.

Grenville, Kate, 'The novelist as barbarian', National Library of Australia, c2005, online at <http://www.nla.gov.au/events/history/papers/Kate_Grenville%20.html>.

——, *Searching for the Secret River*, Melbourne, Text, 2006.

——, 'History and fiction' (response to reviews by Clendinnen and McKenna), January 2007, online at <http://www.users.bigpond.com/kgrenville/index.html>.

Griffiths, Tom, 'Past silences: Aborigines and convicts in our history-making', in Richard White and Penny Russell (eds), *Pastiche I: Reflections on 19th Century Australia*, Sydney, Allen & Unwin, 1994, 5–23.

——, *Hunters and Collectors: The Antiquarian Imagination in Australia*, Melbourne, Cambridge University Press, 1996.

——, 'The poetics and practicalities of writing', in Ann Curthoys and Anne McGrath (eds), *Writing Histories: Imagination and Narration*, Melbourne, Monash Publications in History, 2000, 1–13.

——, *Forests of Ash: An Environmental History*, Melbourne, Cambridge University Press, 2001.

——, 'Truth and fiction: Judith Wright as historian', in *Australian Book Review*, issue 283, 2006.

——, *Slicing the Silence: Voyaging to Antarctica*, Sydney, UNSW Press, 2007.

Grimshaw, Pat, Lake, Marilyn, McGrath, Ann and Quartly, Marian, *Creating a Nation*, Melbourne, McPhee Gribble, 1994.

Grose, Kelvin, 'What happened to the Clergy Reserves of New South Wales?', *Journal of the Royal Australian Historical Society*, vol. 72, part 2, 1986, 92–103.

Gunn, J.S., 'The Australian Bushranging Society', *Journal of the Royal Australian Historical Society*, vol. 68, part 1, June 1982, 59–66.

Gutman, Herbert, *Work, Culture and Society in Industrializing America*, Oxford, Blackwell, 1977.

Hainsworth, D.R., *Builders and Adventurers: The Traders and the Emergence of the Colony 1788–1821*, Melbourne, Cassell, 1968.

——, *The Sydney Traders: Simeon Lord and his Contemporaries 1788–1821*, Melbourne, Cassell Australia, 1972.

Hall, Colin Michael, *Wasteland to World Heritage: Preserving Australia's Wilderness*, Melbourne University Press, 1992.

Hancock, W.K., *Australia*, London, Benn, 1930.

Hansen, David, 'Death dance', *Australian Book Review*, no. 290, April 2007, 27–32.

Harden, J. David, 'Liberty caps and liberty trees', *Past and Present*, no. 146, February 1995, 66–102.

Hardy, Bobby, *Early Hawkesbury Settlers*, Sydney, Kangaroo Press, 1985.

Hawarth, R.J., 'The shaping of Sydney by its urban geology', *Quarternary International*, vol. 103 (2003), 41–55.

Hawkesbury Historical Society, 'Flood levels of the Hawkesbury River recorded at Windsor Bridge for floods 9.15 (30 feet) and over', online at <http://www.hawkesburyhistory.org.au/articles/floods.html>.

Hawkins, Ralph, *The Convict Timbergetters of Pennant Hills: A History & Biographical Register*, Hornsby (NSW), Hornsby Shire Historical Society, 1994.

——, Pullen, Noelene and Wilson, Pam, *Castle Hill and its Government Farm 1801–1811*, Castle Hill, NSW, Hills District Historical Society, 2004.

Hay, Ashley, *Gum: The Story of Eucalypts and their Champions*, Sydney, Duffy & Snellgrove, 2002.

Hayden, Dolores, *The Power of Place: Urban Landscapes as Public History*, Cambridge, Mass., The MIT Press, 1996.

Healey, Chris, *From the Ruins of Colonialism: History as Social Memory*, Melbourne, Cambridge University Press, 1997.

Heney, Helen, *Dear Fanny: Women's Letters to and from New South Wales 1788–1857*, Canberra, Australian National University Press, 1985.

Hetherington, Michelle and Doherty, Seona (eds), *The World Upside Down: Australia 1788–1830*, Canberra, National Library of Australia, 2000.

Hiatt, L.R., 'Mystery at Port Hacking', *Mankind*, vol. 6, no. 7, June 1966, 313–17.

——, 'Bennelong and Omai', *Australian Aboriginal Studies*, no. 2, 2004, 87–9.

Higginbotham, Peter, 'The workhouse', 2006, online at <http://www.workhouses.org.uk/index.html?buildings/buildings.shtml>.

Hills District Historical Society, *The Beginnings of the Hills District*, Castle Hill, Hills District Historical Society, 1987.

Hinkson, Melinda, *Aboriginal Sydney: A Guide to Important Places of the Past and the Present*, Canberra, Aboriginal Studies Press, 2001.

——, 'Exploring "Aboriginal" sites in Sydney: a shifting politics of place?', *Aboriginal History*, vol. 26, 2002, 62–77.

Hirst, John, *Convict Society and its Enemies: A History of Early New South Wales*, Sydney, George Allen & Unwin, 1983.

Hirst, Warwick, *Great Convict Escapes in Colonial Australia*, Sydney, Kangaroo Press, 2003.

Historic Houses Trust of NSW, *Hyde Park Barracks Museum Guidebook*, Sydney, Historic Houses Trust of NSW, 2003.

Hogarth, Murray, 'I've seen the futures, and one works', *Sydney Morning Herald*, 8 March 1999.

Holland, John, *Growing Up on the Hawkesbury: Recollections of a 'River Rat'*, Berowra Heights NSW, Deerubbin Press, 1998.

Holok, Gabriella, 'The evolution of an exhibition: Experiment Farm Cottage cellar display', *National Trust Magazine*, autumn 2007, 14–15.

Horton, David, *The Pure State of Nature*, Sydney, Allen & Unwin, 2000.

Howell, Jocelyn, McDougall, Lyn and Benson, Doug, *Riverside Plants of the Hawkesbury–Nepean*, Sydney, Royal Botanic Gardens, 1995.

Hughes, Joy (ed.), *Demolished Houses of Sydney*, Sydney, Historic Houses Trust of NSW, 1999.

Hughes, Robert, *The Fatal Shore: A History of the Transportation of Convicts to Australia 1787–1868*, London, Collins Harvill, 1987.

Huntington, H.W.H., 'History of Parramatta and District', published as a serial in *Cumberland Argus and Fruitgrower's Advocate*, 19 August 1899 et seq., bound volume of press cuttings, ML.

Huntington, Janice Ruse, *My Mother Reread Me Tenderley: The Life of James Ruse*, Rydalmere (NSW), Valiant Efforts Pty Ltd, 2002.

Hutton, D. and Connors, L., *A History of the Australian Environmental Movement*, Melbourne, Cambridge University Press, 1999.

Hutton Neve, M., *The Forgotten Valley: History of the Macdonald Valley and St Albans NSW*, Sydney, Library of Australian History, 1987.

Illert, Chris, *The Mayran Clan of the Gayn-d'hay-ungara*, East Corrimal NSW, C. Illert and D. Reverberi, 1998.

Ireland, Tracey, 'The absence of ghosts: landscape and identity in the archaeology of Australia's settler culture', *Historical Archaeology*, vol. 37, part 1, 2003, 56–72.

Irvine, Nance, *Mary Reibey, Molly Incognita: A Biography of Mary Reibey 1777–1855 and her World*, Sydney, Library of Australian History, 1982.

—— (ed.), *Dear Cousin: The Reibey Letters: Twenty-two Letters of Mary Reibey, Her Children and their Descendants, 1792–1901*, Sydney, Hale & Iremonger, 1992.

Irving, Robert, 'Georgian Australia', in Robert Irving (ed.), *The History and Design of the Australian House*, Melbourne, Oxford University Press, 1985, 32–63.

Isaac, Rhys, *The Transformation of Virginia, 1740–1790*, Chapel Hill, University of North Carolina, 1982.

Jack, Jan Barkley, 'Early boat building on the upper Hawkesbury', in J.P. Powell (ed.), *Cross Currents: Historical Studies of the Hawkesbury*, 37–64.

Jack, R. Ian (ed.), *A Colonial Scene: The Hawkesbury–Nepean Valley*, Sydney, Department of Adult Education, University of Sydney, 1980.

——, *Exploring the Hawkesbury*, Sydney, Kangaroo Press, 1986.

Jackson, Kenneth T., *Crabgrass Frontier: The Suburbanization of the United States*, New York, Oxford University Press, 1985.

Jackson, Tina, 'Our place—what makes it special', *National Trust Magazine: Our Place*, Sydney National Trust of Australia (NSW), autumn 2008, 7–11.

Jacobs, Jane M., 'Women talking up big: Aboriginal women as cultural custodians, a South Australian example', in Peggy Brock (ed.), *Women, Rites and Sites: Aboriginal Women's Cultural Knowledge*, Sydney, Allen & Unwin, 1989, 76–98.

Jeans, D.N., *A Historical Geography of New South Wales to 1901*, Sydney, Reed Education, 1972.

Jellie, Dugald, 'Metropolis now', *Sydney Morning Herald*, 16 October 1997.

Jeremy, John, *Cockatoo Island: Sydney's Historic Dockyard*, Sydney, UNSW Press, 1998.

Jervis, James, *The Cradle City of Australia: A History of Parramatta*, Parramatta, Council of the City of Parramatta, 1961.

Johnson, A.W., 'Showdown in the Pacific: A remote response to European power struggles in the Pacific, Dawes Point Battery, Sydney, 1791–1925', *Historical Archaeology*, vol. 37, no. 1, 2003, 114–27.

Johnson, Chris, *What is Social Value? A Discussion Paper*, Canberra, Australian Government Publishing Service, 1994.

Johnson, David, *The Geology of Australia*, Melbourne, Cambridge University Press, 2004.

Johnson, Keith A. and Sainty, Malcolm R., *Sydney Burial Ground 1819–1901 (Elizabeth and Devonshire Streets) And History of Sydney's Early Cemeteries from 1788*, Sydney, Library of Australian History, 2001.

Johnson, Matthew, *Housing Culture: Traditional Architecture in an English Landscape*, London, UCL Press, 1993.

——, *An Archaeology of Capitalism*, Oxford, Blackwell, 1996.

Jones, Phillip, *Boomerang: Behind an Australian Icon*, Adelaide, Wakefield Press, 1996.

——, *Ochre and Rust: Artefacts and Encounters on Australian Frontiers*, Adelaide, Wakefield Press, 2007.

Jones, Rhys, 'Ordering the landscape', in Ian Donaldson and Tamsin Donaldson (eds), *Seeing the First Australians*, 181–209.

Jordan, Robert, *The Convict Theatres of Early Australia 1788–1840*, Sydney, Currency House, 2002.

Karskens, Grace, 'Deference, defiance and diligence: three views of convicts in NSW road gangs', *Australian Journal of Historical Archaeology*, vol. 4, 1986, 17–28.

——, 'The house on the hill: the state conservatorium and "First class music" in New South Wales', Lenore Coltheart (ed.), *Significant Sites: History and Public Works in New South Wales*, 1989, 121–41.

——, *Holroyd: A Social History of Western Sydney*, Sydney, UNSW Press, 1991.

——, 'Declining life: on the Rocks in Sydney', *Australian Cultural History*, no. 14, 1995, 63–75.

——, *The Rocks: Life in Early Sydney*, Melbourne University Press, 1997.

——, 'The dialogue of townscape: the Rocks and Sydney 1788–1822', *Australian Historical Studies*, no. 108, April 1997, 88–112.

——, 'Death was in his face: dying, burial and remembrance in early Sydney', *Labour History*, no. 74, May 1998, 21–39.

——, *Inside the Rocks: The Archaeology of a Neighbourhood*, Sydney, Hale & Iremonger, 1999.

——, 'Banished and reclaimed', *Meanjin on Museums: Art or Mart*, vol. 60, no. 4, 2001, 26–34.

——, 'Small things, big pictures: new perspectives from the archaeology of Sydney's Rocks neighbourhood', in Alan Mayne and Tim Murray (eds), *The Archaeology of Urban Landscapes: Explorations in Slumland*, Cambridge, Cambridge University Press, 2002, 69–85.

——, 'Tales of Sydney and the telling of Sydney history', *Journal of Urban History*, vol. 28, no. 6, September 2002, 778–92.

——, 'Engaging artefacts: archaeology, museums and the origins of Sydney', *Humanities Research: Museums of the Future, the Future of Museums*, vol. IX, no. 1, 2002, 36–56.

——, 'Tourists and pilgrims: (re)visiting the Rocks', *Journal of Australian Studies*, January 2003, 29–38.

——, 'Raising the dead: attitudes to European human remains in the Sydney region c1840–2000', *Islands of Vanishment—Historic Environment*, vol. 17, no. 1, 2003, 42–8.

——, 'Revisiting the world view: the archaeology of convict households in Sydney's Rocks neighbourhood', *Historical Archaeology—Journal of the Society of Historical Archaeology*, vol. 37, no. 1, University of Nevada, Reno, 2003, 34–55.

——, 'This spirit of emigration: the nature and meaning of escape in early New South Wales', *Journal of Australian Colonial History*, vol. 7, 2005, 1–34.

——, 'Resurrecting Chapman', *Journal of the Australian Jewish Historical Society*, vol. XVIII, part 1, June 2006, 8–21.

——, 'Water dreams, earthen histories: exploring urban environmental history at Penrith Lakes and Castlereagh', *Environment and History*, vol. 13, no. 2, May 2007, 115–54.

—— and Rogowsky, Melita (eds), *Histories of Green Square*, Sydney, Sydney City Council and School of History, University of New South Wales, 2004.

Kartzoff, M., *Nature and a City: The Native Vegetation of the Sydney Area*, Sydney, Edwards & Shaw Pty Ltd, 1969.

Kass, Terry, Liston, Carol and McClymont, John, *Parramatta: A Past Revealed*, Parramatta City Council, 1996.

Kelly, Max, *Anchored in a Small Cove: A History and Archaeology of The Rocks*, Sydney, Sydney Cove Authority, 1997.

Keneally, Tom, *The Commonwealth of Thieves: The Sydney Experiment*, Sydney, Random House, 2005.

Kercher, Bruce, *An Unruly Child: A History of Law in Australia*, Sydney, Allen & Unwin, 1995.

——, 'Recognition of indigenous legal autonomy in nineteenth century New South Wales', *Indigenous Law Bulletin*, vol. 4, 1998, 7–9.

Kerr, Joan (ed.), *Heritage: The National Women's Art Book*, Sydney, Craftsman House, 1995.

Kerr, Joan and Broadbent, James, *Gothick Taste in the Colony of New South Wales*, Sydney, David Ell Press, 1980.

—— and Falkus, Hugh, *Sydney Cove to Duntroon: A Family Album of Early Life in Australia*, London, Gollancz, 1982.

Kimber, R.G., 'The dynamic century before the Horn Expedition: a speculative history', in S.R. Morton and D.J. Mulvaney (eds)., *Exploring Central Australia: Society, the Environment and the 1894 Horn Expedition*, Surrey Beatty & Sons, Chipping Norton, 1996, 91–102.

King, Hazel, 'Lives in exile: Elizabeth and John Macarthur', in Penny Russell (ed.), *For Richer, for Poorer: Early Colonial Marriages*, Melbourne University Press, 1994, 31–49.

King, Robert J., *The Secret History of the Convict Colony: Alexandro Malaspino's Report on the British Settlement of New South Wales*, Sydney, Allen & Unwin, 1990.

Kingston, Beverley, *The Oxford History of Australia Volume 3 1860–1900 Glad, Confident Morning*, Melbourne, Oxford University Press, 1988.

Kingston, Daphne, *Early Slab Buildings of the Sydney Region*, Sydney, Kangaroo Press, 1985.

Kociumbas, Jan, *The Oxford History of Australia, Volume 2 1770–1860*, Melbourne, Oxford University Press, 1992.

Kohen, James L., 'The importance of archaeology to Aboriginal communities on the Cumberland Plain: an archaeologist's perspective', in Barry Wright, Daniel Moody and Leon Petchkovsky (eds), *Contemporary Issues in Aboriginal Studies: 2*, Proceedings of the Second National Conference on Aboriginal Studies, Sydney, Firebird Press, 1987, 123–34.

——, *The Darug and their Neighbours: The Traditional Aboriginal Owners of the Sydney Region*, Sydney, Darug Link and Blacktown and District Historical Society, 1993.

——, *Aboriginal Environmental Impacts*, Sydney, UNSW Press, 1995.

——, 'Pemulwuy (c1750–1802)', *Australian Dictionary of Biography*, supplementary volume, Melbourne University Press, 2005, 318–19.

——, *A Dictionary of the Dharug Language: The Inland Dialect*, Blacktown, Sydney, Blacktown and District Historical Society, n.d.

—— and Lampert, Ronald, 'Hunters and fishers in the Sydney region', in D.J. Mulvaney and J.P. White (eds), *Australians to 1788*, Sydney, Fairfax, Syme and Weldon, 1989, 343–65.

Kohlhoff, Doug, 'Did Henry Hacking shoot Pemulwuy? A reappraisal', *Journal of the Royal Australian Historical Society*, vol. 99, 2013, 77–93.

Lampert, R., 'Aboriginal life around Port Jackson', in Bernard Smith and Alwyne Wheeler (eds), *The Art of the First Fleet*, 1988, 19–69.

Lawrence, Susan, *Whalers and Freemen: Life on Tasmania's Colonial Whaling Stations*, Melbourne, Australian Scholarly Press, 2007.

Lawson, Henry, *Poetical Works of Henry Lawson*, Sydney, Angus & Robertson, 1968.

Lighthouses of Australia Inc., 'Macquarie Lighthouse: Australia's first lighthouse', 1999, online at <http://www.lighthouse.net.au/lights/NSW/Macquarie/Macquarie.htm#History.

Linebaugh, Peter, *The London Hanged: Crime and Civil Society in the Eighteenth Century*, Harmondsworth, Penguin, 1991.

—— and Rediker, Marcus, *Many Headed Hydra: The Hidden History of the Revolutionary Atlantic*, London, Verso, 2000.

Lines, William, *Taming the Great South Land: A History of the Conquest of Nature in Australia*, Sydney, Allen & Unwin, 1991.

Lippard, Lucy, *The Lure of the Local: Senses of Place in a Multicentered Society*, New York, The New Press, 1997.

Lisle, Phillip, 'Rum beginnings: towards a new perspective of the Grose years', *Journal of the Royal Australian Historical Society*, vol. 91, part 1, 2005, 15–28.

Liston, Carol, *Campbelltown: The Bicentennial History*, Sydney, Allen & Unwin, 1988.

——, *Sarah Wentworth: Mistress of Vaucluse*, Sydney, Historic Houses Trust of NSW, 1988.

——, 'The Dharawal and Gandangara in colonial Campbelltown, New South Wales, 1788–1830', *Aboriginal History*, vol. 12, 1988, 49–62.

——, 'Colonial society' in James Broadbent and Joy Hughes (eds), *The Age of Macquarie*, 1992, 19–34.

Local Government and Shires Association, Cultural Award Nominations, Wollondilly Shire Council, 'Scar Tree Plan of Management Bridgewater Estate 2006', 2007, online at <http://www.culturalawards2007.lgsa-plus.net/showcasedentries.html>.

Low, Tim, 'Foods of the First Fleet: convict food plants of old Sydney town', *Australian Natural History*, vol. 22, no. 7, 1987–88, 292–7.

——, *The New Nature: Winners and Losers in Australia*, Melbourne, Penguin, 2002.

Lynravn, Joan, 'Catchpole, Margaret (1762–1819)', *Australian Dictionary of Biography*, vol. 1, Melbourne University Press, 1966, 215–16.

McAfee, Robert J., *Dawes' Meteorological Journal*, Canberra, Bureau of Meteorology, Australian Government Printing Service, 1981.

McAuley, Gay, 'Remembering and forgetting, place and performance in the memory process', in Gay McAuley (ed.), *Unstable Ground: Performance and the Politics of Place*, Brussels, P.I.E. Peter Lang, 2006, 149–76.

McBryde, Isabel, 'To establish a commerce of this sort: Cross-cultural exchange at the Port Jackson settlement', in John Hardy and Alan Frost (eds), *Studies from Terra Australis to Australia*, Canberra, Occasional Papers no. 6, Highland Press and Australian Academy of the Humanities, 1989, 169–82.

——, *Guests of the Governor: Aboriginal Residents of the First Government House*, Sydney, Friends of the First Government House Site, 1989.

——, 'Barter . . . immediately commenced to the satisfaction of both parties: cross-cultural exchange at Port Jackson 1788–1828', in Robin Torrence and Anne Clarke (eds), *The Archaeology of Difference: Negotiating Cross-cultural Engagement in Oceania*, London, Routledge, 2000, 238–77.

McCarthy, F.D., 'The Lapstone Creek excavation', *Records of the Australian Museum*, vol. 22, 1948, 1–34.

——, 'Culture succession in south eastern Australia', *Mankind*, vol. 5, no. 5, 1958, 177–90.

——, 'Aboriginal cave art on Woronora and Cordeaux Catchment Areas', *The Sydney Water Board Journal*, vol. 10, no. 4, January 1961, 97–103.

McClymont, John, 'Toongabbie', *Dictionary of Sydney*, 2006, online at <http://www.dictionaryofsydney.org/resources/documents/Toongabbie_long.pdf>.

McCormick, Tim, *First Views of Australia 1788–1825*, Sydney, David Ell Press, 1987.

MacDonald, Josephine, Rich, Elizabeth and Barton, Huw, 'The Rouse Hill Infrastructure Project (Stage 1) on the Cumberland Plain, Western Sydney', in Marjorie Sullivan, Sally Brockwell and Ann Webb (eds), *Archaeology in the North: Proceedings of the 1993 Australian Archaeological Association Conference*, Darwin, North Australia Research Unit (ANU), 1994, 260–93.

MacDonald, Patricia, 'By whom and for whom? British reactions to the landscape of New South Wales, 1788–1830', in Michelle Hetherington and Seona Doherty (eds), *The World Upside Down: Australia 1788–1830*, Canberra, National Library of Australia, 2000, 27–33.

MacFie, Peter, 'Dobbers and cobbers: informers and mateship among convicts, officials and settlers on the Grass Tree Road, Tasmania 1830–1850', *Tasmanian Historical Research Association*, vol. 35, no. 3, September 1988, 112–27.

McGrath, Ann, 'The white man's looking glass: Aboriginal colonial gender relations at Port Jackson', *Australian Historical Studies*, vol. 24, no. 95, 1990, 189–206.

——, 'Birthplaces', in Patricia Grimshaw, Marilyn Lake, Ann McGrath and Marian Quartly, *Creating a Nation 1788–1990*, Melbourne, McPhee Gribble, 1994, 7–26.

—— (ed.), *Contested Ground: Australian Aborigines Under the British Crown*, Sydney, Allen & Unwin, 1995.

McIntyre, Julie, 'Between the wines of Madeira and those of the Côtes du Rhone: the Macarthur family and a forgotten colonial industry', *History*, no. 90, December 2006, 4–7.

——, 'Not rich and not British: Philip Schaeffer, a "failed" colonial farmer', *Journal of Australian Colonial History*, forthcoming 2009.

MacKellar, Maggie, *Core of My Heart, My Country*, Melbourne University Press, 2004.

McKendrick, Neil, 'Home demand and economic growth: a new view of women and children in the Industrial Revolution', in N. McKendrick (ed.), *Historical Perspectives: Studies in English Thought and Society in Honor of J.H. Plumb*, London, Europa Publications, 1974, 152–210.

——, Brewer, John and Plumb, J.H., *The Birth of a Consumer Society: The Commercialisation of Eighteenth-Century England*, Bloomington, Indiana University Press, 1982.

McKern, J., 'State industrial activities of Australia, 1822–23', *Journal of the Royal Australian Historical Society*, vol. 10, part 1, 1924, 224–30.

McLoughlin, Lynette, 'Landed peasantry or landed gentry', in Graeme Aplin (ed.), *A Difficult Infant: Sydney Before Macquarie*, 1988, 120–47.

——, *An Island of Bush: The Field of Mars Reserve*, North Ryde, NSW Department of School Education, c1993.

——, 'Seasons of burning in the Sydney region: the historical records compared with recent prescribed burning', *Australian Journal of Ecology*, vol. 23, 1998, 393–404.

——, 'Estuarine wetland distribution along the Parramatta River, Sydney, 1788–1940: implications for planning and conservation', *Cunninghamia*, vol. 6, no 3, 2000, 579–610.

McMahon, John, 'Not a rum rebellion but a military insurrection', *Journal of the Royal Australian Historical Society*, vol. 92, part 2, 125–44.

BIBLIOGRAPHY

McMartin, Arthur, 'Rose, Thomas (1754?–1833)', *Australian Dictionary of Biography*, vol. 2, Melbourne University Press, 1967, 394.

MacMillan, David S., 'Erskine, James (1765?–1825)', *Australian Dictionary of Biography*, vol. 1, Melbourne University Press, 1966, 358–9.

McNeill, Donald, Dowling, Robyn and Fagan, Bob, 'Sydney/global/city: an exploration', *International Journal of Urban and Regional Research*, vol. 29, part 4, 2005, 935–44.

McPhee, John (ed.), *Joseph Lycett Convict Artist*, Sydney, Historic Houses Trust of NSW, 2006.

Madden, Brian and Muir, Lesley, *Canterbury Farm 200 Years*, Canterbury and District Historical Society, 1993.

Mander-Jones, Phyllis, 'Dawes, William (1762–1836)', *Australian Dictionary of Biography*, vol. 1, Melbourne University Press, 1966, 297–8.

Maral, Louise, 'Making history real through fiction—a talk by Kate Grenville' (Herman Blacklock Memorial Lecture, University of Sydney, 2005), *University of Sydney News*, 19 September 2005, online at <www.usyd.edu.au/news/84.html?newsstoryid=687>.

Martin, Michael, *On Darug Land: An Aboriginal Perspective*, St Marys NSW, published by the author, 1988.

Martin, Stephen, *A New Land: European Perceptions of Australia 1788–1850*, Sydney, Allen & Unwin and State Library of NSW, 1993.

Matthews, R.H., 'Some mythology of the Gundungurra Tribe New South Wales', *Zeitschrift für Ethnologie*, Heft 2, 1908.

Maxwell-Stewart, Hamish, *Closing the Gates of Hell: The Death of a Convict Station*, Sydney, Allen & Unwin, 2008.

—— and Duffield, Ian, 'Skin deep devotions: religious tattoos and convict transportation to Australia', in Jane Caplan (ed.), *Written on the Body: The Tattoo in European and American History*, London, Reaktion, 2000, 118–35.

Meagher, Margaret, *Painted Panorama 1800–1870*, Sydney, The Blaxland Gallery, 1985.

Mear, Craig, 'The smallox outbreak in Sydney 1789', *Journal of the Royal Australian Historical Society*, vol. 94, part 1, June 2008, 1–22.

Megaw, J.V.S., 'The excavation of an Aboriginal rock shelter on Gymea Bay, Port Hacking, NSW', *Archaeology and Physical Anthropology in Oceania*, vol. 1, no. 1, 1966, 25–30.

——, *The Recent Archaeology of the Sydney District: Excavations 1964–1967*, Canberra, Institute of Aboriginal Studies, 1974.

Merwick, Donna, *Possessing Albany 1630–1710: The Dutch and English Experiences*, Cambridge University Press, 1990.

Milliss, Roger, *Waterloo Creek: The Australia Day Massacre of 1838—George Gipps and the British Conquest of New South Wales*, Melbourne, McPhee Gribble, 1992.

Monash University, Centre for GIS and Centre for Indigenous Archaeology, 'Sahul Time', online at <http://sahultime.monash.edu.au/explore.html>.

Moore, Clive, 'Blackgin's Leap: a window into Aboriginal–European relations in the Pioneer Valley Queensland in the 1860s', *Aboriginal History*, vol. 14, part 1, 1990, 61–79.

Morris, Colleen and Britten, Geoffrey, 'Colonial cultural landscapes of the Cumberland Plain and Camden—the challenge to manage a disappearing legacy', *Locality*, vol. 10, no. 2, 1999, 8–11.

Morrissey, Philip, 'Dancing with shadows: erasing Aboriginal self and sovereignty', in Aileen Moreton-Robinson (ed.), *Sovereign Subjects: Indigenous Sovereignty Matters*, Sydney, Allen & Unwin, 2007, 65–74.

Mrozowski, Stephen, 'Landscapes of inequality', in Randall H. McGuire and Robert Paynter (eds), *The Archaeology of Inequality: Material Culture, Domination and Resistance*, Oxford, Blackwell, 1991, 79–101.

Mulvaney, John and Kamminga, Johan, *Prehistory of Australia*, Sydney, Allen & Unwin, 1999.

Murray, Robert, and White, Kate, *Dharug and Dungaree: The History of Penrith and St Marys to 1860*, Melbourne, Hargreen Publishing and Penrith City Council, 1988.

Myers, Peter, 'The third city: Sydney's original monuments and a possible new metropolis', *Architecture Australia*, January/February 2000, online at <http://www.archmedia.com.au/aa/aaissue.php?article=18&issued=200001&typon=2>.

Nanson, G.C., Cohen, T.J., Doyle, C.J. and Price, D.M., 'Alluvial evidence of major Late-Quaternary climate and flow-regime changes on the coastal rivers of New South Wales, Australia', in K.J. Gregory and G. Benito (eds), *Palaeohydrology: Understanding global change*, Chichester: John Wiley & Sons, 2003, 233–58.

National Library of Australia, 'George Raper, First Fleet artist', online at <http://nationaltreasures.nla.gov.au/ExhibitionChecklist.pdf/Treasures/item/nla.int-ex6-s31>.

National Museum of Australia, 'The scourge of smallpox', Collections catalogue entry, online at <http://www.nma.gov.au/advancedSearchResultsItemDetail.jsp?irn=430>.

National Trust of Australia (NSW), 'Places to visit: Experiment Farm Cottage', online at <http://www.nsw.nationaltrust.org.au/properties/efc/default.asp>.

Neville, Richard, *A Rage for Curiosity: Visualising Australia 1788–1830*, Sydney, State Library of New South Wales, 1997.

——, 'Eager curiosity: engaging with the new colony of New South Wales', in Michelle Hetherington and Seona Doherty (eds), *The World Upside Down: Australia 1788–1830*, Canberra, National Library of Australia, 2000, 7–12.

Newman, J. and Pevsner, N., *Buildings of England: Dorset*, London, Penguin, 1972.

New South Wales Board of Studies, 'Incidents between British and Koori people Stage 2: British colonisation of Australia', K–6 Education Resources, 2007, online at <http://bosnsw-k6.nsw.edu.au/go/hsie/background-sheets/incidents/>.

New South Wales Department of Environment and Climate Change, 'Threatened species in New South Wales', online at <http://www.threatenedspecies.environment.nsw.gov.au/tsprofile/about_ts.aspx>.

New South Wales Environment Protection Authority, *New South Wales State of the Environment 1997*, Sydney, the NSW EPA, 1997, online at <http://www.epa.nsw.gov.au/soe/97/index.htm>.

——, *New South Wales State of the Environment 2003*, Sydney, the NSW EPA, 2003, online at <http://www.epa.nsw.gov.au/soe/soe2003/index.htm>.

New South Wales Heritage Office, Chinese Market Gardens, La Perouse, *State Heritage Register*, online at <http://www.heritage.nsw.gov.au/07_subnav_02_2.cfm?itemid=5044696>.

BIBLIOGRAPHY

New South Wales National Parks and Wildlife Service, 'Turquoise parrot—threatened species information', 2005, online at <http://www.nationalparks.nsw.gov.au/pdfs/tsprofile_turquoise_parrot.pdf>.

——, 'Scheyville National Park and Pitt Town Nature Reserve: plan of management', September 2000, online at <http://www.nationalparks.nsw.gov.au/PDFs/pom_final_scheyville_pitttown.pdf>.

Nicholas, F.W. and Nicholas, J.M., *Charles Darwin in Australia*, Cambridge, Cambridge University Press, 2002.

Nicholas, Stephen (ed.), *Convict Workers: Reinterpreting Australia's Past*, Melbourne, Cambridge University Press, 1988.

Nix, Irene, *Glimpses of Glenhaven*, Glenhaven (NSW), Glenhaven Progress Association, 1992.

Nugent, Maria, *Botany Bay: Where Histories Meet*, Sydney, Allen & Unwin, 2005.

Nye, Joseph, *Soft Power: The Means to Success in World Politics*, New York, Perseus Book Group, 2004.

O'Farrell, Patrick, *The Irish in Australia*, Sydney, UNSW Press, 1993 (f.p. 1986).

O'Loughlin, Ed, 'Art find lifts veil on an African dreaming', *Sydney Morning Herald*, 17 March 2001.

Onslow, Sibella Macarthur, *Some Early Records of the Macarthurs of Camden*, Adelaide, Rigby, 1975 (f.p. 1914).

Oppenheim, Peter, *The Fragile Forts: The Fixed Defences of Sydney Harbour 1788–1963*, Canberra, Australian Army History Unit, 2004.

Oxley, Deborah, 'Female convicts', in Stephen Nicholas (ed.), *Convict Workers: Reinterpreting Australia's Past*, Melbourne, Cambridge University Press, 1988, 85–97.

——, 'Packing her (economic) bags: convict women workers', *Australian Historical Studies*, vol. 26, no. 102, April 1994, 57–76.

——, *Convict Maids: The Forced Migration of Women to Australia*, Melbourne, Cambridge University Press, 1996.

Parry, Naomi, 'Musquito (c1780–1825)', *Australian Dictionary of Biography*, supplementary Volume, Melbourne University Press, 2005, 299.

——, 'Lock, Maria (c1805–1878)', *Australian Dictionary of Biography*, supplementary volume, Melbourne University Press, 2005, 236–7.

——, ' "Hanging no good for blackfellow": looking at the life of Musquito', in Ingereth Macfarlane and Mark Hannah (eds), *Transgressions: Critical Australian Indigenous Histories*, Canberra, ANU Press, 2007, online at <http://epress.anu.edu.au/aborig_history/transgressions/mobile_devices/index.html>.

Parsons, George, 'The commercialisation of honour: early Australian capitalism 1788–1809', in Graeme Aplin (ed.), *A Difficult Infant: Sydney Before Macquarie*, 1988, 102–19.

——, 'Soldiers and specialisation: The NSW Corps on the Hawkesbury', in J.P. Powell (ed.), *Cross Currents: Historical Studies of the Hawkesbury*, Berowra Heights (NSW), Deerubbin Press, 1997, 11–14.

Parsons, Vivienne, 'Brooks, Richard (1765?–1833)', *Australian Dictionary of Biography*, vol. 1, Melbourne University Press, 1966, 156–7.

——, 'Broughton, William (1768–1821)', *Australian Dictionary of Biography*, vol. 1, Melbourne University Press, 1966, 157–8.

——, 'Throsby, Charles (1777–1828)', *Australian Dictionary of Biography*, vol. 2, Melbourne University Press, 1967, 530–1.

——, 'Wiseman, Solomon, (1777–1838)', *Australian Dictionary of Biography*, vol. 2, Melbourne University Press, 1967, 617–18.

Pedersen, Howard and Woorunmurra, Banjo, *Jandamarra and the Bunuba Resistance*, Broome, Magabala Books Aboriginal Corporation, 2000 (f.p. 1996).

Perkins, John and Thompson, Jack, 'Cattle theft, primitive capital accumulation and pastoral expansion in early New South Wales, 1800–1850', *Australian Historical Studies*, no. 111, October 1998, 289–302.

Perrott, Monica, *A Tolerable Good Success: Economic Opportunities for Women in New South Wales 1788–1830*, Sydney, Hale & Iremonger, 1983.

Perry, T.M., *Australia's First Frontier: The Spread of Settlement in New South Wales*, Melbourne University Press, 1963.

Peters, Merle, *Bankstown's Northern Suburbs*, Sydney, published by the author, 1977.

Petrie, Brian M., 'The French-Canadian convict experience, 1840–1848', *Journal of the Royal Australian Historical Society*, vol. 81, part 2, 1995, 167–83.

Pickett, Charles and Lomb, Nick, *Observer and Observed: A Pictorial History of Sydney Observatory and Observatory Hill*, Sydney, Powerhouse Museum, 2001.

Picton Phillips, Tina, 'Family matters: bastards, orphans and baptisms—New South Wales, 1810–1825', *Journal of the Royal Australian Historical Society*, vol. 90, part 2, December 2004, 122–35.

Plater, Diane (ed.), *Other Boundaries*, Sydney, Jumbunna Aboriginal Education Centre, University of Technology, 1993.

Pleij, Herman, translated by Diane Webb, *Dreaming of Cockaigne: Medieval Fantasies of the Perfect Life*, New York, Columbia University Press, 2001.

Porter, R., 'Science, provincial culture and public opinion in Enlightenment England c1680–1760', in Peter Borsay (ed.), *The Eighteenth Century English Town*, 243–67.

Powell, J.M., *Environmental Management in Australia 1788–1914, Guardians, Improvers and Profit: An Introductory Survey*, Melbourne, Oxford University Press, 1976.

——, 'Snakes and cannons: water management and the geographical imagination in Australia', in Stephen Dovers (ed.), *Environmental History and Policy: Still Settling Australia*, Melbourne, Oxford University Press, 2000, 47–69.

Powell, J.P. (ed.), *Cross Currents: Historical Studies of the Hawkesbury*, Berowra Heights (NSW), Deerubbin Press, 1997.

Powell, Jocelyn (ed.), *The Improvers' Legacy: Environmental Studies of the Hawkesbury*, Sydney, Deerubbin Press, 1998.

Price, Jenny, 'Thirteen ways of seeing nature in LA', *The Believer*, April 2006, online at <http://www.believermag.com/issues/200604/?read=article_price>.

Proudfoot, Helen, *Colonial Buildings—Macarthur Growth Centre: Campbelltown, Camden, Appin*, Campbelltown, Macarthur Development Board, 1977.

——, *Exploring Sydney's West*, Sydney, Kangaroo Press, c1987.

——, 'Fixing the settlement upon a savage shore: planning and building', in Graeme Aplin (ed.), *A Difficult Infant: Sydney Before Macquarie*, 1988, 54–71.

——, 'Opening towns: public virtue and the interior', in James Broadbent and Joy Hughes (eds), *The Age of Macquarie*, 1992, 60–74.

——, Bickford, Anne, Egloff, Brian and Stocks, Robyn, *Australia's First Government House*, Sydney, Allen & Unwin and the NSW Department of Planning, 1991.

Pullen, Noeline, *Traditional Aboriginal Names for the Natural Regions and Features in Baulkham Hills Shire*, Baulkham Hills Shire Council, 2004, online at <http://www. baulkhamhills.nsw.gov.au/IgnitionSuite/uploads/docs/Traditional_Aboriginal_ Names_Natural_Regions.pdf>.

Purtell, Jean, *The Mosquito Fleet: Hawkesbury River Trade and Traders 1794–1994*, Berowra Heights (NSW), Deerubbin Press, 1995.

Pybus, Cassandra, *Black Founders: The Unknown Story of Australia's First Black Settlers*, Sydney, UNSW Press, 2006.

Pye, Michael, *Maximum City: The Biography of New York*, London, Sinclair-Stevenson, 1991.

Pyne, Stephen J., *Burning Bush: A Fire History of Australia*, Sydney, Allen & Unwin, 1992.

Raby, Geoff, *Making Rural Australia: An Economic History of Technical and Institutional Creativity, 1788–1860*, Melbourne, Oxford University Press, 1996.

Ramson, W.S. (ed.), *The Australian National Dictionary: A Dictionary of Australianisms on Historical Principles*, Melbourne, Oxford University Press, 1997 (f.p. 1988).

Read, Peter, *Belonging: Australians, Place and Aboriginal Ownership*, Melbourne, Cambridge University Press, 2000.

——, 'Clio or Janus? Historians and the Stolen Generations', *Australian Historical Studies Special Issue—Challenging Histories: Reflections on Australian History*, vol. 33, no. 118, 2002, 54–60.

——, *Haunted Earth*, Sydney, UNSW Press, 2003.

Rees, Sian, *The Floating Brothel: The Extraordinary Story of the Lady Julian and its Cargo of Female Convicts Bound for Botany Bay*, Sydney, Hodder Headline Australia, 2001.

Reynolds, Henry, *The Other Side of the Frontier: Aboriginal Resistance to the European Invasion of Australia*, Penguin, Melbourne, 1983 (f.p. 1981).

——, *This Whispering in Our Hearts*, Sydney, Allen & Unwin, 1998.

——, *The Question of Genocide in Australia's History: An Indelible Stain?*, Melbourne, Viking, 2001.

Rhodes, Jon, *Cage of Ghosts*, Exhibition, National Library of Australia, 27 September–25 November 2007.

——, 'Finding cages of ghosts', exhibition brochure, Canberra, National Library of Australia, 2007 and online at <http://www.nla.au/exhibitions/cageofghosts/>.

Richardson, Ruth, *Death, Dissection and the Destitute*, London, Routledge & Kegan Paul, 1987.

Ritchie, John, *Punishment and Profit: The Reports of Commissioner John Bigge on the Colonies of New South Wales and Van Diemen's Land 1822–1823: Their Origins, Nature and Significance*, Melbourne, Heinemann, 1970.

Ritchie, Rod, 'The red cedar timber industry in New South Wales and Queensland', in Historic Houses Trust of NSW, *Red Cedar in Australia*, Sydney, Historic Houses Trust, 2004.

Roberts, David, 'Bell's Falls massacre and Bathurst's history of violence', *Australian Historical Studies*, no. 105, October 1995, 615–33.

Robinson, Portia, *The Hatch and Brood of Time: A Study of the First Generation of Native-born White Australians 1788–1828*, Melbourne, Oxford University Press, 1985.

——, *The Women of Botany Bay: A Reinterpretation of the Role of Women in the Origins of Australian Society*, Melbourne, Oxford University Press, 1995.

Robinson, R.W., 'Land', in G.J. Abbot and N.B. Nairn (eds), *Economic Growth of Australia 1788–1821*, (1979), 74–104.

Rodger, N.A.M., *The Wooden World: An Anatomy of the Georgian Navy*, Annapolis, Naval Institute Press, 1986.

Rolls, Eric, *A Million Wild Acres: 200 Years of Man and an Australian Forest*, Melbourne, Nelson, 1981.

——, 'Country and city', in Eric Rolls, *From Forest to Sea: Australia's Changing Environment*, St Lucia, University of Queensland Press, 1993, 18–25.

——, 'More a new planet than a new continent', in Eric Rolls, *From Forest to Sea: Australia's Changing Environment*, St Lucia, University of Queensland Press, 1993, 161–76.

Rose, Deborah Bird, 'The Year Zero and the North Australian frontier', in Deborah Bird Rose and Anne Clark (eds), *Tracking Knowledge in North Australian Landscapes: Studies in Indigenous and Settler Ecological Knowledge Systems*, Canberra, North Australia Research Unit, School of Pacific and Asian Studies, Australian National University, 1997, 19–36.

——, *Dingo Makes Us Human: Life and Land in an Australian Aboriginal Culture*, Melbourne, Cambridge University Press, 2000.

Rosen, Sue, *Losing Ground: An Environmental History of the Hawkesbury–Nepean Catchment*, Sydney, Hale & Iremonger, 1995.

——, *Bankstown: A Sense of Identity*, Sydney, Hale & Iremonger, 1996.

Rosenthal, Michael, 'The extraordinary Mr Earle', in Michelle Hetherington and Seona Doherty (eds), *The World Upside Down: Australia 1788–1830*, Canberra, National Library of Australia, 2000, 35–42.

Rosenzweig, Roy, *Eight Hours for What We Will; Workers and Leisure in an Industrial City, 1870–1920*, New York, Cambridge University Press, 1983.

Ross, Anne, 'Tribal and linguistic boundaries: a reassessment of the evidence', in G. Aplin (ed.), *A Difficult Infant: Sydney Before Macquarie*, 42–53.

Ross, Valerie, *Matthew Everingham: A First Fleeter and His Times*, Sydney, Library of Australian History, 1980.

——, (ed.), *The Everingham Letterbook*, Sydney, Anvil Press, 1985.

——, *A Hawkesbury Story*, Sydney, Library of Australian History, 1989.

Rowland, E.C., 'Simeon Lord: a merchant prince of Botany Bay', *Journal of the Royal Australian Historical Society*, vol. 30, part 3, 1944, 157–95.

Rowse, Tim, *White Flour, White Power: From Rations to Citizenship in Central Australia*, Melbourne, Cambridge University Press, 1998.

——, 'Transforming the notion of the urban Aborigine', *Urban Policy and Research*, vol. 18, no. 2, 2000, 171–90.

Royal Botanic Gardens Sydney, 'Indigenous people of Sydney', n.d., online at <http://www.

rbgsyd.nsw.gov.au/education/for_students_and_teachers/indigenous_people_of_sydney>.

Rusden, G.W., *Curiosities of Colonisation*, London, W. Clowes and Sons, 1874.

Ryan, Lyndal, 'Waterloo Creek northern New South Wales, 1838', in Barn Attwood and S.G. Foster (eds), *Frontier Conflict: the Australian Experience*, Canberra, National Museum of Australia Press, 2003, 33–43.

Ryan, R.J., *Land Grants 1788–1809: A Record of Registered Grants and Leases in New South Wales, Van Diemen's Land and Norfolk Island*, Sydney, Australian Documents Library, 1974.

Ryde City Council, 'Parks and park name history: Field of Mars Reserve', 2008, online at <http://www.ryde.nsw.gov.au/services/parks_gardens_sports/park.htm>.

Sargeant, Doris A., *The Toongabbie Story*, Toongabbie Public School Parents and Citizens Association, 1991 (f.p. 1964).

Schlunke, Katrina, *Bluff Rock: Autobiography of a Massacre*, Fremantle, Curtin University Books/Fremantle Arts Centre Press, 2005.

Scott, Ernest, *A Short History of Australia*, Melbourne, Humphrey Milford, Oxford University Press, 1920.

Scott, Jeannie Caroline, 'The Hall estate or "firm" ', in Russell MacKenzie Warner (ed.), *Over-Halling the Colony*, Sydney, Australian Document Library, 1990.

Seal, Graham, *These Few Lines: A Convict Story The Lost Lives of Myra and William Sykes*, Sydney, ABC Books, 2006.

Seddon, George, 'The evolution of perceptual attitudes', in George Seddon and Mari Davis (eds), *Man and Landscape in Australia: Towards an Ecological Vision*, papers from a symposium held at the Australian Academy of Science, Canberra, 1974, Canberra, Australian Government Printing Service, 1976, 9–17.

——, 'Environmental and social problems of cities', in George Seddon (ed.), *Urbanisation: 12 papers delivered at the 48th ANZAAS Congress*, Centre for Environmental Studies, University of Melbourne, 1977.

Sharpe, Alan, *Pictorial History of Newtown*, Sydney, Kingsclear Books, 1999.

Sheehan, Bernard, *Savagism and Civility: Indians and Englishmen in Colonial Virginia*, Cambridge, Cambridge University Press, 1980.

Silver, Lynette, *The Battle of Vinegar Hill: Australia's Irish Rebellion, 1804*, Sydney, Doubleday, 1989.

Slessor, Kenneth, *Selected Poems*, Sydney, Angus & Robertson, 1977.

Smith, Bernard, *European Vision and the South Pacific*, Sydney, Harper & Row, 1984 (f.p. 1960).

——, 'The artwork', in Bernard Smith and Alwyne Wheeler (eds), *Art of the First Fleet and other Early Australian Drawings*, 1988, 198–236.

——, 'History and the collector—1974', in Bernard Smith, *The Death of the Artist as Hero: essays in History and Culture*, Melbourne, Oxford University Press, 1988, 95–100.

—— (ed.), *Documents on Art and Taste in Australia*, Melbourne, Oxford University Press, 1975.

—— and Wheeler, Alwyne (eds), *Art of the First Fleet and other Early Australian Drawings*, New Haven, Yale University Press, 1988.

Smith, Jeremy, 'The burning bush', in Jeremy Smith (ed.), *The Unique Continent*, St Lucia, University of Queensland Press, 1992, 111–38.

Smith, Jim, *Aborigines of the Burragorang Valley 1830–1960*, Glebe, NSW, Wild & Woolley, 1991.

Smith, Keith Vincent, *King Bungaree: A Sydney Aborigine meets the Great South Pacific Explorers, 1799–1830*, Sydney, Kangaroo Press, 1992.

——, 'The white headhunters of Sydney Cove', *The Republican*, 2 May 1997.

——, *Bennelong: The Coming In of the Eora Sydney Cove 1788–1792*, Sydney, Kangaroo Press, 2001.

——, 'Australia's oldest murder mystery', *Sydney Morning Herald*, 1 November 2003.

——, *Wallumedegal: An Aboriginal History of Ryde*, Ryde, Ryde City Council, 2005.

——, 'Moowattin, Daniel (c1791–1816)', *Australian Dictionary of Biography*, supplementary volume, Melbourne University Press, 2005, 286–7.

——, 'Gooseberry, Cora (c1777–1852)', *Australian Dictionary of Biography*, supplementary volume, Melbourne University Press, 2005, 148.

——, *Eora: Mapping Aboriginal Sydney 1770–1850*, exhibition, State Library of NSW 2006, and catalogue, Sydney, State Library of New South Wales, 2006.

——, 'Moorooboora's daughter', *NLA News*, June 2006, vol. XVI, no. 9, June 2006, 1–4, online at <http://www.nla.gov.au/pub/nlanews/2006/jun06/article5.html>.

——, 'Bennelong, ambassador of the Eora', *Australian Heritage*, autumn 2006, 79–81.

——, 'Bundle (c1787–c1844)', *Journeys in Time*, Sydney, Macquarie University, 1998–2007, online at <http://www.lib.mq.edu.au/all/journeys/people/profiles/bundle.html>.

Souter, Gavin, *Mosman: A History*, Melbourne University Press, 1995.

Spooner, Peter, 'History of gardening', in George Seddon and Mari Davis (eds), *Man and Landscape in Australia: Towards an Ecological Vision*, 1976, 82–9.

Stacker, Lorraine, *Chained to Soil on the Plains of Emu*, Penrith, Nepean District Historical Society, 2000.

Stanbury, Peter and Clegg, John, *A Field Guide to Aboriginal Rock Engravings with Special Reference to Those Around Sydney*, Sydney, Sydney University Press and Oxford University Press, 1990.

Stanner, William, 'The history of indifference thus begins', *Aboriginal History*, vol. 1, no. 1, 1977, 2–26.

State Library of New South Wales, '[Chinese export ware punchbowl featuring a scene of Sydney Cove before 1820]', Webcat entry, online at <http://libapp.sl.nsw.gov.au/cgi-bin/spydus/FULL/PM/BSEARCH/2212/421505,2>.

Stephens, Tony, 'Admired by Macquarie but ignored for a sailing cat', *ENIAR NEWS*, 2002, online at <http://www.eniar.org/news/hist.html>.

Steven, Margaret, *Merchant Campbell 1769–1846: A Study of Colonial Trade*, Melbourne University Press, 1965.

——, 'Public credit and private confidence', in James Broadbent and Joy Hughes (eds), *The Age of Macquarie*, 1992, 48–59.

Stockton, E.D. and Holland, W., 'Cultural sites and their environment in the Blue Mountains', *Archaeology and Physical Anthropology in Oceania*, vol. 9, part 1, 1974, 36–65.

Stone, Lawrence, *The Family, Sex and Marriage in England 1500–1800*, Harmondsworth, Penguin, 1982 (f.p. 1977).

Summers, Anne, *Damned Whores and God's Police*, Melbourne, Penguin, 1975.

Swain, Tony, *A Place for Strangers: Towards a History of Australian Aboriginal Being*, Melbourne, Cambridge University Press, 1997 (f.p. 1993).

Sydney Prehistory Group, *In Search of the Cobrakall: A Survey of Aboriginal Sites in the Campbelltown Area South of Sydney Part 1*, Sydney, National Parks and Wildlife Service, 1983.

Sykes, Geoff, *The History of the Sykes Family in Australia*, self-published, 1971, online at <http://www.sykesfamily.com.au/william.htm>.

Symes, James G., *The Castle Hill Rebellion of 1804*, Castle Hill, Hills District Historical Society, 1990 (f.p. 1979).

Taylor, Amanda, 'Henry Lamb', n.d., Genealogy Search Australia, online at <http://www.searchwhateveraustralia.com.au/articles.html>.

Taylor, Rebe, *Unearthed: The Aboriginal Tasmanians of Kangaroo Island*, Adelaide, Wakefield Press, 2002.

Thomas, Martin, *The Artificial Horizon: Imagining the Blue Mountains*, Melbourne, Melbourne University Press, 2003.

Thomas, Nicholas, *Possessions: Indigenous Art, Colonial Culture*, New York, Thames & Hudson, 1999.

Thompson, Jack and Perkins, John, 'The Wild Cowpastures Revisited', *Journal of the Royal Australian Historical Society*, vol. 77, part 4, 3–19.

Thompson, John, 'A First Fleet treasure trove: a comment on the acquisition by the National Gallery of Australia of the Ducie Collection of George Raper artworks', *(Re)Collections: Journal of the National Museum of Australia*, vol. 1, no. 1, 2006, 93–7.

Thrush, Coll, *Native Seattle: Histories from the Crossing-over Place*, Seattle, University of Washington Press, 2007.

Tick, Stanley, 'Samuel Sidney 1813–1883', *Australian Dictionary of Biography*, vol. 2, Melbourne University Press, 1967, 444–5.

Tobin, Christopher, *The Dharug Story: An Aboriginal History of Western Sydney from 1788*, Penrith City Council, 1997.

Tollard, Clifford, *The Years of Endeavour: Bankstown*, Pyrmont, Today Publications, 1970.

Troy, Jakelin, 'The role of Aboriginal women in the development of contact languages in New South Wales: from the late eighteenth to the early twentieth century', in Anne Pauwels (ed.), *Women and Language in Australian and New Zealand Society*, Sydney, Australian Professional Publications, 1987, 155–69.

——, 'The Sydney language notebooks and responses to language contact in early colonial New South Wales', *Australian Journal of Linguistics*, vol. 12, no. 1, June 1992, 145–70.

——, *The Sydney Language*, Canberra, Australian Dictionaries Project and Australian Institute of Aboriginal and Torres Strait Islander Studies, 1993.

Tucker, James, *Ralph Rashleigh*, London, Folio Society, 1977 (f.p. 1929).

Tuckerman, James, 'No. 189: The Hawkesbury River and Broken Bay', in E.M. Curr (ed.), *The Australian Race: Its origins, languages, customs, place of landing in Australia and the* routes by which it spread itself over that continent, Melbourne: John Farnes, Government Printer, 1887, 359–60.

Turbet, Peter, *The Aborigines of the Sydney District Before 1788*, Sydney, Kangaroo Press, 2001 (f.p. 1989).

Turnbull, Lucy Hughes, *Sydney: Biography of a City*, Sydney, Random House, 1999.

Turner, John, *Joseph Lycett: Governor Macquarie's Convict Artist*, Newcastle, Hunter History Publications, 1997.

Twidale, C.R. and Campbell, E.M., *Australian Landforms: Understanding a Low, Flat, Arid and Old Landscape*, Sydney, Rosenberg Publishing, 2005.

Upton, Ken, 'A Darug discussion', in *The Pemulwuy Dilemma: The Voice of Koori Art in the Sydney Region*, Emu Plains, Lewers Bequest & Penrith Regional Art Gallery, 1990.

Urquhart, Paul, *The New Native Garden: Designing with Australian Plants*, Sydney, New Holland, 1999.

Urry, James, 'Savage sportsmen', in Ian Donaldson and Tamsin Donaldson (eds), *Seeing the First Australians*, Sydney, George Allen & Unwin, 1985, 51–67.

Varley, Jane, 'Australian clays in the Sydney pottery industry', *Journal of the Royal Australian Historical Society*, vol. 71, part 3, 218–28.

Vlach, John Michael, *Back of the Big House: The Architecture of Plantation Slavery*, Chapel Hill, University of North Carolina Press, 1993.

——, *The Planter's Prospect: Privilege and Slavery in Plantation Paintings*, Chapel Hill, University of North Caroline Press, 2002.

Walsh, G.P., 'The geography of manufacturing in Sydney, 1788–1855', *Business Archives and History*, vol. 3, no. 1, 1963, 22–31.

——, 'Manufacturing', in G.J. Abbott and N.B. Nairn (eds), *Economic Growth of Australia 1788–1821*, 1979, 245–66.

——, 'Reibey, Mary (1777–1855)', *Australian Dictionary of Biography*, vol. 2, Melbourne University Press, 1967, 373–4.

Walters, Ian, 'Fish hooks: evidence for dual social systems in southeastern Australia?', *Australian Archaeology*, vol. 27, 1988, 98–114.

Walton, John, *Storied Land: Community and Memory in Monterey*, Berkeley, University of California Press, c2001.

Ward, Russel, *The Australian Legend*, Melbourne, Oxford University Press, 1958.

——, 'The Australian Legend revisited', *Australian Historical Studies*, vol. 18, no. 71, October 1978, 171–83.

Warner, Russell MacKenzie (ed.), *Over-Halling the Colony*, Sydney, Australian Document Library, 1990.

Warren, Jilly, Wilson, Pam and Pullen, Noelene, *Rouse Hill Village: A Step Back in Time*, Castle Hill, Hills District Historical Society, 2006.

Waterhouse, Richard, *From Minstrel Show to Vaudeville: The Australian Popular Stage 1788–1914*, Sydney, UNSW Press, 1990.

——, *Private Pleasures, Public Leisure; A History of Australian Popular Culture Since 1788*, Melbourne, Longman, 1995.

BIBLIOGRAPHY

——, *The Vision Splendid: A Cultural History of Rural Australia*, Fremantle, Fremantle Arts Press/Curtin University Books, 2005.

Watt, Sir James, 'The colony's health', in John Hardy and Alan Frost (eds), *Studies from Terra Australis to Australia*, Canberra, Australian Academy for the Humanities, 1989, 137–51.

Weingarth, John, 'The Head of Sydney Cove', *Journal of the Royal Australian Historical Society*, vol. 10, part 3, 1924, 287–300.

West, Susan, 'The role of the "bush" in 1860s bushranging', *Journal of the Royal Australian Historical Society*, vol. 91, part 2, 2005, 131–47.

——, 'Spiders in the centre of their webs: the NSW police and bushranging in the 1860s', *Journal of Australian Colonial History*, vol. 8, 2006, 1–22.

White, Mary E., *The Greening of Gondwana*, Sydney, Reed Australia, 1986.

White, Richard, *The Middle Ground: Indians, Empires and Republics in the Great Lakes Region 1650–1815*, Cambridge, Cambridge University Press, 1992 (f.p. 1991).

Whittaker, Anne-Maree, 'Mrs Paterson's keepsakes: the provenance of some significant colonial documents and paintings', *Journal of the Royal Australian Historical Society*, vol. 90, part 2, December 2004, 136–51.

——, *Appin: The Story of a Macquarie Town*, Sydney, Kangaroo Press, 2005.

Willey, Keith, *When the Sky Fell Down: The Destruction of the Tribes of the Sydney Region 1788–1850s*, Sydney, Collins, 1979.

Williams, Glyndwr, 'Far happier than we Europeans: reactions to the Australian Aborigines on Cook's voyage', *Australian Historical Studies*, vol. 19, no. 77, 1981, 499–512.

—— and Frost, Alan, 'New South Wales: expectations and reality', in Glyndwr Williams and Alan Frost (eds), *Terra Australis to Australia*, Melbourne, Oxford University Press, 1988, 161–207.

Willmot, Eric, *Pemulwuy: The Rainbow Warrior*, Sydney, Weldons, 1987.

Wilson, Edwin (ed.), *Discovering the Domain*, Sydney, Hale & Iremonger and the Royal Botanic Gardens, c1986.

Wilson, Pam and Pullen, Noeline, *North Rocks: A Brief History and Guided Tour*, Castle Hill, Hills District Historical Society, 2003.

Wilson, William Hardy, *Old Colonial Architecture in New South Wales and Tasmania*, facs. ed., Sydney, Ure Smith and the National Trust of Australia (NSW), 1975 (f.p. 1924).

Wood, Chris Leslie, *A History of Bankstown 1788–1888*, Sydney, Pioneer Productions, 1985.

Wrigley, E.A., 'Urban growth and agricultural change: England and the continent in the early modern period', in Peter Borsay (ed.), *The Eighteenth Century English Town*, 1990, 39–82.

Wright, Judith, *Half a Lifetime*, Melbourne, Text Publishing, 1999.

Yarwood, A.T., 'Marsden, Samuel (1765–1838)', *Australian Dictionary of Biography*, vol. 2, Melbourne University Press, 1967, 207–12.

Yelling, J.A., *Common Field and Enclosure in England in England 1450–1850*, London, Macmillan, 1977.

Young, Anne, *Environmental Change in Australia from 1788*, Melbourne, Oxford University Press, 1996.

Young, Linda, *Middle Class culture in the Nineteenth Century: America, Australia and Britain*, New York, Palgrave Macmillan, 2003.

Theses

Blair, Sandy, 'Newspapers and their Readers in Early Eastern Australia: The *Sydney Gazette* and its Contemporaries', PhD thesis, School of History, University of New South Wales, 1990.

Goodall, Heather, 'A History of Aboriginal Communities in New South Wales 1909–1939', PhD thesis, Department of History, University of Sydney, 1984.

Johnson, Paul-Alan, 'The Phillip Towns: Formative Influences in Towns in the NSW Settlement from 1788–1810', PhD thesis, Graduate School of the Built Environment, University of New South Wales, 1985.

Karskens, Grace, 'The Grandest Improvement in the Country: An Historical and Archaeological Study of the Great North Road, NSW 1825–1836', MA thesis, University of Sydney, 1985.

McKinnon, Jennifer A., 'Convict Bushrangers in New South Wales 1824–1834', MA thesis, La Trobe University, 1979.

Miller, R.D., 'Bull Cave: Its Relevance to the Prehistory of the Sydney Region', BA (Hons) thesis, Department of Anthropology, University of Sydney, 1983.

Newling, Jacqueline, 'Foodways Unfettered: Eighteenth Century Food in the Sydney Settlement', MA (Gastronomy) thesis, University of Adelaide, 2007.

Pryke, Olwyn, 'Old Sydney Town: More than History', BA (Hons) thesis, Department of History, University of Sydney, 1998.

Thompson, J.R., 'Cattle and Cattlemen in Early New South Wales', PhD thesis, School of History, University of New South Wales, 1990.

Young, Linda, 'The Struggle for Class: The Transmission of Genteel Culture to Early Colonial Australia', PhD thesis, Flinders University, 1997.

Conference papers

Goodall, Heather, 'Visions: Wild Places in the Suburbs', paper presented at the Australian Historical Association Conference, Newcastle, 5 July 2004, courtesy of the author.

Pickering, Mike, 'Lost in time', paper given at School of Philosophical and Historical Inquiry, University of Sydney, November 2007, courtesy of the author.

Rediker, Marcus, 'How to Escape Bondage: The Atlantic Adventures of the "Fugitive Traytor" Henry Pitman, 1687', paper given at Escape conference (School of History and Classics, University of Tasmania and International Centre for Convict Studies), Strahan, Tasmania, 26 June 2003.

Unpublished reports

Archaeological & Heritage Management Solutions Pty Ltd, 'Castle Hill Heritage Park: Archaeological Assessment Research Design and Excavation Methodology for Proposed Monitoring of Landscaping and Test Investigation at the Barracks & Schoolhouse Sites', report prepared for Baulkham Hills Shire Council, Stanmore, NSW, 2003.

Bennet, Michael, 'Concord and District Aboriginal History', in 'Archaeological Survey of Land within Canada Bay', report prepared for Michael Therin, Archaeologist, 2004, copy courtesy the author.

Britton, Geoffrey and Morris, Colleen, 'Castlereagh Cultural Landscape Study: Assessment and Recommendations', report prepared for the Penrith Lakes Development Corporation Ltd, July 1999.

Dallas, Mary, 'Aboriginal Context', in Godden Mackay Logan Pty Ltd, 'The Rocks Heritage Management Plan', report prepared for the Sydney Harbour Foreshore Authority, Sydney, 2001, vol. 2, 11–23.

——, Mackay, Richard and Karskens, Grace, 'Archaeological Study of the Land within the Shire of Baulkham Hills in the Parklea Release Area', report prepared for Baulkham Hills Shire Council, November 1989.

Flynn, Michael, 'Place of Eels', report prepared for Parramatta City Council, 1995.

——, 'Holroyd History and the Silent Boundary Project', report prepared for Holroyd Council, August 1997.

Godden Mackay Logan Pty Ltd, 'Angel Place Project 1997: Archaeological Excavation', vol. 1 Main Report and vol. 3 Prehistory Report, prepared for AMP Asset Management Australia Ltd, the NSW Heritage Council and the National Parks and Wildlife Service (NSW), Sydney, 1998.

Karskens, Grace, 'The Gem of Port Jackson: History of Admiralty House', report prepared for Edward Higginbotham, 1986.

Kohen, James L., Knight, A. and Smith, Keith Vincent, 'Uninvited Guests: An Aboriginal Perspective on Government House and Parramatta Park', report prepared for the National Trust of Australia (NSW), August 1999.

Lee, Emma and Darwala-Lia, 'Aboriginal History of Homebush Bay Olympic Site', report prepared for the Metropolitan Local Aboriginal Land Council and Olympic Co-ordination Authority c1998.

MacPhail, M.K., 'Blackwattle Creek Catchment: Statement of Significance', report prepared for Dana Mider & Associates, 2003, courtesy of the author.

——, 'Pollen Analysis of Samples from the Quadrant Site, Broadway, Sydney. Part 2: Middle to Late Holocene Deposits', report prepared for Dana Mider & Associates, 2003.

——, 'Pollen Analysis of Samples from the Quadrant Site, Broadway, Sydney. Part 3: Late Pleistocene Deposits', report prepared for Dana Mider & Associates, 2003.

Murray, Tim and Crook, Penny, 'Exploring the Archaeology of the Modern City Database', Archaeology of the Modern City Project, Department of Archaeology, La Trobe University, online at <http://www.latrobe.edu.au/amc/database.html>.

National Parks and Wildlife Service, 'Meeting Place Precinct Master Plan, Botany Bay National Park, Kurnell', Sydney, April 2003, <http://www.nationalparks.nsw.gov.au/PDFs/botany_bay_masterplan.pdf>.

Proudfoot, Helen, 'Hyde Park Sydney: Statement of Significance and Historical Analysis', report prepared for the Council of the City of Sydney, 1987.

Steele, Dominic, 'Animal Bone and Shell Artefact Report', report prepared for Godden Mackay and the Sydney Cove Authority, 1996, published in Godden Mackay Logan, *The Cumberland/Gloucester Streets Site, The Rocks: Archaeological Investigation Report*, vol. 4 Specialist Artefact Reports, Sydney, Godden Mackay Logan Pty Ltd, 1999, part 2, 139–237.

Sydney Harbour Federation Trust, 'Management Plan, Mosman No. 2, Chowder Bay', 24 November 2003, <http://www.harbourtrust.gov.au/topics/mgmtplancb.html>.

Varman, Robert, 'Early Settlement Site', report, 1997, Hills District Historical Society Collection.

Wilson, Graham, 'Ceramics and Tobacco Pipes Artefact Report', in Godden Mackay Logan, *The Cumberland/Gloucester Streets Site, the Rocks: Archaeological Investigation Report*, vol. 4, part 1, Sydney, Godden Mackay Logan, 1999.

——, 'Castle Hill Heritage Park: Archaeological Excavation Report for the Stage 1 Redevelopment Area', report prepared for Baulkham Hills Shire Council, Stanmore, NSW, Archaeological & Heritage Management Solutions, 2005.

Wollondilly Shire Council, 'Scar Tree Plan of Management, Bridgewater Estate 2006', Picton NSW, the council, 2006, online at <http://www.wollondilly.nsw.gov.au/files/15663/File/CorporateScarTreeManagementPlan1–34.pdf>.

Unpublished research and papers

Bodkin, Frances, 'Boora Birra: The Story of the Sow and Pigs Reef', courtesy of the author, 2001.

Gapps, Stephen, 'Mobile monuments: historical re-enactment and commemoration', 2007, courtesy of the author.

Hawkins, Ralph, 'Timbergetting in the Bluegum High Forest 1788–1830', draft manuscript, courtesy of the author, 2007.

——, 'Geary's Gang: Gangs, Government and Bushranging', typescript research 2007, courtesy of the author.

——, 'Solomon Wiseman', typescript research and narrative, copy courtesy of the author, 2007.

Historic Houses Trust of New South Wales, 'Hyde Park Barracks Guidebook', draft copy, 2003, courtesy John Petersen.

PICTURES

(see also List of illustrations)

Anon., 'Major Johnston with Quartermaster Laycock One Serjeant and twenty-five Private of ye New South Wales Corps defeats two hundred and sixty six armed Rebels, 5th March 1804', ('Convict uprising at Castle Hill, 1804'), National Library of Australia, PIC T2495 NK10162, online at <https://wwwnla.gov.au>.

Anon., 'View of Government Farm, Castle Hill', c1806, Mitchell Library.

Earle, Augustus, 'A Native Family of New South Wales Sitting Down on an English Settlers Farm', watercolour, c1826, National Library of Australia, T83 NK12/45.

Fernyhough. W.H., *Series of Twelve Profile Portraits of the Aborigines of New South Wales*, Sydney, J.G. Austin, 1836, National Library of Australia, PIC S2293-S2305 LOC 4061-A.

Hunter, John, 'Birds and Flowers of New South Wales drawn on the spot 1788, '89 and '90', sketchbook, National Library of Australia, online at <http://www.nla.gov.au/apps/cdview?pi=nla.pic-an3148509&chunk=4&x=11&y=15>.

Lycett, Joseph, 'Convict Barracks Sydney NSW', c1820, watercolour, SLNSW PX*D41 f.5.

Nicholas, William, *Profiles of the Aborigines of New South Wales*, Sydney, Barlows, 1840.

Phelps, P.H.F., 'A Present for One's Friends', in *Native Scenes* [snakes, birds & marine life], 1840–49?, Dixson Library, DL PX 58, <http://image.sl.nsw.gov.au/cgi-bin/ebindshow. pl?doc=dlpx58/a1429;seq=7>.

Rae, John, 'Elizabeth St from Lyons Terrace', 1842, SLNSW, DG SV*/Sp.Coll./Rae/13.

Templar, James Lethbridge, 'Skeletine by Skeleton, July 1844', ML SV*/Hors/3.

MAPS

Ashton, Paul and Waterson, Duncan, *Sydney Takes Shape: A History in Maps*, Brisbane, Hema Maps, 2000.

Balcombe, Thomas, 'Sketch Shewing the Situation of Huts in the Parish of Botany Belonging to Boatswain Maroot', Surveyor General's Sketch Book, vol. 1, SRNSW CG13886, X751 F76, 245.

Bemi, P.L., 'Plan of Laing's Clear', 1838, ML, online at <http://image.sl.nsw.gov.au/cgi-bin/ebindshow.pl?doc=maps/a559;seq=34>.

Burrowes, P., 'Petersham', 1840, online at <http://image.sl.nsw.gov.au/cgi-bin/ebindshow. pl?doc=maps/a559;seq=29>.

Cartwright, C., 'Map of Governor's Desmesne', 1816, ML M3/811.172/1816/1.

Department of Lands New South Wales, Appin 9029–15 Topographic & Orthophoto Map 1:25000, Sydney, 2000.

Harper, W., 'Plan of the Allotments of Ground in Sydney', 1823, SRNSW Map SZ 469.

Meehan, James, 'Plan of the Town of Sydney', 1807, ML ZM2 811.17/1807/1.

Raper, George, 'Chart of Port Jackson New South Wales as Survey'd by Captn John Hunter . . . 1788', ML M2 811.15/1788/1.

Russell, Robert, section maps 1835, SRNSW.

UBD 2003 Professional Drivers Sydney & Blue Mountains Street Directory, Universal Press Ltd, Sydney, 2003.

Parish maps
Available online at <http://parishmaps.lands.nsw.gov.au/pmap.html>

Parish of Appin, County of Cumberland, 1867, AO Map no. 186, Lands Department image ID 14071601.

Parish of Botany, County of Cumberland, 1898, AO Map no. 24500, Lands Department image ID 14040401.

Parish of Bringelly, County of Cumberland, n.d. c1830, AO Map no. 193, Lands Department image ID 14071201.

Parish of Cook, County of Cumberland, n.d. c1830, AO Map no. 211, Lands Department image ID 14069701 and 14069601.

Parish of Cornelia, County of Cumberland, n.d. c1830, AO Map no. 212, Lands Department image ID 14090301.

Parish of Kurrajong, County of Cook, 1893, AO Map no. 39767, Lands Department image ID 14096501.

Parish of Melville, County of Cumberland, n.d. AO Map no. 245, Lands Department image ID 14067101.

Parish of Mulgoa, County of Cumberland, n.d. c1850, AO Map no. 255, Lands Department image ID 14073301.

Parish of Prospect, County of Cumberland, n.d. c1840, AO Map no, 265, Lands Department image ID 14072601.

Parish of Saint Matthew, County of Cumberland, n.d. c1830, AO Map no. 354, Lands Department image ID 14076801.

Parish of Wilberforce, County of Cook, 1896, AO Map no. 39791, Lands Department image ID 14027801.

FILMS

ABC TV, *Rewind—Vinegar Hill*, broadcast 3 October 2004, transcript online at <http://www.abc.net.au/tv/rewind/text/s1209455.html>.

Andrikidis, Peter (director), *The Incredible Journey of Mary Bryant*, drama series, television mini-series, Granada Television International, 2005, National Film & Sound Archive no. 665423.

Lewis, Mark (director), *The Floating Brothel: The Extraordinary Tale of the* Lady Juliana *and the Unlikely Founding Mothers of Modern Australia*, Film Australia/Essential Viewing, 2006, copy held in National Film & Sound Archive, no. 679457.

Miller, George T. (director), *Against the Wind*, drama series, television mini-series, 13 Episodes, Pegasus Productions, 1978, National Film & Sound Archive no. 138030.

Petty, Bruce (director and producer), *Australian History*, animation, narrated by Leonard Teale, 1971, Bruce Petty, National Film & Sound Archive no. 46741.

NEWSPAPERS AND MAGAZINES

Age
Australian
Bell's Life in Sydney
Monitor
Penrith Press
Sydney Gazette
Sydney Morning Herald

INDEX